Advanced Financial Accounting

Richard Lewis
David Pendrill

Second Edition

PITMAN PUBLISHING
128 Long Acre, London WC2E 9AN

© Richard Lewis, David Pendrill and David S Simon 1981 and 1985

Second edition first published in Great Britain 1985
Reprinted 1987

British Library Cataloguing in Publication Data
Lewis, Richard, 1941, Sept 30—
  Advanced financial accounting.—2nd ed.
  1. Accounting
  I. Title   II. Pendrill, David
  657'.48   HF5635

  ISBN 0–273–02287–3

Printed at The Bath Press, Avon

Contents

Preface

When this book was first published in 1981, it was intended primarily for students preparing for the final professional examinations of the major accounting bodies in the UK. It has undoubtedly met a need in this area but has also proved popular with students following the more practically orientated advanced sections of degree courses in accounting and business studies.

In an area of knowledge which changes as fast as financial accounting, any advanced textbook needs to be updated far more regularly than authors and publishers would prefer and, in this second edition, we have incorporated the enormous number of changes which have taken place since 1981. The book now includes relevant provisions of the Companies Act 1981 and considers all Statements of Standard Accounting Practice and Exposure Drafts extant at 1st January 1985. In view of the subsequent consolidation of company law in 1985, we have provided a brief Table of Destinations on page xii; this shows where sections of the Companies Acts 1948–1981, to which we have referred, may be found in the Companies Act 1985.

As well as updating the text, we have taken the opportunity to make many improvements and, in response to requests from users of the first edition, we have now included a large selection of questions taken from the professional examination papers of the Chartered Association of Certified Accountants and the ICAEW. We gratefully acknowledge the permission of these bodies to reproduce their questions and hope that the inclusion of these questions, together with the provision of a separate solutions manual, will provide a more complete package for users.

In all but introductory textbooks, it is necessary for the authors to decide what level of knowledge is to be assumed of readers. We have assumed a thorough knowledge of double entry bookkeeping and of the principles underlying the preparation of accounts for limited companies and groups of companies. We have also assumed extensive knowledge of the detailed legal disclosure requirements relating to the accounts of limited companies. The ICAEW Financial Accounting II examination has recently included a heavy weighting on the preparation of accounts and detailed notes to accounts, and students should not neglect this part of their studies. However, we do not concentrate on such rote learning of company law requirements in this book. Nor do we waste space reproducing accounting standards and exposure drafts. We assume that readers have access to these documents and quote from them only when it aids our exposition. Here we concentrate on the problems which have led to the publication of a statement, the particular solutions proposed and the strengths and weaknesses of these solutions in comparison with available alternatives.

The first edition of this book was written by three authors, Richard Lewis, David Pendrill and David S. Simon who, at the time of its conception, were employed by two colleges of the University of Wales. Although David Pendrill still holds his post at University College, Cardiff, Richard Lewis and David Simon left the University College of Wales at Aberystwyth before the first edition was published. Given our geographical dispersion in London, Cardiff and Hull, respectively, and the consequent difficulties which this entails, we have decided that the second edition should be written by just two authors. Obviously much of David Simon's work in the first edition appears in this revised edition and we gratefully acknowledge the contribution that he has made.

We would very much like to thank Eric Dalton of Pitman for his advice and support and for the intermittent pressure which he puts upon us. Finally we are heavily indebted to Pamela and Louise for their continuous encouragement and tolerance of the many evenings we spend on the telephone discussing accounting problems.

RWL   1 April 1985
DP

1985 Consolidation of Company Law Table of Destinations

Sections referred to in text	*Sections in 1985 Legislation*
Companies Act 1948	Companies Act 1985
56	130
66	135
150	229, 239, 245, 736
151	229
154	736, 744
196	231, Sch. 5 Part V
206	425
207	426
208	427
287	582
319	614, Sch. 19
Sch. 8	Sch. 4
	Companies Act 1985
Companies Act 1967	235, 261(5), Sch.7, Sch.10.
16	261(6), Sch. 10.
17	Sch. 9
Sch. 2	Companies Act 1985
	263, 275
Companies Act 1980	264, 275
39	265, 266, 267
40	Companies Act 1981, or, where marked
41	CP, Companies Consolidation
	Consequential Provisions) Act 1985.
Companies Act 1981	227, 228, 245, 742
1	Sch. 8, Part I.
6	130–134, CP. 12.
36–41	162–170, 380
46–53	170, 171, 172
54	173, 174
55	175
56	176, 177
57	503, 504, 507, 519
58	Sch. 4.
Sch. 1	

Source: Consolidation of the Companies Acts 1948–1983:
Table of Destinations, HMSO, London, 1985.

1 Introduction

One of the most difficult tasks facing an author is deciding how to start his book. An elegant epigram or an eye-catching sentence might well fix the attention of prospective readers or, more importantly, potential purchasers of the book, but such devices do not seem appropriate in this case. We feel that it would be best to start the book in a fashion which reflects its approach, i.e. we shall adopt a practical stance and start by discussing what we mean by the three words which constitute the title of the book – *Advanced Financial Accounting*. It will be convenient to start at the end of the title and then work back.

A number of definitions of accounting are available in the literature, and of these we will select the oft-quoted description provided by the Committee of the American Accounting Association (AAA), which was formed in order to prepare a statement of basic accounting theory. In its report, which was published in 1966, the Committee defined accounting as 'the process of identifying, measuring, and communicating economic information to permit informed judgments and decisions by users of the information'.[1] The Committee went on to point out that the concept of economics referred to in the definition 'holds that economics is concerned with any situation in which choice must be made involving scarce resources'.[2]

We feel that the definition is a useful one in that it focuses not on the accounting process itself but on the reasons why information is required. It is all too easy for accountants to become obsessed with the techniques of their craft and to forget that the application of these techniques is not an end in itself but merely a means to an end. In this book we will constantly reiterate such questions as 'Why is this information required?' or 'How will this data be used?' We believe that a proper study of accounting must start with an examination of the needs of decision makers. Unfortunately, many accounting students start from the other end: there is a transaction – record it. To employ

1 *A statement of basic accounting theory*, AAA, New York, 1966, p. 1.
2 *Ibid.*, p. 1.

1

the jargon of budgeting, we believe in a 'top down' and not the 'bottom up' approach.

The distinction between financial and management accounting is a convenient one to make, but it must not be regarded as one which divides the two areas of study into water-tight compartments. In many ways it would be better if the phrases financial and management accounting were replaced by external and internal accounting as management accounting has financial implications while managers have more than a passing interest in financial accounting. However one describes the dichotomy, it is generally agreed that financial, or external, accounting is primarily concerned with the communication of information about an entity to those who do not share in its management, while management, or internal, accounting refers to the communication of information to the managers of the particular entity. Thus the American Financial Accounting Standards Board (FASB) has defined financial reporting as activities which are intended to serve 'the informational needs of external users who lack the authority to prescribe the financial information they want from an enterprise, and therefore must use the information that management communicates to them'.[3] This is a helpful definition which indicates that in this book we will be concerned with financial information that is given to users rather than information which is required by an individual or group of individuals who are in a position to enforce their request.

We should also make it clear that we shall concentrate on the question of accounting for limited companies. We, of course, recognize that there are many other forms of entity which are of importance, including nationalized industries, charities and central and local government and their associated agencies. Our reason for deciding to concentrate on the topic of limited companies is not because we do not think that the other forms of entities do not merit the concern of financial accountants, but it is because we recognize that, at least at present, most accounting courses are concerned with the private profit-seeking (sadly a more accurate description than profit-making) sector of the economy. More attention is now being paid to the problems of accounting for other forms of entities, and we hope that this work will soon be reflected in the content of accounting courses. In the meantime our readers will appreciate that many of the topics that will be discussed in the context of limited companies are of direct relevance to other forms of economic entity.

3 Statement of Financial Accounting Concepts (SFAC) 1, '*Objectives of financial reporting by business enterprises*' FASB, Stamford, Conn., 1978, Para. 28.

We should also provide some indication of the interpretation that should be placed on the adjective 'advanced' in the title of this book. It does not mean that the text will concentrate on detailed and complex manipulations of debits and credits, although we will of course have to deal with such matters from time to time. In the context of this book, 'advanced' means that we will concentrate on the identification, measurement and communication of economic information in the light of our acceptance of the view of the AAA that such information is required to help in decision making. Thus we will concentrate on such questions as what information is relevant to decision makers, how the information is relevant to decision makers, how the information should be measured, and the manner in which it should be communicated. In so doing we will describe and evaluate alternative approaches to the solution of accounting problems.

The definition of accounting which we quoted above stops at the 'communication' of information. However, it must be emphasized that the interpretation of information is a vital part of an accountant's work, and it is clear that this aspect must be regarded as being an integral part of the process of communication. It should be noted that the definition of accounting does not extend to decision making. Of course, many accountants do become involved in decision making, but when they do so they are performing a managerial rather than an accounting role. We would not for one moment wish to argue that accountants should not become involved in management, but it is essential to distinguish between accounting and decision making. It is important that information provided by accountants should be as free as possible from personal bias (*see* the discussion of the meaning of objectivity on page 13, but if the accountant does not keep the distinction between accounting and decision making clear in his own mind, there is a great danger that he might, possibly quite unconsciously, bias the information provided towards the decision which he would wish to see made.

The above discussion might suggest that we see the work of an accountant as being of a purely technical nature in which he is allowed little latitude for professional judgement. This is not the case, because we believe that the accountant must strive to find out and attempt to satisfy the information needs of decision makers and, as we shall show, this is no easy task.

Accounting theory

Academic accountants tend to bemoan the lack of generally accepted accounting theory. This is understandable because theory is the stock in trade of academics. Some 'practical' accountants are probably rather pleased that there is no generally agreed theory of accounting because some practical men are suspicious of theory and theorizing as they believe that it gets in the way of 'real work'. However, those who take this view are probably ignorant of the role that theory can play in practical matters and do not realize that an absence of theory does give rise to many real and practical difficulties.

The description of accounting theory provided by Hendriksen shows clearly the practical uses of theory. Hendriksen defines accounting theory as 'logical reasoning in the form of a set of broad principles that (i) provide a general frame of reference by which accounting practice can be evaluated and (ii) guide the development of new practices and procedures'.[4] Expressed in this way, it is obvious that the function of theory is to assist in the resolution of practical problems. The existence of a theory would mean that we could say and explain why, given a number of assumptions, method X (perhaps current cost accounting) is to be preferred to method Y (say historical cost accounting).

There have been numerous attempts to construct a theory of accounting.[5] In the early stages of development an *inductive* approach was employed. Thus the practices of accountants were analysed in order to see whether patterns of consistent behaviour could be derived from the observations. If a general principle could be observed, then procedures which deviated from it could be castigated as being unsound. These first attempts were mainly directed towards the establishment of explanatory theories, i.e. theories which explained why certain rules were followed.

This approach failed for two main reasons. One is the difficulty of distinguishing consistent patterns of behaviour from a mass of procedures which had developed with the growth of accountancy and the problem of establishing any general set of explanatory statements. The second, and possibly more important, reason was that the approach did not help to improve accounting practice in any significant way. The approach only allowed the theorist to say 'what is' and not 'what ought to be'.

In response to these problems a different method of theory construction emerged in the 1950s. This method was normative in nature, i.e. it was directed towards the improvement of accounting practice. The

---

4 E. S. Hendriksen, *Accounting Theory*, 4th edn, R. D. Irwin, Homewood, Ill., 1982, p. 1.

5 Hendriksen, *op. cit.*, provides a detailed and authoritative description of these attempts.

methods also included elements of the *deductive* approach, which essentially consists of the derivation of rules on the basis of logical reasoning from a basic set of objectives. The theories generally consisted of a mixture of the deductive and inductive approaches: the latter being used to identify the basic objectives. These approaches to theory construction were extremely valuable in that they generated a number of books and papers which have had a profound effect on the development of accounting practice, in particular in the area of current value accounting.[6] More recently the FASB in the USA has mounted a major exercise which, in part, appears to be attempting to seek a general theory (*see* page 10).

The attempts to formulate a general theory of accounting have been criticized on a number of grounds; the main one being the difficulty of specifying objectives which would represent anything more than the authors' opinion.

Attention has recently been directed towards a less ambitious and more specific approach to theory construction. One such approach is based on the suggestion that accounting theory should be developed by first identifying the users of accounts and then finding out what information they require. It is suggested that the framework would allow us to judge current accounting practice and to help guide the development of new procedures, i.e. satisfy the objectives of accounting theory which were specified by Hendriksen. This is an essentially practically oriented approach, and this is a point which was made explicitly by Professor B. Carsberg and his co-authors when they wrote, 'usefulness for specified purposes is the criterion by which the merits of accounting practice must finally be judged'.[7]

This approach has been endorsed in the two most significant reports on the subject of financial accounting produced in the United Kingdom in recent years – *The Corporate Report* (*see* page 8) and the report of the Sandilands Committee (*see* page 11) – in that a central feature of both these reports was the identification of user groups and their needs.

The various stages in this approach, which has been termed a user decision-oriented approach, has been summarized by Arnold as follows:[8]

6 Some of the more important developments are summarized in Chapter 4.
7 Carsberg *et al*, 'The objectives of published accounting reports', *Accounting and Business Research*, Winter 1974.
8 J. Arnold, 'Information requirements of shareholders', in *Current Issues in Accounting* (B. Carsberg and T. Hope, eds), Philip Allan, Oxford, 1977.

(a) Identify the various user groups and determine the information requirements of each group.

(b) Identify alternative accounting methods which might be employed for reporting to users.

(c) Specify ways of testing the extent to which the alternative accounting methods satisfy the needs of the different user groups.

(d) Using the methods developed in (c) above, select the best methods of reporting to each group paying regard to the costs of each alternative.

(e) Consider the extent to which the method selected in (d) can be combined in a general report.

Arnold points out that the outcome of the above procedure is unlikely to remain stable over time and that it will be necessary to repeat the process at regular intervals. One reason why this would be necessary is that users' understanding of accounting information may change, perhaps as a result of the introduction of new concepts in published financial accounts. Another possible reason may be social changes which might have an effect on the balance between the different user groups. Thus a method of accounting which might be considered suitable in an era where the objective of limited companies is the maximization of shareholders' wealth may well not prove to be acceptable in a period when the interests of employees of limited companies are given greater consideration.

The above approach is intuitively appealing, but it does beg a large number of questions, some of which will be considered later in the book. First, let us consider the way in which accountants should react if they believe that users are basing their decisions on the wrong data. Should they simply supply decision makers with the information for which they are asking, or should accountants supply them with the information for which they should be asking? For the management accountant, the problem is not a difficult one for he usually has a direct link with the decision maker and he can supply the information for which he has been asked, but he can also tell the decision maker how, in the accountant's opinion, the decision-making process could be improved. The problem for the financial accountant is very much greater because there is nothing like the same direct link between the supplier and user of information and because of the impact of legal and other regulatory influences on financial accounting. This question must be considered as part of the broader issue of who should write the rules for financial accounting, and we shall consider this question in Chapter 2.

Another matter which merits further consideration is whether it is desirable that accountants should attempt to produce one 'all purpose' form of report, i.e. whether step (e) on page 6 is necessary. It may be that the information needs of the different user groups are so disparate that little will be gained by attempting to produce one form of accounting report. A related question is how intergroup conflicts of interests can be handled. An obvious example of such potential conflict is provided by the employee user group as they might well request information which the shareholder group might prefer them not to have. Less obvious perhaps, but equally important, is the question of intragroup conflict. It may very well be that the different user groups are by no means homogeneous and that within each group there might be found subgroups with different needs for information and with conflicting interests. To take an extreme example, a short-term creditor might not wish long-term creditors to be made aware of the unhealthy financial state of the particular company if that company is relying on the acquisition of long-term finance in order to pay off the short-term creditors.

The resolution of conflicts such as these means that some group or body will need to consider the costs and benefits in so far as they effect each group or subgroup and fix on a compromise. The obvious candidates for this role are the government and the accountancy profession. This is a controversial issue to which we will return when reviewing the current position concerning the establishment of rules in the financial accounting area.

User groups

The approach to the construction of an accounting theory which we described above has only just started to develop. A number of attempts have been made to identify user groups but, as yet, little progress has been made in respect of the remaining steps.

The traditional view was that the most significant or, in the extreme case, the only user groups were those comprising the company's shareholders and creditors, and this view was dominant, until recent times, in the development of company law. Given this attitude, one should ask why the law requires the publication of financial accounts of limited companies, for it could be argued that shareholders and creditors only need invest in or lend to those companies which agree to provide them with the desired amount of information. The intervention of the State would seem to be an abrogation of the *laissez faire* principle upon which the development of company law was based.

There are perhaps a number of reasons, including the paternalistic attitude of governments which is exhibited by the desire to stop people making fools of themselves by investing in, say, gold mines in Dorking. But perhaps the most important factor is the belief founded in classical economic theory that under conditions of perfect competition the interests of society are best served if all individuals seek to maximize their own wealth. This point was elegantly made in 1850 by the Society for Promoting Christian Knowledge in its *Easy Lessons on Money Matters for the Use of Young People* when it wrote 'it is curious to observe how, through the wise and beneficent arrangement of Providence, men thus do a greatest service to the public when they are thinking of nothing but their gain'.[9]

One of the necessary conditions for perfect competition is perfect knowledge, and thus it is argued that in order for the 'wise and beneficent arrangement of Providence' to come to fruition, it is necessary amongst other things for shareholders to know where they will be able to earn the greatest returns; this can be brought about by the publication of financial accounts by limited companies. While the argument is an important one, justifying the existence of laws requiring the publication of accounting information, it must be admitted that most markets are not perfectly competitive and that the information supplied by financial accounts can in no way be described as supplying the participants of the markets with perfect knowledge.

Another factor which can justify the role of the State in the regulation of the publication of accounting information is the existence of other user groups whose interests need to be protected by the State. Recent developments have stressed the existence of these other user groups such as employees and the general public, and this view was expressed strongly in a discussion document entitled *The Corporate Report.*

The Corporate Report

In 1974 the Accounting Standards Committee (ASC) set up a working party to re-examine the scope and aims of published financial reports in the light of modern needs and conditions. The conclusion of the working party was published in June 1975 as a discussion document entitled *The Corporate Report.* This is an important document which

---

9 A somewhat more modern exposition of this view which deals with its implications for financial accounting will be found in H. B. Rose, *Disclosure in company accounts*, Eaton Paper 1, Institute of Economic Affairs, London, 1965.

did not perhaps receive the attention it deserved because its publication was followed closely by the arrival of the Sandilands report on inflation accounting which was considered to have greater immediate impact. All serious students of accounting should read *The Corporate Report* and we will not attempt to summarize its conclusions here but will confine ourselves to a discussion of the user groups which were identified by the report. The report listed seven user groups,[10] and these groups were:

(a) The equity-investor group, which includes existing and potential shareholders as well as holders of convertible securities, options and warrants.

(b) The loan-creditor group, existing and potential holders of debentures and loan stock as well as providers of short-term secured and secured loans.

(c) The employee group, including existing, potential and past employees.

(d) The analyst–advisor group. This group includes financial analysts and journalists, and other providers of advisory services such as credit-rating agencies.

(e) The business-contact group, which includes customers, trade creditors and suppliers and competitors, business rivals and those interested in mergers, amalgamations and takeovers.

(f) The government, including tax authorities, local authorities and those departments and agencies concerned with the supervision of commerce and industry.

(g) The public. This is perhaps the most controversial group and includes, according to the authors of *The Corporate Report*, tax-payers, rate-payers, consumers and other special-interest groups such as political parties.

It might be said that of the above groups the analyst–advisor group does not constitute a separate group in so far as advisors act on behalf of one or more of the main user groups. The importance of the recognition of the analyst–advisor group relates to the way in which information is presented, because the existence of this group might justify the publication of information which would not be readily understood by the members of other groups unless such information could be interpreted for them by their advisors.

As mentioned earlier in the chapter, the identification of user groups

10 The Sandilands Committee produced a similar list.

is only the first stage in the development of accounting theory. The next step is the identification of their needs, but unfortunately we are still not clear about these despite the considerable attention that has been paid to the decision models employed by, in particular, shareholders. We will, in the course of this book, refer to the present state of knowledge in this area and should emphasize that any discussion of alternative accounting methods in such areas as depreciation, the treatment of foreign currency, etc., should be prefaced by consideration of the likely relevance of the information supplied to those who use the accounts.

FASB conceptual framework project

In the United States the FASB has, since the mid-1970s, been engaged in a major project whose aim is to develop a 'conceptual framework' for accounting which it defined as 'a constitution, a coherent system of interrelated objectives and fundamentals that can lead to consistent standards and that prescribes the nature, function and limits of financial accounting and financial statements'.[11] Whilst it appears that the FASB sets itself the ambitious task of identifying a 'coherent system of interrelated objectives and fundamentals' in practice its approach is close to the user-oriented approach we have discussed above.

Thus with regard to financial reporting in business enterprises the Board arrived at a number of initial conclusions which were published in November 1978 in Statement of Financial Accounting Concepts (SFAC) 1, 'Objectives of financial reporting by business enterprises'. The conclusions have been summarized by Macve[12] as follows:

1. The users on whose decisions attention is focused are investors and creditors, but other users have similar needs.
2. The main factor of importance for the decision they have to take is the assessment of the amount, timing and uncertainty of the future cash flows of the business enterprises in which they are interested.

11 *Scope and Implications of the Conceptual Framework Project*, FASB, Stamford, Conn., 1976, p. 2.

12 Richard Macve, *A Conceptual Framework for Financial Accounting and Reporting*, ICAEW, London, 1981, p. 55. In this report which was commissioned by the ASC, Professor Macve *inter alia* reviewed current literature and opinion in the UK, US and elsewhere on the possibility of developing an agreed conceptual framework. He provides a very useful summary of the work of the FASB as well as commenting on other endeavours including *The Corporate Report*. Macve's conclusion is that whilst the quest for a conceptual framework or general theory is important in identifying questions which need to be answered, it would be idle to hope that a framework could be developed which will give explicit guidance on practical problems.

3. The primary focus of financial reporting is on the provision of measures of enterprise income together with information about enterprises' economic resources, obligations and owners' equity. Information about past cash flows is also useful, and so are explanations by management about the accounts.

Whilst the main users have been identified as investors and creditors many other user groups were identified in SFAC 1 which correspond fairly closely with those enumerated in *The Corporate Report*. The suggestion that the assessment of future cash flows is the major factor is, of course, well rooted in economic theory but still leaves open the question of the extent and the manner by which this need can be satisfied by the publication of financial reports. Based on its initial conclusion, much of the FASB's ambitious programme is concerned with how financial accounts can be constructed in such a way as to make them useful in helping investors, creditors and others assess the magnitude, timing and risk of future cash flows.

Desirable characteristics of financial accounting reports

In the absence of a fully developed theory of accounting many researchers and committees have approached the task of reforming accounting practice by enumerating the characteristics which they believe should be exhibited by financial accounting reports.

Table 1.1 lists those qualities which were selected by three of the more important reports published in recent years: *The Corporate Report* (1975), the report of the Sandilands Committee on Inflation Accounting (1975) and SFAC 2, 'Qualitative characteristics of accounting information' published by the FASB in 1980.

The identification of a list of characteristics will not be of much help in producing a theory of accounting which would yield clear and unambiguous rules of procedure especially as the lists include potentially conflicting characteristics such as prudence and objectivity and understandability and realism. The FASB extended their approach beyond those of the other groups in that instead of merely listing their characteristics they presented them as a hierarchy of characteristics (Table 1.2) which it should be noted includes a number of subcharacteristics not included in Table 1.1. For example predictive value and feedback value.

The FASB list of characteristics is headed by usefulness for decision making with relevance and reliability being regarded as the two primary qualities. This, subject to two overriding requirements, that the benefits exceed the costs and that the information is material, the more relevant and reliable the more desirable it is.

Table 1.1

	The Corporate Report	The Sandilands Report	SFAC 2 (FASB)
Understandable	✓	✓	✓
Objective	✓	✓	✓
Comparable	✓	✓	✓
Realistic	✓	✓	✓
Relevant	✓		✓
Reliable	✓		✓
Consistent		✓	✓
Timely	✓		✓
Prudent		✓	
Economy of presentation		✓	✓
Materiality			✓
Usefulness			✓

Table 1.2

Sources: *The Corporate Report*, ASC, London, 1975; *Report of the Inflation Accounting Committee*, Cmnd 6225 (the Sandilands report) HMSO, London, 1975; SFAC 2, 'Qualitative characteristics of accounting information', FASB, Stamford, Conn., 1980.

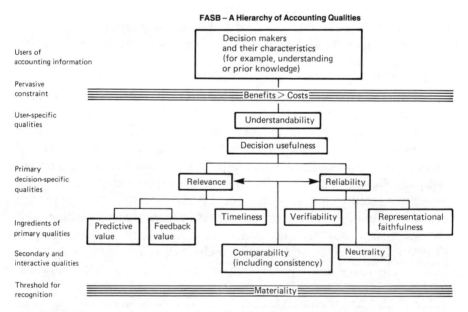

FASB – A Hierarchy of Accounting Qualities

Whilst the ennumeration of desirable characteristics may not contribute directly to the development of a theory of accounting the lists are potentially useful because those who are responsible for the regulation and guidance of accounting practice have to make judgements, and it may be that the identification of desirable features of financial accounting reports may help them in their task.

We will now briefly discuss the implications of the more important of the characteristics listed in Tables 1.1 and 1.2.

Understandable

The Corporate Report clearly states that understandability does not necessarily mean the same as simplicity. Understandability:

> calls for the provision, in the clearest possible form, of all the information which the reasonably instructed reader can make use of and the parallel presentation of the main features for the use of the less sophisticated. [13]

In the various reports stress is placed on the need to supply information in such a way that it would be comprehensible to the less-informed user of accounts without omitting information which would be of value to the informed user.

Objective

Most accountants appear to believe that objectivity is one of the most important of the desirable qualities. Unfortunately, it is not clear that all accountants attach the same meaning to the word. It is probably true that most accountants believe that objectivity is virtually synonymous with verifiability, i.e. that accounts should, so far as it is possible, be based on information which is capable of independent verification and should exclude items which depend on personal opinion or judgement. However, it is clear that the authors of the reports attached different meanings to the word objectivity. In both *The Corporate Report* and FASB's SFAC 2 (which uses the term neutrality) objectivity is defined as the avoidance of bias towards any particular user group. This point is made in *The Corporate Report*, where it is stated:

> The information presented should be objective or unbiased in that it should meet all proper user needs and neutral in that the perception of the measurer should not be biased towards the interest of any one user group. This implies the need for reporting standards which are themselves neutral as between competing interests. [14]

The difference between the 'traditional' (objectivity equals verifiability) and the more recent interpretation of objectivity is an extremely

13 *The Corporate Report, op. cit.*, p. 29.
14 *Ibid.*, p. 29.

important one which might have a considerable impact on the development of accounting practice. For example, in the past objectivity was claimed as the justification for the use of historical cost accounting as opposed to current value accounting on the grounds that the historical cost of an asset was more objective than its current value. However, to the extent that historical cost financial statements are conservative in that they understate the values of assets, it is likely that they will be biased in favour of potential shareholders at the expense of existing shareholders and could thus be said to fail the test of objectivity applied in *The Corporate Report* and SFAC 2.

The Sandilands Committee did not define objectivity in the same way as the other two committees, but it did to some extent reject the traditional interpretation of objectivity. The Sandilands Committee accepted that it was highly desirable that accounts should be based on information which is capable of independent verification but went on to state that the principle should not be rigidly applied as it believed that an element of subjective judgement may be necessary if accounts are to show a true and fair view. The Sandilands Committee's conclusion was that

> However, while objectivity for its own sake may not necessarily be desirable, the scope for the exercise of subjective judgement should be kept to reasonable levels. In general the principle should be not to exclude the exercise of subjective judgement provided it is made clear where and to what extent it has been used.[15]

Comparable

Comparability is seen to be vital because users of accounts will want to be able to compare a company's results both with the results achieved by that company in previous periods and with the results achieved by other companies. The first aspect is important because it helps users to form judgements about the progress of an entity while the importance of the second aspect stems from the need to compare various opportunities.

It is all very well to state that comparability is desirable, but it is not clear how comparability is best achieved. It is not necessarily true that the adoption of the same accounting policies by all companies will achieve comparability if it is found that an accounting policy which might be appropriate to the circumstances faced by one company is inappropriate in the case of another company facing different circumstances. We will return to this point when discussing consistency below

15 The Sandilands report, *op. cit.*, p. 63.

and in the next chapter when considering the extent to which accounting practices should be standardized.

Realistic

In the view of the Sandilands Committee, the requirement that accounts should show a realistic view of a company's affairs is almost synonymous with the legal requirement that they should show a 'true and fair view'. The committee went on to produce an interesting corollary to realism by stating that accounts should avoid giving the impression of absolute precision when such precision cannot exist and that users should be made aware of the degree of precision that can be attached to the information presented and the extent to which items represent attempts by the company to estimate the position on a realistic basis.

Relevant

The importance of relevance has been stressed throughout the chapter. Because of the view taken by the FASB that financial accounts should assist users in making judgements about the magnitude, timing and risk of future cash flows, it is argued in SFAC 2 that 'predictive value' and 'feed-back value' are the main factors which distinguish relevant from irrelevant information. The first factor is concerned with those aspects of accounts which enable users to predict cash flows whilst the second feature refers to the way in which financial accounting information can be used to confirm or correct earlier predictions.

Reliable

This may seem an obviously desirable characteristic but the special meaning placed on the word by *The Corporate Report* should be noted. The report stated that 'information should be reliable in that users should be able to assess what degree of confidence may be reposed in it'.[16] The committee went on to state that the credibility of information is enhanced if it is independently verified but that there may be circumstances where it is useful for an entity to supply information which is not verifiable in this way.

Consistent

This is included in both the Sandilands and SFAC 2 lists but reservations were expressed about excessive adherence to this feature. All other

---

16 *The Corporate Report, op. cit.*, p. 29. Note that a similar point was made by the Sandilands Committee in their discussion of realism.

things being equal the consistent application of the selected accounting treatment over time is desirable in that it aids comparability but when the needs of users change or better accounting techniques are developed then the accounting methods should also change. The Sandilands Committee emphasized the possible conflict between realism and consistency and stated that, in general, realism was the more important of the two. Similarly in the SFAC 2 hierarchy of qualities comparability (including consistency) is shown as being a second-order quality when compared with relevance and reliability.

Whilst it is important to ensure that the new methods are introduced when it is appropriate to do so, it is desirable in such cases to report the results using both the old and new methods for at least 1 year in order to aid comparability.

Timely

Both *The Corporate Report* and SFAC 2 refer to the need for reports to be published quickly on the grounds that up-to-date information is of more value to users than stale news.

Prudent

This characteristic is only found in the Sandilands report list. The Sandilands Committee quoted the definition of prudence in Statement of Standard Accounting Practice (SSAP) 2, which is as follows:

> Revenue and profits are not anticipated, but are recognised by inclusion in the Profit and Loss Account only when realised in the form either of cash or of other assets the ultimate cash realization of which can be assessed with reasonable certainty: provision is made for all known liabilities (expenses and losses) whether the amount of these is known with certainty or is a best estimate in the light of the information available.[17]

It is by no means obvious that prudence is a desirable quality in that prudence by its very nature introduces a bias into accounting. The Sandilands Committee took a somewhat ambiguous view in that it agreed that accounts should be prudent in the manner described in SSAP 2 but went on to warn that care needs to be taken to avoid applying the concept with an undue degree of conservatism and quoted, with approval, the conclusion of an earlier report that 'conservatism for its own sake may actually introduce bias'. It is not clear how an unduly conservative application of a concept can be identified, and

17 SSAP 2, 'Disclosure of accounting policies', ASC, 1971.

it is the view of the authors that this particular feature should not be included as a desirable feature of accounts. It is believed that objectivity, realism and relevance are much surer guides for the development of accounting practice and will encompass the desirable feature of prudence without running the risk of introducing the bias which seems to be inherent in the application of prudence.

A similar position is taken in SFAC 2 where it is declared that conservatism should be regarded as a 'prudent reaction to uncertainty to try and ensure that uncertainties and risks inherent in business situations are adequately considered'[18] and not be interpreted as the 'deliberate, consistent understatement of net assets and profits'.

Economy of presentation
This practical feature is found in both the Sandilands and SFAC 2 lists, in the latter case this feature is regarded as a major factor. It does seem reasonable to suggest that the cost of preparing accounting information must be taken into consideration in the formulation of accounting practice.

Summary

We have in this chapter stressed the need for 'theory' to guide and underpin 'practice'. We have also, very briefly, pointed out that the attempts to formulate general theories have not yet proved to be successful and have suggested that less ambitious methods linked directly to the needs of users of accounts may prove to be more fruitful.

In the absence of any generally agreed theory of accounting, the identification of the desirable characteristics of accounting reports may be regarded as a necessary 'second best' solution and a possible set of characteristics derived from the reports of three important committees has been discussed.

We have reiterated the necessity to relate the provision of accounting information to the needs of the decision makers, and this point has influenced the way in which this book has been written. Some of the chapters, especially those relating to problems of valuation, directly address the way in which accounting information is used. Other chapters, e.g. those concerned with current value accounting and the

18 SFAC 2, 'Qualitative characteristics of accounting information', FASB, Stamford, Conn., 1980, Para. 95.

problems of group accounts, place greater emphasis on technical accounting matters, but even in these chapters our discussion of the relative merits of different methods would be sterile if the needs of users were ignored.

The questions of who does and who should set the rules by which the accounting game is played are important and complex issues which form the subject of the next chapter.

Recommended reading

E. S. Hendriksen, *Accounting Theory* (4th edn), R. D. Irwin, Home-wood, Ill., 1982.
A statement of basic accounting theory, AAA, New York, 1966.
The Corporate Report, ASC, London, 1975.
Report of the inflation accounting committee, Cmnd 6225, HMSO, London, 1975 (the Sandilands report).
Richard Macve, *A Conceptual Framework for Financial Accounting and Reporting*, ICAEW, London, 1981.

Questions

1.1 'The fundamental objective of corporate reports is to communicate economic measurements of and information about the resources and performance of the reporting entity useful to those having reasonable rights to such information.' (*The Corporate Report*)
Required:
Analyse the above quotation and discuss each part in relation to financial reporting.   **(20 marks)**
A. Cert. A. The Regulatory Framework of Accounting, June 1982.

1.2 (a) **Who were considered to be the potential users of financial reports in *The Corporate Report*?**   (8 marks)
       (b) **What do you consider to be their information needs?**   (8 marks)
       (c) **How would you expect a consideration of user needs to influence financial reporting?**   (9 marks)
                                                                      (25 marks)
A. Cert. A. The Regulatory Framework of Accounting, December 1982.

1.3 *The Corporate Report* states that accounting information should be useful.

Required:

   (a) Identify the characteristics of useful information and discuss each briefly.   (10 marks)

   (b) Explain whether or not you consider that identification of desirable characteristics helps to improve financial reporting.   (6 marks)

   (c) It has been suggested that corporate reports which possess these desirable characteristics sometimes recognize the economic substance of a transaction in preference to its legal form.

      Describe two examples of where this may occur.   (4 marks)

                                                              (20 marks)

A. Cert. A. The Regulatory Framework of Accounting, June 1983.

2 Sources of Authority

Introduction

UK statute law imposes a requirement for companies to prepare regular accounts and provides detailed rules on the minimum information which must be disclosed in those accounts. The Companies Act 1981, which implemented the EEC Fourth Directive, not only substantially increased the minimum information which must be disclosed but also laid down prescribed formats for accounts and specified valuation rules which must be applied in preparing accounts.

The Stock Exchange requires the disclosure of certain additional information by listed companies.

Neither statute law nor the Stock Exchange rules specify completely how the various amounts disclosed in the accounts should be calculated. For this the accountant must turn to such sources of authority as accounting principles and conventions established over many years and recommendations and standards issued by relevant professional bodies, both national and international.

This chapter looks at each of these sources of authority and concludes by looking at relevant parts of the EEC company law harmonization programme, which is beginning to have such a large impact on financial accounting in the UK.

Legislation

Background

The advent of the limited liability company by registration under general Act of Parliament in the mid-nineteenth century made possible the widespread separation of management from ownership, which is such a dominant feature of business organization today. With this separation came the need for directors to render accounts to shareholders to show the performance and financial position of the company. It followed that it was necessary to determine what should be included in such accounts and how they should be prepared.

It would have been possible for the law to have left the specification of the form and contents of such accounts to be determined by contract between the shareholders and directors or even to have left the directors to decide what information should be made available in the particular circumstances. However, the law initially flirted with the regulation of accounting disclosure in the period 1844–56 and then became permanently involved with regulating the contents of company accounts early in this century. The Companies Act 1929 increased the information which companies had to disclose whilst extensive disclosure has been required since the Companies Act 1948.

Since it became involved with regulating accounting disclosure, the law has been concerned with the supply of what was considered to be adequate information to shareholders and creditors. Thus it has required directors to lay accounts before the company in general meeting and has tried to ensure that certain minimum information was made available on public record to help a potential creditor to determine whether or not he was likely to be paid if he lent money to or supplied goods and services to the particular company.[1]

As we have explained in the previous chapter, in recent years there has been a recognition that limited companies have an accountability to many other interested parties as well as to shareholders and creditors. Not surprisingly this wider accountability is being increasingly recognized by the law.[2]

Before the implementation of the Companies Act 1981, the accounting requirements of company law were less prescriptive than they have now become. The directors were required to prepare accounts which showed a true and fair view and which contained the minimum information set down in the various Companies Acts. These accounts, together with the accompanying auditors' and directors' reports, had to be laid before the shareholders and filed with the Registrar of Companies within certain time limits. Whilst the basic position is unchanged, substantial alterations have been made by the Companies Act 1981.

1 Readers who wish to study the historical development of accounting further are referred to H. C. Edey, 'Company accounting in the nineteenth and twentieth centuries', in *The Evolution of Corporate Financial Reporting* (T. A. Lee and R. H. Parker, eds), Nelson, London, 1979
2 Examples are the requirement to give details concerning the disclosure of information to and consultation of employees (Companies Act 1967, Sect. 16(1)(b), as introduced by the Employment Act 1982) and the requirement to disclose information on the company's policy regarding disabled employees (Statutory Instrument 1980, No. 1160). Both these provisions require disclosure in the directors' report where a company employs more than 250 employees.

The Companies Act 1981 was mainly concerned with the implementation of the EEC Fourth Directive, and this directive was heavily influenced by the more prescriptive approach to accounting which is taken by the law in France and Germany. As a consequence, the Companies Act 1981 is much more prescriptive than previous legislation in the UK. Although it still contains the overriding principle that accounts should give a true and fair view, it increases substantially the amount of information which must be disclosed and reduces considerably the flexibility which companies previously enjoyed. Thus, whereas directors were previously able to choose the particular formats and valuation rules which seemed most appropriate in the circumstances, the Companies Act 1981 specifies much more tightly the formats and valuation rules which must now be used.

Although the Companies Act 1981 requires that all companies lay full accounts before its shareholders, it permits small- and medium-sized companies to file modified accounts with the Registrar of Companies. These modified accounts will contain less information than the full accounts. Thus a small company need not file a profit and loss account or directors' report and may file a summarized balance sheet and much abridged notes to the accounts. The medium-sized company may file a modified profit and loss account in which certain items are combined and exclude the note which contains details of turnover.[3]

In this book we assume that readers are familiar with the disclosure requirements of the Companies Acts although, for revision purposes, we have included a number of questions requiring the preparation of accounts in accordance with statute law at the end of this chapter.

The current position

The Companies Act 1981 requires that the accounts of a company must give the information specified in the First Schedule to that Act using one of the formats supplied. However, compliance with this requirement and the other disclosure requirements of the Companies Acts 1948–81 is not sufficient to ensure compliance with the law for there is an overriding requirement that every balance sheet shall give a true and fair view of the state of affairs of the company and that every profit and loss account shall give a true and fair view of the profit or loss of the company for the financial year.[4]

3 Companies Act 1981, Sec. 6.
4 Companies Act 1981, Sec. 1.

Hence, having prepared the accounts containing the required disclosure, the accountant must then step back and decide whether or not the overall impression created is true and fair. If the accounts do not give such an impression, additional information must be provided. If the provision of additional information still does not result in a true and fair view, then the accounts must be changed even if this means that they do not comply with the other statutory rules although particulars of any departure, the reasons for it and its effect must be disclosed in the notes to the accounts.

The statutory requirement outlined above poses a number of problems for the accountant. Firstly, he must be thoroughly familiar with the disclosure requirements of the Companies Acts. Secondly, he must know what valuation rules to apply in arriving at the figures to be disclosed. Thirdly, he must determine what is meant by the words 'true and fair'. Let us look at each of these in turn.

The first problem involves painstaking study of the Companies Acts and the various guides thereto and considerable practice in applying those rules in various circumstances. We assume that readers have already undertaken a course of study which has given them this knowledge although, where relevant, we shall reproduce the statutory rules in later chapters.

The second problem involves the selection of valuation rules to apply in arriving at the various figures which appear in the set of accounts. This requires a considerable knowledge of accounting, which this book will help to provide.

Until the Companies Act 1981 accountants would have looked to accounting principles, conventions, recommendations and standards to help them with this task. Although, as we shall see, such sources are still extremely important, the Companies Act 1981 has now incorporated certain basic accounting principles into the law. Thus the law now requires that accounts should be prepared in accordance with four principles:

(1) Going concern.
(2) Consistency over time.
(3) Prudence.
(4) Accruals.

Statute law now requires that these principles must be applied unless there are special reasons for departing from them. Where such special reasons exist, a note to the accounts must state the details of the departure, the reason for it and its effect.[5] We shall discuss these concepts in the section on accounting standards below.

The Act provides that companies may prepare their accounts using either historical cost accounting rules or alternative accounting rules.[6]

The alternative accounting rules are so framed to permit companies to use partial revaluations in their historical cost accounts or to prepare current cost accounts as their main accounts, although, in either case it is necessary to provide certain information to enable partial reconstruction of the historical cost accounts.

Many UK accountants are strongly opposed to the inclusion of such accounting principles and valuation rules in the law. They argue that it provides a straitjacket which may impede accounting development. Two examples will illustrate their argument.

As we explain below it is now being suggested with increasing frequency that accountants should depart from the prudence convention and remove the bias which it produces in accounts. It will be much harder for accountants to effect such a departure now that the prudence convention has been enshrined in statute law.

The alternative accounting rules permit the preparation of current cost accounts as the company's main accounts. Whilst this may have been the system of accounting which was in vogue when the Act was passed, this may not be the case in 10 years time. The reference to current cost accounting in the Act makes it much more difficult for accounting to evolve.

When he has prepared the accounts, the accountant must decide whether they show a true and fair view and, if not, in what respects they need to be altered. In undertaking this task it is essential that he understands what is meant by the expression 'true and fair'.

These words were first introduced together in the Companies Act 1948, following the recommendations of the Cohen Committee.[7] They have never been defined by statute but, rather, their meaning has become established by usage. A good definition has been provided by G. A. Lee:[8]

> Today, 'the true and fair view' has become a term of art. It is generally understood to mean a presentation of accounts, drawn up according to accepted accounting principles, using accurate figures as far as possible, and reasonable estimates other-

---

5 Companies Act 1981, Schedule 1, Part II, Paras. 9–15.
6 The historical cost accounting rules are contained in Schedule 1, Paras. 16–28, whilst the alternative accounting rules are contained in Schedule 1, Paras. 29–34.
7 *Report of the Committee on Company Law Amendment*, Cmnd 6659, HMSO, London, 1945.
8 G. A. Lee, *Modern Financial Accounting*, 3rd edn, Nelson, London, 1981, p. 270.

wise; and arranging them so as to show, within the limits of current accounting practice, as objective a picture as possible, free from wilful bias, distortion, manipulation or concealment of material facts.

So, in order to decide whether or not a set of accounts presents a true and fair view, it is necessary for the accountant to have recourse to a body of accounting principles which have developed over many years, wedded mainly to the historical cost basis of valuation.[9]

Stock Exchange rules

Where companies are listed on the Stock Exchange or have shares which are dealt with on the Unlisted Securities Market, they must comply with additional disclosure requirements laid down by the Stock Exchange. In the former case the requirements are contained in the Stock Exchange Listing Agreement which is to be found in the official publication *Admission of securities to listing* (the Yellow Book). In the latter case, they are set out in *The Stock Exchange unlisted securities market* (the Green Book).

The rules require the provision of both greater and more frequent information than that required by law and two examples will suffice to illustrate them.

Firstly, listed companies are required to provide additional information in respect of certain creditors, namely, (i) bank loans and overdrafts and (ii) other borrowings of the company. Such companies must show the aggregate amounts repayable:

(a) in 1 year or less, or on demand;
(b) between 1 and 2 years;
(c) between 2 and 5 years;
(d) in 5 years or more.[10]

This is a more detailed analysis than that required by statute law.[11]

Secondly, listed companies and those which have shares dealt in on the Unlisted Securities Market must prepare and publish an interim report which contains certain minimum information. In the former case, the report must be sent to shareholders and debenture holders

9 For a fuller discussion of the term 'true and fair' readers are referred to David Flint. *A True and Fair View in Company Accounts*. Gee & Co., London, 1982.
10 Listing Agreement. Para. 10(f).
11 Companies Act 1981. Schedule 1. Para. 48.

or inserted as a paid advertisement in two leading newspapers whilst, in the latter case, the report must be circulated to shareholders or published in one newspaper.

Accounting principles and conventions

Accounting concepts

We have seen how statute law requires companies to disclose a considerable amount of information and lays down broad principles which must usually be applied in arriving at the figures disclosed. We have also seen how this information is extended for companies subject to the rules of the Stock Exchange.

In order to prepare the accounts complying with the law and, where appropriate, the Stock Exchange rules, an accountant must turn to what are referred to as generally accepted accounting principles or generally accepted accounting conventions. These were developed during the latter part of the nineteenth century but have been the subject of continuous development as new situations have arisen.[12]

Many such principles or conventions could be listed but a useful starting point would seem to be the fundamental accounting concepts of SSAP 2, 'Disclosure of accounting policies'. These are defined as 'the broad basic assumptions which underlie the periodic financial accounts of business enterprise'.[13]

Four concepts are listed and these are almost identical to those included in the Companies Act 1981. Users of the accounts may assume that the concepts have been applied in the preparation of a set of accounts unless warning is given to the contrary.

The four concepts are as follows:

(a) *Going concern*   Following the application of this concept, the accounts are drawn up on the basis that the enterprise will continue in operational existence for the foreseeable future. Thus the accountant does not normally prepare the accounts to show what the various assets would realize on liquidation or on the assumption of a fundamental change in the nature of the business. He assumes that the business will continue to do in the future the same sort of things that it has done in the past. If, of course, such continuation is not expected, then

12 *See* B. S. Yamey, 'The development of company accounting conventions', *Three Banks Review*, 1960.
13 SSAP 2, 'Disclosure of accounting policies', Para. 14.

the going concern concept must not be applied. So if, for example, liquidation seems likely then the valuation of assets on the basis of sale values would be appropriate. The accountant must then give warning to the users that the usual going concern concept has not been applied.

(b) *Accruals* This is a rather difficult concept to describe although most accountants understand clearly what is meant by it, at least in situations which are commonly encountered. Revenues and costs are not calculated on the basis of cash received or paid. Revenues are recognized when they are earned usually at the date of a transaction with a third party. Against such revenues are charged, not the expenditures of a particular period, but the costs of earning the revenue which has been recognized.

(c) *Consistency* As we have already seen, the Companies Act 1981 requires that accounting policies must be applied consistently from one period to another. The consistency concept of SSAP 2 goes further than this; it requires like items to be treated in the same manner both within one set of accounts and from one period to another.

Such a concept could easily prevent progress if applied too rigidly for, if a better accounting treatment than the existing method was discovered, it could never be applied because it would be inconsistent with the past! Obviously, it will be necessary to depart from this concept on occasions but then it is necessary to give warning that such departure has occurred and what the effect has been.

(d) *Prudence* This concept requires that accountants do not take credit for revenue until it has been realized in cash or near cash but do provide for all known liabilities. The intention of this asymmetrical approach is to introduce a bias which will tend to understate profit and undervalue assets. Although such a concept might at first sight be thought to benefit users, it may instead damage their interests. Thus a shareholder may sell his shares at a low price because the accounts show low profits and low asset values. In addition we shall see that the failure of accountants to come to grips with changing prices had led to overstatement of profits in an inflationary period. In these circumstances adherence to historical cost-based measures has the very opposite effect to that which a prudence concept would seem to require.

It is, of course, possible to have a conflict between two of the above concepts, and SSAP 2 explicitly deals with the situation where a conflict exists between the accruals concept and the prudence concept. In such a case prudence is stated to prevail although, as we shall see, it has been difficult and indeed sometimes unreasonable for the ASC to comply with this instruction in later Exposure Drafts and standards.[14]

We have looked at the four fundamental accounting concepts listed in SSAP 2, although it is important to realize that other possible concepts could have been listed. Thus, in International Accounting Standard (IAS) 1, 'Disclosure of accounting policies', the International Accounting Standards Committee (IASC) lists only three fundamental accounting assumptions: going concern, consistency and accruals. Prudence, substance over form and materiality are then relegated to a secondary level as governing the selection and application of accounting policies.

Even though an accountant follows the four fundamental accounting concepts, he still has considerable flexibility in the way in which he values assets and determines profit. There are, for example, many methods of depreciating fixed assets or of valuing stocks and work-in-progress; there are many ways of accounting for deferred taxation and for translating the accounts of overseas subsidiaries. From the many such accounting bases available, an accountant must choose the appropriate policy to apply in the circumstances of his particular company.

As we have seen in Chapter 1, we do not have any agreement on the fundamental objectives of accounts; in addition, as we have seen in this chapter, we have no clear-cut ideas of what is meant by the words 'true and fair'. Add to this the fact that the valuation of any asset or liability by its very nature, even under the historical cost system, involves taking a view of the future, and it is not surprising that different accountants will arrive at different views of the same business reality and hence report different figures.

Recommendations and freedom of choice

In order to help their members to choose the appropriate accounting policies, the various professional bodies have issued recommendations on accounting principles. For example, the Institute of Chartered Accountants in England and Wales (ICAEW) issued 29 such recommendations between 1942 and 1969 and these provided guidance on all manner of accounting matters.[15] These recommendations were persua-

14 *See*, for example, the problem of accounting for foreign currency transactions discussed in Chapter 13 and the problem of accounting for research and development discussed in Chapter 15.
15 Some examples are as follows: No. 10, 'The valuation of stock in trade' (1945); No. 12, 'Rising price levels in relation to accounts' (1949); No. 23, 'Hire purchase, credit sale and rental transactions' (1964); No. 25, 'The accounting treatment of major changes in the sterling parity of overseas countries' (1968).

sive rather than mandatory and often permitted a choice from various methods of accounting for a particular set of transactions.

To most accountants the existence of such flexible recommendations was useful. In the majority of cases they could be followed, but if their application was not appropriate in a particular set of circumstances an alternative treatment could be used. Most thoughtful accountants appreciated that there was a multitude of accepted accounting principles and that, if two or more accountants independently prepared accounts for the same company, it was unlikely that they would produce the same results.

A number of incidents in the late 1960s brought the existence of such flexibility to the attention of the general public. Thus in 1968 Sir Frank Kearton, Chairman of Courtaulds and the Industrial Reorganisation Corporation, wrote to the President of the ICAEW to complain about 'the plethora of generally accepted accounting principles'. The problem was brought to a head in 1968 in connection with the GEC/AEI and Pergamon/Leasco affairs.[16]

On 11 September 1969 Professor Edward Stamp wrote a letter to *The Times* in which he was very critical of some aspects of the accountancy profession, in particular its lack of independence and its lack of a theoretical foundation for the preparation of accounts. His well-written letter provoked an angry reaction from the accountancy profession in the person of Ronald Leach, President of the ICAEW. Suffice it to say that the criticism and ensuing debate led to the issue of a 'Statement of intent on accounting standards in the 1970s' by the ICAEW in 1969 and to the subsequent formation of the Accounting Standards Steering Committee.

Standardization

The moves towards standardization and its advantages

The 'Statement of intent on accounting standards in the 1970s' issued by the Council of the ICAEW in 1969, set out a plan to advance accounting standards along the following lines: (a) narrowing the areas of differences and variety in accounting practice; (b) disclosure of accounting bases; (c) disclosure of departures from established definitive accounting standards; (d) wider exposure for major new proposals on

16 These are dealt with in E. Stamp and C. Marley, *Accounting Principles and the City Code: the Case for Reform*, Butterworths, London, 1970.

accounting standards; (e) continuing programme for encouraging improved standards in legal and regulatory matters.

To this end, an Accounting Standards Steering Committee was set up by the Institute of Chartered Accountants in England and Wales, the Institute of Chartered Accountants of Scotland and the Institute of Chartered Accountants in Ireland. The Committee was later joined by representatives of the Association of Certified Accountants and the Institute of Cost and Management Accountants in 1971 and by representatives of the Chartered Institute of Public Finance and Accountancy in 1976. From 1 February 1976 its name was changed to the Accounting Standards Committee and it was reconstituted as a joint committee of the six member bodies acting through the Consultative Committee of Accountancy Bodies (CCAB). By 1 January 1985 the committee had issued 35 Exposure Drafts and 22 Statements of Standard Accounting Practice.

One of the difficulties faced by the Accounting Standards Steering Committee was the problem which we have discussed in Chapter 1, the lack of a conceptual framework for accounting.

The committee recognized that many people have an interest in the financial accounts of a company and that different information may be required for different purposes by those people. As we shall see in later chapters, there are many ways in which assets and liabilities may be valued and a number of associated ways of measuring profit for a period. Some may be relevant to certain users for certain decisions which they must make, whilst others may be useful for decision making by others.[17]

The lack of an agreed conceptual framework has made it difficult to issue standards and many have argued that standards should not have been issued without it. One thing is certain, there would have been few statements of standard accounting practice issued if their preparation had awaited agreement on a conceptual framework. Indeed, as we have argued in Chapter 1, it is becoming more widely recognized that the search for one conceptual framework is a search for the Holy Grail and that ultimately we may have to accept that there are many conceptual frameworks, with the consequent implications for the adoption of multicolumn reporting.

Given the current state of knowledge, it is not possible to say that, given a particular situation, only one accounting treatment is appro-

---

17 Such views are included in *The Corporate Report*, a study by the Scope and Aims Committee of the Accounting Standards Steering Committee, published in July 1975. See Chapter 1.

priate. So, in view of this, the ASC has merely attempted to select one possible treatment from many available as best practice to be followed by all companies.[18]

Users, it is argued, are then in a better position to understand the information communicated by the accounts and to make valid comparisons between companies. Given the current state of knowledge, the standard treatment may not be appropriate in some cases and hence directors are permitted to depart from that treatment provided that they disclose and explain such a departure.[19]

The standards issued so far in the UK can be broadly divided into three categories, although there is some overlap between these:[20]

(a) *Informational – tell people what you are doing*   Recognizing that there are many possible accounting treatments for a given set of 'facts', companies are required to show which treatment is being used in the particular set of accounts. SSAP 2 requires companies to disclose the accounting policies which have been selected for dealing with items which are judged to be critical in the determination of profit such as depreciation, valuation of stock, treatment of research and development and foreign currencies. In practice, the information disclosed in accordance with this statement has often been rather unhelpful.[21]

(b) *Additional disclosure*   Some standards require information to be provided which is not required by law. In such a category fall such statements as SSAP 3, which requires listed companies to publish figures for earnings per share, and SSAP 10, which requires all but small companies to publish a 'statement of source and application of funds'. Such standards may pave the way for changes in legislation and, in the Green Paper *Company accounting and disclosure,*[22] the government indicated its intention to introduce a legislative requirement for large companies to prepare a statement of source and applica-

---

18 In some cases it has not been possible to agree even on one accounting treatment as representing best practice; *see*, for example, SSAP 4, 'The accounting treatment of government grants', which permits two different treatments of capital grants received.

19 Paragraphs 9 and 10, *Explanatory foreword to British standards*, published by the ASC.

20 *See* H. C. Edey, 'Accounting standards in the British Isles', in *Studies in Accounting*, 3rd edn (W. T. Baxter and S. Davidson, eds), ICAEW, London, 1977, pp. 294–305. Professor Edey, in fact, identifies a fourth type of standard, that requiring some uniformity of presentation of accounting statements. Although British standards have sometimes included such formats in non-mandatory appendices, these have not been required in order to comply with the standard. As discussed above, formats have now, of course, been introduced by law.

21 *See*, for example, R. W. Perks and L. Butler, 'Accountancy standards in practice: the experience of SSAP 2', *Accounting and Business Research*, Winter 1977.

22 *Company accounting and disclosure*, Cmnd 7654, HMSO, London, 1979.

tion of funds, although no such requirement has been enacted at 1 January 1985.

(c) *Specification of appropriate methods of valuation*   In this category are standards which tell directors and accountants how to arrive at values and hence profit figures for the accounts. The best examples are SSAP 9, 'Stocks and work-in-progress'; SSAP 12, 'Depreciation'; SSAP 15, 'Deferred taxation'; although SSAPs 4, 5 and 8, which deal with government grants, value added tax and taxation under the imputation system, respectively, also fall into this category. It is not perhaps surprising that it is this category of statement which has provoked the most discussion and criticism.

Before we look at some criticisms of standardization, it is perhaps worth summarizing what seem to be the major advantages of such an approach.

Accounting may be described as the language of business. As with any communication, it is important that the preparers of a document and the users adopt the same language. Standards may be regarded as the generally accepted language. The ASC recognizes that in some cases it will not be appropriate and therefore rightly permits departure.

When directors prepare accounts for their companies, they are not likely to be indifferent to the position shown by those accounts for, after all, they will be judged on the basis of the results disclosed. Thus, given many generally accepted accounting bases, the choice of a particular policy may not be free from bias. The establishment of accounting standards, with the consequent need to justify departures from them, limits the possibility of exercising such bias and strengthens the hands of the auditor.

In addition, it is also clear that the issue of exposure drafts and standards in the 1970s, and early 1980s, has provoked considerable thought and discussion among members of the accounting profession, which has made accounting an exciting area of study.

Some criticisms of standardization

The present approach to accounting standardization is not without its critics, although such critics would attack on different levels. Some would have grave reservations about any form of standardization whilst others accept a need for standardization but criticize the way in which standards are being set in the British Isles. Let us look at each of these in turn.

One of the most pertinent criticisms of the process of standardization was made by Professor W. T. Baxter writing about recommendations on accounting principles in 1953,[23] long before the Accounting Standards Steering Committee was formed. He argued that authoritative backing for one particular accounting treatment may have adverse effects. Although it may help practical men in their day-to-day work, in the longer run it may hinder experimentation and progress. An accountant or auditor may become loath to depart from a particular recommendation or standard and the educational process may become one of learning rules rather than searching for theories or truth. Indeed, if truth subsequently shows a recommendation or standard to have been wrong, then it may be hard for authoritative bodies to admit that they were wrong.

The ASC recognized the force of such criticisms and is clear in pointing out that a standard may not be appropriate in some circumstances and that Statements of Standard Accounting Practice are not the final word on any topic but may be subject to change as a result of future progress. Thus the *Explanatory foreword* makes it clear that where a standard is not appropriate, the directors must depart from it in order to give a true and fair view.[24] It also recognizes that the standards are not absolute but will require amendment as accounting thought evolves.[25]

As stated above, where an accounting standard is not considered appropriate, the directors are required to depart from it and to quantify the effect. Such an approach has been criticized by Morison in an excellent article covering, *inter alia*, the problems of standardization.[26] Having decided that a particular standard is not applicable in the circumstances and having disclosed a figure which they consider best provides a true and fair view of the operations, the directors are forced by this approach to disclose a figure which by definition they consider completely inappropriate. Many would consider such a position to be indefensible.

Such arguments as the above are general arguments against standardization in accounting. Further criticisms have been made of standard

---

23 W. T. Baxter, 'Recommendations on accounting theory', in *Studies in Accounting Theory*, 2nd edn (W. T. Baxter and S. Davidson, eds), Sweet & Maxwell, London, 1962, pp. 414–27.

24 *Explanatory foreword to British standards*, Para. 10.

25 Such changes have already occurred with, for example, SSAP 15 superseding SSAP 11 and the issue of a revised SSAP 1.

26 A. M. C. Morison, 'The role of the reporting accountant today', in *Studies in Accounting*, 3rd edn (W. T. Baxter and S. Davidson, eds), ICAEW, London, 1977, pp. 265–93.

setting in the British Isles, in particular of the way in which standards are formulated and the way in which they are or are not enforced.

Until July 1982, the ASC consisted of 23 members. All of these were qualified accountants, whose membership of the committee was part-time and unpaid. Once a standard had been set by the committee and approved by the councils of the six CCAB members, individual members of the various professional accounting bodies were required to comply with that standard. Thus we had a body of professional accountants imposing rules above those required by the law of the land and attempting to enforce them through the constituent member bodies. The process of standard setting can be criticized on both of these counts.

The people who can be expected to benefit from standards are the users of accounts. If such is the case then should they not have a larger say in the formulation of standards? Indeed accounting standards may have considerable impact on economic behaviour which some would argue should, in a democratic state, be taken into consideration by duly elected Members of Parliament.[27]

To give an example, a standard requiring companies to write off all research and development expenditure as it is incurred may cause firms to stop undertaking research and development due to its adverse effects on the profit figure. This may have severe consequences for the progress and competitive position of the nation.

Only if there are adequate penalties for non-compliance will it be possible to enforce standards. As we have seen, the ultimate penalty for non-compliance is disciplinary action against members. Professional bodies have been loath to take such action and, as a result, there has been a tendency for the rule makers to frame standards and potential standards in such a flexible way as to keep all potential critics and defaulters happy.[28]

The ASC was aware of these and other criticisms and, in 1978, published a draft consultative document as a basis for public discussion and comment.[29] It subsequently considered the 132 written submissions and held formal public meetings in London, Glasgow and Dublin at which interested parties could put their points of view. Following these

---

27 For an account of the effect of standard setting on economic behaviour *see* S. A. Zeff, 'The rise of "economic consequences"', *Journal of Accountancy*, December 1978.

28 *See* M. Lafferty, 'How good are the standards we now have?', in *British Accounting Standards: The First 10 years* (Ronald Leach and Edward Stamp, eds), Woodhead-Faulkner, Cambridge, 1981.

29 *Setting accounting standards: a consultative document*, ASC, London, 1978.

it published, in 1981, a document *Setting accounting standards: report and recommendations by the Accounting Standards Committee*, which has become coloquially known as the 'Watts Report' after the then chairman of the ASC, Mr Tom Watts.

This report came to the conclusion that accounting standards should continue to be set by an ASC operating in the private sector, rather than by a government body. However, it recommended that the wider public interest and the needs of uses should be more clearly recognized in the membership of the ASC. In particular non-accountants should be appointed to its membership in appropriate cases and standards should only be set after the widest and most open consultation. With regard to enforcement it recommended the establishment of a joint panel to review non-compliance with accounting standards by listed companies.

As we shall see in the next section, considerable progress has been made in 'opening up' the membership and procedures of the ASC although no panel to review non-compliance has been set up.

The 1983 *Review*

When he took up office as its chairman, Ian Hay Davidson set in motion a major reorganization of the ASC.

The constitution of the ASC was changed to ensure that, rather than having a set number of seats for each of the CCAB members, the seats were allocated in such a way as to ensure, as far as possible, that the committee has the best men for the job. In addition, the membership of the committee was reduced from 23 to 20, and, of these, five are to be 'users' of accounts who need not be accountants.

At the same time a working party was set up to develop certain of the recommendations in the Watts Report, to seek ways of shortening the standard setting process and to consider whether there was a need for an alternative or new type of pronouncement. The conclusions of this working party, *Review of the standard setting process*, were published in June 1983.

The *Review* summarizes the essential characteristics of future accounting standards as follows:

(a) As at present, they will be prepared by the ASC, but issued by and subsequently enforced by the six CCAB bodies.

(b) They will deal only with those matters which are of major and fundamental importance and affect the generality of companies. They will therefore be few in number.

(c) As at present, accounting standards will apply to all accounts which are intended to show a true and fair view of financial position and profit or loss.[30]

Most accountants will be pleased to see, from the second characteristic, that accounting standards are to be few in number and will be delighted that they are to be spared the 'standards overload' of their colleagues in the USA.[31] The third of the characteristics is likely to pose many problems for the ASC and has already done so in the search for a successor to the standard on current cost accounting, SSAP 16. Whilst it is undoubtedly theoretically correct that accounting standards should apply to all accounts which are intended to give a true and fair view, this is just not possible politically at the present time.[32]

The law already imposes lesser disclosure obligations on small- and medium-sized companies and it is increasingly being recognized that it will be difficult to produce appropriate standards for listed companies if those same standards must be applied to small proprietary companies. The *Review* envisaged possible exemptions in specific standards as the answer to this problem, but this is not a wholly satisfactory approach.[33]

In connection with standards the *Review* also considered the process of setting and revising accounting standards and introduced a new document, the Statement of Intent (SOI), in addition to the Discussion Paper, the Exposure Draft (ED) and the Statement of Standard Accounting Practice (SSAP) with which we were already familiar. The Statement of Intent is a public statement, much shorter than an Exposure Draft, explaining how the ASC proposes to deal with a particular accounting matter. It may be issued instead of a Discussion Paper or an Exposure Draft or may be issued in addition to such documents. The first Statement of Intent was issued in 1983, in connection with accounting for goodwill and, in this particular case, followed the issue of two Discussion Papers and an Exposure Draft on the subject.

---

30 *Review of the standard setting process*, ASC, 1983, Para. 3.5.

31 At 1 January 1985 the FASB has issued more than 80 statements of financial accounting standards as well as many other documents.

32 This point is neatly made by Tom Watts in 'The Role of the Accounting Standards Committee', Deloitte Haskins and Sells Lecture at University College Cardiff, 1983.

33 Such a piecemeal approach to exemptions has already been used in SSAP 3, 'Earnings per share', which only applies to listed companies, and SSAP 10, 'Statements of source and application of funds', which only applies to companies with a turnover or gross income greater than or equal to £25 000 per annum.

A major innovation proposed in the *Review* was a completely different type of statement to be issued on certain topics which are not of sufficient importance to warrant the issue of an accounting standard. The new statement is called a Statement of Recommended Practice (SORP) and harks back to the earlier recommendations of the professional accountancy bodies. As the name implies, the new pronouncement is non-mandatory and there is to be no requirement for a company to disclose any departure from such a statement.

It is intended that such statements will be issued for matters which are of widespread application but not of fundamental importance or for matters which are of limited application, for example, in respect of specific industries or particular areas of the public sector. In the case of statements of limited application it is intended that the Statement of Recommended Practice be prepared by the specific industry or particular area of the public sector and then 'franked', that is approved, by the ASC.

No Statement of Recommended Practice had been issued at 1 January 1985 but ED 34 on pension scheme accounts was issued as the first Exposure Draft of a Statement of Recommended Practice in April 1984.

International standardization

Introduction

It may be argued that, if standards have merit within the boundaries of one country, so too they must have merit if applied more generally. In a period in which investors based in one country choose between investments in many countries, a lack of comparability between accounts drawn up in different countries may well lead to incorrect decision taking and thereby to an inefficient allocation of scarce resources.

As individual countries have pursued a policy of standardization, so too a number of bodies have become concerned with international standardization.

Both the United Nations and the Organisation for Economic Co-operation and Development have studied and issued publications on the regulation of accounting.[34] As might be expected these bodies are mainly concerned with the regulation of disclosure by large multinational companies.

34 *International standards of accounting and reporting for transnational corporations*, UN, 1977. *Guidelines for the disclosure of information by multinationals*, OECD, 1976.

Two more general attempts at standardization are relevant in this country; those of the International Accounting Standards Committee (IASC) and of the European Economic Community (EEC). We first look at the work of the IASC and then consider the work of the EEC in the final section of this chapter.

The International Accounting Standards Committee and its progress

Although the possibility of international standards has been debated since early this century, the most successful programme began with the formation of the IASC in June 1973.

The founder members were drawn from professional accountancy bodies in the following countries: Australia, Canada, France, Germany, Japan, Mexico, the Netherlands, the UK, the Republic of Ireland and the USA. Since that time the professional accountancy bodies from more than 50 countries have been admitted to membership and these include developed countries, such as the Scandinavian countries, as well as many developing countries, including, for example, India, Nigeria and Trinidad. Not surprisingly, the membership does not include countries from the communist bloc.

The objectives of the IASC as stated in the original 1973 agreement were:

> to formulate and publish in the public interest basic standards to be observed in the presentation of audited accounts and financial statements and to promote their worldwide acceptance and observance.

Under a revised agreement entered into in 1982 the reference to basic standards was removed and the revised objectives became:

> (a) to formulate and publish in the public interest accounting standards to be observed in the presentation of financial statements and to promote their worldwide acceptance and observance, and
> (b) to work generally for the improvement and harmonization of regulations, accounting standards and procedures relating to the presentation of financial statements.

In order to achieve these objectives, members joining the IASC enter into the following undertaking:

> to support the work of IASC by publishing in their respective countries every International Accounting Standard approved for issue by the Board of IASC and by using their best endeavours:
> (i) to ensure that published financial statements comply with International Accounting Standards in all material respects and disclose the fact of such compliance;

   (ii) to persuade governments and standard-setting bodies that published financial statements should comply with International Accounting Standards in all material respects;

  (iii) to persuade authorities controlling securities markets and the industrial and business community that published financial statements should comply with International Accounting Standards in all material respects and disclose the fact of such compliance;

  (iv) to ensure that the auditors satisfy themselves that the financial statements comply with International Accounting Standards in all material respects;

  (v) to foster acceptance and observance of International Accounting Standards internationally.

The undertaking emphasizes the fact that the IASC has no direct power to implement or enforce its standards. Rather it must rely on its members to persuade the relevant institutions in their particular countries to adopt and enforce the standards.

Given the very different ways which countries use to regulate accounting, in some countries this will involve persuading the relevant standard-setting bodies to comply whilst, in other countries, it will involve the much more difficult task of persuading the government that changes to the law are necessary.

Even before the IASC had been established, Irving Fantl identified three major barriers to international standardization:[35]

  (a) differences in background and traditions of countries;

  (b) differences in the needs of various economic environments;

  (c) the challenge to the sovereignty of states in making and enforcing standards.

These are enormous problems for the IASC although it has taken steps to try and overcome the barriers. Thus it tries to work closely with the major standard-setting bodies to ensure that it is involved before a country's position becomes entrenched. In addition, like the ASC, it is attempting to consult more widely and has formed a consultative committee drawn from a number of international bodies including the International Association of Financial Executives Institutes, the International Confederation of Trade Unions and World Confederation of Labour and the World Bank.

What then has been the progress of the IASC?

At 1 January 1985 it has issued 24 International Accounting Standards. This is a remarkable output in a little over 10 years and, although many of the documents may be criticized for leaving far too much

---

35 I. L. Fantl, 'The case against international uniformity', *Management Accounting*, May 1971.

choice, some are of particular value here, in so far as there are as yet no equivalent Statements of Standard Accounting Practice in this country.[36] Although it is necessary for the IASC to create its collection of standards, this is by no means sufficient to achieve international standardization. Full international standardization requires that the standards are adopted and enforced although, even if not formally adopted, partial standardization may be achieved if companies begin to comply with them voluntarily. At present there is very little evidence to evaluate the effectiveness of the IASC.[37] What is likely is that implementation of the standards will be much slower than the development of the standards and that even the development of its standards will be slower in future as the committee tackles more and more controversial subjects.

Harmonization in the EEC

The use of Directives
When the European Economic Community was established by the Treaty of Rome on 25 March 1957 one of the objectives to be achieved by member states was 'the approximation of their respective national laws to the extent required for the common market to function in an orderly manner'.[38] To achieve this objective a number of programmes of law harmonization have been undertaken. One of these is the company law harmonization programme under the provisions of Article 54(3)(g) which calls for 'the co-ordination of the safeguards required from companies in the Member States, to protect the interests both of members and of third parties'.

When the EEC Commission has obtained agreement on a set of proposals on a particular topic, it places a Draft Directive before the Council of Ministers. If the Directive is adopted, governments of member states then have a specified period to enact legislation and incorporate the provisions of the Directive into their national law.

---

36 Some examples are: IAS 14, 'Reporting financial information by segments'; IAS 18, 'Revenue recognition'; IAS 19, 'Accounting for retirement benefits in the financial statements of employers'.
37 One piece of evidence is a study based on the Price Waterhouse International Surveys of Accounting Principles and Reporting Practices: R. D. Nair and W. G. Frank, 'The harmonisation of international accounting standards 1973–1979', *The International Journal of Accounting*, **17**, No. 1, Fall 1981. This comes to the tentative conclusion that the IASC had a significant impact over the period studied.
38 Treaty of Rome, Article 3(h).

In practice, many countries have been unable to keep to the timetable imposed by particular Directives and, for the Seventh Directive, the time limits set are much longer than for previous Directives. This is, however, to a large extent necessary to accommodate fundamental changes which are required in some member states.[39]

There are now many Draft Directives and proposals for Directives under discussion but only seven, including the Eighth on qualification of auditors but not the Fifth on structure and management of plcs, have been adopted at 1 January 1985. Of these the two of most concern to accountants are the Fourth Directive on company accounts and the Seventh Directive on consolidated accounts.[40] The former was adopted on 25 July 1978 and has been implemented in the UK by the Companies Act 1981. The latter was adopted on 13 June 1983 and member states must bring into force the laws, regulations and administrative provisions necessary to comply with it before 1 July 1988, although they may provide that the provisions only apply for financial years beginning on 1 January 1990 or during the calendar year 1990.[41]

In this section of the chapter we look briefly at these two Directives.

The Fourth Directive
The original draft of the Fourth Directive was published in November 1971, some time before the UK became a member of the EEC. Not surprisingly the draft was, as it still is, heavily influenced by the current law and practice in France and Germany. When the UK joined the EEC in March 1973, it pressed for certain changes to the draft and, as a result, an amended draft was issued in February 1974. Although not all of the changes suggested by the UK were accepted, the requirement to give a 'true and fair view' was admitted as an overriding objective of accounts and the Directive was eventually adopted by the Council of Ministers on 27 July 1978.

As we have seen early in this chapter, the major changes prescribed by the Fourth Directive were as follows:

(a) limited companies have to adopt compulsory formats for both the balance sheet and the profit and loss account;
(b) defined methods of valuing assets, the so-called 'valuation rules', must be followed.

39 *See* below.
40 These directives may be found in the *Official Journal of the European Communities*. The text of the Fourth Directive is in Volume 21, L222, 14 August 1978, whilst the text of the Seventh Directive is in Volume L193/1, 18 July 1983.
41 Seventh Directive, Article 49.

In addition, the Directive provided definitions of small- and medium-sized companies and permitted member states to offer such companies exemptions from complying with certain requirements of the Directive.[42]

We have already seen how the provisions of the Fourth Directive have been implemented in the UK but it is worth spending a little time looking at the likely impact of the Fourth Directive in the EEC as a whole.

Given the very different accounting systems which exist in member countries, it is perhaps not surprising that it took some 10 years for the Fourth Directive to be adopted. Although this Directive undoubtedly moves the accounting requirements of the various countries closer together, there are two major factors which will limit its effectiveness in achieving harmonization.

Firstly, as we have seen, the Directive contains an overriding requirement that accounts must give a 'true and fair view'. Although it is difficult to define such a term, accountants in the UK have long experience of working with it and are thoroughly familiar with what it means. In many EEC countries the term is unknown and, although it will be translated and included in their respective national legislation, it is by no means certain that it will be interpreted or applied in the same way in those countries as it is in the UK.

Secondly, in order to be able to obtain agreement, it was necessary to include a large number of options in the Fourth Directive and there are over 60 points on which EEC countries are able to exercise a choice.[43] Member states must decide whether or not to incorporate the particular options in their national legislation and may, in fact, even permit individual companies a choice from alternative treatments under the national legislation. Examples of such options are as follows.

One example is the possible exemptions for small- and medium-sized companies. Some countries, such as the UK, will give most of these whilst other countries will not. In such a case the information provided by small companies in different countries will not be comparable.

A second example is that countries may adopt historical cost valuation rules or may either permit or require the applications of alternative accounting rules. In the UK the Companies Act 1981 permits the use of such alternative accounting rules whilst it is highly unlikely that all other countries will do so. Given the requirement for information

---

42 Fourth Directive, Articles 11, 27 and 47.
43 T. R. Watts, ed., *Handbook on the EEC Fourth Directive*, ICAEW, London, 1979, p. 1.

to reconstruct historical cost accounts when alternative accounting rules are used, this will mean that most international comparisons will only be possible on the basis of the historical cost figures.

A third example is provided by the possible choice of formats. The Directive provides two balance-sheet formats and four profit-and-loss-account formats. Although part of the choice is between a horizontal or a vertical format, there are differences between the information disclosed in the two pairs of profit-and-loss-account formats.

Member states may either impose one balance-sheet format and one profit-and-loss-account format on all companies or it may specify all formats and permit companies to choose between them. The Companies Act 1981 has given the widest possible choice with the result that, even in this country, different companies will disclose somewhat different information. Other countries may be more rigid and, if different countries adopt different formats, there will be a lack of comparability.

Even if all countries were to adopt the same formats, the inability to define terms with precision will mean that there is a superficial comparability only. For example, the profit-and-loss format of Article 25 requires the disclosure of, *inter alia*, cost of sales, distribution costs and administrative expenses. Even if we ignore the flexibility of the underlying valuation rules, it is highly likely that different companies will analyse similar expenses between these three categories in different ways and, hence, although the same descriptions are used, the figures will not be comparable.

The above examples are not given to belittle the efforts which have been made to try and achieve harmonization in the EEC but rather to ensure that readers do not overestimate their likely impact.

The Seventh Directive
Although a proposed Seventh Directive was first issued in May 1976 and an amended proposal was issued in December 1978, it was not until June 1983 that the Seventh Directive was actually adopted.[44] As with the Fourth Directive it has been a long and difficult task to reach agreement on when consolidated accounts should be prepared and what they should contain. This should not surprise us when it is realized that some continental countries have no legal requirement for consolidated accounts at all.[45] One of the major difficulties has been in defining

---

44 *Official Journal of the European Communities*, Volume L193/1, 18 July 1983.
45 Examples are Greece and Luxembourg.

the circumstances in which consolidated accounts should be required and a large part of the Directive is devoted to this problem.[46]

In the UK the basic legal position is that group accounts are required when one company has the legal power of control over another company irrespective of whether the parent company exercises this power. The proposed Directive was initially concerned to ensure that information was provided about concentrations of economic power and, as a consequence, consolidated accounts were required when companies were managed in practice by a 'central and unified management'. Ownership was only important to the extent that it led to a presumption that such central management might exist.

A criterion based on the existence of an economic unit is much more difficult to apply than one based on the legal power of control and accountants in the UK are relieved to find that the Directive has come down in favour of a definition based on the existence of this legal power of control.[47]

Some other problems which have had to be resolved in this connection are whether or not consolidated accounts should be required when an individual or partnership controls companies, whether consolidated accounts should be required for subgroup holding companies where the ultimate parent company is in another EEC country or non-EEC country and whether horizontal consolidations should be required for companies in the EEC where, for example, two French companies are both under the control of a US company.[48]

The second part of the Directive is concerned with the preparation of consolidated accounts. As is the case for the accounts of individual companies, there is an overriding requirement that consolidated accounts give a 'true and fair view' as well as the requirement that they give the information specified by the Directive using the valuation rules and formats specified in the Fourth Directive as far as appropriate.

Although the Seventh Directive will have a very large impact in many EEC countries, it is likely to have a relatively small effect in practice in the UK as most of its provisions are already contained in our law or in SSAP 14, 'Group accounts'. However, as was the

---

46 Seventh Directive, Sec. 1, 'Conditions for the preparation of consolidated accounts' (Articles 1–15).

47 Seventh Directive, Sec. 1. As we shall see in Chapter 12 it is still possible for member states to require consolidated accounts where there is unified management but no legal power of control (Article 1, Para. 2).

48 Readers who wish to pursue these topics are referred to Sharon M. McKinnon, *Consolidated Accounts: The Seventh EEC Directive* (Alan D. H. Newham, ed.), AMSA, 1983. Chapter 15 is particularly relevant.

case with the Fourth Directive, many matters which are at present regulated by standard will become part of the law of the land.

As was also the case with the Fourth Directive, member states are given a large number of options, including the possibility of delaying the introduction of certain of the provisions even beyond the starting date of 1990. The way in which member states exercise these options will determine the ultimate degree of harmonization of consolidated accounts achieved by this directive.

Recommended reading

H. C. Edey, 'Accounting standards in the British Isles', in *Studies in Accounting*, 3rd edn (W. T. Baxter and S. Davidson, eds), ICAEW, London, 1977, pp. 294–305.

R. Leach and E. Stamp, eds, *British Accounting Standards: The First Ten Years,* Woodhead-Faulkner, Cambridge, 1981.

Setting accounting standards: a consultative document, ASC, London, 1978.

Review of the standard setting process, ASC, London, 1983.

Questions

2.1 SSAP 2 *Disclosure of Accounting Policies* states that there are four fundamental accounting concepts which have general acceptability.
Required:
   (a) **State and briefly explain each of these four fundamental concepts.**
                                                                                        (8 marks)
   (b) **State and briefly explain three other accounting concepts.**   (6 marks)
   (c) **In what circumstances might you abandon one of the concepts stated in either part (a) or part (b) when preparing a financial statement?**
                                                                                        (6 marks)
                                                                                        (20 marks)
A. Cert. A. The Regulatory Framework of Accounting, June 1982.

2.2 During the examination of the financial records of various company clients you find the following material items:

(1) The profit and loss account of Albatross Ltd for the year ended 30 June 1983 has charged therein £16 400 being general rates payable for the year commencing 1 April 1983, and £15 000 being rent paid for the quarter to 30 September 1983.

(2) Eagle Ltd has included in the work in progress valuation as on 31 July 1983, for the first time, a sum of £60 000, which represents apportioned overheads at 10% on direct costs. In the accounts for the year ended 31 July 1982, the work in progress has been stated at £450 000.

(3) In the accounts for the year ended 31 May 1983, Birdie Ltd has included in sales £40 000 which represents goods sent to customers on a sale or return basis.

(4) Underpar Ltd has stocks and work in progress in the balance sheet at cost on 31 August 1983, including apportioned overheads, amounting to £110 000. Information available indicates that sales have been falling rapidly in the last six months following the introduction to the market of a rival product of improved specification and lower price. The company has an issued share capital of £20 000 and a debit balance on reserves of £2500 as on 31 August 1983.

You are required to write short memoranda to the directors of each of the above companies explaining the fundamental accounting concepts involved and the adjustments, if any, to their accounts which you consider necessary.

(16 marks)

ICAEW Financial Accounting I, November 1983.

2.3 The setting of mandatory accounting standards by a semi-official body representative of the accountancy profession began in the United Kingdom and the Republic of Ireland in 1970. Doubts have recently been expressed about the practical workings of the standard-setting process, and about the usefulness of standard-setting in general.

You are required:
(a) to set out arguments BOTH for AND against the setting of mandatory accounting standards by bodies representative of professional accountants; and (10 marks)
(b) to appraise the 1983 proposals of the UK/Irish Accounting Standards Committee for the issuing of Statements of Intent (SOI) and Statements of Recommended Practice (SORP), in addition to the documents already issued by the ASC. (10 marks)
(20 marks)

A. Cert. A. Advanced Financial Accounting, December 1984.

2.4 The need to conform to two sets of Accounting Standards – International and UK-Irish – may create problems for accountants.

You are required:
(a) to set out the objectives of the International Accounting Standards Committee in preparing International Accounting Standards, and the obligations of the Members in support of those objectives;

(6 marks)

(b) **to explain the difficulties that arise from the existence of two sets of Standards; and** (3 marks)

(c) **to explain what has been done to reconcile the demands of the two sets of Standards.** (6 marks)

(15 marks)

A. Cert. A. Advanced Financial Accounting, December 1982.

Note: Questions 2.5–2.9 are included to enable readers to revise the statutory disclosure requirements and the additional requirements of the Stock Exchange.

2.5 The Companies Act 1981 lays down more formalized accounting rules and disclosure requirements than has hitherto been the practice. In particular, in relation to historical cost accounts, the Act covers the following subjects:

(1) Depreciation
(2) Development costs
(3) Goodwill
(4) Current assets
(5) Purchase price and production costs of assets
(6) Stocks and fungible items

You are required to write brief notes on the requirements of the Companies Act 1981 in respect of each of the above six subjects comparing them, where appropriate, with existing SSAP's. (18 marks)

ICAEW Financial Accounting II, December 1982.

2.6 Sellby Ltd, a trading company, employing 15 people, has an authorized share capital of £200 000 divided into 100 000 8% preference shares of £1 each and 1 000 000 ordinary shares of 10p each. A trial balance extracted from the books of the company as on 30 April 1983 showed the following position:

	£'000	£'000
Preference share capital		100
Ordinary share capital (fully paid)		50
Profit and loss account, as on 30th April 1982		15
Corporation tax		12
Creditors		154
Debtors	324	
Sales (all in United Kingdom)		1250
Purchases	880	
Stocks, as on 30 April 1982	75	
Distribution expenses	129	
Administrative expenses	139	
Audit fees	2	
Carried forward	1 549	1 581

	£'000	£'000
Brought forward	1 549	1 581
Fixtures and fittings	10	
Motor vans	27	
Directors' remuneration	39	
Preference dividend paid	4	
Interim ordinary dividend paid	3	
Advance corporation tax	3	
Bank medium term loan		50
Bank loan interest	6	
Hire purchase balances not yet due		20
Hire purchase interest paid	4	
Bank balance	6	
	1 651	1 651

The following information is also relevant:

(1) Directors' remuneration consists of managing director's salary £12 000, chairman's salary £15 000 and fees paid equally to all four directors of £3000 each.

(2) Fixtures and fittings had originally cost £20 000 and motor vans had cost £36 000. Depreciation is to be provided on cost at 20% and 25% respectively.

(3) Stocks as on 30 April 1983 amounted to £80 000.

(4) Provision is to be made for Corporation Tax based on the results of the year (calculated at 38%) estimated at £17 000, payable on 1 January 1985.

(5) The bank medium-term loan was granted on 1 May 1980 for a fixed term of 10 years.

(6) The hire purchase agreements were for 3 years with effect from 1 May 1982.

(7) The directors recommend payment of the second half-year's dividend on the preference shares and a final ordinary dividend of 2p per share. The related Advance Corporation Tax is considered to be recoverable.

(8) The directors have decided that the financial statements shall be prepared in accordance with the appropriate Companies Act 1981 formats.

You are required to prepare:
   (a) the company's financial statements for the year ended 30 April 1983 in accordance with generally accepted accounting principles and in a form suitable for presentation to members (22 marks), and

(b) the modified accounts which the company can present to the Registrar of Companies (8 marks).

The information given may be taken as if it included all that is necessary to satisfy the requirements of the Companies Acts 1948 to 1981.

Note: Ignore the requirements to disclose accounting policies and to prepare a statement of source and application of funds. **(30 marks)**

ICAEW Financial Accounting I, May 1983.

2.7 The trial balances of Buildall plc, a listed company, and of its wholly owned subsidiary, Constructahut Ltd, include the following balances at 30 November 1983.

	Buildall plc		Constructahut Ltd	
	Dr. (£)	Cr. (£)	Dr. (£)	Cr. (£)
Sales ledger control account	487 600	1 200	308 400	600
Purchase ledger control account	300	133 200	200	83 100
Bills of exchange	14 100	3 000		10 200
Sundry items		74 600		39 200
Current account with Constructahut Ltd		1 200		
Current account with Buildall plc			1 200	
Roofers Ltd		1 400		
Proposed dividend		23 600		
Taxation		44 300		900
10% mortgage debenture		126 000		
Hire purchase account				19 000
Bank overdraft				187 500
VAT		16 200		8 900
Rents received in advance		21 000		
Advance corporation tax recoverable	10 100			

The following additional information is given:

(1) The 10% mortgage debenture is repayable in equal annual instalments of £14 000 up to 1992.

(2) Certain motor vehicles are acquired on hire purchase. The balance of £19 000 above represents the following monthly instalments.

Agreement No. 1	37 of £300
No. 2	23 of £200
No. 3	12 of £175
No. 4	8 of £150

(3) Buildall plc owns 24% of the issued voting share capital of Roofers Ltd.

(4) An analysis of the taxation balances shows:

	£
Corporation Tax on results of the year ended 30 November 1983	40 900
Advance Corporation Tax—on interim dividend paid 1 May 1983	(6 700)
—on proposed dividend	10 100
	44 300

The payment date for Corporation Tax is fifteen months after the year end.

The subsidiary has no taxable profits but has a liability to pay £900 income tax which has been deducted from patent royalties.

(5) Sundry items consist of the following:

	Buildall plc £	Constructahut Ltd £
Outstanding PAYE and NI	22 600	16 800
Accrued expenses	18 900	8 400
Outstanding expense creditors	33 100	14 000
	74 600	39 200

(6) Buildall plc has been served with a writ demanding £75 000 damages in respect of a painting contract carried out over 3 years ago. This is the first intimation that the customers concerned were dissatisfied with the work and the directors strongly believe the claim to be without foundation. No provision is included in the above balances.

(7) Constructahut Ltd occupies premises under a 21-year lease granted in 1976 at a fixed rental of £40 000 per annum. In addition it rents a yard under a licence expiring in 1986 at a cost of £12 000 per annum.

(8) The parent company has guaranteed the overdraft of its subsidiary up to a limit of £250 000.

You are required to produce, in a form suitable for inclusion in the group's financial statements, the appropriate notes for creditors and contingent liabilities in respect of both the group and the parent company. Ignore comparatives.

(23 marks)

ICAEW Financial Accounting II, December 1983.

2.8 Cumberland Group plc is a manufacturing company with retail trading subsidiaries. Its accounting reference date is 31 May and it now has to adopt the new disclosure requirements of the Companies Act 1981 for its financial statements at 31 May 1984.

The following balances are included in the consolidation summaries:

	Dr. £	Cr. £
Purchased goodwill:		
cost	25 000	
amount written off—brought forward		15 000
—year		1 250
Freehold property:		
factory cost—building—brought forward	117 363	
—additions	42 147	
—land brought forward	45 000	
—depreciation—brought forward		54 230
—year		3 190
former warehouse cost	235 167	
Leasehold property:		
Retail shops—cost—brought forward	52 042	
—additions	12 148	
—depreciation—brought forward		21 973
—year		2 649
Office building—valuation 1978	97 000	
—depreciation—brought forward		5 215
—year		1 043

The following additional information is available:

(1) The freehold interest in the factory was acquired in 1952 and the land cost of £45 000 is not depreciated. The buildings are being written off over 50 years.

(2) The former warehouse is no longer used by the group but is let to a third party at a market rental. It is not depreciated. It is the directors' intention to have this property formally revalued at 31 May 1985. They intend to treat this as an investment property.

(3) There were three retail leasehold shops as follows:

Shop	A	B	C
lease expires (all 31 March)	2008	1997	1998
	£	£	£
Cost brought forward	18 146	33 896	—
additions	897	—	11 251
Depreciation brought forward	5 703	16 270	—
year	544	1 355	750

The cost of the leases is being written off over the period of the lease.

(4) The leasehold office building was built in 1972 at a cost of £89 343 on leasehold land. At 31 May 1984 the building was revalued by Chesballs & Partners, Chartered Surveyors, on an open market basis at £85 000. The directors resolve to incorporate the valuation into the financial statements. The lease was granted in June 1972 and expires in 2071.

(5) The directors are confident that all the other properties are worth not less than book value.

You are required to prepare the appropriate notes including the accounting policies covering properties and goodwill in a form suitable for publication in the consolidated financial statements of Cumberland Group plc at 31 May 1984. You are not required to give separate figures relating to the parent company. **(21 marks)**

ICAEW Financial Accounting II, July 1984.

2.9   The Stock Exchange's 'Admission of Securities to Listing' imposes upon listed companies disclosure requirements in addition to those required by statute and SSAPs.

Required:
   (a) Give examples of such additional disclosure requirements from the Stock Exchange regulations. (8 marks)
   (b) Identify the objectives the Stock Exchange is pursuing when regulating the reporting requirements of listed companies. What means, in addition to increased disclosure, does the Stock Exchange adopt in pursuit of these objectives? (12 marks)
   (20 marks)

A. Cert. A. The Regulatory Framework of Accounting, December 1982.

3 What is Profit?

The layman has no doubt about the way in which the question should be answered. Profit is the difference between the cost of providing goods or services and the revenue derived from their sale. If a greengrocer can sell for 5p an apple which cost him 3p, his profit must be 2p. Accountants also used to inhabit this seemingly comfortable world of simplicity, but they are now aware that such a world is not only uncomfortable but downright dangerous. We can perhaps agree that profit is the difference between cost and revenue, but we can now see that there is more than one way of measuring costs. Historical cost is only one alternative, which may indeed be one of the least helpful for many purposes. Furthermore, it is not even obvious that we should measure the difference between costs and revenue in monetary terms, for other measurement units have been suggested, e.g. current purchasing power units.

In order to answer the question 'what is profit?' it is perhaps best to start by considering that most useful of hypothetical examples in accounting theory – the barrow boy who trades for cash and rents his barrow.

Consider such a barrow boy whose only asset at the start of a day's trading is cash of £2000. Let us suppose that the barrow boy rents a barrow and a pitch for the day which together cost him £20. Let us further assume that he spends £80 in the wholesale market for a barrow-load of vegetables, all of which are sold for £130. The trader therefore ends the day with cash of £2030 and we can all agree that his profit for that day's trading is £30.[1] In other words we have taken the barrow boy's profit to be the increase in monetary wealth resulting from his trading activities.

Let us extend the illustration by supposing that the barrow boy has changed the style of his operation. He now owns his barrow and trades

---

1 Actually this is not strictly true for one might wish to impute a charge for the labour supplied by the barrow boy and would say that his profit is the excess of £30 over the imputed labour charge.

in household sundries of which he can maintain a stock. If we wish to continue to apply the same principle as before in calculating his profit, we would need to measure his assets at the beginning and the end of each day. Thus we would need to place a value on his stock and his barrow at these two points of time as well as counting his cash.

All this may appear to be very simple, but it is by no means trivial, for the above argument contains one important implication, that profit represents an increase in wealth or 'well-offness', and one vital consequence, that in order to measure the increase in wealth it is necessary to attach values to the assets owned by the trader at the beginning and end of the period.

Let us now consider the implied definition of profit in a little more detail. The argument is that a trader makes a profit for a period if either he is better off at the end of the period than he was at the beginning (in that he owns assets with a greater monetary value) or would have been better off had he not consumed the profits. This essentially simple view was elegantly expressed by the eminent economist Sir John Hicks, who wrote that income – the term which economists use to describe the equivalent, in personal terms, of the profit of a business enterprise – could be defined as 'the maximum value which [a man] can consume during a week and still expect to be as well off at the end of the week as he was at the beginning'.[2]

This definition cannot be applied exactly to a business enterprise since such an entity does not consume. The definition can, however, be modified to meet this point, as was done by the Sandilands Committee,[3] who defined a company's profit for a year by the following adaptation of Hicks' dictum: 'A company's profit for the year is the maximum value which the company can distribute during the year, and still expect to be as well off at the end of the year as it was at the beginning'.[4]

The key questions that have to be answered in arriving at such a profit are 'How do we measure "well-offness" at the beginning and end of a period?' and 'How do we measure the change in "well-offness" from one date to another?'

This is not the end of the matter for we may wish to make a distinction between that part of the increase in 'well-offness' which is available for consumption and that which should not be so regarded. In tra-

2 J. R. Hicks, *Value and Capital*, 2nd edn, Oxford University Press, Oxford, 1948, p. 172.
3 *Report of the Inflation Accounting Committee*, Cmnd 6225, HMSO, London, 1975.
4 *Ibid.*, p. 29.

ditional accounting practice a distinction is made between realized and unrealized profits such that only the former is normally available for distribution. Recent company legislation[5] introduced into statute law the concept of distributable profits and the legal aspects of the assessment of this element of profit will be discussed in the final section of this chapter.

Turning to our two questions, we will first examine the question of how we may measure 'well-offness' or 'wealth' of a business at a point in time. There are two approaches. The wealth of a business can be measured by reference to the expectation of future benefits; in other words the value of a business at a point of time is the *present value* of the expected future net cash flow to the firm. The second approach is to measure the wealth of a business by reference to the values of the individual assets of the business. Actually these two approaches can be linked by the recognition of an intangible asset, often called goodwill, which can be defined as the difference between the value of the business as a whole and the sum of the values of the individual assets less liabilities.

Present-value approach

We will assume that readers are familiar with the principles and mechanics of discounted cash flow techniques.

With the present-value approach the value of a business is regarded as being the present value of the expected net cash flows that will be generated in the future. This approach is often attacked as being 'too theoretical'. It is rather difficult to see why a method should be attacked on these grounds in that it could be argued that the more theoretical is the method the greater is its logical justification. The point here is that the phrase 'too theoretical' is used to describe methods which are difficult to apply; a better description of the method's defect would be that it is impractical. It is, of course, true that the present-value method is difficult to apply, involving as it does the estimation of the future cash flows of the business and the selection of an appropriate rate of discount. In one sense, however, the expected present value of future benefits is an essentially practical figure in that an individual or group considering the sale or purchase of a business must make some subjective judgement of its value in order to decide whether the transaction is worth while. As will be shown in Chapter 8, a number

5 Companies Acts 1980 and 1981.

of proxy measures might be calculated, but it is clear that, whether the users recognize it or not, the figures produced by the use of the alternative methods should, if they are to give anything like the correct answers, be approximations to the present value of the businesses.

Clearly the present-value approach is an important and useful one when it is applied to the valuation of shares or an entire business for the purposes of determining whether their sale or purchase would be worthwhile at a given price, and the methods used for such purposes will be discussed in Chapters 8 and 9. At this stage, however, we are concerned with the problem of valuing a business for the purpose of measuring the entity's periodic profit.

We do not have sufficient space to explore the 'present-value method' of profit determination[6] but we should point out that the approach has been attacked on grounds other than those concerned with the difficulties associated with estimates involved. This additional criticism goes to the heart of the method itself in that it is suggested that the regular reporting of profit should not be based on future expectations. The present-value approach is, of course, based entirely on expectations of the future and depends on decisions involving the way in which assets will be employed. It is argued that one of the objectives of accounting is to aid decision making and that is hardly appropriate if the fundamental measure of profit should be based on the assumption that all decisions have already been made. This point was made by Edwards and Bell, who wrote:

> A concept of profit which measures truly and realistically the extent to which past decisions have been right or wrong and thus aids in the formulation of new ones is required. And since rightness or wrongness, must, eventually, be checked in the market place, it is changes in market values of one kind or another which should dominate accounting objectives.[7]

This quotation provides a neat introduction to the asset by asset approach.

Measurement of wealth by reference to the valuation of individual assets

In this section we will discuss some of the different possible methods that may be used to value assets. We will at this stage concentrate

6 Interested readers can refer to T. A. Lee, *Income and Value Measurement*, 2nd edn, Nelson, London, 1980.
7 E. O. Edwards and P. W. Bell, *The Theory and Measurement of Business Income*, University of California Press, Stanford, Calif., 1961, p. 25.

on the problems associated with the determination of an asset's value using the different bases and will defer the question of the suitability of the different bases of asset valuation for profit measurement until later.

Historical cost

The historical cost of an asset can usually be determined with exactitude so long as the records showing the amount paid for the asset are still available. The matter, however, is not all that simple. The historical cost of a fixed asset when new may well be known, but it will usually be impossible to say what proportion of the original total cost should be regarded as being applicable to that portion of the asset which remains unused at a point in time. For example, imagine that we are dealing with a 2-year-old car which cost £10 000 and which we expect to have a total life of 5 years, do we say that the historical cost of the unused portion of the car is three-fifths of £10 000, i.e. £6000? This is, of course, the class of question which is answered by the use of some more or less arbitrary method of depreciation. As we will show later, much the same sort of expedient is used in various forms of current value accounting.

Readers will be aware of the difficulties involved in the determination of historical cost of trading stock – whether stock should be valued on the basis of 'average', FIFO, etc. The problem is even more acute when trading stock involves work in progress and finished goods as the question of the extent to which overheads should be included in the stock figure must be considered. Similar problems arise when determining the cost of fixed assets which are constructed by a firm for its own use.

There is another class of assets for which it may be difficult to find the historical costs. These are assets which have been acquired through barter or exchange, a special case of which are assets which are purchased in exchange for shares in the purchasing company. In such instances it may be necessary to estimate the historical cost of the assets acquired. This is usually done by reference to the amount that would have been realized had the assets which had been given in exchange been sold for cash. In some cases it might prove to be extremely difficult to make the necessary estimates as there may not be a market in the assets concerned.

Yet further problems occur where a number of assets are purchased together, for example, where a company purchases the net assets of another company or unincorporated firm. For accounting purposes it is necessary to determine the historical cost of the individual assets and liabilities which have been acquired and this involves an allocation of the global price to the individual assets and liabilities which are separately identified in the accounting system. Any balancing figure represents the amount paid for all assets and liabilities not separately identified in the accounting system and is described as goodwill.[8] Such an allocation is made using 'fair values', a rather poorly defined concept which usually results in the individual assets being valued at their replacement cost and liabilities being valued at their face value. Replacement cost may be thought of as the cost of buying individually assets of similar age and condition to those acquired as part of the collection although, as we shall see, this is a gross oversimplification of the term replacement cost.

The contents of this section may seem fairly obvious, but it is important to remember that the determination of an asset's historical cost is not always an easy task.

'Adjusted' historical cost

By 'adjusted' historical cost we mean the method whereby the historical cost of an asset is taken to be its original acquisition cost adjusted to account for changes in the value or purchasing power of money between the date of acquisition and the valuation date. This method of valuation forms the basis of current purchasing power accounting (*see* Chapter 4).

The practical difficulties of this approach include all those which were discussed in the preceding section on historical cost and to these must be added the problems involved in measuring the changes in the value of money. This is done by using a price index, which is an attempt to measure the average change in prices over a period.

Great care must be taken when interpreting the figures produced by the adjusted historical cost approach. It must be remembered that this method does not attempt to revalue (i.e. state at current value) the assets; it is money and not the asset which is revalued. The adjusted historical cost method can be contrasted with those approaches under which assets are stated at their current values which are the subjects of the following sections.

---

8 Such an approach is also necessary when preparing the consolidated accounts and is discussed in Chapter 12.

Replacement cost

Replacement cost (RC) is often referred to as an entry value because it is the cost to the business of acquiring an asset. In crude terms it may be defined as the estimated amount that would have to be paid in order to replace the asset at the date of valuation.

This is a useful working definition, but it *is* crude as it begs a good number of questions, some of which will be discussed below.

The definition includes the word 'estimated' because the exercise is a hypothetical one in that the method is based on the question 'How much would it cost to replace this asset today?' Since the asset is not being replaced the answer has to be found from an examination of the circumstances prevailing in the market for the asset under review. If the asset is identical with those being traded in the market the estimate may be reasonably objective. Thus, if the asset is a component which is still being manufactured and used by a business, its replacement cost may be found by reference to manufacturer's or supplier's price lists. However, even in this apparently straightforward case, there may still be difficulties in that the replacement cost may depend on the size of the order. Typically a customer placing a large order will pay a lower price per unit than someone buying in small lots. In some types of business the difference between the two sets of prices may be significant, as is evidenced by the different prices paid for food by large supermarkets and small grocery shops. This observation leads to the conclusion that in certain instances it will be necessary to add to the above definition of replacement cost that the estimate should assume that the owner of the asset would replace it in 'the normal course of business', in other words that the replacement would be made as part of the normal purchasing pattern of the business.

The difficulties inherent in the estimation of replacement cost loom very much larger when we turn our attention to assets which are not identical to those which are currently being traded in the market, including those which have been made obsolete by technological progress. A special, and very important, class of non-identical assets are used assets because all used assets will differ in some respect or other from other used assets of a similar type.

A more detailed discussion of the way in which the replacement cost of assets, which are not identical with those traded in the market are found, will be provided later in the book in the chapter on current value accounting (Chapter 6), but it will be helpful if we indicate some of the possible approaches at this stage:

(a) *Market comparison*   In some cases, such as used motor vehicles, the asset in question may be sufficiently similar to assets which are being traded in the market to allow the value to be determined by comparing the asset in question with those being traded. It may prove necessary to adjust the value found by direct comparison to account for any special features pertaining to the particular asset. Thus the approach includes a subjective judgement element which is combined with the reasonably objective comparison with the market.

(b) *Units of service*   With this approach a value is placed on the units of service which the asset is capable of providing rather than on the asset itself. This line of attack is especially useful when valuing obsolete assets. In order to use the method the future productive capacity of the asset must be estimated so that an attempt can be made to find how much it would cost, at the date of valuation, to purchase an asset which is capable of providing the same capacity. One might take as an example a machine which is expected to be able to operate for another 2000 hours. In certain circumstances it might be appropriate to say that the replacement cost of the machine was half the cost of new machines which had an expected life of 4000 hours, so long as it could be assumed that the operating costs of the two machines were identical. If this assumption could not be made an adjustment would have to be made to take account of the difference between the operating costs.

(c) *Replacement cost of inputs*   In certain cases, particularly fixed assets manufactured by the owner for his own use and work in progress and finished goods, it might be possible to determine an asset's replacement cost by reference to the current replacement cost of the various inputs used in the construction of the asset. Thus the necessary labour input could be costed at the wage rates prevailing at the valuation date with similar procedures being applied to the other inputs – raw materials, bought-in components and overheads.

Net realizable value

The net realizable value of an asset may be defined as the estimated amount that would be received from the sale of the asset less the anticipated costs that would be incurred in its disposal. It is sometimes called an exit value as it is the amount realizable when assets leave the firm.

One obvious problem with this definition is that the amount which would be realized on the disposal of an asset depends on the circumstances in which it is sold. It is likely that there will be a considerable difference between the proceeds that might be expected if the asset was disposed of in the normal way and the proceeds from a forced and hurried sale of the assets. Of course, it all depends on what is meant by the 'normal course of business', and while the phrase may be useful enough for many practical purposes it must be remembered that it is often not possible to think in terms of the two extreme cases of 'normal' and 'hurried' disposals. There may be all sorts of inter-mediate positions between these extremes. It can thus be seen that there may be a whole family of possible values based on selling prices which depend on the assumptions made about the conditions under which they are sold and that, particularly in the case of stock, great care must be taken when interpreting the phrase that the net realizable value of an asset is £x.

As was true for the replacement cost basis of valuation, the difficulties associated with the determination of an asset's net realizable value are less when the asset in question is identical, or very similar to, assets which are being traded in the market. In such circumstances the asset's net realizable value can be found by reference to the prevail-ing market price viewed from the point of view of a seller in the market. The replacement cost is, of course, related to the purchaser's viewpoint. If there is an active market the difference between an asset's replace-ment cost and its net realizable value may not be very great and will depend on the expenses and profit margins of traders in the particular type of asset.

The relationship of the business to the market will determine whether, in the case of that business, an asset's replacement cost exceeds its net realizable value or vice versa. It is likely that the barrow boy to whom reference was made earlier would find that the replace-ment cost of his barrow could be greater than its net realizable value, while the reverse is likely to hold for his vegetables. It is generally, but not universally, true that a business will find that the replacement costs of its fixed assets will exceed their net realizable values while in the case of trading stock the net realizable value will be the greater.

Generally the estimation of the net realizable value of a unique asset is even more difficult than the determination of such an asset's replace-ment cost. It may be possible to use the units of service approach in that one could examine what the market is prepared to pay for the productive capacity of the asset being valued, but the process is likely to be more subjective. In the replacement cost case the owner is the potential purchaser and will base his valuation on his own estimate of the productive capacity of the asset, but in the net realizable value case the hypothetical purchaser will have to be convinced of the asset's productive capacity.

A further difficulty involved in the estimation of net realizable value is the last phrase in the definition – 'less the anticipated costs that would be incurred in its disposal'. This sting in the definition's tail can be extremely significant, especially in the case of work in progress, in relation to which the estimation of anticipated additional costs may be difficult and subjective.

Present value

It might be possible to apply the present-value approach to the valuation of individual assets. To do so would require the valuer to attach an estimated series of future cash flows to the individual asset and select an appropriate discount rate. We will discuss the problems inherent in this approach in Chapter 5, which outlines the proposals of the Sandilands Committee. At this stage it is perhaps sufficient to point out that it is usually difficult to attach cash flows to a particular asset since the typical business consists of a number of assets which are used in combination to generate revenue.[9] Thus a factory purchases raw materials which are processed by many machines to produce the finished goods which are sold to earn revenue. In such circumstances as these it would seem impossible to say what proportion of the total net cash flow should be assigned to a particular machine.

Capital maintenance

Let us for a while ignore the practical problems associated with the valuation of assets at an instant in time and assume that one can generate a series of figures (depending on the basis of valuation selected) reflecting the value of the bundle of assets which constitutes a business and hence, after making appropriate deduction for creditors, arrive at a series of figures showing the owners' equity or capital in the enterprise at an instant in time.

If this can be done is the profit for a period found by simply deducting the value of the assets (less liabilities) at the start of the period from the corresponding value at the end of the period? In other words if, using the selected basis of valuation, the value of the assets at time

9 We will return to this problem in Chapter 15 when discussing the question of depreciation.

t_0 was £1000 and the value at time t_1 £1500 is the profit for the period £500? The answer is, probably not.

We must remember that we have defined profit in terms of the amount that can be withdrawn or distributed whilst leaving the business as well-off at the end as it was at the beginning of the period. Now assume that in this simple example the valuation basis used is replacement cost and, for the sake of even more simplicity, that no capital has been introduced or withdrawn during the period and that the firm only holds one type of asset, the replacement cost of which has increased by 50%. (Thus the company holds the same number of assets at the end as it did at the beginning of the period.) Let us also assume that prices in general have not increased over the period.

The question which has to be answered is how much could be distributed by way of a dividend at the end of the period without reducing its 'well-offness' below that which prevailed at the start of the period. It could be argued that £500 could be paid as that would leave the value of the assets constant. It could also be argued that nothing should be paid because in order to pay a dividend the company would have to reduce its holding of assets. If the latter view is accepted it means that the whole of the increase in the value of the assets should be retained in the business in order to maintain its 'well-offness'. It will be seen that each of the approaches described in the simple example will be found in different accounting models but at this stage we simply want to show that it is not sufficient to find the difference between values at two points in time. The profit figure will also depend on the amount which it is deemed necessary to retain in the business to maintain its 'well-offness', that is on the concept of *capital maintenance* which is selected. We shall describe the various approaches to capital maintenance in a little more detail below.

There are thus two choices to be made – the basis of asset valuation and the aspect of capital which is to be maintained. In theory each of the possible bases of valuation can be combined with any of the different concepts of capital maintenance with each combination yielding a different profit figure. In practice the two choices are not made independently of each other in that, as we will show, there are some combinations of asset value/capital maintenance which are mutually consistent and yield potentially helpful information whilst others appear not to provide useful information usually because the two choices are made on the basis of an inconsistent approach to the question of the objectives served by the preparation of financial accounts.

We can summarize the argument thus far by stating that the profit figure depends on (a) the basis of valuation selected, and (b) the concept of capital maintenance used, and is found in the following way:

(i)   Find the difference between the value of the assets less liabilities at the beginning and end of the period after adjusting for capital introduced or withdrawn.
(ii) Decide how much of the difference (if any) needs to be retained in the business to maintain capital.
(iii) The residual is then the profit for the period.

We will now turn to a more detailed examination of the possible ways of viewing the capital of the company (or of its owners) which is to be maintained. It will be helpful to categorize the various approaches to capital maintenance in the following way:

> Money capital maintenance
>> Not adjusted for inflation
>> Adjusted for inflation ('real money capital maintenance')
> Physical capital maintenance
>> From the standpoint of the entity
>> From the standpoint of the equity shareholders' interest.

We shall deal with the above in turn.

Money capital maintenance

With money capital the bench mark used to decide whether a profit has been earned is the book value of the shareholders' interest at the start of the period.

If money capital is to be maintained then, in the absence of capital injections or withdrawals,[10] the profit for the period is the difference in the values of assets less liabilities at the start and end of the period with no further adjustment. Money capital maintenance is used in traditional historical cost accounting which is not to say that, as we will show in Example 3.1, it cannot be combined with other bases of asset valuation.

Real (money) capital maintenance

With real money capital (which is often referred to simply as real capital maintenance) the bench mark used to determine whether a profit has

---

10 In order to save repeating this phrase readers should, for the remainder of this section, continue to assume the absence of capital injections and withdrawals.

been made is the *purchasing power* of the equity shareholder's interest in the company at the start of the period. Thus, if the equity share-holders' interest in the company is £1000 at the start and the general price level increases by 15% in the period under review a profit will only arise if, on the selected basis, the value of the assets less liabilities, and hence the equity shareholders' interest,[11] at the time amounts to at least £1150.

Both the money capital and real money capital maintenance approaches concentrate on the equity shareholders' interest in the company and are hence sometimes referred to as measures of profit based on *proprietary capital maintenance*.

Physical capital maintenance

The physical capital maintenance concept is less clear-cut than the money and real money approaches. Broadly it is concerned with the physical assets of the enterprise and suggests that capital is maintained if at the end of the period the company has the same level of assets as it had at the start. A very simple example of the physical capital approach is provided by the following example.

Suppose a business starts the period with £100 in cash, 20 widgets and 30 flanges and ends the period with £130 in cash, 25 widgets and 32 flanges. Then the profit for the period, using the physical capital maintenance approach could be regarded as being:

Profit = £30 in cash + 5 widgets + 2 flanges.

For certain purposes one could stop here, for the list of assets given above shows the increase in wealth achieved by that business over the period. To state profit in this way does provide a very clear picture of what has happened and shows in an extremely objective fashion the extent to which the business has grown in physical terms. Account-ancy, however, is concerned with providing information stated in monetary terms.

In order to take this additional step it is necessary to select a basis of valuation, for this would then enable the accountant to place a single monetary value on the profit.

Let us assume that it is decided that replacement cost is the selected valuation basis and that the replacement costs at the end of the year are widgets £100 each and flanges £150 each. The profit for the period would then be stated as follows:

---

11 Preference shares being treated as liabilities for this purpose.

	£
Increase in cash	30
Increase in widgets, 5 × £100	500
Increase in flanges, 2 × £150	300
Profit	£830

The above example is obviously simplistic in so far that companies hold a large number of different sorts of assets and, only in the most static of situations, will the assets held at the end of the year match those which were owned at the start of the period. However, the example does illustrate the sort of thinking which will be developed in later chapters.

The example was based on the variant of the physical capital maintenance measure which states that a company only makes a profit if it has replaced (or is in a position to replace) the assets which were held at the start of the period and which have been used up in the course of the period. An alternative approach is to consider the output which is capable of being generated by the initial holding of assets and design an accounting model which would only disclose a figure for profit if the company is able to maintain the same level of output. An approach of this nature is found in the SSAP 16 version of current value accounting (*see* Chapter 6) where the aspect of capital which has to be maintained is the operating capability of the business.

Most variants of the physical capital maintenance approach relate the determination of profit to the assets held by the business, i.e. look at the problem from the standpoint of the business. The physical capital approach is thus often referred to as a measure of *entity capital*. It is, however, possible to combine elements of physical capital mainten-ance with the proprietary concept. This is done, for example, in SSAP 16 when arriving at the current cost profit attributable to shareholders. In essence when deriving this profit figure only a proportion of the capital maintenance charge required to maintain the operating capa-bility of the firm is charged, reflecting the point that some part of the increased investment required by the company, due to increases in the prices of its assets, will be supplied by creditors.

An extended illustration is provided in Example 3.1, in which the combinations of three different bases of valuation and three different concepts of capital maintenance are shown.

EXAMPLE 3.1: DIFFERENT PROFIT CONCEPTS
In this example the three valuation bases used are historical cost (HC),

replacement cost (RC) and net realizable value (NRV), and the three measures are capital maintenance money capital, real money capital and physical capital.

Suppose that a trader has an inventory consisting of 100 units at the start of the year (all of which were sold during the year) and 120 units at the end of the year, but has no other assets or liabilities.

Assume that the trader has neither withdrawn nor introduced capital during the period.

Suppose that the following prices prevailed:

Opening position (100 units)

Basis of valuation	Unit price (£)	Total capital (£)
Historical cost	1.00	100
Replacement cost	1.10	110
Net realizable value	1.15	115

Closing position (120 units)

Basis of valuation	Unit price (£)	Total capital (£)
Historical cost	1.50	180
Replacement cost	1.70	204
Net realizable value	1.80	216

In order to use the real money capital approach it is necessary to know how a suitable general price index moved over the year. We will assume that an index moved as follows:

	Index
Beginning of the year and date on which the opening inventory was purchased	100
Date on which the closing inventory was purchased	118
End of year	120

(a) *Money capital* In this case the opening money capital depends on the selected basis of asset valuation and hence profit is the difference between the value of the assets at the end of the period and the corresponding figure for opening money capital.

Basis of valuation	Closing value of assets (£)	Opening money capital (£)	Profit (£)
Historical cost	180	100	80
Replacement cost	204	110	94
Net realizable value	216	115	101

(b) *Real money capital*

(i) *Historical cost*   The closing inventory of £180 (as measured by its historical cost) was acquired when the general price index was 118. The index has risen to 120 by the year end and thus the historical cost of inventory expressed in terms of pounds of year-end purchasing power is £180 × 120/118 = £183.

Opening money capital based on historical cost was £100. The index stood at 100 at the beginning of the year and rose to 120 by the year end. Thus the real money capital which has to be maintained is £100 × 120/100 = £120.

The profit derived from the combination of historical valuation and real money capital is hence £183 − £120 = £63 (expressed in 'year-end pounds').

(ii) *Replacement cost*   As the replacement cost is a current value it is automatically expressed in year-end pounds and hence the closing value of inventory is £204.

Opening money capital using replacement cost was £110 which, expressed in year-end pounds, is equivalent to £132 (£110 × 120/100). The profit for this particular combination is thus £204 − £132 = £72.

(iii) *Net realizable value*   The argument is similar to that which was used above and the profit derived from net realizable value–current purchasing power combination is calculated as follows:

	£
Closing inventory at net realizable value (automatically expressed in pounds of year-end purchasing power)	216
Opening money capital (based on net realizable value) restated in year-end pounds, £115 × 120/110	138
Profit	£78

(c) *Physical capital*   In this simple example it can be seen that the wealth of the business has increased by 20 units and the only question is how the 20 units should be valued:

Basis of valuation		Profit (£)
Historical cost (using first in, first out)	20 × £1.50	30
Replacement cost	20 × £1.70	34
Net realizable value	20 × £1.80	36

The various profit figures are summarized in the following table:

	Capital maintenance concept		
Basis of valuation	Money (£)	Real money (£)	Physical units (£)
Historical cost	80	63	30
Replacement cost	94	72	34
Net realizable value	101	78	36

The usefulness of different profit measures

In Example 3.1 nine different profit figures emerged. It is impossible to say that one of these is the 'correct' figure. They are all 'correct' in their own terms, although it may be argued that some of them may be generally more useful than others. The different measures reflect reality in different ways. We will meet some of these measures later in this book in the context of the various proposals that have been made for accounting reform.

It might be useful if at this stage we examined a number (but by no means all) of the different objectives which are served by the preparation of financial accounts and consider which of the different profit measures would appear to be the more useful in each case.

We will first discuss the question of whether a business should be allowed to continue in existence. For simplicity we will assume that the business is a sole proprietorship. Consider the profit figure of £78 derived from the combination of the net realizable value asset valuation method and real capital maintenance. This figure shows the potential increase in purchasing power which accrued to the owner of the business by virtue of his decision not to liquidate the business at the beginning of the year. Had he taken that option the owner would have received £115, which expressed in terms of year-end pounds amounts to £138, i.e. he could at the beginning of the year purchase an 'average' combination of goods and services amounting to £115 but it would cost £138 to purchase the same quantity of goods and services at the end of the year. By allowing the business to continue the owner has increased his wealth by £78 in that should he liquidate the business at the end of year he would release purchasing power amounting to £216. Now this analysis does not enable the owner to tell whether he was right to allow the business to continue in operation, but the figures do allow him to compare his increase in wealth with that which he would have achieved had he liquidated the business at the beginning of the year and invested his funds elsewhere. In the words of Edwards and Bell (*see* page 56) the owner has been able to check in the market place his decision not to wind up the business.

But, of course, the past is dead and it is current decisions which are important, the decision to be taken in this case being whether or not the business should be liquidated at the end of the year. It would be naive to assume that the figure of past profit can be expected to continue in the future. However, the decision maker has to start somewhere and most people find it easier to think in incremental terms. With this approach the decision maker might say: 'In the conditions which prevailed last year I made a profit of £x. I accept that next year there will be a number of changes in the circumstances facing the business, and I estimate that the effect of these changes will be to change my profit by £y.' It is clear that if this approach is adopted a profit figure related to the decision maker's objectives (in this case assumed to be the maximization of his potential consumption) is a valuable input to the decision making process.

Let us now consider the subject of taxation. A government might well take the view that companies should be able to maintain the productive capacity and that taxation should only be levied on any increase in the company's wealth as measured against that particular yardstick. In that case, one of the set of profit figures derived from the application of physical capital maintenance might be thought to be most suitable on the grounds that, to use the figures given in our example, if the company started the year with 100 units then in order to maintain the productive capacity it should hold 100 units at the end of the year. The government would, if it took this view, wish to base its taxation levy on the physical increase of wealth of 20 units. Arguments for and against the use of one of the three members of the physical capital maintenance set could be deployed, but these will not be pursued at this stage. There are obviously severe practical difficulties in the use of the physical units approach where the company owns more than one type of asset and, as will be discussed later, other more practical methods have been suggested which would allow governments to apply a taxation policy which closely approximates to that postulated above.

Later in this book we will point out the limitations of the historical cost approach and, in fairness, we should now consider whether the profit derived from the traditional accounting system (historical cost asset values and money units of comparison) could be said to be particularly apposite for any purpose. It is sometimes suggested that the traditional profit figure is of use in questions concerned with distribution policy, for, to quote Professor W. T. Baxter,

> The ordinary accounting concept has obvious merits; it is familiar and (inflation apart) cautious, and most of its figures are based on objective data; its widespread use has therefore been sensible where the decisions are about cash payments (e.g. tax and dividends), since it reduces the scope for bickering and the danger of paying out cash before the revenue has been realized. [12]

How do we choose?

We have identified nine different methods of measuring profit and pointed out that many other different methods are available. Clearly it would not be practical nor helpful from the point of view of the users of accounts to include in a company's annual published accounts a long series of different profit figures. The next question is, therefore, which basis or bases is/are the most suitable for inclusion in published accounts. The reference to the plural 'bases', holds upon the possibility that it might be found desirable to include more than one profit concept in the published accounts.

A sensible approach to this question would be a consideration of the purposes for which a knowledge of a company's profits are used, which is in effect the consideration of the aims and objectives of published financial accounts. A very long list of such purposes can be provided, but it might be helpful if these were analysed under four

12 W. T. Baxter, *Accounting Values and Inflation*, McGraw-Hill, London, 1975, p. 23. It may be strange to quote the words of one of the foremost advocates of current value accounting in support of historical cost accounting. However, Professor Baxter, on whose work this section of the book is largely based, was seeking to show that different profit concepts may be useful for different purposes.

different heads, i.e. control, consumption, taxation, valuation. It must, however, be recognized that the divisions between these heads are not watertight and that they share numerous common features.

The limitations of historical cost accounting

The following chapters of the book deal with the subject of current purchasing power and current value accounting and will, by implication, highlight some of the deficiencies of the traditional form of accounting, i.e. historical cost basis of valuation and money capital maintenance. It might, however, be helpful if by way of introduction we tested the traditional system against the objectives enumerated above.

Control

It is a widely held view that the prime objective of the preparation and publication of regular financial reporting is – so far as public limited companies are concerned – to provide a vehicle whereby the directors can account to the owners of the company on their *stewardship* of the resources entrusted to their charge. This involves providing shareholders with information about the progress of the company as well as details of the amounts paid to directors by way of remuneration. In theory shareholders can, when supplied with this information, take certain steps to remedy the position if the information suggests that all is not well. One mechanism that is available to shareholders is to effect a change in directors, but in practice it is rare for shareholders directly to oust directors because of the publication of unfavourable results. This end might be achieved by the indirect process of a take-over, in that shareholders might accept an offer for their shares on the grounds that they believe that the new management will be more effective than existing management. An individual shareholder can, of course, achieve similar ends by selling his shares but in so doing he must compare what he considers to be the value of the shares with the existing management with the current market price (*see* the section on valuation below).

The above discussion is based on the view that the directors need only account for their stewardship to their shareholders, but it has been suggested that the concept of stewardship should be extended – at least so far as large companies are concerned – to cover the need to report to the community at large. This view, propounded for example in *The Corporate Report*,[13] is based on the view that large companies control the use of significant proportions of a country's scarce resources and that consequently large companies should report to the community at large on the way in which the resources have been used. It will be realized that such a view does not attract the support of all business-men and accountants, who may well be concerned with the nature of the control devices which might follow if this view was adopted. The pressure of public opinion might be an acceptable control device, but many would be concerned that this might not be regarded as being sufficiently strong and that recourse might be made to government intervention or 'interference' or, ultimately, nationalization.

If stewardship is narrowly defined to cover simply the reporting by directors to shareholders of how they have used shareholders' funds, then it is possible to argue that historical cost accounting is reasonably adequate. An historical cost balance sheet lists the assets of the company and the claim by outsiders (liabilities) on the company; however it will not identify *all* the assets, as it will usually omit many intangible assets such as the skill and knowledge of the employees, degree of monopoly power, etc. The main point, however, is whether stewardship should be narrowly defined in the manner suggested above. If share-holders, and others, are to apply effective control they should be helped to form judgements about how well the directors have used the resources entrusted to them.

As we indicated earlier in the chapter there are a number of different possible approaches to the question of how one can measure how successful a company – and by implication its managers – has been over a period. A further discussion of this topic will be provided later in the book, but at this stage it is perhaps sufficient to point out that historical cost accounting will not – except in the simplest of cases where a high proportion of a company's assets is made up of cash – be of much assistance. Historical cost accounts, in general, simply show the acquisition cost or the depreciated historical cost of a company's assets and not their current values, let alone the value of the company as a whole.

It is sometimes argued that even if historical cost accounts do not provide an absolute measure of success they can at least allow comparisons to be made between the quality of performance achieved by different companies. This statement is sometimes justified by argu-

---

13 Scope and Aims Committee of the Accounting Standards Steering Committee, *The Corporate Report*, Accounting Standards Steering Committee, London, 1975.

ments such as, 'Inflation affects all companies to more or less the same extent and therefore a comparison of profitability measured on a historical cash basis, e.g. rate of return on capital employed, enables a rough comparison to be made of relative success.'

Two points need to be made. The first concerns inflation. As will be shown the problem is not just inflation – a general increase in prices or fall in the value of money – but includes the treatment of changes in relative prices. For, even in an inflation-free economy, there will be changes in individual prices. The limitations of historical cost accounting in the context of changes in relative prices can be seen by considering the following simple example.

Suppose that two companies start operations as commodity dealers, in an inflation-free environment, with £1000 each. Company A spent its £1000 on commodity A while Company B invested its £1000 in commodity B. Assume that neither company bought or sold any units during the period and that over the period the market value[14] of commodity A increased by 2% and commodity B increased by 20%. Historical cost accounts will not show that Company B performed better in the sense that it has chosen to invest in a commodity which experienced a greater increase in value.

The second point which should be made about the argument advanced above is that it is not true that inflation affects all companies to more or less the same extent. This point will be developed later when we will show that price changes (both general and relative) affect different companies in very different ways and that it is in fact the case that historical cost accounts are most unhelpful when it comes to the comparison of performance.

Consumption

Probably one of the most important uses of the profit figure is in determining the amount of any increment of wealth which is available for distribution and how it should be shared between the various groups entitled to share in such a distribution, i.e. the different classes of shareholders, the directors and employees (either directly through profit-sharing schemes or indirectly through wage claims) and the community through taxation. There are what might be called 'legal' and

---

14 For simplicity we will ignore transaction costs and assume, in the case of both commodities, that there is no difference between the commodities' replacement costs and net realizable values.

'economic' aspects to this question. Company law requires that dividends may only be paid out of profits and tax law specifies the amount of taxation which has to be paid; however, subject to these constraints, plus any other legal limitations arising from such things as profit-sharing agreements, it is for the directors to make economic judgements about the level of dividends and, again subject to numerous institutional and possibly legal constraints, the level of wages. Empirical evidence suggests that, in the absence of dividend restraint, companies' dividends are related to the level of profit. It is also safe to suggest that sole traders and partners act in a similar fashion in that, when deciding on the level of their drawings, they will be influenced by the profits of their businesses.

The concept of capital maintenance based on historical cost accounting principles has, in periods of anything but modest price changes, proved to be a dangerous bench mark when used to assess the amount which a company can pay out by way of dividend or through taxation. For example, the maintenance of historical cost capital is not, except in the simplest of cases, the same as the maintenance of the company's productive capacity. The point is an obvious one, for we could visualize a company which started business with £10000 which it invested in 1000 units of stock. If the price of the stock increases and if the whole of the company's historical cost profit is taxed or consumed away, its historical cost capital will be maintained, but it is clear that the company will have to reduce the physical quantity of stock.

It should be recognized that there is a great deal of difference between using the capital maintenance approach as a bench mark to measure profit and requiring companies to maintain their capital. Presumably distribution decisions should be made on the basis of consumption needs and perceived future investment opportunities inside and outside the company, and in many cases it would be sensible not to restrict distributions to profits. It is necessary that company law should attempt to provide a measure of protection to creditors, but this should not be done in an inflexible way.[15]

It will be argued in the following chapters that there is a need to devise a measure of profit that will provide a signal that if more than the amount of profit is consumed or taxed away then the substance of the business – however that may be defined – will be eroded. However, this is not to say that the substance of the business should never

---

15 Current legal practice regarding distributable profit is outlined in the final section of this chapter.

be reduced by way of dividend – in other words a partial liquidation of the business might in certain circumstances be beneficial to shareholders without being detrimental to the interests of creditors and employees.

Taxation

In Britain, as in many other countries, a company's tax charge is based on its accounting profit, although numerous adjustments might have to be made when computing the profit subject to taxation. The general rule is, however, clear – the higher the accounting profit, the higher, all other things being equal, the amount that will be paid in tax.

For reasons similar to those discussed in the above section on consumption, the historical cost accounting system does not constitute a suitable basis for the computation of the taxation obligations of businesses. This view depends on the not unreasonable assumption that governments would wish companies to be at least able to maintain the substance of their businesses. As we have shown, it is possible for historical cost accounting to generate a profit figure even when there has been a decline in the productive capacity of the business or, in less extreme cases, the reported profit might far exceed the growth in the company's productive capacity. Thus the use of historical cost accounting as the basis for taxation means that in periods of rising prices the proportion of the increase in a company's wealth which is taken by taxation may be very much larger than that which is implied by the nominal rate of taxation. In extreme cases taxation might be payable even where there has been a decline in the productive capacity of the business.

The rapid and extreme inflation of the mid 1970s made governments and others very much aware of the inadequacy of historical cost accounting for the purposes of taxation; this recognition resulted in the introduction of Stock Appreciation Relief in November 1974. The effect of the combination of this relief and the availability of 100% first year allowances was such that for many, especially manufacturing, companies the amount of tax actually paid is related to the size of its dividend, because of the incidence of Advance Corporation Tax, rather than its accounting profit. In contrast, the deficiencies of historical cost accounting were not reflected in financial accounting practice prior to the introduction of SSAP 16, 'Current cost accounting', except in so far as piecemeal revaluations were included in the historical cost accounts or supplementary statements based on current purchasing power (CPP) and current value accounting principles were published along with the main, historical cost, financial statements.

Valuation

The information contained in a company's accounts is a significant, but not the sole, input to decisions concerning the valuation of a business or of a share in the business. This subject will be discussed in detail in Chapters 8 and 9. At this stage it is perhaps sufficient to point out that the value of any asset, including a business or a share, depends on the economic benefits which *will* flow to the asset's owner. It requires neither much space nor forceful argument to suggest that a knowledge of the historical cost of a company's assets will not be of much help in assessing the value of a company or of its shares. Indeed, it was never the view of accountants that historical cost accounts should be used in this way. However, this view has never fully been accepted by the users of accounts, who have, understandably from their point of view, believed that the information provided by a company's accounts should help them form judgements concerning valuation. In fact it can be argued that the case for accounting reform does not simply rest on the existence of inflation, which still appears to be a permanent feature of our economy. A second plank in the argument is the recognition that the wish of users to be supplied with information which will help them assess the value of companies and shares thereof is a legitimate demand and one which will be better served by accounts based on current value principles than by historical cost accounts.

Summary

So far in this chapter, we have considered the meaning of profit and have shown that there are very many ways of measuring this elusive concept. These depend essentially on the choice made regarding the basis of asset valuation and the aspect of capital which is to be maintained. We have also discussed the limitations of historical cost accounting when tested against the more important purposes which a 'reasonable man' might expect financial accounts to serve. In the chapters which follow we will consider in some detail a number of the more important accounting models which have been developed and used in practice. But before doing so we will turn our attention to the subject of distributable profits.

Distributable profits

We will conclude this chapter with a discussion of the meaning of distributable profit. Dividends can only be paid out of profits but, surprisingly, until the passage of the Companies Act 1980 statute law offered no guidance as to what constituted profits available for distribution. There were a number of leading cases, some of which are distinguished by their age rather than their economic rationale, which combined to produce some rather odd and confusing results.[16]

The implementation of the Second and Fourth EEC Directives necessitated the inclusion of provisions relating to distributable profits in UK statute law and hence the Companies Act 1980 contained the following definition:

> a company's profits available for distribution are its accumulated, realized profits, so far as not previously utilized by distribution or capitalization, less its accumulated realized losses, so far as not previously written off in a reduction or reorganization of capital duly made.[17]

The above represents the only legal requirement placed on private companies. Additional demands are placed on public companies and investment companies.

A public company may not pay a dividend which would reduce the amount of its net assets below the aggregate of its called-up share capital plus its undistributable reserves.[18] For this purpose the Act defines undistributable reserves as:

(a) The share premium account.

(b) The capital redemption reserve fund.

(c) Excess of accumulated unrealized profits over accumulated unrealized losses (to the extent that these have not been previously capitalized or written off).

(d) Any other reserve which the company may not distribute.

Before turning to the special case of investment companies we will discuss the implications of the above to public and private companies. Note that no distinction is made between revenue and capital profits, both are distributable; the key element is whether the profits have been *realized*, a term which will be discussed in further detail below.

A private company can, legally, pay a dividend equal to the accumulated balance of realized profits less realized losses irrespective of the existence of unrealized losses. In contrast, the effect of the 'net asset

16 Interested readers are referred to E. A. French, 'Evolution of the Dividend Law of England' in *Studies in Accounting* (W. T. Baxter and S. Davidson, eds), ICAEW, London, 1977.

17 Companies Act 1980, Sec. 39(2).

18 Companies Act 1980, Sec. 40(1).

rule' imposed on public companies is to require such a company to cover any net unrealized losses which are reflected in its balance sheet. Thus, suppose a company's balance sheet is as given below:

	£	£
Share capital		50
Share premium		25
Unrealized profits	20	
Unrealized losses	(35)	(15)
Realized profits less realized losses		40
Net assets		100

If the concern were a private company it could pay a dividend of £40, but if it were a public company the maximum possible dividend would be restricted as follows:

	£	£
Net assets		100
less Share capital and undistributable reserves		
Share capital	50	
Share premium	25	
Excess of unrealized profits over unrealized losses[19]	0	75
Maximum dividend payable by public company		25

The effect of this net asset rule is to reduce the possible dividend by the net unrealized losses:

	£
Realized profits less realized losses	40
less Excess of unrealized losses over unrealized profits	15
Maximum dividend	25

An investment company is a listed public company whose business consists of investing its funds principally in securities with the intention of spreading the risk and giving its shareholders the benefits of the results of its management of funds. Such a company can, if it satisfies

19 Note that the excess of unrealized profits over unrealized losses is zero rather than the 'mathematical' excess of minus 15.

a number of other conditions,[20] give notice to the Registrar of Companies of its intention to be regarded as an investment company, in which case it must also indicate its status on its letters and order forms.[21]

An investment company may calculate its maximum dividend on the same basis as any other public company but it is afforded greater flexibility by Sec. 41 of the Companies Act 1980 in that it can ignore any capital losses in determining the maximum dividend payable. An investment company can, subject to a number of conditions, pay a dividend equal to the amount of its accumulated realized revenue profits less its accumulated revenue losses (both realized and unrealized). The most important restriction is that after the payment of the dividend the company's assets must be equal to or greater than $1\frac{1}{2}$ times its liabilities. Thus, if an investment company wishes to take advantage of the provision in Sec. 41 of not restricting its dividend by virtue of the existence of capital losses, it (a) cannot then distribute capital profits, and (b) must apply the 'asset ratio test'.

It should be noted that the asset ratio test will be affected by the way in which it is proposed to fund the dividend in that the result will depend on whether the dividend will reduce assets (if paid out of a positive cash balance) or increase liabilities (if paid from an overdraft). Suppose, for example, that an investment company has assets of £1200 and liabilities of £600. Then:

(a) Dividend paid out of cash (i.e. liabilities held constant).

	Initial position (£)	After dividend (£)	Maximum dividend (£)
Assets	1200	900 (3)	300
Liabilities	600	600 (2)	

(b) Dividends paid out of an overdraft (assets held constant).

	Initial position (£)	After dividend (£)	Maximum dividend (£)
Assets	1200	1200 (3)	
Liabilities	600	800 (2)	200

20 For a detailed list of conditions readers should refer to Sec. 41 of the Companies Act 1980.
21 European Communities Act 1972, Sec. 9(7), as amended by Companies Act 1980, Third Schedule, Para. 45.

The various provisions outlined above are summarized and illustrated in Example 3.2.

EXAMPLE 3.2
The balance sheet of Company A is summarized below:

		£
Total assets		4000
less Total liabilities		1000
		3000
Share capital		200
Share premium account		800
Unrealized profits		
Revenue	200	
Capital	100	
		300
Unrealized losses		
Revenue	(200)	
Capital	(800)	
		(1000)
Realized profits		
less Realized losses		
Revenue	2300	
Capital	400	
		2700
		£3000

We will now work out the maximum dividend on the assumption that Company A is (a) a private limited company, (b) a public limited company and (c) an investment company.

(a) *Private company* Maximum dividend is the total of the realized profits less losses, i.e. £2700.

(b) *A public company* In addition to the above restriction a public company is subject to the capital maintenance rule that, after distribution, the net assets must equal the share capital plus undistributable reserves. In this case the unrealized profits are more than offset by the unrealized losses and thus do not need to be included as part of the undistributable reserves. Hence, in this case the maximum dividend is given by:

	£	£
Net assets		3000
less Share capital	200	
Share premium	800	
	——	1000
Maximum dividend		2000

(c) *An investment company*   On the basis of the capital maintenance test the maximum dividend is £2000 (as would be the case for any public company). Using the alternative allowed by Sec. 41 the maximum dividend is the excess of the realized revenue profits over all revenue losses, i.e. £2300 − £200 = £2100, subject to the application of the asset ratio test.

   (i) If a dividend of £2100 was paid by cash, total assets would fall from £4000 to £1900 which is more than 1.5 times the liabilities of £1000.

  (ii) If the dividend was paid by overdraft liabilities would increase to £3100 which would require asset cover of 1.5(£3100) = £4650, i.e. more than £4000.

Hence the maximum dividend is £2100 but only if such a payment did not increase the liabilities. The lower limit of the maximum dividend is £2000 (as this can be justified on the alternative capital maintenance role) whilst a dividend of between £2000 and £2100 would be possible if only a proportion of the dividend was paid out of an overdraft.

Realized profits

It is clear from the above that the most important element in assessing a company's distributable profits is deciding on what constitutes realized profits and losses. Neither the Companies Act 1980 nor the Companies Act 1981 gives specific guidance on this matter, the former Act does however provide some help in specific circumstances whilst the latter Act gives some general guidance.

   The 1980 Act states that a provision, as defined by the Companies Act 1948,[22] i.e. an amount set aside for depreciation or diminution in value of assets or retained in order to provide a known liability whose amount cannot be determined with substantial accuracy, is to be treated as a realized loss. There is only one exception which is

22 Companies Act 1948, Eighth Schedule, Para. 27.

that any provision to take account of the diminution of the value of a fixed asset that arose on the revaluation of *all* the company's fixed assets may be regarded as an unrealized loss.[23]

On a related issue – the consequence of a surplus on the revaluation of a fixed asset which is being depreciated – the Act permits companies to convert unrealized profits to realized profits as the asset is depreciated.[24] For example, a company purchased a fixed asset for £50 000 when its expected life was 10 years and its expected residual value was zero. Using the straight-line method of depreciation the annual charge would be £5000 and, after 2 years, the net book value would be £40 000. If after those two years, this asset were revalued to £72 000 there would be a revaluation surplus of £32 000, that is £72 000 less £40 000. The revised future annual depreciation charge would be £72 000 ÷ 8 = £9000.[25]

The additional annual depreciation charge of £4000 will then be added to the realized profits of the company year by year for the purposes of determining its distributable profit. Thus, by the end of 8 years the original unrealized profit of £32 000 would have been regarded as fully distributable.

As stated above the 1981 Act provides some general guidance which amplifies but does not amend the position stated in the 1980 Act. The 1981 Act states that realized profits are:

> such profits of the company as fall to be treated as realized profits for the purposes of those accounts in accordance with principles generally accepted with respect to the determination for accounting purposes of realized profits at the time when those accounts are prepared.[26]

The key phrases in the above are 'principles generally accepted' and 'at the time when these accounts are prepared'.

As explained in Chapter 2, the main sources of authority in deciding what are 'principles generally accepted' are the legal principles laid down in the First Schedule of the Companies Act 1981 and the pronouncements of the accountancy professional bodies through, in particular, the various statements of standard accounting policies. In this context an important document is a *Statement of Guidance* published by the ICAEW in 1982.[27]

23 Companies Act 1980, Sec. 39(4).

24 Companies Act 1980, Sec. 39(5).

25 This is in accordance with the provisions of SSAP 12, 'Accounting for depreciation', discussed in Chapter 15.

26 Companies Act 1981, First Schedule, Para. 90.

27 *Statement of Guidance – The determination of realized profits and disclosure of distributable profits in the context of the Companies Acts 1948 to 1981*, ICAEW, September 1982.

The statement draws particular attention to the prudence and accruals concepts outlined in SSAP 2, 'Disclosure of accounting policies', and the parallel provisions of the 1981 Act.[28] It is assumed that readers are familiar with the four fundamental accounting concepts discussed in Chapter 2 and at this stage we can restrict ourselves to quoting from the definition of the prudence concept which states:

> revenues and profits are not anticipated, but are recognized for inclusion in the profit and loss account only when realized in the form either of cash or of other assets the ultimate cash realization of which can be assessed with reasonable certainty . . .[29]

In the guidance statement stress is placed on the phrase 'reasonable certainty' which is stated to be the limiting factor in assessing whether profit may be regarded as being 'realized'.

The legal definition of realized profits refers to the application of principles generally agreed at the time the accounts are prepared. This implies that a subsequent change in accepted principles will not be accompanied by a reclassification of realized and unrealized profits. The definition also holds out the prospect that the principles might change over time by, for example, the issue of new or amended Statements of Standard Accounting Practice and would not require legislative changes.

The guidance statement avers that, in general, a profit required by a Statement of Standard Accounting Practice to be recognized in the profit and loss account should be treated as realized profit, unless the statement specifically indicates the contrary. In future as statements are revised and new ones issued, it is expected that they will deal specifically with matters relating to the determination of realized profit. The guidance statement refers to an earlier Statement of Standard Accounting Practice – SSAP 9, 'Stocks and work in progress' – which had, following its issue in 1975, generated some controversy in that it requires that, under certain circumstances, profit should be recognized on uncompleted long-term contracts. Doubts had been expressed as to whether such profits could be treated as realized under the terms of the Companies Acts. The view expressed in the guidance statement is that such a profit could be so treated because the relevant principle for recognizing profit in SSAP 9 was the 'reasonable certainty' of the final outcome which meant that the requirements of SSAP 9 were not in conflict with the statutory provisions.

---

28 Companies Act 1981, First Schedule, Paras. 12 and 13.
29 SSAP 2, 'Disclosure of accounting policies', Para. 14.

One of the more common examples of an unrealized profit is the surplus on revaluation of fixed assets. ED 16 (supplement to SSAP 6, 'Extraordinary items and prior year adjustments') proposes that all such surplus be credited to reserves. If, later, the asset is sold the profit and loss account would only be credited with the difference between the sale proceeds and the book value of the asset but the previously recognized unrealized profit which had now, by virtue of the sale, become realized, would not be reflected in the profit and loss account. The sale would of course increase the distributable reserves of the company and although neither statute nor any Statement of Standard Accounting Practice requires companies to distinguish between distributable and non-distributable reserves, it is necessary, if a 'true and fair' view is to be provided to indicate by way of note any significant realizations of previously recognized unrealized profits. The effect of these proposals, which are in accord with general practice, is that some elements of realized profit will not be recognized in the profit and loss account. This is not thought to be a wholly satisfactory position and is a subject of further review by the ASC.[30]

Summary

Statute law in respect of distributable profits places considerable stress on the question of realization with the overriding principle being that profits that have been, or are soon expected to be, converted into cash, can be paid as dividends. Thus the law does not require private companies, which comprise the vast majority of companies, to maintain capital and such companies can pay a dividend even if the fixed asset base has been eroded by unrealized losses. If the directors of a private company wish to act in this way it is a matter for them, or their share-holders, to decide. In the case of public companies creditors and minority shareholders are afforded greater protection because of the existence of the provision to maintain the capital base (share capital plus undistributable reserves) which is, however, in practice calculated by reference to historical accounting principles.

This liberal approach to the determination of the profit available for dividend is, from an economic point of view, a good thing in so far as it allows funds to flow from unprofitable and marginally profitable enterprises to companies where they can be put to better use. Whilst

---

30 'A review of SSAP 6', Para. 2.12, a Discussion Paper issued by the ASC in 1983. *See* page 671.

it is right that directors should be allowed to reduce the size of their companies through the payment of dividends this freedom does reinforce the need for financial accounts to show the effect of such decisions and hence provides a further justification for the case for requiring the publishing of accounts based on current value principles.

This section has concentrated on legal and pseudolegal considerations but we should conclude with one practical point drawn from the world of financial management. In the vast majority of cases the limiting factor in fixing a dividend policy is the availability of cash and the alternative uses to which that cash can be put rather than the availability of distributable profit.

Recommended reading

R. H. Parker and G. C. Harcourt (eds.), *Readings in the Concept and Measurement of Income*, Cambridge University Press, Cambridge, 1969.

T. A. Lee, *Income and Value Measurement: Theory and Practice*, 2nd edn., Nelson, London, 1980.

Questions

3.1 (a) State what you understand by the term 'capital maintenance' and give examples of TWO capital maintenance concepts. (10 marks)

(b) Outline the practical reasons for measuring and reporting profit.
(10 marks)
(20 marks)

A. Cert. A. The Regulatory Framework of Accounting, December 1984.

3.2 (a) Explain how far the measurement of income may be considered to be related to the measurement of capital. (10 marks)

(b) What do you understand by the entity and proprietory concepts of capital, and what are their implications for capital maintenance?
(10 marks)
(20 marks)

A. Cert. A. The Regulatory Framework of Accounting, June 1982.

3.3 In recent years some accounting theorists have lost faith in (1) Historical Cost (HC) accounting, and now propound, in particular, three alternative accounting systems, based on (2) Current Purchasing Power (CPP), (3) Replacement Cost (RC), and (4) Net Realizable Value (NRV).

You are required to compare and contrast the four systems, with regard to their usefulness and reliability, in an inflationary period, for:

(a) income measurement; and (8 marks)

(b) capital maintenance. (8 marks)

(16 marks)

A. Cert. A. Advanced Financial Accounting, June 1982.

3.4 The following are details of three separate companies' summarized balance sheets at 31 March 1982.

	Angie plc	Betty plc	Cathy Ltd
	£'000	£'000	£'000
Fixed assets	2500	380	500
Current assets	900	180	300
Current liabilities	(700)	(160)	(200)
	2700	400	600
Share capital	200	300	2000
Reserves:			
Revaluation	1100	(200)	—
Realized capital profit	800	—	—
Brought forward realized revenue profit (loss)	400	500	(1600)
Current year realized revenue profit (loss)	200	(200)	200
	2700	400	600

Angie and Betty are public companies and Cathy a private company under the Companies Act 1980.

Angie's property, previously included in the financial statements at original cost of £900 000, was revalued on 1 April 1981 at £2 million. This revalued amount is included in the figures above, subject to the full amount being written off equally over the next 50 years from 1 April 1981. Prior to this date, no depreciation had been provided on property. At 31 March 1982, no transfer had been made between revaluation reserve and realized revenue profit.

You are required to:

(a) **compare briefly the bases for calculating the maximum distribution under the provisions of the Companies Act 1980 in respect of public, private and investment companies** (8 marks),

(b) calculate the maximum distribution that Angie, Betty and Cathy could each make under the Companies Act **1980** (8 marks)**, and**

(c) calculate the maximum distribution if Betty plc is an investment company and its dividend is to be paid from bank overdraft (3 marks).

(19 marks)

ICAEW Financial Accounting II, July 1982.

4 Accounting for Inflation

Introduction

In Chapter 3 we suggested that the historical cost asset valuation/capital maintenance system (which we will refer to as conventional accounting) suffers from numerous shortcomings when tested against the aims and objectives of financial accounting. This observation is not a new one,[1] but the case for accounting reform has only been generally accepted within the last 5–10 years, and it may be instructive to consider the possible reasons for the change in the attitude of many accountants.

The most obvious factor is the high rate of inflation which has been a feature of economies of the industrialized countries in recent years. The British economy provides a good – a far too good – example of this. The rates of inflation for the UK in recent years as measured by the changes in the Index of Retail Prices are shown in the following table:

Year	Inflation (%)
1983	5.2
1982	5.2
1981	12.0
1980	14.1
1979	17.8
1978	8.8

Source: Derived from the Index of Retail Prices.

It was not always thus. The price increase for the whole of the 10 years to 1962 was only of the order of 28%.

1 See Sir R. Edwards, 'The nature and measurement of income', originally published as a series of articles in The Accountant, July–October 1938; reprinted in Studies in Accounting (W. T. Baxter and S. Davidson, eds), ICAEW, London, 1977, pp. 96–140. This is only one, and by no means the earliest, of many references that could have been selected. In this classic paper Sir Ronald Edwards, an accountant who was both a university professor and a successful businessman, clearly outlined many of the problems inherent in conventional accounting and discussed many important matters which are still controversial issues.

The apparently permanent increase in the rate of inflation has highlighted the shortcomings of conventional accounting which we discussed in the previous chapter.

While rapid and sustained inflation was undoubtedly the major cause of the general acceptance of the need for accounting reform, there are other possible reasons which should not be overlooked. One factor which may well have been significant is the fact that financial accounting information now plays a far more important part in the economy than it did in the days when the main purpose of published accounts was the transmission of information by directors to shareholders. This change is evidenced by the extent to which accounting information is used by groups other than shareholders; for example, by employees in wage negotiations. The reporting of a profit which is largely illusory due to the effect of inflation is especially dangerous if the profit figure is used as an excuse to demand wage increases which will have to be paid in real pound notes.

The increasing involvement of government in companies' affairs is another important factor. The profit figure is an important element in this relationship in that it not only provides the basis for taxation, but is also used for such other purposes as price and dividend controls and antimonopoly legislation. In an extreme case a company whose profits are overstated because of the defects of the conventional accounting system may find itself faced by wage claims it cannot pay, be prevented from increasing its prices, be accused of exploiting its market position by making excessive profits and be required to pay too much tax. It is therefore not surprising that the business community was prepared to accept accounting reform.

The path towards accounting reform has been tortuous and is, as far as Britain is concerned, outlined in Figure 4.1, which can be used as a guide to the contents of this and the following chapters. There are two lines shown on Figure 4.1. One represents the current purchasing power method, i.e. the adjusted historical cost asset valuation basis combined with the maintenance of real money capital. The second path reflects the progress towards the adoption of a system of current value accounting which, so far as Britain is concerned, combines a variant of the replacement cost approach to valuation with a physical capital maintenance measure of profit.

In this chapter we will briefly outline the existing state of play and discuss the current purchasing power (CPP) model; current value accounting will be the subject of the next two chapters.

CPP accounting retains most of the significant features of historical

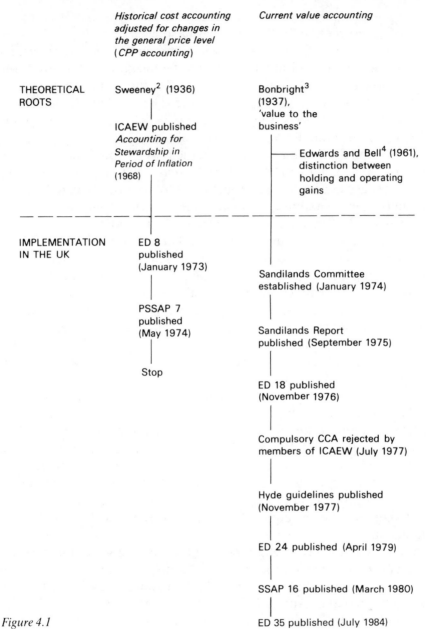

Figure 4.1

2 F. N. Sweeney, *Stabilized Accounts*, Harper, New York, 1936 (reprinted by Arno Press, New York, 1977).

3 J. C. Bonbright, *The Valuation of Property*, Michie, Charlottesville, Va., 1937 (reprinted 1965).

4 E. O. Edwards and P. W. Bell, *The Theory and Measurement of Business Income*, University of California Press, Stanford, Calif., 1961.

cost accounting, and the only real change is the replacement of money unit of measurement by the purchasing power unit. It can be seen that when compared to a system which attempts to measure current values the CPP model involves a far less radical departure from the conventional method, and it is perhaps not surprising that the first tentative steps on the path to accounting reform taken by the British accountancy profession were on the CPP route; much the same occurred in the United States and Australia.[5]

In 1968 the Research Foundation of the ICAEW published *Accounting for Stewardship in a Period of Inflation*. The title is instructive in that it suggests a far more restrictive view of the objectives of financial accounts than is accepted nowadays and does illustrate the extent of the changes that have since taken place. The methods outlined in that document were not original. They had been described in English by Sweeney in 1936[6] and his work was itself based on work done in Germany during the period of hyperinflation which followed the First World War. The significance of the publication was that it was produced by a body associated with a leading professional accounting institute and indicated that that body was apparently prepared to initiate reform. The seeds took a long time to germinate, and we had to wait until 1973 for the publication of ED 8 by the ASC. ED 8 proposed that companies should be required to publish, along with their conventional accounts, supplementary statements which would, in effect, be their profit and loss accounts and balance sheets based on CPP principles. ED 8 was followed by the issue of Provisional Statement of Standard Accounting Practice (PSSAP) 7, in May 1974. The inclusion of the word 'provisional' in the title of this standard (the only occasion on which this has been done by the ASC) reflected the uncertainties in the mind of the accountancy profession on this matter, since it meant that companies were requested rather than required to comply with the standard.

Many users of accounting reports, including the government, were dissatisfied with this approach. Consequently, the government established its own committee of enquiry into inflation accounting in January 1974, i.e. after the issue of ED 8. The committee was chaired by Mr, now Sir, Francis Sandilands and its report (usually referred to as the

---

5 For example, in the United States the FASB (the US equivalent of the British ASC) produced an Exposure Draft in December 1974 which was similar in content to ED 8, but the Securities Exchange Commission (a US Government Agency) in 1976 called for the disclosure by larger companies of additional information concerning the replacement costs of fixed assets and stock.

6 F. N. Sweeney, *op. cit.*

Sandilands Report) was issued in September of 1975.[7] The committee recommended the adoption of a system of accounting known as 'current cost accounting' which is, as will be shown later, a very different creature from CPP accounting. As a result of the publication of the Sandilands Report, the ASC abandoned its own proposals and set up a working party, the Inflation Accounting Steering Group (IASG) to prepare an initial Statement of Standard Accounting Practice based on the Sandilands' proposals. The outcome of this group's labours was ED 18, 'Current cost accounting', which was published in November 1976. This publication came under a good deal of attack from many quarters, including those who supported the main principles of current cost accounting (CCA). The Exposure Draft was considered by many to be unnecessarily complicated and to deal with too many subsidiary issues. The draft was also attacked by many rank and file – some would say backwoods – members of the ICAEW, and their efforts resulted in the passing of a resolution in July 1977 by members of the Institute which rejected any compulsory introduction of CCA.

This did not halt the advance of CCA. The government, in a discussion document issued in July 1977 (*The future of company reports*), reiterated its support for the adoption of CCA, while in November 1977 the accountancy profession issued a set of interim recommendations to cover the period until a revised set of detailed proposals could be formulated. These recommendations are commonly called the Hyde guidelines after the name of the chairman of the committee responsible for the recommendations. A second Exposure Draft, ED 24, was published in April 1979 which was followed by the issue of SSAP 16 in March 1980. SSAP 16 was allowed to prevail for 3 years while the effect of the introduction of CCA was evaluated. Following this period ED 35 was published in July 1984. SSAP 16 and ED 35 will be discussed in more detail in Chapters 6 and 7.

CPP accounting

The elements of CPP accounting have already been introduced, i.e. the adjusted historical cost basis of valuation coupled with profit measurement based on the maintenance of real money capital. Before describing how these can be combined to produce a coherent accounting model it will be as well to consider how, and from whose point of view, the purchasing power of money should be measured.

7 *Report of the Inflation Accounting Committee*, Cmnd 6225, HMSO, London, 1975.

The prices of different goods and services change by different amounts, and the problem faced by those responsible for measuring changes in the purchasing power of money is to find a suitable average value to reflect the different individual price changes which have taken place during the period under review. This could be done by considering all the different goods and services which are traded in the country during the period and to compare their prices with those prevailing in the comparison or base period. This is a massive task, but it is possible to arrive at the required answer by indirect methods as is done in the United States in the calculation of the gross domestic product implicit price deflator.

An alternative approach is to select a sample of goods and services, measure the changes in their prices, and then average them. This method is used to construct the Index of Retail Prices (RPI), which is based on the price changes which affect 'middle income' households. In order to construct the index it is necessary to assign weights to the various price changes to take account of their relative importance. These weights are based on the spending patterns of a sample of householders which is drawn so as to exclude households with incomes which are significantly higher and significantly lower than the average.

One of the major provisions of PSSAP 7 was the stipulation that changes in the purchasing power of money should be measured by reference to the RPI. The consequence of this proposal was that changes in purchasing power were not to be measured from the point of view of the individual firm or even all firms but from the point of view of individual consumers. Thus it was the intention that CPP accounts should not be regarded as providing proxies to current value accounts, but rather as restatements of the conventional historical cost accounts in terms which attempted to adjust for the effect of inflation on shareholders and other individuals.

The basic principle underlying CPP accounts is that all monetary amounts should be converted to pounds of CPP in a manner which is analogous to the way in which sums expressed in different foreign currencies are translated to a common base. Assume that we are attempting to measure the CPP profit for a transaction which involved the purchase of goods for £200 in January 1983 and their sale for £300 in December 1983. The RPI was 325.9 at the date of purchase and 342.8 at the date of sale. If we wish to measure the profit in terms of purchasing power at December 1983 we would need to convert the £200, which represented January 1983 purchasing power, in terms of December 1983 purchasing power. In order to carry out such calculations it will be helpful if we use symbols which indicate the purchasing power associated with the monetary amount; we will do this by specifying that £(Jan. 83) means January 1983 pounds and so on.

The calculation of CPP profit for the above transaction could then be shown as follows:

	£(Dec. 83)
Sales	300.00
Purchases, $£(Jan. 83)\ 200 \times \dfrac{342.8}{325.9}$	210.37
	£(Dec. 83) 89.63

The equation

$$£(\text{Jan. }83)\ 200 \times \frac{342.8}{325.9} = £(\text{Dec. }83)\ 210.37$$

means that a consumer would require £210.37 in December 1983 in order to be able to command the same purchasing power as was available from the possession of £200 in January 1983.

The consequence of the extension of the basic CPP principle to the profit and loss account is that all items will be expressed in terms of current (i.e. year-end) purchasing power, while the same will be true in the balance sheet. Thus all items in the balance sheet will have to be converted in terms of year-end purchasing power except the so-called monetary assets and liabilities which are automatically expressed in such terms. Example 4.1 illustrates the preparation of CPP accounts in the absence of monetary assets and liabilities.

EXAMPLE 4.1
Bell Limited's historical cost and CPP balance sheets at 31 December 19X6 (on which date the RPI was 120) are given below:

Bell Limited
Balance sheet as at 31 December 19X6

	Historical cost £	Note	CPP £(31 Dec. X6)
Fixed assets			
Cost	10 000	(a)	12 000
Accumulated depreciation	4 000	(b)	4 800
	6 000		7 200
Stock	3 300	(c)	3 600
	9 300	£(31 Dec.19X6)	10 800
Share capital	4 000	(d)	4 800
Retained earnings	5 300	(e)	6 000
	9 300	£(31 Dec.19X6)	10 800

Notes

(a) The fixed assets were purchased for £10 000 on 1 January 19X3 when the RPI = 100:

$$£(1 \text{ Jan. X3}) \; 10\,000 \times \frac{120}{100} = £(31 \text{ Dec. X6}) \; 12\,000.$$

(b) Bell Limited depreciates its fixed assets on a straight-line basis over 10 years (assuming a zero scrap value). Thus at the end of 19X6 four-tenths of the asset has been written off and the accumulated depreciation figure is thus

$$4/10 \text{ of } £(31 \text{ Dec. X6}) \; 12\,000 = £(31 \text{ Dec. X6}) \; 4800.$$

(c) The company's stock was purchased for £3300 on 30 September 19X6 when the RPI was 110:

$$£(30 \text{ Sep. X6}) \; 3300 \times \frac{120}{110} = £(31 \text{ Dec. X6}) \; 3600.$$

(d) The share capital consists of 4000 £1 ordinary shares which were issued on 1 January 19X3 when the RPI was 100:

$$£(1 \text{ Jan. X3}) \; 4000 \times \frac{120}{100} = £(31 \text{ Dec. X6}) \; 4800.$$

(e) Had CPP accounts been prepared in the past the CPP retained earnings would have emerged in the same way that retained earnings emerge in the historical cost accounts. In this case the CPP retained earnings can be found by treating it as the balancing figure in the CPP balance sheet. It is not possible to find the CPP retained earnings from its historical cost equivalent as the relationship between them depends on the aggregate of the differences between the CPP and historical cost figures of all the balance sheet items.

During 19X7 Bell Limited engaged in the following transactions:

(a) On 31 March 19X7 it sold half its stock for cash of £(31 Mar. X7) 5500. £(31 Mar. X7) 4400 of the proceeds were used to purchase additional stock while the balance was paid out as a dividend.

(b) On 1 July 19X7 one-quarter of the 1 January 19X7 stock was sold for £(1 July X7) 2750; the proceeds were used to pay for the overhead expenses which may be assumed to accrue evenly over the year.

The RPI moved as follows:

Date	Index
1 January 19X7	120
31 March 19X7	121
1 July 19X7 (which may be assumed to be the average value for the year)	132
31 December 19X7	143

The CPP profit and loss account for the year ended 31 December 19X7 is given below:

Bell Limited
Profit and loss account

	£(31 Dec. X7)	£(31 Dec. X7)
Sales, £(31 Mar. X7) $5\,500 \times \frac{143}{121}$	6 500	
Sales, £(1 Jul. X7) $2\,750 \times \frac{143}{132}$	2 979	9 479
less Opening stock, £(30 Sep. X6) $3\,300 \times \frac{143}{110}$	4 290	
Purchases, £(31 Mar. X7) $4\,400 \times \frac{143}{121}$	5 200	
	9 490	
less Closing stock, £(30 Sep. X6) $825 \times \frac{143}{110}$		
$+$ £(31 Mar. X7) $4\,400 \times \frac{143}{121}$	6 272	3 218
Gross profit		6 261

Gross profit b/f		6 261
less Overheads,		
£(1 Jul. X7) $2\,750 \times \dfrac{143}{132}$	2 979	
Depreciation,		
£(1 Jan. X3) $10\,000 \times \dfrac{1}{10} \times \dfrac{143}{100}$	1 430	4 409
Net profit		1 852
less Dividends,		
£(31 Mar. X7) $1\,100 \times \dfrac{143}{121}$		1 300
		552
Retained earnings, 1 Jan. X7,		
£(1 Jan. X7) $6\,000 \times \dfrac{143}{120}$		7 150
Retained earnings, 31 Dec. X7	£(31 Dec. X7)	7 702

Bell Limited
CPP balance sheet as at 31 December 19X7

	£(31 Dec. X7)	£(31 Dec. X7)
Fixed assets:		
Cost, £(1 Jan. X3) $10\,000 \times \dfrac{143}{100}$	14 300	
Accumulated depreciation,		
£(1 Jan. X3) $5\,000 \times \dfrac{143}{100}$	7 150	7 150
Stock:		
£(30 Sep. X6) $825 \times \dfrac{143}{110}$	1 072	
£(31 Mar. X7) $4\,400 \times \dfrac{143}{121}$	5 200	6 272
	£(31 Dec. X7)	13 422
Share capital,		
£(1 Jan. X3) $4\,000 \times \dfrac{143}{100}$		5 720
Retained earnings		
(from the profit and loss account)		7 702
	£(31 Dec. X7)	13 422

Example 4.1 illustrates the necessity of identifying the dates on which the different transactions took place in order to determine the denominator of the conversion factor (i.e. the RPI at the date of the transaction): the numerator is always the same – the RPI at the balance sheet date. In the example it was practicable to deal with each sale separately, but in practice it would usually be found necessary to make some simplifying assumption, e.g. that the sales accrued evenly over the year, which would mean that the average value of the RPI would be taken as the denominator in the conversion factor. A similar approach would probably have to be taken in respect of purchases and overhead expenses.

The treatment of depreciation merits special attention. Note that in Example 4.1 the conversion factor used in the calculation of the depreciation expense in the profit and loss account and the fixed asset items in the balance sheet is $143/100$. The denominator, 100, is the RPI at the date on which the fixed asset was acquired. It is sometimes suggested that when calculating the depreciation expense the denominator should be the average value of the RPI for the year on the grounds that 'depreciation is written off over the year'. This is indeed so, but the vital point which is missing in this argument is that the pound of depreciation which is being written off in 19X7 is a pound of 1 January 19X3 as it was pounds with a 1 January 19X3 purchasing power which were given up in exchange for the asset.

Monetary assets and liabilities

A common feature of inflation is that debtors gain in purchasing power while creditors lose.[8] And, because free lunches are not a common feature of our economy, it is – to use the terminology of game theory – a zero-sum game; the debtors' gains equal the creditors' losses. In other words, all other things being equal one effect of inflation is to transfer purchasing power from creditors to debtors.

The reason for this is that if a person borrows money in a period of inflation he will repay it in pounds of lower purchasing power (value) than those which he obtained when he was granted the loan. The longer the loan then, so long as the inflation continues, the greater will be the difference between the values of the pound notes borrowed and of the pound notes repaid. Thus, a houseowner with a mortgage whose

8 It is possible for the contracts between lenders and borrowers to be drawn up in terms of purchasing power instead of monetary units. These are often called index-linked agreements.

income has kept step with inflation may well be amongst those hard-faced men who 'have done well out of inflation' in that his mortgage payments constitute a continually declining percentage of his income.

It is, of course, possible for creditors to protect themselves in some cases by increasing the interest rate to take into account the expected rate of inflation. If this is done the market rate of interest will be based upon the market's view of the likely future rates of inflation. Thus, a quoted rate of interest may be broken down into two parts, one, which we may term the 'real' interest rate, is that which would have been charged in the absence of inflationary expectations; the balance represents the inflation premium. This point has a good deal of relevance to some important questions about the treatment of gains and losses on monetary items. We will return to this point later.[9]

If the above analysis is extended to a company it can be said that a company will lose purchasing power in a period of inflation if, taking the year as a whole, it holds net monetary assets (in simple terms if its cash plus debtors exceeds its creditors). Conversely, it will gain in purchasing power if, on average, it is in a net monetary liability position. The calculation depends on the meaning of monetary assets and liabilities.

In PSSAP 7 monetary items were defined as 'Assets, liabilities, or capital, the amounts of which were fixed by contract or statute in terms of numbers of pounds regardless of changes in the purchasing power of the pound'.[10]

Let us first consider the distinction between monetary and non-monetary liabilities. A non-monetary liability would be one in which the payment of interest, or the return on capital, or both, are not subject to a limit expressed in terms of a given number of pound notes. Such liabilities are rare in the private sector of the economy, but the British Government has issued a number of securities in which the returns are dependent on movements of the RPI. In contrast, the obligations on the part of the borrower of a monetary liability are fixed and are not affected by changes in purchasing power.

We will now turn to the distinction between monetary and non-monetary capital. Preference shares which do not entitle their owners to a share of any surplus on liquidation of the company are clearly monetary items in that the rights associated with them – the annual dividend and the repayment of principal – are subjected to upper limits which are expressed in monetary terms. Conversely, equity capital is

9 *See* page 114.
10 PSSAP 7, 'Accounting for changes in the purchasing power of money', Para. 28.

a non-monetary item because no limits are placed on the amounts that can be paid to the owners of this type of capital. The effect of inflation on the relationship between equity and preference shareholders is similar to that on the relationship between debtors and creditors, i.e. equity shareholders will gain in purchasing power at the expense of preference shareholders because the latters' interests are fixed in money terms and will decline with a fall in the value of money. This point will be illustrated in Example 4.3.

Monetary assets are those assets the values of which are fixed in monetary terms, e.g. cash and debtors. Non-monetary assets, such as stock and fixed assets, are those assets whose values may be expected to vary according to changes in the rate of inflation. Consider as examples debtors and stock and suppose that a company has £100 invested in each of these assets. Assume that as a result of some catastrophe the RPI increases by 100% (or the purchasing power of money falls by 50%) overnight. The violent change in the RPI will not affect the debtors figure in that the asset will still only realize 100 £1 notes, but it is highly probably that it will have an effect on the stock figure as the cost of the stock will be likely to rise. In other words it would take $(100 + x)$ £1 notes to buy the stock using the less valuable pounds.

The classification of investments into monetary and non-monetary categories often appears to be difficult, but this is not really so because we can employ the same analysis as was used in our discussion of capital. If the investment is in a fixed interest security where the dividend or interest and the repayment of principal is fixed in monetary terms, then it is a monetary item. An investment in equity shares where there is no limit on the amount that can be received is a non-monetary item.

The computation of gains and losses on a company's net monetary position

We showed earlier that one effect of inflation is to transfer purchasing power from creditors to debtors; we will now show how the amount of the creditors' loss and debtors' gain can be calculated. We will at this stage concentrate on interest-free credit and hence ignore the possibility of creditors reducing or eliminating their loss by incorporating an inflation premium in the rate of interest charged.

Suppose that A Limited borrowed £(1 Jan. X4) 300 from B Limited on 1 January 19X4 which it repaid on 30 September 19X4. The year end for both companies is 31 December 19X4. Assume that the RPI moved as follows:

Date:	1 January X4	30 September X4	31 December X4
Index no.:	120	150	160

We will first consider the position from A Limited's point of view. The company borrowed 300 £1 notes when the index was 120 and repaid the same number of £1 notes when the index was 150. In order to calculate the gain on purchasing power involved we need to convert one or other of the pounds borrowed or repaid so that the comparison can be made in terms of common purchasing power. We will convert the pounds borrowed in terms of 30 September 19X4 purchasing power. The calculation could then be made as follows:

$$£(30 \text{ Sep. X4})$$

Purchasing power acquired,

$£(1 \text{ Jan. X4}) \, 300 \times \dfrac{150}{120}$ 375

Purchasing power given up on repayment of the loan   300

Gain $£(30 \text{ Sep. X4})$ 75

The gain in purchasing power, expressed in 30 September 19X4 purchasing power, is thus $£(30 \text{ Sep. X4})$ 75. If the company's year end is 31 December then for the purpose of the annual accounts the gain will have to be converted to 31 December 19X4 purchasing power:

$$\text{Gain} = £(30 \text{ Sep. X4}) \, 75 \times \frac{160}{150}$$

$$= £(31 \text{ Dec. X4}) \, 80.$$

Note that the analysis has been confined to the borrowing made by A Limited. If A Limited has used all or part of the borrowing to invest in monetary assets (which would include keeping the cash in a bank) it would experience a loss in purchasing power due to the holding of a monetary asset in a period of inflation.

If we consider the creditor, B Limited, a similar analysis will show that its loss of purchasing power resulting from the loan is $£(31 \text{ Dec.} X4)$ 80. In making the loan B Limited gave up purchasing power amounting to $£(1 \text{ Jan. X4}) \, 300$ or $£(31 \text{ Dec. X4}) \, 400$. The repayment of the loan increased B Limited's purchasing power by $£(30 \text{ Sep. X4})$

300 or £(31 Dec. X4) 320. Thus its loss of purchasing power is £(31 Dec. X4) 80.

The above analysis can be generalized as follows:

Suppose that a monetary asset of £(1)A was acquired at time 1 when the RPI was I_1, was sold at time 2 when the RPI was I_2 and that the year end is considered to be time 3 when the RPI was I_3. Then the purchasing power given up by virtue of the investment in the monetary asset is given by

$$£(1)A = £(2)A\frac{I_2}{I_1}.$$

The purchasing power regained from the disposal of the asset is given by £(2)A. The loss of purchasing power in time 2 purchasing power is

$$£(2)A\frac{I_2}{I_1} - £(2)A = £(2)A\left(\frac{I_2}{I_1} - 1\right),$$

and the loss of purchasing power in time 3 (year end) purchasing power is

$$£(3)A\left(\frac{I_2}{I_1} - 1\right)\frac{I_3}{I_2} = £(3)AI_3\left(\frac{1}{I_1} - \frac{1}{I_2}\right).$$

In the special case where the asset is still in existence at the year end, $I_2 = I_3$ and the loss can be stated as follows:

$$\text{Loss} = £(3)AI_3\left(\frac{1}{I_1} - \frac{1}{I_3}\right) = £(3)A\left(\frac{I_3}{I_1} - 1\right). \tag{4.1}$$

If £A is replaced by $-£A$ the above approach can be used to calculate the gain in purchasing power resulting from holding a monetary liability in a period of rising prices.

In the above analysis we concentrated on a single monetary item, but in practice a company's net monetary position will fluctuate on a daily basis. The foregoing method can be adapted to deal with this problem in the following way.

Suppose that a company starts the year on 1 January with net monetary assets of £200, reduces its net monetary assets by £280 on 1 April and finally increases its net monetary assets by £100 on 1 October. If this were the case the company would have held net monetary assets of £200 for 3 months (January–March), net monetary liabilities of £80 for the next 6 months (April–September) and been a net monetary creditor of £20 for the last 3 months of the year. An alternative way of viewing the position, which we will use to calculate the total loss or gain on the company's monetary position, is to say that it: (a) held a monetary asset of £200 for the whole of the year; (b) held a monetary liability of £280 for the 9-month period from April to December; (c) held a monetary asset of £100 for the 3-month period from October to December.

Assume that the appropriate index numbers are:

Date:	1 January	1 April	1 October	31 December
Index no.:	100	140	150	180

The loss or gain on each of the three hypothetical items can then be calculated by substituting the appropriate values in equation (4.1) as follows:

(a) Loss = £(31 Dec.) $200 \times \left(\dfrac{180}{100} - 1 \right)$;

(b) Loss = $-$£(31 Dec.) $280 \times \left(\dfrac{180}{140} - 1 \right)$;

(c) Loss = £(31 Dec.) $100 \times \left(\dfrac{180}{150} - 1 \right)$.

The total loss is given by:

$$£(31 \text{ Dec.}) \left\{ 200\left(\frac{180}{100} - 1 \right) - 280\left(\frac{180}{140} - 1 \right) + 100\left(\frac{180}{150} - 1 \right) \right\}$$

$$= £(31 \text{ Dec.}) \left\{ -200 + 280 - 100 + 200 \times \frac{180}{100} - 280 \times \frac{180}{140} + 100 \times \frac{180}{150} \right\}$$

$$= £(31 \text{ Dec.}) \left(200 \times \frac{180}{100} - 280 \times \frac{180}{140} + 100 \times \frac{180}{150} \right) - £(31 \text{ Dec.}) \, 20.$$

Note that the second term in the right-hand side of the above expression, £(31 Dec.) 20, is the balance of the company's net monetary assets at the year end. We can now see that it is possible to calculate a company's total gain or loss by first converting all changes to the company's net monetary assets to year-end purchasing power (this gives us the first term on the right-hand side of the expression) and then subtracting the actual balance of net monetary assets.

The loss in this case will be

£(31 Dec.) 120 $-$ £(31 Dec.) 20 = £(31 Dec.) 100.

The above result may be interpreted as follows. If the company had been in a position to arrange its affairs so that cash, debtors and creditors had been in the form of non-monetary items whose values had changed exactly in step with inflation, it would have had 'net monetary assets' of £120 at the year end. It could have achieved this result had it been able to get its debtors to agree that they would repay the company with pounds which represented the same purchasing power as was represented by the amount of the debt at the date at which it was established, and had made a similar arrangement with its creditors. The company's bank balance is a special case of a creditor or debtor depending on whether or not the account is overdrawn.

The hypothetical £120 is then compared with the actual closing balance of £20 and it can be seen that the company's policy of holding net monetary assets over the year has resulted in a loss of purchasing power of £(31 Dec.) 100.

The above argument can be generalized in the following fashion:

Let a_1 be the opening balance of net monetary assets plus the increase in net monetary assets for the first day of the year and let a_j, $j = 2$, ..., 365, be the increase in net monetary assets for day j. Then the loss of the holding of net monetary assets expressed in terms of year-end purchasing power, £(day 365), using equation (4.1), is given by

$$\text{Loss} = £(\text{day } 365)\left[a_1\left(\frac{I_{365}}{I_1} - 1\right) + a_2\left(\frac{I_{365}}{I_2} - 1\right) + a_3\left(\frac{I_{365}}{I_3} - 1\right) + \ldots + a_{365}\left(\frac{I_{365}}{I_{365}} - 1\right)\right]$$

$$= £(\text{day } 365)\left(I_{365}\sum_{j=1}^{365}\frac{a_j}{I_j} - \sum_{j=1}^{365} a_j\right).$$

Note that $\sum_{j=1}^{365} a_j$ represents the actual closing balance of net monetary assets which we can call A. Therefore

$$\text{Loss} = £(\text{day } 365)\left(I_{365}\sum_{j=1}^{365}\frac{a_j}{I_j} - A\right).$$

The use of computing facilities would make the above approach feasible in practice, but in preparing CPP accounts it is customary to take averages and assume that, depending on the circumstances, the increases in net monetary assets due to sales took place evenly either over the year as a whole or over each month or quarter, etc. If the annual assumption were made, the increase in net monetary assets would be assumed to have taken place at a date on which the general price index was at the average value for the year. If the calculation were done on a quarterly basis, the average values of the general price index for the quarters would be used.

Example 4.2 shows how one can calculate the loss or gain on a company's net monetary position.

EXAMPLE 4.2

On 1 January 19X2 Match Limited's monetary items were as follows:

	£
Balance at bank	8 000
Trade debtors	2 000
Trade creditors	6 000
Proposed dividend	1 000

A summary of the company's cash book for 19X2 revealed the following:

Cash book

		£			£
1 Jan.	Opening balance	8 000	1 Jan.	Purchase of fixed	
Jan.–Jun.	Cash sales	5 000		assets	50 000
	Trade debtors	18 000	Jan.–Jun.	Trade creditors	16 000
1 Jul.	Issue of ordinary		1 Jul.	Payment of 19X1	
	shares	30 000		dividend	1 000
Jul.–Dec.	Cash sales	8 000	Jul.–Dec.	Trade creditors	20 000
	Trade debtors	24 000	31 Dec.	Closing balance	6 000
		£93 000			£93 000

Credit sales for the year were

January–June	£21 000
July–December	£28 000

Credit purchases for the year were

January–June	£14 000
July–December	£21 000

The values of a suitable general price index at appropriate dates were

Date:	1 January	Average Jan.–Jun.	1 July	Average Jul.–Dec.	31 December
Index:	140	148	160	162	165

We must identify the changes in the company's net monetary balances. Note that the sale of goods results in an immediate increase in the company's net monetary assets regardless of whether the sale was made for cash or credit. If the sale was made on credit the increase in debtors will increase the company's net monetary assets, but the consequence of this is that the payment of cash by debtors will not affect the total net monetary position of the company. Similarly the payment of the proposed dividend does not affect the net monetary position of the company. It merely reduces cash and the liability of proposed dividends, both of which are monetary items.

The changes in the company's net monetary assets may be summarized as follows:

		Increase (£)	Decrease (£)	Net (£)	Balance (£)
1 Jan.	Opening balance				
	Bank	8 000			
	Debtors	2 000			
	Creditors		6 000		
	Proposed dividend		1 000		
		£10 000	£7 000	£3 000	3 000
1 Jan.	Reduction in cash (purchase of fixed assets)		£50 000	£(50 000)	(47 000)
Jan.–Jun.	Increase in cash (cash sales)	5 000			
	Increase in debtors (credit sales)	21 000			
	Increase in creditors (credit purchases)		14 000		
		£26 000	£14 000	£12 000	(35 000)
1 Jul.	Increase in cash (issue of shares)	£30 000		£30 000	(5 000)
Jul.–Dec.	Increase in cash (cash sales)	8 000			
	Increase in debtors (credit sales)	28 000			
	Increase in creditors (credit purchases)		21 000		
		£36 000	£21 000	£15 000	£10 000[11]

11 The closing balance of the net monetary assets is made up as follows:

	£
Bank	6 000
Debtors	9 000
	15 000
less Creditors	5 000
	£10 000

The company's loss or gain on its monetary position can now be found by converting all changes in net monetary items to year-end purchasing power.

		Conversion factor	Increase	Decrease
1 Jan.	Opening balance, £(1 Jan. X2) 3000	$\frac{165}{140}$	3536	
1 Jan.	Decrease, £(1 Jan. X2) 50000	$\frac{165}{140}$		58929
Jan.–Jun.	Increase, £(Jan.–Jun.) 12000	$\frac{165}{148}$	13378	
1 Jul.	Increase, £(1 Jul. X2) 30000	$\frac{165}{160}$	30938	
Jul.–Dec.	Increase, £(Jul.–Dec.) 15000	$\frac{165}{162}$	15278	
31 Dec.	Balance			4201
			£63130	£63130

	£(31 Dec. X2)
Actual balance of net monetary assets	10000
Balance from above	4201
Gain	
£(31 Dec. X2)	5799

Note that the company gained in purchasing power even though it disclosed positive net monetary assets in both the opening and closing balance sheets because it was, over the year as a whole, a net monetary debtor.

Example 4.3 combines the features of Examples 4.1 and 4.2 in that it demonstrates how a set of CPP accounts can be produced in a case where a company holds net monetary items. It also shows how a set of historical cost accounts can be 'converted' into CPP accounts.

EXAMPLE 4.3

(A) Parker Limited's historical cost and CPP balance sheets as at 1 January 19X5 (when the RPI was 150) are given below:

Parker Limited
Balance sheets as at 1 January 19X5

	Historical cost		Notes, conversion factors	CPP	
	£	£		£(1 Jan. X5)	£(1 Jan. X5)
Fixed assets					
Net book value		8 000	(a) $\frac{150}{100}$		12 000
Current assets					
Stock	1 200		(b) $\frac{150}{140}$	1 286	
Debtors plus cash	600	1 800	(c)	600	1 886
		£9 800		£(1 Jan. X5)	13 886
Share capital					
£1 10% preference shares	2 000		(c)	2 000	
£1 ordinary shares	4 000	6 000	(d) $\frac{150}{80}$	7 500	9 500
Reserve		2 400	(e)		2 986
Owner's equity		8 400			12 486
15% debentures		1 000	(c)		1 000
Current liabilities		400	(c)		400
		£9 800		£(1 Jan.X5)	13 886

Notes
(a) The fixed assets were acquired when the RPI was 100.
(b) The stock was purchased over a period for which the average value of the RPI was 140.
(c) Monetary items.
(d) The ordinary shares were issued on a date at which the RPI was 80.
(e) The 'CPP reserve' is the balancing figure in the CPP balance sheet.

(B) During 19X5, Parker Limited issued 2000 £1 ordinary shares at a premium of 25 pence per share on 1 April when the RPI was 160 and purchased fixed assets of £(1 Sep. X5) 3000; the RPI on 1 September 19X5 was 175.

Parker Limited's historical cost profit and loss account for 19X5 is given below:

Parker Limited
Profit and loss account

	£	£
Sales		12 000
less Opening stock	1 200	
Purchases	7 000	
	8 200	
less Closing stock	1 600	6 600
Gross profit		5 400
less Sundry expenses	1 450	
Debenture interest	150	
Depreciation (20% reducing balance)	2 200	3 800
Net profit		£1 600

No dividends were declared during the year.

A full year's depreciation has been provided on the fixed assets purchased on 1 September 19X5.

(C) In order to prepare the CPP accounts it is necessary to make certain assumptions about the dates on which the various transactions took place. It will be assumed that sales, purchases, expenses and debenture interest all accrued evenly over the year and that the average RPI for the year was 170. It will further be assumed that the average age of the closing stock was 2 months and that the RPI on 30 October 19X5 was 178. The RPI at the year end will be taken to be 180.

For convenience the RPI at appropriate dates are summarized below:

Date	Index
Issue of original ordinary shares	80
Purchase of original fixed assets	100
Purchase of opening stock	140
1 January 19X5	150
1 April 19X5 (issue of 2 000 ordinary shares)	160
Average for 19X5	170
1 September 19X5 (purchase of fixed assets)	175
30 October 19X5 (purchase of closing stock)	178
31 December 19X5	180

(D) We will now calculate the losses or gains resulting from the company's monetary position. The loss or gain on short- and long-term items will be calculated separately. The calculations are usually done separately because of the different factors which give rise to a company's holding of short-term and long-term monetary items. The short-term items depend on the company's policy regarding its investment in working capital; in most cases the short-term items are equivalent to a company's net current assets excluding stock. The longer-term position is a consequence of the company's overall financing strategy and depends on the level of gearing at which the company operates.

The short-term position may be calculated as follows:

		Actual +	Actual −	Conversion factor	Year-end pounds +	Year-end pounds −
1 Jan.	Opening balance	200		$\frac{180}{150}$	240	
1 Apr.	Issue of shares	2 500		$\frac{180}{160}$	2 812	
Average for year	Sales *less* purchases, expenses + interest	3 400		$\frac{180}{170}$	3 600	
1 Sept.	Purchase of fixed assets		3 000	$\frac{180}{175}$		3 086
31 Dec.	Closing balance		3 100			3 566
		£6 100	£6 100		(31 Dec. X5) £6 652	(31 Dec. X5) £6 652

The company's actual balance of short-term monetary items is £3100, but had the company been able to maintain the purchasing power of these items it would have had £3566. Hence, the loss on holding short-term monetary items for the year is £(31 Dec. X5) [3566 − 3100] = £(31 Dec. X5) 466.

The company's long-term monetary liabilities consist of the preference shares and the debentures. The opening balances for these items are:

	£(1 Jan. X5)
Preference shares	2 000
Debentures	1 000
	£(1 Jan. X5) 3 000

The above balance is equivalent in year-end pounds to

$$£(31 \text{ Dec. X5}) \left[3\,000 \times \frac{180}{150} \right] = £(31 \text{ Dec. X5}) \, 3\,600.$$

However, since we are dealing with monetary items these values are not affected by the changes in the price level and the value at the year end is £(31 Dec. X5) 3000.

The company has therefore gained in purchasing power from holding monetary liabilities and the gain is given by

$$£(31 \text{ Dec. X5}) \left[3\,000 \times \frac{180}{150} - 3\,000 \right]$$

$$= £(31 \text{ Dec. X5}) \, 3\,000 \left[\frac{180}{150} - 1 \right]$$

$$= £(31 \text{ Dec. X5}) \, 600.$$

(E)   We are now in a position to prepare the CPP profit and loss account and balance sheet.

Parker Limited
CPP profit and loss account for the year ended 31 December 19X5

	£(31 Dec. X5)	£(31 Dec. X5)
Sales, $12\,000 \times \dfrac{180}{170}$		12 706
less Opening stock, $1\,200 \times \dfrac{180}{140}$	1 543	
Purchases, $7\,000 \times \dfrac{180}{170}$	7 412	
	8 955	
less Closing stock, $1\,600 \times \dfrac{180}{178}$	1 618	7 337
Gross profit		5 369
less Sundry expenses, $1\,450 \times \dfrac{180}{170}$	1 535	
Debenture interest, $150 \times \dfrac{180}{170}$	159	

Depreciation,

$0.20 \times 8\,000 \times \dfrac{180}{100}$	2 880	
$0.20 \times 3\,000 \times \dfrac{180}{175}$	617	5 191

Net trading profit		178
Gain on long-term monetary items	600	
less Loss on short-term monetary items	466	134
Profit for the year		£(31 Dec. X5) 312

CPP balance sheet as at 31 December 19X5

	£(31 Dec. X5)	£(31 Dec. X5)
Fixed assets		
Net book value:		
$(8\,000 - 1\,600) \times \dfrac{180}{100}$	11 520	
$(3\,000 - 600) \times \dfrac{180}{175}$	2 469	13 989
Current assets		
Stock, $1\,600 \times \dfrac{180}{178}$	1 618	
Cash *plus* debtors *less* creditors	3 100	4 718
		£(31 Dec. X5) 18 707
Share capital		
£1 10% preference shares		2 000
£1 ordinary shares:		
$4\,000 \times \dfrac{180}{80}$	9 000	
$2\,000 \times \dfrac{180}{160}$	2 250	11 250
		13 250
Reserves		
Share premium account,		
$500 \times \dfrac{180}{160}$	562	

Reserves, 1 January 19X5,

$$2986 \times \frac{180}{150}$$ 3 583

Profit for 19X5   312   4 457

Owners' equity   17 707

15% Debentures   1 000

£(31 Dec. X5) 18 707

The nature of the loss or gain on a company's net monetary position

One of the more important features of a set of CPP accounts is its disclosure of the loss or gain arising from the company's net monetary position. It attempts to show the results, from the point of view of the equity shareholders, of the financing policy adopted by the company in a period of changing prices.

The figures disclosed by CPP accounts have, however, been criticized on a number of grounds. One cause for criticism stems from the observation that the nominal interest normally includes some compensation for the fact that in a period of rising prices the debtor will discharge his debt in pounds of a lesser value than the pounds which he borrowed. If, at the time the debt was issued, the market correctly assessed the future course of inflation, the 'gain' which apparently accrues to the borrower will be equal to the compensation for inflation which is included in the nominal rate of interest. If this were the case it would seem sensible to set off the gain against the interest payable in the accounts of the borrower and to set off the corresponding loss against the interest receivable in the accounts of the lender. If this were done the accounts would disclose the 'real' interest payable and receivable.

In practice the market will not be correct in its assessment of the future course of inflation and there will be a real loss or gain arising from the company's net monetary position. The loss or gain will depend on the difference between the anticipated and actual rates of inflation and thus, so far as interest-bearing loans are concerned, the debtor will not automatically gain nor the creditor automatically lose. The debtor will only gain if inflation turns out to be greater than that which was anticipated when the borrowing was made.

Suppose that £10 000 debentures were issued at a nominal rate of interest at 12% and let us suppose that it is known that the market believed that prices would rise by 9% each year for the period of the loan. It could thus be argued that the real rate of interest is 3%.

Assume that the actual rate of inflation in 19X7 was 15%. The items relating to the loan which would appear in the CPP profit and loss account for 19X7 would be:

Interest payable, 12% of £10 000	£1 200[12]
Gain on long-term borrowing, $£10\,000 \left(\dfrac{115}{100} - 1\right)$	£1 500

It could, however, be argued that the following would provide a more realistic description of what in fact took place:

Interest payable, 3% of £10 000	£300
Gain on long-term borrowing, $£10\,000 \left(\dfrac{115}{100} - 1\right) - 9\% \text{ of } £10\,000$	£600

In practice it is not possible to break down the nominal interest rate into the two elements – the real interest rate and the compensation for anticipated inflation – and hence it is not possible to present the CPP accounts in the above manner. However, it is clear that in the case of interest-bearing loans the loss and gains on the company's net monetary position will be overstated in the CPP accounts of the borrower and lender. There is thus a strong case for the suggestion that the loss or gain should be shown in the same section of the CPP profit and loss account as interest payable or receivable, and that the criticism referred to above is more concerned with the format of the CPP profit and loss account as proposed in PSSAP 7 than with the principles involved.

It must be emphasized that the above discussion refers only to interest-bearing items. The CPP profit and loss account will not overstate the loss or gain on such items as cash at bank on current account or trade creditors.

It has also been argued that it is misleading to measure the loss or gain by reference to changes in the RPI as this assumes that the alternative of putting, say, £10 000 into a bank account is the payment

---

12 For simplicity it has been assumed that interest is paid at the year-end and the question of whether the interest should be deemed to have accrued evenly throughout the year, which would require the interest payment to be converted to pounds of year-end purchasing power, has been ignored.

of a dividend of that amount. In reality only a very small proportion of the cash generated by a company is used to pay dividends; the greater proportion is recirculated in the business and is used to purchase stock and fixed assets and to pay wages and other overheads. It has been suggested that the loss in purchasing power experienced if a company deposited £10 000 in a bank account for 1 month should be measured by reference to the increase in prices of those items which will be purchased by the company.

The above argument can be countered by the assertion that the purpose of business activity is to increase future consumption and that physical assets are not acquired for their own sake. The objective of CPP accounts is to show the effect of changing prices on the consumption opportunities of the equity shareholders and not on the potential asset purchases of the firm.

Suppose that a slothful company starts the year with £100 000 in the bank and does nothing until the end of the year when it purchases assets the cost of which have increased by 10% over the year. Let us also assume that the RPI has increased by 15% over the same period. Is the loss on holding money £10 000 or £15 000? From the point of view of the equity shareholders it is £15 000. Had the £100 000 been distributed at the beginning of the year the shareholders could have consumed goods and services amounting to £100 000. As prices had on average gone up by 15% over the year they would have required £115 000 at the year end to purchase an equivalent bundle of goods and services.

At the year end the directors of the company must decide how best to maximize the total potential consumption over time of their shareholders. If the directors decide to invest the whole of the £100 000 in assets it must be on the basis of the belief that such action will be more beneficial to the shareholders than would the distribution of the cash. The shareholders would sacrifice immediate consumption in return for what is hoped will be greater consumption opportunities in the future.

It can be seen that there are two steps in the argument. First, the potential consumption opportunities of the shareholders has fallen by £15 000 (measured in year-end pounds) over the year. Second, a sacrifice of the consumption opportunity of £100 000 at the year end which is required if the investment is to be made.

To show the loss on holding money as £10 000 would not reflect the fact that the potential consumption opportunity of the equity shareholders had fallen by £15 000 over the year.

Strengths and weaknesses of the CPP model

As we pointed out in Chapter 3, an accounting model can be appraised in terms of the selected capital maintenance test and asset valuation basis. We will now evaluate the CPP model in this way.

The real money capital maintenance test appears to be a sensible choice. Money is not of itself a valuable commodity – its utility depends on what can be done with it or, in other words, what it can buy either now or in the future. Thus, given that the purchasing power of money does vary over time, it seems reasonable to suggest that it is more helpful for many purposes to use a bench mark based on the maintenance of real money capital rather than money capital. In particular, the use, in CPP accounting, of a price index based on changes in consumer prices does seem to be the appropriate basis for the preparation of financial statements which serve to show the impact of an entity's operations on the economic welfare of its owner. The case for the use of the real money capital test in such circumstances can be highlighted by the presentation of a simple example.

Suppose that a sole trader conducts all his business on a cash basis such that his only business asset is cash and that the business has no liabilities. Assume that he starts the year with £10 000 and has £12 000 at the end of the year, during which time he has neither introduced nor withdrawn any cash.

The profit which would be disclosed by the conventional accounting method which uses the money capital test is £2000, but does this represent the owner's increase in 'well-offness' over the year? The question cannot be answered in the absence of any knowledge of the change in the purchasing power of money over the year. If the rate of inflation was less than 20% then it seems reasonable to suggest that the owner was better off at the end of the year than he was at the beginning of the year in the sense that he could purchase more goods and services. Similarly, if the rate of inflation was more than 20% the owner would be worse off.

Let us now turn to the CPP basis of asset valuation. It is here that the CPP model is weak. As has already been stated, the CPP model does not purport to show the current economic value of assets since the basis of valuation is historical cost. With CPP accounting it is money and not the asset which is 'revalued'. Thus the CPP model suffers from much the same limitations as historical cost accounting which were outlined in Chapter 3, and most authorities appear to agree that the CPP approach is not an adequate response to the criticisms of the conventional method.

Given the obvious usefulness of the real money capital test and the weakness of the CPP asset valuation basis, many people, including the authors, believe that it would be sensible to combine the profit measure based on real capital maintenance with a basis of asset valuation which does reflect current values. This view was not, however, shared by the Sandilands Committee, who saw no need to include adjustments for changes in general purchasing power in CCA. We will return to this topic in Chapter 7.

Recommended reading

See list at end of Chapter 7.

Questions

4.1   The accounts for the year ended 31 March 1974 of a public quoted company are reproduced below together with an index of prices of consumer goods and services.

Consolidated Profit and Loss Account

	£	£
Group turnover		25 003 606
Group trading profit		5 835 357
Depreciation		919 773
		4 915 584
Interest paid		485 549
Profit before taxation		4 430 035
Taxation		2 112 904
		2 317 131
Dividends		
Paid 31 December 1973	272 790	
Proposed	350 731	
		623 521
Balance, transferred to reserves		1 693 610

Consolidated Balance Sheet	£	£
Fixed assets		11 036 492
Trade investment at cost (purchased 15 April, 1973) (market value £149 385)		241 308
Current assets		
Stock and work in progress	8 177 351	
Debtors	4 990 709	
Quoted investments at cost 1961 (market value £80 530)	55 010	
Bank balances	696 532	
	13 919 602	
Current liabilities		
Trade creditors	2 404 859	
Bank overdrafts		
secured	499 386	
unsecured	292 807	
Taxation	1 417 869	
Dividend proposed	350 731	
	4 965 652	
Net current assets		8 953 950
Net tangible assets		20 231 750
Financed by		
Share capital		4 639 292
Reserves		10 179 429
Total capital and reserves		14 818 721
8% Unsecured loan stock		2 034 576
Secured loans		2 594 274
Deferred taxation		549 539
Investment grants in suspense		234 640
		20 231 750

An Index of Consumer Goods and Services

Year	Index (average)	1973 (month)	Index	1974 (month)	Index
1961	97.9	Jan.	171.3	Jan.	191.8
1962	101.6	Feb.	172.4	Feb.	195.1
1963	103.6	March	173.4	March	196.8
1964	107.0	April	176.7	April 1973/	
1965	112.1	May	178.0	March 1974	
1966	116.5	June	178.9	average	182.0
1967	119.4	July	179.7		
1968	125.0	Aug.	180.2		
1969	131.8	Sept.	181.8		
1970	140.2	Oct.	185.4		
1971	153.4	Nov.	186.8		
1972	164.3	Dec.	188.2		
1973	179.4				

Enquiry into the accounts had disclosed that the fixed assets consist of two large items of plant which cost £5 million in 1972 and £2 million in 1967 and sundry small items bought over the last 10 years. All these items are depreciated over a ten year life.

Bank interest is debited by the bank on 30 June and 31 December but debenture and loan interest is paid on 31 March and 30 September. The dividends are normally paid on 30 June and 31 December.

Stock and work in progress represent expenditure made in January (2/5ths), February (1/5th) and March (2/5ths); Debtors represent invoices in February and March; Creditors were for goods supplied in February and March. There was no change in the issued share capital during the year.

You are required to state the factors you would use to convert, as on 31 March 1974, the items in the profit and loss account and balance sheet for use in CPP accounts. You are NOT required to calculate the current pounds.

(12 marks)

ICAEW Advanced Accounting II, November 1974.

4.2   Export and Import (Moorgate) Ltd was formed on 1 January 1974 with a fully subscribed share capital of £100 000. On the 31 March 1974 a loan of £50 000 was received from a finance company requiring interest at 15% p.a. and repayment at the end of 1977.

Storage facilities with a life of 10 years were purchased at a cost of £20 000 on 31 March 1974 and on the same date 2000 boxes of a new eastern spice 'Musky' were imported at a total cost of £120 000. Sales of Musky during the year to 31 March 1975 were for cash and consisted of 200 boxes at £100 per box on 30 April, 500 boxes at £110 per box on 31 December, and 500 boxes at £130 per box on 31 March 1975.

Any cash in excess of immediate requirements was placed on deposit and during the year to 31 March 1975 gross interest received exceeded all the expenses (including loan interest payable), apart from the cost of Musky, by £5000. In the period to 31 March 1974 the interest received exactly offset the expenses to that date, and accounts for the 3 months were completed.

The inflation during the life of the company is represented by the following factors:

	Price Index	Factor to convert to 31 March 1975 £'s
1 January 1974	100	1.5
31 March 1974	107	1.4
30 April 1974	107	1.4
31 December 1974	125	1.2
31 March 1975	150	1.0
Average 1 April 1974 to 31 March 1975	115	1.3

You are required to prepare (omitting comparative figures):
 (a) **accounts for the year ended 31 March 1975 on the historical basis,**
 (b) **accounts for the same period on the Constant Purchasing Power (CPP) basis in accordance with the provisional standard,**
 (c) **a supplementary statement which reconciles the two statements as suggested by the provisional standard, and**
 (d) **a statement to the shareholders explaining the significance of the difference between (a) and (b).**
Taxation should be provided at the rate of 55%.   **(23 marks)**
ICAEW Financial Accounting II, July 1975.

5 Current Value Accounting I: Developments up to SSAP 16

The contribution of Edwards and Bell

In Chapter 4 we identified two main theoretical sources of current cost accounting (CCA) – the work of Edwards and Bell and the work of Bonbright. We will first discuss the ideas of Edwards and Bell.

Their seminal work, *The Theory and Measurement of Business Income*,[1] was published in 1961. The book represented a major advance in the development of current value accounting, and its particular contribution to the CCA model was the recognition of the distinction between holding and operating gains and we will concentrate on this aspect of their work.

The distinction between holding and operating gains

For the purposes of determining business profit[2] Edwards and Bell divided the activities of a company into holding intervals and sales moments – the latter being assumed to be instantaneous (*see* Figure 5.1). A sales moment is the instant in time when the company sells goods while a holding interval is the interval between successive sales moments.

Suppose that a company starts an accounting period with assets with a replacement cost of £40, and that at the end of the first holding period its assets have a replacement cost of £60. These are not necessarily the same assets, as the company might well have exchanged assets during the period. Thus a manufacturing company might have reduced its cash and increased its holding of raw materials, work in progress

1 E. O. Edwards and P. W. Bell, *The Theory and Measurement of Business Income*, University of California Press, Stanford, Calif., 1961.
2 Edwards and Bell, *op. cit.*, used the phrase 'business profit' to refer to the profit measurement related to assets valued at current cost. As defined by Edwards and Bell an asset's current cost is usually (but not always) the same as its replacement cost. For simplicity, we will assume that there is no difference between current cost and replacement cost.

and finished goods. Since, by definition, the company has made no sales during the holding interval, the change in replacement cost must be due to an increase in the replacement cost of assets owned by the company.

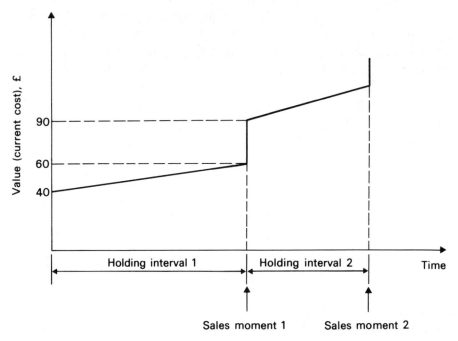

Figure 5.1

Immediately after the first sales moment the replacement cost of the company's assets equals £90. These assets will consist of the receipts from sales plus those of the company's assets which were not sold. The total business profit so far (assuming that no capital has been introduced or withdrawn) is £50; the difference between the replacement cost of the assets immediately after the first sales moment and the equivalent value at the start of the accounting period.

The total business profit of £50 can be divided into two elements. Part of the profit, £20, is due to the increase in the replacement cost of the assets during the holding period. This, Edwards and Bell called the realizable cost saving although other terms used to describe it are holding gain and revaluation surplus. We will use the term holding gain. The replacement cost of assets at the moment of the first sale was £60, but as they were acquired with assets which had a current cost of £40, the company has gained, or saved, £20 by virtue of acquiring or manufacturing the goods sold in advance of the date of sale.

The remainder of the business profit, £30, is termed the current operating profit. This is the difference between the replacement cost of the assets before and after the sales moment. Now many of company's assets will remain unchanged during the sales moment (i.e. will not be sold) and the current operating profit can be stated in terms of the assets that do change. Thus, the current operating profit can be said to be equal to the receipts from sales less the replacement cost of assets used up (or exchanged) in the sales moment.

The same approach can be used for each sales moment and, if we consider the accounting period as a whole, then, if it is assumed that no capital is introduced or withdrawn,

Business profit for period = Replacement cost of assets at end of period – replacement cost of assets at beginning of period
= Sum of current operating profits for all sales moments + Sum of holding gains for all holding intervals.

The approach described above is illustrated in Example 5.1.

EXAMPLE 5.1
Bow Limited started the year with the following assets:

	£
Stock, at replacement cost	600
Cash	400
	£1 000

and finished the year with

	£
Stock, at replacement cost	900
Cash	500
	£1 400

It will be assumed that the company has no operating expenses and that no capital was introduced or withdrawn. The total business profit is thus: £1400 − £1000 = £400.

The company's activities for the year were as follows:

			Stock	Cash
First holding interval	1 Jan.	Opening balances	600	400
	17 Feb.	Purchased stock for £200	200	(200)
		Stock had an RC of £900 at		
		31 March	HG 100	
	31 Mar.		900	200
First sales moment	31 Mar.	Stock with an RC of £300		
		sold for £450 (COP = £150)	(300)	450
			600	650
Second holding interval	1 Apr.		HG 80	
		Stock had an RC of £680 on	—	—
	30 Jun.	30 June	680	650
Second sales moment	30 Jun.	Stock with an RC of £280		
		sold for £300 (COP £20)	(280)	300
			400	950
Third holding interval	1 Jul.	Purchased Stock for £450	450	(450)
	30 Sep.	Stock had an RC of £900 at		
		31 Dec. (the year end)	HG 50	
	31 Dec.	Closing balances	£900	£500

where RC is the replacement cost, HG is the holding gain and COP is the current operating profit.

The total business profit of £400 can be analysed as follows:

Current operating profits		
First sales moment £(450 − 300)	150	
Second sales moment £(300 − 280)	20	170
Holding gains	—	
First holding interval £(900 − 800)	100	
Second holding interval £(680 − 600)	80	
Third holding interval £(900 − 850)	50	230
Business profit		£400

We will discuss the problems involved in distinguishing between holding and operating gains later when we introduce the CCA model.

However, it might be useful if we commented that a company's holding gains might be argued to give some indication of its success in the acquisition or manufacture of inputs, e.g. the extent to which it benefited by purchasing stock before a price increase. In contrast, the current operating profit might be said to provide information about the company's success as a seller of goods – the extent to which, because of its efficiency or position in the market, it can sell goods for a price which is greater than the current cost of replacing them.

The distinction between realized and unrealized holding gains

The total holding gain for a period may be split into two elements – the realized holding gain (RHG) and the unrealized holding gain (UHG). The RHG is that part of the total which is associated with the assets which have been used up or consumed in the period; that is, the RHG is the difference between the current value of the asset at the date at which it is consumed (e.g. the date of sale in the case of stock) and the historical cost of the asset. Conversely, the UHG arises from the increase in value of the assets which remain on hand at the end of the period and is equal to the difference between the current value of the assets at the end of the period and their historical cost or, in the case of assets owned at the beginning of the period, their value at that date.

The position is complicated slightly when we consider the consumption of assets which were owned at the beginning of the period because part of the RHG is effectively the realization of part or the whole of the UHG of earlier periods.

Example 5.2 illustrates these points.

EXAMPLE 5.2

Clive purchased 100 units of stock for £10 each on 1 December 19X7. No sales were made in December 19X7 and the RC of the units at 31 December 19X7 (Clive's year end) were £11 each.

Clive sold 60 units for £18 each on 30 June 19X8, at which date the RC of each unit was £13. No more sales were made in 19X8 but Clive purchased 20 units for £15 each on 10 October. The RC of stock on 31 December 19X8 was £16 per unit.

In 19X7 the only element of business profit is the UHG of £1 per unit or £100.

Now let us consider the year 19X8. Clive's assets at the start of the year, measured at RC, amounted to 100 units at £11 each or £1100. His assets at the end of the year were

	£
Cash $(60 \times 18) - (20 \times 15)$	780
Stock 60 units at £16	960
	£1 740

Clive's business profit for 19X8 was therefore £1740 − £1100 = £640. Clive's COP for the year is given by

	£
Sales $60 \times £18$	1 080
less RC of stock at the date of sale, $60 \times £13$	780
COP	£300

His RHG is given by

	£
RC of stock at the date of sale	780
less Historical cost of stock, $60 \times £10$	600
RHG	£180

But of the above RHG of £180 a part represents the realization of a portion of the 19X7 UHG, the amount involved being $60 \times £1 = £60$. Clive's UHG in 19X8 is given by

	£	£
RC at year end of closing stock of 60 units		960
less RC at 1 January of unsold closing stock held on 1 January, $40 \times £11$	440	
Historical cost of stock purchased in the year, $20 \times £15$	300	740
UHG		£220

The total business profit (BP) for the year is given by

BP = COP + RHG + UHG − (that part of the RHG which was
                        included in the UHG of previous years).

Substituting the monetary values, we have

$$BP = £(300 + 180 + 220 - 60)$$
$$= £640.$$

The relationship between historical cost profit and business profit

The relationship can be easily seen if we resort to some simple algebra.

Let R be the revenue from sales, C be the current value of assets used up in generating sales, and H be the historical cost of those assets. Then the COP is given by $R - C$ while the RHG is equal to $C - H$.

The historical cost profit (HCP) is of course the difference between revenue and the historical cost of the assets consumed or, to use the above symbols,

$$HCP = R - H$$
$$= (R - C) + (C - H)$$
$$= COP + RHG.$$

In other words the historical cost profit is the sum of the current operating profit and the realized holding gains.

Let us now consider the implications of the above statement. The following discussion will serve as an introduction to the CCA model which will be developed later in this chapter, as well as providing further evidence of the weaknesses of the historical cost accounting model.

It can be seen that historical cost profit has, when compared with business profit, two possible defects. First, historical cost profit combines two arguably distinct elements, COP and RHG, and the conventional accounting model makes no attempt to separate them. Second, the historical cost approach ignores UHG, i.e. it takes no account of the current value of the assets held at the end of the period.

The significance of these two observations depends on the view that is taken of the most suitable concept of capital for the purposes of profit determination. If the view is taken that the enterprise should be able to replace its assets as they are used up if it is to maintain its wealth or capital, then it might be argued that RHG should not be regarded as being part of the profit for the period. It will be seen that CCA is based, in part, on the view that RHG should not be included in the company's profit. The reason for this was that the designers of CCA believed that, all other things being equal, a company should be able to replace the assets used up in a period if it is to maintain its 'well-offness'.

Of course if one takes a different view of what constitutes 'well-offness' then it might be that RHG could be regarded as being part of profit. Such a view is implicit in the historical cost approach. However, it might still be argued that one of the defects of historical cost accounting is its failure to disentangle COP and RHG. This argument is based on the view that a company's COP and RHG are the result of different circumstances, and knowledge of the two elements might help the user of accounts to understand how the company obtained its historical cost profit. In particular, it might assist users to estimate future profits. For example, it might be that in a given year a company makes a very much greater profit than it had achieved in previous years because of the existence of RHGs. Those wishing to predict future profits would then no doubt consider the extent to which they believe that the opportunities to achieve RHGs will continue in the future.

To the extent that accounting practice in the UK and other countries allows companies to revalue assets for balance sheet purposes, UHGs are to be found in what are otherwise historical cost accounts. It will, however, be noted that UHGs are not shown in the historical cost profit and loss account, but are carried directly to reserves.

The recognition of UHGs in historical cost accounting is partial, irregular (in the chronological and not moral sense) and is generally dependent on the whims of the directors.[3] Most adherents of current value accounting would not wish to include UHG as part of a company's profit and, as we shall see, this was a view that was adopted by the designers of CCA. Even so, there is still a strong case for valuing assets at the current value, or in other words, systematically recognizing UHGs. This is in fact an important feature of CCA in which UHGs are, more or less, dealt with in the same manner as they are in historical cost accounts. The real difference is that in CCA all UHGs on stocks and fixed assets are systematically recorded and reflected in the accounts.

The purpose of this section is to discuss the contribution of Edwards and Bell to the developments of CCA. This can perhaps best be understood by noting that CCA makes a sharp distinction between current cost operating profit and holding gains.

It must, however, be noted that not all authorities agree that it is possible to make a clear and sharp distinction between operating and

---

3 The Companies Act 1967 does, however, require directors to make a suitable statement in the directors' report when, in their opinion, the difference between the book and market value of land, when it is held as a fixed asset, is significant.

holding gains or that, even if it were possible, it would be desirable so to do. We will return to this point in Chapters 6 and 7 where we will review SSAP 16 and ED 35.

Which 'current value'?

In Chapter 3 we pointed out that there are several ways of valuing an asset, each of which are of relevance in the determination of periodic accounting profit. In other words there is not one unique measure of profit but a whole set depending on the basis of asset valuation employed and the selected capital maintenance concept.

Let us for a moment ignore the problems associated with the choice of the capital maintenance concept and accept the argument that the present value approach to asset valuation should be rejected for the theoretical and practical reasons outlined in Chapter 3. We are then – if we are to use current values – left with the choice between the replacement cost and net realizable value approaches.

Clearly both are of relevance and a strong case can be made for requiring companies, or at least larger companies – to publish multi-columnar accounts which would show both the replacement costs and the net realizable values of their assets and, possibly, their historical costs. Thus, companies would be required to report profit on more than one basis. Against this the view has been expressed that the approach would be too costly on the part of the producers of accounts and too complicated for the users of accounts.

The cost argument can easily be countered for, as will be seen, the proposals of SSAP 16 would require companies to be aware of both the replacement cost and net realizable values of virtually all their assets. The second aspect of the argument can – at least in the authors' view – be dealt with almost as easily. If it can be shown that there are a number of ways of measuring profit then it surely is confusing and misleading to imply that there is only one. Considerations of practicability must limit the number of different profit figures which are reported, but it does seem reasonable to suppose that users of accounts should be able to cope with and benefit from the publication of two or three views of a company's results.

The foregoing argument has, it must be admitted, not been accepted by those charged with the task of reviewing accounting practice except in so far as it has been advocated that the current value accounts should be published along with historical cost accounts. Conventional wisdom has it that one set of current value accounts is enough. Thus the question of which asset valuation method should be adopted is central to the current value accounting debate.

The net realizable value (NRV) approach possesses a number of virtues. The total of the net realizable values of a company's assets does provide some measure of the risks involved in lending to or investing in the company in that the total indicates the amount that would be available for distribution to creditors and shareholders should the business be wound up. This point is of course dependent on the problems associated with the determination of net realizable values which were discussed in Chapter 3, and in particular the assumptions that are made about the circumstances surrounding the disposal of the assets. It has also been argued, notably by Professor R. J. Chambers, that the profit derived from a variant of the net realizable value asset valuation basis,[4] shows, after adjusting for changes in the general price level, the extent to which the potential purchasing power of the owners of an enterprise has increased over the period. However, the potential would only be realized if all the assets were sold and it must be noted that in reality companies do not sell off all their assets at frequent intervals.

In practice companies continue in the same line or lines of business for a considerable time, making only marginal changes to the mix of their activities. It is therefore argued that if only one current value profit is to be published then it should be based on the replacement cost approach. For if it is assumed that a company is going to continue in the same line of business then it should only be regarded as maintaining its 'well-offness' if it has generated sufficient revenue to replace the assets used up. Thus, replacement cost is the preferred choice of those groups in the UK and most overseas countries which have recommended the introduction of current value accounting. A strict adherence to the use of replacement cost, however, would not allow accounts to reflect the fact that companies *do* change their activities or the manner in which they conduct their present activities and that all the assets owned at any one time would not necessarily be replaced. Thus some modification of the replacement cost approach is required.

---

4 The method which is known as CoCoA or continuously contemporary accounting also has the merit of avoiding the need to make arbitrary 'allocations' such as depreciation where the cost of the asset is allocated to different time problems (*see* page 575). Readers interested in studying this method should refer to R. J. Chambers, *Accounting for Inflation – Methods and Problems*, University of Sydney Press, Sydney, 1975.

Deprival value (value to the business)

A suitable basis of asset valuation which would lead to the use of replacement cost in those circumstances where the owner would – if deprived of the asset – replace it and the use of a lower figure if the asset was not worth replacement was suggested by Professor J. C. Bonbright in 1937. Professor Bonbright wrote, 'The value of a property to its owner is identical in amount with the adverse value of the entire loss, direct and indirect, that the owner might expect to suffer if he were deprived of the property.'[5]

Professor Bonbright's main concern was with the question of the legal damages which should be awarded for the loss of assets. He was not concerned with the impact of asset valuation on the determination of accounting profit. Others, notably Professor W. T. Baxter in the UK, recognized the relevance of this approach to accounting and developed the concept in the context of profit measurement. Professor Baxter coined the term 'deprival value', which neatly encapsulates the main point that the value of an asset is the sum of money which the owner would need to receive in order to compensate him exactly if he were deprived of the asset. It must be emphasized that the exercise is of a hypothetical nature; the owner need not be physically dispossessed of his asset in order for its deprival value to be determined. This approach was adopted by the Sandilands Committee and has, more or less, survived the various modifications to the original proposals and remains as the asset valuation basis underlying current cost accounting. Thus, in a current cost balance sheet, assets are shown at their deprival value while a current cost profit and loss account would show the current operating profit (or current cost operating profit), which is the difference between the revenue for the period and the deprival value of the assets consumed in the generation of revenue.

Before turning to a discussion of CCA, it might be helpful if we explored the meaning of deprival value in a little more detail. Ignoring non-pecuniary factors, the deprival value of an asset cannot exceed its replacement cost, for if the owner were deprived of an asset he could restore his original position through the asset's replacement. The owner might of course incur additional costs (e.g. a loss of potential profit) if there was any delay in replacement – the indirect costs referred to in Professor Bonbright's original definition. There may be circum-

---

5 J. C. Bonbright, *The Valuation of Property*, Michie, Charlottesville, Va., 1965.

stances where these additional costs may be so substantial that they will need to be included in the determination of the replacement cost, but generally these additional factors are ignored.

The owner might not feel that the asset was worth replacing, in which case the use of the asset's replacement cost would overstate its deprival value. Suppose that a trader owns 60 widgets whose current replacement cost is £3 per unit. Let us also assume that the trader's position in the market has changed since he acquired the widgets, that he will only be able to sell them for £2 each, and that this estimate can be made with certainty. The trader's other assets consist of cash of £100.

The trader's wealth before the hypothetical loss of the widgets is £220 (actual cash of £100 plus the certain receipt of £120). Let us now assume that the trader is deprived of his widgets. It is clear that he would only need to receive £120 in compensation, i.e. the net realizable value of the widgets, to restore his original position. If the trader were paid £180 (the replacement cost) he would end up better off.

In order for an asset's deprival value to be given by its net realizable value the net realizable value must be less than its replacement cost. Otherwise a rational owner (and in this analysis it is assumed that owners are rational) would consider it worth while replacing the asset.

We must now consider a different set of circumstances under which the owner would not replace the asset but has no intention of selling it. The asset may be a fixed asset which is obsolete in the sense that it would not be worth acquiring in the present circumstances of the business. The asset is still of some benefit to the business and it is thought that this benefit exceeds the amount that would be obtained from its immediate sale – i.e. its net realizable value. This benefit will, at this stage, be referred to as the asset's 'value in use'.

An example of this type of asset might be a machine which is used as a standby for when other machines break down. The probability of breakdowns may be such that it would not be worth purchasing a machine to provide cover because the replacement cost is greater than the benefit of owning a spare machine. It must be emphasized that the relevant replacement cost in this analysis is the cost of replacing the machine in its present condition and not the cost of a new machine. The machine may have a low net realizable value (which may be negative if there are costs associated with the removal of the machine) which is less than its value in use. In such circumstances an asset's deprival value will be given by its value in use, which would be less than its replacement cost but greater than its net realizable value.

As will be seen, the determination of an asset's value in use often proves to be a difficult task. In certain circumstances it may be possible to identify the cash flows that will accrue to the owner by virtue of his ownership of the asset and thus, given that an appropriate discount rate can be selected, its present value can be found. In other instances the amount recoverable from further use may have to be estimated on a more subjective basis. However, this estimate will approximate to the asset's present value and hence we will at this stage, use the term present value (PV) for simplicity. It should, however, be noted that the phrase is not used in SSAP 16 or ED 35.

The above discussion is summarized in Figure 5.2.

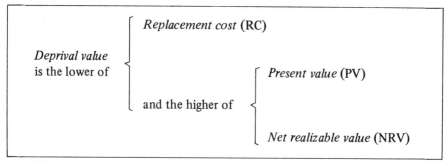

Figure 5.2   A definition of deprival value.

We will discuss the meaning of the terms replacement cost (RC), present value and net realizable value in the context of SSAP 16 and ED 35 in Chapters 6 and 7, but at this stage we should emphasize that the relevant values are the lowest possible replacement cost and the highest possible net realizable value.

In the case of a fixed asset the replacement cost is the lowest cost of replacing the services rendered by that asset rather than the cost of the asset itself. The replacement cost of stock will depend on the normal pattern of purchases by the business and thus it will be assumed that the usual discount for bulk purchases will be available.

The net realizable value of work in progress which would, in the normal course of business, require further processing before they are sold needs careful interpretation. The conventional definition of net realizable value in relation to stock is the 'actual or estimated selling price (net of trade but before settlement discounts) less (a) all further costs to completion and (b) all costs to be incurred in marketing, selling and distributing'.[6] There is an alternative definition which is the amount

6 SSAP 9, 'Stocks and work in progress', Para. 21.

that would be realized if the asset were sold in its *existing* condition less the cost of disposal. For the purposes of determining the asset's deprival value the higher of the two possible net realizable values will be taken.

Assume that a business holds an item of work in progress which could be sold for £200 in its existing condition, but which could, after further processing costing £30, be sold for £250. Also assume that its replacement cost is £350 and thus that the asset's replacement cost does not yield its deprival value.

In this case the asset's deprival value is £220 so long as the period required to complete and market the stock is brief enough for us to be able to ignore the effect of discounting. It is clear that before the hypothetical deprival of the asset the business would expect to receive £220 from its sale after taking account of the additional processing costs. If, on the other hand, the increase in the sales proceeds that would be expected if the asset were processed was less than the additional manufacturing costs, a rational owner would sell the asset in its existing condition and the net sales proceeds under these circumstances would give its deprival value.

In the context of Figure 5.2 six different situations can be envisaged:

(a) $RC < NRV < PV$; then the deprival value is given by the RC. In this case the asset's RC is less than both its NRV and PV. It is worth replacing and because its PV is greater than its NRV it is likely that the asset involved is a fixed asset which will be retained for use within the company.

(b) $RC < PV < NRV$; then the deprival value is given by the RC. As (a) except that as the asset's NRV exceeds its PV the asset will be sold and is probably part of the trading stock of the business.

(c) $PV < RC < NRV$; then the deprival value is given by the RC. The asset would be replaced and then sold. It is almost certain to be part of the trading stock.

(d) $NRV < RC < PV$; then the deprival value is given by the RC. This is likely to be a fixed asset. It is worth replacing since its PV is greater than its RC.

(e) $NRV < PV < RC$; then the deprival value is given by the PV. This asset is not worth replacing, but given that it is owned it will be retained since its PV is greater than its NRV. This is likely to be a fixed asset which would not now be worth purchasing but is worth retaining because of its comparatively low NRV.

(f) $PV < NRV < RC$; then the deprival value is given by the NRV.

This is the second case where the asset's value to the business is not its RC. The asset is not worth replacing nor is there any point in keeping it. It is obviously an asset which should be sold immediately. It might be an obsolete fixed asset whose scrap value is now greater than the benefit that would be obtained from its retention. Alternatively, the asset might be an item of trading stock in respect of which there has been a change in the business's place in the market, i.e. it can no longer acquire or manufacture the stock for an amount which is less than its selling price net of expenses.

It is clear that the deprival value of a fixed asset can only be given by its replacement cost or present value. The deprival value of an asset is based on its net realizable value only when it would be in the interest of the business to dispose of the asset. Thus, following the conventional definition of a current asset – an asset which will be used up within a year of the balance sheet date or within the operating cycle of the business, whichever is the longer – an asset whose deprival value is given by the net realizable value should be classified as a current asset.

The trading stock of a business is, by definition, an asset which is held for sale and hence its deprival value will either be its replacement cost or its net realizable value but not its present value (although in the case of stock which will not be sold for a considerable time its net realizable value may itself be based on the present value of future cash flows).

The deprival value of other current assets[7] may be any of the three possible figures. Consider, as an example, the case of an unexpired insurance premium. Its deprival value is the loss which would be suffered if the insurance company could no longer honour its obligations. If the business felt that it was worth replacing the asset and would take out a new policy to cover the risk the asset's deprival value would be given by its replacement cost. But suppose that it was believed that the cost of the new policy would outweigh the benefits that would be afforded by the policy. It the perceived benefits from the policy exceed the amount that could be obtained if the business surrendered the policy the asset's deprival value would be its 'present value' (or value in use), which would be an amount which is less than the replacement cost but greater than its net realizable value (or surrender value

---

7 Whilst it is instructive to examine the application of the deprival value concept to current assets, it should be noted that both SSAP 16 and ED 35 provide that current assets (other than stock) should be included in a current cost balance at their historical cost.

of the policy). It may be that the net realizable value exceeds the perceived benefit that would flow from the retention of the policy. In this instance the deprival value of the asset is its net realizable value but, if this was indeed the case, the business should in any event surrender the policy.

It is now necessary to make another change in terminology. The Sandilands Committee used the phrase 'value to the business' to describe deprival value and this phrase was repeated in subsequent publications up to and including SSAP 16. However, in ED 35 the phrase 'current cost' is used. Whilst the definitions of the term vary to some degree the basic principle of deprival value is maintained. In general we will, when discussing the various reports, use the description selected by the authors of the particular report.

It can be seen that the value to the business basis of valuation includes elements of both the entry and exit price approaches. However, it should be emphasized that it is regarded as being a modified replacement cost approach. The Sandilands Committee, for example, were of the view that 'it is reasonable to assume, where the replacement cost can be ascertained or estimated, that in the great majority of cases it will correctly represent the value of an asset to a business'.[8]

This is, however, an empirical matter, but it does not appear that the necessary empirical work has been carried out. It may be found that the Sandilands Committee has overstated the relevance of replacement cost.

From Sandilands to SSAP 16

The chronology of the development of CCA in the UK was set out in Chapter 4. It will be our task to explain the provisions of SSAP 16 and ED 35, but in order to do this it is necessary for us to explain the main principles which emerged in their various precursors. In so doing we will differentiate between those principles which have survived the succeeding modifications and those which fell by the wayside. One unfortunate feature of the various reports is the changes which were made in terminology. For example, Sandilands referred to holding gains (or losses) while SSAP 16 describes these as revaluation surpluses (or deficits).

8 *Report of the Inflation Accounting Committee*, Cmnd 6225, HMSO, London, 1975, p. 60.

The Sandilands Report

Two of the main principles of the Sandilands Report have already been considered in the preceding sections. However, for convenience, all the major proposals are summarized below:

(a) A system of accounting based on current values and known as current cost accounting should be introduced. This remains the position in SSAP 16 and ED 35.

(b) The asset valuation basis should be 'value to the business'. This was defined by Sandilands in terms similar to that provided earlier in this book. SSAP 16 retained the basic principle but modified the definition. Thus assets were to be shown in the balance sheet at their value to the business. The Sandilands Committee stated that liabilities should also be dealt with in a similar fashion, but that, as an interim measure until future studies had been carried out, they should continue to be shown at their nominal value. Under the provisions of SSAP 16, assets are shown in the balance sheet at their value to the business while liabilities are shown at their nominal value.

(c) That no adjustment be made for changes in general purchasing power. This is one of the more contentious aspects of the report; it must be remembered that the Sandilands Report was published after the accountancy profession had indicated its preference for CPP accounting in Provisional SSAP 7. We will discuss this issue in a little more detail later.

(d) The current cost profit and loss account should show the company's current operating profit or, as it was called in Sandilands, the company's current cost profit, i.e. the difference between revenue and the value to the business (measured at the dates of consumption) of the assets consumed during the period. All revaluation surpluses and deficits (referred to in Sandilands as holding gains and losses) should be transferred to a reserve account. This basic principle is maintained in SSAP 16 and ED 35 but, as will be seen, certain other adjustments are laid down in these documents.

(e) The current cost accounts should be the only form of published accounts; the committee did not believe that two sets of accounts should be presented except for a limited transitional period during which both historical cost and current cost accounts would be published. The committee's view was that 'if current cost accounts were presented as supplementary statements to historic cost accounts confusion could legitimately arise as to which set of accounts showed a true and fair view.[9] This proposal was subsequently modified. SSAP 16 allowed companies to present either the historical cost or the current cost accounts as the 'main accounts' with the alternative accounts being presented as supplementary information. In producing ED 35 the ASC to some extent returned to the Sandilands position in that they proposed that the published accounts should only include one set of accounts. If companies decide (as will the vast majority) to prepare their accounts under the historical cost convention, certain current cost information should be presented as a note to the accounts. This information comprises sufficient elements to enable the current cost profit for the year to be determined whilst the current costs of certain assets, noteably fixed assets and stock, need also to be disclosed.

(f) That the accountancy profession should be called on to produce a statement of standard accounting practice which would implement the Sandilands proposals.

The differences between historical cost and current cost accounts based on the Sandilands proposals can be summarized as follows:

Item	Historical cost accounts	Current cost accounts
Profit and loss accounts		
1. Cost of goods sold	Historical cost of goods sold	Value to the business, measured at the date of sale of goods sold
2. Depreciation expense	Charge based on the fixed asset's historical cost or later valuation	Charge based on the fixed asset's value to the business at the balance sheet date
Balance sheets		
3. Fixed assets	Historical cost (or later valuation) less accumulated depreciation	Value to the business at the balance sheet date
4. Revaluation reserve	A revaluation reserve is only found where there has been a generally isolated revaluation of assets	All revaluation surpluses, both realized and unrealized, are credited to the reserve account while revaluation deficits are debited to the account

In principle the Sandilands current cost balance sheet should show stock at its value to the business, but the committee was of the view

9 *Report of the Inflation Accounting Committee, op. cit.*, p. 164.

that the historical cost of stock, if calculated on the first-in first-out (FIFO) basis, would provide a reasonable approximation to its value to the business in those cases where the net realizable value of stock exceeded its historical cost. In those instances where the net realizable value falls below cost stock would be written down to net realizable value in both the historical and current cost accounts. In this context the committee restricted its proposals to the suggestion that where there was a significant difference between the value to the business and historical cost of stock the fact should be stated in a note to the accounts. In contrast the SSAP 16 and ED 35 provisions apply the 'value to the business' concept to the treatment of stock.

The essential features of the Sandilands proposals are illustrated in Example 5.3. This example will be extended in the course of the chapter to show the effect of the development of the CCA model. In order to concentrate on the essential points a number of simplifying assumptions will be made. In particular it will be assumed that the company has no overheads or fixed assets. This means that depreciation will not appear in the examples. It should, however, be noted that the same principles are applied to both the depreciation and cost of goods sold expenses. Thus, the calculation of the cost of goods sold expense is based on the proportion of the stock consumed during the period while the depreciation expense is based on the proportion of a fixed asset which is assumed to have been used up during the period, i.e. on the selected depreciation pattern.

An extended example of CCA will be provided after we have introduced the provisions of SSAP 16.

EXAMPLE 5.3

X Limited's opening historical cost balance sheet is given below:

	£		£
Capital and sundry reserves	220	Stock (100 units)	100
Loan (interest free)	220	Debtors	240
		Cash	100
	£440		£440

X Limited buys for cash and sells on 1 month's credit.

A monthly dividend equal to the reported profit, which depends on the method of accounting selected, is distributed.

The company incurs no overhead expenses and owns no fixed assets.

The mark up is constant at 20% on historical cost; all price increases are passed on immediately. The company uses the first-in first-out method of stock valuation.

Stock is held constant at 100 units; the monthly sales are 200 units.

The cost of stock at the end of the previous month is £1 per unit; the cost of purchases increase by 10% at the beginning of the month.

We will first present the historical cost accounts:

Historical cost profit and loss account for month 1

	£	£
Sales, 200 × £1.1 × 1.2		264
less Opening stock	100	
Purchases, 200 × £1.1	220	
	320	
less Closing stock	110	210
Profit		54
less Dividend		£54

Historical cost balance sheet as at the end of month 1

	£
Stock	110
Debtors	264
Cash, £(100 + 240 − 220 − 54)	66
	£440
Capital and sundry reserves	220
Loan (interest free)	220
	£440

The current cost accounts (Sandilands' version) are as follows:

CCA (Sandilands) profit and loss account for month 1

	£	£
Sales		264
less Historical cost of sales		
(see historical cost profit and loss account)	210	
Cost of sales adjustment (*see* note (a))	10	220
Current cost profit		44
less Dividend		£44

CCA (Sandilands) balance sheet as at the end of month 1

	£
Stock	110
Debtors	264
Cash	76
	£450
Capital and sundry reserves	220
Revaluation reserve (*see* note (b))	10
	230
Loan (interest free)	220
	£450

Notes

(a) The cost of sales adjustment is the difference between the value to the business and the historical cost of goods sold, i.e. the realized revaluation surplus.

(b) The realized revaluation surplus is credited to the revaluation reserve (referred to by Sandilands as the stock adjustment reserve). If the company had owned fixed assets both the realized and unrealized revaluation surplus would have been credited to a revaluation reserve (which Sandilands called the fixed asset revaluation reserve).

ED 18

Following the publication of the Sandilands Report in September 1975 the ASC set up a group, under the chairmanship of Douglas Morpeth, known as the Inflation Accounting Steering Group (IASG), which was charged with the task of preparing a Statement of Standard Accounting Practice which would implement the Sandilands proposals. The work of the IASG led to the publication by the ASC in November 1976 of ED 18, 'Current cost accounting' as well as the publication of a *Guidance Manual on Current Cost Accounting.*[10] The aim of the guidance manual was to assist both in the preparation of published accounts using CCA principles and in the implementation and operation of a complete CCA system.

The guidance manual is a fairly lengthy work of some 280 pages

10 Inflation Accounting Steering Group, *Guidance Manual on Current Cost Accounting,* Tolley, London, on behalf of the ICAEW, 1976.

while ED 18 itself was, at 94 pages, considerably longer than other statements, including PSSAP 7. It is to be expected that the introduction of a new system of accounting should require lengthy explanation, but many people thought that ED 18 was an unnecessarily long and complex document, a fact which might have contributed to its ultimate rejection. ED 18 was ambitious in that it attempted to deal with items, such as deferred taxation, which were strictly outside its brief and this too provoked some criticism.

The IASG's brief was to apply the Sandilands proposals and they were therefore not able to question the basic principles promulgated in the report. They did, however, make a number of fundamental changes (as well as numerous detailed alterations) to the proposals made by Sandilands.

There is little point in spelling out the detailed changes, but it will be useful to indicate their general nature. In general the ED 18 proposals would have made the current cost accounts significantly more subjective than the Sandilands version. For example, Sandilands proposed that the replacement cost of plant and machinery should generally be measured by reference to a suitable external price index applicable to the fixed assets used in the particular industry. In contrast, ED 18 provided for five possible methods of determining the replacement cost which were ranked in order of preference. The preferred basis was the use of suppliers' price lists, the next was the company's own estimate based on 'expert opinion' while the least preferred was the industry specific price index as recommended by Sandilands.

The Sandilands Committee's view was that the loss of accuracy that would result from the use of externally produced price indexes should be accepted in return for the greater objectivity that would be achieved by the use of such indexes. They asserted that if accounts are to have sufficient objectivity to be generally acceptable, the necessary valuations should be made on bases external to the company. In contrast the IASG, in this and other areas, appeared to be more prepared to trade objectivity for the use of data which was specific to the company and the subjective nature of the proposals was a further aspect of ED 18 which was the subject of major criticism.

In drafting ED 18 the IASG took a different view to that of the Sandilands Committee in connection with the treatment of stock in the balance sheet. The ED 18 proposal was that stock should be included at its value to the business at the balance sheet date (the lower of the stocks' replacement cost and net realizable value) instead of historical cost. Hence the ED 18 version of current cost accounts includes an additional unrealized revaluation surplus, the difference between the historical cost and value to the business of closing stock. This proposal was also included in SSAP 16.

One major difference between the Sandilands and ED 18 proposals was the treatment of revaluation surpluses (and deficits). The Sandilands Committee adopted what some people regarded as an inconsistent line with regard to the determination of profit and, in particular, the extent to which revaluation surpluses could be regarded as part of a company's profit. It may be helpful if we summarize the analysis provided in the Sandilands Report.

The committee stated that its definition of profit was equivalent to that of Sir John Hicks and it modified Hicks' statement (*see* page 54, Chapter 3) to fit the circumstances of a company as follows: 'A company's profit for the year is the maximum value which the company can distribute during the year, and still expect to be as well off at the end of the year as it was at the beginning'.[11]

The next step in the process is to decide how to measure 'well-offness'. The committee stated, 'If we were granted perfect knowledge of the future, the quantification of this capital ("well-offness") would be fairly clear. It would be the discounted net present value of future net cash flows arising for the company'.[12]

These views led the committee to define a company's annual profit in economic terms as:

> The discounted net present value of all future net cash flows at the end of the year, less the discounted net present value of the future net cash flows at the beginning of the year, plus the net cash flow arising within the year after making adjustments for the introduction of new capital during the year.[13]

The committee appeared to have accepted the above as its 'ideal' measure and then went on to examine methods which approximated to this approach but which were capable of practical application. A number of different approaches were examined and the committee finally decided that the method which combined the maintenance of physical capital measured by reference to the 'value of the business' of the company's assets was 'the most useful method of accounting for inflation in the longer term'.[14] However, as has been pointed out by a number of critics of the Sandilands Report, the committee did

---

11 Sandilands, *op. cit.*, p. 29.
12 *Ibid.*, p. 29. It might be pedantic to note that one of two nets in the last sentence is redundant.
13 *Ibid.*, p. 29.
14 *Ibid.*, p. 41.

not attempt to show the extent to which the selected approach approximated to the 'ideal' method referred to above.[15]

A consequence of the committee's view was that a CCA profit and loss account should only include the company's current operating profit (or gain) and that all revaluation surpluses should be credited to non-distributable revaluation reserves. This implies that a company's current operating profit represents the maximum dividend that could be distributed if the company is to maintain its capital.

In apparent contrast to this approach the committee also adopted the view we discussed in Chapter 3 that profit is not a single concept; that there is no such thing as the 'right' basis for the determination of profit and that each basis is 'correct' in terms of its own assumptions. In the context of the question of the extent to which revaluation surpluses (or holding gains) might be regarded as part of profit (i.e. could be distributed without diminishing the 'well-offness' of the company) the committee stated:

> A further division of total gains (current operating profit plus holding gains) may be made between gains regarded as 'profit' for the year and gains which are not so regarded. Many different views may be taken of the extent to which gains of all kinds may be regarded as profit for the year, according to circumstances. In different situations, any part of total gains may be regarded as profit. The measurement of profit is thus not an objective process in the sense that within a given amount of total gain the amount of profit is fixed by independent factors. The extent to which given amount of total gain is regarded as profit may vary between nil and 100 per cent, depending on the point of view of the individual or company involved and on the conventions of the accounting system adopted.[16]

However, as was pointed out above, the proposals of the Sandilands Committee would not have permitted companies any latitude in the question of the extent to which revaluation surpluses could be regarded as part of the annual profit. The IASG in drafting ED 18 adopted a contrary position.

The appropriation account

ED 18 included a proposal that a company's financial statements should include an appropriation account. The account would be credited with the current cost profit for the year, carried from the current cost profit

15 R. J. Chambers, *Current cost accounting: a critique of the Sandilands Report*, ICRA Occasional Paper No. 11, University of Lancaster, Lancaster, 1976, p. 54.
16 Sandilands, *op. cit.*, p. 23.

and loss account, and with all revaluation surpluses (and debited with revaluation deficits). The appropriation account would be debited with the transfer to the revaluation reserve plus the dividends for the year and the balance on the account would be credited to distributable reserves.

The structure of the appropriation account is as follows:

Appropriation account for the year ended 31 December 19XX

	£000s	£000s
Current cost profit		2 500
Net surplus for the year on the revaluation of assets	3 700	
Appropriated to revaluation reserve (say)	3 500	200
		2 700
Dividends		1900
Amount taken to general reserve		£ 800

It was proposed that the initial presumption should be that the net surplus on the revaluation of assets would need to be retained in the business and hence that the amount transferred to the revaluation reserve should equal the net surplus. However – and this is where the proposals differed substantially from those of Sandilands – directors could, depending on their views of the circumstances of the company, transfer a lesser or greater amount. The amount of the transfer would be left to the discretion of the directors, although they would have been required to explain the basis and the reasons for the amounts appropriated to or from the revaluation reserve.

It will be noted that these provisions would have allowed directors to select from a number of different capital maintenance concepts and this does seem to indicate a lack of certainty on the part of the IASG as to the most appropriate way of measuring 'well-offness' or the substance of the business. The group recognized this; in its introduction to ED 18 the IASG expressed its belief that the proposals of ED 18 should be regarded as representing an interim solution, and that one of the major problems which prevented the publication of a more definite statement, was the lack of consensus on how to measure the substance of a business.

The very wide range of choice which would have been available under the proposals give rise to the accusation that under ED 18 companies would be able to choose their own profit;[17] profit in this context

---

17 *The Economist*, 2 July 1977.

being the current operating gain plus or minus the difference between the net revaluation surplus and the transfer to the revaluation reserve. The criticism may well have been too harsh in that the ED 18 proposals would have required companies to report on their various gains and directors to explain the rationale for the transfer to the revaluation reserve. However, the general view was that the ED 18 model would have made it difficult to compare the results of different companies and the appropriation account does not appear in the SSAP 16 model. The ASC in drafting SSAP 16 did deal with the need to make an additional investment in net monetary assets in a period of rising prices and the problems associated with the gearing adjustment. The difference is that SSAP 16 requires all companies to make the necessary adjustments although, as will be seen in Chapter 6, directors would be allowed a fair amount of discretion in deciding how the adjustments should be made.

The IASG's terms of reference were such that they could not depart from the basic model proposed by the Sandilands Committee which, it will be remembered, did not include an adjustment for changes in the value of money. Even so, the IASG did seek to go beyond the basic Sandilands model in that ED 18 proposed that companies should be required to publish, by way of a note to the current cost accounts, a statement showing the effect of changes in the value of money. This statement would have served two purposes. It would have provided a comparison of the actual change in the owners' interest with the changes that would have been required to maintain the owners' purchasing power. The statement would also have shown the profit or loss on holding net monetary items (*see* pages 101–105 of Chapter 4). SSAP 16 included the statement showing the effect of changes in the general price level on shareholders' interest as one of the voluntary statements which companies are invited, but not required, to publish as notes to the current cost accounts.

EXAMPLE 5.4

Because of the simplifying assumptions used in our running example (*see* Example 5.3) there are a few differences between the Sandilands and ED 18 versions of the current cost accounts. The presentation is different and the ED 18 model allows the directors to decide how much should be transferred to the revaluation reserve.

The ED 18 accounts based on the data given in Example 5.3 would be as follows:

CCA (ED 18) profit and loss account for month 1

	£	£
Sales		264
less Historical cost of sales	210	
Cost of sales adjustment	10	220
Current cost profit		£44

Appropriation account for month 1

	£	£
Current cost profit		44
Net surplus for the month on the revaluation of assets	10	
Appropriated to revaluation reserve	x	$10 - x$
		$54 - x$
Dividend		$54 - x$
Amount taken to general reserve		£ 0

Note £x is the amount which the directors deem should be transferred to the revaluation reserve given the circumstances of the company.

CCA (ED 18) balance sheet as at the end of month 1

	£
Stock	110
Debtors	264
Cash	$66 + x$
	£$(440 + x)$
Capital and sundry reserves	220
Revaluation reserve	x
	$220 + x$
Loan (interest free)	220
	£$(440 + x)$

The rejection of ED 18

As was described in Chapter 4, the members of the ICAEW passed a resolution in July 1977 which rejected the compulsory introduction of CCA and, as a result, ED 18 was withdrawn. The views of those who supported the resolution covered a wide spectrum. Some people were (and no doubt still are) against the introduction of CCA in any form. There were others who, while sympathetic to CCA, believed that the basic CCA model as proposed by the Sandilands Committee contained a number of serious weaknesses. We will concentrate on the views of the second group.

Three major problem areas were identified: (a) the absence of any adjustments for changes in the value of money; (b) the treatment of monetary assets; (c) the absence of a gearing adjustment, i.e. the failure to recognize that a proportion of the additional amounts that would be required to be invested in the business as a result of the increased cost of stock and fixed assets might be financed by creditors.

The first problem was not dealt with in SSAP 16 and we will defer a discussion of this subject until Chapter 6. The other two problems are addressed in SSAP 16 and it might be helpful if they were considered at this stage. The ED 18 proposals would have allowed directors to take the factors into account when deciding the amount to be transferred to the revaluation reserve. However, it was felt that this proposal left too much to the discretion of directors and that it would be better if the need to make the adjustments were made an integral part of the proposals.

Monetary assets

The capital maintenance concept on which the Sandilands version of CCA is based is a company's ability to maintain the value to the business of its non-monetary assets. Thus, if 100% of a company's current operating profit was paid out by way of dividends or taxation the company would still be able to replace the non-monetary assets consumed during the period which it wished to replace (i.e. those assets whose value to the business is equal to their replacement costs). This formulation may appear to be acceptable when applied to a manufacturing concern the vast proportion of whose assets are in non-monetary form, but there are, however, numerous examples of companies whose assets are almost wholly or at least substantially of a monetary nature. A bank is an obvious example of a case of a company whose assets are mainly monetary (cash and various forms of debtors), but many manufacturing and trading concerns also need to hold appreciable quantities of monetary assets. A manufacturing company might, for example, have to grant its customers extended periods of credit and hence require to maintain its debtors at a high level. Let us assume that a company has, because of the nature of the market in which it operates, to allow all its customers 2 months credit.

Suppose that there is a 50% increase in the cost of manufacturing the product sold by the company. The result of this increase is that the company would have to increase its investment in stock and debtors. The Sandilands version of CCA allows the company to reduce its current operating profit by the extra amount that would need to be invested in stock but would permit no such, or similar, adjustment for the additional amount that would need to be invested in debtors.

It was argued that the failure to recognize that a company might need to increase its holding of monetary assets in periods of rising prices was a basic weakness of the Sandilands proposals and subsequent developments – the Hyde guidelines, SSAP 16 and ED 35 – attempt to overcome this problem.

We will return to this point later when dealing with SSAP 16, but at this stage it might be helpful if we presented a simple example of a situation where an adjustment of the type described is required.

EXAMPLE 5.5
This example is based on the data presented in Example 5.3. The opening balance sheet is, for convenience, given below:

	£		£
Capital and sundry reserves	220	Stock (100 units)	100
Loan (interest free)	220	Debtors	240
		Cash	100
	£440		£440

The opening cash balance, i.e. £100, is equal to half the company's monthly purchases (at the old prices) and we will assume that the company considers that, in its particular circumstances, it is necessary to maintain the relationship between the opening cash balance and the monthly cost of purchases. During the month under review the cost of the trading stock increases by 10% and thus the company would, if it is to maintain the required cash balance, need to have £110 at the start of the following month.

In practice a similar target would be set for debtors, but in this simplified example the closing debtors figure already includes the effect of the increased price.

It was shown in Example 5.3 that, if it is assumed that the whole of the profit is distributed, the closing cash balance was £66 using historical cost accounting and £76 if the accounts were prepared and profit calculated using the Sandilands version of CCA. This means that even on the latter basis the reported profit is too high if the company wishes to distribute all its reported profit and maintain both its monetary and non-monetary assets at the required level. The Sandilands current cost profit, and dividend, was £44 and it is clear that this must be reduced by £34 if the required balance of monetary assets is to be maintained.

This could be achieved by charging against current cost profit a 'monetary adjustment' of £34, i.e. 10% of £340. The company's opening balance of monetary assets (cash and debtors) equals £340 and 10% represents the increase in cost faced by this particular company. The monetary adjustment would be credited to a non-distributable reserve which might be called a 'monetary reserve'.

The modified version of the current cost accounts incorporating the monetary adjustment is shown below:

Profit and loss account

	£	£
Sales		264
less Historical cost of sales	210	
Cost of sales adjustment	10	
Monetary adjustment	34	254
Current cost profit		10
less Dividend		£ 10

Balance sheet

	£		£
Capital and sundry reserve	220	Stock	110
Revaluation reserve	10	Debtors	264
Monetary reserve	34	Cash	110
	264		
Loan (interest free)	220		
	£484		£484

The gearing adjustment

Virtually all companies are financed by a mixture of debt and equity, for even those companies which do not include any long-term debt as part of their capital structure will purchase goods and services on credit and will hence be partly financed by trade creditors. It is argued that creditors will generally finance part of the increased investment in assets that will be caused by price increases, and it is therefore not necessary for a company to set the whole of the additional sums required to finance the increase cost of assets against the profit available for distribution.

Suppose that a retailing company holds stock of 600 units, representing 3 months trading, which are all purchased on credit with the supplier allowing 2 months credit. Let us also assume that stock originally cost £2 per unit and that the price per unit is increased to £3. Then, if we ignore other items, the company's investment in working capital before the price increase was

Stock	1 200
less Trade creditors	800
Working capital	£ 400

While the position after the price change is

Stock	1 800
less Trade creditors	1 200
Working capital	£ 600

Thus, if it is assumed that the suppliers will continue to allow the company the same credit terms, it can be seen that the company will only require to make a net additional investment of £200 (£600 − £400) and not £600 (£1800 − £1200) in stock as a result of the price increase.

The original Sandilands proposals took no account of the extent to which creditors would provide part of the additional investment, and it was hence argued that the Sandilands profit was too conservative (low) when viewed from the standpoint of the owners of the company. The validity of this criticism depends on the view that is taken of the nature of accounting reports and in particular whether the reports should simply consider the firm as an entity or whether they should pay regard to the position of its owners. To return to the above example, the company has to invest £600 more in stock if it is to continue to hold the same physical volume and the Sandilands model would reflect the need to make the additional investment. However, all other things being equal, the trade creditors would provide £400 of this amount and hence only £200 would have to be retained from the amount that would otherwise be available for distribution to shareholders.

Similar considerations apply to those companies which maintain an element of debt in their capital structure. If it can be assumed that the existing debt/equity or gearing ratio can be maintained then only a proportion of the total additional investment will need to be withheld from the shareholders. The argument here is that the recognition of revaluation surpluses for the period will increase the equity interest in the company and that − all other things being equal − creditors might be expected to be willing to increase the amount of their loan in proportion to the increase in equity interest. If they did so the debt/equity ratio after the credit to the revaluation reserve and the receipt of the additional funds from the creditors would be equal to the original debt/equity ratio.

The purpose of the gearing adjustment is to reflect that proportion of revaluation surpluses which will be financed by creditors. As will be seen, the gearing adjustment is then credited to the profit and loss account and (or in some circumstances debited) and the resulting figure may be considered as being the current cost operating profit attributable to shareholders.

The gearing adjustment is debited to the revaluation reserve, in other words the net credit to the revaluation reserve is the difference between the additional investment required less the amount that it is assumed will be provided by creditors.

A simplified version of the gearing adjustment is illustrated in Example 5.6.

EXAMPLE 5.6
Opening balance sheet

	£		£
Capital and sundry reserves	220	Stock	100
Loan (interest free)	220	Debtors	240
		Cash	100
	£440		£440

The company's gearing ratio (Debt divided by Debt plus Equity) is 50% or, in other words, half the long-term capital was, at the start of the period, provided by creditors. However, this simple example does not include trade creditors.

We showed in Example 5.5 that, with the assumptions stated therein, the company would need to charge £10 as the cost of sales adjustment and £34 as the monetary adjustment in the CCA profit and loss account if the current cost profit is to represent the maximum dividend that could be paid while still maintaining the required volume of assets. It was assumed in Example 5.5 that there would be no increase in loan capital and that the additional investment would be made entirely from the funds that would otherwise be available for distribution to shareholders. This extra retention led to a reduction in the gearing ratio which fell to 45% (($£220/£484) \times 100$) (*see* page 151).

The rationale for the incorporation of a gearing ratio into the profit and loss account is the assumption that part of the additional investment will be made by creditors. For the purposes of this example we will assume that the company will maintain its gearing ratio at 50%. Thus the gearing adjustment will be 50% of the total of the cost of sales adjustment and monetary adjustment, i.e. 50% of £(10 + 34) = £22.

The CCA profit and loss account incorporating the cost of sales, monetary and gearing adjustments would then appear as follows:

Profit and loss account

	£	£
Sales		264
less Historical cost of sales	210	
Cost of sales adjustment	10	
Monetary adjustment	34	254
Current cost operating profit		10
add Gearing adjustment		22
Current cost operating profit attributable to shareholders		32
less Dividend		£ 32

Balance sheet

	£		£
Capital and sundry reserves	220	Stock	110
Revaluation reserve,		Debtors	264
£(10 + 34 − 22)	22	Cash	88
	242		
Loan (interest free)	220		
	£462		£462

It will be noted that the cash balance is £88 and not the £110 which is the balance which the company wishes to hold (*see* Example 5.5). The reason for the shortfall is that creditors have not yet increased their loan by the required amount of £22; for the same reason the gearing ratio is 48% and not 50%. If we now assume that the additional loan is forthcoming the balance sheet would appear as follows:

Balance sheet

	£		£
Capital and sundry reserves	220	Stock	110
Revaluation reserve	22	Debtors	264
	242	Cash	110
Loan (interest free),			
£(220 + 22)	242		
	£484		£484

The Hyde Committee guidelines

The ICAEW resolution of July 1977 rejecting the compulsory introduction of CCA placed the leaders of the accountancy profession in an embarrassing position. They had very strongly argued the urgent need for reform, but the resolution of the members of the ICAEW meant that fresh proposals would have to be formulated and it was clear that this would take some time. In one sense the ASC did not feel itself bound by the vote of the members of the English Institute as the resolution was regarded as being a rejection of ED 18 rather than the rejection of CCA on anything other than a voluntary basis. The ASC therefore set to the task of producing a new exposure draft, but also established a special committee under the chairmanship of William Hyde. The task of this committee was to produce a simplified set of guidelines which could be used by companies in the interim until an appropriate standard could be promulgated. The committee's report was published in November 1977 under the title *Inflation accounting – an interim recommendation.*

The ASC recommended that the proposals be adopted by all listed companies starting with accounting periods ending on or after 31 December 1977 but also urged the wider adoption of the proposals 'in the interests of more informative reporting'.[18]

The Hyde Committee recommended that companies should include in their published accounts a prominent separate statement which would in effect be a CCA profit and loss account. Companies were not required to publish a CCA balance sheet, although it would have been necessary to prepare such a balance sheet in order to calculate the required adjustments.

The basic outline of the supplementary statement is shown below:

Current cost statement for the year ended 31 December 19XX

	£000	£000
Turnover		6000
Profit before taxation and interest as in the historical cost accounts		800
less Adjustments		
Depreciation	140	
Cost of sales	160	300
Operating profit		500
Interest payable less receivable		80
		420

(cont. next page)

---

18 *Inflation accounting – an interim recommendation*, ICAEW, London, 1977, Para. 4.

Current cost statement cont.

Gearing adjustment	120
Adjusted profit before taxation and extraordinary items	540
Taxation	80
Adjusted profit before extraordinary items	460
Extraordinary items (net of tax)	40
Adjusted profit attributable to shareholders	420
Dividends	220
Adjusted retained profit	£200

The above format would apply to an individual company and a slightly modified version would be used for group accounts.

The depreciation adjustment is the difference between the depreciation charge based on historical cost and the charge calculated by reference to the value to the business of the fixed assets, i.e. the realized revaluation surplus on fixed assets. The cost of sales adjustment is similarly the realized revaluation surplus on stock consumed during the period; the difference between the historical cost of goods sold and their value to the business at the date of sale.

The gearing adjustment had not been included in either the Sandilands or ED 18 proposals and, as has been discussed above, its absence had been one of the grounds of criticism of these proposals. The Hyde Committee accepted the argument in favour of the introduction of such an adjustment but their proposals in this area were not wholly satisfactory. In effect the committee conflated the monetary and gearing adjustments which were illustrated in Examples 5.5 and 5.6. They divided companies into two groups, depending on whether or not a company's monetary liabilities exceeded its monetary assets. In the case of a company which had an excess of monetary liabilities the gearing adjustment would be similar to the adjustment illustrated in Example 5.6, i.e. it would be a credit (in times of rising prices) to the profit and loss account representing the proportion of the depreciation and cost of sales adjustments which might be financed by creditors. In the alternative situation (where a company's monetary assets exceeded its monetary liabilities), the adjustment would be similar to the monetary adjustment illustrated in Examples 5.5 and 5.6. The adjustment would then be a debit to the profit and loss account representing the additional amount that would be required to be retained by the company in order to maintain its investment in net monetary assets.

The reasoning behind the Hyde approach appears to be the view that there is a special relationship between monetary liabilities and monetary assets in that it is assumed that monetary liabilities are the source of finance for the monetary assets and that only the excess of monetary liabilities over monetary assets can be regarded as providing a source of finance for non-monetary assets. Thus in the case of a company with excess monetary liabilities the 'credit gearing adjustment' is restricted because it is calculated by reference to the excess monetary liabilities and not, as was done in Example 5.6, the whole of the monetary liabilities. Similarly, it was argued that the need of a company to retain funds in order to finance an increase in monetary assets to take account of increased costs applies only to the extent that monetary assets are not covered by monetary liabilities.

Suppose that a company's balance sheet is as follows:

	£		£
Equity	100	Non-monetary assets	150
Monetary liabilities	200	Monetary assets	150
	£300		£300

and assume that the total of the depreciation and cost of sales adjustments is £90.

The basic Hyde assumption is that £150 of the monetary liabilities is used to finance monetary assets. One implication of their assumption is that the company does not need to retain funds in order to increase monetary assets as these will automatically be provided by creditors and that the company therefore does not need to make a monetary adjustment. A second implication is that only £50 (£200 − £150) of the monetary liabilities can be regarded as a source of finance for the non-monetary assets and that the whole of the equity is used for this purpose. Thus two-thirds (100/150) of the non-monetary assets (which of course include the fixed assets and stock) is financed by the shareholders and one-third by the creditors. Thus the gearing adjustment is a credit of one-third of £90, i.e. £30.

Let us now consider the case of a company whose monetary assets exceed its monetary liabilities. Suppose that such a company has the following asset and capital structure:

	£		£
Equity	200	Non-monetary assets	150
Monetary liabilities	100	Monetary assets	150
	£300		£300

In this case the Hyde assumption is that the whole of the monetary liabilities is the source of finance of the monetary assets and that the non-monetary assets are wholly financed by the equity shareholders. The consequence of this assumption is that there is no 'credit gearing adjustment' because the additional investment required as a result of the increased cost of stock and fixed assets must be provided by the shareholders. The shareholders must also finance any required increase in the company's net monetary assets which is shown above to be £50. In order to make the required adjustment it is necessary to decide how much extra is required in order to cope with increased prices. It may be thought appropriate, in the absence of a more suitable index, to base the adjustment on the change in the RPI; if this is the case, and if we assume that the RPI has increased by 10% over the period, then the debit gearing adjustment is 10% of £50, i.e. £5.

The above represents a highly simplified version of the Hyde guidelines, but a number of proposals reappear in SSAP 16 and these will be discussed in the next chapter.

ED 24

As the differences between ED 24 and SSAP 16 are comparatively minor and involve no matters of principle, we will not describe the provisions of ED 24 but instead proceed directly to a consideration of SSAP 16.

Recommended reading

See list at the end of Chapter 7.

Questions

See end of Chapter 6 for Current Cost Accounting questions.

6 Current Value Accounting II: The SSAP 16 Approach

In this chapter we will describe the version of current cost accounting (CCA) which formed the subject of SSAP 16, 'Current cost accounting', published in March 1980. The standard required certain companies, essentially listed companies and other large entities, to publish a current cost profit and loss account and current cost balance sheet. The current cost accounts could either be presented as the main accounts (in which case certain historical cost information would also have to be disclosed in the notes) or as supplementary statements to the main, historical cost accounts.

We will discuss some of the criticisms of the SSAP 16 version of CCA in Chapter 7, where we will also discuss post SSAP 16 developments.[1]

Contemporaneously with the issue of SSAP 16 the ASC published a booklet entitled *Guidance notes on SSAP 16: current cost accounting*, which is intended to help in the application of the standard. The methods outlined in the booklet were not mandatory, but it is apparent that it has a considerable impact on the way in which the standard is applied. Numerous references will be made in this chapter to both the guidance notes and the standard; references to the guidance notes will be of the form (GN, Para. *x*) while references to the standard will take the form (SSAP 16, Para. *x*).

The basic approach adopted in SSAP 16 is rooted in the Sandilands proposals, but to these have been added the gearing and monetary working capital adjustments.

Scope of SSAP 16

The standard applies to all entities which have any class of share or loan listed on the Stock Exchange and other 'large' entities (SSAP

---

1 For example, ED 35, issued in July 1984, which proposes that companies which produce their accounts under the historical cost convention should not be required to publish an additional set of current cost accounts but instead include certain elements of current cost information in the notes to the accounts.

16, Para. 46). Certain types of entities are, however, specifically excluded. The excluded entities are wholly owned subsidiaries, entities whose aim is not the earning of profit, e.g. charities, and what have been termed 'value-based' companies. Value-based companies comprise (a) authorized insurers, (b) property investment and dealing companies and (c) investment trust companies, unit trusts and similar enterprises. Value-based companies are excluded because of the difficulty in defining their 'operating capability' (see page 161). As we shall show the concept of capital maintenance which is the basis of the SSAP 16 version of CCA is the need to maintain the operating capability of the business.

Method of presentation

The method of presentation is outlined in SSAP 16, Paras 47 and 48. The basic principle is that the annual financial statement of entities falling within the scope of the standard must include current cost accounts prepared in accordance with the provisions of SSAP 16 together with historical cost accounts or historical cost information. The current cost accounts should contain a profit and loss account and balance sheet together with certain explanatory notes which will be detailed later in the chapter.

The current cost profit and loss account

An example of the format of a current cost profit and loss account is provided below. A striking feature of the account is the presentation of two profit figures – the *current cost operating profit* and the *current cost profit attributable to shareholders:*

X Limited
Current cost profit and loss account for the year ended 31 December 19XX

	£	£
Turnover		xxx
		—
Profit before interest and taxation on the historical cost		
basis		xxx
less Current cost operating adjustments		xxx
		—
CURRENT COST OPERATING PROFIT		xxx
Gearing adjustment	(xxx)	
Interest payable less receivable	xxx	xxx
	—	—

Current cost profit before taxation	xxx
Taxation	xxx
	—
CURRENT COST PROFIT ATTRIBUTABLE TO SHAREHOLDERS	xxx
Dividends	xxx
	—
Retained current cost profit for the year	£xxx
	═

Statement of retained profits/reserves

Retained current cost profit for the year	xxx
Movements on current cost reserve	xxx
Movements on other reserves	xxx
	—
	xxx
Retained profits/reserves at the beginning of the year	xxx
	—
Retained profits/reserves at the end of the year	£xxx
	═

Notes

(a) The above is based on an example included in the Appendix to SSAP 16. An alternative treatment is illustrated in the Appendix in which the gearing adjustment is shown after taxation.

(b) The three current cost operating adjustments are the depreciation adjustment, the cost of sales adjustment and the monetary working capital adjustment. It has been assumed that the total of the adjustments is a debit and that, in consequence, the gearing adjustment is a credit.

(c) Corresponding amounts for the preceding period must be shown. These need not be provided in the first period for which current cost accounts are prepared if the current cost accounts are not the main accounts and if the information is not readily available.

Since the measurement of profit is dependent on the selected basis of capital which is required to be maintained, a discussion of profit must start with a consideration of capital. SSAP 16 states that 'the CCA system is based upon a concept of capital which is represented by the net operating assets of a business' (SSAP 16, Para. 3). The paragraph goes on to state that the '*Net operating assets* can be said to represent, in accounting terms, the *operating capability* of the business'. Thus it appears that capital is really regarded as the operating capability of the business and that the maintenance of net operating assets is regarded as a proxy measure.

The key terms are defined as follows:

> The *operating capability* of the business is the amount of goods and services which the business is able to supply with its existing resources in the relevant period. These resources are represented in accounting terms by the net operating assets at current cost. (SSAP 16, Para. 39)

> *Net operating assets* comprise the fixed assets (including trade investments), stock and monetary working capital dealt with in a historical cost balance sheet. (SSAP 16, Para. 38)

A more detailed discussion of the nature of monetary working capital will be provided later in the chapter, but at this stage it can broadly be defined as trade debtors and prepayments plus stock which is not subject to a cost of sales adjustment less trade creditors and accruals. In certain circumstances monetary working capital will include cash and balances at bank (including overdrafts).

The *current cost operating profit* is then the surplus arising from the ordinary course of business in the period after allowing for the impact of price changes on the funds needed to continue the existing business and maintain its operating capability. It is to be calculated before interest on net borrowings[2] and taxation (SSAP 16, Para. 6).

The current cost operating profit is the historical cost profit plus, or minus, three adjustments, which comprise the current cost operating adjustments referred to in the format above. The three adjustments are as follows: (a) a depreciation adjustment which is the difference between the value to the business of the fixed assets consumed in the period and the depreciation charged in the historical cost accounts; (b) a cost of sales adjustment which is the difference between the value to the business of the stock consumed in the period and the cost of stock charged in the historical cost accounts; (c) a monetary working capital adjustment which is to allow for the effect of price changes on the monetary working capital needed to support the operating capability of the business – this adjustment is similar to the monetary asset adjustment which was discussed in Chapter 5.

It can be seen that the current cost operating profit is analogous to the Sandilands current cost profit, with the only difference being the addition of the monetary working capital adjustment. In particular the objective of the two profits is similar. The purpose of the Sandilands current cost profit was to report the amount which could be distributed as taxation and dividends after providing for the maintenance of the

---

2 A discussion of the meaning of net borrowings will have to be deferred until later in the chapter, but at this stage interest on net borrowings can be said to constitute all interest except that which may be payable on certain current liabilities.

physical assets of the business (fixed assets and stock) while the SSAP 16 current cost operating profit may be regarded as the sum that may be distributed as interest, taxation and dividends while maintaining the business investment in physical assets plus its net investment in monetary working capital.

Current cost profit attributable to shareholders

In calculating the current cost operating profit no account is taken of the way in which the net operating assets of the business are financed, i.e. the extent of the entity's gearing. It is argued that regard should be taken of the extent to which the shareholders will gain (in periods of rising prices) because the repayment rights of creditors are fixed in monetary terms.

As was pointed out in Chapter 5, one effect of increases in the prices of operating assets is a decrease in the gearing ratio or, in other words, an increase in the proportion of the assets which are financed by shareholders. In order to deal with this point the CCA profit and loss account discloses the current cost profit attributable to shareholders, which is defined as follows:

> The current cost profit attributable to shareholders is the surplus for the period after allowing for the impact of price changes in the funds needed to maintain their [the shareholders] proportion of the operating capability. It is calculated after interest, taxation and extraordinary items. (SSAP 16, Para. 41)

In order to arrive at the current cost profit attributable to shareholders it is necessary to commence with the current cost operating profit and to take into account interest on net borrowings, taxation and extraordinary items. In addition, it is necessary to make a gearing adjustment. The gearing adjustment included in SSAP 16 is an abatement of the total of the current cost operating adjustments depending upon the proportion of the net operating assets financed by net borrowings. This form of adjustment will be discussed in further detail on page 199. It should, however, be noted that this approach to calculating the gearing adjustment was subject to considerable criticism. These criticisms and alternative approaches which were later adopted by the ASC will be described in Chapter 7.

Distributable profits

A fairly simple-minded interpretation of the two measures of profit can be presented in terms of distribution policy.

The current cost operating profit is the maximum that could be paid out by way of interest on net borrowings, dividends to shareholders and taxation without eroding the net operating assets of the business. The current cost profit attributable to shareholders is the maximum amount which could be paid out as dividends, without eroding the shareholders' investment in the net operating assets of the business. Alternatively, it can be regarded as the maximum that could be paid out by way of dividends without eroding the net operating assets of the business on the assumption that additional finance (equal to the gearing adjustment) could be raised.

Presumably the ASC did not define the two measures of profits in these terms because they did not wish to give the impression that they could be used as simple indicators of the amount that could be distributed. This point is made forcefully in SSAP 16, Para. 23, where it is emphasized that, as with all systems of accounting, the amount that can prudently be distributed depends not only on profitability but also on the availability of funds. The ASC goes on to point out that when determining the amount to be distributed 'consideration must be given to factors not reflected in profit, such as capital expenditure plans, changes in the volume of working capital, the effect on funding requirements of changes in production methods and efficiency, liquidity and new financing arrangements' (SSAP 16, Para. 23).

Another reason for the ASC's rejection of an interpretation based on distribution policy is the interpretation's reliance on the assumption that additional funds will be provided by net borrowings. The ASC wished to show that the current cost accounts are mainly based on past events and do not depend on assumptions about the ability of the company to obtain additional finance in the future (SSAP 16, Para. 19). It appears that their interpretation of current cost profit attributable to shareholders is on the following lines.

It is true that, if a credit gearing adjustment is made, the distribution of the whole of the current cost profit attributable to shareholders will lead to an erosion of a company's total operating capability. However, the existing shareholders' interest in the (diminished) business will be maintained if the dividend is restricted to the current cost profit attributable to shareholders.

Clearly no objection can be made to the wish of the ASC to show that the information produced by current cost accounts can be interpreted in the light of past events. It is, however, unfortunate that the committee did not make clear the point concerning the potential erosion of the total operating capability of the business. The definition of current cost profit attributable to shareholders could have been improved for it is capable of misinterpretation as 'proportion' could be taken to mean the proportion of shareholders interest *vis-à-vis* the interest of the suppliers of the net borrowings. It is clear that this is not intended and it would have been better had the current cost profit attributable to shareholders been defined as: 'the surplus for the period after allowing for the impact of price changes on the funds needed to maintain the shareholders' interest in the operating capability of the business'.

The statement of changes in retained profits/reserves

The format shown on page 160 follows that of the current cost profit and loss account included in the Appendix to SSAP 16. As an appendix the methods outlined are illustrative and not prescriptive and the statement of retained profits/reserves which appears at the foot of the present example is not referred to in the standard itself. However, its inclusion in the appendix meant that it was used widely. The purpose of the statement is to show the total of the retained gains for the year. Thus it shows the retained current cost profit for the year (i.e. the current cost attributable to shareholders less the dividends payable in respect of the year) and any movements on the current cost reserve and any other reserves.

Current cost reserve

The current cost reserve is the owners' equity account to which all the various revaluation surpluses are credited and deficits debited. The account is also debited or credited with the monetary working capital and the gearing adjustments.

The cost of sales adjustment (if positive) is a realized revaluation surplus in that it represents the difference between the cost of stock and its value to the business at the date of consumption. The monetary working capital adjustment is in contrast not a gain but rather an additional sum which needs to be retained in the business if it is to operate at the same level of activity despite the increase in prices.

The gearing adjustment is an abatement of the three current cost accounts adjustments and is debited (or in periods of falling prices credited) to the current cost reserve.

In addition to the above, the unrealized revaluation surpluses are credited and deficits debited to the current cost reserve account. Thus, as with the conventional historical cost accounting system and in accordance with the terms of SSAP 6 ('Extraordinary and prior year adjustments'), revaluation surpluses are not taken to the profit and loss account but are instead taken directly to a reserve.

The adjustments which are required to transform a set of historical cost accounts into a set of current cost accounts are summarized as follows:

Cost of sales adjustment	Debit	P and L account
	Credit	Current cost reserve
Depreciation adjustment	Debit	P and L account
	Credit	Accumulated depreciation
Monetary working capital adjustment	Debit	P and L account
	Credit	Current cost reserve
Gearing adjustment	Debit	Current cost reserve
	Credit	P and L account
Difference between value to the business and the historical cost net book value of fixed assets at the balance sheet date (taking into account any depreciation adjustments credited to accumulated depreciation account in arriving at value to the business)[3]	Debit	Fixed asset account
	Credit	Current cost reserve
Difference between value to the business and historical cost of stock at the balance sheet date	Debit	Stock account
	Credit	Current cost reserve

It has been assumed in the above that the appropriate prices have increased during the period.

The balance sheet

There are two major differences between a current cost balance sheet and a historical cost balance sheet. First, assets are shown at their value to the business on the balance sheet date rather than at a figure based on historical cost or a past revaluation. Thus balance sheet values for certain assets will differ. Second, the current cost balance sheet includes a current cost reserve account.

---

3 The adjustment to accumulated depreciation is known as 'backlog depreciation'. (*see* page 172).

SSAP 16 definition of value to the business

The main difference between the definitions as presented in Sandilands and in SSAP 16 relates to the situation where replacement cost does not provide the value to the business. In the Sandilands presentation (*see* page 134) this would occur when the replacement cost was higher than both the asset's value in use (or present value) and its net realizable value. In SSAP 16 the value to the business of an asset is defined as follows: the value to a business is either (a) net current replacement cost;[4] or, if a permanent diminution to below net current replacement cost has been recognized, (b) recoverable amount, which is the greater of the net realizable value of an asset and, where applicable, the amount recoverable from its further use (SSAP 16, Paras 42 and 43).

There may not appear to be very much difference between the two approaches, but reference to the guidance notes shows that the ASC has attempted to answer one of the criticisms that was made of the ED 24 proposals: the subjective nature of any present value measure. The ASC have done this in two ways. They have emphasized the point that the need to estimate the 'recoverable amount' exists under historical cost accounting in those situations where the book value of assets have to be written down. In addition it is suggested that in order to estimate the recoverable amount it would not normally be necessary to discount future cash flows (GN, Para. 29).

The standard itself is silent on the question of the circumstances which would warrant the recognition of a 'permanent diminution to below net current replacement cost'. The guidance notes are not all that much more helpful. In the case of fixed assets the guidance notes suggest that the need to estimate the recoverable amount will usually occur in one of two cases (GN, Para. 29). First, the asset concerned may already have been put out of use and be held for sale, in which case the recoverable amount is the current realizable amount net of realization expenses. The second situation is where the asset continues in use (i.e. it must be assumed that its value to the business is greater than the asset's realizable amount). In this case the asset's recoverable amount is 'the total estimated amount which can be recovered from its use'. This, it is suggested in the guidance notes, would 'normally [be] calculated by reference to the estimated cash flows arising from its future use and its ultimate disposal' (GN, Para. 29). The cash flows

---

4 The phrase net current replacement cost is used to describe the depreciated current cost of an asset. Thus the net current replacement cost of a fixed asset which is 25% written off will be 75% of the replacement cost of a new asset (*see* page 168).

should be calculated in terms of existing price levels and would not normally be discounted.

The application of the definition of value to the business in the case of stock is simpler in that there is no need to consider the 'amount recoverable' from the further use of stock. The only possible bases of valuation are the replacement cost and net realizable value. The guidance notes state clearly that, 'the value to the business of an item of stock is the lower of its current replacement cost and its recoverable amount (i.e. net realisable value)' (GN, Para. 68).

It can thus be seen that the valuation basis is basically the same as was proposed by Sandilands. In order for the concept to be made operational the requirement for discounting, which is undoubtedly necessary in theory, has been removed. The upper limit of an asset's value to the business is its net current replacement cost while the lower limit is its net realizable value. In many instances the value to the business of an asset will be one of these limits; however, in certain cases the value may be placed somewhere between the two, and in such cases the estimation of the asset's value to the business is bound to be subjective.

We will now turn to a more detailed discussion of the various elements of a set of current cost accounts.

Fixed assets

Plant and machinery, etc.

We will first consider physical assets other than land and buildings. The introduction of current cost accounting does not eliminate the problems associated with depreciation. It is still necessary to estimate the proportion of the asset which has been assumed to have been used up in the period.

In normal circumstances the value to the business of an existing fixed asset is the net current cost of a replacement asset which 'has a similar useful output or service potential' (GN, Para. 10).

The net current replacement cost of an asset is normally based on its gross current replacement cost (i.e. the replacement cost of a new asset) and the proportion of the asset that has been deemed to be used up. Thus assume that an asset has a gross current replacement cost of £20 000 and as at 31 December 19XX, that 40% of it has been used up (say, for example, it has been depreciated at 10% per annum on a straight line basis for four years assuming a zero scrap value).

Its net current replacement cost will be £12 000 and it will be included in a current cost balance sheet at 31 December 19XX as follows:

	£
Gross current replacement cost	20 000
less Accumulated depreciation	8 000
Net current replacement cost	£12 000

It might be appropriate at this stage to consider the question of the estimates of asset lives. It has been suggested that conservative estimates of asset lives have been made in the past in the context of historical cost depreciation in order to make some crude allowance for inflation. This will clearly only help when the assets are relatively new. The guidance notes recognize this point and emphasize the importance of reviewing estimates of asset lives and rates of depreciation on the introduction of CCA and the need in subsequent periods to make regular reviews of these matters (GN, Paras 55 and 56).

The standard does not specify how the gross current replacement cost of an asset should be determined. Companies are allowed considerable latitude and the guidance notes simply observe that the most convenient method of calculating the gross current replacement cost is normally through the application of relevant indices to existing gross book values (GN, Para. 17). The indices could be those prepared by government agencies[5] or be generally recognized privately produced indices or even indices compiled by a company on the basis of its own purchasing experience.

The effects of the freedom that will be allowed to companies in deciding on the method of arriving at gross current replacement costs will only be appreciated after some experience of the use of CCA has been obtained. However, it does seem likely that any distortions that result from the application of different methods will be less than those that obtain under historical cost accounting where asset values and depreciation are heavily dependent on the year in which the asset was acquired.

It is recognized that there may be circumstances where the use of an index of asset prices may not be appropriate; in such cases the gross current replacement cost should be based on expert opinion or other evidence of the current cost of assets (GN, Para. 20).

5 The government regularly issues two volumes of index numbers, *Price Index Numbers for Current Cost Accounting* and *Current Cost Accounting: Guide to Price Indices for Overseas Countries*. Both volumes are published by Her Majesty's Stationery Office.

In addition to the general problem that no suitable price index may be available, the guidance notes (GN, Para. 20) put forward three situations where the use of an index may be rejected: (a) where there has been substantial technological change in the class of assets concerned; (b) where it is known that the costs of specific assets have changed in a substantially different way from the change in the index; (c) where the historical purchase cost of the asset to which the index is applied was affected by special circumstances which are unlikely to be repeated and for which allowance cannot accurately be made by adjusting the index. The second and third of these reasons are self-evident and need not concern us, but the first is of considerable importance, especially to companies engaged in industries which are subject to rapid technological changes. The unthinking use of an index which has been substantially affected by changes in technology could lead to misleading results. Supppose, for example, that the price index for machines used in a particular industry had doubled over the four years in which the asset whose value is being sought has been owned. Let us also suppose that the operating costs of the machines had been reduced by 50% over the same period. The use of the index without correction would mean that the value of the asset would be overstated. It would also mean that the current cost operating profit for the period would be understated because it would be charged with both a high depreciation charge (which would be based on a machine with low operating costs) and the higher operating costs associated with the old machine.

The problem is discussed in some depth in the guidance notes and is the subject of Appendix (i), 'Modern equivalent asset'. It is pointed out in that appendix that a modern substitute for the existing asset may differ not only in its initial capital cost but also in terms of operating costs, life and output. It is suggested that in some instances the problem may be overcome by the use of a broadly based price index which might reflect a gradual change in technology. Alternatively, in extreme cases where major assets are involved, it may be necessary to check the results against calculations which make allowances for the differences in service potential. An example of the type of calculation which might be required is given below:

Original cost of asset	£100 000
Price index	
(a) at date of acquisition of asset	100
(b) at the date of valuation	225

Gross replacement cost of asset based on the movement
  of the price index, £100 000 × 225/100   £225 000
Estimated total life of machine   5 years

However, let us suppose that the current cost of a modern asset which may be deemed to be a modern equivalent of the asset being valued is £250 000 and also suppose that the annual operating costs of the new machine is £16 000 a year less than the old machine and that the life of the new machine is 5 years.

On a comparable basis the value of the asset is clearly less than £250 000. The difference is the capital value which is attributable to the saving of £16 000 per year in operating costs. If conventional discounting theory is used, the capital value is the present value of £16 000 per year discounted at the appropriate rate of discount. Let us suppose that the rate of discount is 15%, then using annuity tables the capital value is £16 000 × 3.3522 = £53 635. Thus the gross replacement cost of the asset under review is £196 365 (£250 000 − £53 635).

We therefore have three possible values of the gross current replacement cost:

	£
Gross current replacement cost based on movements of the price index	225 000
Current cost of a modern asset without adjustment	250 000
Current cost of a modern asset after adjustment	196 365

Now, as has already been stated (page 168), the value to the business of a fixed asset should be related to the current cost of a replacement of an asset which has a similar useful output or service potential. Thus, the gross current replacement cost of the asset is £196 365. The value to the business of the asset is its net current replacement cost, which is based on the proportion of the asset which has been considered to have been used up; this will depend on the estimated life of the asset and the method of depreciation used by the business.

It must be emphasized that the guidance notes suggest that calculations of the type illustrated above need only be made when 'major assets are involved' (GN, Appendix (i), Para. 5) and that it is only necessary to discount savings where the amounts are substantial and there is no other way of estimating the capital value of the new asset which is attributable to the savings. It is suggested that in many cases the problem of technological change can be overcome by the use of the appropriate index (GN, Appendix (i), Para. 4).

Depreciation

Under CCA the depreciation charge is based on the value to the business of that part of the asset used up in the period. In principle the value to the business should be measured by reference to the value at the date of consumption of the asset, but the guidance notes suggest that in practice the value may be based on the fixed asset's average value for the period or its value at the end of the period.

CCA does, however, present one additional complication – *backlog depreciation*. This arises from the need to revalue accumulated depreciation, i.e. that part of the asset which has already been written off. This may appear to be a strange and unnecessary procedure, but it is required because the value of the asset is based in the first instance on the restatement of the gross current replacement cost of the asset. In so far as part of the asset has been used up, the increase in gross current replacement cost of the asset will overstate the holding gain made in the year. A deduction must therefore be made in respect of that part of the asset which has already been used up. Thus, the accumulated depreciation at the start of the period must also be 're-valued' and the increase in this value (backlog depreciation) must be deducted from the increase in the gross current replacement cost to give the net holding gain for the period.

To illustrate the point, suppose that an asset was purchased for £10 000 on 1 January 19X2 when the appropriate price index was 100. Let us also suppose that: (a) the index remained constant until 31 December 19X4 when it rose to 120; (b) the asset is depreciated on a straight-line basis over 5 years with a zero scrap value, i.e. 20% of the asset is assumed to be used up each year; (c) the company's year end is 31 December. The book value of the asset on 31 December 19X3 is as follows:

	£
Gross current replacement cost (which is also the historical cost)	10 000
less Accumulated depreciation (2 years)	4 000
Net current replacement cost	£ 6 000

The gross current replacement cost of the asset at 31 December 19X4 is £10 000 × 120/100 = £12 000. Given that sales revenue has accrued throughout the year, the current cost depreciation should be calculated using average values of the fixed assets. However, SSAP 16 permits the use of closing values as an approximation to this and, in this first illustration, we shall use the closing value.

The CCA depreciation charge for 19X4, if based on the end of year value, is 20% of £12 000, i.e. £2400. The value to the business, or net current replacement cost, of the asset at 31 December 19X4 is two-fifths of £12 000, i.e. £4800, as two-fifths of the asset remains to be used at that date.

Consider that portion of the asset which was deemed to be in existence at the beginning of the year (three-fifths of the original asset). Its value at the start of the year was £6000 and since the index increased by 20% its year end value was £7200. Thus the company experienced a holding gain or revaluation surplus of £1200 and this is the amount which is to be credited to the current cost reserve account.

The gross current replacement cost of the asset increased by £2000 (£10 000 to £12 000) and to take this amount, without adjustment, to the current cost reserve would be to overstate the gain.

The difference of £800 between £2000 and £1200 is the increase in value of that part of the asset which had been used up at the start of the year, i.e. two-fifths of £2000 = £800.

The argument can be illustrated graphically if it is assumed that the asset was made up of five equal blocks one of which is used up each year. The position at 1 January 19X4 was

Gross replacement cost, £10 000

2 000	2 000	2 000	2 000	2 000

Accumulated depreciation, £4 000 | Net replacement cost, £6 000

The position at 31 December 19X4 *before* recording the depreciation charge for 19X4 was

Gross replacement cost, £12 000

2 400	2 400	2 400	2 400	2 400

Accumulated depreciation, £4 800 | Net replacement cost, £7 200

	£
Increase in gross replacement cost, £12 000 − £10 000	£2 000
less Backlog depreciation, £4 800 − £4 000	800
Net surplus on revaluation	£1 200

The position at 31 December 19X4 *after* recognizing the depreciation charge for the year was

Gross replacement cost, £12 000

2 400	2 400	2 400	2 400	2 400

Accumulated
depreciation, £7 200

Net replacement
cost, £4 800

In practice a convenient way of calculating backlog depreciation is to follow the steps set out below:

(1) Estimate the asset's gross current replacement cost at the year end.

(2) Calculate the depreciation charge for the year.

(3) Calculate the required balance on the accumulated depreciation account at the year end – $x\%$ of (1) where $x\%$ is the proportion of the asset which has been assumed to have been used up.

(4) Backlog depreciation is then the difference between (3) and the sum of the opening accumulated depreciation and the depreciation charge for the year.

Depreciation based on average values

If the depreciation charge for the year is based on values other than those which apply at the year end, there will be another element of of backlog depreciation. This element may be described as current year backlog to distinguish it from the prior year backlog which was discussed in the above section.

The current year backlog arises from the fact that, for the purposes of the balance sheet, accumulated depreciation is based on the year-end value while the depreciation charge will be based on a different value, a lower value if prices are rising. To illustrate this let us assume that the company which was the subject of the above illustration decides to base its depreciation charge on average values and that the appropriate price index increased from 120 to 150 in 19X5.

If use is again made of the blocks, the position at 31 December 19X5 can be illustrated as follows:

Gross replacement cost, £15 000

£2700 depreciation for 19X5

3 000	3 000	3 000	3 000	3 000

Accumulated depreciation,
£12 000

Net replacement
cost, £3000

The gross current replacement cost at 1 January 19X5 was £12 000 and so the depreciation charge for 19X5 based on average values is

$$\frac{\frac{1}{2}£(15\,000 + 12\,000)}{5} = £2\,700.$$

Thus, of the portion (block) of the asset used up during the year which is valued at year-end prices at £3000, only £2700 has been charged to the current cost profit and loss account. The difference of £300 is the current year backlog. The prior year backlog is $3£(3\,000 - 2\,400) = £1\,800$ and the net credit to the current cost reserve account is then given by

	£	£
Increase in gross current replacement cost, £15 000		
− £12 000		3 000
less Prior year backlog	1 800	
Current year backlog	300	2 100
Net surplus		£ 900

If the quick method of calculating backlog depreciation is used the figures are as follows:

	£	£
Gross current replacement cost of asset at		
31 December 19X5		£15 000
Required balance of accumulated depreciation at		
31 December 19X5, 80% of £15 000		12 000
less Accumulated depreciation at 31 December 19X4	7 200	
Depreciation charge of 19X5	2 700	9 900
Backlog depreciation		£ 2 100

It is sometimes suggested that it would be more sensible to charge the backlog depreciation to the profit and loss account rather than debiting it to the current cost reserve. This suggestion is, however, based on a misunderstanding of the basic principle of CCA that revenue for the period should be matched with the current cost of the inputs to the manufacturing/trading process which were required to generate that revenue, i.e. the current cost of the assets used up in the accounting period. If backlog depreciation was charged to the profit and loss account, the effect would be to charge the current year's profits with the increased cost of assets which were consumed in previous years.

The consesquence of not charging backlog depreciation must also be noted. This is that, even if the company had each year set aside cash equal to the depreciation charge, it would not have sufficient funds (from this process alone) to replace the asset. Suppose that the asset which has been the subject of the earlier illustration was sold on 31 December 19X5 for its net current replacement cost of £3000. Then, assuming that cash equal to the annual depreciation charges had been set aside, and ignoring any interest that might have been earned on the investment, the cash available for the replacement of the asset would be

	£	£
Cash from sale of asset		3 000
Cash set aside equal to annual depreciation charges		
19X2	2 000	
19X3	2 000	
19X4	2 400	
19X5	2 700	9 100
Cash available		12 100
Shortfall		2 900
Cash required to replace asset		£15 000

The shortfall is equal to the total backlog depreciation which arose in respect of the asset, £800 in 19X4 and £2100 in 19X5.

Land and buildings

In the standard itself, no distinction is made between land and buildings and plant and machinery; however, the guidance notes suggest that a different approach to valuation be used for land and buildings. A distinction is drawn between specialized and non-specialized buildings. Specialized buildings are those which by their nature are rarely sold except as part of the sale of the business in which they are used. Non-specialized buildings are, in contrast, generally sold as units in their own right. While it is easy to classify certain types of buildings – oil refineries are clearly specialized buildings, while office blocks are usually non-specialized – there are many instances where it will be difficult to make the distinction between the two types of buildings.

It is suggested that specialized buildings should be valued in the same way as plant and machinery[6] but that the underlying land should be valued on the same basis as non-specialized buildings (GN, Para. 32).

Non-specialized buildings, such as the majority of offices, shops and general industrial units, are those which are commonly bought and sold, as one unit, together with the underlying land. Since the normal method of acquiring such assets is purchase in the open market, it is suggested that their net current replacement cost should be valued by reference to the estimated cost of purchasing the property on the open market and not by reference to the updated value of the cost of the building plus the current cost of the land. The use of indices is considered to be inappropriate because the market value of properties will often move in an individual way depending on their location, and the use of the individual valuations is therefore called for (GN, Para. 34). In the case of land and buildings which will continue to be used by the business, their value can be increased by the cost of acquisition and adaptation, although adaptation costs should be valued on the same principles as plant and machinery (GN, Paras 34 and 39). In contrast, land and non-specialized buildings which are surplus to the present and future needs of the business should be valued at their open market value less costs of disposal, i.e. at their net realizable value (GN, Para. 38).

Valuation need not be made annually, but it is expected that not more than 5 years should elapse between valuations, and should be made by professionally qualified and experienced valuers who could be in the employ of the company owning the asset (GN, Paras 40 and 41).

It should be noted that because the values of non-specialized buildings and land are found by reference to their existing condition, only the net current replacement cost is shown in the current cost balance sheet, i.e. the gross current cost and accumulated depreciation are not recorded.

Depreciation of non-specialized buildings

In accordance with the provisions of SSAP 12, depreciation must be

6 An exception to this rule is suggested in the case of buildings such as hotels, petrol filling stations and public houses which are conventionally recorded in the historical cost accounts at figures which include 'inherent trading potential' (or goodwill element). It is suggested that these buildings should be treated as non-specialized buildings because the method of valuation suggested for such buildings is a better basis of valuation of the goodwill element (GN, Para. 33).

provided on buildings. Thus, it is necessary to apportion the total valuation of a property between land and buildings. Neither SSAP 16 nor the guidance manual include any details about the method which should be used to depreciate non-specialized buildings. It appears that, if depreciation is to be provided on a straight line basis, in a year in which the property is not revalued the depreciation charge will be found by dividing the net current replacement cost at the beginning of the year by the remaining life of the asset measured from that date. Thus, if there are no subsequent revaluations, the asset would be written off evenly over its remaining life. The only advice that is given as to the method which should be adopted in a year in which a revaluation is made is provided in the guidance notes, which state that 'Any transfer to or from current cost reserve, when these assets [non-specialized buildings] are again revalued, will be calculated by reference to the net figure after depreciation' (GN, Para. 49).

Thus it is suggested that the closing value should first be determined, the depreciation charge for the year should then be calculated and finally the transfer to the current cost reserve should be made which would be equal to the difference between the net current replacements costs at the end and the beginning of the year plus the depreciation charge. This approach was included in the ED 18 proposals and the following example is based on a numerical example included in the guidance manual to ED 18 (Para. 6.20).

Suppose that XYZ Limited owned buildings which had a net current replacement cost of £550 000 on 1 January 19X3 and an estimated life of 21 years from 1 January 19X3. Let us assume that the buildings were revalued on 31 December 19X3, at which date a value of £600 000 was placed on the building but no change was made in the estimated life of the asset.

The depreciation charge is calculated by dividing the depreciable amount (estimated value of the buildings) by the life of the asset from the year end. The life is measured from the year end rather than the beginning of the year because the building was valued on the basis of its condition at the end of the year (i.e. after depreciation for the period).

The depreciation charge is thus £600 000/20 = £30 000. If the net current replacement cost of the building at 31 December 19X3 is £600 000 then the figure before charging depreciation for the year is £630 000. As the net current replacement cost at 1 January 19X3 was £550 000, the transfer to the current cost reserve is £80 000.

These adjustments can be conveniently summarized as follows:

	£
Debit land and buildings	50 000
Debit profit and loss account (depreciation expense)	30 000
Credit current cost reserve	80 000

Let us assume that the buildings are not revalued in 19X4. The depreciation charge for 19X4 will thus be the same as in 19X3, £30 000. The figure can be obtained by dividing the asset's net current replacement cost at the beginning of the year by the building's life measured at that date. This method can be used for all periods in which there is not a revaluation of the asset. Thus, if there is no revaluation in 19X5, the depreciation charge for the year is given by

$$\frac{\text{Net current replacement cost at 1 January 19X5}}{<\text{Estimated life as at 1 January 19X5}>}$$

$$= \frac{£570\,000}{19} = £30\,000.$$

The straight-line method of depreciation has been used in the above illustration. There is nothing in the standard which precludes the use of other methods of depreciation, but use of the straight-line method avoids many problems when there are frequent revaluations of the asset.

Wasting and intangible assets

Wasting assets are fixed assets which cannot be renewed in their existing location, e.g. mineral-bearing land. Under historical cost accounting such assets may or may not be treated as capital assets to be amortized over their useful lives. If such an asset is recorded in the historical cost accounts, then it should be stated in the current cost balance sheet at its value to the business. In arriving at net current replacement cost, the best estimate of the current costs should be used.

Similarly, intangible assets such as patents and copyrights but excluding goodwill should, where possible, be stated at value to the business, but if this is not possible they can be included in the current cost accounts at their historical cost (GN, Para. 45).

Goodwill arising on consolidation

Goodwill should be calculated on the basis set out in SSAP 14 ('Group accounts'). This standard is discussed in Chapter 12, but at this stage we need to point out that SSAP 14 requires that the net asset of a subsidiary be valued at the date of acquisition. Thus the asset of 'goodwill on consolidation' will relate only to the premium or discount on acquisition and will not include an element due to the difference between the current value and book value of net assets at the date of acquisition. An adjustment will have to be made if goodwill on consolidation is carried at an amount established prior to the introduction of SSAP 14 and includes an element which can be related to the difference between current value and book value. In such a case goodwill should be reduced to the extent that it represents revaluation surpluses relating to assets held at the date of acquisition (SSAP 16, Para. 53(e)). The adjustment is necessary to avoid double counting the revaluation surpluses and is made by crediting goodwill and debiting the current cost reserve account (GN, Para. 125).

Investments

An investment in an associated company should be shown in the balance sheet of the investing company or in the group balance sheet on the basis of the applicable proportion of the associated company's net assets based on the principles of SSAP 16 plus, if applicable, any goodwill (SSAP 16, Para. 53(b); GN, Para. 133). If the associated company does not produce current cost accounts, the amounts should be stated on the basis of the directors' best estimate.

Other investments (excluding those which are treated as current assets) should be stated at the directors' valuation. Where the investment is listed and the directors' valuation is materially different from the mid-market price, the basis of the valuation and the reasons for the difference should be stated (SSAP 16, Para. 53(c)).

Investments which are treated as current assets should, like all other current assets other than stock subject to a cost of sales adjustment, be shown on the historical cost basis (SSAP 16, Para. 53(f)).

Profits and losses on disposal of fixed assets

When an asset is sold, the difference between the net current replacement cost shown at the last balance sheet date and the net current replacement cost at the date of sale should be taken to current cost reserve. If there remains a difference on disposal, it is charged or credited in the profit and loss account, where appropriate, as an extraordinary item (GN, Para. 53).

Changes in the basis of valuation of fixed assets

Our description of the treatment of fixed assets and depreciation has, in the main, been based on the assumption that the value to the business is found by reference to the replacement cost of the asset. We must now consider how to deal with an asset in respect of which a permanent diminution to below net current replacement cost has been recognized. If an asset's value to the business is written down from its current replacement cost to its net realizable value, or an amount recoverable from further use, the difference is charged to the profit and loss account and is not debited to the current cost reserve account. This follows from the principle that all changes in net book value, arising from changes in the asset's service potential, such as depreciation, are taken to the profit and loss account while only changes to the net book value which are due to movements in prices are taken to the current cost reserve account (GN, Para. 12). In principle, therefore, in a period in which a change is made, the net currrent replacement cost at the balance sheet date should first be established and this will give rise to a credit or debit to the current cost reserve account because it is caused by a movement in prices. The difference between the year-end net current replacement cost and the net realizable value is then debited to the profit and loss account on the grounds that the recognition of permanent diminution below net current replacement cost must be based on the view that there has been a decline in the asset's service potential.

Stock

A distinction is made between stock which is, or is not, subject to the cost of sales adjustment (COSA). The distinction, however, is not clearly made, and the classification will in many instances depend heavily on judgement. As was discussed in Chapter 5, the COSA is the difference between the historical cost of stock and its value to the business at the date of sale. A more detailed discussion of stock not subject to the COSA will be provided later, but in general such stock may be said to consist of items whose replacement costs cannot be determined and those where such a valuation would be inappropriate because there is no intention to replace them by the purchase of substantially similar items.

Valuation of stock subject to the COSA

The value to the business of an item of stock is the lower of its current replacement cost and the recoverable amount (in the case of stock, its net realizable value).

The current replacement cost may be obtained from any of a number of sources, including suppliers' price lists and the use of indices. In appropriate cases use can be made of standard costs updated where necessary by the allocation of price variances (GN, Para. 73 and Appendix (ii)). The current replacement cost of work in progress and finished goods is obtained by calculating the current replacement costs of the inputs (raw materials, labour and overheads) which have been required to bring the asset to its condition at the date of valuation. The existence of a suitable standard costing system would obviously help this process.

The problem of deciding whether stock should be written down to its net realizable value is little different from that which is experienced under historical cost accounting when the decision as to whether stock should be written down from cost to net realizable value has to be made. Strictly, each item of stock should be considered individually, but in practice the assessment might have to be made on the basis of the different categories of stock. If stock is written down to its recoverable value, the difference should be charged to the current cost profit and loss account and not debited to the current cost reserve account.

In many instances stock cannot be replaced immediately because there is a delay between the date of the order and the date on which the goods will be delivered. In such a case, the relevant replacement cost is the one prevailing on the day on which the order would have had to have been placed to secure delivery on the date of valuation (GN, Para. 69). Thus, if there is a 3-month delay in delivery, stock on hand at 31 December 19X4 should in principle be valued by reference to its cost on 30 September 19X4, but in practice considerations of materiality may allow this nicety to be ignored.

Value to the business of stock must be determined in respect of the stock in hand at the balance sheet date as well as at the dates of sale of the stock sold during the period. The difference between the historical cost of stock held on the balance sheet date and its value to the business on that date is an unrealized holding gain which, if prices have risen, is debited to the stock account and credited to the current cost reserve account.

Transfer to current cost reserve account

The difference between the value to the business at the date of sale of stock and the historical cost of the stock is a realized gain which is debited to the current cost profit and loss account and credited to the current cost reserve account. In so far as part of the realized gain relates to stock which was in hand at the beginning of the period, some of the realized holding gain will already have been credited to the current cost reserve account as part of the unrealized gain recognized at the last balance sheet date, and account has to be taken of this. The net transfer to the current cost reserve account for a period is then given by: the unrealized holding gain on stock held at the end of the period plus the holding gain realized during the year less the unrealized holding gain in respect of opening stock which was recognized at the last balance sheet date.

COSA

The COSA is the difference between the value to the business of the stock sold and its historical cost (i.e. the realized holding gain).

In principle the current cost profit and loss account should be charged with the value to the business of each item of stock sold measured at the date of sale. The informational needs if this were to be done for any but the smallest entities would be enormous, so in practice proxy measures are normally used. In most instances the assumption is made that the objective of charging the profit and loss account with the current cost of replacement will be adequately served by charging the profit and loss account with the average cost of purchases.

If the volume of stock has remained reasonably constant over the year, or has changed at a more or less constant rate, the average cost for the period can be used. If these conditions do not hold, perhaps because stock is purchased or manufactured at a fairly constant rate while sales are made in large parcels at infrequent intervals, the calculations should be based on shorter periods, e.g. monthly.

The averaging method

The averaging method (which is the subject of Appendix (ii) of the guidance notes) is commonly employed to calculate the COSA because it is simple to calculate and requires the minimum of additional data over and above that which is part of the historical cost system. In essence, with the averaging method the opening and closing stocks (based on the first in first out (FIFO) convention) are expressed in terms of the average price for the period. No adjustment is made to the purchases figure on the grounds that this is automatically expressed in terms of the average price for the period. Thus, the three elements in the cost of goods sold expense (opening stock, closing stock and purchases) are all expressed in terms of the average cost for the period.

In order for the averaging method to be used the stock volume must either have been constant or increased (or decreased) at a constant rate over the period for which the calculation is made. The average purchase price may be calculated by using a simple average of the period's prices selected at regular intervals. The use of the averaging method is illustrated below.

Suppose that the following historical cost of stock information is available (based on the FIFO convention): opening stock, £30 000; purchases, £140 000; closing stock, £40 000. Let us also assume that the appropriate price indices for the stock in question were as follows: opening stock 100; average for the year, 130;[7] closing stock, 150. The cost of goods sold expenses based on both historical cost and current cost principles are shown below:

	Historical cost (£)		Current cost (£)
Opening stock	30 000	(£30 000 × 130/100)	39 000
Purchases	140 000		140 000
	170 000		179 000
less Closing stock	40 000	(40 000 × 130/150)	34 667
	£130 000		£144 333

The COSA is then £144 333 − £130 000 = £14 333.

Note that the COSA does not depend on knowledge of the purchases figure and that it can be found by simply adjusting the opening and closing stocks as long as the three price index numbers are available.

The opening stock element of the COSA is

$$£30\,000 \times \frac{130}{100} - £30\,000 = £9\,000,$$

i.e. the difference between the opening stock valued at average price and its historical cost. Similarly, the closing stock element is

$$£40\,000 - £40\,000 \times \frac{130}{150} = £5\,333,$$

7 The average for the year will be the average value of a series of index numbers for a number of dates spaced at regular intervals over the year. It is not necessarily the simple average of the indices applicable at the beginning and end of the year.

i.e. the difference between the historical cost of closing stock and its value based on the average price for the period.

In times of rising prices the historical cost of closing stock will be greater than the closing stock figure based on average prices because, using FIFO, the units comprising the closing stock will have been deemed to have been purchased at more recent prices, which will be higher than the average. However, since closing stock is deducted in order to arrive at the cost of goods sold the reduction in the value placed on closing stock will add to the COSA.

The formula for calculating the COSA can be expressed as follows. Let S_1 and S_3 be the historical cost (based on the FIFO convention) of opening and closing stock, respectively. Let P_1, P_2 and P_3 be the price indices applicable to opening stock, the average cost for the period and closing stock, respectively. The COSA is then given by

$$\text{COSA} = S_1 \left(\frac{P_2}{P_1}\right) - S_1 + S_3 - S_3\left(\frac{P_2}{P_3}\right)$$

$$= \frac{S_1}{P_1}(P_2 - P_1) + \frac{S_3}{P_3}(P_3 - P_2).^{[8]}$$

The above formula is also applicable in periods when prices are falling. In this case the COSA will represent a realized holding loss which will be credited to the current cost profit and loss account and debited to the current cost reserve account.

In principle the indices applied to both opening and closing stocks should relate to the date on which the stock was acquired (or more precisely to the date on which stock would have to have been ordered for delivery on the date of acquisition). However, the guidance notes suggest that the year-end indices can be used if the results so derived are not significantly different from those which would be obtained from the use of the indices applicable to the dates of acquisition.

In the above example the COSA was calculated for the year as a whole. This is acceptable if the volume of stock remains approximately constant or increases or decreases gradually. If the volume of stock is subjected to severe fluctuations, the calculations should be made at more frequent intervals, possibly monthly.

8 In the examples which follow the formula will be used in the above form. The formula presented in Appendix (vii) of the guidance notes is identical but is presented in a different way:

$$\text{COSA} = \frac{S_1}{P_1}(P_2 - P_1) + \frac{S_3}{P_3}(P_3 - P_2) = (S_3 - S_1) - P_2\left(\frac{S_3}{P_3} - \frac{S_3}{P_1}\right).$$

One important practical difficulty is the extent to which stock needs to be disaggregated for the purposes of calculating the cost of sales adjustment. No specific guidance is given on this matter either in the standard or in the guidance notes. The latter (in Appendix (ii)) simply says that, 'It may be necessary for some businesses to use different methods of calculating the effect of price changes (on stock) for different sections of the business or for different cost elements of the stock'. It will be recognized that, especially in the case of businesses which operate in a number of different areas, the balance sheet value of stock and the COSA will depend greatly on the extent to which stock is disaggregated for the purposes of the calculations.

It must be emphasized that the averaging method is only one method which can be used to arrive at the COSA. In the case of large units it may be possible to identify the value to the business of specific items when they are sold. In other cases the LIFO method may be used to arrive at the charge to the profit and loss account, but this method should not of course be used to find the balance sheet value of stock.

Stock not subject to a COSA

The discussion of stock has so far been based on the assumptions of a simplistic world in which stock when sold is replaced by more or less identical items. In such instances it is possible to make a clear distinction between a realized revaluation surplus (which is represented by the COSA) and an operating gain.[9] However, there are many situations where it would either be impossible or misleading to make such a distinction, and the standard deals with the problem by distinguishing between stock which is and which is not subject to a COSA.

An obvious example of a case where the use of a COSA would not be appropriate is provided by a trader who does not deal with a limited range of goods but instead is prepared to switch from one line to another whenever he senses the opportunity of making greater profits. He might, for example, start the period with a warehouse full of carpets but use the cash flow generated from the sale of the carpets

9 It may be argued that this approach does not really arrive at the operating gain. After all, the decision to operate of necessity involves holding stock and hence price changes in the period of stock holding are just as much a part of the operations of the firm as the differences between sales and revenue and the current cost of goods sold. For a consideration of this point readers are referred to D. F. Drake and N. Dopuch, 'On the case for dichotomising income', *Journal of Accounting Research*, Autumn 1965 and P. Prakash and S. Sunder, 'The case against separation of current operating profit and holding gain', *The Accounting Review*, January 1979.

to purchase refrigerators. In such a case it would not be sensible to charge the current cost profit and loss account with the replacement cost of carpets as the carpets will not be replaced. In such a case the cost of goods sold will be charged to its current cost account at its historical cost. Thus, so far as stock which is bought and sold in the same period is concerned, the total CCA profit will be the same as the historical cost profit.

Stock not subject to the COSA will also be shown in the current cost balance sheet at its historical cost. The reason for this is not immediately obvious. A current value can be placed on the stock and it could be argued that the inclusion of stock in the balance sheet at its current value rather than historical cost would be more in line with the principles of CCA. But what variant of current value would be appropriate? The use of current replacement cost would not be sensible as the stock will not be replaced. Net realizable value would at first sight seem to be more appropriate. The difference between the net realizable value of the stock at the balance sheet date and its historical cost does represent a gain, but it is an unrealized gain and it therefore cannot be credited to the current cost profit and loss account as this account is restricted to realized gains. A possible alternative would be to credit the gain to the current cost reserve account, but this would also not be in accord with the general principles underlying CCA. The reason for this is that the current cost reserve account represents the amount that must be retained if the operating capability of the business is to be maintained. But since the stock is not to be replaced it is clear that the price movements relating to the particular line of stock is not a relevant factor in determining the amounts that need to be retained in order to maintain operating capability.

Something, however, does need to be done, because, if prices are in general increasing, the trader will need to retain additional funds in order to maintain the substance of the business. The answer to the problem in terms of the CCA model adopted in SSAP 16 is to include stock not subject to a COSA as part of the entity's monetary working capital, and hence its existence will affect the monetary working capital adjustment (MWCA).

This adjustment will be discussed in more detail later in this chapter. At this stage it is sufficent to point out that the MWCA is generally based on the average price movements for a range of goods rather than – as is the case with the COSA – the prices of specific goods. In the instance of a carpet trader who is switching to refrigerators and who might then start to sell fur coats, or possibly turnips, the

MWCA might very well be based on a very broadly based price index such as the Index of Retail Prices.

In general, it can be stated that stock is included as part of monetary working capital and hence not subject to a COSA when either the stock will not be replaced or when, because stock will only be replaced after an interval, it is not possible to estimate the future replacement cost. Specific examples of these situations include the following:

(a) *Seasonal products* (GN, Para. 76)   By their nature many agricultural products cannot be replaced until the next season. Thus a farmer who sells his wheat cannot replace his stock until the next harvest and may not be in a position to estimate the costs of replacing the wheat. In addition he may decide to grow another crop and this decision may not have been made at the time when the accounts are prepared.

The guidance notes (GN, Para. 76) suggest that, when it is known that replacement of seasonal products is intended, a COSA should, if practicable, be made based on a price index which corresponds with the long-term trend in replacement prices.

In many cases the managers of the business will defer the decision about whether the stock will be replaced and choose, each season, from the range of opportunities available to them. In this case stock should be treated as monetary working capital and the MWCA should be of an amount that will broadly maintain the ability of the business to continue to take advantage of such opportunities.

(b) *Dealing stock* (GN, Para. 78)   The *raison d'être* of some businesses, e.g. commodity dealers, is the making of revaluation surpluses rather than operating gains; that is stock is purchased in anticipation of price increases in an attempt to earn dealing profits. Since such companies are not generally in a position to acquire their stock at a practice which is lower than the price which is available to other purchasers at the time of sale, the replacement cost of stock will be almost equal and possibly marginally greater than the net realizable value (the sales proceeds). The application of a COSA would thus effectively eliminate all or most of the profit on the deal, which would give an extremely misleading view of the activities of the business. Thus a COSA should not be applied and the required adjustment should be effected through the MWCA.

(c) *Contract work in progress* (GN, Paras 83–87)   A COSA based on the prices of specific inputs calculated in the same way as the adjustment for the generality of manufactured goods can be applied to contracts which are broadly repetitive in nature.

Non-repetitive contracts present greater difficulties. The answer suggested in the guidance notes is the same as the method outlined for seasonal products. If possible a COSA based on indices covering prices relevant to the business should be applied, otherwise the contract should be included in monetary working capital.

The treatment of progress payments should be noted. Progress payments relieve the business from part of the burden of financing its stock and thus progress payments should be deducted from the value of the contract and the appropriate adjustment should be based on the net value.

Readers will have noted that the rules for distinguishing between stock which is and which is not subject to a COSA are by no means clear cut. This problem is not as great as it might appear because the cost of sales and monetary working adjustments may be regarded as complementary. Indeed the standard specifically permits businesses to combine the COSA and the MWCA (SSAP 16, Para. 56). Advocates of CPP would no doubt point out that the need to recognize special cases, some examples of which are given above, casts doubt on the validity of the CCA model. It does seem that the CPP approach, with certain modifications, might well be the most appropriate method for a trader who is prepared to switch from one type of business to another without restriction.

MWCA

The basic principle underlying the MWCA was discussed in Chapter 5. The adjustment is required to represent the amount of additional (or reduced) finance needed to maintain monetary working capital following changes in the input prices of goods and services used and financed by the business. Thus, if prices are rising, a business will, all other things being equal, have to increase its investment in debtors as well as its investment in stock. However, the additional investment will be reduced to the extent that the investment in debtors and other monetary assets is financed by creditors.

The standard defines monetary working capital as the aggregate of

(a) trade debtors, prepayments and trade bills receivable, plus
(b) stock not subject to a cost of sales adjustment, less
(c) trade creditors, accruals and trade bills payable,

in so far as they arise from the day-to-day operating activities of the business as distinct from transactions of a capital nature (SSAP 16, Para. 44).

The standard goes on to point out that bank balances and overdrafts may fluctuate with the volume of stock or the items in (a), (b) and (c) above. That part of bank balances or overdrafts arising from fluctuations should be included in monetary working capital together with any cash floats required to support day-to-day operations, if to do so would have a material effect on the current cost operating profit.

One obvious example of a situation where bank balances or overdrafts would be included in monetary working capital is provided by a business which, because of the seasonal nature of activities, exhibits considerable fluctuations in its holding of stock and its investment in debtors. The most likely consequence of the business's net reduction in its investment in stock plus debtors less creditors is an increase in its bank balance (or reduction in its overdraft). If prices rise in the period during which the business's bank balance is high, the business will only be able to purchase a lesser quantity of stock, etc., unless additional working capital is obtained. In such an example the temporary increase in bank balance should be included as part of the monetary working capital and the MWCA should be calculated by reference to the total amount of working capital required in the circumstances of the business, irrespective of its composition.

By excluding bank balances and overdrafts from the main definition of monetary working capital, SSAP 16 has attempted to reduce the subjectivity involved in making the MWCA. However, in certain cases such an approach is undoubtedly inadequate and hence exceptions have had to be made. Given the difficulties involved, it follows that, even though they are in the same business situation, different firms may come to different conclusions about whether or not cash balances, etc., should be included. If such is the case, interfirm comparison in this area may be difficult.

Calculation of the MWCA

The MWCA is calculated in the same way as the COSA and the averaging method described on pages 183–185 is usually found to be the most convenient approach. If the averaging method is used the calculation will be based on the opening and closing balances of items included in monetary working capital, appropriate price indices relating to the beginning and end of the period and the average price index for the period.

The calculations can be done for the year as a whole or separate calculations may be made for lesser periods. It is important to ensure that the MWCA is calculated by reference to the same periods as the COSA. The reason for this is the relationship between stock and the remaining elements of working capital. In general, if stock is decreased the other elements of working capital are increased and vice-versa.

In principle separate index numbers should be used to calculate the various elements of the MWCA. The index for debtors should be based on the movements of the costs of the goods and services sold which gave rise to the debtors.

In many cases the index used for the stock of finished goods will be suitable for debtors, but adjustments may be required if, for example, certain products are sold primarily for cash while others are sold on credit, since it is the costs of the inputs used in the manufacture of the goods sold on credit which are relevant to the debtors adjustment. Strictly, the calculation should be based on the debtors figure less the profit element, but it is suggested that the total debtors can be used where this 'gives a fair approximation' (GN, Para. 96).

The index for creditors should be based on movements of these items which are financed by creditors. Thus, changes in wage rates which should in general be included in the debtors index will often be immaterial so far as the index for creditors is concerned. Despite the fact that these two indices will normally reflect different price movements, the guidance notes suggest that, where the percentage changes in debtors and creditors indices over the period are similar, a single index can be used and the debtors and creditors can be dealt with by making a single adjustment. In appropriate cases the single index may be the same as the one applied to stock (GN, Para. 95).

As is the case with the COSA, regard must be paid to the average age of the debtors and creditors when applying the index if to do so would yield a materially different adjustment than would be obtained by the index numbers relating to the ends of the periods over which the calculation is made. Thus, if, for example, the average age of debtors is 1 month, the value of the appropriate index number at 30 November should be applied to the closing balance of debtors if the business has a 31 December year end.

If stock not subject to a COSA is included in monetary working capital, the appropriate index should be based on price changes 'most appropriate to the stock in question and the general nature of the business' (GN, Para. 102). In the absence of a more suitable index a general index should be applied.

If cash or overdrafts are included in monetary working capital, the index should be based on the price movements of the items which will be purchased by the cash.

Special mention should be made of banks and other financial enterprises. In such instances cash will normally be included in monetary working capital. If the financial institution is of a specialized nature, the index applied to cash and the other elements of monetary working capital should be based on the prices of the assets for which the business provides finance (GN, Para. 103). The rationale for this procedure can be seen if one considers a finance company which specializes in financing the purchase of motor vehicles. If the price of motor vehicles does not increase, no MWCA will be required irrespective of changes in other prices because the company would still be able to sustain its level of business with its existing investment in monetary working capital.

In a general banking business a widely based index such as the Index of Retail Prices should be used.

If a business's monetary working capital is a net liability and if the net liability exceeds the value of stock subject to a COSA, the excess is not regarded as financing working capital and should be excluded from the MWCA calculation. The excess is included in the net borrowing figure and will therefore affect the gearing adjustment (GN, Para. 98).

We will now present an example to illustrate the calculation of both the COSA and MWCA.

EXAMPLE 6.1

Suppose that Fowl Limited's current assets and current liabilities at 1 January, 30 June and 31 December 19X5 are as follows:

	1 January		30 June		31 December	
	£	£	£	£	£	£
Current assets						
Stock at historical cost		60 000		130 000		90 000
Trade debtors		20 000		60 000		65 000
Prepayments		1 200		1 500		1 400
Cash in hand		2 000		1 800		2 200
		83 200		193 300		158 600

less Current liabilities

Trade creditors	30 000		90 000		80 000	
Accrued expenses	5 000		4 000		7 000	
Dividends payable	16 000		—		20 000	
Corporation Tax	20 000		12 000		44 000	
Bank overdraft	22 000	93 000	67 000	173 000	15 000	166 000
Net current assets		£(9 800)		£20 300		£(7 400)

We will calculate the MWCA and the COSA on the basis of two alternative sets of assumptions. The first set will enable us to calculate the adjustments in a very simple fashion while the second set of assumptions will require a much more complex series of calculations.

Assumptions A are as follows:

(a) That the price movements relevant to stock, debtors and creditors follow the same path, thus enabling us to use the same index for all these items.

(b) That in view of the rapid turnover of stocks, debtors and creditors the index numbers at the beginning and end of the period can be used.

(c) That the business is not subject to any seasonality and that the COSA and MWCA can be calculated for the year as a whole.

(d) That the company's bank overdraft does not fluctuate with the level of stock, trade debtors and creditors and that it does not require cash floats to support its day-to-day operations. Thus, cash and overdrafts are excluded from the MWCA calculation.

(e) That the appropriate index numbers referred to in paragraph (a) are: 1 January, 120; average for the year, 125; 31 December, 140.

Under these assumptions, the cost of sales adjustment using the formula for the averaging method given on page 185 is

$$\text{COSA} = \frac{£60\,000}{120}(125 - 120) + \frac{£90\,000}{140}(140 - 125) = £12\,143.$$

On the basis of the definition of monetary working capital given on page 189 and the above assumptions, monetary working capital at 1 January and 31 December is

	1 January		31 December	
	£	£	£	£
Trade debtors		20 000		65 000
Prepayments		1 200		1 400
		21 200		66 400

	1 January		31 December	
	£	£	£	£
b/f		21 200		66 400
less Trade creditors	30 000		80 000	
Accrued expenses	5 000	35 000	7 000	87 000
		£(13 800)		£(20 600)

Note that the cash, dividends payable, Corporation Tax and the bank overdraft have not been included.

At both 1 January and 31 December the monetary working capital is a net liability, but, as the net liabilities are less than the stock subject to the COSA at both dates, nothing has to be added to net borrowings.

Using the averaging method the MWCA is given by

$$\text{MWCA} = \frac{-£13\,800}{120}(125 - 120) + \frac{-£20\,600}{140}(140 - 125) = -£2782.$$

As the MWCA is negative, £2782 will be credited to the current cost profit and loss account and debited to the current cost reserve account.

In a case such as this, when the same index numbers are used in the COSA and MWCA calculations, the combined figure of £9361 (£12 143 − £2782) could be shown in the current cost profit and loss account.

Assumptions B are as follows:

(a) That although the same index number series can be used for stock (except for the stock referred to in paragraph (d) below) and debtors (including prepayments), a different series need be used for creditors (including accrued expenses). This might reflect a position where there was a high labour content in stock and the goods sold.

(b) That the business is seasonal in that the company builds up its stock towards the end of June and then gradually runs it down over the following 12 months. Thus the COSA and MWCA will each be calculated separately for the periods January to June and July to December.

(c) That the profit element in debtors averages 60% and it is considered that the exclusion of this amount will have a significant effect on the MWCA. Thus only 40% of the debtors figure will be included in monetary working capital.

(d) Of the stock in hand on 30 June, £30 000 represents a special purchase which will not be repeated; most of the stock was sold in the following 6 months and only £5000 remained on 31 December. It is not intended that the cash generated from the sale of the stock should be used to expand the normal business operations. Instead it will be used to finance special projects as and when they arise. The stock in question should therefore not be made subject to a cost of sales adjustment but included in monetary working capital. It is likely that an index covering a broader range of prices than those which relate to the normal stock purchased by the company would be used to calculate the stock element of the MWCA. For convenience, the index relating to the company's normal trading stock and debtors will be referred to as index A while the index applicable to the special purchase will be described as index B. Index B might very well cover the price movements of a range of industries in which the company would be prepared to undertake special projects. The debtors in the main arise from the sale of the company's normal stock; if this were not the case, part of the debtors should, in principle at least, be adjusted for the purposes of the MWCA by index B.

(e) That the nature of the business is such that it requires to maintain some cash in hand and therefore the cash figures should be included in monetary working capital and, for simplicity, it will be assumed that index A is the appropriate index.

(f) Given the assumptions made about the special stock purchase it is clear that the business is now in effect divided into two parts and separate COSA and MWCA should be made for each section of the business. We have not done so; our reason for this is not only our wish not to further complicate an already detailed example, but also to indicate that it is likely that the simplification used in this example will often be found in practice.

(g) That the bank overdraft does fluctuate with the level of stock, debtors and creditors. However, the overdraft is also regarded as a medium-term source of finance. The base level of the overdraft is about £20 000 and the variations about that figure should be included in monetary working capital. (Note that in these circumstances £20 000 would be included in net borrowings for the purpose of the gearing adjustment.) The overdraft at 31 December is less than £20 000 because the cash generated from the sale of the special stock has not been reinvested. In principle the overdraft figure at 31 December should be analysed and the amount of the cash generated from the special purchase should be adjusted by index B while the difference between the actual balance (excluding the cash from the sale of the special purchases) and £20 000 should be adjusted by index A. For simplicity this adjustment will not be made and index A will be used for that part of the bank overdraft which is included in monetary working capital.

(h) That the average age of stock at 1 January and 31 December is 3 months and at 30 June 1 month. This assumption is consistent with a substantial increase in the stock purchased towards the end of the first half-year. Thus the index numbers of stock will refer to 1 October 19X4, 31 May 19X5 and 1 October 19X5. It is assumed that the debtors collection and creditors payments are short enough to be ignored and thus the index numbers at the start and end of each period can be used.

(i) That the appropriate index numbers are as given below:

	Normal stock and debtors (+ cash) (index A)	Special stock (index B)	Creditors
1 October 19X4	112	—	—
1 January 19X5	120	—	110
Average for January–June	123	130*	115
31 May 19X5	124	130	—
30 June 19X5	126	—	120
Average for July–December	133	165	125
1 October 19X5	135	170	—
31 December 19X5	140	—	130

* Since none of the 'special stock' had been sold prior to 30 June, the appropriate index number representing the average purchases for the period must be the same as the one applied to the stock held on 30 June.

Using assumptions B, the COSA may be calculated as follows. The 'normal stock' figures are

	1 January (£)	30 June (£)	31 December (£)
Stock per accounts	60 000	130 000	90 000
less Special stock	—	30 000	5 000
Normal stock	£60 000	£100 000	£85 000

The COSA for the period January–June (for the normal stock only) is then given by

$$\text{COSA} = \frac{£60\,000}{112}(123 - 112) + \frac{£100\,000}{124}(124 - 123) = £6\,699$$

and for the period July–December

$$\text{COSA} = \frac{£100\,000}{124}(133 - 124) + \frac{£85\,000}{135}(135 - 133) = £8\,517.$$

The total COSA is thus £15 216.

Also under assumptions B, the MWCA may be computed by the following means:

	£	£
1 January		
Stock, not subject to COSA		—
Trade debtors, 40% of £20 000	8 000	
Prepayments	1 200	
Cash in hand	2 000	
Overdraft, £22 000 − £20 000	(2 000)	
Total, debtors, etc.		9 200
Trade creditors	(30 000)	
Accrued expenses	(5 000)	
Total, creditors		(35 000)
Total MWC		£(25 800)
30 June		
Stock, not subject to COSA		30 000
Trade debtors, 40% of £60 000	24 000	
Prepayments	1 500	
Cash in hand	1 800	
Overdraft, £67 000 − £20 000	(47 000)	
Total, debtors, etc.		(19 700)
Trade creditors	(90 000)	
Accrued expenses	(4 000)	
Total, creditors		(94 000)
Total MWC		£(83 700)

31 December	£	£
Stock, not subject to COSA		5 000
Trade debtors, 40% of £65 000	26 000	
Prepayments	1 400	
Cash in hand	2 200	
Overdraft, £15 000 − £20 000	5 000	
Total, debtors, etc.		34 600
Trade creditors	(80 000)	
Accrued expenses	(7 000)	
Total, creditors		(87 000)
Total MWC		£(47 400)

Note that in each instance the negative balance of monetary working capital is less than the cost of the stock subject to the COSA.

	£

MWCA for January–June

Stock not subject to COSA, $\dfrac{£30\,000}{130}(130 - 130)$ 0

Debtors, prepayments, cash and overdrafts,

$\dfrac{£9200}{120}(123 - 120) + \dfrac{£(-19\,700)}{126}(126 - 123)$ −239

Creditors and accrued expenses,

$-\dfrac{£35\,000}{110}(115 - 110) - \dfrac{£94\,000}{120}(120 - 115)$ −5508

−£5747

MWCA for July–December

Stock not subject to COSA,

$\dfrac{£30\,000}{130}(165 - 130) + \dfrac{£5\,000}{170}(170 - 165)$ 8 224

Debtors, prepayments, cash and overdraft,

$-\dfrac{£19\,700}{126}(133 - 126) + \dfrac{£34\,600}{140}(140 - 133)$ 636

Creditors and accrued expenses,

$$-\frac{£94\,000}{120}(125-120)-\frac{£87\,000}{130}(130-125) \qquad\qquad -7\,263$$

$$£1\,597$$

The total MWCA for the year is thus $-$ £5747 + £1597 = $-$£4150, and thus £4150 should be credited to the current cost profit and loss account and debited to the current cost reserve account.

The very long Example 6.1 illustrates that, unless a fair number of simplifying assumptions can be made, the MWCA will require quite complex calculations. The amount of detail could in practice be even greater in the case of a business which deals in a range of products whose prices have changed by different amounts.

We have now completed our discussion of the three adjustments – cost of sales, depreciation and monetary working capital – which distinguish current cost operating profit from the historical cost profit. We will now turn to the adjustments that are made to the current cost operating profit to arrive at the current cost profit attributable to shareholders. The adjustments are interest on or income relating to the items comprising net borrowings on which the gearing adjustment is based, the gearing adjustment itself, taxation and extraordinary items.

Unless and until the Inland Revenue agrees that tax should be based on the profit derived from current cost accounts, the tax charge will depend on the historical cost results and hence the tax charge included in the current cost profit and loss account is the same as the historical cost profit and loss charge.

SSAP 6 ('Extraordinary items and prior year adjustments') applies to current cost accounts as well as historical cost accounts and so there is no difference in the principles that should be applied in identifying extraordinary items. The figures might, however, be different, in so far as the extraordinary items are based on changes in the book values of stock and fixed assets.

The gearing adjustment

The gearing adjustment was introduced in Chapter 5 and discussed in the context of the definition of the current cost profit attributable to shareholders on page 168.

In order to avoid the accusation that the gearing adjustment is based on the assumption of what will happen, the ASC interpret the adjustment in the light of past events and state that it is a reflection of a gain which has accrued to shareholders as assets are used or sold. The point is made in the guidance notes:

> The fixed assets and the working capital commonly will have been financed in part by borrowing. Where such borrowing is fixed in monetary amount, any liability to repay remains unaltered, even when price changes affect the operating assets of the business financed by it. If prices rise, the value to the business of assets exceed the borrowing that has financed them. The excess (less interest payable on the borrowings) in effect accrues to the shareholders, and is realised as the assets are used or sold in the ordinary course of business. The existence of borrowing during a period of rising prices thus provides a benefit to shareholders which offsets to a greater or lesser extent, the cost of servicing the borrowing and conversely when prices decline. (GN, Para. 106)

If, in a period of rising prices, the dividends are restricted to the current cost operating profit less taxation, interest, etc., the shareholders' interest in the business would increase and hence this amount would not be in accord with the definition of current cost profit attributable to shareholders. Thus the gearing adjustment serves to increase (in periods of rising prices) the current cost profit attributable to shareholders.

The gearing adjustment is the product of the *gearing proportion* and the sum of the three current cost adjustments.

The gearing proportion is the ratio of net borrowings (as defined below) to the average net operating assets for the year taken at their current cost. The net operating assets is the sum of: (a) fixed assets, including investments which are not regarded as current assets, and (b) stock and monetary working capital (GN, Para. 111). Net borrowing is defined as follows:

> Net borrowing is the excess of:
>
> (a) the aggregate of all liabilities and provisions fixed in monetary terms (including convertible debentures and deferred tax but excluding proposed dividends) other than those included within monetary working capital and other than those which are, in substance, equity capital[10] over
>
> (b) the aggregate of all current assets other than those subject to a cost of sales

---

10 An example of a case where a loan may be regarded as being equivalent to equity is provided by the wholly owned subsidiary, e.g. of an overseas company, where part of the loans advanced by the parent company is in effect part of that company's equity stake in the subsidiary. In that case the loans should be treated as equity capital for the purposes of calculating the subsidiary's gearing adjustment.

adjustment and those included within monetary working capital. (SSAP 16, Para. 45)

The definitions cover all the balance sheet items such that

Net operating assets = Net borrowings plus shareholders' interest (including proposed dividends).

Thus the ratio of net borrowings to net operating assets is the same as the ratio of net borrowings to shareholders' interest plus net borrowings. If, following the terminology used in the guidance notes, we let net borrowings be represented by L and shareholders' interest by S, then

$$\text{Gearing proportion} = \frac{L}{L + S}$$

Net borrowings would be negative if the aggregate of relevant current assets exceeds the total liabilities and provisions as defined above. In such cases net borrowings is taken to be zero and hence no gearing adjustment is made (SSAP 16, Para. 22). Further, no adjustment is made for the excess current assets as it is not regarded as forming part of net operating assets (GN, Para. 112). This provision has been subject to some criticism and its implications will be discussed on page 246.

Some readers, having noted that one needs the shareholders' interest from the current cost balance sheet in order to calculate the gearing adjustment, may be puzzled about how to proceed given that one needs the gearing adjustment in order to complete the current cost balance sheet. The answer to this apparent paradox is that the gearing adjustment simply represents a transfer between the current cost reserve account and the profit and loss account, which are both part of the shareholders' interest. It is therefore necessary initially to prepare draft current cost accounts without the gearing adjustment in order to find the shareholders' interest and net borrowings; the inclusion of the gearing adjustment will then be a final adjustment which will change the composition but not the total of shareholders' interest.

The inclusion of the above version of the gearing adjustment in SSAP 16 provoked considerable criticism and we will return to the subject in Chapter 7 where we will outline the alternatives which were subsequently considered by the ASC.

The calculation of the SSAP version of the gearing adjustment is illustrated in Example 6.2.

EXAMPLE 6.2

Suppose that the current cost balance sheets (before the calculation of the gearing adjustment in the case of 19X7) at 31 December 19X6 and 19X7 are as follows:

	19X6		19X7	
	£000	£000	£000	£000
Fixed assets		11 200		11 400
Investments				600
Net current assets				
Stock	3 000		4 300	
Monetary working capital	500		2 200	
	3 500		6 500	
Proposed dividends	(200)		(300)	
Other current liabilities (incl. tax)	(600)	2 700	(400)	5 800
		£13 900		£17 800

	19X6		19X7	
	£000	£000	£000	£000
Share capital and reserves				
Preference shares		1 000		1 000
Ordinary shares		4 000		5 000
Share premium		—		500
Current cost reserve		3 200		3 800
Other reserves		1 100		2 800
		9 300		13 100
Debentures	4000		4000	
Deferred tax	600	4 600	700	4 700
		£13 900		£17 800

The total of the three current cost adjustments for 19X7 is £600 000 debit to the current cost profit and loss account.

In order to calculate the gearing proportion, it will be helpful to recast the balance sheets to show the totals of net operating assets, shareholders' interest and net borrowings:

	19X6 (£000)	19X7 (£000)
Fixed assets	11 200	11 400
Investments	—	600
Stock	3 000	4 300
Net monetary working capital	500	2 200
Total net operating assets	£14 700	£18 500
Share capital and reserves	9 300	13 100
Proposed dividends	200	300
Total shareholders' interest	£ 9 500	£13 400
Other current liabilities	600	400
Debentures	4 000	4 000
Deferred tax	600	700
Total net borrowings	£ 5 200	£ 5 100

The average net borrowings is given by

$$L = \frac{£5200 + £5100}{2} = £5150$$

and the average shareholders' interest by

$$S = \frac{£9\,500 + £13\,400}{2} = £11\,450.$$

The gearing proportion is then given by

$$\frac{L}{L+S} = \frac{£5\,150}{£5\,150 + £11\,450} = 0.31$$

and the gearing adjustment by $0.31 \times £600\,000 = £186\,145$.

The gearing adjustment will be credited to the current cost profit and loss account and debited to the current cost reserve.

The gearing adjustment is particularly intended for limited companies where a clear distinction between creditors and shareholders can be made. There are, however, many instances where it is not possible to make a clear-cut distinction. In some cases there may be investments which, although they are legally in the form of loans, are, from an economic standpoint, part of the owners' long-term investment in the enterprise (e.g. advances made by a parent company to a subsidiary). It is suggested that in such cases the gearing adjustment should be based on the view that the loan capital is actually part of equity. A note to the accounts should be provided which would explain the treatment adopted and, if possible, specify the gearing adjustment based on the assumption that all loans are treated as such and not included with equity (GN, Paras 109 and 110).

Care must be taken when considering the treatment of interest receivable and payable in order to ensure that it is dealt with in the current cost profit and loss account in a manner which is consistent with the treatment of the underlying assets and liabilities.

Interest which is related to assets and liabilities which are included in monetary working capital should be credited or debited to the current cost profit and loss account before arriving at the current cost operating profit. Other interest should be shown in arriving at the current cost profit attributable to shareholders, distinguishing between interest on borrowing which has been included in the gearing adjustment and that which has not been so included possibly because it has been treated as part of the equity (GN, Paras. 119 and 120).

Notes to the accounts

We have now completed our review of the main features of current cost accounts prepared in accordance with SSAP 16. In addition to the points to which we have referred above, the standard requires the publication of a number of notes to the accounts. These are to be found in Paras 56–59 of the standard.

CCA and group accounts

In general, group current cost accounts should be prepared in accordance with the principles set out in SSAP 16. The actual standard makes few specific references to group accounts. It is stated (SSAP 16, Para. 46) that when a parent company which is exempted from the need to publish current cost accounts because of the nature of its trade has subsidiaries which are engaged in non-exempt businesses and which collectively exceed the numerical limits set out in the standard, then the group accounts should include current cost information in respect of such subsidiaries. A parent company of a group which is required to publish group current cost accounts need not publish current cost accounts for itself as a single company where historical cost accounts are the main accounts (SSAP 16, Para. 60).

Part IV of the guidance notes is devoted to the subject of group accounts. This section of the notes mainly consists of matters of a practical nature and we will not attempt to summarize it in any detail. We will, however, briefly discuss the monetary working capital and gearing adjustments in the context of group accounts and the problems associated with minority interests at this stage. The treatment of goodwill was dealt with on page 179.

The group MWCA should be the total of the adjustments for each company in the group. Care should be taken when intercompany debt is included in monetary working capital to ensure that it is consistently treated in the accounts of the two companies (GN, Para. 141).

In contrast it is suggested that the gearing adjustment should normally be calculated on a group basis to avoid anomalies which could occur where the pattern of intercompany financing differs from the group's external financial arrangements (GN, Para. 142). Thus the gearing proportion should be based on the group balance sheet, but this would be applied to the aggregate of the current cost adjustments derived from the accounts of the individual companies.

When there are substantial minority interests, the proportion of the current cost adjustments (including the gearing adjustment) applicable to minorities is the aggregate of the figures derived from the accounts of the individual companies (GN, Para. 143). This method does create problems in that the group gearing adjustment is based on the group figures and is not the total of the individual gearing adjustments.

The method suggested by the guidance notes (GN, Para. 144), is first to calculate the group gearing adjustment before making allowance for minority interests. In this stage of the calculation the minority interest is treated as if it were part of the shareholders' interest. The total of the gearing adjustments relating to minorities derived from the subsidiaries' accounts is then deducted from the group total adjustment to leave the adjustment relating to the shareholders of the parent company. In some circumstances a simplified method can be used whereby the group gearing adjustment is apportioned between minority interest and the shareholders of the parent company on the basis of the ratio of group share capital and reserves to the minority interest disclosed in the group balance sheet.

Statement of change in shareholders' equity interest

This statement is not referred to in SSAP 16 but is included as a possible voluntary additional statement in Appendix (vi) of the guidance notes. CCA does not of course deal with the maintenance of capital in terms of general purchasing power, and the purpose of the statement is to show the extent to which shareholders' interest measured by reference to general purchasing power has been maintained. The format of the statement will be illustrated in Example 6.3.

We are now in a position to present a comprehensive example illustrating the preparation of a set of current cost accounts.

COMPREHENSIVE EXAMPLE 6.3

The historical cost and current cost balance sheets of Ant Limited as at 31 December 19X4 are given below:

	Historical cost (£)	Current cost (£)	Difference (£)
Fixed assets			
Cost	180 000	212 400	
less Accumulated depreciation	18 000	21 240	
	162 000	191 160	29 160
Current assets			
Stock	50 000	52 174	2 174
Debtors	60 000	60 000	
Current liabilities			
Creditors and account expenses	(30 000)	(30 000)	
Dividends payable	(5 000)	(5 000)	
Overdraft	(50 000)	(50 000)	
	£187 000	£218 334	£31 334
Share capital			
£1 ordinary shares	100 000	100 000	
Current cost reserve	—	36 466	36 466
Profit and loss account	27 000	21 868	−5 132
	127 000	158 334	
10% debentures	60 000	60 000	
	£187 000	£218 334	£31 334

Ant Limited started trading on 1 January 19X4. As a current cost balance sheet has been prepared at the end of its first year of trading, the balance on the current cost reserve account at 31 December 19X4 can be analysed as follows:

	£	£
Unrealized surpluses		
Fixed assets	29 160	
Stock	2 174	31 334
Realized surpluses – the cumulative total of the current cost adjustments that have been passed through the profit and loss account including the gearing adjustment		5 132
		£36 466

Normally when current cost accounts are prepared for the first time the current cost reserve will include only unrealized surpluses at the date of introduction of the system and it would not be possible to identify past realized surpluses.

Ant Limited's historical cost trading and profit and loss account for the year ended 31 December 19X5 and balance sheet as at that date are given below:

Ant Limited
Trading and profit and loss account for the year ended 31 December 19X5

	£	£
Sales		500 000
less Opening stock	50 000	
Purchases	390 000	
	440 000	
less Closing stock	90 000	350 000
Gross profit		150 000
less Sundry expenses	56 000	
Debenture interest	6 000	
Depreciation	28 000	90 000
Profit before taxation		60 000
less Corporation Tax		16 000
		44 000

	£	£
b/f		44 000
less Dividends		
Paid	8 000	
Proposed	15 000	23 000
		21 000
Retained profits 1 January 19X5		27 000
Retained profits 31 December 19X5		£48 000

Balance sheet as at 31 December 19X5

	£	£	£
Fixed assets			
Cost		380 000	
Accumulated depreciation		46 000	334 000
Current assets			
Stock		90 000	
Debtors		100 000	
Balance at bank		9 000	
		199 000	
less Current liabilities			
Creditors	50 000		
Accrued expenses	4 000		
Dividends payable	15 000		
Corporation tax	16 000	85 000	114 000
			£448 000
Share capital			
£1 ordinary shares			300 000
Share premium account			40 000
Profit and loss account			48 000
			388 000
10% debentures			60 000
			£448 000

Notes
(a) On 1 July 19X5 the company issued 200 000 £1 ordinary shares at a premium of 20 pence per share.
(b) On 1 July 19X5 the company purchased fixed assets costing £200 000.

There were no sales of fixed assets in the year. The company depreciated its fixed assets at 10% per annum on a straight-line basis assuming a zero scrap value.

The workings required in order to prepare the current accounts will be organized in the following sections:

A. Fixed assets and depreciation;
B. COSA and stock;
C. MWCA;
D. Gearing adjustment;
E. Movement on the current cost reserve account;
F. Statement of changes in shareholders' equity interest after allowing for changes in the general purchasing power of money (this is one of the voluntary statements mentioned in SSAP 16).

A   *Fixed assets and depreciation*

A1   The appropriate price index for fixed assets moved as follows:

Date:	1 January 19X5	1 July 19X5	31 December 19X5
Index:	118	132	144

A2   An analysis of the fixed assets held on 1 January 19X5 revealed that they had all been purchased on 1 January 19X4 at a cost of £180 000.

A3   The gross replacement cost of fixed assets at 31 December 19X5 is

	£
Opening balance per current cost balance sheet,	
£212 400 × 144/118	259 200
Assets purchased on 1 July 19X5, £200 000 × $\frac{144}{132}$	218 182
	£477 382

A4   The curent cost depreciation charge for 19X5 based on the average gross current replacement cost is

	£
On fixed assets held on 1 January 19X5,	
10% of $\frac{1}{2}$ (£212 400 + £259 200)	23 580
On fixed assets purchased on 1 July 19X5,	
5% of $\frac{1}{2}$ (£200 000 + £218 182)	10 455
	£34 035

A5   The depreciation adjustment is then

	£
Current cost depreciation	34 035
less Historical cost depreciation	28 000
Depreciation adjustment	£ 6 035

A6   Required balance on accumulated depreciation at 31 December 19X5:

	£
Fixed assets held on 1 January 19X5 (and purchased on 1 January 19X4), 20% of £259 200	51 840
Fixed assets purchased on 1 July 19X5, 5% of £218 182	10 909
	£62 749

A7   Backlog depreciation:

	£	£
Accumulated depreciation at 31 December 19X5		62 749
less Accumulated depreciation (per current accounts) at 1 January 19X5	21 240	
CCA depreciation charge for 19X5	34 035	55 275
Backlog depreciation		£ 7 474

A8   The CCA balance sheet figures are then

	£
Gross replacement cost (A3)	477 382
less Accumulated depreciation (A6)	62 749
Net replacement cost	£414 633

A9   The net credit to the current cost reserve is

	£
Increase in gross replacement cost	
Assets held on 1 January 19X5, £259 200 − £212 400	46 800
Assets purchased on 1 July 19X5, £218 182 − £200 000	18 182
	64 982
less Backlog depreciation	7 474
Net credit	£57 508

B   *COSA and stock*

B1   Assume (i) that all the stock is subject to a COSA; (ii) that the averaging method can be used and that the adjustment can be made for the year as a whole (note that this can only be done if similar assumptions can be made about the MWCA); (iii) that the average age of stock is 3 months; (iv) that the appropriate price index for stock moved as follows:

Date:	1 October 19X4	Average for 19X5	1 October 19X5	31 December 19X5
Index:	115	128	140	150

B2   The COSA for 19X5 is given by

$$\text{COSA} = \frac{£50\,0000}{115}(128 - 115) + \frac{£90\,000}{140}(140 - 128) = £13\,366.$$

B3   The unrealized revaluation surplus on the stock held on 31 December 19X5 is given by

	£
Current replacement cost at 31 December 19X5, $£90\,000 \times \frac{150}{140}$	96 429
less Cost of stock	90 000
Unrealized surplus	£ 6 429

B4   The credit to the current cost reserve account is

	£	£
Realized surplus, i.e. COSA		13 366
Increase in unrealized surplus		
Unrealized surplus at 31 December 19X5	6 429	
Unrealized surplus at 1 January 19X5	2 174	4 255
		£17 621

C   *MWCA*

C1   Assume (i) that the overdraft and balance at bank do not fluctuate with the level of stock, debtors or creditors, and hence should not be included in monetary working capital; (ii) that the ages of debtors and creditors can be ignored and the year-end index numbers can be used in the calculation; (iii) that the appropriate price indices as follows:

Date	1 January 19X5	Average for 19X5	31 December 19X5
Debtors index	120	133	146
Creditors and accrued expenses index	115	125	135

C2   The MWCA is then given by

£

$$\text{Debtors,} \quad \frac{£60\,000}{120}(133-120) + \frac{£100\,000}{146}(146-133) \quad = \quad 15\,404$$

Creditors and accrued expenses,

$$\frac{-£30\,000}{115}(125-115) - \frac{£54\,000}{135}(135-125) \quad = \quad -6\,609$$

£ 8 795

D   *Gearing adjustment*

D1   In order to calculate the gearing proportion it is necessary to construct a draft CCA balance sheet as at 31 December 19X5. It will be helpful if we first summarize the adjustments that have been made to shareholders' interest current cost reserve:

	£
Balance 1 January 19X5	36 466
add Increases for 19X5	
Fixed assets (A9)	57 508
Stock (B4)	17 621
MWCA (C2)	8 795
Balance before gearing adjustment at 31 December 19X5	£120 390

The balance on the CCA profit and loss account as at 31 December 19X5 (before making the gearing adjustment) is

	£	£	£
Balance on CCA profit and loss account at 1 January 19X5			21 868
Increase in retained earnings in 19X5, historical cost profit and loss account		21 000	
less Current cost adjustments			
Depreciation adjustment (A5)	6 035		
COSA (B2)	13 366		
MWCA (C2)	8 795	28 196	(7 196)
Balance of CCA profit and loss account at 31 December 19X5 before the gearing adjustment			£14 672

D2 A draft CCA balance sheet (before the gearing adjustment) can now be prepared. For convenience the balance sheet will be arranged so as to disclose the totals of net operating assets, shareholders' interest and net borrowings.

CCA balance sheet as at 31 December 19X5
(before making the gearing adjustment for 19X5)

	£	Workings
Net operating assets		
Fixed assets	414 633	A8
Stock	96 429	B3
Debtors	100 000	
Creditors	(50 000)	
Accrued expenses	(4 000)	
	£557 062	
Shareholders' interest		
Share capital	300 000	
Share premium	40 000	
Profit and loss account	14 672	D1
Current cost reserve	120 390	D1
Proposed dividends	15 000	
	£490 062	

	£
Net borrowings	
Balance at bank	(9 000)
Corporation Tax	16 000
Debentures	60 000
	£ 67 000

Only the shareholders' interest and net borrowings are required to calculate the gearing proportion. In practice it will often be simplest to calculate the net operating assets and net borrowings thus deriving shareholders' interest as the balancing figure.

D3   As the gearing proportion is based on average values it is necessary to analyse the opening balance sheet to derive the required totals:

Analysis of CCA balance sheet as at 1 January 19X5

	£
Net operating assets	
Fixed assets	191 160
Stock	52 174
Debtors	60 000
Creditors	(30 000)
	£273 334

	£
Shareholders' interest	
Share capital	100 000
Profit and loss account	21 868
Current cost reserve	36 466
Proposed dividends	5 000
	£163 334

Net borrowings	
Overdraft	50 000
Debentures	60 000
	£110 000

D4   The required averages are then calculated as follows:

Shareholders' interest (S) = £0.5 $(163\,334 + 490\,062)$ = £326\,698;

Net borrowings (L) = £0.5 $(110\,000 + 67\,000)$ = £88\,500.

The gearing proportion is then given by

$$\frac{L}{L+S} = \frac{88\,500}{88\,500 + 326\,698} = 0.21.$$

D5   The total of the current cost adjustments (*see* D1) is £28\,196 and the gearing adjustment is therefore $0.21 \times £28\,196 = £5921$.

E   *Movements on the current cost reserve*

E1   The standard requires that the balance sheet be supported by a statement showing the movement on reserves (SSAP 16, Para. 57) but does not specify the form the statement should take. A statement is illustrated in the appendix to SSAP 16, and this example will be based on the format of that statement. One important feature is that the statement analyses the balance on the current cost reserve between the realized and unrealized elements.

E2   The balance on the current cost reserve account at 31 December 19X5 is

	£
Balance (excluding gearing adjustment) from D1	120\,390
less Gearing adjustment (D5)	5\,921
Balance at 31 December 19X5	£114\,469

E3   The above balance can be analysed in the manner described below, which will enable the realized and unrealized elements to be identified. Special reference needs to be made to the treatment of the depreciation adjustment for the year, i.e. the difference between the current cost and the historical cost depreciation charges. The excess depreciation is credited to the accumulated depreciation account and not the current cost reserve. It does, however, have an impact on the current cost reserve as it represents a transfer from the unrealized to the realized section of the account. This is because depreciation is a measure of the consumption of an asset and hence is a measure of the surplus on the fixed assets which has been realized during the year.

	Unrealized (£)	Realized (£)	Total (£)
Fixed assets			
Line 1: Balance at 1 January 19X5	29 160		
Line 2: Increase for year (A9)	57 508		
Line 3: Depreciation adjustment (A5)	(6 035)	6 035	
Stock			
Line 4: Balance at 1 January 19X5	2 174		
Line 5: Increase in unrealized surplus (B4)	4 255		
Line 6: COSA (B2)		13 366	
Line 7: Realized surpluses at 1 Janary 19X5		5 132	
Line 8: MWCA (C2)		8 795	
Line 9: Gearing adjustment (D5)		(5 921)	
	£87 062	£27 407	£114 469

E4   Using the above table a statement of the form illustrated in the appendix to SSAP 16 can be prepared:

Current cost reserve

	£	£	£
Balance at 1 January 19X5 (Lines 1, 4 and 7)			36 466
Revaluation surpluses reflecting price changes			
Fixed assets[11] (Line 2)	57 508		
re Stocks and work in progress (Lines 4, 5 and 6)	17 621	75 129	
MWCA (Line 8)		8 795	
Gearing adjustment (Line 9)		(5 921)	78 003
			£114 469
Of which:			
Realized			27 407
Unrealized			87 062
			£114 469

11 Note that in the statement included in the appendix separate figures are given for land and other fixed assets.

F   *Statement of changes in shareholders' equity interest after allowing for changes in the general purchasing power of money*

F1   The format of the statement is illustrated in Appendix (vi) of the guidance notes. The objective of the statement is to compare equity interest as shown in the current cost accounts at the beginning and end of the year after adjusting for any capital introduced. The difference enables shareholders and others to judge whether the increase in the equity interest has been sufficient to compensate the equity shareholders for the increase in the general price level. Note that the closing balance is stated before dividends.

F2   The Index of Retail Prices is the most suitable index and it is assumed that it moved as follows:

Date:	1 January 19X5	30 June 19X5	31 December 19X5
Index:	150	172	188

F3   The statement will now be presented:

Statement of change in shareholders' equity interest after allowing for change in the general purchasing power of money for the year ended 31 December 19X5.

	£	Workings
Equity interest at the beginning of the year, as shown in the current cost accounts	158 334	
Proceeds of share capital issued on 1 July 19X5	240 000	
	398 334	
Amount required to compensate for the change in the general purchasing power of money during the year	62 437	F4
	460 771	
Equity interest before dividends at the end of the year, as shown in the current cost accounts	498 806	F5
Excess	£ 38 035	

The excess can be analysed as follows:

	£	
Current cost profit attributable to share-holders	21 725	F6
Effect on equity interest of price changes experienced by the company being greater than the general rate of UK inflation	16 310	
	£ 38 035	

F4   Amounts required to compensate for the change in general purchasing power:

	£
Opening capital, £158 334 $(188/150 - 1)$	40 111
Share capital issued on 1 July 19X5, £240 000 $(188/172 - 1)$	22 326
	£ 62 437

F5   Equity interest at 31 December 19X5:

	£
Shareholders' interest (D2)	490 062
add Interim dividend paid (assume the payment was made on 30 June 19X5), £8000 × 188/172	8 744
	£498 806

F6   Current cost profit attributable to shareholders:

	£
Profit after tax per historical cost accounts	44 000
less Current cost operating adjustments (D1)	28 196
	15 804
add Gearing adjustment (D5)	5 921
	£21 725

We can present the current cost accounts. It will be assumed that the historical cost accounts are the main accounts and the following accounts will not contain all the information which is required by statute. The current cost profit and loss account is the alternative form presented in the Appendix to SSAP 16 which is slightly different from the format illustrated on pages 160–1.

Ant Limited
Current cost profit and loss account for the year ended 31 December 19X5

	£	Workings
Historical cost trading profit before interest	66 000	
less Current cost operating adjustments (note 2)	28 196	D1
Current cost operating profit	37 804	
Interest on net borrowings	6 000	
	31 804	
Taxation	16 000	
Current cost profit after interest and taxation	15 804	
Gearing adjustment	5 921	D5
Current cost profit attributable to shareholders	21 725	
Dividends	23 000	
Retained current cost profit for the year	£(1 275)	
Current cost earnings per share	10.9 pence	

Statement of retained profits/reserves

	£	Workings
Retained current cost profit for the year	(1 275)	
Movements on current cost reserve	78 003	E4
	76 728	
Reserves at the beginning of the year	58 334	
Reserves at the end of the year	£135 062	

Summarized current cost balance sheet as at 31 December 19X5

	£	£	£	Workings
Assets employed				
Fixed assets (note 4)			414 633	A8
Net current assets				
Stock		96 429		B3
Balance at bank		9 000		
Monetary working capital (net)		46 000		D2
Working capital		151 429		
Proposed dividends	15 000			
Other current liabilities	16 000	31 000	120 429	D2
			£535 062	
Financed by				
Share capital and reserves				
Share capital		300 000		
Share premium		40 000		
Current cost reserve (note 5)	114 469			E4
Retained profit	20 593	135 062	475 062	
Debentures			60 000	
			£535 062	

Notes to current cost accounts

1. This note should include details of the following:

   (a) A general description of current cost accounts.
   (b) The bases and methods adopted in relation to: (i) fixed assets and depreciation; (ii) working capital; (iii) the gearing adjustment.
   (c) Other accounting policies.

   An example of a suitable note is provided on pages 48 and 49 of the guidance notes.

2. Current cost adjustments made in deriving the current cost operating profit

		£
Cost of sales		13 366
Money working capital		8 795
Working capital		22 161
Fixed assets (depreciation)		6 035
Current cost operating adjustments		£28 196

3. The following shows the net current replacement costs of the net operating assets and the method by which the assets were financed:

	£
Fixed assets	414 633
Working capital	151 429
Net operating assets	£566 062
Share capital and reserves	475 062
Proposed dividends	15 000
Total shareholders' interest	490 062
Debentures	60 000
Other current liabilities (net)	16 000
Net borrowing	76 000
	£566 062

4. Fixed assets:

	Gross current replacement cost	Accumulated depreciation	Net current replacement cost
Fixed assets	£477 382	£62 749	£414 633

5. Current cost reserve. This note is displayed in working E4.
6. Changes in shareholders' equity interest after allowing for changes in the general purchasing power of money. This note is displayed in working F3.

Recommended reading

See list at the end of Chapter 7.

Questions

6.1 'The Standard does not deal with the maintenance of financial capital in general purchasing power terms.' *SSAP 16.*

> **Required:**
> (a) **What is the underlying concept of capital in SSAP 16** Current Cost Accounting? **Define any terms you use in your explanation.**
> (10 marks)
>
> (b) **What voluntary disclosure does SSAP 16** Current Cost Accounting **suggest for reporting the impact of changes in general purchasing power on shareholders' equity interest? Explain whether you consider this to be necessary.** (10 marks)
> **(20 marks)**

A. Cert. A. The Regulatory Framework of Accounting, December 1982.

6.2 The historical cost plant register summary of British Doorknobs plc at 30 June 1982 showed the following:

Year of purchase 30 June		Cost £	Estimated scrap-value £	Depreciable amount £	Expected life years
1975		42 196	196	42 000	7
1976		36 482	482	36 000	12
1977		31 153	1 153	30 000	10
1978		42 987	987	42 000	7
1979		168 502	3 502	165 000	11
1980		787 346	7 346	780 000	15
1981	Special	123 406	1 406	122 000	10
	Other	64 492	1 492	63 000	7
1982		16 118	118	16 000	8

It is the company's policy to depreciate for a full year in the year of purchase and not to provide in the year of disposal.

It is not the general policy to revise asset lives for current cost accounts but the plant purchased in the year ended 30 June 1975 is a special case.

It is still in use and it is now accepted that the original estimate of its expected life was unduly pessimistic and that, solely for current cost accounts, it should have a further life of 5 years which should be applied retrospectively.

During the year ended 30 June 1982 certain plant, excluded from the above plant register and purchased in the year ended 30 June 1978 at a cost of £16 146, was scrapped. This plant had a written down value at 30 June 1981 of £5 146. There were no disposal proceeds.

The following indices supplied by the Central Statistical Office are used by the company for its current cost accounts:

30 June 1974	66.1
1975	71.9
1976	86.5
1977	109.7
1978	131.1
1979	149.9
1980	166.1
1981	183.7
1982	195.1

The special machinery, purchased in the year ended 30 June 1981, is used for forming ovaloid brass door knobs of which the company is the only manufacturer in the world outside the USA. It is considered by the directors that there is no appropriate index available but they have obtained a quotation dated 30 June 1982 for a similar new machine from the original suppliers for £147 000.

You are required to:

(a) calculate at 30 June 1982:

  (i) the current cost value of plant and machinery,
  (ii) the depreciation adjustment, and
  (iii) the disposal adjustment (22 marks), **and**

(b) comment on the significance of the use of different asset lives in the historical cost and current cost accounts (3 marks).

Note: Ignore taxation.   **(25 marks)**

ICAEW Financial Accounting II, December 1982.

6.3 The recently issued consolidated balance sheet and profit and loss account of a public company, prepared on a historical cost basis, are summarized below.

	30 September	
	1980	1979
	£m	£m
Consolidated balance sheet		
Capital and reserves	631	499
Loans	149	29
	780	528
Fixed assets		
Cost	1016	590
Depreciation	232	130
Net	784	460
Current assets		
Stocks	502	304
Debtors	332	211
Liquid funds for day to day use	25	23
	859	538
Current liabilities		
Creditors	405	208
Taxation	20	15
Overdraft	418	234
Dividends	20	13
	863	470
Net current assets/(liabilities)	(4)	68
	780	528

	£m
Consolidated profit and loss account for year to 30 September 1980	
Turnover—Home	1246
Export	532
	1778
Trading profit	303
Depreciation (the same rate on all fixed assets)	102

Profit before interest	201
Interest	13
	188
Taxation	30
Profit after taxation	158
Ordinary dividends	26
Retained profit	132

The directors have asked you to prepare current cost accounts in accordance with SSAP 16.

A loan of £120 000 was raised halfway through the year.

The cost of sales adjustment for 1980 has been calculated as £21m and the monetary working capital adjustment as £9m.

There have been no sales of fixed assets during the last five years and those held at the beginning of the year represent purchases of £100m, 130m, 150m, 210m in 1976, 1977, 1978 and 1979 respectively, spread equally throughout each year. They have been depreciated at 10% p.a. including the year of purchase.

The stocks at the year end represent purchases made at the year end (50%) and equally over the year (50%), and similarly for trade creditors. The age analysis for debtors showed that 75% represented year end sales and 25% equally over the year.

The indices which represent the price changes experienced by the particular assets held by the company and the general price index over the years were:

		Year ended 30 September				
		1980	1979	1978	1977	1976
Beginning of year	Fixed assets	165	144	121	110	100
	Stocks	180	160	140	120	100
	Other current assets and liabilities	180	160	140	120	100
	General prices	188	168	146	117	100
Average during year	Fixed assets	172	154	133	116	105
	Stocks	190	170	150	130	110
	Other current assets and liabilities	190	170	150	130	110
	General prices	197	182	157	135	108

End of year		Year ended 30 September				
		1980	1979	1978	1977	1976
	Fixed assets	180	165	144	121	110
	Stocks	200	180	160	140	120
	Other current assets and liabilities	200	180	160	140	120
	General prices	204	188	168	146	117

You are required to:

(a) calculate the depreciation adjustment for **1980** (10 marks),

(b) calculate the gearing adjustment for **1980** (10 marks), **and**

(c) present the current cost reserve account (10 marks).   **(30 marks)**

ICAEW Financial Accounting II, December 1980.

6.4   SSAP 16 deals with current cost accounting. Wigwam Ltd trades as agricultural merchants and contractors. Its stocks at two successive year ends were as follows:

	31 October	
	1981	1980
	£000	£000
Goods for resale	884	675
Seasonal stocks	87	121
Wheat futures	55	54
Contract work in progress	—	47
	1026	897

The following further information is given:

(1) The goods for resale consist of the normal stocks of the business which are offered for sale via the warehouse and retail outlets. They have been valued on a unit cost basis. They include certain old stocks which have been valued at their net realizable value at 31 October 1981 of £138 000 (1980 £123 000). It has been estimated that the remaining stock, valued at cost, was purchased equally over the preceding four months in 1981 and three months in 1980.

(2) It has always been Wigwam's policy to buy produce when there has been a particularly good year and to store it by the appropriate means so that it can be released to the processor later during the winter. The seasonal stocks at 31 October 1980 consisted of raspberries purchased during August 1980 and at 31 October 1981 consisted of apples purchased during October.

(3) The company deals on the commodity futures market. At each year end, the stocks consist of wheat purchases which have been made on the commodity futures market and for which delivery has not been taken. These stocks have been valued consistently at the price paid for the futures contracts. Subsequent to each year end, and prior to delivery date, the contracts have been sold at a profit on the futures market.

(4) From time to time the company also undertakes construction contracts for farmers using mainly subcontract labour. At 31 October 1980 there was a single contract for the construction of grain silos and driers.
   The contract ledger for this job showed the following entries:

			Dr.	Cr.
1980	October 31	Balances brought forward	47 340	—
	November 30	Costs	15 167	—
	December 31	Costs/cash	14 183	10 000
1981	January 31	Costs	10 300	—
	February 28	Costs (final)	2 250	—
	March 31	Cash	—	90 000
	October 31	Balance to profit and loss account	10 760	—
			100 000	100 000

The opening balance on the contract arose equally over the preceding 5 months.

(5) The relevant mid-month indices supplied by the Central Statistical Office are:

	Stocks held by corn, seed and agricultural merchants		Construction stocks	
	1980	1981	1980	1981
January	105.2	142.0	109.4	137.2
February	106.7	143.9	111.6	139.8
March	107.0	145.5	113.0	141.0
April	110.6	146.1	115.3	142.4
May	115.7	146.6	119.2	144.8
June	117.7	148.3	121.6	145.9
July	120.8	147.7	124.6	148.5
August	124.3	144.0	126.8	149.0
September	127.6	141.8	128.2	149.0
October	132.6	138.7	131.1	150.4
November	136.1	137.5	133.4	151.1
December	138.5	136.9	134.6	151.3

You are required:

(a) for those items for which it is appropriate, to calculate the cost of sales adjustment using the averaging method for the year ending 31st October **1981** (14 marks),

(b) to state where it would not be appropriate to use a cost of sales adjustment in Wigwam Ltd and to give the alternative approach you would adopt (6 marks), **and**

(c) to explain briefly the term 'purchasing skills' and state how this affects the application of SSAP 16 (5 marks).

Make calculations to the nearest £ hundreds.   **(25 marks)**

ICAEW Financial Accounting II, July 1982.

6.5   The current assets and current liabilities of a high class retail company at the beginning and end of the year to 31 December 1980 are summarized below.

		Opening		Closing	
Current assets		£'000	£'000	£'000	£'000
	Stock	54		75	
	Debtors	40		50	
	Cash	21		15	
		—	115	—	140
less Current liabilities					
	Trade creditors	50		60	
	Bank overdraft	30		50	
		—	80	—	110
Net current assets			35		30

The bank overdraft is considered a permanent source of finance. Stock at the end of each year represents purchases made equally during the preceding three months. Debtors represent sales in the preceding two months.

The monthly index of stock prices and the general price index was:

	Stock Price Index	General Price Index
1979 October	115	162
November	117	164
December	118	167
1980 January	120	170
February	124	174
March	126	178
April	129	175
May	132	176

	Stock Price Index	General Price Index
June	132	177
July	134	179
August	134	180
September	135	181
October	138	182
November	140	184
December	141	186
Average for year	132	177

You are required to:
(a) explain the purpose of the monetary working capital adjustment (3 marks),
(b) calculate the monetary working capital adjustment in accordance with SSAP 16 by reference to the data given above (work to the nearest £100) (4 marks), and
(c) explain briefly why some authorities do not consider that a monetary working capital adjustment is necessary (3 marks).   **(10 marks)**

ICAEW Financial Accounting II, July 1981.

6.6 Below are the historical cost profit and loss account of Achilles plc. for the year ended 31 December 1981, and its balance sheet as at that date, with corresponding figures for the previous year.

Achilles plc
Historical Cost Profit and Loss Account for the year ended 31 December 1981

	£'000s	£'000s
Turnover		6 000
Net trading profit, after charging:		550
Depreciation:		
Buildings	58	
Vehicles and equipment	575	
Losses (gains) on disposal of fixed assets:		
Buildings	15	
Vehicles and equipment	(20)	
Investment income (gross of tax credits)		50
Net profit before interest		600
Debenture interest.(gross)		150
Net profit before taxation		450
Taxation		225
Net profit for year—carried forward		225

	£'000s	£'000s
Net profit for year—brought forward		225
Dividends:		
Cumulative preference – paid	25	
Ordinary – paid	50	
Ordinary – proposed	75	
		150
Retained earnings for year		£75

Historical Cost Balance Sheet, 31 December 1981

31.12.1980						
	Cost or			Cost or	Depre-	
Net	valuation	Net assets		valuation	ciation	Net
£'000s	£'000s			£'000s	£'000s	£'000s
		Fixed assets				
300	300	Land		300	–	300
700	1 000	Buildings		1 150	273	877
1 150	2 000	Vehicles and equipment		2 300	1 125	1 175
2 150	£3 300			£3 750	£1 398	2 352
400		*Long-term investments,*				400
		at cost				
		(Market value £500 000;				
		1980, £450 000)				
		Current assets				
	425	Stocks			650	
	475	Debtors and prepayments			700	
	4	Bank and cash balances			295	
	904				1 645	
		Less: Current liabilities				
	350	Bank overdraft			–	
	250	Creditors and accruals			350	
	100	Corporation Tax, 1981 (*less* ACT)			116	
	50	Proposed dividend			75	
	21	ACT on proposed dividend			32	
	771				573	
133		*Net current assets*				1 072
£2 683						£3 824

£		Financed by	£
		Share capital authorized, issued and Fully paid	
	250	10% Cumulative preference (£1 shares)	250
	1 000	Ordinary (£1 shares)	1 000
1 250			1 250
		Reserves	
	300	Share premium account	300
	232	Fixed assets revaluation reserve	232
	751	Retained earnings	826
1 283			1 358
2 533			2 608
–		15% Debentures	1 000
150		Deferred taxation	216
£2 683			£3 824

Notes

(1) Land was revalued in the books of account at £300 000 as at 1 January 1979.

(2) Buildings (original cost £800 000, accumulated depreciation £160 000) were also revalued in the books at the same date, on the basis of £1 000 000 replacement cost as new. Depreciation is at the rate of 5% per annum on gross book value, with a full year's charge in the year of acquisition and none in the year of disposal.

(3) Professional valuations for CCA purposes were:
   Land (market value): 31 December 1980, £360 000; 31 December 1981, £400 000.
   Buildings (gross replacement cost as new): 31 December 1980, £1 250 000; 31 December 1981, £1 600 000 (including 1981 additions, valued at £275 000). During 1981 some buildings were demolished, their valuations being: 1 January 1979 (for historical cost purposes), £100 000 gross, £25 000 net; 31 December 1980 (for current cost purposes), £120 000 gross, £18 000 net.

(4) The Vehicles and equipment on hand at 31 December 1980 were acquired as follows, on average at the middle of each year:

	Cost	Accumulated depreciation
	£	£
1978	400 000	300 000
1979	600 000	300 000
1980	1 000 000	250 000
	£2 000 000	£850 000

In 1981 all the 1978 items were sold for £120 000, and new items were bought for £700 000. The company's policy is to charge depreciation at 25% per annum on gross book value, with a full year's charge in the year of acquisition and none in the year of disposal. Of the 1979 equipment, £200 000 (at cost) was by 31 December 1981 deemed to be obsolescent. The directors of Achilles plc had contracted to replace it in 1982 with modern equipment costing £350 000, and having a service capacity 40% greater than that of the old equipment.

(5) For CCA purposes, the relevant price index numbers for vehicles and equipment (taken as at the month-end) were as follows:

1978	June	100
1979	June	115
1980	June	135
1980	December	150
1981	June	175
1981	December	200

(6) The stocks were on average one month old as at 31 December in both years. The relevant price index numbers were:

1980	November	99
1980	December	100
1981	November	123
1981	December	125

(7) The 15% Debentures were issued at par on 1 January 1981.

(8) For CCA purposes, the profit and loss account adjustments were:

	£
Depreciation adjustment (including allowance for gains and losses on disposal of fixed assets)	208 000
Cost of sales/Monetary working capital adjustment	177 000
Gearing adjustment	68 000

You are required to prepare the current cost balance sheet of Achilles plc as at 31 December 1981, with corresponding figures, on the same basis, for 31 December 1980 (without a general inflation adjustment).

Current cost reserve balances are to be inserted as balancing figures, and no extra marks will be given for computing them directly. **(30 marks)**

A. Cert. A. Advanced Financial Accounting, December 1982.

6.7 Shown below is the group profit and loss account (current cost basis) for a public quoted company, together with related notes.

Profit and loss account for the year ended 31st December 1980

1979	1979 restated in 1980's £'s		1980
£ million	£ million		£ million
5 368	6 334	Sales	5 715
374	441	Trading profit before financing costs and taxation (Note 5)	119
(8)	(9)	Interest and other financial items	(46)
(80)	(94)	As in historical costs accounts	(110)
72	85	Gearing adjustment (Note 6)	64
366	132	Profit before taxation	73
(123)	(145)	Taxation	(123)
(20)	(24)	Minority interests	(11)
223	263	Profit (loss) attributable to parent company	(61)
(16)	(19)	Extraordinary items	(173)
207	244	Profit (loss) attributable to parent company after extraordinary items	(234)
(134)	(158)	Dividends	(101)
73	86	Profit (loss) retained for year	(335)

Note A: Current cost adjustments reduced the historical cost trading profit as shown below:

	1980	1979 restated in 1980 £'s	1979
	£ million	£ million	£ million
Trading profit – historical cost accounts	358	787	667
Cost of sales	(109)	(164)	(139)
Monetary working capital	(3)	(70)	(59)
Supplementary depreciation	(165)	(148)	(125)
Indexation of government grants	38	36	30
Trading profit – current cost accounts	119	441	374

The amount of depreciation charged and government grants credited in the current cost accounts were:

Depreciation	456	440	373
Government grants	59	58	49

Note B: Gearing adjustment

Under SSAP 16 the gearing adjustment in respect of fixed assets is related to the charge for supplementary depreciation (after making allowance for the difference between historical and CCA asset lives). The adjustment thus excludes revaluation surpluses not yet treated as realized. The company believes that this results in mis-stating the amount by which the interests of the equity stockholders have been affected by loan and other external financing, the interest on which has been charged against profits.

Under the company's method, the gearing adjustment represents the total holding gains less losses for the year on assets effectively financed by borrowings less cash; the exchange gains on the non-sterling part of these net borrowings are then added to the adjustment.

The cost of interest and other financial items calculated in accordance with the company's method would be:

	1980	1979 restated in 1980 £'s	1979
	£ million	£ million	£ million
As in historical cost accounts	(110)	(94)	(80)
Gearing adjustment	86	117	99
Exchange gains on financial items	118	81	69
The company's method	94	104	88

You are required to:

(a) explain the second column of figures, the one that is headed **1979 restated in 1980 £'s**, (3 marks),

(b) comment upon the three figures given for sales, (3 marks),

(c) explain the entry in Note A 'indexation of government grants', (4 marks),

(d) explain and comment upon the phrase in Note B 'the charge for supplementary depreciation (after making allowance for the difference between historical and CCA asset lives)' (4 marks),

(e) explain and comment upon the statement in Note B 'excludes revaluation surpluses not yet treated as realized' (4 marks),

(f) comment upon the difference between the gearing adjustment in the accounts and that preferred by the company (3 marks), and

(g) comment upon the three figures given for dividends (3 marks).

(24 marks)

ICAEW Financial Accounting II, December 1981.

7 Current Value Accounting III: Evaluation and Post SSAP 16 Developments

In this chapter we will evaluate current cost accounting (CCA) paying special attention to the SSAP 16 version. We shall also chart the evaluation of the ASC's thinking following the publication of SSAP 16 and discuss the provisions of ED 35. Finally we will contrast current purchasing power (CPP) and CCA and show why, in our view, the next major step in accounting reform should involve incorporating the best elements of both approaches.

Criticisms of SSAP 16

Asset valuation

There are those who attack the basic principles of current value accounting based on 'value to the business'. The attacks come from a number of quarters including adherents of historical cost accounting, CPP accounting and systems of accounting based on variants of the net realizable value approach to asset valuation.

The strength of the attack from those who advocate the retention of historical cost accounting seems to fluctuate with the level of inflation. When inflation is high the attacks are muted, but they tend to intensify when there is a fall in the rate of inflation. The authors contend, for the reasons given in Chapter 3, that the defects of historical cost accounting do not disappear with inflation because there will be substantial and, from the point of view of users of accounts, significant changes in relative prices even if there is only a modest change in the general price level.

The CPP saga, in which the method was originally proposed by the accountancy profession only to be quickly dropped following the recommendations of a committee (Sandilands Committee) of which the majority of members were non-accountants, was not a particularly edifying chapter in the profession's history. The fact that the ASC could publish PSSAP 7 ('CPP accounting') in May 1974 and then, less than 2 years later, publish ED 18 is a reflection of the lack of an agreed conceptual framework which leads many non-accountants to wonder whether accountants are as knowledgeable as they would have the public believe. There are still those who believe that the basic CPP approach would provide the most informative accounts,[1] especially as, from the point of view of shareholders, CPP accounts do indicate the extent to which the shareholders' interest has been maintained in terms of those price changes which are of relevance to individuals. This view is not held by those who are influential in professional circles in the UK, but the method does still attract considerable support in the USA.

While there are relatively few advocates of the pure form of CPP accounting there are many who believe that the basic CCA approach, as advocated by Sandilands and subsequently developed to emerge as SSAP 16, is seriously deficient in its treatment of inflation. We will return to this point later when discussing some specific criticisms of SSAP 16.

The most widely known advocate of a system of current value accounting in which the selling price of assets would form the basis of asset valuation is Professor R. J. Chambers of the University of Sydney. Professor Chambers has published a number of trenchant papers on CCA[2] in which he has made valid and important criticisms of the methodology of the Sandiland's report and drawn attention to a number of weaknesses in the original proposals, some of which have been corrected in subsequent developments. Most people, including the authors, are not convinced by Chambers' case that CCA should be rejected or even that it is inferior to his own approach. However, it is clear that there are many virtues in Professor Chambers' approach – which he calls 'continuously contemporary accounting' – and a possible long-term development is the publication of accounts based on the two approaches which would accord with the fact that there is more than one way of reflecting a company's position.

We will now discuss a number of specific criticisms of SSAP 16 – its scope and method of presentation; the gearing adjustment; the problem of negative net borrowing and its treatment (or non-treatment) of inflation. We also describe the extent to which the weaknesses identified have been resolved by the proposals in ED 35.

1 D. R. Myddelton, *On a Cloth Untrue*, Woodhead-Faulkner, Cambrdige, 1984.
2 *See*, for example, R. J. Chambers, *Current cost accounting – a critique of the Sandilands report*, Occasional Paper No. 11, International Centre for Research in Accounting, University of Lancaster, Lancaster, 1976.

Scope of CCA

SSAP 16 applies (with certain exceptions) to all listed companies and other large profit-seeking entities. When reviewing SSAP 16 the ASC had to consider whether any new standard should have the same scope or whether it should be applied to a smaller or larger group of entities. In so doing it had to balance two factors. The first was its belief that nearly all businesses are affected by price changes and that, ideally, such changes should be reflected in their accounts.[3] Against this had to be set the complaints that the costs of preparing current cost accounts outweighed the benefits as perceived by the entities who had to prepare the accounts and who incurred the cost. In the event the ASC moved towards restricting the scope of mandatory CCA in that ED 35 proposes that the new standard should apply only to public companies. This change was justified by the view that the benefits from providing CCA is most apparent with public companies where one or more of the following prevail:

(a)　Separation of ownership and management.
(b)　A market for the capital of the company.
(c)　A large number and wide range of users of the accounts.[4]

As is the case with SSAP 16 wholly owned subsidiaries and value-based companies are exempt from the provisions of ED 35.

Method of presenting CCA information

SSAP 16 requires that companies which fall within its scope should publish two sets of accounts one based on the historical cost convention and the other on current costs (SSAP 16, Para. 48). The only exception from this requirement is that companies are allowed to present current cost accounts as the only accounts so long as they are accompanied by adequate historical cost information. However, since very few companies opt to take advantage of this provision, in almost all cases the introduction of SSAP 16 has meant that companies which comply with its provisions present two separate sets of accounts. The ASC noted that 'the inclusion of two separate sets of accounts prepared on different bases in the annual report did not commend general support' (ED 35,

3　ED 35, Para. 25.
4　ED 35, Para. 26.

Para. 1.4). On a related point the ASC identified an element of misunderstanding on the users of accounts who, it appears, often believe that a current cost balance sheet shows the current value of the business. In the light of these findings it is proposed in ED 35 that the revised statement should require a single set of accounts with information about the effect of changing prices[5] shown in a note to the accounts other than where it is shown in the accounts themselves. We will introduce the detailed provisions later (page 250) but at this stage we would mention that the information is such as to show the current cost profit for the year and how it is derived from the historical cost profit but, so far as the balance sheet is concerned, only the current cost of fixed assets and stocks need to be shown.

The gearing adjustment

The principle behind the gearing adjustment was introduced on page 163 whilst the particular form of gearing adjustment adopted in SSAP 16 was discussed on pages 199–201.

The gearing adjustments is one of the most unsatisfactory and unclear elements of the SSAP 16 version of CCA as evidenced by the inclusion of ED 35 of no less than three types of gearing adjustment (including the SSAP 16 version) with the proposal that companies could select any one of them as long as they did so on a consistent basis. The three types of adjustment included in ED 35 are not given names but it would be helpful for the purposes of discussion if they were christened. Hence the authors have devised the following terms which indicate the nature of the various adjustments: *partial specific*, *full specific* and *purchasing power* gearing adjustments.

With the SSAP 16 approach, which the authors have called the partial specific method, the adjustment is found by multiplying the gearing proportion[6] by the current cost adjustments, i.e. the realized holding surpluses (the cost of sales and depreciation adjustments) and the extra finance needed to be invested in monetary working capital (the MWCA). The adjustment may be interpreted, in periods of rising prices, as the reduction in the amount that has to be retained in the business to maintain operating capability due to the fact that some

---

5 It is of interest to note that whilst SSAP 16 is entitled 'Current cost accounting', ED 35 is called 'Accounting for the effects of changing prices'.

6 The gearing proportion is the ratio of net borrowing to the total of not borrowing plus shareholders' interest.

of the additional finance will be provided by borrowing. The full specific gearing adjustment[7] is found by applying the gearing proportion to the total of the current cost adjustments plus the change in the unrealized revaluation surpluses for the year which may be regarded as being financed by borrowings. Thus a measure of distributable profit derived from the use of the full specific gearing ratio would disclose the total that could be distributed which would maintain operating capability on the assumption that sufficient additional finance could be obtained to maintain the balance sheet gearing ratio.

ED 35 does not spell out how the full specific gearing adjustment should be calculated. For that we will have to wait for the SSAP or, more probably, the associated Guidance Notes. However, the general principal is clear and that full specific gearing adjustment can be derived as follows:

Gearing adjustment = Gearing ratio × [Closing balance on the current cost reserve (before calculating the gearing adjustment) less the opening balance on the current cost reserve].

The partial specific (SSAP 16) approach does not fully reflect the impact of price increases on shareholders' interest as it depends on the nature of the assets held and the extent to which they are deemed to be realized in the course of the year which *inter alia* depends on the method of depreciation adopted. The partial specific method is also inconsistent in that it applies the current gearing proportion to gains that were made in the past when there may have been a different capital structure while, in contrast, the full specific method applies the current gearing proportion to current gains. Thus the full specific method appears to be based on a more clearly defined and logical concept of capital maintenance than the partial specific method.

The differences between the two methods can be illustrated as follows:

Consider two companies, A Limited and B Limited. At 1 January 19X8 they have identical balance sheets with the one exception, that A's assets are in the form of stock while all of B's assets are represented by land. The balance sheets are

---

7 This method has been called the 'ICI method' because it was used by ICI in its current accounts. The approach was first proposed by Wynne Godley and Francis Cripps in *The Times*, 1 October 1975. Another principal advocate was Martin Gibbs, a research partner of the stockbroking firm of Phillips and Drew and a member of the ASC. *See ICI's Current Cost Accounts*, Phillips and Drew, London, 1978.

		£
Assets		
(A Stock, B Land)		£1 000
Shareholder's interest		600
Net borrowing		400
		£1 000

Note that the gearing ratio for each company at 1 January 19X8 was 40%.

Let us suppose that A Limited held its stock for the year and sold it all for £1800 on 31 December 19X8, at which date the replacement cost was £1200, i.e. the price of stock had increased by 20%. Let us also suppose that A replaced its stock on 31 December 19X8. A Limited's cost of sales adjustment was £200 and its gearing adjustment calculated on the basis of the gearing proportion at 1 January was £80.

Finally, assume that on 31 December 19X8 A paid a dividend equal to the current cost profit attributable to shareholders.

The current cost accounts, in summary form, for the year would then be as follows:

A Limited
CCA profit and loss account 19X8

	£
Historical cost profit	800
less Cost of sales adjustment	200
Current cost operating profit	600
add Gearing adjustment	80
Current cost profit attributable to shareholders	680
less Dividends	£680

CCA balance sheet at 31 December 19X8

	£	£
Stock		1 200
Shareholders' interest		
At 1 January 19X8	600	
Increase in current cost reserve, £200 − £80	120	720
Net borrowings, £400 + £80		480
		£1 200
Gearing ratio at 31 December 19X8		40%

Note that the dividend could only have been paid if it was possible (as has been assumed) to increase net borrowings by £80 (the amount of the gearing adjustment). The 'cash account' for the year being

	£	£
Cash from sales		1 800
less Cost of replenishing stock	1 200	
Dividend	680	1 880
Decrease in cash		£80

Let us now consider B Limited. We will assume that it rented the land out for £600 (which is equal to A Limited's current cost operating profit) and that the value of the land increased by 20%. There is no SSAP 16 gearing adjustment because the revaluation surplus is unrealized. We will also assume that B Limited pays a dividend equal to the current cost profit attributable to shareholders. B Limited's current cost accounts would then appear as follows:

B Limited
CCA profit and loss account 19X8

	£
Current cost operating profit and current cost profit attributable to shareholders	600
less Dividend	£600

CCA balance sheet at 31 December 19X8

	£	£
Asset		
Land		£1 200
Shareholders' interest at 1 January 19X8	600	
Increase in current cost reserve	200	800
		400
Net borrowings		£1 200
Gearing ratio at 31 December 19X8		33⅓%

We can now compare the position of the two companies at the year end. In the case of A Limited it can be seen that after the distribution of the dividend the volume of the company's assets has been maintained, as has the gearing ratio. In contrast, in the case of B Limited, while the assets have been maintained, the gearing ratio has declined from 40% to 33⅓%.

It is difficult to suggest any sound justification for the differences between the two results. In both companies the shareholders' interest has been maintained after taking account of the price changes of those assets held by the company.

A Limited is allowed a gearing adjustment by SSAP 16 because its revaluation surplus was realized while B Limited is not permitted a credit gearing adjustment and hence is not allowed to recognize the gain which arises from using net borrowing to finance real assets which have increased in value.

If the full specific method were used, B Limited would have been allowed a gearing adjustment and it too would have been able to pay a dividend of £680 (subject to the same assumptions which applied to A Limited that net borrowings could be increased).

The two examples used above represent the extreme condition: 100% realized revaluation surplus and 100% unrealized revaluation surplus. If the examples had included a depreciating asset, the proportion of the surplus deemed to have been realized during the year, and hence the gearing adjustment, would have depended on the depreciation pattern employed.

The ASC's rationale for the inclusion in SSAP 16 of the partial specific method was that a gearing adjustment based on realized surpluses satisfies more closely the fundamental accounting concepts of accruals and prudence. The partial specific method is certainly more prudent than the full specific method in that the gearing adjustment cannot exceed the sum of the current cost operating adjustments. The counterargument is that the result of this interpretation is a current cost profit attributable to shareholders which is based on an unclear concept of capital maintenance; in other words, it is one which is dependent on the nature of the assets held. It is perhaps worth pointing out that although the ASC's method can be said to be more prudent it can still, as was shown in the example of A Limited, result in a situation where a dividend equal to the current cost profit attributable to shareholders can only be paid by increasing net borrowings.

The authors' view is that of the two, the full specific method is preferred on the grounds of logic and, perhaps more importantly from a practical point of view, comparability. In that the method treats all revaluation surpluses in the same way, its use would enable more realistic comparisons to be made between the results of different companies. It is difficult to see the advantages that are to be gained from the more 'prudent' approach of SSAP 16, and even if it is felt that such advantages exist, it is unlikely that they would outweigh the disadvantage of the loss of comparability.

An alternative approach

The third type of gearing adjustment identified in ED 35 – which we have termed the purchasing power gearing adjustment — is of a very different nature to the full and partial specific methods. The purchasing power gearing adjustment reflects the effect of general price changes on net borrowing (or net monetary assets other than those included in monetary working capital). It will be recognized that this adjustment is essentially the same as is found in CPP accounting, where it is described as the profit or loss on net monetary items. The adjustment is found by applying the rate of increase in general prices to the average net borrowings[8] (or net monetary assets) during the year.

As is pointed out in ED 35 (Para. 20), when the purchasing power gearing adjustment is combined with the interest payable or receivable during the period, the resultant figure will show the 'real' interest or credit for the yearr (*see* page 115). Thus the ASC has interpreted this form of gearing adjustment in terms of the loss or gain accruing to shareholders as a result of their net monetary position (other than those items which are included in monetary working capital and hence the subject of the MWCA).

The purchasing power gearing adjustment does have attractive features in so far that it does show the extent to which shareholders have gained or lost because of the company's net monetary position and does pay some regard to the change in value of money. However, its use in a system which otherwise pays scant regard to the need for accounting for inflation is inconsistent and destroys the basic notion of capital maintenance underlying CCA – the maintenance of operating capability. Consider, for example, a highly geared company operating in an industry where the specific prices have increased at a far lower rate than the rate of inflation. The realized and unrealized surpluses may be quite modest in amount but the credit gearing adjustment may be very large. In such a case the inclusion of a purchasing power gearing adjustment in the calculation of the distributable profit may result in an excessive payment taking into regard the need to replace assets. To illustrate this point let us return to the example of A Limited on page 241 and assume that the increase in the general price level for the year was 80%. The credit purchasing power gearing adjustment would be £320 and thus it might appear that a dividend of £920 could be paid. It is, however, clear that a dividend of this amount could

---

8 The average is not necessarily found by finding the arithmetic means of the opening and closing net borrowings (although this approach will often be used in practice). If the net borrowings have fluctuated over the year it might be necessary to calculate a weighted average.

not be paid without reducing the operating capability of the business. The point is that whilst the gain on owing money in a period of rapid inflation has been recognized no account has been taken of the fact that the company has suffered a 'real' loss in holding assets whose price increases have been far below the rate of inflation. Thus, it does seem strange to include one element of accounting for inflation while ignoring all the others (*see* pages 248–250). We will show at the end of the chapter how the purchasing power gearing adjustment (in its guise of the loss or gain on net monetary position) can be incorporated in an accounting system based on both CPP and current cost principles.

Whilst for the reasons suggested above use of a purchasing power gearing adjustment might well produce odd results when monetary liabilities exceed monetary assets thus producing a credit gearing adjustment there are some advantages in the approach where the net monetary assets exceed the liabilities. The debit gearing adjustment which would result would appear to be more consistent with CCA principles as will be shown in the following section.

The following example shows how to calculate the three different versions of the gearing adjustment using the data given in Example 6.3 (pages 206–221).

EXAMPLE 7.1

  (i) *Partial specific gearing adjustment* (the SSAP 16 version)

Total of the other current cost adjustments	£28 196	(page 213)
Gearing ratio	0.21	(page 215)
Partial specific gearing adjustment	$= 0.21 \times £28\,196$	
	$= £5\,921$	

 (ii) *Full specific gearing adjustment*

	£
Increase in current cost reserve	
Closing balance before gearing adjustment	120 390
Opening balance	36 466
Increase	£83 924
Full specific gearing adjustment	$= 0.21 \times £83\,924$
	$= £17\,624$

(*cont. next page*)

EXAMPLE 7.1 (*cont.*)

(iii) *Purchasing power gearing adjustment*

Opening net borrowing	£110 000	(page 214)
Closing net borrowing (in opening prices),[9]		
+ £67 000 × 150/88	£53 457	(page 214)
Average net borrowing (in opening prices)	£81 728	
Retail Price Index 1 January 19X4	150	
Retail Price Index 31 December 19X4	188	
Increase in 19X4	= 25.3%	
Purchasing power gearing adjustment	= 0.253 = £81 728	
	= £20 677	

Negative net borrowing

Net borrowing was defined in Chapter 6 on page 200. In that chapter we also pointed out that when net borrowing was negative, i.e. when current assets (other than those included in monetary working capital) exceed liabilities and provisions fixed in monetary terms, no gearing or any other sort of adjustment would be made in the SSAP 16 version of CCA. It was assumed that where there was an excess of non-monetary working capital monetary assets[10] such excess is financed by the non-monetary working capital liabilities leaving nothing to help finance any necessary additions to stock, fixed assets or monetary working capital. Whilst this may be a reasonable view it leaves open the question of whether an adjustment should be made to take account of the fall in the 'real value' of the excess non-monetary working capital monetary assets.

SSAP 16 stated that such assets are not covered by the current cost framework and are analogous to assets held for investment, i.e. no

---

9 Paragraph 20 of ED 35 states that the gearing adjustment 'is calculated by applying the rate of increase in general prices to the average net borrowing (or net monetary assets other than those included in monetary working capital) during the year'. However, if the rate of increase for the year is to be applied to the average net borrowing then, to be consistent, the average must be expressed in purchasing power as at the start of the year.

10 Unfortunately if we are not to depart from the terminology employed in SSAP 16 and ED 35 we have to use this clumsy title.

adjustment was required to take account of the need to maintain operating capability.

The ASC adopted a tentative approach to this issue stating that: 'This situation raised complex issues which have not yet been subject to adequate public debate and no adjustment is therefore required in the Standard.' The statement does, however, go on to state that 'entities are encouraged to include information on any changes in the value to the business of such excess assets and in their effective purchasing power. This should be given and described in a note to the accounts' (SSAP 16, Para. 22). The ASC also suggested that the voluntary statement showing the effect of the change in shareholders' equity after allowing for a change in the general purchasing power of money might be particularly helpful in the case of a company which holds excess monetary assets (SSAP 16, Para. 36).

The failure of SSAP 16 to include a requirement that adjustment be made for the impact of price changes on excess monetary assets will lead to an overstatement of profit in some instances. Consider a company which sells off part of its business and holds cash preparatory to a new major acquisition. An increase in the price of the assets which it is intended to acquire could well be regarded as a loss suffered in the cash holding.[11]

SSAP 16 would allow some adjustment to be made in this case in so far as the increase in cash which may be regarded as arising from the temporary reduction in stock and debtors could be included in monetary working capital and hence give rise to a debit MWCA. However, the cash released from the sale of fixed assets would be regarded as arising from a capital transaction and this could not be regarded as part of monetary working capital.

As we have seen the ED 35 proposals would allow companies to include a gearing adjustment when they hold excess monetary assets. Thus it would be possible to reflect to some extent the loss experienced in the situation described above. However, in so far as ED 35 proposes the use of a general price index in such situations it is clear that the purchasing power gearing adjustment is not seen as a measure of the extent to which a company might experience a specific loss related to its own circumstances from holding excess monetary assets (other than those included in monetary working capital).

---

11 It is like someone who sells a house before going overseas for a couple of years with the intention of buying a new house on his return. If, as has often happened, house prices increase by more than could be earned by interest, the traveller may well find that he will have to purchase a smaller house on his return.

CCA and inflation

One of the more controversial aspects of the report of the Sandilands Committee was its treatment of inflation. It was suggested that although the committee was described as the 'Inflation Accounting Committee' its proposals did not account for inflation in any way if inflation is regarded as describing a situation where there is a general increase in prices. The Sandilands proposals were concerned only with changes in specific prices, and hence any accounts produced based on the proposals would have been independent of changes in the general price level.

This 'weakness' is also to be found in the various developments of the Sandilands proposals up to and including SSAP 16. However, many of the changes that have been made to the original proposals have narrowed the gap between CPP and current cost accounts.

It is difficult, especially for those who are not in sympathy with this aspect of the Sandilands proposals, to summarize the reasons why the Sandilands Committee acted as it did, but it may be helpful if one or two strands of their argument were presented.

The committee listed five principal criteria for the unit of measurement to be used in accounts, although the reasons for their choice were not clearly stated. The criteria were as follows:

1. The unit should be equally useful to all users of accounts.
2. The unit should not change from year to year.
3. The unit should be the same for all enterprises presenting financial statements.
4. The unit should preferably be a physical object which could be exchanged by the users of the accounts.
5. The unit should represent a constant 'value' through time.[12]

It was argued that the monetary unit (the pound) satisfied the first four of the criteria,[13] although not everyone would agree with this view. The CPP unit was also examined and found to be wanting the respect of all five criteria.[14] It was argued that the CPP unit completely failed to satisfy the first four criteria and only 'very imperfectly' satisfied the last criterion.

It would require more space than is available to discuss this issue properly, and readers are invited to study the Sandilands report to consider whether the above criteria should be used to assess the relative desirabilities of different units and the extent to which they are satisfied by the monetary and CPP units. We will, however, consider the reason

12 *Report of the Inflation Accounting Committee*, Cmnd 6225, HMSO, London, p. 43.
13 *Ibid.*, p. 57.
14 *Ibid.*, pp. 122–3.

why the Sandilands Committee felt that the CPP unit did not represent a constant value over time.

The Sandilands Committee's view was that it is not possible to measure inflation except on an individual basis because inflation is a personal matter depending on an individual's particular pattern of consumption. They wrote:

> Inflation does not exist as a quantifiable phenomenon independent of the price movement in any specific group of goods and services or of the spending pattern of any specific group of individuals or entities and is not a phenomenon capable of independent and objective measurement, affecting all individuals and entities in the same way. The rate of inflation will vary for different individuals and entities in the country according to the selection of goods and services which they buy.[15]

The Sandilands proposals therefore eschewed the use of any broadly based price index.

The climate of the time during which the Sandilands Committee sat may also be of relevance as it was established after the introduction, by the Heath Government, of an incomes policy which encouraged wage and salary agreement which included threshold clauses. The effect of such clauses was to increase wages by amounts which depended on increases in the Index of Retail Prices. The index increased by very much more than had been expected when the policy was formulated, thus triggering substantial wage increases. As a result many people argued that this type of incomes policy was a grave mistake and, more generally, that 'indexation' was inflationary and should be avoided. Indexation may be simply defined as automatic adjustments in response to changes in a general price index, and perhaps CPP was regarded as being likely to exacerbate the problems of inflation. It is possible that had the Sandilands Committee sat at another time it might not have rejected CPP so comprehensively.

The total reliance of the Sandilands Committee on specific price indices might have been partly responsible for certain defects in their model; for example, the failure to provide for any adjustments for those items, such as monetary working capital, to which specific price indices cannot be applied. In developing the CCA model the ASC has made use of broadly based indices including, in certain instances, the Index of Retail Prices and have, implicitly at least, rejected the more extreme views of the Sandilands Committee.

It is possible to combine the CPP and CCA methods. An approach which would totally integrate the two approaches has been suggested

15 *Report of the Inflation Accounting Committee*, Cmnd 6225, HMSO, London, p. 13.

by Professor William Baxter,[16] but it is possible to envisage a more modest integration. There is a case for crediting the shareholders' equity each year by the amount necessary to compensate for the increase in real terms during the year, i.e. the adjustment would be the opening balance of shareholders' interest by the percentage change in the Index of Retail Prices. If this change were made it would mean that shareholders would be able to see very clearly whether their interest in the enterprise had been maintained in real terms, and whether the increase in the prices of the specific assets used by the enterprise had increased by a greater or lesser extent than the increase in the general rate of inflation.

A very serious consequence of the failure to incorporate adjustments for changes in the general purchasing power of money in CCA is that the comparability over time is lost. It is impossible to make any realistic assessment of a 5-year summary of results based on current cost accounts if no account is taken of inflation. For example, what interpretation should be placed on a 5-year summary which showed an average annual increase of CCA earning per share of, say 5%? The answer must depend on the rate of inflation. An average annual increase of 5% might well be acceptable if there was no inflation, but would represent a very disappointing set of results if inflation was running at 20% per annum.

In a discussion paper issued in 1982, the ASC recommended that corresponding amounts and 10-year summaries should be adjusted to a common price base using the Retail Price Index.[17]

ED 35, 'Accounting for the effects of changing prices'

ED 35 was published in July 1984 and comments on its proposals were requested for submission by 31 December 1984 with the expectation that the new standard would operate in respect of accounting periods beginning on or after 1 January 1985. The standard when published will be accompanied by guidance notes; notes were not published with the Exposure Draft and hence some of the details of its proposals are a little unclear. The main principles underlying the draft are, however, very clear. The basic principle of CCA as set out in SSAP 16

16 *See*, for example. W. T. Baxter, *Accounting Values and Inflation*, McGraw-Hill, London, 1975. *See* also the section at the end of this chapter.
17 *Corresponding amounts and ten-year summaries in current cost accounting: a discussion paper*, ASC, London, 1982.

is to be maintained. The only significant differences are, as we have shown, in the style of presentation, its scope and the treatment of the gearing adjustment.

The fact that companies subject to the standard are no longer required to publish a complete set of current cost accounts may, at first sight, be regarded as a response to criticisms that the work of preparing such accounts was too costly and time consuming. This is not, however, the case in that the ASC specifically stated its belief that for publicly accountable companies the benefits of providing current cost information exceeds the costs of provision (ED 35, Para. 1.8). In addition in order to calculate the current cost adjustments which it is proposed should be published a full current cost balance will have to be prepared even if it is not included in the published accounts.

In one respect the apparent alleviation of the burden proposed by ED 35 might result in more work on the part of companies and their auditors, as is usually the case, as an unqualified audit report is desired. Under the terms of SSAP 16 current cost information could be regarded as being supplementary to information given in the main historical cost accounts. If, as some companies chose, the current cost data was not provided, the auditors merely had to include in their audit opinions a reference to its exclusion. Such a reference is not regarded as a qualification. In drafting ED 35 it appears that the ASC is adopting a firmer stance in that it is stated that compliance with the proposals is regarded to be essential if the financial statement is to give a true and fair view.[18] Thus, if the required current cost information is not provided the auditors' could not simply comment on the omission, they would have to qualify their opinion by stating that the accounts did not provide a true and fair view.

In adopting this position the ASC feared that they may have produced a logical and legal paradox. If current cost information is necessary for a true and fair view to be given for one class of companies (i.e. public companies subject to ED 35) why is it not necessary in the case of other companies (private and value-based companies)? The ASC sought counsel's approval on this point which it made publicly available prior to the publication of ED 35. In outline the view of counsel was that 'true and fair' is not a hard and fast concept and that in deciding what is necessary to provide a true and fair view the 'cost-effectiveness' of any provision is a relevant consideration. Hence, in the view of the lawyers it would be reasonable to say that something

---

18 ED 35, p. 9.

was necessary to provide a true and fair view in the case of one class of companies which was not required in the case of another class of company. Whilst this may well be a sensible pragmatic view it does add even greater elasticity to that already flexible concept of 'true and fair'.

Amended definitions

ED 35 proposed relatively few changes to the way in which terms are defined in SSAP 16. It is true that the definitions section (Part 2) of ED 35 is somewhat longer than the equivalent section of SSAP 16 but that is only because a number of terms which were only explained in Part 1 of SSAP 16 are specifically defined in the Exposure Draft. One important change in terminology should, however, be noted. Whilst its definition remains the same the phrase 'value to the business' used in SSAP 16 is replaced by 'current cost' in ED 35. This is a potentially misleading change in that there are situations where the 'current cost' will not be based on 'cost' but rather be derived from the 'recoverable amount'. The use of the phrase 'value to the business' does have the advantage of implying that its determination is not based entirely on a measure of the cost of an asset.

We will not reproduce, at this stage, the definitions which can be found in ED 35 and which have been explained previously in this book. However, we will touch upon those definitions which are either new or which have been changed materially.

Working capital adjustment

> A working capital adjustment is the increase in working capital required during the period (or the decrease possible during the period, when current costs are falling) in order to maintain the operating capability of the net operating assets. It comprises two elements, a cost of sales adjustment and a monetary working capital adjustment.[19]

As can be seen above the phrase working capital adjustment comprises both the cost of sales adjustment and the MWCA.

Monetary working capital

There has been a change in the definition of monetary working capital which is defined in ED 35 as follows:

> Monetary working capital comprises all current assets used in the day-to-day operating activities of the business other than stocks which are subject to a cost of sales

---

19 ED 35, Para. 38.

adjustment less current liabilities other than those which do not finance the operating capability of the business or which arise from transactions of a capital nature.[20]

In contrast the SSAP 16 definition is:

Monetary working capital is the aggregate of:

(a) trade debtors, prepayments and trade bills receivable, plus
(b) stocks not subject to a cost of sales adjustment, less
(c) trade creditors, accruals and trade bills payable,

in so far as they arise from the day-to-day operating activities of the business as distinct from transactions of a capital nature.[21]

As we described on page 190 the SSAP 16 definition is extended by a discussion of the circumstances where it would be appropriate to include bank balances and overdrafts as part of monetary working capital and noted that the treatment of bank balances would necessarily be subjective but that the ASC had attempted to minimize the subjectivity by excluding bank overdrafts from the definition of monetary working capital. Hence, a bank overdraft which was used essentially as a medium-term source of finance would, under SSAP 16, be excluded from monetary working capital and included in net borrowing.

Although the point is not made specifically in ED 35 (although it might be expected to be discussed in the guidance notes) bank overdrafts which constitute part of the company's capital structure which have provided a source of finance for fixed assets (which are part of the operating capability of the business) are to be included in monetary working capital.[22]

Thus it appears that the initial presumption of SSAP 16 is that overdrafts will be excluded whilst ED 35 presumes that they will be included in monetary working capital. Whatever stance is taken the problem of overdrafts remains in that whilst an overdraft and a medium-term liability might serve exactly the same economic function, their treatment in the accounts might differ simply because the overdraft is regarded as a current liability.

---

20 ED 35, Para. 37.
21 SSAP 16, Para. 44.
22 The ED 35 definition of monetary working capital states that current liabilities arising from transactions of a capital nature should be excluded. It is not clear what is meant by 'of a capital nature'. If this is interpreted strictly as liabilities arising from the purchase of fixed assets, it would follow that the reference to operating capability would only apply to the non-capital portion of the net operating assets of the business. This does not appear to be the intention of the ASC and, hence, it appears that items of a capital nature are short-term liabilities arising from the purchase of fixed assets which will shortly be extinguished by a cash payment.

A similar situation exists in relation to bank balances. These were excluded from monetary working capital in the SSAP 16 definition but could be included if they fluctuated with the volume of stock or the other elements of monetary working capital. The ED 35 definition includes cash balances so long as they are used 'in the day-to-day operating activities of the business'. Readers will appreciate that it will usually be impossible to state with exactitude what proportion of the bank balance is needed for day-to-day operations and hence a good deal of subjectivity remains.

Gearing adjustment and gearing ratio
The three types of gearing adjustment which are proposed in ED 35 have been explained above but for convenience the definitions are reproduced below:

A gearing adjustment is either:

(a) that part of the adjustments made to allow for the impact of price changes on the net operating assets (including the depreciation, cost of sales, monetary working capital, fixed asset disposals, minority interest and extraordinary items adjustments) that may be regarded as associated with items that are financed by net borrowing; or

(b) those parts of the total adjustments made to allow for the impact of price changes on the net operating assets, including the net surplus on the revaluation of assets arising during the period, that may be regarded as associated with items that are financed by net borrowing; or

(c) the effect of general price changes on net borrowing (or net monetary assets other than those included in monetary working capital). (ED 35, Para. 39)

Whilst the gearing ratio is the ratio of net borrowing to the current cost of net operating assets.[23]

Wholly owned subsidiaries
Wholly owned subsidiaries were not defined in SSAP 16 but that standard clearly states that if companies are to be exempt from its scope because they are wholly owned subsidiaries, the parent company must be registered in the UK. In which case, unless the parent company itself was exempt, current cost information would be provided in the group accounts.

In contrast ED 35 defines a wholly owned subsidiary as 'a company all of whose equity share capital is held by another company' (ED 35,

---

23 There is a change of terminology here in that in SSAP 16 the gearing ratio is called the gearing proportion.

Para. 45). No mention is made of the need for the other company to be registered in the UK and hence wholly owned subsidiaries of overseas companies which were covered by SSAP 16 are outside the scope of ED 35.

Disclosure requirements

1. In so far as profit and loss items are concerned the following current cost information should be shown:

   (a) a depreciation adjustment,
   (b) a cost of sales adjustment,
   (c) a monetary working capital adjustment,
   (d) a gearing adjustment,
   (e) any other material adjustments to the profit or loss on ordinary activities consistent with the current cost convention (showing each separately),
   (f) the effect of the above current cost adjustments on the profit or loss on ordinary activities,
   (g) the current cost adjustment or adjusted amount in respect of minority interests,
   (h) the current cost adjustment or adjusted amount in respect of extraordinary items, and
   (i) the effect of all the above current cost adjustments on the profit or loss for the financial year.

The cost of sales and monetary working capital adjustments may be combined as a working capital adjustment.

2. The financial statements should show the gross and net current cost of fixed assets, as well as the accumulated current cost depreciation.

3. The gross current cost of intangible fixed assets should be derived, as far as it is practicable, on the following bases:

   (a) Intangible assets (excluding goodwill) – at the best estimate of their current cost.
   (b) Goodwill – at cost at the date of acquisition, based on the difference between the fair value of the consideration given and the aggregate of the fair values of the separable net assets required.
   (c) Investments in associated companies – at the applicable proportion of the current cost of the associated companies' net assets or, where such information is not readily available, at the best estimate thereof.

(d) Other investments – at market price or, where such information is not readily available, at the directors' best estimate thereof.

4. The current cost of stock should also be shown.

5. Companies that prepare their financial statements under the historical cost (or modified historical cost) convention should show the required current cost information in a note to the accounts. Companies that use the current cost convention for the financial statements will automatically include the required information in their accounts.

6. The accounting policies adopted in arriving at the current cost information should be described in the note to the accounts. These policies should normally be consistent with those adopted for the rest of the accounts; when they are not, details of the differences and the reasons for the variations should be disclosed.

7. The accounting policies should be consistently applied from one year to the next.

8. In the case of group accounts the parent company should present the information required in respect of the group; it need not present the information in respect of itself as a single company.

The disclosure requirements do not include any references to the need to disclose, using the terminology of SSAP 16, either a current cost operating profit or the current cost profit attributable to shareholders. In effect the ED 35 proposals require the publication of a list of ingredients which would allow the user to construct his own current cost accounts by combining the required current cost information with the published historical cost accounts. In addition, as we shall show, ED 35 does not attempt to specify the way in which the data should be disclosed so it is likely that there will be considerable variations in the way in which any standard based on ED 35 is applied. Such a liberal approach might be justified on the grounds that no generally accepted approach has yet been established. However, it does appear that the very wide range of practice that is likely to emerge will hinder the learning process necessary if users are to understand the meaning of current cost accounts. In particular the failure to require the publication of the various current cost profit figures does appear to be a retrograde step.

Presentation of the required information

In the appendix to ED 35 three examples of methods of presentation are provided but it is emphasized that these are not to be regarded as prescriptive and that other methods may equally comply with the provisions of the statement. One of the examples provides only the minimum information whilst the other examples include additional information which it is thought. may be of value to the users of the accounts.

We will present two examples; the first (based on Example A in the Appendix) provides only the minimum information whilst the second (based on Example C) provides additional data. In each case the figures will be based on those used in Example 6.3. We will, however, also show how information not included in Example 6.3, in particular in relation to group accounts, would be shown.

EXAMPLE 7.2

	£
Working capital adjustment	22 161
Depreciation adjustment	6 035
Adjustment to profit on disposal of fixed assets	–
Adjustment to income from associated companies	–
	28 196
Gearing adjustment	(5 921)
Amount of profit on ordinary activities after taxation required to meet current cost adjustment	34 117
Adjustment to minority interests	–
Adjustment to extraordinary items	–
Amount of profit for the financial year required to be retained to meet the effects of changing prices	£34 117
Gross current cost of fixed assets	477 382
Accumulated current cost depreciation	62 749
Net current cost of fixed assets	£414 633
Current cost of stocks	£96 429

EXAMPLE 7.3

	£	£
Profit on ordinary activities before taxation		60 000
Add:		
Interest payable less receivable		6 000
		66 000

(cont. next page)

EXAMPLE 7.3 (*cont.*)	£	£
b/f		60 000
Cost of sales adjustment	13 366	
Monetary working capital adjustment	8 795	
	22 161	
Depreciation adjustment	6 035	
Adjustment to profit on disposal of fixed assets	–	
Adjustment to income from associated companies	–	28 196
Current cost operating profit		37 804
Gearing adjustment	(5 921)	
Interest payable less receivable	6 000	79
		37 725
Taxation		16 000
		21 725
Minority interests after making current cost adjustment		–
Extraordinary items after making current cost adjustment		–
		£21 725

The information included in respect of balance sheet items is as given in Example 7.2 except that the data relating to fixed assets is analysed between tangible fixed assets, intangible fixed assets and investments whilst the current costs of the three elements of stocks are provided, viz. raw materials and consumables, work in progress and finished goods for resale.

The utility of current cost accounts

In Chapter 3 we analysed the purposes which were served by the publication of periodic financial statements under four heads, viz. control, taxation, consumption and valuation. We will, in concluding this chapter, assess the virtues and limitations of current cost accounts in terms of these objectives.

It must, first, be recognized that there is more than one way of measuring the performance of a company and that a set of accounts based on a single system is bound to fail to include all the information that might be of interest to users of accounts. Thus it is difficult to envisage the development of any single system of accounting which could be regarded as an ideal system serving all needs of all users.

Whilst this section of the chapter will focus on a discussion of the advantages and disadvantages of producing a complete set of current cost accounts, many of the comments will also apply to the publication of less comprehensive current cost information along the lines of ED 35.

Control

Current cost accounts are likely to be more helpful than historical cost accounts or current purchasing power accounts in helping share-holders and others to assess how well or badly the directors have employed the resources which have been entrusted to them, especially through the use of such measures as return on capital employed. The current cost accounts attempt to show the current values of the assets of the company and whether or not the net assets have increased during a period after allowing for specific price changes. Thus it may be argued that the current cost accounts will provide a better vehicle for the exercise of control by shareholders and others. There are obvious weak-nesses in the current cost approach which have been mentioned in this chapter, including its failure to adjust for changes in the general price level. A further defect, which is inherent in any system of account-ing which is based on the valuation of individual assets, is that the balance sheet total of assets less liabilities will not be equal to the valuation of the business as a whole. We will return to this point in the valuation section on page 261.

Taxation

If one makes the not unreasonable assumption that a government would only wish to levy taxation on any surplus that is generated after the substance of the business has been maintained, then it can be seen that CCA is likely to provide a better basis for taxation than the histori-cal cost and CPP methods.

It must be recognized that the amount of taxation payable by a com-pany depends not only upon the way in which its taxable profit is calculated, but also upon the nominal tax rate applied to that taxable profit. Even if the government were to adopt current cost profits, rather than historical cost profits, as the basis for the computation of taxable profits, it might still wish to raise the same amount from the taxation of business profits. If such were the case there would be a redistribution of the tax burden within the business sector, with no change in the total burden on that sector.

In general it could be said that those companies which use large quantities of depreciating assets, carry substantial stocks, make considerable investments in monetary working capital and which possess low gearing ratios will experience the greatest decline in reported profits following a switch from historical cost accounting to CCA.

The admittedly imperfect concept of capital maintenance underlying CCA does make it a potentially attractive basis for taxation, and a number of discussions on the possibility of levying taxation on the basis of the profit on current cost profits were initiated following the publication of SSAP 16. However, many problems will have to be resolved before CCA can take the place of historical cost accounting as the basis of assessing a business enterprise's liability for taxation. There is first the matter that only a minority of entities are required to provide current cost information. It may be considered desirable to introduce a two-tier tax system with different nominal tax rates such that larger companies are taxed on current cost principles with smaller companies continuing to be taxed on their historical cost results. It this were done there would, of course, be considerable pressure from those smaller companies who would gain from the switch to CCA to be taxed on this basis.

It is unlikely that the Inland Revenue would accept the numerous subjective elements which are to be found in the SSAP 16 or ED 35 versions of CCA, e.g. the selection of price indices and the definition of monetary working capital, and consideration would have to be given to these matters. The treatment of the gearing adjustment is also likely to require careful consideration. It is reasonable to include the gearing adjustment in arriving at the profit subject to taxation as it does offset the total nominal cost of interest which is charged to the accounts; in other words, ignoring for a moment the unsatisfactory nature of the SSAP 16 gearing adjustment, only the real cost of interest as opposed to the nominal charge would be allowed against tax. However, if this were done there would be a strong case for not taxing the whole of the interest payments received by lenders, thus allowing them some relief from inflation. Such a change would have serious consequences for the whole of the tax system – both personal and corporate – and is unlikely to be taken without a good deal of discussion.

Consumption

Many of the points made in the above section on taxation can be applied with equal force to the question of consumption. The introduction of CCA will make it less likely that dividends will be paid unwittingly out of capital.

Valuation

The sum of the values of the assets less liabilities of a business as shown in a current cost balance sheet will not, other than in the simplest of cases, be the same as the value of the business as a whole, but it is likely that the current cost total will give a better approximation to this value than the figures that are disclosed by the historical cost accounts.

It is not necessary at this stage to spell out the reasons why there is a difference between the total of the values of the individual assets less liabilities and the value of the business as a whole, as the subject of the valuation of a business is discussed in detail in a later section of this book. The main reason for the difference is that which is covered by the concept of goodwill, which recognizes that an existing business will usually possess substantial but intangible assets such as reputation, established relationships with suppliers and customers, and managerial skill, which are not recorded on a balance sheet.

The liabilities section of the balance sheet provides another possible reason for the difference. It must be remembered that, under the provisions of SSAP 16, liabilities are included at their nominal amounts and not at their current values.

The above discussion of goodwill was based on the assumption that the value of the business was greater than the total of the values of the assets less liabilities. The reverse can also be true, and a potential weakness of the CCA model is that it can overstate the value of the assets in particular because of the existence of interdependent assets. This problem arises from the fact that assets will be valued at their replacement cost unless a permanent diminution in value has been recognized. If each asset is considered in isolation it may well be that no permanent diminution is recognized and the proper basis of valuation would be the replacement cost. However, if a particular bundle of assets is considered as a whole it may be seen that they are collectively not worth replacing and thus that a value less than the sum of their replacement values should be placed on them. An often quoted hypothetical example of this problem is that of a railway line which runs through two tunnels. Assume that the present value of the railway line is £400 000 and the replacement costs of each tunnel is £250 000. If each tunnel is considered in isolation it is clear that if it was destroyed it would be worth replacing, and thus it would be valued for CCA purposes at £250 000. However, it is clear that if both tunnels were simultaneously destroyed they would not be replaced because the total replacement cost would exceed the benefit that would be obtained from the action.

The above example is highly artificial, but the principles can obviously be extended to more complex and practical examples. The sum of the replacement costs of machines and other assets situated in a factory may easily be greater than the price that would be paid for the factory as a whole. Indeed, this position may be only too common in the case of declining industries, e.g. steel, shipbuilding, etc.

It is of course true that the position described above can and does exist under historical cost accounting. Accountants are reasonably good at ensuring that there is a write down in the book value of individual assets where their recoverable value falls below their net book value, but often fail to make the corresponding adjustment when there is a severe decline in the fortunes of the business as a whole. The application of the going concern concept is relevant to these instances where the ability of the company to continue in business is in question, but does not cover the intermediate position where the business can still survive but where its value has fallen below the total book value of the assets less liabilities. Clearly, given the fact that the total of the assets will be higher in current cost accounts, this particular problem will occur more frequently than is the case with historical cost accounting.

Thus, while it will generally be true that the current cost balance sheet totals will provide a closer approximation to the value of the business than historical cost information, there will still be substantial differences between the two values. This is not to be taken as a criticism of CCA in that the designers of the system did not set this as one of the objectives of CCA. However, it is likely that many laymen will not fully appreciate this point, and there may well be some confusion on the part of the general public, who may believe that a system of current cost accounts should tell them how much a business is worth. It was for this reason that the ASC in drafting ED 35 proposed the removal of the requirement to publish a current cost balance sheet.

Summary

CCA is certainly not *the* perfect system of accounting in that there is more than one way of reflecting the activities of a business. Neither is it *a* perfect system of accounting in that, even within its own parameters, it is capable of improvement. The important practical test of whether the work that has gone into the development of CCA and the effort that is required in preparing the accounts are worth while is whether the provision of such accounts will enable better decisions to be made.

Attempts have been made to answer this question including the studies commissioned by ASC on the implementation of SSAP 16. The conclusion was that there were some advantages to be gained from the publication of current cost data in that their availability provided a better basis for decision making than a complete reliance on historical cost information. However, the CCA model as presently developed does not represent the final stage in the reform of accounting practice and further changes can be expected to occur over the next decade.

CPP and CCA combined

The major weakness of CCA is that it ignores inflation whilst the most serious flaw in CPP accounting is that it pays no regard to the current value of assets. If these statements are accepted the obvious conclusion is that accountants should seek to design a system which combines the useful features of both CPP and CCA or, to put it more negatively, eliminates their major weaknesses. The adoption of such a system has been advocated for many years by a number of accountants, mostly of the academic variety[24] but the cause has recently been espoused by accountants of a more practical bent such as the Institute of Cost and Management Accountants.

In essence the system can be described as one which is based on the current cost of assets[25] and the measurement of profit based on the maintenance of real money capital. The basic principles are illustrated in the following example:

Suppose that Guy started busines on 1 January 19X3 with £1000 which he used to purchase 100 units of stock for £10 each. Trading was not overactive during the year and the only sales he made were 60 units for £18 each on 31 December 19X3.

24 W. T. Baxter, *Accounting Values and Inflation*, McGraw-Hill, London, 1975.

25 In a complete system liabilities would also be valued so that, for example, it would be recognized that – all other things, including the rate of interest, being equal – a £1000 of debenture stock repayable in 5 years is a more onerous obligation than £1000 of stock repayable in 50 years. In other words, using the deprival value concept the debtor would be far happier if he were 'deprived' of the need to repay the 5-year debenture as opposed to the 50-year loan.

For simplicity we will assume that he incurred no overheads during the year. Let us suppose that the general price level increased by 10% over the year whilst the replacement cost of stock increased by 15%. Then Guy's only sales transaction can be analysed as follows:

	£
Cost of sales	600
Inflation increase	60
Cost of sales restated in current pounds	660
Price increase in excess of inflation	30
Replacement cost of date of sale	690
Sales	1 080
Profit	£ 390

Now if we had prepared a standard CCA profit and loss account we would also have shown a profit of £390 as this is the difference between the sales proceeds and the current cost of the stock consumed. The major difference between the CCA approach and the above is that in the latter the CCA cost of sales adjustment of £90 has been broken down into two elements, (a) £60, which represents the amount by which the cost of the stock held needed to increase in order to keep step with inflation, and (b) £30, the amount by which the increase in the current cost of the stock exceeded inflation. The justification for disaggregating the CCA cost of sales adjustment in this way is that, if account is taken of the fall in the value of money, then the whole of £90 cannot be regarded as a realized holding gain as £60 merely represents that which is required to keep step with inflation and is not a 'real gain'. In consequence that element of the nominal gain which is required to keep step with inflation (£60 in this case) is sometimes known as the *fictitious holding gain* while the *real realized holding gain* (or loss) is the difference between the current cost of the asset at the date at which it is consumed and the restated historical cost (i.e. the historical cost adjusted for the change in the general price level).

If we now turn our attention to the closing stock the same approach can be used, i.e.:

	£	£
Current cost of closing stock £400 × 1.15		460
Historic cost of closing stock	400	
Inflation adjustment (fictitious unrealized holding gain) 10%	40	440
Real unrealized holding gain		£ 20

Opening money capital was £1000 and if real money capital is to be maintained this amount must be enhanced by 10% to take account of the fall in the value of money.

On the basis of the above considerations Guy's accounts for 19X3 would appear as follows:

Profit and loss account 19X3

	£
Sales	1 080
Current cost of goods sold	690
Operating profit	£ 390

Statement of gains/losses 19X3

	£
Operating profit	390
Realized real holding gain	30
Unrealized real holding gain	20
	£440

Balance sheet as at 31 December 19X3

	£	£
Capital 1.1.X3	1 000	
Inflation adjustment 10%	100	1 100
Reserves		
Realized gains		
Operating	390	
Holding	30	420
Unrealized gains		20
		£1 540
Stock at current cost (40 items @ £11.50)		460
Cash (60 @ £18)		1 080
		£1 540

The capital and reserves section of the balance sheet well illustrates the different views that may be taken with regard to distribution. If it is accepted that capital is maintained if assets less liabilities at the balance sheet date equal opening capital after adjusting for inflation, then the maximum that could be distributed without diminishing capital is £440. If it is argued that only realized profits should be distributed then the dividend should be restricted to £420. If it is argued that the business must retain sufficient funds to maintain the same level of activity (i.e. be able to replace the 60 units sold) the maximum dividend is equal to the realized operating gain of £390.

This last line of argument brings us to the current cost account approach that it is the operating capability of the business that must be kept intact if capital is to be maintained. Thus it can be seen that within the combined CCA/CPP approach it is possible to focus on a profit calculated on the basis of physical capital maintenance. The authors, along with most other writers on the subject, would not, however, advocate this be done as they believe that the concept of 'operating capability' is unclear, ambiguous and leads to unnecessary complexities – such as the monetary working capital and gearing adjustments. However, even if the maintenance of real money capital is taken to be the bench mark used to measure profit it may still be of value to show what proportion of the operating profit has been paid out by way of dividend so that users can see the extent to which the reserves of the business have increased or decreased after setting aside a sum to allow for increases in specific prices over the rate of inflation. The formulation used in the above simple example would allow this assessment to be made as well as showing the extent to which the total gains are realized.

Before turning to a slightly more complex example, we will discuss those issues which we were able to sidestep in our very simple example – the monetary working capital and gearing adjustments.

The monetary working capital and gearing adjustments arise from the attempts to measure changes in operating capability. The first because it attempts to show the increased investment required in monetary working capital while the second strives to show the extent to which the increased investment in stocks, fixed assets and monetary working capital would be provided by creditors.[26] These adjustments are not required in an accounting system based on the maintenance of real money capital. In such a system the impact of inflation on monetary items is the loss or gain on both the business' short- and long-term monetary positions as described in Chapter 4.

Example 7.4 illustrates one way of combining current cost asset valuation with the maintenance of real money capital.

---

26 This, of course, does not apply to the third type of gearing adjustment (purchasing power) specified in ED 35.

EXAMPLE 7.4

Suppose that Park Limited started business on 1 January 19X2. On that date the company issued 12 000 £1 shares and £4000 of debentures and purchased fixed assets for £12 000 and stock of £6000. The purchases were partly financed by an overdraft of £2000.

Park's balance sheet at 1 January 19X2 is then

	£		£
Share capital	12 000	Fixed assets	12 000
Debentures	4 000	Stock (100 units)	6 000
		Overdraft	(2 000)
	£16 000		£16 000

We will assume that all transactions took place on 1 July 19X2. On that date Park Limited purchased another 400 units for £75 (total £30 000) and sold 380 units for £36 000. Closing stock at FIFO cost is thus £9000.

Overhead expenses, including debenture interest, all paid for cash on 1 July 19X2, amounted to £5000. On 1 July the company paid its suppliers £27 000 and received £31 000 from its customers; thus trade creditors at 31 December 19X2 amounted to £3000 and trade debtors equalled £5000. The company's overdraft at the year end was

	£
Overdraft at 1 January 19X2	2 000
add Paid to suppliers	27 000
Paid for overheads	5 000
	34 000
less Received from customers	31 000
Overdraft at 31 December 19X2	£ 3 000

Depreciation is to be provided at 20% per annum on a straight line basis.

Assume that the appropriate price indices moved as follows:

Date	1 January	1 July	31 December
General price index	90	100	110
Stock price index	80	100	120
Fixed asset price index	95	100	105

Note that the stock price index increased by more than the rate of inflation while the fixed asset price index rose by less (i.e. the price of the fixed assets fell in real terms).

In order to see clearly how certain elements of CCA can be combined with a set of CPP accounts, it is helpful to prepare first the CPP accounts. These will appear as follows:

CPP accounts

Profit and loss account for 19X2

	£(31 Dec.)	£(31 Dec.)	Workings
Sales, 36 000 × 110/100		39 600	
less Opening stock, £6000 × 110/90	7 333		
Purchases, £30 000 × 110/100	33 000		
	40 333		
less Closing stock, £9000 × 110/100	9 900	30 433	
Gross profit		9 167	
less Overheads, £5000 × 110/100	5 500		
Depreciation, £2400 × 110/90	2 933	8 433	
		734	
Gain on short-term monetary items	344		A1
Gain on long-term monetary items	889	1 233	A1
CPP profit for the year		£ 1 967	

Balance sheet as at 31 December 19X2

	£(31 Dec.)	£(31 Dec.)
Fixed assets		
Cost, £12 000 × 110/90	14 667	
less Accumulated depreciation,		
£2400 × 110/90	2 933	11 734
Current assets		
Stock, £9000 110 100	9 900	
Debtors	5 000	
Current liabilities	14 900	
Creditors	(3 000)	
Overdraft	(3 000)	8 900
		£20 634
Share capital, £12 000 × 110/90		14 667
Retained profits		1 967
		16 634
Debentures		4 000
		£20 634

CPP workings

A1 Loss on short-term monetary items is given by

	Actual £		Conversion factor	£(31 Dec.)	
1 Jan. Opening balance		2 000	110/90		2 444
1 Jul. Sales	36 000		110/100	39 600	
Purchases		30 000	110/100		33 000
Overheads		5 000	110/100		5 500
31 Dec. Closing balance	1 000			1 344	
	£37 000	£37 000		£40 944	£40 944

Gain on short-term monetary items is

$$£(31 \text{ Dec.}) (1344 - 1000) = £(31 \text{ Dec.}) \ 344.$$

Gain on long-term monetary liabilities is

$$£(31 \text{ Dec.}) \ 4000\left(\frac{110}{90} - 1\right) = £(31 \text{ Dec.}) \ 889.$$

Current cost adjustments

Four adjustments need to be calculated, the realized and unrealized real gains (or losses) on stock and fixed assets expressed in closing pounds.

(a) *Real realized gain on stock (the cost of sales adjustment)* Stock with a historical cost of £27 000 was sold on 1 July by which date the stock price index had moved to 100, i.e. the replacement cost of date of sale was:

Opening stock, £(1 Jan.) 6000 × 100/80	= £(1 July) 7 500
1 July purchases	£(1 July) 21 000
	£(1 July) 28 500

These are 1 July pounds and have to be converted to year-end pounds:

£(1 July) 28 500 × 110/100	= £(31 Dec.) 31 350
Cost of goods sold per CPP profit and loss account	= £(31 Dec.) 30 433
Cost of sales adjustment	£(31 Dec.) 917

(b) *Real realized loss on fixed assets (depreciation adjustment)*

	£(31 Dec.)
Depreciation charge based on movement in specific prices, £2400 × 105/95	2653
Depreciation charge per CPP accounts	2933
Depreciation adjustment (loss) £(31 Dec.)	280

Note;
(i) Depreciation is based on year-end prices.
(ii) The loss means that the cost of the asset consumed (deemed to be 20% of the fixed assets) increased by less than the rate of inflation.

(c) *Real unrealized gain on stock*

	£(31 Dec.)
Closing stock	
At replacement cost, £9000 × 120/100	10 800
At adjusted historical cost £9000 × 110/100	9 900
Real unrealized gain £(31 Dec.)	900

(d) *Real unrealized loss in fixed assets*

	£(31 Dec.)
Net book value at 31 Dec.	
At replacement cost 80% of £12 000 × 105/95	10 611
At adjusted historical cost (per CPP accounts), 80% of £12 000 × 110/90	11 734
Real unrealized loss[27] £(31 Dec.)	1 123

We are now in a position to present the accounts, which we will do in summarized form:

Profit and loss account

	£(31 Dec.)	£(31 Dec.)
Sales		39 600
less: Current cost of goods sold	31 350	
Overheads	5 500	
Depreciation	2 653	39 503
Current cost operating profit £(31 Dec.)		97

27 Since this is the first year in the life of the assets and as depreciation is based on year-end values, there is no backlog depreciation.

Statement of gains and losses

	£(31 Dec.)	£(31 Dec.)
Current cost operating profit		97
Gains/losses on assets		
Realized		
Gain on stock	917	
Loss on fixed assets	(280)	637
Unrealized		
Gain on stock	900	
Loss on fixed assets	(1123)	(223)
Gains on monetary items (per CPP accounts)		
Short term	344	
Long term	889	1223
	£(31 Dec.)	1774

Balance sheet as at 31 December

	£(31 Dec.)	£(31 Dec.)
Fixed assets, net current replacement cost		10 611
Current assets		
Stock at replacement cost	10 800	
Debtors	5 000	
	15 800	
Current liabilities		
Creditors	(3 000)	
Overdraft	(3 000)	9 800
	£(31 Dec.)	20 411
Share Capital		
Issued	12 000	
Inflation adjustment[28]	2 667	14 667
Reserves		1 744
		16 411
Debentures		4 000
	£(31 Dec.)	20 411

Our example included a fully stabilized set of CPP accounts, i.e. all items were converted to pounds of year-end purchasing power.

---

[28] In years other than the first, the inflation adjustment would be applied to the opening balance of shareholders equity. In this case the inflation adjustment is £12 000 $(110/90 - 1)$ = £2667.

It is possible to avoid the need to adjust all items and instead deal only with the major impact of inflation by, for example, not converting all the profit and loss items and only applying an inflation factor to the opening balance of owners' equity. A number of different variants on the theme of combining CPP and CCA can be found in Whittington and Tweedie's book *The Debate on Inflation Accounting*.[29] The title of the book is apt because the debate will continue. It may be somewhat foolhardy to predict exactly how the debate will end but it may be reasonable to suggest that in the not too distant future the financial statements of, at least, the larger enterprises, will account for changes in both the value of assets and the value of money.

Recommended reading

E. O. Edwards and P. W. Bell, *The Theory and Measurement of Business Income*, University of California Press, Stanford, Calif., 1961.

Report of the inflation accounting committee, Cmnd 6225, HMSO, London, 1975 (the Sandilands report).

Provisional Statement of Standard Accounting Practice 7, 'Accounting for changes in the purchasing power of money', ICAEW, London, 1974.

H. C. Edey, 'Deprival value and financial accounting', in *Debits, Credits, Finance and Profits* (H. C. Edey and B. S. Yamey, eds), Sweet & Maxwell, London, 1974.

D. Tweedie, *Financial reporting, inflation and its capital maintenance concept*, ICRA Occasional Paper No 19, Lancaster, 1979.

D. R. Myddelton, *On a Cloth Untrue*, Woodhead-Faulkner, Cambridge, 1984.

G. Whittington, *Inflation Accounting – An Introduction to the Debate*, Cambridge University Press, Cambridge, 1983.

G. Whittington and D. Tweedie, *The Debate on Inflation Accounting*, Cambridge University Press, Cambridge, 1984.

W. T. Baxter, *Inflation Accounting*, Philip Allan, Oxford, 1984.

Questions

7.1 Experience with current cost accounting (CCA) since the issuance of SSAP 16: *Current Cost Accounting* (1980) suggests that it may not have been

---

29 G. Whittington and D. Tweedie, *The Debate on Inflation Accounting*, Cambridge University Press, Cambridge, 1984.

a success, and that the standard may have to be drastically modified, or even abandoned.

You are required:
(a) to suggest ways in which SSAP 16 may have failed to justify the expectations with which it was launched; and (10 marks)
(b) to point out weaknesses in the conception and in the practice of CCA which may have contributed to its failure to commend itself to the business community. (10 marks)
(20 marks)

A. Cert. A. Advanced Financial Accounting, December 1984.

7.2   In recent years several accountants in the U.K. have attacked the system of Current Cost Accounting (CCA), as outlined in SSAP 16: *Current Cost Accounting* (1980), and some have demanded its abandonment.
You are required to set out arguments both FOR and AGAINST:
(a) the abandonment of CCA; and (10 marks)
(b) the introduction of Current Purchasing Power Accounting (CPP).
(6 marks)
(16 marks)

A. Cert A., Advanced Financial Accounting, First paper, December 1983.

7.3   SSAP 16: *Current Cost Accounting* states that 'where a proportion of the net operating assets is financed by net borrowing, a gearing adjustment is required in arriving at the current cost profit attributable to the shareholders.'
Required:
(a) Outline the reasons for the inclusion of a gearing adjustment in current cost accounts. (10 marks)
(b) The gearing adjustment described in SSAP 16 has been criticized because:
   (i) it is based only on the current cost operating adjustments, and
   (ii) it ignores negative net borrowings.
   Discuss each of these criticisms. (10 marks)
(20 marks)

A. Cert. A. The Regulatory Framework of Accounting, June 1983.

7.4   The principal features of ED 35: *Accounting for the Effect of Changing Prices*, are:
(1) It will apply only to public companies.
(2) Compliance will be essential for accounts to give a true and fair view.
(3) Disclosure of the information required is to be made in notes to the accounts.
(4) The only balance sheet information that is required is on fixed assets and stocks.
(5) The profit and loss account information to be disclosed is similar to that required by SSAP 16.

You are required to discuss the proposals embodied in these principal features comparing them with those in SSAP 16 and comment on whether, in your opinion, they meet the criticisms raised against SSAP 16 with regard to these particular features. (18 marks)

ICAEW Financial Accounting II, December 1984.

8 The Valuation of a Business

Introduction

A business is an asset, and the same theoretical underpinnings can be applied to the valuation of a business as were applied to the valuation of individual assets in earlier chapters. There is, however, one very important difference between a single asset and a business: this is that a single asset usually represents only a small proportion of the owner's wealth. It is unlikely that this will be so in the case of a business and hence its valuation will depend in part on the other assets owned by the person or group on whose behalf the valuation is being made. In other words the value of a business could be said to be given by: the value of the owner's total stock of assets on the assumption that the business is owned less the value of the owner's total stock of assets without the business.

The significance of the effect of the potential or existing owner's other assets can be seen by considering the example of valuation of a pharmaceutical business. Let us suppose that there are two potential purchasers – a photographic company and an engineering company. It is likely, all other things being equal, that the photographic company would place a higher value on the business than the engineers if, as is probable, the pharmaceutical and photographic businesses have common outlets which would enable the photographic company to use the same representatives to sell both types of product. This is an example of what is called positive *synergy*, i.e. the interaction of assets so that the combined earnings of two or more assets will exceed the sum of their potential separate earnings.

The bases of valuation of a business will be dependent on the circumstances in which the valuation is being made, and we should therefore commence this chapter by considering the reasons why a valuation of a business is required.

Taxation

Tax legislation dictates that a business will have to be valued for the purposes of Capital Transfer Tax and Capital Gains Tax when the proprietor of a business dies or transfers part or all of his interest in the business during his life.

Insurance

A prudent management will wish to insure its business. This is often done by reference to the tangible assets of the business only, and the problem then reduces to deciding on the value to be attached to the business's tangible assets, a subject which was dealt with in some detail earlier in the book.

There are, however, many businesses where such an approach would result in a significant undervaluation of the business because tangible assets constitute only a small proportion of its assets. Examples of such enterprises include management consultancies, advertising agencies and firms of accountants. In these and similar cases the major asset of the business is the skill and enterprise of its owners and employees and in many, especially smaller, concerns the greater proportion of these assets is provided by the owner himself. If this is the case the owner should carefully consider the amount of life and disability insurance required to ensure that the value of the assets of the owner, or of his estate, will not decline should the owner be unable, by death or otherwise, to continue to work. In theory the amount of the insurance, the insurable risk, should, if we ignore the contribution of employees and other elements of 'goodwill', be equal to the value of the business less the value of the tangible assets.

Transfer of ownership

Both the potential vendor and the potential purchaser of a business will require valuation from their own particular standpoint and would, for the purposes of negotiation, wish to estimate the value which is in the minds of the other party to the transaction. We will discuss this topic in detail later in the chapter, but at this stage we will point out the particular problems faced by the potential purchaser.

A potential purchaser cannot be sure of retaining the trained labour force and management which are currently a part of the business. Also, the potential purchaser may not be interested in the business as a whole but only in a part of it which he intends to keep as a going concern, selling off the other assets. In contrast, he may not wish to persist with any part of the business and may only be interested in one or a number of the assets of the business which he would find more expensive to acquire in any other way.

There is also the question of synergy to be considered; thus the degree of interaction between the business being acquired and the purchaser's present business may be such that the value of the business to the purchaser bears little relation to the value of the business on its own. The potential purchaser also faces the practical problem that he may not be able to obtain all the necessary information.

In addition to the above circumstances, which apply to most forms of business enterprise, a number of special factors apply in the cases of partnerships and companies.

Partnerships

If the business is a partnership the problems of valuation may be acute and frequent. Whenever there is a change in the partnership arrangements a valuation of both the 'old' and 'new' partnerships is required, for the ongoing partners will give up a share in the old partnership in return for a share in the new partnership. In practice the difficult problems involved are often dealt with in so far as the valuation of the old partnership is concerned by the addition to the tangible assets of a figure for goodwill based on such arbitrary formulae as x years purchase of the average profits of a past period. Such an approach is theoretically unsound because it is based on past results rather than future expectations, but the method is usually easy to apply and will reduce the possibility of disagreement arising between the partners.

The contribution of the partners to the new partnership is dealt with in the first instance by the selection of a profit-sharing agreement based on the capital and labour inputs of the partners, but this will, of course, only encompass the profits recognized by the accounting system and will ignore changes in the valuation of assets, especially goodwill. Thus, when there is next a change in the partnership arrangements the problem of the valuation of the business will again have to be faced.

Companies

When a company requires new capital and proposes to raise this by the issue of new shares it will be necessary to value the company in order that an appropriate and equitable price will be derived for the new issue. Often, when a company is faced with a takeover bid, it will be advantageous to obtain a valuation in order that the bid may either be defended or a fair price agreed for the company's shares.

In addition, there is also a need for the shareholders of the company to have some indication of the current value of the company in order that they may judge the stewardship of the directors by reference to the rate of return which they obtain on their investment. Indeed, it is argued that this knowledge should be in the possession of all investors on the grounds that the most efficient use of the nation's resources will be achieved if investment is steered towards those companies which offer the greatest return.

A valuation model based on earnings

The standard valuation model for any asset is based on the cash flows that will be generated by the use of the asset – the 'present value model', i.e.

$$V_0 = \sum_{j=0}^{\infty} \frac{Y_j - X_j}{(1 + K)^j},\tag{8.1}$$

where V_0 is the value of the asset at time t_0, K is the discount rate, Y_j are the cash receipts generated by the asset in year j, X_j are the cash expenses associated with the asset in year j. In practice, however, the models employed in the valuation of businesses are often based on the net profits of the business as disclosed by the accounts of the enterprise rather than on the cash flows generated by the business.

Such earnings-based models are not as conceptually sound as cash flow models and are, with the increasing use of discounted cash flow techniques in business, of less importance nowadays than in the past. They are, however, still used and do have the advantage of simplicity as fewer adjustments have to be made to the figures reported in a company's accounts than is the case when cash flow models are employed. It therefore seems appropriate to consider the circumstances under which the differences between the two approaches may not be significant.

Now if C_j is the expenses of the business in year j on an accruals basis and R_j is the revenue of the business in year j on an accruals basis, than the profit of the business in year j is given by

$$P_j = R_j - C_j.$$

Over the life of the business the cash receipts from sales must be the same as the revenue accrued (if bad debts and discounts are ignored), i.e.

$$\sum_{j=0}^{\infty} Y_j = \sum_{j=0}^{\infty} R_j,$$

and the cash payments must be the same as the expenses calculated on an accruals basis (again ignoring bad debts and discounts), i.e.

$$\sum_{j=0}^{\infty} X_j = \sum_{j=0}^{\infty} C_j.$$

If the net expenditure on fixed assets per year is approximately the same as the annual depreciation charge, and if the business investment in net current assets is approximately constant, then it follows that

$$Y_j \simeq R_j \quad \text{and} \quad X_j \simeq C_j.$$

The valuation model, equation (8.1), can then be restated as follows:

$$V_0 = \sum_{j=0}^{\infty} \frac{Y_j - X_j}{(1 + K)^j}$$

and thus

$$V_0 \simeq \sum_{j=0}^{\infty} \frac{R_j - C_j}{(1 + K)^j} = \sum_{j=0}^{\infty} \frac{P_j}{(1 + K)^j}.$$

Therefore the value of the firm can be stated in terms of the discounted value of the expected profits to be earned over the firm's lifetime.

The nature of the discounting process is such that the later terms in the series have less impact on the overall valuation V_0 than the earlier terms. In other words, for a given P_j and K, $P_j/(1 + K)^j$ becomes smaller as j becomes larger. Thus the importance of the assumptions referred to above relating to the purchase of fixed assets and investment in working capital is reduced as the years pass.

It might be argued that this formulation overstates the value of the business because not all the profit is paid to the proprietor, but some is re-invested in the business. Thus the cash flow to the proprietor is less than the profit flow to the business. This is generally true, but the recognition of this point leads us to modify but not abandon our approach. A rational proprietor with a discount rate K would only re-invest the profits of the business where the expected rate of return on that investment was greater than K. Consider, for example, the re-investment of I from the profits in year 1. Then the profit paid to the proprietor falls from P_1 to $P_1 - I$. However, this investment must earn at least rate K, so the profits in year 2 must be increased from P_2 to at least $P_2 + I(1 + K)$ if this was a 1-year investment.

Thus, in place of the valuation

$$V_0 = P_0 + \frac{P_1}{1 + K} + \frac{P_2}{(1 + K)^2} + \ldots + \frac{P_n}{(1 + K)^n} + \ldots,$$

we have, if it is assumed that the amount invested earns a return of K (i.e. that profits of year 2 are $P_2 + I(1 + K)$), a value, V_0', which is given by

$$V_0' = P_0 + \frac{P_1 - I}{(1 + K)} + \frac{P_2 + I(1 + K)}{(1 + K)^2} + \ldots + \frac{P_n}{(1 + K)^n} + \ldots,$$

$$= P_0 + \frac{P_1}{(1 + K)} + \frac{P_2}{(1 + K)^2} + \ldots + \frac{P_n}{(1 + K)^n} + \ldots$$

$$= V_0.$$

The same analysis can be applied to investments made in later years.

If it is assumed that the amounts invested will earn a greater return than K then the value V_0 can be regarded as providing a lower limit of the range of values of the business.

We have thus established a theoretical model for the valuation of a business as a going concern, based upon the discounted value of the future earnings of the business.

Valuation of a business as a going concern

Initially, in formulating a solution to the valuation problem, we will confine the discussion to the case of a business which is being valued as a going concern and whose management and assets will be unchanged as a result of the circumstances leading to the requirement for a valuation.

The direct application of our theoretical model poses several problems. The first and most obvious problem is that the model requires us to forecast earnings for the business for the remainder of its life. This, it will readily be recognized, is an impossible task. The second problem arises in the estimation of the discount rate, K, which should be used to carry out this calculation. Thus, in practice, the theoretical model is rarely applied as we have derived it, but rather various rule of thumb approximations are used to establish a range of values for the business which experience has shown might be indicated by the theoretical model were we able to use it.

Asset valuation approach

Our first approach to the problem of valuation will be an asset valuation approach. It can be argued that if a business is acquiring or retaining an asset, then the value of that asset to the business must, in the case of acquisition of the asset, be greater than the cost of that asset and, in the case of retention of the asset, be greater than the net realizable value of the asset. If, therefore, all the assets of the business are valued at their net realizable values, then the sum of those values will clearly be less than their value to the business and can be regarded as providing the lower bound to the range of values based on the asset valuation approach. This point is not as simple as it appears because of the difficulty in determining the net realizable value of assets and, as described in Chapter 3, the net realizable value of an asset depends on the circumstances under which it is assumed that the asset will be sold.

The upper bound of the range of assets will be the sum of the replacement costs of the company's assets so long as it is recognized that the assets include intangibles such as goodwill. The determination of the replacement cost of both tangible and in particular intangible assets does produce substantial practical difficulties.

Discounted earnings approaches

These approaches are related to the present value method, but contain a number of simplifying assumptions which facilitate their use. There is, however, a danger that the crudity of the assumptions may in certain circumstances mean that the links between the methods described and the present value method become tenuous.

A common theme of the simplified approaches is that one figure is selected as representing what is termed the *maintainable profit* of the business. This figure is sometimes based on the average profit for the recent past; in which case adjustments need to be made for changes in capital employed, inflation, etc. Alternatively, the profits of the most recent year or the forecast profit of the current year may be used to provide a first estimate of the maintainable profit. The first estimate, however derived, may then be adjusted on a more or less subjective basis by the valuer. He might feel that the current year, or recent past, does not provide a reasonable indication of the future and may, therefore, inflate or deflate the first estimate depending on his view of the likely future trend in profits.

The valuer will, especially in the case of smaller businesses, have to consider the extent to which profit is being distributed by way of remuneration. For example, the directors of a family-owned limited company may be paid a great deal more than the economic value of their services and part of their remuneration should be regarded as profit. In such an instance the reported accounting profit is understated in the sense that – all other things being equal – a higher profit could have been obtained if the family directors were replaced by professional managers paid at the market rate.

We are now in a position to consider a simple discounted earnings approach.

Let us assume that an estimate of the maintainable profit has been obtained. The next step is to determine the capitalization rate which will be necessary to fix the current value of an anticipated stream of future earnings. This is usually done by comparing the business concerned with a similar business the current value of which is known and whose maintainable profit can be estimated. The capitalization rate derived from the relationship between current value and earnings in this case can be applied, after making any necessary adjustments, to the business which is to be valued.

One very convenient basis of comparison is the share price and earnings of a publicly quoted company undertaking a similar type of business since this will give a readily available price to earnings (P/E) ratio which can be applied to the earnings of the business. It is usual to apply a lower P/E ratio to the earnings of the business being valued than is currently applied to the earnings of a publicly listed company and the discount to cover the lack of marketability would usually be in the region of 25 to 33%. In addition it will be necessary to make suitable adjustments to this P/E ratio to take into account differences, in such matters as asset backing and earnings growth, between the quoted company and the unquoted business.

One disadvantage of this approach is that the P/E ratio derived from the market is based on marginal transactions, i.e. the price which is associated with the transfer of a relatively small proportion of the shares in issue. This price is not obviously applicable for the valuation of the business as a whole because, on the one hand, the purchase of the business would mean that a larger parcel of shares was acquired (which would suggest that a lower P/E rate should be used), while on the other hand the purchaser would be gaining control of the whole business (which might justify the use of a higher P/E ratio).

The above approach, together with the asset valuation method, is illustrated in Example 8.1. The data of this example will be used as the basis of a running example which will appear later in the chapter.

EXAMPLE 8.1

ABC Limited is an unquoted company which has been trading for 10 years in an inflation-free environment and has been earning profits consistently. It is required, for some reason whose tax effects and influence upon the path of the business will be negligible, to arrive at a valuation for the business. The following information is known about the business as at 31 December 19X9:

Profits for ABC Limited			
19X0	£ 1 000	19X5	£15 000
19X1	£ 2 000	19X6	£14 000
19X2	£ 5 000	19X7	£16 000
19X3	£ 8 000	19X8	£14 000
19X4	£12 000	19X9	£17 000

The book values of the assets of the business in 19X0 were £10 000 and are now £70 000.

The book values of the assets of the business are believed to be reasonable approximations of their net realizable values, apart from the business premises, which have a book value of £20 000 but an estimated net realizable value of £60 000.

The net realizable value of ABC's assets is thus £70 000 + £(60 000 − 20 000) = £110 000 which, as argued above, might be regarded as the lower band of the range of values based on an asset valuation approach.

The maintainable profit of the business could be based on the average of the last 5 years' profits, which appear to be reasonably stable, hence the maintainable profit is £15 200.

Let us assume that the quoted shares of a similar business sell at a P/E ratio of 10 and that it is appropriate to discount this figure by 25% to take account of the reduced marketability of the shares of ABC Limited, i.e. the P/E ratio would be 0.75 of 10 = 7.5.

The simple discounted earnings method valuation of the business is then 7.5 × £15 200 = £114 000.

Super-profits method

It is sometimes suggested that the earnings stream of a business can be divided into two elements – the first is the expected return on the value of the tangible assets employed on the business while the second is an additional amount, known as the *super-profit*. The super-profit is therefore the difference between the maintainable profit and the expected return on the tangible assets employed. The essence of the super-profit method is that the additional profits are regarded as riskier than the expected return and that the super-profit should therefore be capitalized at a lower multiple (or higher capitalization rate) than the expected return.

A number of arguments can be advanced to support the view. One is based on the standard economic theory that in a perfectly competitive market, profits that are higher than the norm for the type of assets employed in the business will be eroded away because the existence of excess profits will encourage new entrants into the market. The new firms will drive down the price until the excess profits are eliminated. The strength of this argument does depend on the structure of the market involved and it has to be recognized that there may be barriers to entry whereby a monopolist can continue to reap excess profits in the long term.

The super-profits method has also been justified by reference to the transient nature of goodwill. It can be argued that the super-profits represent the profits generated by the existence of goodwill. Consider a new business which has tangible assets of £80 000 and that the normal return on assets of the type employed by the business is 12%. Then the expected profit is £9600. An existing business with identical tangible assets may be earning a profit of £12 000. The difference between the two profits which may be regarded as the super-profit is due to the fact that the existing business has created 'goodwill', e.g. has established good relationships with customers, a skilled workforce, etc. Now by its very nature goodwill will disappear if no steps are taken to ensure its survival. Thus, new employees will have to be trained, customers will have to be provided with satisfactory service and so on. When an existing business is acquired its goodwill will gradually disappear and it will, in effect, have to be replaced by the activities of the new owners. This view, if accepted, can be used as an argument for applying a lower multiple to the super-profits.

The theoretical weakness of the super-profits method is that the separation of maintainable profits into the two elements is artificial. The associated practical difficulty is the determination of the expected rate of return on assets of the type employed in the business. All businesses have some goodwill (although in very badly run firms goodwill may be negative) and thus it is unlikely that reference to similar businesses will yield the required return. It is sometimes suggested that the expected return might be related to the return on government securities, but an investment in a business will carry a greater risk and it will therefore be necessary to adjust for this difference.

The super-profits method is perhaps superficially attractive, but on more detailed consideration it does seem to suffer from severe theoretical and practical shortcomings. Given its difficulties a valuer might well be advised to use the present value approach described earlier in the chapter, which would mean that he would not be confined to one figure of maintainable profit. He could estimate the future trend of profits, which would enable him to consider the possibility of growth. The required discount rate could be obtained from an examination of similar businesses and would avoid the need to make the artificial distinction between normal and super-profits.

The mechanics of the super-profits method are illustrated in Example 8.2.

EXAMPLE 8.2
Data are assumed to be the same as those given for Example 8.1.

Let us suppose that the 'normal' rate of return on assets of the type used by ABC Limited is 10%. The 'super-profits' can then be calculated as follows:

	£
Expected maintainable profits (from Example 8.1)	15 200
less Normal return, 10% of £110 000	11 000
Super-profits	£4 200

Let us assume that it is believed that the super-profits should be valued at 4 years' earnings, i.e. a multiple of four or a capitalization rate of 25% should be applied to the figure of £4200. It should be noted that one of the major defects of the super-profits method is that it is by no means clear how the required multiple should be determined.

The value of ABC Limited would then be determined as follows:

	£
Value of tangible assets	110 000[1]
Value of super-profits 4 × £4 200	16 800
	£126 800

1 This is of course equivalent to capitalizing the expected return of £11 000 by 10%.

Valuation of a business for amalgamation with another

The valuation of a business which is to be amalgamated with another business is a more complex process because it cannot be made in isolation. From the point of view of the potential purchaser the maximum price that he would be prepared to pay is the difference between the value of the combined business and the value of his existing business.

If the amalgamation gives rise to positive synergy the value of the amalgamated business will be greater than the sum of the values of the individual business taken in isolation. The basic principle can be simply stated but the practical problems are immense in that the purchaser has to place a value on a business which has yet to be established. The purchaser will usually not only have to consider the tangible assets, which can be valued with relative ease, but also the intangible assets which may be particularly influenced by the synergical effect of the amalgamation.

In many amalgamations some of the assets of the acquired business will not be retained in the new business. The first step therefore in valuing a business for acquisition will be to determine the asset structure of the business and identify the assets which will not be required in the future. These assets must be valued at their net realizable value at the time at which they are expected to be sold and these figures discounted to the present time to ascertain the present value of the superfluous assets. In many cases, the sale of the superfluous assets will take place immediately and therefore no discounting will be necessary and the value of these assets may be considered to be a deduction from the purchase price of the business.

In practice the valuation figure must be the net realizable value of the surplus assets which are to be sold plus the present value of the additional earnings which will accrue to the acquiring business as a result of the acquisition. It is of course apparent that a major problem arises in determining the rate of interest at which the earnings of the business must be discounted, and this has already been discussed.

We will consider an example in order to assist with the explanation of this analysis.

EXAMPLE 8.3

ADG is a business which produces and sells to retailers a certain range of fashion clothes. It has made the following estimates of potential earnings for the next 10 years:

Year no.	1	2	3	4	5	6	7	8	9	10
Earnings (£000s)	120	140	170	200	210	220	240	260	280	300

XYZ is a business which owns a series of boutiques in a certain locality. The boutiques buy clothes from various suppliers and retail them. Each boutique has a manager and an assistant but all purchasing and policy decisions are taken centrally by the owner and his staff.

XYZ independently estimates its earnings for the next 10 years to be

Year no.	1	2	3	4	5	6	7	8	9	10
Earnings (£000s)	10	15	20	25	28	31	33	34	35	35

The net assets of XYZ have a book value of £100 000, which includes 10-year leases on retail shops valued at about £60 000, a freehold shop and office valued at £20 000, stock worth £20 000 at retail prices, on which £12 000 is owing to suppliers.

ADG is interested in acquiring XYZ in order to provide some additional retail outlets. If it were to do this it would retain most of the shops with their staff, but would not retain the owner, his staff nor the freehold shop and offices. It would use the shops to sell only its own clothes, and so improve its turnover and profit margin.

ADG have made the following estimates of costs and earnings if it were to acquire XYZ. Initially, it would sell the freehold shop and office for £20 000 and the leases on two of the ships for a further £10 000. This would entail the dismissal of 10 staff who would need to be compensated for loss of employment, which would cost ADG about £25 000. The entire stock of the shops would be sold as quickly as possible and replaced with clothing supplied by ADG. The estimated trading earnings of ADG with XYZ for the next 10 years are as follows:

Year no.	1	2	3	4	5	6	7	8	9	10
Earnings (£000s)	125	150	200	230	255	270	280	300	320	350

Thus, ADG can assess the differences between its performance without XYZ and with XYZ. These differences are

Year no.	1	2	3	4	5	6	7	8	9	10
Difference in earnings (£000s)	+5	+10	+30	+30	+45	+50	+40	+40	+40	+50

Additional gains to ADG would be the sale of the freehold and the leasehold shops (£30 000) and of the stock (£20 000) less the liabilities due to suppliers (£12 000) and the cost of laying off the excess employees (£25 000): an immediate net gain of £13 000.

It is assumed that all other assets of the business would be retained. Thus, the figures to be discounted to give a present value for the acquisition are as follows:

Year no.	0	1	2	3	4	5	6	7	8	9	10
Earnings (£000s)	13	5	10	30	30	45	50	40	40	40	50

In practice it may be difficult to decide upon the appropriate discount rate. The problem may be overcome by considering a range of discount rates within which it is likely that the appropriate rate will fall. We will assume that the selected range is 15–20%.

The present values of the earnings stream are £157 620 when discounted at 15% and £127 063 when discounted at 20%, whilst the present values of the earnings of XYZ for the next 10 years should it continue as an independent business are £116 926 when discounted at 15% and £93 598 when discounted at 20%. The value of the business of XYZ on its own can therefore be seen to be less than its value to ADG at any given discount rate between 15% and 20%, therefore agreement should readily be reached as to a purchase price since it will be advantageous for the owner of XYZ to sell at £117 000 or above and for ADG to buy at £127 000 or below, given that 15% and 20% represent the extremes of the possible discount rates applicable to this type of business.

As can be seen in the example, if the business can be put to a more profitable use by the new management and if there is not a substantial difference between the discount rates used by the parties, it is likely that a price for the business will be agreed. If we retain the assumption about the comparability of the discount rates, it is clear that the converse holds and that if the business would be employed less profitability by the potential purchaser it is not likely that agreement could be reached as the business would be worth more to the potential seller than it is to the potential buyer. If the parties employ widely different discount rates the above conclusions may not apply.

Suppose for example that the owner of XYZ was content with a return of 10% on his capital. Then, discounting the earnings stream of XYZ at 10%, he would derive a present value of £149 606. If ADG expected a 20% return on their investment then the value they would put upon the acquisition of the business would be £127 064. In such a case it would be impossible to fix a price which would not lead to a worsening of the perceived positions of one or both parties.

The value of control of a business

For a sole proprietor there is no question of ownership of a business without control, but for a partnership or a company it is possible to share in the ownership of a business without having control of the business. In using the word 'control' in this context we mean that the individual in question is able to determine the business policy or any particular action of the business without resort to persuading other owners of the business that this course of action is desirable.

When a business is jointly owned the value of the business to the controlling owner is in most cases greater, proportionately to his holding, than to the other owners. This has been clearly established in law in valuing shares for Capital Transfer Tax purposes where a controlling interest in a company is recognized as carrying a higher proportionate value than a minority interest. The law, however, merely follows upon observed fact, since the valuation is based upon what a potential purchaser would be likely to pay for the holding being valued, given that he had access to all the information that would be available to a prudent potential purchaser. Thus we must examine the underlying reasons for which a controlling interest in a business is proportionately more valuable than a minority interest.

The most obvious reason for this higher valuation is that the controlling interest enables the owner of that interest to arrange the affairs of the business in a way that best suits his own circumstances. This may appear to offend the profit maximization principle which is assumed to apply to businesses, but it does in fact take us one step further in the analysis. The assumption of profit maximization for a business is a rationalization of the principle of the maximizing of utility for the individual. These two criteria do not necessarily coincide, but provided there are many owners with many preferences it is a practicable solution to suggest that if maximum profit is available then the individuals will be able to get the most utility from spending it. However, the crux of the problem can be illustrated by supposing there is only one owner and examining the maximizing of his utility and the profit of the firm separately.

Assume that there are two possible paths for the business to follow producing the following dividend flows given differing re-investment patterns:

Year no.	1	2	3	4	5
Path 1 dividends (£000s)	5	7	12	17	20
Path 2 dividends (£000s)	11	11	11	11	11

If the cost of capital to the business is 10% then the present value of these dividends will be £43 376 if path 1 is followed and £41 700 if path 2 is followed. The profit maximization assumption would indicate that path 1 should be followed.

Suppose, however, that the owner of the business requires more money in the early years, and if he is not able to take this money from the business he must borrow it at 25% interest, and he is prepared to do so. This means that the owner's discount rate is 25% and therefore the present value of the dividends streams to him are £28 140 if path 1 is followed and £29 580 if path 2 is followed. He will choose to follow path 2.

Thus the value to this individual from controlling the business, and thereby directing the business to follow path 2 rather than path 1 is £29 580 − £28 140 = £1440.

Now it is clear that if this business was owned by many shareholders and run by a professional manager it should follow path 1 because the manager could show that by re-investing profits at a high rate in the early period the firm would be better off by £43 376 − £41 700, i.e. by £1676 in present value terms, whilst the individual we have considered would be worse off by £1440 if he were the sole recipient of these dividends.

Thus we have shown that the net present value of the dividends stream from the business is dependent upon the rate at which the stream is discounted. Therefore the value which will be placed by an individual upon a business will depend upon his expected income stream and his own time preference rate. The control of a firm enables an individual to co-ordinate the discount rate used by the firm with that which optimizes his own welfare.

There are, of course, other advantages to having control of a business which are concerned with status and the ability to use the business to help to achieve personal goals, but the difference in value between a minority and controlling interest stems from the difference between the individual's utility maximizing position and profit maximization. The difference will in nearly all cases make a controlling interest in a business proportionately more valuable than a minority interest.

The valuation of a business represents therefore much the same type of problem as does the valuation of other assets, but because the business is a complex asset and its ownership is often diverse the estimation involved is even more difficult.

Recommended reading

See list at the end of Chapter 9.

Questions

See end of Chapter 9 for valuation questions.

9 The Valuation of Securities

Introduction

We will follow the chapter on the valuation of a business by a chapter on the valuation of securities, concentrating upon the value of small holdings of the securities of companies. Where securities which give a controlling interest in a business are to be valued, the valuation procedures dealt with in the previous chapter should be used.

It is convenient to distinguish between the *ex post* (after) and *ex ante* (before) need to value securities, although as we shall show similar principles apply in each case. In an *ex post* valuation the purpose of the exercise is the determination of the value of the securities at a current or past date, whilst in an *ex ante* valuation the requirement is to estimate the value of the security at some future date.

Ex post valuations have to be made for the purposes of Capital Transfer Tax when securities are transmitted by death or otherwise from one person to another. The need to include investments at a valuation in current cost accounts has increased the need for *ex post* valuations of securities.

Ex ante valuations are also of considerable importance. The management of a company should consider the effect on the value of the company's securities of alternative courses of action available to them when deciding upon such matters as the company's investment policy or capital structure. It is possible, for example, that diversification into a new area may influence the stock market's perception of the risk associated with the company's earnings. Thus it seems reasonable that when management is contemplating such diversification it should consider the likely impact on security prices and not confine itself to an assessment of the change in the company's cash flow.

Valuation of fixed interest securities

Fixed interest securities which are quoted on the Stock Exchange present few problems in *ex post* valuation since their value at some past time may be determined by the price at which those securities were traded. However, where *ex ante* valuations are required or where the securities are not quoted or where the securities are quoted but there has been no trading we must use a valuation model.

The model which we shall use will be the present value model, to which we made reference in the last chapter. This model discounts to the present time all the expected future cash flows of the security and states that this is the value of that security.

The rate of discount will be the appropriate cost of capital for income streams of similar risk characteristics to the one being appraised which may be based on the discount rate applied to quoted securities in the market. Redeemable fixed interest securities will yield the same sum of money each year as income until their redemption date is reached when a return of capital, on some prescribed basis, will take place. Irredeemable securities will yield the same money sum as income in perpetuity. It must, however, be borne in mind that where the fixed interest security is issued by a company there will be some risk of insolvency leading to a loss of income and capital for the holder.

Consider therefore a security which will pay an annual sum of £s for n years, at which time a return of capital of £C will be made. The first payment of interest will take place in one years' time from the date of valuation. The appropriate cost of capital is $100k\%$.

Now the ex interest price which that security should command will be the present value of the income stream, i.e.

$$P_0 = \sum_{j=1}^{n} \frac{s}{(1+k)^j} + \frac{C}{(1+k)^n}$$

$$= s\frac{(1+k)^n - 1}{k(1+k)^n} + \frac{C}{(1+k)^n}$$

where P_0 is the current price which represents the value of the security, s is the annual interest paid and C is the redemption value of the security.[1]

---

1 The derivation of this equation is as follows. Given that

$$P_0 = \sum_{j=1}^{n} \frac{s}{(1+k)^j} + \frac{C}{(1+k)^n},$$

let

$$\sum_{j=1}^{n} \frac{s}{(1+k)^j} = X.$$

(cont. next page)

Loans and preference shares

Loans and preference shares are usually valued as fixed interest securities since both usually specify a rate of interest or dividend which is regarded as the fixed annual payment to the security holders. In using the same analysis for loans and for preference shares it must be remembered that the payment of loan interest and the repayment of loan capital is a contractual liability of the company whilst the payment of preference share dividends and the repayment of preference share capital is at the directors' discretion, except in so far as they are bound by the articles of association of the company. Thus it is clear that in adverse financial circumstances for the company, the loan holders can be more certain of their income and capital than can the preference shareholders, and therefore they are likely to apply a lower discount rate in arriving at a valuation of their securities than are the preference shareholders.

We will deal first with the valuation of irredeemable securities. These are securities whose capital will not be repaid unless the company is wound up or is subject to a capital reconstruction. If the company is currently a going concern then the repayment of any capital is sufficiently far in the future, and sufficiently unlikely that we may disregard it. We can also consider that there will be a perpetual income stream of the annual sum. For such a security we can state that its value

1 *(cont.)*

Then

$$X = s\left[\frac{1}{1+k} + \frac{1}{(1+k)^2} + \ldots + \frac{1}{(1+k)^{n-1}} + \frac{1}{(1+k)^n}\right]$$

and

$$X(1+k) = s\left[1 + \frac{1}{1+k} + \ldots + \frac{1}{(1+k)^{n-1}}\right].$$

Therefore

$$X\left[(1+k) - 1\right] = s\left[1 - \frac{1}{(1+k)^n}\right],$$

so that

$$X = s\frac{(1+k)^n - 1}{k(1+k)^n}$$

and thus

$$P_0 = s\frac{(1+k)^n - 1}{k(1+k)^n} + \frac{C}{(1+k)^n}.$$

is given by its annual income divided by the appropriate discount rate, i.e. s/k.[2]

For redeemable loans and preference shares it is necessary to use the full formulation as derived:

$$P_0 = s\frac{(1+k)^n - 1}{k(1+k)^n} + \frac{C}{(1+k)^n}.$$

Although this formulation may appear complex, it is simple to use in practice. Most finance textbooks reproduce tables which show, for different values of k and n, the values of

$$\frac{(1+k)^n - 1}{k(1+k)^n} \quad \text{and} \quad \frac{1}{(1+k)^n};$$

the former would appear in a table entitled the present value of an annuity while the latter can be found from the table of 'present values'.

Remember that the above formulae assume that the next dividend or interest payment will be made one year after the date of valuation. In practice the interest and dividend payments on fixed interest securities are made every half year, and therefore the payments should be discounted for the appropriate number of half years at the half-yearly discount rate.

The major problem involving fixed interest securities is therefore the choice of appropriate discount rates where, because of the lack of a market value, the valuation model described above has to be used.

The valuation of ordinary shares

We will first consider the usually simple task of valuing quoted shares. We will then introduce a theoretical model and show how it may be applied to unquoted shares.

2 In proving this statement we are able to use the formulation derived above:

$$P_0 = s\frac{(1+k)^n - 1}{k(1+k)^n} + \frac{C}{(1+k)^n},$$

Recognizing that $C/(1+k)^n \to 0$ as $n \to \infty$, we can state that

$$P_0 = s\frac{(1+k)^n - 1}{k(1+k)^n} = s\left(\frac{1}{k} - \frac{1}{k(1+k)^n}\right).$$

Now as $n \to \infty$, $1/(1+k)^n \to 0$ and therefore $P_0 \to s/k$.

Quoted shares

In most circumstances the *ex post* valuation of quoted shares will present few difficulties as the valuation can be made by reference to the prices at which the shares were traded on the required valuation date. Such prices can be found listed in the Stock Exchange Daily List. Typically, there will be a number of different prices quoted for any one day since prices will fluctuate during the day and the normal practice, for valuation purposes, is to take the average of the highest and lowest prices marked.

There are circumstances when the Stock Exchange price will not give a reliable guide to the value of a holding of shares. This will occur when the block of shares to be valued is large compared with the number of shares which are actively traded on the Stock Exchange. Clearly, if the normal level of activity in a company share runs at about 10 000 shares per day it is extremely likely that the hypothetical sale of 100 000 shares would only have been achieved at a lower price than that which actually prevailed on the appropriate date. Similarly, a purchase of a large block of shares would probably have to have been made at a higher price. Thus, in such circumstances, the realizable value of a large block of shares will be less than the product of the number of shares and the Stock Exchange price per share while the replacement cost of the shares would be greater than that figure. Valuation of such large blocks of shares therefore requires a considerable element of subjective judgement about the circumstances leading to the need for evaluation and about the likely effect on the market of a transaction of unusual size.

True and market value

We shall now consider whether it can be said that a share has a true or intrinsic value which may be different from its market value. There are different opinions on this matter. Some argue that there cannot be a difference between the two because (ignoring the problem of large blocks of shares) the value of a quoted share must be the same as the price at which it was traded and that it is not meaningful to talk of a 'true' value which differs from its market value. Advocates of this view believe that the price of a share is determined by the interaction of buyers and sellers, who are influenced by many factors, including speculative motives, and that there is little point in attempting to analyse the results of any particular company in any great detail. The investment strategy of this school is to attempt to determine when share prices will change and to buy or sell depending upon whether they think that the share price will rise or fall. An extreme, and well known, example of this approach is provided by the chartists, who claim that it is possible to identify patterns of past share price movements which may be used to determine whether the share price will rise or fall. It must be said that not everyone agrees that this is a valid approach.

An alternative view is that the share does have a true value based on the economic value of the company which, if the company is a going concern, will be based on the company's prospective dividends since they must ultimately be available to the shareholders. It is argued that due to differences in expectations and other market imperfections it is likely that the market price will not be the same as the true value but that over time the difference will be eroded as the participants in the markets come to share the same expectations. This view suggests that it would be profitable to attempt to identify and purchase those shares which are currently 'undervalued'.

We will concentrate on the second approach not only because of its importance in its own right but also because it provides a theoretical underpinning to the whole subject of the valuation of shares, whether quoted or unquoted.

Dividend valuation models

The first assumption we must make is that investors are only interested in the cash flows that will accrue to them as a result of their ownership of shares, i.e. we will assume that investors will ignore any non-pecuniary benefits (such as prestige from holding shares in the company or other perquisites available to shareholders).

We will consider initially a potential purchaser of a share who intends to hold that share for only a year and then to resell it. His outlay is the current purchase price; he will receive a dividend in one year's time and will then sell the share. We will assume that the purchaser could alternatively put his money in a risk-free bank account and leave it there to earn interest. There is, therefore, a cost to the individual, that is the lost interest. We can consider this lost interest as his cost of capital.

Let us suppose that the price he pays to purchase the share is $£P_0$, the price for which he sells the share is $£P_1$, the dividend he receives at the year end is $£D_1$ and the cost of capital (expressed as a decimal) is k.

Now if the potential investor had deposited the purchase price in a risk-free interest-earning bank account at the beginning of the year (time t_0) he would at the end of the year (time t_1) have £$P_0(1+k)$. Alternatively, if he purchases the share he would at time t_1 receive £$(P_1 + D_1)$. He will only purchase the share if he expects the purchase to make him at least as well off as his deposit in the interest earning account, i.e. if $P_0(1+k) < P_1 + D_1$ or $P_0 < (P+D)/(1+k)$.

Let us assume that the participants in the market all make the same estimates of P_1, D_1 and k. Then a share which is cheaply priced, i.e. where $P_0 < (P_1 + D_1)/(1+k)$, will be purchased and the price will be bid up until equilibrium is achieved when, $P_0 = (P_1 + D_1)/(1+k)$.

We have thus derived a simple model of the value of a share based on its expected dividend for the year and its expected price in one year's time. Readers will note that it is a present value model.

If we consider the subsequent purchaser (who will hold the share for one year only), then the same considerations will apply at time t_1, so that we can say that P_1 will be given by $P_1 = (P_2 + D_2)/(1+k)$, where P_2 is the selling price of the share at time t_2, and D_2 is the dividend to be paid at time t_2. Thus we could state that

$$P_0 = \frac{D_1}{1+k} + \frac{D_2}{(1+k)^2} + \frac{P_2}{(1+k)^2},$$

and so, by extending the analysis for the whole life of the company,

$$P_0 = \frac{D_1}{1+k} + \frac{D_2}{(1+k)^2} + \frac{D_3}{(1+k)^3} + \dots + \frac{D_n}{(1+k)^n}$$

$$= \sum_{j=1}^{n} \frac{D_j}{(1+k)^j}$$

$$= D_j \frac{(1+k)^n - 1}{k(1+k)^n}.[3]$$

If, therefore, we can estimate the dividends to be paid out for the rest of the life of the company, including the final or liquidating dividend and also the cost of capital, we can make an estimate of the equilibrium value of the share.

This represents a laborious calculation, quite apart from the fact that it is a difficult forecasting problem. To simplify this, it is sometimes

3 *See* footnote 1 on pages 293–4.

possible to assume that the dividend can be expected to grow at a constant rate (less than the cost of capital) each year.

Let the rate of growth of the dividend be g and the cost of capital be k, which is greater than g; also let the dividend at time t_0 be D_0. Then we can state that the value of the share at time t_0 will be given by the expression

$$P_0 = \frac{D_0(1+g)}{(k-g)},\,[4]$$

Thus, if we use the assumption that the company will have a reasonably long life with dividends increasing at $100g\%$ per year and has a constant cost of capital of $100k\%$, we can use the last declared dividend to estimate the value of a share.

[4] We may derive this equation by the following procedure.

The growth rate of the dividend is g and the dividend at time t_0 is D_0; thus the dividend at time t_1 is given by $D_1 = D_0(1+g)$. Analogously, the dividend at time t_2 is given by $D_2 = D_0(1+g)^2$, and so on; so the dividend at time t_n, $D_n = D_0(1+g)^n$. Hence

$$P_0 = \frac{D_0(1+g)}{1+k} + \frac{D_0(1+g)^2}{(1+k)^n} + \frac{D_0(1+g)^3}{(1+k)^3} + \ldots + \frac{D_0(1+g)^n}{(1+k)^n},$$

i.e.

$$P_0 = D_0\left[\frac{1+g}{1+k} + \frac{(1+g)^2}{(1+k)^2} + \ldots + \frac{(1+g)^n}{(1+k)^n}\right]. \qquad (*)$$

Multiplying each side of the equation by $(1+k)/(1+g)$, we obtain

$$P_0\frac{(1+k)}{(1+g)} = D_0\left[1 + \frac{1+g}{1+k} + \frac{(1+g)^2}{(1+k)^2} + \ldots + \frac{(1+g)^n}{(1+k)^{n-1}}\right]; \qquad (**)$$

then taking $(*)$ from $(**)$ we obtain

$$P_0\left[\frac{(1+k)}{(1+g)} - 1\right] = D_0\left[1 - \frac{(1+g)^n}{(1+k)^n}\right].$$

Therefore if the rate of interest, k, is greater than the rate of growth, g, then as $n \to \infty$, $(1+g)^n/(1+k)^n \to 0$.

In simple terms this means that if $k > g$ then $(1+g)/(1+k) < 1$. Any number less than one when multiplied by itself becomes smaller. In the equation given, $(1+g)^n/(1+k)^n$ means $(1+g)/(1+k)$ multiplied by itself n times, thus as n becomes large, tending towards infinity, the value of $(1+g)^n/(1+k)^n$ will become very small, tending towards zero, and thus the term can be ignored as it is of little significance. This phenomenon can be illustrated by multiplying 0.4 by itself 10 times. $(0.4)^{10} = 0.0001$, which can be seen to be of very little significance compared with 1.

Therefore

$$P_0\left[\frac{(1+k)}{(1+g)} - 1\right] = D_0, \qquad \text{or} \qquad P_0\left[\frac{(1+k)-(1+g)}{1+g}\right] = D_0,$$

i.e.

$$P_0 = D_0\frac{(1+g)}{(k-g)}.$$

If, however, the rate of growth of the dividend is greater than the cost of capital, we must discount the forecast dividends for the desired time horizon in order to arrive at a value for the share.

Estimation of the variables

There remains the problem of estimating the growth rate (g) and the cost of capital (k). Of these g is the simpler to estimate as it is usually possible to examine past data for the company and so estimate its past dividend growth rate. This, of course, assumes that the past rate will provide a good estimate of future growth. If other information about the expected future dividend pattern is available, extrapolation from past data may not be necessary.

Care should be taken to ensure that the dividends per share are adjusted to take account of any rights issue or other capital changes that may have taken place in the period under review.

EXAMPLE 9.1

Consider a company which has paid the following dividends:

Year	Dividend (pence per share)
1970	6.0
1971	6.2
1972	6.4
1973	6.8
1974	6.8
1975	7.2
1976	7.3
1977	7.5
1978	7.8

Graphically the above can be represented as shown in Figure 9.1.

Sophisticated mathematical techniques are available which can be used to estimate the average percentage growth in dividends for the period, but we will describe a simple and quick method which will often give a reasonable first approximation.

We can see that dividends have increased from 6.0p per share in 1970 to 7.8p per share in 1978. A visual inspection of the graph indicates that these observations are reasonably close to the trend and it therefore seems safe to use them. The average increase in dividends is

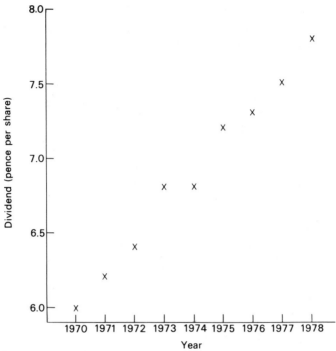

Figure 9.1

$1.8/8 = 0.22\text{p}$ per year, but we are seeking the average percentage growth g, which can be calculated as follows:

$$D_0(1+g)^8 = D_8,$$

where D_0 is the 1970 dividend and D_8 is the 1978 dividend, i.e.

$$6.0(1+g)^8 = 7.8,$$

$$\frac{1}{(1+g)^8} = \frac{6.0}{7.8} = 0.77.$$

$(1+g)^8$ and hence g can be calculated by the use of logarithms, but an easier way is to make use of present value tables which give the value of $1/(1+g)^n$ for different values of g and n. If we use the tables where $n = 8$ we find that

g	Present value
0.02	0.853
0.03	0.789
0.04	0.731

We can see that g lies between 0.03 and 0.04 and we could probably accept an estimate of say 0.035 ($3\frac{1}{2}\%$). Given the other problems of estimation there seems little point in interpolating between 0.03 and 0.04 to find a more exact figure.

Where, however, the growth rate of the annual dividend is not constant in the period under consideration, some approximation must be made, such as taking a geometric mean[5] of the growth rates in the period under consideration.

Alternatively it may be possible to identify a cyclical trend in the dividend pattern and this could be used to forecast the dividends for the next 5 years, using a mean growth rate thereafter. In this way it is often possible to obtain a reasonable estimate of value from the dividend valuation model, i.e.

$$P_0 = \frac{D_1}{(1+k)} + \frac{D_2}{(1+k)^2} + \frac{D_3}{(1+k)^3} + \frac{D_4}{(1+k)^4} + \frac{D_5 + D_5\frac{(1+g)}{(k-g)}}{(1+k)^5}$$

(Since $P_5 = D_5[(1+g)/(k-g)]$ this is simply the discounting of expected cost flows over a 5-year time horizon.)

Throughout the analysis which has been carried out so far it has been assumed that the cost of capital can be determined, and the proposition that it is the return which could be achieved by investment in a bank deposit account has not been retracted. It will, however, be clear that in the absence of unexpected inflation an investment in a deposit account with a sound bank can be regarded as a risk-free investment while it is evident that investment in the shares of a limited company is not risk free.

The risk associated with investment in the shares of a limited company can be explained in two main ways. First, the interest element, or dividend for ordinary shares, is not guaranteed but may fluctuate with the fortunes of the company and the whim of the directors. Second, the ability to recover one's capital at the end of the 'investment period' is dependent upon the sale of those shares. Since the sale of shares requires a market transaction the recovery of capital is dependent upon the state of the market and is by no means guaranteed.

5 The geometric mean of n items is the nth root of the product of those items, e.g. the geometric mean, g, of the growth rates for periods 1 and 2, g_1 and g_2 is given by $g = \sqrt{g_1 \times g_2}$. This mean is appropriate for our analysis since the mean g for which we are searching is such that

$$D_0(1+g)^n = D_0(1+g_1)(1+g_2)\ldots(1+g_n)$$
$$= D_0 \prod_{j=1}^{n} (1+g_j).$$

It therefore seems reasonable that an investor will require a higher return from a risky investment compared with a risk-free investment. Strictly this depends on the assumption that the investor is risk averse, i.e. that he would prefer the certainty of receiving £X rather than enter an arrangement whereby he has a 50% chance of receiving £$(X + Y)$ and a 50% chance of receiving £$(X - Y)$. A risk preferer might favour the risky prospect and therefore expect a lower rate on a risky investment because he enjoys the uncertainty and is attracted by the possibility of higher returns. Most investors may be assumed to be risk averse, an assumption that is evidenced by the taking out of insurance policies to reduce the level of risk experienced in life.

The introduction of risk into this analysis makes the estimation of the cost of capital more difficult. In practice the problem is often tackled by inflating the cost of capital based on a risk-free investment by a premium determined on some subjective basis depending on the investor's view of the riskiness of the investment. There are theoretical objections to this approach which are based upon the subjectivity of the risk assessment, and theoretical models[6] have also been formulated relating the premium to some objective measure of the risk of the proposed investment.

A further complicating factor in determining the cost of capital is that of a changing price level. If the price level of goods and services which would otherwise be bought with the capital that is invested is subject to change, then the value of the capital invested by the individual will change as its purchasing power will change. There are basically two ways of dealing with inflation in the valuation model.

The first is to adjust all items to real terms by expressing all cash flows in terms of purchasing power of a common, usually the current, date. However, if this is done then the cost of capital should also be measured in real terms to ensure that inflation is not counted twice.

The real cost of capital (for an investment of given level of risk), r, can be estimated as follows:

Let k be the 'nominal' cost of capital (i.e. the actual rate of return which is required on an investment of the given level of risk) and let m be the annual rate of inflation. Assume that £1.00 is invested at the start of the year; this is equivalent to an investment of £$1(1 + m)$ in year-end pounds. However, at the year end the investor will receive

---

6 One such well-documented model is the 'capital asset pricing model'. This model is described in most finance textbooks, e.g. J. C. Van Horne, *Financial Management and Policy*, 6th edn, Prentice-Hall, Englewood Cliffs, N.J., 1983; H. Levy and M. Sarnat, *Capital Investment and Financial Decisions*, 2nd edn, Prentice-Hall, London, 1982.

£1$(1 + k)$, therefore the real rate of interest, r, is given by the equation

$$£1(1 + m)(1 + r) = £1(1 + k)$$

or

$$1 + m + r + mr = 1 + k.$$

If we assume that mr is very small, since it is the product of two very small numbers, both much less than 1, then we can state that $r = k - m$.

The estimate, therefore, of the real cost of capital is the nominal cost less the expected change in the price index.

The second alternative for valuing the investment in ordinary shares is to express all the cash flows which have been predicted in money terms at their expected price levels and to discount these cash flows at the money ('nominal') cost of capital. This method is probably simpler to understand since money figures will be used throughout the analysis, reducing the conceptual problems of identifying 'real' monetary units.

The determination of the cost of capital does, in the final analysis, depend upon the opportunity cost approach. The opportunity cost of an investment is the best alternative return which has been foregone by selecting this specific investment. This approach to determining the cost of capital is one of the most useful approaches available to those involved in the valuation of securities since it enables an estimate of the cost of capital to be made by comparison with other available investments. When such a comparison is being made it is important that the risk characteristics of the alternative investments are sufficiently alike to make the comparison meaningful.

This opportunity cost method of comparison is then the dominant approach used by market participants in their valuation calculations, especially in the case of shares in unquoted companies or in the search for underpriced shares in quoted companies. The typical procedure that would be followed would be to identify a comparable quoted company and to obtain its dividend yield (see below) which represents the first approximation to the opportunity cost of capital. This dividend yield will then be adjusted upwards by about a quarter to a third to reflect the lack of marketability of the unquoted shares. Additional adjustments will usually be made to reflect other differences between shares in the quoted company and those in the unquoted company. These might include differences in dividend cover, asset backing or growth prospects. The adjusted dividend yield will then be used as the cost of capital in order to capitalize the dividends of the unquoted share.

The opportunity cost method is therefore theoretically justifiable and applicable in practice: there are, however, two main practical problems inherent in this approach. There is the problem that no two companies are exactly alike, and great care must be taken when selecting a company with which comparisons are to be made. Ideally companies being compared should be in the same industry, be of approximately the same size and operate in the same market as a company whose shares are being valued. It is unlikely that the ideal company will be found. The other problem is that comparison can be made in respect of more than one aspect of a company's performance. It is rather like the problem faced by a judge in a beauty contest. Most people would not rank the participants in terms of only one of their attributes; they are likely to consider faces, figures, complexion, hair, etc., and balance these factors in their own minds before coming to a ranking decision. Similarly, when comparing the results of two companies, one would have to consider a number of factors in addition to the level of dividends upon which we have concentrated so far. These factors would be the assets and earnings of the companies because these will influence the expectation of future dividends. Only if the companies have sufficient earnings will they be able to maintain their dividend pay out.

The valuation of unquoted shares

In this section of the chapter we will first consider the main stock exchange indicators which provide a basis for comparison of companies. We will then present an example dealing with the valuation of the shares of an unquoted company.

In order to discuss the main stock exchange indicators we will make use of a hypothetical quoted company whose summarized accounts for the year t_0 to t_1 are given below:

Profit and loss account for the period t_0 to t_1

	£000s
Turnover	2000
Earnings	200
less Corporation Tax (at 52% of taxable profit)	80
	120
Dividends paid	60
Unappropriated earnings for the period	60
Retained earnings at t_0	400
Retained earnings at t_1	460

Balance sheets

	t_0 £000s	t_1 £000s
Net assets	£1000	£1060
Financed by		
1 million 50p ordinary shares	500	500
Retained earnings	400	460
	900	960
9% debentures 1990	100	100
	1000	1060

At time t_1 the companies' share are quoted at £1.50. For the period t_0 to t_1 the basic rate of Income Tax is 30% and the rate for Advance Corporation Tax (ACT) is three-sevenths.

In this section we will examine five ratios – the dividend yield, the dividend cover, the earnings per share, the price/earnings ratio and the earnings yield. Four of these ratios include the price of the company's shares and this can be used to make a direct comparison between the price of one share with another; the dividend cover ratio is different in that it serves as an indicator of risk associated with the dividend as well as giving some indication of the management's distribution policy.

Dividend yield
The dividend yield provides a measure of the return that the investor will receive on his investment. It is calculated on a pre-tax basis (for the recipient) and hence the dividend figure included in the calculation will be the gross dividend, i.e. the net cash payment received by the shareholder plus the tax credit.

In our example the net dividend per share is given by £60 000/1 000 000 = 6p and, as the rate of ACT is 3/7, the gross dividend is $6 + 6 \times 3/7 = 8.57$p. The dividend yield is then given by

$$\text{Dividend yield} = \frac{\text{Gross dividend per share}}{\text{Market price per share}} \times 100\%$$

$$= \frac{8.57}{150} \times 100 = 5.7\%.$$

It should be noted at this point that companies may declare a dividend of a certain percentage of the ordinary share capital. This means that the dividend per share is that percentage of the nominal value of the ordinary share capital and should not be confused with the dividend yield. Thus, the dividend declared by the company in our example was 6p per share, and the shares have a nominal value of 50p each. The percentage dividend declared would therefore have been 12%.

Dividend cover
The purpose of this ratio is to help assess the likelihood that management will not have to reduce the dividend from its current level. The dividend cover is the ratio between the profit, excluding extraordinary items, attributable to the ordinary shareholders (i.e. profit after tax and any preference dividends) and the current dividend.

In the case of our example, profit attributable to shareholders is £120 000 and the dividend declared is £60 000. Therefore dividend cover = 120 000/60 000 = 2.

In the USA the reciprocal of the dividend cover, the payment ratio, is a more commonly used statistic.

The position is more complicated where distribution of the full earnings would involve irrecoverable ACT and hence increase the taxation charge in the profit and loss account. In such cases a better method of calculating dividend cover would be:

$$\frac{\text{Dividend}}{\text{cover}} = \frac{\text{Maximum dividend payable out of profits for the year}}{\text{Actual dividend for year}}.$$

To give an example, let us consider a company which has both UK and overseas trading income. Let us assume that the rate of UK Corporation Tax is 50%, the rate of ACT is three-sevenths and the rate of overseas tax is 60%. The summarized profit and loss account is as follows:

	£000s	£000s
Profit before taxation		
UK		130
Overseas		76
		206
less Taxation (based on taxable profits)		
UK (50% × £100 000)	50	
Overseas (60% × £60 000)	36	86
Profit after taxation		120
less Dividend proposed		60
Retained profit for year		60

The ACT payable is three-sevenths of any dividend, but the maximum ACT which may be relieved in this year is 30% of the UK taxable profit, that is 30% of £100 000. The maximum dividend payable is therefore calculated as follows:

$$D = £120\,000 + £30\,000 - (3/7)D,$$
$$(10/7)D = £150\,000,$$
$$D = £105\,000.$$

Payment of a dividend of £105 000 would involve a payment of ACT of £45 000, of which only £30 000 would be relieved. Hence an hypothetical profit and loss account would appear as follows:

	£000s	£000s
Profit before taxation (as above)		206
less Taxation (as above)	86	
Unrelieved ACT	15	101
	—	
		105
less Maximum dividend payable		105

On this basis our dividend cover is given by

$$\text{Dividend cover} = \frac{\text{Maximum dividend payable}}{\text{Dividend for year}}$$
$$= \frac{105}{60}$$
$$= 1.75.$$

Earnings per share
The earnings per share ratio is one that is very simple in concept, but which is often difficult to calculate in practice. The basic concept is that the earnings of the company for the year should be apportioned to the ordinary shares in issue to give an indication of the amount of earnings which would be available to the holder of one ordinary share. This simple concept thus enables the earnings associated with holding an ordinary share in one company to be compared with those associated with holding an ordinary share in another company.

It is, however, on this matter of comparability that complications can and do arise. If the ratio is to be used meaningfully then it must be calculated on a similar basis for every company, and the earnings must be representative of the company's earnings potential. It is clear that the earnings stated in companies' reports are not necessarily comparable with one another because different accounting policies may have been applied as there will have been differing levels of earnings from non-trading transactions which will not be representative of the companies' earnings potentials, also the levels of taxation incurred may not have been consistent, and one of the main reasons for the inconsistency of tax charges is because a company may have incurred irrecoverable ACT, thus increasing its tax charge because of its dividend policy.

In order to increase comparability, the earnings per share figure should be calculated on the consolidated profit of the period (after tax and after deducting minority interests and preference dividends but before taking into account extraordinary items) divided by the number of equity shares in issue and ranking for dividend in respect of the period.[7]

This still leaves the problem of irrecoverable ACT or unrelieved overseas tax arising from the payment or proposed payment of dividends. It can be argued that if such tax reduces the earnings available then this is a management decision and the reduced level of earnings should be shown in the calculation. This calculation using the higher tax charge in arriving at earnings is known as the net basis of calculating earnings per share.

The alternative argument is that the reported earnings per share should not be affected by the level of dividends actually payable when the figure is desired for the comparison of the performances of companies. In this case the lower tax charge that would have occurred had no dividend been declared is used in calculating the ratio and is known as the nil distribution earnings per share.

For companies that do not suffer irrecoverable ACT or unrelieved overseas tax there will be no difference between the net basis and the nil distribution basis of calculating earnings per share. We will ensure that this is the situation which we face in our example (*see below*), where there are also no extraordinary items.

Hence, if the earnings for the year attributable to the ordinary shareholders is £120 000 and the number of shares in issue is 1 000 000, then the earnings per share ratio is 12p.

Some of the other problems which may occur in the calculation of the earnings per share, and a discussion of SSAP 3, will be found in the appendix to this chapter (p. 316).

---

7 *See* SSAP 3, Para. 10.

Price to earnings ratio

While the security valuation model developed so far rightly concentrates upon the dividend to be expected, consideration is given in practice to the company's earnings. This has been found to be useful because earnings represent an upper limit for dividend distribution and because dividend restraint has been imposed upon companies, from time to time, distorting the valuation calculations.

The most common valuation tool based on earnings is the price to earnings (P/E) ratio, which is calculated as follows:

$$P/E \text{ ratio} = \frac{\text{Price per share}}{\text{Earnings per share}}.$$

In the case under examination, the earnings per share is 12p, as we showed previously, and the share price is £1.50. Hence

$$P/E \text{ ratio} = \frac{150}{12} = 12.5.$$

The P/E ratio shows the investor the numbers of years' earnings that he will purchase with his investment and enables him to compare this investment with alternatives. The flaw in the argument is, of course, that the P/E ratio is based on the last known earnings figure while the investor is 'buying' future earnings. Thus the shares of a company whose earnings are expected to grow will, all other things being equal, have a higher P/E ratio than the shares of a company whose earnings are not expected to increase. Similarly, a company whose earnings are considered by the market to be risky will have shares with a lower P/E ratio than a company with a more certain earnings stream.

Earnings yield

The earnings yield is an alternative way of relating the company's earnings to its share price and is given by

$$\text{Earnings yield} = \frac{\text{Earnings per share}}{\text{Share price}} \times 100\%.$$

Unfortunately, the value of earnings per share most commonly used in such calculations is based on different assumptions from the value of earnings per share used to calculate the P/E ratio. For the purposes of calculating the earnings yield the earnings per share figure is the maximum dividend that could have been declared from the profits for the year, i.e. the grossed up earnings to allow for the tax credit; the so-called 'full distribution' basis (*see* page 308). It is therefore necessary to determine whether the figure being used for valuation purposes is gross or net of tax so that consistent comparisons may be made.

EXAMPLE 9.2: VALUATION OF THE SHARES OF AN UNQUOTED COMPANY

The basic principle is that the value is the price that the shares would fetch if sold on the open market on the date in respect of which the shares are being valued. As was stated earlier this is done by looking at the price of shares of similar, but quoted, companies.

X Limited is an unquoted company whose accounts for the last 4 years disclose the following:

Balance sheets

End of year	1	2	3	4
	£000s	£000s	£000s	£000s
Net assets	£850	£1 000	£990	£1 110
Share capital				
£1 ordinary shares	500	500	500	500
Retained earnings	200	300	390	510
Loans	150	200	100	100
	£850	£1 000	£990	£1 110

Results

	Year 1	Year 2	Year 3	Year 4
	£000s	£000s	£000s	£000s
Earnings after tax	150	160	180	220
Dividend	50	60	90	100

We will attempt to place a value on the shares of X Limited as at the end of year 4 on the assumption that the shares being valued represent only a small proportion of the total issue.

There are two quoted companies, A plc and B plc, which appear to be similar to X Limited. The *Financial Times* listing at the end of year 4 shows the following:

High	Low	Stock	Price	+ or −	Div. net	Cover	Div. yield gross	P/E
135	100	A plc 50p ord.	130	+ 2	4.9	1.857	5.4	10
90	60	B plc 25p ord.	80	− 1	2.5	3.689	4.5	6

The 'price' is, of course, the price per share quoted in pence at the end of the day's business while 'high' and 'low' are the highest and lowest prices achieved during the preceding 12 months '+ or −' shows the change from the closing price on the preceding day. 'Div net' is the net dividend, i.e. before the addition of the tax credit while 'Cover' is the dividend cover. The yield is the dividend yield, which is calculated on the value of the dividend and associated tax credit, while the P/E ratio is calculated on the 'net' distribution basis (i.e. the earnings per share figure is computed after deducting the whole of the tax charge including irrecoverable ACT and irrecoverable overseas tax arising from a dividend distribution).

We will assume that none of the companies involved in the analysis has suffered irrecoverable ACT or overseas tax during the period under review.

We will now calculate the earnings per share, dividend per share and dividend cover for X Limited for the last four years:

| | Year | | | |
	1	2	3	4
Earnings per share	30p	32p	36p	44p
Dividends per share, net	10p	12p	18p	20p
Dividends per share, gross	14.6p	17.2p	25.7p	28.5p
Dividend cover	3.0	2.7	2.0	2.2

Note that the dividend cover calculation is based on the net dividend and that it has been assumed that the rate of ACT has been $3/7$ throughout the period.

We can see that both the earnings and dividends per share have grown steadily over the period. These are expressed in monetary terms and in a full analysis we should attempt to eliminate the effect of inflation. However, we will assume that the figures for year 4 which will be used in the comparison are not unrepresentative of the period.

The dividend cover has declined over the period from 3.0 to 2.2. The most recent figure is still acceptable and the decline should not, all other things being equal, affect the valuation, since it would appear that the dividend can be maintained given that it is more than twice covered.

Now it is clear from comparisons of dividend cover that X Limited lies between A plc and B plc. We will carry out calculations in order to estimate the price of X Limited in comparison to A plc and B plc, and it is worth noting that it will be necessary for the comparison company to have similarly assessed growth prospects for the valuations derived to be useful.

First we shall make an estimate of the share value using a dividend yield approach.

The gross dividend per share for X Limited is 28.5p. The gross dividend yield for A plc is 5.4%. In order to adjust the figure for X Limited being an unquoted company we might increase it by about a third, giving a level of comparison of about 7%. Thus we could produce a value for the shares of X Limited of £(0.285/0.07) = £4.07. Alternatively, if we compare X Limited with B plc we would expect a gross dividend yield of about 6% (4.5% × 1.33). Thus we would produce a value for the shares of X Limited of £(0.285/0.06) = £4.75.

The dividend valuation approach therefore gives values of £4.07 and £4.75.

We may similarly attempt to carry out a valuation using an earnings approach. Again we must adjust the P/E ratios of the quoted companies by about one-third to allow for the fact that X Limited is unquoted. Thus we would apply P/E ratios of about 7 and 4 in comparison with A plc and B plc.

The earnings per share of X Limited is 44p, thus the application of an earnings-based approach gives valuations for X Limited's shares of £3.08 and £1.76.

We would also look at the asset backing of X Limited's shares. This can be done using the net book value of the assets as disclosed by the historical cost accounts:

Net book value of assets at the end of year 4	= £1 110 000
Loans outstanding	= £ 100 000
Net book value of assets less liabilities	= £1 010 000
Number of shares	= £ 500 000
Net book value per share	= £2.05

If the shares are being valued on the assumption that the business is a going concern then the above figure may be of dubious value, but it might give some indication of the lowest possible share valuation. An examination of the current value of the assets may also be of interest, but this is likely to be of much greater relevance to a potential purchaser of a controlling interest in the business, which was discussed in detail in the preceding chapter.

Thus, we have five possible valuations of a share in X Limited:

(a) book value per share   £2.05

    (b) comparison with A plc

        (i) on dividend yield   £4.07

        (ii) on P/E ratio   £3.08

    (c) comparison with B plc

        (i) on dividend yield   £4.75

        (ii) on P/E ratio   £1.76

These figures represent a very large range, and it is obvious that if the company being considered is not comparable on a dividend cover basis with the quoted company a large discrepancy of prices between the earnings-based figure and the dividend-based figure will result, even though the growth prospects might be similarly assessed.

The wide range produced in the above analysis probably stems from the different individual cover between X Limited and B plc although it will be necessary to consider whether there are other significant differences between the three companies. It seems unlikely that X Limited will increase its dividend cover to approximate with that of B plc, and therefore in the absence of evidence of comparability of other factors we will ignore the comparison with that company. It is also unlikely that X Limited will be broken up, and therefore a reasonable range for the valuation of the shares of X Limited would seem to be between £3.00 and £4.00.

Whilst it is often necessary to value unquoted shares by reference to the market value of otherwise comparable quoted shares it must be noted that the method does suffer from many severe limitations in that (a) the dividend policies of unquoted companies tend to be different from and less stable than those of their quoted counter-parts: (b) the asset base and its financing of unquoted companies is likely to be different from the quoted companies with which they will be compared, the quoted companies being on the whole less volatile; (c) the value of quoted companies' shares is dependent upon the market and therefore will be volatile and not necessarily equal to their intrinsic worth; (d) quoted companies have been subject to dividend restraint in certain periods whilst private companies have not been so much affected, especially where the close company provisions have applied.

The valuation of shares cannot be made simply by application of formulae. The valuer must balance the information derived from an analysis such as that described above with other information and, ultimately, apply his intuition and judgement before arriving at his conclusion.

Some, but by no means all, of the other factors which might be considered are as follows: (a) whether there are any restrictions upon the transfer of shares and the nature of any such restrictions; (b) the history and prospects of the company and the industries in which it operates; (c) the nature and quality of the company's management; (d) the prospects of a takeover or a merger; (e) the impact of inflation; (f) the results of a more detailed analysis of the company's accounts as discussed in Chapter 18.

The valuation of shares for statutory purposes

In valuing shares for statutory purposes such as the calculation of the liability of an individual to Capital Gains Tax or Capital Transfer Tax, an agreement of valuation must be reached with the Shares Valuation Division of the Inland Revenue. This body has shown that it tends to calculate the value of an unquoted shareholding by comparison with the value of shares in similar quoted companies, making allowance for the differing circumstances of the companies and also discounting the share price so derived by between 10% and 35% on the basis of the restrictions of the articles of association of the company and the size of the shareholding in question.

In negotiations for the statutory valuation of shares it is necessary to consider the possibility of capital appreciation in addition to the points made in the previous section. Potential capital appreciation will be taken into account in the statutory valuation when it can be shown that it is likely to occur, such would be the case if, for example, the directors were already considering a new issue of shares at a higher price than the current valuation.

It must be remembered that the requirement for the valuation of shares for Capital Gains Tax, as laid down in Schedule 10 of the Finance Act 1975, is that the value is the assumed price of an armslength transaction given all the information a prudent purchaser might reasonably acquire. This is open to many interpretations and serves to illustrate the large range of values which could be maintained in the negotiations for the statutory valuations of shares in unquoted companies.

Readers who are faced with the problem of statutory valuation are urged to make reference to recent appeals dealt with by the Special Commissioners and the High Court to acquaint themselves with current precedent. These are frequently reported in the weekly and monthly accounting journals.

Appendix: SSAP 3, 'Earnings per share'

The importance of the earnings per share (EPS) measure and the uses to which it is put was discussed in the main body of the chapter. EPS is the subject of SSAP 3 which requires all companies having a listing on a recognized stock exchange for any class of equity to display *on the face* of its audited profit and loss account its EPS on a net basis (*see* page 309) for both the current year and the corresponding previous period. The importance placed by the ASC on the EPS measure can be gauged from the specific requirement that it be shown in a prominent position and not buried in the notes of accounts. The basis on which the figures are calculated, in particular the earnings and the number of equity shares, must also be shown but this may be done either on the profit and loss account or in the notes.

Since the primary use of the EPS measure is in decisions regarding the valuation of equity shares the relevant earnings figure is that which is relevant to equity shareholders (i.e. after the preference dividend and any minority interest) on 'normal' activities, i.e. the earnings figure before the addition (or subtraction) of extraordinary items (as defined in SSAP 6[8]).

Thus the definition of EPS as stated in Para. 10 of SSAP 3 is:

> The profit in pence attributable to each equity share, based on the consolidated profit of the period after tax and after deducting minority interests and preference dividends, but before taking into account extraordinary items, divided by the number of equity shares in issue and ranking for dividend in respect of the period.

In many instances the EPS figure can be calculated with ease but there are some potentially complicating factors including situations where the tax charge is affected by the level of distributions, when losses are incurred and where there either have been or there might be, changes in a company's capital structure involving equity capital. Each of these will be discussed below.

Taxation and the level of dividends

Whilst in most cases the bulk or the whole of a company's liability to taxation is unaffected by the size of its dividends, there are some instances where this will not be the case. The exceptions occur either because the level of dividends are such as to make it impossible to recover, in the immediate future, ACT paid, or because the dividends

---

8 SSAP 6, 'Extraordinary items and prior year adjustments'.

restrict the amount of overseas taxation that can be relieved.[9] In these exceptional cases the question arises as to what should be included as the tax deduction in arriving at the earnings figure – the actual tax charge or that which would have been charged if no distribution had been made.

If the actual tax charge is used we have what is termed the *net* basis of calculating EPS while if the alternative is adopted the result is called the *nil distribution* basis. The latter term is self-explanatory but it should be noted that even if the nil distribution basis is adopted any tax resulting from the payment of a preference dividend should be deducted in calculating the earnings figure.

The main argument in favour of the use of the nil distribution basis is that it aids comparability between companies in that the EPS is not dependent on the level of distribution. Use of the net basis is justified by the view that it takes into account all relevant factors including the additional tax liabilities inherent in the dividend policy adopted by the directors for which they should be accountable to shareholders. The ASC obviously believe that stewardship is more important than comparability as SSAP 3 specifies that the net basis should be used. However, the desirability, but not obligation, of also showing the EPS using the nil basis where the two methods would yield significantly different results is stressed.

Losses and unpaid preference dividends

If the earnings attributable to equity shareholders is negative the EPS should be calculated in the normal way with the result shown as a loss per share.

A related issue is the treatment of unpaid preference dividends. If the shares are cumulative the dividend for the period should be taken into account in arriving at the EPS whether or not it has been declared. In the case of non-cumulative preference shares only the dividend paid or proposed should be included.

Actual changes in equity share capital

It will be helpful to use a simple example. Let us assume that MM plc's earnings attributable to equity shareholders for 19X5 is £2.0

9 Readers who are unfamiliar with this subject should consult any standard text on Corporation Tax such as S. W. Mayson, *A Practical Approach to Revenue Law*, Financial Training Publications Limited, London, 1983.

million and that at 1 January, the start of its financial year, it had in issue 20 million ordinary shares of 25p each and that on 1 October it issued a further 4 million 25p ordinary shares. What is the EPS for 19X5? The answer depends on the source of the issue, specifically whether it was a scrip (or bonus) issue or whether the issue was for cash (or other consideration) and, if for cash, etc., whether the issue was at, or below, the market price.

A scrip issue does not raise extra cash and merely represents a re-arrangement of the equity interest in a company in that a transfer is made from reserves to equity share capital. There are simply more shares in issue at the end of the year than there were at the beginning and, hence, to show the EPS appropriate to the new capital structure all that is required is to apportion the earnings over the shares in issue at the year end, 24 million and thus the EPS is $(£2\,000\,000/24\,000\,000) \times 100 = 8.0$p.

To assist comparability, the EPS for the corresponding period should be adjusted accordingly. Similar considerations apply if shares are split into shares of a smaller nominal value.

Let us now assume that the issue of shares was made at the full market price, whilst recognizing that in practice such an issue is nowadays a rare event, as most issues for cash take the form of rights issues to existing shareholders at a price below that which prevails on the market. To calculate the EPS where there has been an issue at the full market price all that is necessary is to calculate the *weighted* average number of shares in issue in the course of the year and divide the result into the total earnings of the year. The average is weighted to take account of the timing of the share issue.

In this case the company had 20 million shares in issue for 9 months and 24 million for 3 months. The appropriate weightings to be applied are hence $\frac{3}{4}$ and $\frac{1}{4}$ and the weighted average is $\frac{3}{4} \times 20\,000\,000 + \frac{1}{4} \times 24\,000\,000 = 21\,000\,000$ with the new EPS $(£2\,000\,000/21\,000\,000) \times 100 = 9.5$p.

It will be noted that this figure exceeds the 8.0p per share in the scrip issue example and it will be instructive to consider why this is so. A company which makes a scrip issue raises no extra resources and hence, all other things being equal, will not increase its earnings. Thus the only effect of the scrip issue is to divide the earnings over a greater number of shares. In contrast if shares are issued for cash, extra resources are obtained which, it is hoped, will increase earnings in the future. If the new investment generates the same rate of return as the existing assets of the business, then, all other things being equal, the EPS after an issue at the full market price will be the same as that which prevailed before the issue. However, in practice it will take some time to deploy the additional resources and in the first instance the additional cash will earn a small or even a negative return, hence the issue of shares for cash will normally reduce the EPS (from that which applied before the issue) until the new investment comes on stream.

A rights issue lies somewhere between the two extremes of a scrip issue and an issue at the full market price in that it combines elements of both since whilst additional cash is raised the original shares lose some of their value.

In order to distinguish between the two elements of a rights issue it is necessary to find what is called the *theoretical ex-rights price*. This is the price per share following the issue which would make the stock market value of the company immediately after the rights issue equal to the sum of the market value before the announcement of the issue and the proceeds of the rights issue.[10] Once the theoretical ex-rights price is determined the EPS calculation can be made on the assumption that there were two transactions a scrip issue followed by an issue at the new market price.[11]

Let us assume that a company has in issue 12 000 shares which had a market price of £2 and 8 months after the start of the year makes a rights issue of 1 for every 3 shares held (a 1 for 3 issue) at a discount of 25%, i.e. 4000 shares were issued at a price of £1.5 each raising £6000. The theoretical ex-rights price, x, is given by:

$$16\,000x = 12\,000 \times £2 + 4\,000 \times £1.5$$
$$16\,000x = £24\,000 + £6\,000$$
$$x = £1.875.$$

We need to find the size of a hypothetical scrip issue which would, all other things being equal, have reduced the market price per share from £2 to £1.875.

10 The actual price per share following the issue is not likely to be equal to the theoretical ex-rights price as the actual price is likely to be affected by the market's expectations of future results and dividend policy. It might, for example, be thought that the total dividend per share would at least be held constant following the issue and hence the total dividend payable increased and this expectation might, of itself, increase the market price.

11 The same result would be achieved if it was assumed that the transactions were made in the reverse order, i.e. an issue at the market price followed by a scrip issue. The above method, however, accords with the description given in SSAP 3 and we will hence concentrate on that alternative.

Let x be the number of shares in issue following the scrip issue

then $x \times £1.875 = 12\,000 \times £2$

$$\text{or } x = 12\,000 \times \frac{£2}{£1.875} = 12\,800.$$

Thus the scrip issue would be such as to increase the number of shares in issue from $12\,000$ to $(12\,000 \times 2/1.875)$. We should note that the factor $2/1.875$ is the:

$$\frac{\text{Actual market price before the issue}}{\text{Theoretical ex-rights price}}.$$

We can now divide the rights issue into its two elements (a) the scrip issue and (b) the issue at the market price (or, in this case, at the theoretical ex-rights price). Thus:

(i) The company started with	12 000 shares
(ii) The hypothetical scrip issue increased the shares to $12\,000 \times 2/1.875$ or an additional	800 shares
(iii) The hypothetical issue of 3200 shares at £1.875 raised £6000	3 200 shares
Thus the company finished with	16 000 shares

To calculate the EPS it is necessary to remember that in the case of a scrip issue the earnings were simply divided by the number of shares ranking for dividend at the end of the year (irrespective of the date of the scrip issue) whilst in the case of an issue at market price the average number of shares was used (weighted on the basis of the time of the issue). To combine these two methods we draw a line after the hypothetical scrip issue and say that at the end of 8 months there were $12\,800$ ($12\,000 \times 2/1.875$) shares in issue but as the increase was due to a scrip issue we will calculate the EPS on the assumption that the company had $12\,800$ shares for the whole of the 8-month period. Thus the weighted average number of shares will be calculated on the basis that the company had $12\,000 \times 2/1.875$ shares for 8 months and $16\,000$ shares for 4 months. The weighted average number of shares is then:

$$12\,000 \times \frac{2}{1.875} \times \tfrac{2}{3} + 16\,000 \times \tfrac{1}{3} = 13\,867$$

and, if the earnings for the year were £1664, the EPS would be 12p.

The method described above is that recommended in Para. 18 of SSAP 3 which states that the factor which should be used to inflate the number of shares prior to the issue to adjust for the bonus element should be:

$$\frac{\text{Actual cum rights price on last day of quotation cum rights}}{\text{Theoretical ex-rights price}}.$$

In order to aid in comparability the EPS figure for the prior year needs to be adjusted to take account of the hypothetical scrip issue, if 12 000 shares were in issue for the whole of the proceeding year then for the purposes of restating the EPS this figure will be increased to 12 800, i.e. to 12 000 × (cum rights price)/(theoretical ex-rights price). Actually, a short cut can be taken as the same result can be obtained by multiplying the original EPS by the reciprocal of the above ratio, i.e. by (theoretical ex-rights price)/(cum rights price).[12]

Possible future changes in capital structure

If at the balance sheet date the company has contracted to issue shares at some time in the future the effect may be to dilute (reduce) the EPS in future. The same might happen if at the balance sheet date the company has already issued shares which have not yet ranked for dividend (and hence which have been excluded from the EPS calculation) but which may do so in the future. In such cases SSAP 3 requires that the fully diluted EPS be shown on the face of the profit and loss account together with the basic EPS so long as the dilution is material (5% is stated to be material for this purpose). Where there is a material dilution the standard requires that:

(a) equal prominence should be given to both the basic and fully diluted EPS,
(b) the basis of calculation of the diluted EPS figure should be disclosed and

12 Let P be the original EPS, P' the restated EPS, E the earnings, S the original number of shares in issue and F the ratio of the cum rights price to the theoretical ex-rights price. Then

$$P = \frac{E}{S}$$

and

$$P' = \frac{E}{SF} = P \times \frac{1}{F}.$$

(c) the fully diluted EPS for the corresponding period should only be shown if the assumptions on which it was based still apply.

The contract to issue further shares may be in the form of warrants or options to subscribe for equity shares in the company or may be in the form of convertible debentures, loan stock or preference shares.

The basic principle is to show the maximum effect of the possible dilution and hence if the terms of the issue of the options or convertible securities are such that the conversion ratio varies, e.g. if the number of equity shares which will be issued in respect of the conversion of each £1000 of convertible loan stock reduces over time, the greatest possible number of potential additional shares should be used in the calculation. Further it should be assumed that the conversion had been effected on the first day of the accounting period or, if later, the date of issue of the security.

It would clearly be misleading to treat, say, convertible loan stock as both loan stock and equity capital and hence when calculating the fully diluted EPS it is necessary to add to the basic earnings the interest (less taxation thereon) payable in respect of the convertible stock. Similarly it would be misleading to assume that the cash received from the exercise of an option to purchase equity shares would not increase earnings and hence in such circumstances SSAP 3 states that the earnings for the period should, for the purposes of the calculation, be increased by an amount equivalent to that which would have been earned had the proceeds of the exercise of the option been invested in $2\frac{1}{2}\%$ Consolidated Stock on the first day of the period at the closing price of the previous day. Note that if convertible loan stock is finally converted during the year it is still necessary to show the fully diluted EPS for the year.

When calculating the fully diluted EPS the denominator will always be greater than that used in the basic EPS calculation whilst in some circumstances the numerator will also be increased. Hence in some circumstances, such as a company with a low basic EPS and a large volume of convertible loan stock, the diluted EPS may actually be greater than the basic figure. In such cases SSAP 3 states that the conversion right would not be exercised and hence a fully diluted (or actually inflated) EPS figure should not be shown. If there is more than one type of security which falls to be treated as part of the calculation of the diluted EPS and if the inclusion of security would be to increase the basic EPS then that security should be totally excluded from the calculation.

In summary, SSAP 3 requires, in appropriate circumstances, the presentation of two figures for EPS on the face of the profit and loss account (with corresponding figures for the preceding period) – the basic and fully diluted figures and recommends the inclusion of a further figure in the notes to the accounts – with the basic EPS calculated on the nil distribution basis.

Some of the points covered in the Appendix are illustrated in Example 9A.1.

EXAMPLE 9A.1

A. PB plc's capital structure for the whole of the year ended 31 December 19X2 was as follows:

	£
200 000 £1 deferred ordinary shares	200 000
2 000 000 ordinary shares, 50p each	1 000 000
	1 200 000
Convertible loan stock (10%)	600 000
	£1 800 000

Notes
(a) The deferred ordinary shares will not rank for dividend until 1 January 19X9 at which date they will each be divided into two 50p ordinary shares which will rank *pari passu* with the ordinary shares then in issue.
(b) The loan stock is convertible into 50p ordinary shares on the following terms. Each £100 of loan stock is convertible into 60 shares if the option is exercised on 1 January 19X6 or 50 shares if exercised on 1 January 19X7.
(c) Under the terms of a share incentive scheme certain executives have the option to purchase a total of 100 000 ordinary shares for £1.2 each.
(d) PB plc's earnings per share for 19X7 was £320 000/£2 000 000 = 16.0p.

B. On 30 September 19X3 the company made a 1 for 4 rights issue for £1.4 per share. The actual cum rights price on the last day of quotation cum rights was £2.0. No shares were issued under the terms of the share incentive scheme in 19X3 nor was there any increase in the company's obligations under the scheme.

C. A summary of PB plc's profit and loss account for the year ended 31 December 19X3 is given below:

	£
Profit before interest and tax	860 000
less Interest	60 000
	800 000
less Corporation Tax at, say, 50%	400 000
Profit attributable to ordinary shareholders	£400 000

D. *Basic EPS* In order to calculate the basic EPS it is necessary to work out the theoretical ex-rights price, x.

$$2\,500\,000 \times £x = 2\,000\,000 \times £2 + 500\,000 \times £1.4$$
$$2\,500\,000 \times £x = £4\,000\,000 + £700\,000$$
$$x = £1.88.$$

The weighted average number of shares in issue for 19X3 is given by:

$$2\,000\,000 \times 2/1.88 \times 9/12 \quad = \quad 1\,595\,744$$
$$2\,500\,000 \times 3/12 \quad\quad\quad = \quad\;\; 625\,000$$

Weighted average $\quad\quad\quad\quad\; 2\,220\,744$

The basic EPS for 19X3 is

$$\frac{£400\,000}{2\,220\,744} = \underline{\underline{18.0p}}$$

and the restated EPS for 19X2 is

$$16 \times \frac{1.88}{2} = \underline{\underline{15.0p}}.$$

E. *Fully diluted EPS*

	19X3 (£)	19X2 (£)
Earnings attributable to ordinary shareholders	400 000	320 000
Add: Interest on convertible loan stock (less tax)	30 000	30 000
Earnings from proceeds of share option scheme (£120 000) at 9% in 19X3, 8% in 19X2 less tax		
(*see below*)	5 400	4 800
	£435 400	£354 800

(It has been assumed that the yield on $2\frac{1}{2}\%$ consolidated stock was 9% on 1.1.19X3 and 8% on 1.1.19X2.)

	19X3	19X2
Average number of ordinary shares	2 220 744	2 127 659[13]
Maximum increase due to:		
(i) Conversion of deferred shares	400 000	400 000
(ii) Conversion of loan stock	360 000	360 000
(iii) Options under incentive scheme	100 000	100 000
	3 080 744	2 987 659
Fully dilated EPS	14.1p	11.9p

Recommended reading

Janette Rutterford, *Introduction to Stock Exchange Investment*, Macmillan, London, 1984.

N. Eastway and H. Booth, *Practical Share Valuation*, Butterworths, London, 1983.

Christopher G. Glover, *The Valuation of Unlisted Shares*, Accountants Digest No. 132, ICAEW, London, 1983.

Statement of Standard Accounting Practice No. 3, *Earnings per Share*, ASC, London, 1972.

Questions

9.1 The valuation of unlisted shares is highly subjective, especially when the object is to fix a fair price for acquisition by the company or by the owner's fellow-shareholders.

You are required:
   (a) to set out the principal bases commonly used for valuing unlisted shares, distinguishing the situations in which such bases are most appropriate; and   (9 marks)
   (b) to evaluate critically the theoretical soundness of the said bases of valuation, and the extent to which they achieve approximate justice as between buyer and seller.   (7 marks)
                                                                     (16 marks)

A. Cert. A., Advanced Financial Accounting, Second paper, December 1983.

---

13 $2\,000\,000 \times 2/1.88 = 2\,127\,659.$

9.2 Engineering Products Ltd is a family business which has proved successful. Existing shareholders are planning to sell some of their shares to the public by way of an offer for sale. The directors have examined quoted companies making similar products and have decided that Machine Components Ltd provides a relevant comparison.

Summarized information relating to Machine Components Ltd (adjusted to reflect the current tax law) over the last five years includes

Earnings per share – current	3.00p
– average 1970–1974	2.00p
Price per share – current	24.00p
– range 1970–1974	10.00 to 40.00p
Dividend per share – current	1.50p
– average 1970–1974	1.20p
Book value of net assets per share – 1974	20.00p

Summarized financial data for Engineering Products Ltd includes

Balance Sheet as on 31 December 1974

	£
Authorised and issued share capital	
5 000 000 shares of 10p each	500 000
Accumulated reserves	600 000
Long term loans	400 000
	1 500 000
Fixed assets at cost, less depreciation	1 000 000
Net current assets	500 000
	1 500 000

Profit and Loss Accounts 1970 to 1974
(adjusted to current tax law)

	1970 £	1971 £	1972 £	1973 £	1974 £
Profit after tax	150 000	175 000	200 000	200 000	225 000
Dividend	50 000	50 000	50 000	100 000	100 000
Retention	100 000	125 000	150 000	100 000	125 000

You ascertain that:
(1) there has been no change in the issued share capital.
(2) the fixed assets include land which cost £50 000 and has recently been

revalued by professional experts at £150 000 in its current use and at £250 000 as housing land.

(3) it is expected that planning permission for the change of use will be obtained and that alternative premises can be obtained at an inclusive rent of £15 000 p.a.

You are required to:

(a) **calculate information in respect of Engineering Products Ltd similar to that relating to Machine Components Ltd,**

(b) **recommend a price range for the sale of 2 million shares to the public clearly indicating the factors that you have used in arriving at your recommendation, and**

(c) **explain briefly how (or if) and why (or why not) your recommendation would change if a sale to a single buyer of 3 million shares was being considered.** **(20 marks)**

ICAEW Financial Accounting II, July 1975.

9.3 It has been announced that Avaricious Ltd, a quoted company, has undertaken to purchase the whole of the issued share capital of Parochial Ltd, a private company carrying on business as wholesalers and retailers of wines and spirits.

The following are extracts from the accountants' report on Parochial Ltd.

Profit and Loss Accounts

Year ended 31 March	Note	1974 £'000	1975 £'000	1976 £'000	1977 £'000	1978 £'000
Sales		5 157	6 489	8 651	13 026	18 042
Cost of sales	1	5 013	6 299	8 375	12 647	17 520
		144	190	276	379	522
Interest on bank deposits		—	11	6	29	78
Profit before taxation		144	201	282	408	600
Taxation	2	55	106	125	223	306
Profit after taxation		89	95	157	185	294
Dividends – ordinary		27	17	22	15	20
Retained profits for year		62	78	135	170	274

Notes:

1. Cost of sales is stated after charging:

Depreciation	11	13	23	25	29
Directors' remuneration	57	52	59	77	80
Finance charges	5	6	17	3	4

2. Taxation comprises:

Corporation Tax	55	—	—	13	—
Deferred taxation	—	106	125	202	310
Prior year adjustments	—	—	—	2	(4)
Advance Corporation Tax written off	—	—	—	6	—
	55	106	125	223	306

Statement of Net Assets at 31 March 1978

	Note	£'000	£'000
Fixed assets	1		1 430
Investments			18
Current assets			
Stock		3 256	
Debtors		348	
Cash		4	
		3 608	
Current liabilities			
Creditors		2 378	
Loans		68	
Bank overdraft		617	
		3 063	
Net current assets			545
Deferred taxation	2		(696)
Net assets at 31 March 1978			1 297

Notes:

1. Fixed assets

	At cost £'000	Aggregate depreciation £'000	Net book value £'000
Freehold land and buildings –			
Warehouses etc.	241	—	241
Retail outlets	1 032	—	1 032
	1 273	—	1 273
Short leasehold property	58	14	44
Plant and motor vehicles	200	87	113
	1 531	101	1 430

2. Deferred taxation
   The balance at 31 March 1978 comprises:

	£'000
Stock relief	1335
Unutilized losses arising from	
stock relief claims	(606)
Advance corporation tax	(33)
	696

The liability to tax for accelerated capital allowances and capital gains rolled over, not included above, is estimated at £38 000 and £5500 respectively.

Two companies which are considered to be in the same line of business as Parochial Ltd are quoted and the most recent data from the *Financial Times* relating to them is shown below:

1978					+ or −	Div	Cover	Yield	
High	Low	Stock		Price		net		Gross	P/E
117½	87	Company	K						
		50p		103	+2	4.25	3.5	6.3	6.9
390	225	Company	L						
		10p		340	−1	4.4	4.8	2.0	16.2

You are required:
  (a) **to calculate for Parochial Ltd the dividend per share and cover, assuming that there are 400 000 shares of £1 each in issue** (4 marks),
  (b) **with the disclosed information to estimate, and justify, a value for Parochial Ltd** (15 marks), **and**
  (c) **to state, and explain the necessity for, three additional topics you would expect to find dealt with in the accountants' report** (6 marks). **(25 marks)**

ICAEW Financial Accounting II, December 1978.

9.4   Cosmos Limited is an unlisted private company, manufacturing electronic equipment. You have been its auditor for the three years ended 31 March 1982.

On 1 June 1982 you are consulted by S. Moon, a shareholder-director of Cosmos Limited and your personal client, who is thinking of selling his shareholding and leaving the company. The articles of association require him to offer his shares first to his fellow-shareholders. Only if none offers a reasonable price may he seek an outside purchaser. Moon estimates that his earnings in alternative employment are unlikely to exceed £15 000 in the first year.

You are required (on the basis of information given below):
  (a) **to estimate the highest, and lowest, prices per share that S. Moon can reasonably hope to obtain if he offers his holding of 50 000 £1 ordinary shares to his fellow-shareholders;** (15 marks)

(b) **to estimate the highest price per share that he can reasonably hope to obtain from an outside purchaser; and** (5 marks)

(c) **to advise S. Moon as to whether he should sell his shares and leave Cosmos Limited, or remain with it; his relations with his fellow-directors are good.** (10 marks)

(30 marks)

In your files you have the confidential profit and loss accounts submitted to the directors for the three years ended 31 March 1982, as summarized below.

Cosmos Limited
Profit and Loss Accounts

	Year ended 31 March		
	1980	*1981*	*1982*
	£'000s	£'000s	£'000s
Sales	3 000	3 600	4 000
Cost of sales (excluding depreciation)	(2 400)	(2 700)	(3 000)
Gross profit	600	900	1000
Directors' emoluments	(80)	(100)	(115)
Other cash overheads	(120)	(150)	(185)
Depreciation (straight line basis):			
Freehold buildings (5% p.a.)	(5)	(5)	(5)
Plant, fixtures and vehicles (25% p.a.)	(200)	(250)	(320)
Surpluses on disposal of plant, fixtures			
and vehicles	10	15	25
Net trading profit	205	410	400
Interest payable (gross):			
On 15% debentures	—	—	(38)
On bank overdraft	(10)	(25)	—
Net profit before taxation	195	385	362
Taxation (net)	(100)	(200)	(180)
Net profit after taxation	95	185	182
Extraordinary items (after taxation)	(2)	—	10
Net profit for year	93	185	192
Goodwill amortized	(2)	(2)	(2)
Dividends (net):			
On 10% Cumulative preference shares	(20)	(20)	(20)
On ordinary shares	(50)	(80)	(100)
Retained earnings for year	21	83	70

The latest balance sheet of the company (with corresponding figures for the previous year) is as follows, in summary form:

Cosmos Limited
Balance Sheet, 31 March 1982

Net Assets	Cost £'000s	Depre-ciation £'000s	Net £'000s	31.3.81 Net £'000s	Cost £'000s
Fixed assets					
Freehold land	50	—	50	50	50
Freehold buildings	100	50	50	55	100
Plant, fixtures and vehicles	1 280	640	640	600	1 000
	1 430	690	740	705	1 150
Goodwill unamortized			4	6	
			744	711	
Current assets					
Stocks:					
Raw materials	60				50
Work in progress	180				160
Finished goods	500				450
	740				660
Debtors *less* Provisions	350				315
Bank and cash balances	103				11
Prepayments	10				8
	1 203				994
less: *Current liabilities*					
Bank overdraft	—				75
Creditors and accruals	100				80
Mainstream Corporation Tax	37				179
Proposed dividend (net)	100				80
ACT thereon	43				34
	280				448
Net current assets			923	546	
			1667	1257	

Financed by
Share capital – Issued
   10% Cumulative preference

(£1)	200			200
Ordinary (£1)	500			400
	——	700	600	——
Reserves				
Share premium account	200			300
Retained earnings	420			350
	——	620	650	——
		1320	1250	
15% Debentures				
(repayable 1.4.86)		250	—	
Deferred taxation		97	7	
		1667	1257	

The capital structure of Cosmos Limited has changed as follows, over the last three years:

Issue capital as at 1 April 1979:
   200 000 10% Cumulative preference shares of £1 each, fully paid, issued at par; and
   250 000 Ordinary shares of £1 each, fully paid, issued at par.

Issued for cash at 1 April 1980:
   150 000 Ordinary shares of £1 each, fully paid, at £3.00 per share, ranking for dividend in 1980–81.

Bonus issued at 1 April 1981:
   100 000 Ordinary shares of £1 each, fully paid, capitalized from share premium account, ranking for dividend in 1981–82.

The ordinary shares carry one vote each at general meetings. The preference shares carry no votes unless their dividends are in arrear, when the shares carry one vote each.

The shareholdings and emoluments of the directors and their families, as at 31 March 1982, are shown below. None of the directors has a contract of service.

	Preference Shares	Ordinary Shares	Emoluments (£ p.a.) £
W. Starr (Chairman and Managing Director	—	200 000	40 000
Mrs W. Starr (his wife)	200 000	25 000	—
G. Planett (director)	—	150 000	30 000
R. Sunn (director)	—	75 000	25 000
S. Moon (director)	—	50 000	20 000
	200 000	500 000	£115 000

According to S. Moon, Cosmos Limited is facing strong Japanese competition. It cannot expect to do more than maintain its 1981–82 sales volume, or to raise its average selling prices by more than 10% per annum, the expected rate of inflation. On the basis of this and other information given by Moon, you draw up projected current cost accounts of Cosmos Limited for the year ending 31 March 1983, as follows:

Cosmos Limited
Current Cost Profit and Loss Account (projected)
Year ending 31 March 1983

	£'000s	£'000s	£'000s
Sales			4400
Cost of sales (HC, excluding depreciation)			(3 256)
HC gross profit			1 144
Directors' emoluments		(127)	
Other cash overheads		(203)	
Depreciation (net):			
Freehold buildings	(5)		
Plant, fixtures and vehicles	(300)		
		(305)	
			(635)
HC net trading profit			509
Current cost adjustments:			
Depreciation		(99)	
Cost of sales		(85)	
Monetary working capital		(25)	
			(209)
			300

CC net trading profit
Interest on 15% debentures (gross) (38)
Gearing adjustment 46
                                                            ——   8

CC net profit before taxation   308
Taxation (HC basis)   (240)

CC net profit after taxation   68
Goodwill amortization (HC basis)   (2)
Dividends (net):
  Preference   (20)
  Ordinary   (100)
                                                  ——   (120)
                                                            ——   (122)

CC retained (overdistributed) earnings for year   (54)

Current Cost Balance Sheet (projected)
31 March 1983

Net assets	Valuation £'000s	Depreciation £'000s	Net £'000s
Fixed assets			
Freehold land	132	—	132
Freehold buildings	220	132	88
Plant, fixtures and vehicles	1 650	825	825
	2 002	957	1 045
Goodwill Unamortised			2
			1 047
Current assets			
Stocks		826	
Debtors *less* Provisions		385	
Bank and cash balances		180	
Prepayments		11	
		1 402	

less *Current liabilities*

Creditors and accruals	110	
Mainstream Corporation Tax	202	
Proposed dividend (net)	100	
ACT thereon	43	
	455	
Net current assets		947
		1 994

Financed by
Share capital – issued

10% Cumulative preference (£1)	200	
Ordinary (£1)	500	
		700

Reserves

Share premium account	200	
Current cost reserve	378	
Retained earnings	366	
		944
		1 644
15% Debentures		250
Deferred taxation		100
		1 994

Note: The appropriate (pre-tax) rate of discount to be used in your calculations is 15% per annum. Corporation tax 52%, basic rate of income tax 30%. You may make any further (reasonable) assumptions that you wish, on matters not specifically dealt with in the question.

A. Cert. A. Advanced Financial Accounting, June 1982.

9.5 The boards of directors of three manufacturing companies, Aleph Limited, Beth Limited, and Gimel Limited (all unlisted), decide to amalgamate as from 1 January 1982. A new (listed) company, Daleth plc, is to be formed, of which the existing companies are to become subsidiaries. All three companies revalue their identifiable assets as at 31 December 1981, and their balance sheets then appear as follows (in summary form):

Balance Sheets, 31 December 1981

Net assets	Aleph Limited Valuation £'000s	Net £'000s	Beth Limited Valuation £'000s	Net £'000s	Gimel Limited Valuation £'000s	Net £'000s
Fixed assets						
Land	200	200	250	250	100	100
Buildings	1 000	800	1 100	850	600	500
Plant and Equipment	1 500	863	1 300	750	1 500	741
	£2 700	1 863	£2 650	1 850	£2 200	1 341
Current assets	£		£		£	
Stocks	600		500		400	
Debtors and prepayments	500		420		350	
Bank and cash balances	100		10		50	
	1 200		930		800	
less: *Current liabilities*						
Bank overdraft	—		191		—	
Creditors and accruals	300		280		220	
Corporation Tax – Current year (*less* ACT)	120		80		50	
Proposed dividend	100		20		50	
ACT on proposed dividend	43		9		21	
	563		580		341	
Net current assets		637		350		459
		£2 500		£2 200		£1 800
Financed by share capital (£1 shares)	£'000s	£'000s	£'000s	£'000s	£'000s	£'000s
Preference (10%)	300		—		—	
Ordinary	1 000		800		500	
		1 300		800		500

Reserves						
Share premium a/c	100		200		—	
Revaluation reserve	200		180		150	
Retained earnings	300		940		700	
	——	600	——	1 320	——	850
		1 900		2 120		1 350
Debentures	(10%)	500	— (12½%)			400
Deferred taxation		100		80		50
		£2 500		£2 200		£1 800

The three boards of directors agree on the following projections of results for 1982, 1983 and 1984, on the assumptions:

(1) that Aleph, Beth and Gimel do not merge; and
(2) that they do merge, as subsidiaries of Daleth plc, and that plans for rationalization of their businesses are carried through.

All figures are on the basis of end-1981 price levels, and of the revaluations then made.

Projected Results, 1982–1984

(1) Without amalgamation:

	Aleph Limited			Beth Limited			Gimel Limited		
	1982	*1983*	*1984*	*1982*	*1983*	*1984*	*1982*	*1983*	*1984*
	£'000s	£'000s	£'000s	£'000s	£'000s	£'000s	£'000s	£'000s	£'000s
Turnover	5 000	6 000	7 000	4 000	4 000t	4 500	3 000	2 800	2 500
Net trading profit	500	650	800	350	325	300	250	220	200
Net profit after interest	450	600	750	325	290	250	200	170	150
Net profit after taxation	225	300	375	155	140	120	100	85	75
Dividends	150	200	200	100	80	50	75	60	60
Retained earnings	75	100	175	55	60	70	25	25	15

(2) With amalgamation:

	Daleth plc		
	1982	*1983*	*1984*
	£'000s	£'000s	£'000s
Turnover	14 000	16 000	18 000
Net trading profit	1 400	1 700	2 000

The cost of capital of Aleph, Beth and Gimel is 15% per annum, after taxation, in each case. Inflation during 1982–1984 is expected to average 10% per annum.

You are required:
(a) **to draw up a scheme of amalgamation of the three existing companies, by means of an exchange of securities with the new company, Daleth plc. The scheme must be reasonable, fair to all interested parties, and likely to obtain the consent of a three-fourths majority in value of each class of shareholders and debentureholders, as required by the articles of association of all the companies; and** (16 marks)
(b) **to draft, by the merger method, the Consolidated Balance Sheet of the new group as at 1 January 1982, in accordance with your scheme of amalgamation.*** (9 marks)
(25 marks)

A. Cert. A. Advanced Financial Accounting, December 1982.
* The merger method of accounting is dealt with subsequently in Chapter 11.

9.6 The following data relates to Unsatiable Appetites Ltd for the two years ended 31 December 1980:

	1979	1980
	£	£
Trading profit before tax	67 220	103 580
Taxation (Marginal rate 52%)	27 630	35 760
Profit after taxation	39 590	67 820
Dividends		
Preference paid 31 December	(5 400)	(5 400)
Ordinary paid 14 September	(19 250)	(14 000)
proposed	(9 625)	(16 000)
Retained	5 315	32 420

At 1 January 1979 the issued share capital consisted of 160 000 ordinary shares of 50p each and 100 000 5.4% cumulative preference shares of £1 each.

On 1 April 1979 a bonus issue was made on the basis of one new ordinary share for every four held.

On 1 October 1979 options were granted to the senior executives to subscribe for a total of 100 000 ordinary shares at the current market price of 75p each. These options were exercisable on the 1 December 1980, 1981 or 1982.

An investment of £100 2½% consolidated stock would have given a gross yield of

16% on 1 January 1979, 15% on 1 December 1979,
14% on 1 January 1980, 13% on 1 December 1980.

On 1 January 1980 a previously announced rights issue of ordinary shares was taken up by all eligible shareholders. The basis was one for four at 60p per share and the market price on the last day of dealing, cum rights, was 70p.

On 1 July 1980 the company issued £300 000 of a 15% convertible debenture. The terms of conversion were one ordinary share for each £1 of the debenture exercisable on the 31st December of any year up to and including 1995. Interest was payable each year on 30th June and 31st December.

On 1 December 1980 20 400 ordinary shares were issued on the exercise of the executives share options.

You are required to:
  (a) **explain the purpose of presenting the earnings per share statistic in the annual accounts** (4 marks)**, and**
  (b) **calculate the earnings per share figures that will be disclosed in the published accounts for the year ended 31 December 1980 (the published explanatory note is not required but clear working notes are expected)** (16 marks)**.**

(20 marks)

ICAEW Financial Accounting II, December 1981.

9.7 The consolidated profit and loss account of Sandgrit plc for the year ended 31 December 1981 showed the following:

	£	£
Trading profit before interest		2 498 151
Interest payable		1 948 268
		549 883
Share of profits less losses of associated companies		277 085
Group trading profit before taxation and extraordinary items		826 968
Taxation		110 648
Group profit after taxation and before extraordinary items		716 320
Extraordinary items		188 320
Group profit after taxation and extraordinary items		904 640
Dividends – preference	119 000	
ordinary	386 403	
		505 403
Retained earnings transferred to reserves		399 237

The relevant note in the financial statements on share capital contained the following extract:

Issued and fully paid:	7% Preference shares of £1 each	Ordinary shares of 25p each
At 31 December 1980	1 700 000	11 534 000
Issued in connection with the rights issue on 31 May 1981	—	4 943 000
Issued in connection with conversion of loan stock on 30 June 1981	—	20 000
At 31 December 1981	1 700 000	16 497 000

The middle market price of the company's ordinary shares immediately prior to and after the rights issue on 31 May 1981 was 33p cum rights and 30.6p ex-rights respectively.

You are required to:
(a) **calculate the earnings per share of Sandgrit plc on the net basis for the year ended 31 December 1981 together with a suitable note for inclusion in the financial statements** (10 marks),
(b) **state what you understand by the 'nil distribution basis' of calculating earnings per share** (3 marks), **and**
(c) **explain why earnings per share is often not a meaningful figure in the context of smaller unquoted companies** (3 marks).

(16 marks)

ICAEW Financial Accounting II, December 1982.

10 Capital Reorganization, Reduction and Reconstruction

Introduction

There are many reasons for making changes to a company's capital structure and these range from those which are virtually cosmetic to those where the company's capital base has almost disappeared.

At the cosmetic end of the spectrum is the bonus (or scrip) issue designed to tidy up a balance sheet which might otherwise show a large number of different reserves. At the other end of the spectrum is the capital reconstruction scheme entered into as the only possible alternative to liquidation of the company. In such a case, the value of the company's assets may be less than the value of its liabilities with the probable result that the company will be unable to meet its debts as they fall due. The company must then reach some agreement with its debenture-holders and other creditors about how their liabilities are to be treated. To achieve economic viability, it will often be necessary to raise new capital from existing shareholders and if, as is likely, the company has accumulated losses, the new shares would probably be unattractive to investors. The writing down, or reduction, of share capital removes such losses from the balance sheet and brings a greater likelihood of earlier future dividends, thus making the shares more attractive.

Within this spectrum of reasons for a reorganization of capital, there are numerous possibilities. A company may wish to raise new share capital and use a rights issue as a cheaper alternative to a general offer to the public; conversely it may wish to reduce its share capital in line with a smaller level of operations or perhaps to permit a shareholder director in a family company to retire. A capital reorganization scheme may be used to effect a change in the relative rights of different classes of shareholders, perhaps when a company is involved in a business combination. Taxation considerations are important in leading a company to reorganize its capital so that its earnings may be distributed to members in a tax-efficient way.

In some cases the reason for the reorganization is unique, that is it is only applicable in the circumstances of the particular company. A good example is the scheme of arrangement undertaken by European Ferries plc in 1984. Under this scheme, ordinary shareholders were permitted to convert their ordinary shares into preference shares and only those preference shares now carry the right to discounts on Townsend Thoresen ferries. The purpose of the scheme was to limit any future growth in the number of shareholders entitled to such discounts.

Changes in share capital such as bonus issues and rights issues are dealt with in more elementary textbooks on accounting. Here we concentrate on certain reorganizations of capital permitted under the provisions of the Companies Acts 1981 and 1948.

In the first section we look at the redemption or purchase of its own shares by a company under the provisions of the Companies Act 1981. We deal with both the purchase of shares other than out of capital, which may be made by any limited company with a share capital, and a purchase out of capital, which may only be made by a private limited company. In the following section we examine the more wide-ranging powers to reduce capital contained in the Companies Act 1948. Next we provide the background to other capital reorganizations including those which involve the alteration of creditors' rights. In the final section, we consider the design and evaluation of a capital reconstruction scheme to be undertaken as an alternative to liquidation.

Redemption and purchase of shares

Purchase other than out of capital[1]

Up to 1981 the only class of share that a company was able to redeem was redeemable preference shares, but the Companies Act 1981 now permits limited companies both to issue redeemable shares of any class, and to purchase its own shares, whether or not they were issued as redeemable shares. The difference between a redemption and a purchase is that in the former case the shares will be reacquired on terms specified when the security was issued whilst in the case of a purchase the amount payable will depend on conditions prevailing at the date of purchase. Apart from this, the rules governing redemption and purchase are the same and, in order to avoid repetition, we shall merely

1 The relevant legal provisions are contained in the Companies Act 1981, Paras 46–53.

use the term purchase throughout this section. In both cases the purchased shares are cancelled and cannot be reissued.

The 1981 Act distinguishes two categories of purchase, a market purchase and an off-market purchase. The market purchase is a purchase of shares listed on a recognized stock exchange or dealt in on the Unlisted Securities Market. It follows that such a purchase may only be made by a public company which has shares quoted on the relevant market. The off-market purchase is any other purchase of shares under a contract and may be made by both public and private companies. In view of the possibility that one particular shareholder may be beneficially treated, the Act lays down more onerous conditions for an off-market purchase than for a market purchase. Thus, whereas the market purchase may be made in accordance with a general authority passed by an ordinary resolution in general meeting, the off-market purchase requires approval of a specific contract by a special resolution in general meeting.

Private companies are in certain circumstances allowed to reduce their permanent capital by the purchase of their own shares and we shall deal with these provisions later in the chapter. With this exception the 1981 Act lays down very detailed rules to ensure that the permanent capital is maintained intact following the purchase. The general principle, which has applied for many years on the redemption of redeemable preference shares is that the purchase must be made either out of distributable profits or out of the proceeds of a new issue of shares made for the purpose or by a combination of the two methods.

In many instances the purchase will be made at a premium, i.e. the purchase price will exceed the share's nominal value. Any premium payable on purchase must be paid out of distributable profits unless the shares being purchased were originally issued at a premium,[2] in which case some or all of the premium may come from the proceeds of the new issue.

Where the purchase is made out of distributable profits an amount must be transferred to a capital redemption reserve, which is treated as paid-up share capital of the company. It would appear that the intention of the Act is that the amount of the transfer should be such as to ensure that the permanent capital following the purchase is maintained at the original level. However, probably unintentionally, due to the particular wording used in the Act, circumstances can arise which

2 This means that where some of the shares in issue were issued at par with others having been issued at a premium it will be necessary to identify which particular shares are being purchased.

could result in either an increase or a reduction in permanent capital. The circumstances might occur where shares are purchased at a premium out of the proceeds of a fresh issue of shares itself made at a premium[3] and these will be illustrated in the examples which follow.

First let us assume that a company purchases shares without making a new issue of shares. In such a case the amount payable, including any premium, must come from distributable profits and, in order to maintain the permanent capital of the company, it is necessary to transfer an amount equal to the nominal value of the shares purchased from distributable profits to a capital redemption reserve, which is treated as paid-up share capital of the company. This is illustrated in Example 10.1.

EXAMPLE 10.1
Bratsk plc has the following summarized balance sheet:

	£
Net assets	1500
Share capital – £1 shares	1000
Share premium	200
(Permanent capital)	1200
Distributable profits	300
	1500

It purchases 100 £1 shares for £160 out of distributable profits.

Summarized journal entries together with the resulting balance sheet are as follows:

	£	£
Dr Share capital	100	
Premium on purchase	60	
Cr Cash		160
	160	160
Dr Distributable profits	160	
Cr Premium on purchase		60
Capital redemption reserve		100
	160	160

3 *See*, for example, Donald Jamieson, 'Companies Act 1981 and the maintenance of capital', *Accountancy*, July 1983, pp. 103–5.

Summarized balance sheet after purchase of shares:

		£
Net assets	(1500 − 160)	1340
Share capital	(1000 − 100)	900
Share premium		200
Capital redemption reserve		100
(Permanent capital)		1200
Distributable profits	(300 − 160)	140
		1340

Notice that the permanent capital of the company remains unchanged at £1200.

Next let us assume that a company purchases shares out of the proceeds of a new issue. In the absence of any premium payable on purchase, discussed below, the nominal value of the shares purchased is replaced by the nominal value of and any share premium received on the new issue.

EXAMPLE 10.2
Chita Limited has the following summarized balance sheet:

	£
Net assets	1500
Share capital – £1 shares	1000
Share premium	200
(Permanent capital)	1200
Distributable profits	300
	1500

Chita purchases 100 £1 shares at their nominal value out of the proceeds of an issue of 80 £1 shares at a premium of 25p per share.

Summarized journal entries and the resulting balance sheet are as follows:

	£	£
Dr Cash	100	
Cr Share capital		80
Share premium		20
	100	100
Dr Share capital	100	
Cr Cash		100

Summarized balance sheet after purchase of shares:

	£
Net assets	1500
Share capital (1000 + 80 − 100)	980
Share premium (200 + 20)	220
(Permanent capital)	1200
Distributable profits	300
	1500

Once again, the permanent capital has been maintained at £1200.

Frequently, as in the case of Bratsk (Example 10.1) above, a premium is payable on the shares purchased. Such a premium must be paid out of distributable profits except that where the shares which are being purchased were originally issued at a premium, all or part of the premium now payable may be paid out of the proceeds of the new issue and charged against the share premium account. The amount which may be charged against the share premium account is the lower of

(i) the amount of the premium which the company originally received on the shares now being purchased, and
(ii) the current balance on the share premium account, including any premium on the new issue of shares.

EXAMPLE 10.3
Dudinka Limited has the following summarized balance sheet:

	£
Net assets	1500
	══
Share capital – £1 shares	1000
Share premium	200
	───
(Permanent capital)	1200
Distributable profits	300
	───
	1500
	══

Dudinka Limited purchases 100 £1 shares which were originally issued at a premium of 20p per share. The price paid is £180 and this is financed by the issue of 90 £1 shares at a premium of £1 per share.

Part of the premium payable may be financed from the proceeds of the new issue; the amount is the lower of the original share premium on the shares now being purchased and the balance of the share premium account, including the premium on the new share issue. In this case the amount is the lower of £20 (100 at 20p) and £290 (£200 + £90) and hence £20 may be debited to the share premium account. The balance must come from distributable profits.

Summarized journal entries and the resulting balance sheet are as follows:

	£	£
Dr Cash	180	
Cr Share capital		90
Share premium		90
	───	───
	180	180
	══	══
Dr Share capital	100	
Premium on purchase	80	
Cr Cash		180
	───	───
	180	180
	══	══
Dr Share premium	20	
Distributable profits	60	
Cr Premium on purchase		80
	───	───
	80	80
	══	══

Summarized balance sheet after purchase of shares:

	£
Net assets (1500 + 180 − 180)	1500
Share capital (1000 + 90 − 100)	990
Share premium (200 + 90 − 20)	270
(Permanent capital)	1260
Distributable profits (300 − 60)	240
	1500

So, even where the proceeds of the new issue are exactly equal to the amount payable on purchase, the restriction on the amount of any premium payable which may be charged against the share premium account will often result in part of the premium payable being charged against distributable profits and a consequent increase in the permanent capital of the company.

In the final example of this section, we look at a company which purchases shares but raises only part of the finance by making a new issue of shares. We shall assume that the shares are purchased at a premium and that the new shares are issued at a premium. As we shall see, it is in this situation that a reduction in the permanent capital of the company may occur.

EXAMPLE 10.4

Ivdel plc has the following summarized balance sheet:

	£
Net assets	1500
Share capital – £1 shares	1000
Share premium	200
(Permanent capital)	1200
Distributable profits	300
	1500

It purchases 100 shares which were originally issued at a premium of 50p per share. The agreed price is £180 and the company issues 40 shares at a premium of £1 per share to help finance the purchase.

The premium payable on purchase is £80 and part of this may come from the proceeds of the new issue and be charged to the share premium account. As explained above, this amount is the lower of the original premium (£50) and the balance on the share premium account after the new issue (£240). Hence £50 may be debited to the share premium account and the balance must be debited to distributable profits.

As part of the purchase price is being met from distributable profits, it is necessary to make a transfer to capital redemption reserve. Section 53(2) of the 1981 Act requires the amount to be calculated by deducting the aggregate amount of the proceeds of the new issue from the nominal value of the shares purchased. In this case the amount of the transfer is therefore:

	£
Nominal value of shares purchased	100
less Proceeds of new issue (40 × £2)	80
	—
Necessary transfer	20
	=

Necessary journal entries and the resulting balance sheet are given below:

	£	£
Dr Cash	80	
Cr Share capital		40
Share premium		40
	—	—
	80	80
	=	=
Dr Share capital	100	
Premium on purchase	80	
Cr Cash		180
	—	—
	180	180
	=	=
Dr Share premium	50	
Distributable profits	30	
Cr Premium on purchase		80
	—	—
	80	80
	=	=
Dr Distributable profits	20	
Cr Capital redemption reserve		20
	=	=

Summarized balance sheet after purchase of shares:

	£
Net assets (1500 + 80 − 180)	1400
Share capital (1000 + 40 − 100)	940
Share premium (200 + 40 − 50)	190
Capital redemption reserve	20
(Permanent capital)	1150
Distributable profits (300 − 30 − 20)	250
	1400

In this case, the permanent capital has been reduced from £1200 to £1150 which does not appear to accord with the intended aim of maintaining permanent capital. The reason the reduction occurs is because the proceeds of the new issue are used to finance part of both nominal value and premium payable and yet this is not recognized in making the transfer to capital redemption reserve.

Let us illustrate: the proceeds of the new issue are £80 and, of this, £50 is used to finance the premium on purchase. This leaves only £30 to replace the nominal value of the shares issued. To maintain permanent capital of the company, the transfer to capital redemption reserve should be calculated as follows:

	£	£
Nominal value of shares purchased		100
less Net proceeds of new issue:		
Total proceeds	80	
less Utilized to finance part of premium payable	50	
	—	30
Transfer to capital redemption reserve		70

Such a transfer would maintain permanent capital at £1200 but it is not the transfer required by law. Section 53(2) makes no reference to 'net' proceeds and hence the law seems to permit such a reduction in capital for both public and private companies.

Purchase out of capital[4]

The permissible capital payment
Whereas failure to maintain capital in the circumstances discussed above may be an unintended effect of the legislation, the 1981 Act

---

4 The relevant legal provisions are contained in the Companies Act 1981, Secs 54–58.

specifically permits a private, but not a public, company to purchase its shares out of capital. This provides such a company with a means for reducing its permanent capital without the formality and expense of undertaking a capital reduction scheme under the provisions of the Companies Act 1948, which we discuss in the next section. Such an ability to purchase shares out of capital is of considerable benefit to, for example, a family-owned company where a member of the family wishes to realize his investment but no other member of the family wishes, or is able, to purchase it.

A purchase of shares out of capital results in a fall in the resources available to creditors and the 1981 Act therefore provides a number of safeguards to protect their interests. Before summarizing these safeguards, we will explain the calculation of the permitted reduction in capital, what the Act describes as the 'permissible capital payment'.

The private company is not free to specify the amount of the payment out of capital. Rather the payment is restricted to the amount actually paid for shares less both the distributable profits and the proceeds of any fresh issue of shares made for the purpose of the purchase. Thus a payment from capital may only be made when all distributable reserves have been utilized. Rules are laid down to ensure that the permanent capital of the company is not reduced by more than the permissible capital payment although these rules may still not succeed due to the problem discussed in connection with Example 10.4 above.

If the total of the permissible capital payment and the proceeds of a fresh issue of shares is less than the nominal value of the shares purchased, there would be a reduction in permanent capital in excess of the permissible capital payment. To prevent this, the law requires that the difference be transferred to a capital redemption reserve. If the permissible capital payment together with the proceeds of any fresh issue of shares exceeds the nominal value of the shares purchased, the excess may be eliminated by writing it off against any one of a number of accounts, including accounts for capital redemption reserve, share premium, share capital or unrealized profits. This ability to write off the excess to any one of these named accounts or, indeed, to deal with it in some other way, provides a private company with considerable flexibility to design its own capital reduction scheme.

We shall illustrate the above rules with two examples.

In Example 10.5 the purchase of shares is made partly out of capital and partly out of distributable profits whilst in Example 10.6 the purchase is, in addition, made partly out of the proceeds of a new issue of shares.

EXAMPLE 10.5

Kotlas Limited has the following summarized balance sheet:

	£
Net assets	1250
Share capital – £1 shares	1000
Distributable profits	250
	1250

It purchases 200 £1 shares at a cost of £300. In the absence of a share premium account or a new issue of shares at a premium, the amount of the premium payable must be provided from distributable profits.

The permissible capital payment is:

	£
Amount payable	300
less Distributable profits	250
Permissible capital payment	50

As the permissible capital payment (£50) is less than the nominal value of the shares purchased (£200) it is necessary to make a transfer from distributable profits to a capital redemption reserve.

	£
Nominal value of shares purchased	200
less Permissible capital payment	50
Necessary transfer	150

Necessary journal entries and the resulting summarized balance sheet are given below:

	£	£
Dr Share capital	200	
Premium on purchase	100	
Cr Cash		300
	300	300

	£	£
Dr Distributable profits	250	
Cr Premiun on purchase		100
Capital redemption reserve		150
	250	250

Summarized balance sheet after purchase of shares:

		£
Net assets	(1250 − 300)	950
Share capital	(1000 − 200)	800
Capital redemption reserve		150
(Permanent capital)		950

The permanent capital of the company has been reduced from £1000 share capital to £950. It has fallen by the amount of the permissible capital payment.

EXAMPLE 10.6
Nordvik Limited has the following summarized balance sheet:

	£
Net assets	1250
Share capital – £1 shares	1000
Share premium	200
(Permanent capital)	1200
Distributable profits	50
	1250

Of the £1 shares, 500 were issued at par when the company was formed and 500 were issued at a premium of 40p per share some years later.

Nordvik purchases 200 of the shares which were originally issued at par for an agreed price of £300 and finances the purchase in part by an issue of 50 shares at a premium of 60p per share.

As the shares purchased were not originally issued at a premium, no part of the premium payable may come from the proceeds of the new issue. The whole of the premium payable, that is the whole of the increase in value of these particular shares since their issue, must be charged against distributable profits.

In this case the permissible capital payment is:

	£	£
Amount payable		300
less Distributable profits	50	
Proceeds of new issue (50 × £1.60)	80	
	—	130
Permissible capital payment		170

In order to determine whether or not a transfer to capital redemption reserve is necessary, we must compare the proceeds of the new issue and the permissible capital payment with the nominal value of the shares purchased.

	£	£
Nominal value of shares purchased		200
less Permissible capital payment	170	
Proceeds of new issue	80	
	——	250
		(50)

In this case no transfer to capital redemption reserve is required. Rather the excess £50 may be charged to one of the accounts discussed above and we have chosen to debit it to the share premium account.

Necessary journal entries and the resulting summarized balance sheet are given below:

	£	£
Dr Cash	80	
Cr Share capital		50
Share premium		30
	—	—
	80	80
Dr Share capital	200	
Premium on purchase	100	
Cr Cash		300
	——	——
	300	300

		£	£
Dr Distributable profits		50	
Share premium		50	
Cr Premium on purchase			100
		100	100

Summarized balance sheet after purchase of shares:

		£
Net assets	(1250 + 80 − 300)	1030
Share capital	(1000 + 50 − 200)	850
Share premium	(200 + 30 − 50)	180
		1030
(Permanent capital)		1030
Distributable profits		—
		1030

The permanent capital of the company has been reduced from £1200 to £1030 by the amount of the permissible capital payment of £170.

The safeguards
In view of the fact that there is a reduction in the permanent capital, that is a reduction in the net assets available to creditors and the remaining shareholders, the law provides a number of safeguards where a company wishes to make such an off-market purchase of shares involving a payment out of capital. Thus not only must the payment out of capital be permitted by the company's articles of association and authorized by a special resolution of the company but the directors must also provide a statutory declaration of solvency to the effect that, having made a full enquiry into the affairs and prospects of the company, they have formed the opinion that the company will be able to pay its debts both immediately after the payment and during the following year. As the protection of creditors and shareholders rests on this continuing solvency of the company, the law requires that a report by the company's auditors on the reasonableness of the directors' opinion is attached to the statutory declaration.

After the payment out of capital has been authorized, the company must publicize it in an official gazette and either a national newspaper or by individual notice to each creditor. Any creditor, or any shareholder who did not vote for the special resolution, may then apply to the court for the cancellation of the resolution and the court may then cancel or confirm the resolution and may make an order to facilitate an arrangement whereby the interests of dissenting creditors or members are purchased.

If the directors' optimism subsequently proves not to have been well founded and the company commences to wind up within a year of the payment out of capital and is unable to pay all its liabilities and the costs of winding up, then directors and past shareholders may be liable to contribute. The directors who have signed the statutory declaration and/or past shareholders, whose shares were purchased, may have to pay an amount not exceeding in total the permitted capital payment.

Thus the Companies Act 1981 provides safeguards to protect creditors. The use of its provisions to make a purchase of shares partly out of capital is undoubtedly much cheaper and less burdensome than a reduction of capital under the provision of the Companies Act 1948 to which we turn next.

Capital reduction

The Companies Act 1948 gave companies a much wider power to reduce capital from that discussed above but it also imposed the more onerous condition that any such reduction must be confirmed by the court. In this section we consider the provisions of the 1948 Act with regard to the reduction of capital.

Providing it is authorized to do so by its articles of association, a limited company may reduce its share capital by passing a special resolution, which must be confirmed by the court. The Act gives a general power to reduce share capital but specifically lists three possible ways to reduce capital:[5]

(a) extinguish or reduce the liability on any of its shares in respect of share capital not paid up; or

(b) either with or without extinguishing or reducing liability on any of its shares, cancel any paid-up share capital which is lost or unrepresented by available assets; or

(c) either with or without extinguishing or reducing liability on any of its shares, pay off any paid-up share capital which is in excess of the wants of the company.

5 Companies Act 1948, Sec. 66.

A capital reduction for the first and third of the possible reasons listed would seem to be extremely rare. With regard to the first, few companies now have partly paid shares in existence and hence there is invariably no liability in respect of partly paid capital which could be reduced. With regard to the third, although it might make good economic sense for directors to return 'permanent' capital to shareholders where better investment opportunities exist outside of the company than within it, it appears that most directors have been loathe to relinquish their control over such resources and have usually found some way to employ them within the company.

Both of these capital reductions ((a) and (c)) do, of course, result in a reduction in the potential net assets or actual net assets available to creditors. Thus, in the first case, there is a reduction in the liability of members and hence in the potential pool of net assets available to creditors on a liquidation. In the third case, resources actually leave the company so directly reducing the pool of net assets to which the creditors have recourse. For these reasons the court must give any creditor an opportunity to object to the capital reduction and will only usually confirm the scheme if the debt of such a dissenting creditor is paid or secured.

The second of the three possible capital reduction schemes is the one most commonly found in practice. Thus where a company has made losses in excess of previous profits, its net assets will be lower than its permanent capital. Given that such a position has been reached, it will often be sensible to recognize the fact by reducing the capital and writing off the losses so that a more realistic position is shown by the balance sheet and the company may make a fresh start. In particular, after such a scheme the company will be able to distribute realized profits without the need to first make good the accumulated realized losses and, in the case of a public company, net unrealized losses.[6]

The simplest way such a capital reduction scheme may be carried out is by reducing proportionately the nominal value of the ordinary shares outstanding. This has no effect whatsoever on the real value of the ordinary shareholders' interest since the same number of shares in the same company are held in the same proportions by the same people! Each shareholder has the same proportional interest in the net assets of the company after the scheme as he did before it. This demonstrates the irrelevance of the par value and supports the argu-

6 *See* Chapter 3.

ment that companies should be permitted to issue shares of no par value.[7]

To illustrate such a scheme, let us look at an example.

EXAMPLE 10.7

Perm plc has the following summarized balance sheet:

	£
Net assets	1200
Share capital	
1000 £1 ordinary shares, fully paid	1000
500 £1 10% preference shares, fully paid	500
	1500
Share premium	200
	1700
less Accumulated losses	500
	1200

The preference shares rank for dividend and repayment of capital in priority to ordinary shares. The company wishes to reduce its capital by an amount sufficient to remove the accumulated losses and to write down the net assets to a more realistic book value of £900. Thus it wishes to reduce permanent capital by £800, that is $(500 + (1200 - 900))$.

For illustrative purposes we shall consider two possible capital reduction schemes, the first involving a reduction of ordinary share capital only and the second involving the reduction of both ordinary share capital and preference share capital.

Scheme 1

As explained above, the total amount of the capital reduction is £800. However, for the purpose of a reduction of capital, a share premium account is to be treated as paid-up share capital of the company[8] so that £200 may be written off against the share premium leaving £600

7 A government committee under the chairmanship of Mr Montague Gedge reported in favour of the issue of shares of no par value as long ago as 1954. Cmnd 9112/54, HMSO, London, 1954.

8 Companies Act 1948, Sec. 56(1).

to reduce the ordinary share capital from £1000 to £400, that is from £1 to 40p per share.

The balance sheet after the capital reduction would therefore appear as follows:

Summarized balance sheet after capital reduction

	£
Net assets	900
Share capital	
1000 40p ordinary shares	400
500 £1 10% preference shares	500
	900

The interest of preference shareholders and ordinary shareholders in the liquidation value of the company has not altered. Preference shareholders would receive the first £500 while ordinary shareholders would receive the remainder. If the company continues to trade, both sets of shareholders gain in the sense that the company will be able to pay dividends as soon as profits are made without any need to make good the past losses first.

Scheme 2
Given the fact that preference shareholders as well as ordinary shareholders benefit from the capital reduction scheme, ordinary shareholders might argue that preference share capital as well as ordinary share capital should be reduced. However, as we shall see, a reduction in the par value of a preference share has a much more serious effect than the reduction in the par value of ordinary share capital. Indeed a reduction in the par value of both preference shares and ordinary shares with no other changes, will lead to a fall in the real value of the preference shares, but a rise in the real value of the ordinary shares. This may be illustrated as follows.

As before let us assume that the amount of the capital reduction is £800 and that, of this, £200 may be written off against the share premium account leaving £600 to be written off against share capital. Given that the ordinary share capital is £1000 and that the preference share capital is £500, it might be thought that the amount of £600 should be written off in the ratio 2:1 which would produce a balance sheet as follows:

Summarized balance sheet after capital reduction

	£
Net assets	900
Share capital	
1000 60p ordinary shares	600
500 60p 10% preference shares	300
	900

While this may initially appear fair, a little thought will make it clear that the preference shareholders have been unfairly treated.

Given that the par value of a preference share determines the amount of the preference dividend and the amount which the preference shareholders receive on a liquidation, preference shareholders will have suffered a real loss. They are worse off after the scheme than before. Conversely the ordinary shareholders are better off. Not only would they receive more on an immediate liquidation, as less would be paid to the preference shareholders but they are also likely to receive higher future dividends, as a lesser dividend would be paid to the preference shareholders.

Careful attention must be paid to the likely effect of reducing the par values of different types of share capital. A capital reduction such as Scheme 2 is unlikely to be acceptable to the preference shareholders unless they are given some other benefit such as a holding of ordinary shares which will give them an opportunity to share in any future prosperity.

The legal background to other reorganizations

We have looked in some detail at the ways in which a company may reduce its share capital under the provisions of both the Companies Acts 1981 and 1948. As we saw in the introduction to this chapter, there are many other ways in which a company may wish to reorganize its capital. For example, it may wish to alter the respective rights of different classes of shareholders, while, if it is in financial difficulties, it may need to reduce not only share capital but also the claims of creditors. In this section we look briefly at the legal background to such reorganizations.

First, it is necessary to make it clear that although the term 'capital reduction' has a clear legal meaning, as discussed above, the terms 'capital reorganization', 'capital reconstruction' and, indeed, 'scheme of arrangement' do not. These terms tend to be used interchangeably although there is, perhaps a tendency to use the term 'capital reconstruction' for the more serious changes in capital structure; so in the final section of this chapter we look at a capital reconstruction scheme undertaken as an alternative to liquidation of the company. In the remainder of this section we will use the term reorganization.

Any reorganization which involves creditors will invariably be carried out in accordance with the procedures laid down in Sects 206–7 of the Companies Act 1948. These procedures are designed to protect the various parties involved by requiring court approval for the reorganization. This sounds fine in theory but it must be recognized that our legal system is ill-equipped to pass judgements on the economic merits of schemes and thus the tendency is for courts to concern themselves with deciding whether the scheme satisfies the required legal formalities.[9]

Under Sects 206–7, the company will apply to the court which will then direct meetings of the various parties affected to be held. The company must then send out details of the proposed scheme and, providing a majority in number representing three-quarters in value of those attending the various meetings agree and the scheme is sanctioned by the court, it will become binding on all parties once an office copy is delivered to the Registrar of Companies.

It is sometimes the case that a reorganization entered into in accordance with the above provisions involves the transfer of the whole or part of an undertaking from one company to another. In such a case, Sect. 208 gives the court wide powers to make provision for the transfer of ownership of assets, liabilities, rights and duties to the transferee company.

The above provisions may be used to effect a reorganization even where there is no change in creditors' rights. However, alternative procedures are available in such cases which do not involve the formality and expense of going to court. Thus it may be possible to vary the rights of two or more classes of shareholders by merely holding separate class meetings and obtaining the necessary majority votes, although a dissenting minority is given a right to object to the variation in an application to the court.

9 *See* L. C. B. Gower, *Principles of Modern Company Law*, 4th edn, Stevens and Sons, London, 1979, p. 717.

Another possible means of reorganization is provided by Sect. 287 of the 1948 Act. Under this section, once a voluntary liquidation of the company is proposed, the liquidator may be given authority by a special resolution to sell the whole or a part of the undertaking to another company in exchange for shares or other securities in that other company. Thus, where it is desired to change the rights of two or more classes of its shareholders, the company may be put into voluntary liquidation and a new company may be formed with the desired mix of various classes of shares. The business of the transferor company may then be sold to the new company in exchange for the new shares, which may then be distributed to the shareholders in the transferor company to achieve the desired change. This procedure is much simpler than the use of a scheme under Sects 206–8 of the Act.

Invariably taxation considerations will be extremely important in most capital reorganizations and, in view of the complexity of the tax legislation, specialist advice is almost always necessary.

Capital reconstruction

In this section we shall concentrate on the design and evaluation of a capital reconstruction scheme for a company which is in severe financial difficulties. It will be assumed that, in the absence of a capital reconstruction scheme, the liquidation of the company would be inevitable. This assumption will affect both the design of the scheme and the way in which it will be evaluated by the interested parties.

As the alternative source of benefits to interested parties is the amount receivable on liquidation, it is essential for us to recall the order in which the proceeds from the sale of assets must be distributed by a liquidator.

Distribution on liquidation

It is the duty of a liquidator to sell the assets of a company as advantageously as possible and to pay costs, creditors and shareholders in the following order:

(1) Debts secured by a fixed charge. These must be paid out of the proceeds of sale of the particular assets. In practice a receiver will usually be appointed to sell the assets, which are the subject of the charge, and to pay the secured creditors the amounts due to them.

It will rarely be the case that the proceeds of sale are exactly equal to the costs of the receiver and the amount of the debt. Any excess will be paid over to the liquidator of the company whilst, to the extent of any deficiency, the creditors are treated in the same way as other unsecured creditors.

(2) Costs of the liquidation, in the order specified by law.

(3) Preferential creditors. These are listed in Sect. 319 of the Companies Act 1948 and include such debts as local rates, taxation, wages and salaries of employees, accrued holiday remuneration and national insurance contributions. There are limits to the preferential debts: for example, any liability for taxation may only be treated as preferential to the extent of 1 year of assessment and wages and salaries are only preferential to the extent of £200 per person. To the extent that only part of a debt is preferential, the remainder will be treated as an unsecured creditor.

(4) Creditors secured by a floating charge.

(5) Unsecured creditors, including the amounts mentioned in (1) and (3) above.

(6) Shareholders of the company in accordance with their rights as laid down in the company's articles of association. Preference shares will normally be paid before any amounts are paid to ordinary shareholders.

Where the amounts available are insufficient to pay any of the above groups in full, each member of the particular group receives the same proportion of the amount of his debt. This proportion is determined as the amount available for a particular group divided by the total amounts due to that group.

Design of a capital reconstruction scheme

Given that a company is in financial difficulties, the objective in the design of a capital reconstruction scheme will be to produce an entity which is a profitable going concern. In some cases the financial difficulties may be so severe that this is impossible for, no matter how skilfully a capital reconstruction scheme is designed, it is not possible to turn the sow's ear into a silk purse. Where the financial difficulties are less severe and the company is capable of operating profitably, a capital reconstruction scheme may have a high probability of success. In order to achieve that success, it will usually be necessary to relieve the company of its burden of immediate debts and will often be necessary to raise new finance, probably by a new issue of shares.

Any capital reconstruction scheme which affects the rights of creditors and shareholders will require the necessary majorities of votes in favour of the scheme as required by Sect. 206 of the Companies Act 1948, together with the sanction of the court. Hence, to stand any chance of success the scheme must give each interested party the same or more than he would receive on liquidation of the company. In addition the scheme must be accepted as equitable by the various interested parties. It must ensure that no one class of creditors or shareholders is favoured at the expense of any other so that each creditor and shareholder is treated – and feels that he is treated – fairly.

The design of a capital reconstruction scheme is illustrated in the following example while the resulting scheme is evaluated in the final section of this chapter.

EXAMPLE 10.8: A possible capital reconstruction scheme

The balance sheet of Sakhalin plc on 31 December 19X5 is as follows:

Sakhalin plc
Balance sheet on 31 December 19X5

	£000s	£000s
Fixed assets at cost less depreciation		
Land and buildings	2500	
Plant and machinery	1000	3500
Current assets		
Stock and work in progress	1000	
Sundry debtors	1500	2500
		6000
less Current liabilities		
Arrears of debenture interests	250	
Trade creditors	1000	
Bank overdraft	3000	4250
		1750
Financed by		
10% secured debentures (note (a))		1250
1 million authorized and issued £1		
5% preference shares	1000	
2 million authorized and issued £1		
ordinary shares	2000	
	3000	
less Accumulated losses	2500	500
		1750

The following information is available:

(a) The debentures are secured on the office premises, the net realizable value of which is estimated to be £900 000.

(b) The other land and buildings are estimated to have a net realizable value of £1 900 000.

(c) The net realizable value of the plant and machinery is estimated to be £500 000, of the stock and work in progress £750 000, and the recoverable debts are now estimated to be £1 425 000.

(d) The preference dividend has not been paid for 4 years.

(e) The debenture interest is 2 years in arrears.

(f) The articles provide that, on liquidation, the preference shareholders rank for repayment at par prior to any distribution to the ordinary shareholders.

From preliminary meetings of the directors and soundings of the interested parties the following information has also been obtained:

(g) The debenture holders are prepared to agree to a reconstruction scheme providing the rate of interest is increased from 10 to 15% p.a., and they are given a fixed security on the total land and buildings, rather than just the office premises, of the company. They are also willing to accept ordinary shares in lieu of £125 000, that is one of the 2 years interest in arrears.

(h) The bank is prepared to agree to a reconstruction scheme provided its debt is secured by a floating charge over the assets of the company, thus improving its position *vis-à-vis* any other creditors of the reconstructed company. They would be willing to provide this amount of finance for the medium term.

(i) The trade creditors are unlikely to agree to any reduction in their claims but are thought to be willing to supply the reconstructed company and to continue to grant credit on normal terms.

(j) The preference share holders would be willing to forego their arrears of dividend and to accept ordinary shares instead of preference shares.

(k) The directors consider that, if the company is able to raise an additional £1 million in cash by a rights issue, it will be able to commence trading successfully. Expected annual earnings before debenture interest and dividends will then be at least £300 000 and due to accumulated tax losses, no corporation tax will be payable in the foreseeable future.

(l) Debenture holders, preference shareholders and ordinary shareholders are willing to subscribe for new ordinary share capital in the company.

(m) Costs of the reconstruction scheme are expected to be £60 000.

(n) In the absence of a satisfactory scheme the company will have to be liquidated involving costs of £295 000.

From the above information it is possible to calculate the amount of the capital reduction required, namely:[10]

		£000s
(a)	To correct the value of plant and machinery	500
(b)	To correct the value of stock and work in progress	250
(c)	To correct the value of debtors	75
(d)	To eliminate the adverse balance on the profit loss account	2500
(e)	To provide for the costs of the scheme	60
		3385
(f)	Less surplus on revaluation of land and buildings	300
		3085

In order to begin to decide who must bear this loss in the reconstruction scheme, we must first examine what each class of creditor and shareholder would receive if the company were to be liquidated.

The realizable value of the assets and the way in which they would be distributed are as follows:

	£000s	£000s
Office premises	900	
less Payable to debenture holders secured on office premises	900	
Other premises		1900
Plant and machinery		500
Stock and work in progress		750
Sundry debtors		1425
		4575
less Costs of liquidation		295
Available for unsecured creditors		4280

10 In a balance sheet, assets should be shown at their 'going concern value' rather than their net realizable value. In order to avoid complicating the example by the introduction of another set of values, the realistic going concern values, assets have been written down to their net realizable values.

	£000s	£000s
Unsecured creditors:[11]		
Bank overdraft		3000
Debenture holders		
Capital	1250	
Interest	250	
	1500	
less Paid out of security as above	900	600
Trade creditors		1000
		4600

There would be £4280 available to meet unsecured creditors of £4600 with the result that each of these creditors, including the debenture holders to the extent that they are unsecured, would receive 93p in the £1. The various parties would therefore receive the following amounts on liquidation of the company:

	£000s
Bank (0.93 × £3 000 000)	2790
Debenture holders (900 000 + 0.93 × 600 000)	1460
Trade creditors (0.93 × 1 000 000)	930
Preference shareholders	0
Ordinary shareholders	0
	5180

Thus all parties would lose on a liquidation and there is an incentive for them to agree to a suitable reconstruction scheme. It is clear that any losses under the scheme must fall most heavily on the shareholders.

One possible scheme of reconstruction would be as follows:

	Reduction (£000s)
(a) 2 million £1 ordinary shares to each be reduced to 1p ordinary shares	1980
(b) 1 million £1 preference shares to be cancelled in exchange for 1 million 1p ordinary shares	990
(c) The granting of an increased rate of interest of 15% p.a. and a fixed charge on all premises to the debenture holders and the waiving of £125 000 of interest in arrears in exchange for 1 million 1p ordinary shares	115
Carried forward	3085

11 For simplicity it is assumed that there are no preferential creditors.

	Reduction (£000s)
Brought forward	3085
(d) The granting of a floating charge on the debt due to the bank	—
(e) Consolidation of the 4 million 1p ordinary shares into 40 000 £1 ordinary shares	—
(f) The making of a rights issue of 25 £1 ordinary shares for each £1 ordinary share held thus raising cash of £1 000 000. Thus finance would come from old ordinary shareholders (£500 000), old preference shareholders (£250 000) and old debenture holders (£250 000)	—
Total reduction achieved as required	3085

After such a reconstruction scheme is carried into effect, the balance sheet would appear as shown below:

Sakhalin plc

Balance sheet after scheme	£000s	£000s
Tangible fixed assets – at valuation		
Land and buildings		2800
Plant and machinery		500
		3300
Current assets		
Stock and work in progress	750	
Debtors	1425	
Cash	1000	
	3175	
less Current liabilities		
Bank overdraft (secured)	3000	
Debenture interest (1 year)	125	
Trade creditors	1000	
Cost of reconstruction	60	
	4185	(1010)
		2290
less 15% Debentures (secured on land and buildings)		1250
		1040

	£000s	£000s
Share capital		
1 040 000 £1 ordinary shares, fully paid		1040

Note The apparently poor current ratio is due to the fact that the bank overdraft is included in current liabilities, in accordance with normal practice, whereas it is in fact medium-term capital.

Evaluation of a capital reconstruction scheme

In evaluating a capital reconstruction scheme, as in designing it, the aim must be to establish the equity of the changes in rights as a result of the scheme. In most cases professional advisors are called upon by each class of member and creditor to evaluate the scheme from their point of view and, in order to do this, it is necessary to evaluate the scheme as a whole since the changes of relative rights will be extremely important.

The rights of participants fall into two classes, the capital repayment rights and the income participation rights. In order the make an appropriate comparison of these, it is helpful to set out the interest of the various parties in the company both before and after the proposed reconstruction.

In Example 10.9 we shall do this in respect of the scheme which has been proposed for Sakhalin plc in Example 10.8.

EXAMPLE 10.9
Evaluation of proposed scheme – comparison of interests:

Original class	Interest prior to scheme	Interest after scheme
Bank	£3 000 000 unsecured overdraft	£3 000 000 secured overdraft
Debenture holders	£1 250 000 partly secured 10% debentures plus £250 000 arrears of interest	£1 250 000 fully secured 15% debentures plus £125 000 arrears of interest plus one-quarter of the ordinary shares
Trade creditors	£1 000 000 unsecured debt	£1 000 000 unsecured debt
Preference Shareholders	£1 000 000 £1 5% preference shares	One-quarter of the ordinary shares
Ordinary Shareholders	All ordinary shares	One-half of the ordinary shares

We have already considered the amounts each class would receive should the scheme be rejected and the company forced into an immediate liquidation. These amounts need to be compared with the position following the reconstruction and we shall do so by evaluating three alternative possible outcomes. Firstly, we shall assume that despite the scheme, the company goes into liquidation immediately following the end of the capital reconstruction. Secondly, we will assume that the earnings are as expected, about £300 000 per annum. Finally, we will assume that the earnings are more than anticipated; we will for this purpose, assume a figure of £500 000 per annum.

If we assume that the costs of the reconstruction scheme are paid, the position on the subsequent liquidation would be as follows:

Position on liquidation after scheme

	£000s	£000s
Amount receivable from sale of premises		2800
less Debentures		
Capital	1250	
Interest	125	1375
		1425
Amount realized from other assets:		
Plant and machinery	500	
Stock and work in progress	750	
Debtors	1425	2675
Cash (1 000 000 − 60 000)		940
		5040
less Costs of liquidation		295
		4745
less Bank secured by floating charge		3000
		1745
less Trade creditors		1000
Available for ordinary shareholders		745
Divisible:		
Old debenture holders ($\frac{1}{4}$)		186
Old preference shareholders ($\frac{1}{4}$)		186
Old ordinary shareholders ($\frac{1}{2}$)		373
		745

So, on a liquidation subsequent to the scheme the original parties would receive the following amounts:

	£000s
Bank	3000
Debenture holders (1 375 000 + 186 000)	1561
Trade creditors	1000
Preference shareholders	186
Ordinary shareholders	373
	6120

Debenture holders and preference shareholders have, of course, subscribed £250 000 each for new ordinary share capital whilst ordinary shareholders have subscribed £500 000.

Let us next examine the interests of the various parties in the expected earnings of the reconstructed company.

As we have seen in note (k) on page 365, the annual earnings before debenture interest and dividends are expected to be at least £300 000 and no corporation tax is likely to be paid in the foreseeable future. It follows that these earnings may be divided:[12]

	£	£
Old debenture holders		
Interest 15% × £1 250 000	187 500	
Share of balance ¼(300 000 − 187 500)	28 125	215 625
Old preference shareholders		
¼(300 000 − 187 500)		28 125
Old ordinary shareholders		
½(300 000 − 187 500)		56 250
		300 000

It is helpful to examine the position if earnings turn out to be higher or lower than expected and, for illustrative purposes, we look at the position if earnings are £500 000:

	£	£
Old debenture holders		
Interest – as above	187 500	
Share of balance ¼(500 000 − 187 500)	78 125	265 625

12 For simplicity we have ignored Advanced Corporation Tax.

	£	£
Brought forward	265 625	
Old preference shareholders		
¼(500 000 − 187 500)		78 125
Old ordinary shareholders		
½(500 000 − 187 500)		156 250
		500 000

We are now able to set out the position of each party before and after the proposed scheme in order to draw conclusions about its acceptability:

			Position after scheme		
Original class	Amount receivable on liquidation before scheme (£000s)	New capital introduced (£000s)	Amount receivable on liquidation after after scheme (£000s)	Share of earnings £300 000 (£000s)	Share of earnings £500 000 (£000s)
Bank	2790	—	3000	n/a	n/a
Debenture holders	1460	250	1561	215.625	265.625
Trade creditors	930	—	1000	n/a	n/a
Preference shareholders	—	250	186	28.125	78.125
Ordinary shareholders	—	500	373	56.250	156.250

The scheme would appear to offer advantages to all parties:

The bank converts unsecured debt into secured debt and stands to receive more in a liquidation after the scheme than in one before it.

On an immediate liquidation the debenture holders would receive £1 460 000 whereas if they invest a further £250 000 they will obtain a higher rate of interest on their debentures, a higher level of security and one-quarter of the ordinary share in the reconstructed company. Although they would only receive £1 561 000 on a liquidation after the scheme, their share in future earnings is attractive. If the level of future earnings is £300 000 their rate of return is approximately 12.6%, that is £215 625 divided by the amount of £1 710 000 (1 460 000 + 250 000) effectively invested. If future earnings are £500 000, the rate of return rises to approximately 18.2%.

Trade creditors would receive more in a liquidation after the scheme than in one before it.

Both preference shareholders and ordinary shareholders would appear to benefit considerably from the scheme. Although they would not receive back their new investment if a liquidation occurred immediately after the scheme, their potential earnings yield is high. If future earnings are £300 000, the yield is 11.25% (28.125/250) while, if earnings are £500 000, the yield rises to 31.25% (78.125/250).

If all the parties are happy with the scheme, they will vote in favour of it at their respective meetings. Provided it is then confirmed by the court, the scheme will become operative as soon as a copy of the court order is lodged with the Registrar. If any of the parties are unhappy with the scheme, it will be necessary to amend it. If, at the end of the day, agreement on a satisfactory scheme cannot be reached, the company will be liquidated.

Recommended reading

L. C. B. Gower, *Principles of Modern Company Law*, 4th edn, Stevens and Sons, London, 1979, Chapter 27.

M. Renshall and R. White, *Purchase of Own Shares*, Accounts Digest No. 136, ICAEW, London, 1983.

Questions

10.1 The following companies wish to purchase their own shares in accordance with the provisions of the Companies Act 1981.

(1) Strawberry plc, whose shares are dealt in the USM has the following shareholders' funds:

	£'000
Called up share capital	500
Reserves – Revaluation	100
– Profit and loss account	300
	900

The company intends to purchase 20 000 shares of £1 each at a price of 90p per share on the market. At the same time it is issuing to a merchant bank 13 000 shares at a price of £1 each payable in cash.

(2) Greengage plc has the following shareholders' funds:

	£'000
Called up share capital	200
Share premium account	20
Profit and loss account	50
	270

All the shares, of £1 each, were originally issued at a price of £1.10 each. 100 000 shares are now to be purchased at a price of £1.50 each which will be financed by a new issue to a merchant bank of 100 000 shares at £1.30 per share.

(3) Peach Ltd is a private company with shareholders' funds as follows:

	£
Called up share capital	5000
Share premium account	500
Profit and loss account	50
	5550

It is intended to purchase 1000 shares of £1 each, originally issued at par, at a price of £1.10 per share. A fresh issue of 850 shares will be made at par.

(4) Plum Ltd has the following shareholders' funds:

	£
Called up share capital	2000
Share premium account	500
Profit and loss account	5000
	7500

It is intended to purchase 1000 shares of £1 each, which were originally issued at £1.50 per share, for £1.60 per share. Simultaneously a fresh issue will be made of 500 shares of £1 each at £1.70 per share.

(5) Raspberry plc, a listed company, has the following shareholders' funds:

	£'000
Called up share capital	400
Reserves – Revaluation	120
– Profit and loss account	40
	560

It is proposed to purchase 200 000 50p shares from a venture capital trust at a 5% discount on the current market price of £2 per share. The shares purchased will then be issued to the company's founders at 75p each.

You are required in each of the above five examples to comment, with reasons, on whether the transactions are permitted under the Companies Act 1981 and if so to give the revised shareholders' funds after the share transactions, the necessary journal entries and where appropriate, the permissible capital payment. **(18 marks)**

Note: Ignore all taxation and duties.

ICAEW Financial Accounting II, July 1984.

10.2 Combined Engineering plc, a holding company, makes up financial statements to 31 July. During 1981, the group experienced difficult trading conditions which have strained its finances and its bankers have applied pressure on the directors for a substantial reduction in borrowings. Trading has been particularly bad in the wholly owned subsidiary, Rex Garages Ltd, engaged in the motor trade. The directors therefore resolved early in 1982 to dispose of Rex Garages Ltd.

Management accounts drawn up at 30 April 1982 showed the following:

	Parent £'000		Rex £'000
Fixed assets:			
Properties		3 646	1 352
Plant and machinery		4 201	462
Vehicles		2 948	437
		10 795	2 251
Shares in subsidiaries at cost		1 550	—
(includes £500 000 re Rex)			
Loans to subsidiaries		2 000	—
(includes £1 000 000 re Rex)			
Current assets:			
Stocks	12 529		3 368
Debtors and prepayments	11 620		1 675
Cash	25		8
	24 174		5 051
Current liabilities:			
Trade creditors and accruals	11 206		1 486
Bank overdrafts	17 483		1 817
	28 689		3 303
Net current (liabilities)/assets		(4 515)	1 748
		9 830	3 999

	Parent £'000	Rex £'000
Share capital	2 000	500
Reserves	2 830	499
Loan capital	5 000	3 000
	9 830	3 999

In early May 1982 the following plan of action, relating to Rex, was agreed:

(1) Certain properties with a book value of £950 000 will be sold to a third party for £1.2m. The sale proceeds will be used to repay the loans of £750 000 secured on these properties and the balance used to reduce the loan of £1m from the holding company (included in Rex's loan capital).

(2) The three group executives concerned with the management of Rex will be declared redundant. Under their contracts of employment they will be entitled to £150 000 each which will be paid to them in cash and borne by Combined Engineering plc.

(3) The same three will Purchase Rex at net asset value as shown in the 30 April 1982 management accounts after the adjustments for the properties to be sold and after further adjustments referred to below.

(4) The remaining property is to be written down by £100 000. This will necessitate a repayment of £150 000 of the third party loan secured thereon. This sum will be advanced temporarily by Combined Engineering plc.

(5) Subsequently the loan from Combined Engineering plc, including the temporary advance, will be repaid. To raise the necessary finance for this, sufficient new car stocks will be sold off to the trade at a discount of 30% on the cost price used in 30 April 1982 management figures.

(6) The three executives will acquire Rex's shares using their compensation for redundancy augmented by personal borrowing.

(7) Management Venture Capital Ltd, an independent company, will advance £600 000 loan capital which will be used to reduce Rex's bank overdraft.

(8) The consideration for the Rex shares will be paid in cash by 31 July 1982.

You are required to produce the pro forma balance sheets of Combined Engineering plc and Rex Garages Ltd at 31 July 1982 assuming that the above transactions duly take place and that both companies break even in trading between 30 April 1982 and that date.
Ignore taxation.   **(18 marks)**
ICAEW Financial Accounting II, July 1982.

10.3 The summarized balance sheet of Rejuvenated (1980) Limited and of Rejuvenated (1974) Limited from which it has recently emerged by way of a reorganization are shown below.

	Rejuvenated (1974) £'000s	Rejuvenated (1980) £'000s
Fixed assets	2 450	1 800
Current assets		
Stock	1 300	900
Work in progress	1 300	700
Debtors	400	350
	5 450	3 750
Share capital		
Ordinary shares of £1	1 000	200
Deferred shares of 5p	—	100
5% Preference shares of £1	1 000	—
8% Preference shares of £1	—	500
Reserves	3 250	50
15% Loan 1992	—	1 000
10% Loan 1982	1 000	—
Current liabilities		
Trade creditors	1 250	1 250
Overdraft	850	650
	5 450	3 750

The changes in share capital reflect the writing off of 90% of the ordinary share capital; the issue for cash of £100 000 of deferred shares at par to the existing ordinary shareholders; the writing-off of 50% of the preference share capital and the increase in the rate of interest from 5% to 8%; the issue for cash of 50 000 ordinary shares at par to the existing preference shareholders.

The debenture holders agreed to redate their loan from 1982 to 1992 in consideration of the increase in the rate of interest from 10% to 15%. They also purchased 50 000 ordinary shares at par.

The assets in the balance sheet of Rejuvenated (1980) reflect up to date valuations on a going concern basis.

It is expected that the profit available for payment of interest and dividends in the following year will amount to £300 000, and would have been available whether or not the new company had been organized.

The deferred shares do not participate in any dividend in any year until a dividend of 20% has been paid on the ordinary shares. Thereafter they rank equally with the ordinary shares on a 'per share' basis.

You are required to:

  (a) **show how the £300 000 available would have been paid to the interested parties if Rejuvenated (1974) had survived** (5 marks),

  (b) **show how the £300 000 available would be distributed by Rejuvenated (1980)** (5 marks),

  (c) **calculate and state the amounts available to the original interested parties of Rejuvenated (1974) following the reorganization** (5 marks),

  (d) **calculate one gearing ratio reflecting the capital position and one gearing ratio reflecting the income position, for both companies** (5 marks), **and**

  (e) **comment on the balance sheet structure of Rejuvenated (1980)** (5 marks).

Ignore all taxation matters when anwering this question. No credit will be given for reflecting current taxation legislation. **(25 marks)**
ICAEW Financial Accounting II, December 1980.

10.4   The summarized balance sheets of two companies are as follows:

	Bombedout plc 31 October 1983 £'000	Allgo Ltd 31 October 1983 £'000
Property	40	—
Plant and machinery	25	284
Stocks	140	564
Debtors	80	846
Creditors	(90)	(916)
Bank overdraft	(202)	(287)
	(7)	491
Share capital – ordinary shares of £1 each	220	10
Profit and loss account	(227)	481
	(7)	491

In order for Messrs Quick and Buck, who jointly owned all the shares in Allgo, to realize some cash, a reverse takeover of their company by Bombedout, a listed but almost moribund company, was made in the following manner:

  (1) The £1 shares in Bombedout were quoted at 10p each and Messrs Quick and Buck each purchased over a period of time 13% of the equity at that price in the market.

  (2) They then joined the board of Bombedout and ousted the existing directors.

  (3) The stock of Bombedout was sold, realizing 65% of book value.

(4) A rights issue was made by Bombedout at par on the basis of one new 'A' ordinary share of £1 each for each £1 ordinary share already in issue. The rights issue was fully taken up. With the consent of the Takeover Panel, there was sent with the renounceable allotment letter an offer from Messrs Quick and Buck to pay £1.10 cash for each new fully paid 'A' ordinary share renounced to them. They received acceptances in respect of 95% of the Bombedout shares for which they made an offer.

(5) Bombedout applied to the Court for a write down of the old shares to a nominal value of 10p each writing off part of the debit balance on profit and loss account.

(6) Bombedout obtained a loan of £400 000 from its bankers, secured on its property. £300 000 of the loan was used for capital improvements to the property and the remainder added to bank balances.

(7) After improvement, the Bombedout property was valued at £500 000 and the valuation incorporated in the accounts of the company.

(8) Although the net assets of Allgo on 31 October 1983 were considered to be shown at fair value, with the consent of its shareholders, Bombedout acquired all the shares in Allgo at 6 times the net asset value on 31 October 1983 by issuing further 'A' ordinary shares of £1 each at par, Messrs Quick and Buck sold 75% of this allotment to a finance house at a discount of $12\frac{1}{2}\%$ for cash.

(9) The goodwill arising on the purchase of Allgo was to be written off immediately.

Other than the above transactions, all of which were completed by 31 March 1984, there was no change in the balance sheet of either company between 31 October 1983 and 31 March 1984.

You are required to:
  (a) prepare the summarized consolidated balance sheet of Bombedout at 31 March 1984 (15 marks), **and**
  (b) calculate how much cash, net of the purchase of shares in Bombedout, Messrs Quick and Buck raised (6 marks).

(21 marks)

Note: Ignore taxation and the costs of reorganization.
ICAEW Financial Accounting II, December 1984.

10.5   Ace plc is a holding company, manufacturing electronic office equipment. It has two wholly owned subsidiaries: Deuce Ltd, manufacturing office stationery, and Trey Ltd, manufacturing an advanced line in microcomputers. As at 31 December 1983 (the group's year-end), the balance sheets of the three companies are as summarized on page 382).

After some years of manufacturing problems and poor sales, with many redundancies among the workforce, the group is now experiencing a revival of its fortunes, in the electronic fields though not in stationery. The directors of Ace plc, as at 1 April 1984, are considering an offer by Quart plc to purchase the whole share capital of Deuce Ltd for £1 000 000 in cash. This, they believe, is the best price that they are likely to obtain.

The directors of Ace plc are planning to develop the business of Trey Ltd, and to raise further funds on the London capital market.

You are required, as Ace plc's chief accountant, to make a short report to the directors (utilizing the information below, with such further, reasonable, assumptions as you think necessary) on a scheme for the reconstruction of the Ace Group's financial structure and for the issue of additional securities, including a recommendation on whether or not to sell Deuce Ltd. The scheme is to be carried through, if possible, by 1 January 1985. (40 marks)

Notes

(1) Ace plc acquired the whole ordinary share capital of Deuce Ltd for £1 500 000 in cash, and that of Trey Ltd in return for an issue of 8.8 million of Ace's own ordinary shares at a premium of £300 000.

(2) Consolidation of the financial statements is effected by the acquisition (purchase) method. Pre-acquisition profits: Deuce, £100 000; Trey, £150 000. Goodwill arising on consolidation has not been amortized.

(3) The dividends of Ace's 10% cumulative preference shares are four years in arrear.

(4) The group's debentures (with no intra-group holdings) were issued on the following terms, at par, and are redeemable at par in all cases:
Ace plc: Interest 12% per annum, redemption 1 January 1986.
Deuce Ltd: Interest 14% per annum, redemption 1 July 1985.
Trey Ltd   Interest 15% per annum, redemption 1 January 1990.
All these debentures are secured by floating charges.

(5) Ace plc's bank overdraft is also secured by a floating charge, ranking after that of the debenture holders.

(6) Professional valuers, as at 1 January 1984, have appraised the non-monetary assets of the group as follows:
Ace plc: Freehold property – land (cost £200 000), market value £300 000; buildings, replacement cost (new), £960 000. Plant, replacement cost (new), £3 500 000. Stocks, replacement cost, £1 100 000.
Deuce Ltd: Freehold property – land (cost £50 000), market value £80 000; buildings, replacement cost (new), £490 000. Plant, replacement cost (new), £1 800 000. Stocks, replacement cost, £550 000.
Trey Ltd: Freehold property – land (cost £400 000), market value £500 000; buildings, replacement cost (new), £1 500 000. Plant, replacement cost (new), £2 500 000. Stocks, replacement cost (new), £1 050 000.

Depreciation (straight line): buildings, 5% per annum; plant, 15% per annum – in both cases, with a full year's charge in the year of acquisition and none in the year of disposal.

(7) For 1984, no acquisitions or disposal of freehold property were planned. In relation to plant, acquisitions were expected to be: Ace, £500000; Deuce, £100000; and Trey, £400000. Disposals were expected to be: Ace, £350000 gross value, £50000 written down value, £60000 proceeds; Deuce, £50000, £10000, and £8000 respectively; and Trey, £250000, £40000, and £45000 respectively.

(8) Profit projections have been made for the years 1984 to 1988, on the assumption that there is no reorganization of the group, and after taking account of asset revaluations as at 1 January 1984. The figures below are trading profits/(losses), net of interest and taxation, before consolidation of the accounts and excluding intra-group dividends.

	Ace £'000s	Deuce £'000s	Trey £'000s
1984	80	(30)	100
1985	120	10	150
1986	150	20	180
1987	160	50	200
1988	180	80	220

(9) Corporation Tax rate is to be taken as 50%. Basic rate of income tax, 30%.

Balance Sheets at 31 December 1983

Net assets	Ace plc £'000s	£'000s	Deuce Ltd £'000s	£'000s	Trey Ltd £'000s	£'000s
Fixed assets						
Freehold property:						
Cost	1 000		400		1 600	
Depreciation	(250)		(150)		(540)	
	—	750	—	250	—	1 060
Plant:						
Cost	3 000		1 500		2 000	
Depreciation	(1 500)		(600)		(800)	
	—	1 500	—	900	—	1 200
Shares in subsidiaries	4 000		—		—	
		6 250		1 150		2 260
Current assets						
Stocks	1 200		600		1000	
Debtors	500		200		400	
Intra-group balance	220		—		—	
Bank and cash balances	30		50		20	
	1 950		850		1420	
Current liabilities						
Bank overdraft	(800)		—		—	
Creditors	(600)		(420)		(440)	
Intra-group balances	—		(100)		(120)	
Corporation Tax	(50)		—		(60)	
Proposed dividend	—		—		(100)	
ACT on proposed dividend	—		—		(43)	
	(1 450)		(520)		(763)	
Net current assets	—	500	—	330	—	657
		6 750		1 480		2917
Financed by:						
Debenture loans		3 000		250		800
Deferred taxation		100		70		67
Capital and reserves						
10% Cumulative preference shares (£1)	500		—		—	
Ordinary shares (25p)	3 500		1 000		2 000	
	4000		1 000		2 000	
Share premium account	350		200		—	
Retained earnings	(700)		(40)		50	
	(350)		160		50	
	—	3 650	—	1 160	—	2 050
		6 750		1 480		2917

A. Cert A., Advanced Financial Accounting, June 1984.

11 Business Combinations

Introduction

Words such as merger, amalgamation, absorption, takeover and acquisition are all used to describe the coming together of two or more businesses. Such words do not have precise legal meanings and, as they are often used interchangeably, the American description 'business combinations' perhaps best describes the subject matter of this chapter.

A company may expand either by 'internal' growth or by 'external' growth. In the former case it expands by undertaking investment projects, such as the purchase of new premises and plant, whilst in the latter case it expands by purchasing a collection of assets in the form of an established business. In this second case we have a business combination in which one company is very much the dominant party, acquiring control of that other business either with or without the consent of the directors of that business.

Where such 'external' growth is contemplated, it will be necessary to value the collection of assets it is proposed to purchase. It will usually be necessary to determine at least two values: (a) the value of the business to its present owners (this will determine the minimum price which will be acceptable); (b) the value of the business when combined with the existing assets of the acquiring company (this will determine the maximum price which may be offered). In some cases it may be possible to apply capital budgeting techniques to arrive at these values but often other methods of valuation, such as those discussed in Chapter 8, will be used.

In other circumstances two or more companies may both see benefits from coming together. Thus two companies may consider that their combined businesses are worth more than the sum of the values of the individual businesses. For such a combination, the individual businesses must be valued to help in the determination of the proportionate shares in the combined business, although, of course, the ultimate shares will to a considerable extent depend upon the bargaining ability of the two parties.

The following table gives some indication of the importance of business combinations in the years 1976–1983. It shows acquisitions and mergers of industrial and commercial companies within the UK:[1]

| Year | Number of companies acquired | Consideration (£ million) | | | |
		Total	Cash	Ordinary shares	Pref. shares/ loan stock
1976	353	448	321	120	7
1977	481	824	512	304	8
1978	567	1140	654	463	23
1979	534	1657	934	515	208
1980	469	1475	760	669	46
1981	452	1144	775	338	31
1982	463	2206	1283	701	223
1983	447	2343	1026	1261	57

Some reasons for combining

Purchase of undervalued assets

As we have seen in the chapter on valuation of a business (Chapter 8), the same collection of assets may have different values to different people. As a result, it is often possible for one business to purchase another business, that is a collection of assets, at a price below the value of the underlying assets. If we take limited companies, for example, the shares of a company may be standing at a relatively low price because the current management is making poor use of the assets or has not communicated good future prospects to the shareholders. Even though the acquiring company purchases the shares at a price higher than the existing market price, it may be able to acquire underlying assets which have a much higher value than the price paid. Indeed, as many asset strippers have found, even the sale of assets on a piecemeal basis may generate a sum considerably in excess of the price paid for those assets.

Economies of scale

The combination of two businesses may result in economies of scale, that is to say the cost of producing the combined output will be less

1 The information has been taken from the CSO publication *Financial Statistics*.

than the sum of the costs of producing the separate outputs or, alternatively, the combined output will be greater for the same total cost. Such economies of scale may exist not only in production but also in administration, research and development and financing.

Concentrating first on production, economies of scale may arise for such reasons as the following: set-up costs may be spread over larger outputs; indivisible units of high cost machinery may become feasible at higher levels of output; where capacity is dependent on volume and cost is dependent on surface area, as in the case of storage tanks, such area – volume relationships may result in less than proportionate rises in costs.

When we turn to administration, a large organization may attract and make better use of scarce managerial talent and enable the firm to employ specialists. Large organizations may also be able to attract suitable people to administer research and development programmes and to use the results of those programmes more effectively. In addition, the larger organization is often in a position to raise and service capital more cheaply than a smaller organization.

Economics textbooks devote considerable space to discussions of the theoretical bases for economies of scale and governments have often encouraged and supported combinations on the grounds that they would improve the efficiency of British industry, in particular its competitiveness in international markets. Such encouragement was, for example, the specific role of the Industrial Reorganization Corporation set up by the Labour government in 1960. This body promoted such mergers as those between Associated Electrical Industries and General Electric Company in 1967 and between Leyland Motor Corporation and British Motor Holdings in 1968. The Corporation was abolished in 1970 by a Conservative government less committed to intervention and subsequent governments have, for reasons which will be discussed later, been less confident of the benefits to be obtained from mergers.

Various techniques have been developed to examine whether and to what extent economies of scale exist in practice. Although there appears to be scope for economies of scale in many industries, these do not appear automatically after a business combination, but have to be planned. A number of studies[2] have found that the performances of many combined businesses have been rather disappointing. In

2 *See*, for example, G. Meeks, *Disappointing Marriage: A Study of the Gains from Merger*, Cambridge University Press, Cambridge, 1977, or G. D. Newbould, *Management and Merger Activity*, Guthstead, London, 1970.

particular there are diseconomies of large organizations, due mainly to the problems of administering large units, which may often outweigh the benefits afforded by economies of scale.

Elimination or reduction of competition

By eliminating or reducing competition, it may be possible for a company to make larger profits; combining with another business may be one means of achieving this end. Although integration may occur for many reasons, one reason may be that it is possible to reduce competition both by vertical integration, that is by combining with a firm at an earlier or later stage of the production cycle, or by horizontal integration, that is by combining with a firm at the same stage in the production cycle.

To illustrate, a firm at one stage of production may combine with a firm at an earlier stage of production, that is a supplier, thus ensuring a ready source of supply and perhaps putting it in a position to charge a higher price to competitors at the second stage, and hence squeeze them out of business. The extent to which this is possible would depend upon the structure of the market, that is the extent to which there are monopoly elements or competitive elements present.

Combination with a firm at the same stage of production would reduce the number of competitors by one and again may give rise to higher profits as a result of the increased industrial concentration. Again, much would depend upon the structure of the industry before and after the combination. The combination of two small firms in a very competitive industry might have little effect, whereas the combination of two giants might turn an oligopoly into a virtual monopoly.

There are obvious dangers to the public at large from mergers which reduce the level of competition and it is for this reason that we have legislation on monopolies and mergers.[3] Under such legislation the Secretary of State and Director General of Fair Trading have discretionary powers to refer certain mergers[4] to the Monopolies and Mergers Commission, an independent body of economists, accountants, lawyers, businessmen and trade unionists supported by a full-time staff. This commission decides whether or not a merger is likely to

3 Current law is contained mainly in the Fair Trading Act 1973 which superseded the Monopolies and Mergers Act 1965.
4 These are mergers where the gross value of assets being transferred exceeds £15 million or where the merger would create or enhance a monopoly share (25% or more) of the relevant market in the UK or a substantial part of the UK.

have effects which are against the public interest. If it concludes that the merger is likely to have adverse effects, the appropriate Secretary of State may take various courses of action; thus he may forbid a proposed merger, reverse one which has already taken place or impose restrictions on the future operations of the merged businesses.

Reduction of risk

By combining with a firm which makes different products, a business is often able to reduce risk. Thus one reason for diversification, the combination of businesses in different industries, may be that it often results in an expected earnings stream which is less variable than the separate earnings streams of the two individual businesses. Such a reduction of risk is usually considered to be an advantage and will often lead to an increase in share values, although it may be argued that a shareholder may be better able to reduce risk himself by the selection of his own portfolio of shares.

Use of price/earnings ratios

In many business combinations, one company has been able to increase the wealth of its own shareholders by combining with a company which has a lower price/earnings ratio.

To illustrate let us take a simple example of two companies:

	Company A	Company B
Earnings	£10 000	£10 000
Number of ordinary shares	100 000	100 000
Earnings per share	10p	10p
Current market price	£1.50	£1.20
P/E ratio	15	12

Let us suppose that company A issues 80 000 shares valued at £120 000 (80 000 at £1.50) in exchange for 100 000 shares in company B valued at £120 000 (100 000 at £1.20). If there is no change in earnings after the combination, the earnings of the combined companies as reflected in the group accounts will be £20 000 and the earnings per share 11p, that is £20 000 divided by 180 000 shares in A. If the market continues to use the P/E ratio of company A, that is 15, the price of a share in company A after the combination will be £1.65. This is greater than £1.50, the price of a share in company A before the combination and hence advantageous to the original shareholders in the company. It is also advantageous to the original shareholders in company B who now hold 80 000 shares in company A valued at £132 000 compared with their former holdings of 100 000 shares in company B which were valued at £120 000.

It may be argued that the market is unlikely to apply the same P/E ratio to the combined earnings as they previously did to the earnings in company A as a separate company. An 'average' P/E ratio of 13.5, calculated as shown below, would perhaps be expected:

	Earnings	Values
Company A	£10 000	£150 000
Company B	£10 000	£120 000
Combined	£20 000	£270 000

Hence the average P/E ratio is 270 000/20 000 = 13.5.

This does not appear to happen in practice, and the resulting P/E ratio is usually well above this 'average' P/E ratio because the market anticipates a better future.

Thus, even though benefits such as economies of scale and reduction of competition do not materialize, some companies have been able to increase the wealth of their shareholders by acquiring other companies with lower P/E ratios.

Managerial motives

Under traditional economic theory, the role of management is to respond in a rational, but more or less automatic way, to circumstances which present themselves. Thus if, for example, economies of scale are perceived to be likely if two businesses combine, such a combination will be pursued in order to maximize the wealth of shareholders.

Gerald Newbould,[5] examined all the major mergers which occurred during the UK merger boom of 1967 and 1968 and found that the role of management in these mergers was very different from that suggested by economic theory. Thus, *inter alia*, he found that often the period between preliminary discussions of a merger and the public announcement of intention to proceed was so short that little fundamental analysis of the benefits or disbenefits of such a combination was possible.

5 G. D. Newbould, *op. cit.*

He also found that in many cases no attempts had been made to obtain the benefits of synergy after the merger and that often performance of the merged businesses was disappointing. Other studies have come to similar conclusions.[6]

The above factors suggested that the usual financial and economic reasons put forward for mergers were, in practice, not of prime importance. What seemed to be a more important determinant of mergers amongst large companies was the objectives of managers. In order to cope with increasing uncertainty, managers desired to increase their market power or to defend their market position. Although such activities could well further the interests of shareholders, they may have even greater benefits for the managers themselves. Thus a less uncertain life, a larger empire and perhaps larger remuneration due to control of such an empire may be extremely important motivating forces.

Whatever the ultimate objective, managerial motives seemed to play a much larger role in merger activity than traditional economic theory allows them.

Methods of combining

In order to be able to acount for combinations, we must first explore some of the methods which may be used to effect them. Such methods may best be classified as to whether or not a group structure results from the combination.

Let us take as an example two companies, L and M, and assume that the respective boards of directors and owners have agreed to combine their businesses.

Combinations which result in a group structure

Two such combinations may be considered.

In the first case, company L may purchase the shares of company M and thereby acquire a subsidiary company; alternatively company M may purchase the shares of company L.

The choice of consideration given in exchange for the shares acquired will determine whether or not the old shareholders in what becomes the subsidiary company have any interest in the combined businesses. Thus if company L issues shares in exchange for the shares of company

6 *See* footnote 2 to this chapter.

M, the old shareholders in company M have an interest in the resulting holding company and thereby in the group whereas, if company L pays cash for the shares in company M, the old shareholders in M take their cash and cease to have any interest in the resulting group.

In the second case, a new company, LM, may be established to purchase the shares of both L and M. Thus the shareholders in L and M may sell their shares to LM in exchange for shares in LM. The resulting group structure would then be:

Holding company

Subsidiary companies

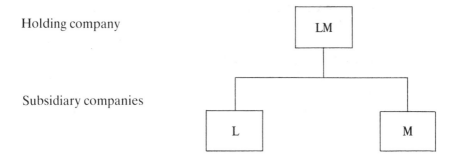

The shareholders in LM would be the old shareholders in the two separate companies and their respective interests would depend, as in all the examples in this section, upon the valuations placed upon the two separate companies, which would in turn depend upon bargaining between the two boards of directors.

It would be possible for company LM to issue not only shares but also loan stock in order to purchase the shares in L and M. It would be difficult for payment to be made in cash as LM is a newly formed company, although it could, of course, issue other shares or raise loans to obtain cash.

Combinations not resulting in a group structure

Again, two such combinations may be considered.

First, instead of purchasing the shares of company M, company L may obtain control of the net assets of M by making a direct purchase of those net assets. The net assets would thus be absorbed into company L and company M would itself receive the consideration. This would in due course be distributed to the shareholders of M by its liquidator.

Once again the choice of consideration determines whether or not the old shareholders in M have any interest in the enlarged company L.

Second, instead of one of the companies purchasing the net assets of the other, a new company may be formed to purchase the net assets of both existing companies. Thus a new company, LM, may be formed to purchase the net assets of company L and company M. If payment is made by issuing shares in LM, these will be distributed by the respective liquidators so that the end result is one company, LM, which owns the net assets previously held by the separate companies and has as its shareholders the old shareholders in the two separate companies.

Preference for group structure

The above are methods of effecting a combination between two, or indeed more, companies. It appears that the majority of large business combinations make use of a group structure rather than a purchase of assets or net assets. Such a structure is advantageous in that separate companies enjoying limited liability are already in existence. It follows that names, and associated goodwill, of the original companies are not lost and, in addition, that it is not necessary to renegotiate contractual arrangements. All sorts of other factors will be important in practice; some examples are the desire to retain staff, the impact of taxation and stamp duty and whether or not there is a remaining minority interest.

Choice of consideration

As discussed above, the choice of consideration will determine who is interested in the single business created by the combination and will therefore be affected by the intentions of the parties to the combination. It will also be affected by the size of the companies and by conditions in the market for securities and the taxation system in force.

The main possible types of consideration are cash, loan stock, ordinary shares or some form of convertible security; all sorts of combinations of these are possible.

Let us look at the use of each of these before turning to some factors which will influence the choice between them.

Cash

Where one company purchases the shares or assets of another for cash the shareholders of the latter company cease to have any interest in the combined businesses.

From the point of view of the selling shareholders, they take a certain cash sum and will be liable to Capital Gains Tax on the disposal of their shares.

From the point of view of the purchasing company, its cash holdings will decrease. It has sometimes been suggested that the use of cash will give a better chance of success if opposition is anticipated and, providing the earnings of the company which is purchased are greater than the earnings which would be made by using cash in other ways, there will be an increase in the earnings per share.

Loan stock

In this case the selling shareholders, either directly or indirectly, exchange shares in one company for loan stock in another company. Hence an equity investment is exchanged for a fixed interest investment, which may or may not be an advantage, depending upon the relative values of the securities and the circumstances of the individual investor. Any liability to Capital Gains Tax will be deferred until ultimate disposal of the loan stock.

From the point of view of the shareholders of the company which is purchasing the shares or net assets, there may be an advantage in that the level of gearing will be increased. In addition, interest on the loan stock will be deductible for Corporation Tax purposes.

Ordinary shares

A share for share exchange is often the method used in combinations involving large companies. Here the shareholder merely exchanges his shares in one company for shares in another company.

From the point of view of the selling shareholder, this may have many benefits, although the extent to which they exist will depend upon the exact terms of the combination and the relative values of the shares. The selling shareholder continues to have an interest in the combined businesses with the benefits mentioned in the second section of this chapter and will not be subject to Capital Gains Tax on the exchange. Against this the value of the security which he receives is not certain but will depend upon market reaction to the combination.

From the point of view of the combined companies a share exchange does not affect their liquidity. The extent to which it is beneficial for the existing shareholders of the company must depend upon the relative values of the shares.

Although shares were a very popular consideration in the late 1960s, the collapse of share prices in the 1970s led to a more widespread use of cash.[7]

Convertible loan stock

In the past decade the issue of convertible loan stock has become more common and has sometimes been used in connection with business combinations. In such a case, the shareholders in one company exchange their shares for convertible loan stock in another company.

From the point of view of a selling shareholder, he exchanges an equity investment for a fixed interest security, but one which is convertible into a equity investment at some time in the future if he so wishes. Thus if in the future share prices move in his favour he will be able to take up his equity interest whilst, if they move against him, he will be able to retain his fixed interest investment. Again, any liability to Capital Gains Tax is deferred until ultimate disposal of the convertible stock or equity shares issued in exchange.

From the point of view of the company issuing such securities, the interest on the loan stock is deductible for taxation purposes and the debt is self-liquidating if loan holders convert loan stock into ordinary shares. If loan holders do convert, the tax deductibility is, of course, lost and in addition there is a reduction in gearing and possible dilution of the existing shareholders' interest.

The choice in practice

As has been seen above, the various forms of consideration which may be used have advantages and disadvantages. The choice in any business combination will depend upon a large number of factors, some of which are discussed in this section.

It is convenient to distinguish between an agreed combination where the two sets of shareholders in the individual companies are to be shareholders in the new or enlarged company and a situation where one party is dominant and is seeking to obtain control of the other company as cheaply as possible.

In the first of these two situations the major part of the consideration must obviously be equity shares although, if a situation of surplus cash or low gearing is expected after the combination, an opportunity may be taken to pay part of the consideration in cash or some form of loan stock.

7 *See* the statistics on page 384 for an analysis of the total expenditure for each of the years 1976–1983 between cash, ordinary shares and fixed interest securities.

In the second situation the choice of consideration will be affected considerably by the nature of the companies involved and the market situation. Where the biddee company is small or opposition is expected, a cash bid may be preferred. Loan stock may be attractive where rates of interest are low and especially if they are expected to rise. Where, however, it is felt that the shares of the dominant company are over-priced relative to those of the other company, then a share issue is likely to be most attractive.

Jim Slater, who rose to fame in the merger boom of the late 1960s, summed up the choice in these circumstances as follows:

> I would like to stress that the question of purchase consideration is another complete subject in itself. If I had to summarize it in a few words, I would say that you should imagine the two businesses together and, if the acquiring company's shares are over-priced, issue as many as possible, and if they are under-priced, use the cheapest loan stock you can issue.[8]

Accounting for business combinations

Accounting for business combinations is a topic which has been the cause of considerable controversy in both the UK and the USA. Most readers will be familiar with the traditional method of accounting, known as the 'acquisition' or 'purchase' method. They may not, however, be familiar with the alternative 'merger' or 'pooling of interests' method. This latter approach is used extensively in the USA and was used in the UK on a number of occasions in the 1960s.[9] ED 3, 'Accounting for acquisitions and mergers', which was published in January 1971, attempted to define the situations in which each method should be used so as to remove any discretion. For reasons explained below, this Exposure Draft never became a Statement of Standard Accounting Practice and, in the UK, the use of the merger method appears to have been extremely rare in recent years. Changes made by the Companies Act 1981 have now made it possible to make progress on this subject and the ASC issued ED 31, with the same title as ED 3, in October 1982.

Acquisition and merger accounting

As stated above, the acquisition method has traditionally been used to account for business combinations and, where the consideration for shares or assets purchased is wholly cash or loan stock, this is agreed to be

8 *See* page 67 in *What is Profit?*, papers presented at the ICAEW Summer Course, 1970.
9 Thus the merger method was used, for example, when British Leyland Motor Corporation Ltd was formed to combine British Motor Holdings Ltd and the Leyland Corporation Ltd in 1968 and also in the combination of Trust House Group Ltd with Fortes Holdings Ltd in 1970.

the correct method of accounting. However, where the consideration given is wholly or predominantly ordinary shares, many accountants would argue that the acquisition method is inappropriate. Here the shareholders in one company exchange their equity holding in that company for an equity interest in another company, a holding company if shares are purchased or an enlarged company if net assets are purchased. In such circumstances, use of the acquisition method frequently produces inconsistencies in the treatment of the two combining companies. These inconsistencies are avoided by the use of the merger method but, as we shall see, consistency is obtained only at a price.

In order to illustrate the differences between the acquisition and merger methods of accounting, let us take a simple example involving a share for share exchange:

EXAMPLE 11.1

Column 1 shows the summarized balance sheets of H Limited and S Limited before combination. H buys the shares in S and gives shares in exchange. Columns 2 and 3 show the results of using, respectively, the acquisition and merger methods of accounting.

Summarized balance sheets

	1 Before combination	2 Acquisition method	3 Merger method
	(£)	(£)	(£)
H Limited			
£1 ordinary shares	1 000	1 800	1 800
Share premium	—	1 600	—
Retained profits	600	600	600
	1 600	4 000	2 400
Net assets	1 600	1 600	1 600
Shares in S Limited, at 'cost'	—	2 400	800
	1 600	4 000	2 400
S Limited			
£1 ordinary shares	800	NO CHANGE	
Retained profits	400		
	1 200		
Net assets	1 200		

In order to concentrate on the essential differences between the methods, we will assume that the current value of each share in both H Limited and S Limited is agreed to be £3, so that H Limited issues 800 shares in exchange for the 800 shares of S Limited.

If the *acquisition method* is used, the shares issued by H Limited will be valued at their value at the date of issue, that is at £3 per share. The investment in subsidiary will be shown at cost of £2400 whilst a share premium of £1600 will be recorded. Column 2 of the summarized balance sheets above reflects these entries.

We now give a consolidated balance sheet for H Limited together with its subsidiary S Limited using the acquisition and merger methods of accounting, respectively:

Consolidated balance sheet of H Limited and subsidiary S Limited

	1	2
	Acquisition method (£)	Merger method (£)
£1 ordinary shares	1 800	1 800
Share premium	1 600	—
Retained profits	600	1 000
	4 000	2 800
Net assets (1600 + £1200)	2 800	2 800
Goodwill on consolidation (£2400 − £1200)	1 200	—
	4 000	2 800

Column 1 shows the consolidated balance sheet immediately after the combination using the acquisition method. In preparing this consolidated balance sheet the excess of the cost of investment in the subsidiary over the value of the net assets acquired is shown as goodwill on consolidation. Good accounting practice would require the net assets of S Limited to be shown at their fair value at the date of acquisition rather than at their book value in the accounts of S Limited but, in order to keep the example simple, this has not been done here. The effect on retained profits and assets of applying this method may be summarized as follows:

(a) *Retained profits* Before the combination, the retained profits of H Limited and S Limited were £600 and £400, respectively. After the combination the profits of S Limited existing at the date of combination are capitalized, so that the retained profits of the group are only £600, those applicable to H Limited.

(b) *Assets* Before the combination the net assets of H Limited and S Limited were shown at book values of £1600 and £1200, respectively. After the combination, although the net assets of H Limited are still included at their historical cost, the net assets of S Limited are included at a global valuation of £2400, that is identified assets of £1200 plus the goodwill of £1200.

Many would question whether this gives a true and fair view of the combination. After all, exactly the same people are interested in the net assets after the combination as before, although their proportionate interests will probably have changed as a result of the bargaining process. All that has happened is that the shareholders in S Limited have exchanged their shares in S Limited for shares in H Limited, which now in turn owns S Limited.

Thus two sets of shareholders have come together for their mutual benefit. Why then should the retained profits of one company be capitalized whilst those of the other are not? Similarly, why should the net assets of one company effectively be shown at their current value whilst those of the other are shown at their historical cost?

A further criticism could be made of the method in that the consolidated balance sheet would look very different if, instead of the acquisition of shares in S Limited by H Limited, S Limited had acquired the shares of H Limited. This is a perfectly feasible alternative means of combination. The results produced will therefore vary depending upon what may in fact be an arbitrary choice of holding company.

Consideration of questions like these have led to the development of the merger method of accounting, which may be said to concentrate on the substance rather than the legal form of the transaction.

Under the *merger method*, shares issued in exchange for other shares are valued not at their fair value, but at their par value. Thus, using our simple example, the 800 shares issued by H Limited would be valued at £1 each, that is £800, rather than at £3 each. Correspondingly, the investment in S Limited would be shown at a 'cost' of only £800. Column 3 of the summarized balance sheets (p. 395) reflects this entry.

Column 2 of the consolidated balance sheets provides the resulting consolidated balance sheet. From this it may be seen that the pre-combination retained profits of the two individual companies are still available while the net assets of both companies are shown at their historical-cost-based valuation. It is as if the companies had been combined since the cradle and it follows that, in preparing the consolidated profit and loss account, the results of both companies would be included for the whole year irrespective of the date on which the combination occurred.[10] In preparing the consolidated accounts necessary adjustments must, of course, be made to reflect uniform accounting policies throughout the group.

While the use of the merger method results in a consistent treatment of the profits and net assets of the two companies, it does, of course, have the result that all the assets are valued on the basis of old historical costs, which are arguably of little relevance to users of the accounts. Under the acquisition method, the assets of at least one company are shown at their fair value at the date of the combination and to move from such a position to one where all assets are shown on the basis of their historical costs to the separate companies, is regarded by some accountants as a step in the wrong direction.

In ED 22, the IASC proposed the use of a method which seemed to offer the advantages of the merger method without this disadvantage. Under this 'New entity method', both companies were required to restate the carrying value of their assets and liabilities to their fair values at the date of combination so that the assets of both companies would be shown on a consistent basis at fair value rather than historical cost. Such a method, which apparently owed much to Dutch thinking, does not appear in International Accounting Standard (IAS) 22[11] although it is mentioned in an appendix to our own ED 31.[12] Instead of requiring the use of such a method, that appendix merely permits its use, regarding it as a variant of merger accounting using current values.

In the above example the total nominal value of the shares issued was the same as the total nominal value of the shares purchased. In most combinations this will not be the case and it is necessary to deal with the situation where these are not equal. Where the par value of the shares issued exceeds the par value of the shares acquired, there has effectively been a capitalization of reserves as far as the combined businesses are concerned. Hence the reserves after the combination will be reduced by this excess. Where the par value of the shares issued

---

10 This is to be contrasted with the position using the acquisition method of accounting where the consolidated profit and loss account should only include the results of a new subsidiary from the date of acquisition. This topic is considered in some detail in the following chapter.
11 IAS 22, 'Accounting for business combinations", IASC, London, 1983.
12 ED 31, 'Accounting for acquisitions and mergers', ASC, London, 1982.

is less than the par value of the shares purchased, a capital reserve is created to maintain the permanent capital, that is the share capital and non-distributable reserves, at the same level after the combination as the aggregate permanent capital of the two companies before the combination.

In the above example a method of combination resulting in a group structure has been illustrated. It is important to bear in mind that the possibility of choice between the acquisition or merger method applies to all the possible methods of combination outlined in the third section of this chapter. Thus providing shares are issued in exchange for shares or the total net assets of a company, so that the two sets of shareholders have an interest in the resulting combined business we have the theoretical possibility of applying the merger method.

Towards an accounting standard

The fate of ED 3
In January 1971 the ASC issued ED 3, 'Accounting for acquisitions and mergers', in which it attempted to distinguish between two types of business combination and specify the appropriate accounting treatment for each. If the combination was an acquisition the acquisition method of accounting had to be used while, if the combination satisfied the definition of a merger, merger accounting had to be applied.

Even when this Exposure Draft was issued, there was some doubt as to the legality of the merger method under the then law. As has been shown, use of the merger method requires that shares issued are recorded as being issued at their nominal value rather than their market or fair values. Although the Exposure Draft referred to legal opinion to the contrary, such a treatment seemed to many to be illegal under Sec. 56 of the Companies Act 1948 which states quite clearly:

> Where a company issues shares at a premium, whether for cash or otherwise, a sum equal to the aggregate amount or value of the premiums on those shares shall be transferred to an account, to be called 'the share premium account', . . .

The recording of shares issued at their par values, when their fair value was in excess of par value, had already been held to be illegal in the case of *Henry Head & Co. Ltd* v. *Ropner Holdings*[13] and, in view of the questionable legality of the proposals in ED 3, the Exposure Draft was first allowed to go out of print and then subsequently withdrawn.

---

13 *Henry Head & Co. Ltd* v. *Ropner Holdings* (1951) All E.R. 994.

The illegality of the merger method was subsequently confirmed in the case of *Shearer* v. *Bercain Ltd*[14] and little progress was possible until the Companies Act 1981 legalized the use of the merger method of accounting in certain circumstances.

The Companies Act 1981
The Companies Act 1981 relieves companies from the need to create a share premium account, which would otherwise be required under Sec. 56 of the 1948 Act, where shares are issued at a value in excess of their nominal value.[15] The relief is available when a company issues equity shares in exchange for equity shares in another (the acquired) company such that, following the transaction, it holds at least 90% of the nominal value of each class of equity share of the acquired company. If these conditions are satisfied, relief from Sec. 56 of the 1948 Act is also extended to any equity shares which are issued in exchange for non-equity shares in the acquired company without restriction on the proportion of non-equity shares acquired.[16]

Thus, if one company issues equity shares to acquire 95% of the equity shares of another company, it is not necessary to create any share premium account in respect of that transaction. If, however, one company already holds 20% of the equity shares in another company and then purchases an additional 75% of those shares, the relief from the need to create a share premium account applies only to the equity shares issued to obtain the 75% holding, that is the purchase which takes the total holding over 90%.

The main consequence of the above provisions is that it permits, although it does not require, the subsequent use of the merger method to account for the combination. In addition, a less restricted retrospective relief is given to companies which have applied merger accounting before 1981, effectively legalizing what was illegal at the time. Relief from the requirement to create a share premium account is also provided in the case of certain group reconstructions which involve the transfer of ownership of a company within a group.

Since the use of the merger method of accounting has been legalized, the ASC has again turned its attention to the circumstances in which this method of accounting should be used. Before we look at the pro-

14 *Shearer* v. *Bercain Ltd* (1980) S.T.C. 359.
15 The detailed law is contained in Companies Act 1981, Secs 36–41.
16 Equity share capital is defined widely to mean 'in relation to a company, its issued share capital excluding any part thereof which, neither as respects dividends nor as respects capital, carries any right to participate beyond a specified amount in a distribution'. Companies Act 1948, Sec 154(5).

posals contained in ED 31, which was issued in October 1982, we shall examine some of the matters which that Exposure Draft has had to resolve.

Criteria for use of the merger method
Use of the merger method of accounting would seem to offer certain advantages where there is a uniting of interests, that is where the equity shareholders in two separate companies pool their interests to become equity shareholders in a combined entity.

As described above, the law now allows (but does not require) the use of the merger method providing at least 90% of the equity shares of the acquired company are part of the pool, or, to put it another way, even when up to 10% of the equity shares do not become part of the pool. Within this legal framework, the ASC must decide what conditions are necessary for the use of the merger method of accounting and whether, if those conditions are satisfied, use of the merger method should be obligatory or optional. In this section some of the factors that will have to be considered are briefly discussed while in the final section of the chapter we will examine the proposals contained in ED 31.

Firstly, although there must be a uniting of interests, to what extent is it necessary to obtain the approval of the two sets of shareholders? Do all the shareholders in the two companies have to agree to the merger or only some minimum proportion? The law requires the holding in the offeree company to exceed 90% but it says nothing about obtaining the agreement of the shareholders in the offeror company. Clearly the ASC could, if it wished, impose much more stringent conditions here.

Secondly, there is the question of relative size. If one company is much smaller than the other then, even though all shareholders in both companies agree to a uniting of interests, the end result may well be a situation in which one set of shareholders is dominant in the combined entity with the other set of shareholders having insignificant influence. Is this really a uniting of interests or merely an 'acquisition' using equity shares as the consideration?

Thirdly, in order for there to be a uniting of interests, the consideration must be equity shares. If the consideration is wholly cash or loan stock, resources leave the combining businesses and one set of shareholders ceases to have any equity interest in the combination and there is definitely no uniting of interests. A difficulty arises where the consideration consists mainly of equity shares but also partly of cash or loan stock. Does this disqualify the combination for treatment as a merger? If it does not do so in principle, then what is the maximum percentage of the consideration which may be given in a form other than equity shares?

These are the main questions which must be addressed in clarifying the circumstances in which merger accounting may or should be used. By the nature of the questions, answers can only involve arbitrary choice and hence it is not surprising that the selection of a suitable set of criteria has posed problems for standard setting bodies here and overseas.

The approach of ED 31

ED 31 requires the use of acquisition accounting for an acquisition and merger accounting for a merger. It defines the conditions for use of the merger method as follows:[17]

> The conditions which must be met in order for a business combination to be accounted for as a merger are as follows:
>
> (a) the business combination should result from an offer to the holders of all equity shares and the holders of all voting shares which are not already held by the offeror; the offer should be approved by the holders of the voting shares of the company making the offer; and
>
> (b) the offer should be accepted by holders of at least 90% of all equity shares and of the shares carrying at least 90% of all votes of the offeree company; for this purpose, any convertible stock is not to be regarded as equity except to the extent that it is converted into equity as a result of the business combination; and
>
> (c) not less than 90% of the fair value of the total consideration given for the equity share capital (including that given for shares already held) should be in the form of equity capital; not less than 90% of the fair value of the consideration given for voting non-equity share capital (including that given for shares already held) should be in the form of equity and/or voting non-equity share capital.

If we concentrate on a situation in which the two companies combining have only voting equity shares in issue, the conditions may be summarized in the following way.

In order to be able to use the merger method of accounting there must be a uniting of interests approved by a majority of shareholders in the offeror company and by at least 90% of the total shareholders in the offeree company.[18] Not less than 90% of the fair value of the

---

17 ED 31, Para. 17.
18 This has the consequence that a merger cannot occur if the offeror company has previously purchased 10% or more of the shares in the offeree company.

consideration given for the total holding in the offeree company, acquired both now and in the past, must consist of equity shares; thus the maximum proportion of the total consideration which may be paid in cash or loan stock is 10%. The ASC did not consider it necessary to impose a size test in ED 31, although such a test had been included in ED 3.

In a Statement of Intent, issued in April 1984, the ASC has subsequently signified its intention to develop a standard using different criteria from those discussed above. It appears that the revised criteria will remove the requirement for approval of the offer by the holders of the voting shares in the offeror company. This, in effect, would have made the use of the merger method of accounting optional in that its use could be avoided it the directors of the offeror company refrained from obtaining the necessary approval. In addition it appears that the standard will contain a limit of 20%, rather than 10%, on the amount of non-equity included in the total consideration and a limit of 20%, rather than 10%, on the proportion of shares which the offeror may hold prior to making the offer for the remaining shares.

At the time of writing it remains to be seen what conditions will be included in the Statement of Standard Accounting Practice. Indeed there is even some doubt as to whether the use of the merger method will be required even if the conditions are satisfied!

Questions

11.1 **(a)** **What differences may arise in the presentation of a consolidated balance sheet if the merger method is used rather than the acquisition method?** (10 marks)

   (b) **State briefly the circumstances in which relief is available under the 1981 Companies Act from the requirements of Sec. 56 of the 1948 Companies Act.** (Section 56 requires the premium on an issue of shares to be transferred to a share premium account). (10 marks)

   (20 marks)

A. Cert. A., The Regulatory Framework of Accounting, June 1983.

11.2   In the United Kingdom, the merger (pooling) method of preparing group accounts was considered illegal until the Companies Act 1981 came into force. Today it is considered permissible, in certain circumstances.

You are required:
(a) to explain the different effects of preparing group accounts by the acquisition (purchase), and merger (pooling) methods in relation to a dynamic

group which acquires and disposes of subsidiaries from time to time over a period of years. (**N.B. You are NOT asked to expound the mechanics of the two methods**); and   (9 marks)

(b) to offer reasons for the use of the two methods in the different circumstances in which they are appropriate.   (6 marks)
                                                                    (**15 marks**)

A. Cert. A. Advanced Financial Accounting, June 1984.

11.3 Consolidated Furniture Group plc wishes to adopt the merger accounting principles in ED 31, *Accounting for Acquisitions and Mergers*, in respect of its combination with Tables & Chairs Ltd on 30 September 1983.

On 1 August 1983 Consolidated Furniture Group plc acquired 5% of the issued share capital of Tables & Chairs Ltd for a consideration of 80 000 shares of 25p each at an agreed value of 125p each.

The terms of the merger on 30 September 1983, which were accepted by all shareholders and declared unconditional on the same day, were that for every 8 shares held in Tables & Chairs Ltd, a holder received 20 shares of 25p each at an agreed value of 135p each in Consolidated Furniture Group plc plus £3 nominal of 13% Unsecured Loan Stock 2002.

All the shares issued were credited as fully paid and ranked *pari passu* with existing shares in issue except that those issued on 30 September 1983 were not to rank for the final dividend in respect of the year ended 30 November 1983.

The draft summarized balance sheet and profit and loss account of the companies for the year ended 30 November 1983, the accounting reference date for Consolidated Furniture Group plc, were:

	Consolidated Furniture Group plc	Tables & Chairs Ltd
Balance sheet	£'000	£'000
Fixed assets	4 563	3 092
Goodwill at cost	—	800
Investments	175	—
Current assets	2 369	3 626
Current liabilities	(2 286)	(4 207)
	4 821	3 311
Share capital	3 000	1 600
Reserves	1 821	1 711
	4 821	3 311

	£'000	£'000
Profit and loss account		
Turnover	36 873	25 003
Profit before tax	1 151	127
Taxation	260	—
Profit after tax	891	127
Dividends paid	288	—
Profits retained	603	127

Additional information is given as follows:

(1) The reserves of Consolidated Furniture Group plc at 30 November 1983 consisted of a share premium account of £140 000 and revenue reserves of £1 681 000. The reserves in Tables & Chairs Ltd are undistributed revenue reserves.

(2) The issue of the shares made on 1 August 1983 is reflected in the draft financial statements.

(3) It is the policy of Consolidated Furniture Group plc to write off goodwill in equal instalments over 5 years.

(4) It is considered that the market value of the 13% loan stock issued is par.

(5) The share capitals of the companies are:
Consolidated Furniture Group plc   —   ordinary 25p each
Tables & Chairs Ltd   —   ordinary £1 each

(6) The directors of Consolidated Furniture Group plc resolve to propose a final dividend of 1p per share. This is not yet reflected in the draft financial statements.

You are required to:
(a) prepare a consolidated balance sheet and profit and loss account, in summary form, of Consolidated Furniture Group plc at 30 November 1983 (14 marks)
(b) give the revised analysis of reserves of Consolidated Furniture Group plc at 30 November 1983 suitable for inclusion in the published financial statements (5 marks), **and**
(c) comment whether you consider merger accounting to be appropriate in the above example giving an indication of advantages which may arise (5 marks)

Note: Make calculations to nearest £'000 and ignore the costs of the merger and Advance Corporation Tax.   **(24 marks)**

ICAEW Financial Accounting II, December 1983

12 Some Problems of Accounting for Intercompany Investments: Associated Companies and Groups

Degrees of investment

Where one company acquires shares in another company, the appropriate accounting treatment depends upon the intention of the investing company's directors.

If the investment is intended to be for the short term it will be treated as a current asset whereas if it is intended for the long term it will be treated as a fixed asset.[1] In a traditional historical cost balance sheet, an investment treated as a current asset will be shown at the lower of cost and net realizable value while an investment treated as a fixed asset will be shown at its historical cost unless its value has fallen permanently below cost when it will be shown at that lower value.

For both short-term and long-term investments, it is usual to take credit in the profit and loss account of the investing company for dividends received and receivable, although dividends receivable are only recognized to the extent that they are in respect of accounting periods ended on or before the accounting year end of the investing company and have been declared prior to approval of the investing company's own accounts. Some companies are even more prudent and take credit only for dividends received in an accounting period.

The above accounting treatments provide limited information to users of the investing company's accounts and, where the investment is long term and substantial, extensive modifications are made. Thus, where the investment is sufficient to give the investing company significant influence over the investee company, that is sufficient influence to constitute it an associated company, SSAP 1 requires a special accounting treatment.[2]

---

1 The balance sheet formats under Companies Act 1981 require, *inter alia*, the separate disclosure of shares in group companies, shares in related companies and other investments other than loans. The term 'related company' includes associated companies but is a somewhat wider category of investment.

2 SSAP 1, 'Accounting for the results of associated companies', was issued by the Accounting Standards Steering Committee in January 1971. Following a review of the operation of the

Where the investment is sufficient to create a holding-company/subsidiary-company relationship, the investing company must, subject to certain exceptions, prepare group accounts.[3] Such group accounts will normally take the form of a set consolidated accounts[4] and readers are assumed to be thoroughly familiar with the basic method of consolidation used in the UK.

This chapter looks first at the methods of accounting for associated companies. It then turns to some of the problems which arise in connection with accounting for groups, paying particular attention to those problems which are the subject matter of SSAP 14, 'Group accounts'. Problems of accounting for associated companies and subsidiaries situated overseas aré left until the next chapter.

Accounting for associated companies

What is an associated company?

Before SSAP 1 specified the appropriate accounting treatment for an associated company, a long-term investment in another company was usually treated in one of two ways. Either it was a simple investment and was treated as a fixed asset, as discussed above, or it was an investment in a subsidiary, in which case it was normal to prepare a separate set of consolidated accounts replacing the investment by the underlying assets and liabilities.

The original SSAP 1 which was issued in January 1971, recognized that there is an intermediate type of investment, an associated company, which it defined as follows:[5]

A company (not being a subsdiary of the investing group or company) is an associated company of the investing group or company if;

(a) the investing group or company's interest in the associated company is effectively that of a partner in a joint venture or consortium or
(b) the investing group or company's interest in the associated company is for the long term and is substantial (i.e. not less than 20 per cent of the equity voting rights), and, having regard to the disposition of the other shareholdings,

standard and the publication of ED 25, a revised SSAP 1, 'Accounting for associated companies', was issued by the ASC in April 1982.
3 Companies Act 1948, Sec. 150.
4 *See* Companies Act 1948, Sec. 151, and SSAP 14, 'Group accounts', ASC, London, 1978, Para. 15.
5 SSAP 1, 'Accounting for the results of associated companies', ASC, London, January 1971, Para. 6.

the investing group or company is in a position to exercise a significant influence over the associated company.

In both cases it is essential that the investing group or company participates (usually through representation on the board) in commercial and financial policy decisions of the associated company, including the distribution of profits.

The essence of the relationship is whether or not the investing company is able to exercise significant influence over the investee company so that the use of an historical-cost-based valuation and the taking of credit for dividends received and receivable is no longer an adequate method of accounting. Whether or not such significant influence exists must depend upon the particular distribution of shareholdings: it could exist with a holding of 16% of the equity shares of a company, if ownership of the remaining shares was highly dispersed, and may not exist with a holding of 40%, if, for example, the remaining 60% of the equity shares are held by one other person or entity.

As can be seen in Para. (b) of the above definition, the original SSAP 1 specifically mentioned a holding of 20% of the equity voting rights and this led to a situation in which some accountants tended to apply a mechanical test, treating any investment of more than 20% as an associated company and any investment of 20% or less as a simple investment. Thus some accountants preferred to use this objective cut-off point rather than to make a subjective judgement taking into account all of the relevant factors.

As part of its normal programme of reviewing standards the ASC reconsidered the principles of SSAP 1 during 1979 and issued ED 25, 'Accounting for the results of associated companies', in September 1979. In due course a revised SSAP 1, 'Accounting for associated companies', was issued in April 1982 and this has provided a more satisfactory definition of an associated company:[6]

An associated company is a company not being a subsidiary of the investing group or company in which:

(a) the interest of the investing group or company is effectively that of a partner in a joint venture or consortium and the investing group or company is in a position to exercise a significant influence over the company in which the investment is made, or

(b) the interest of the investing group or company is for the long term and is substantial and, having regard to the disposition of the other shareholdings, the investing group or company is in a position to exercise a significant influence over the company in which the investment is made.

6 Revised SSAP 1, 'Accounting for associated companies'. ASC, London, April 1982, Part 2, Para. 13.

> Significant influence over a company essentially involves participation in the financial and operating policy decisions of that company (including dividend policy) but not necessarily control of those policies. Representation on the board of directors is indicative of such participation, but will neither necessarily give conclusive evidence of it nor be the only method by which the investing company may participate in policy decisions.

Although no figures appears in the above definition, a holding of 20% of the equity voting rights is still used to provide a cut-off point in helping to determine whether or not an investee company is an associated company. Where the investing company or group holds 20% or more of the equity voting rights, there is a presumption that the investee company is an associated company, which may be rebutted if the investing company or group can clearly demonstrate that it is not in a position to exercise significant influence. Conversely, where the investing company or group holds less than 20% of the equity voting rights, there is a presumption that no significant influence, and hence no associated company, exists. To treat the investee company as an associated company in such circumstances requires the investing company both to demonstrate clearly that it is in a position to exercise significant influence and to obtain the concurrence of the associated company.[7] The revised statement thus provides an objective cut-off point at a holding of 20% of the equity voting rights but quite sensibly recognizes that a classification based on one such figure will not always be appropriate.

Possible methods of accounting for associated companies

Where one company does exercise significant influence over another it seems unreasonable to account for an investment in that company as a simple investment. In order to evaluate the stewardship of the directors of the investing company, users require further information. To take credit in the profit and loss account merely for dividends received and receivable is not really sufficient where the directors of the investing company are able to influence the level of those dividends. In addition, to show the investment in the balance sheet at its historical cost gives no guide to what is happening to the underlying assets, the use of which is influenced by the investing company's directors.

If then treatment as a simple investment is inadequate for associated companies, what method should we use? There would seem to be two closely related possibilities. We could use a method of proportional

---

7 Revised SSAP 1, Paras 14 and 15.

consolidation, with various levels of disclosure, or we could use a method common in the USA, known as the equity method of accounting. SSAP 1 requires the use of the equity method of accounting, but let us also examine the alternative of proportional consolidation.

Using the method of proportional consolidation we would remove the investment in the associated company from the investing company's balance sheet and replace it by the proportionate share of the assets and liabilities of the associated company together with any premium or discount on acquisition. In the profit and loss account of the investing company we would remove any dividends received or receivable already credited and take credit, instead, for the appropriate proportion of profits or losses made by the associated company. The consolidated retained profits would then include the appropriate proportion of the post-acquisition profits retained by the associated company. Having adopted this approach we would disclose the resulting figures in a number of ways. Thus it is possible to show the share of the assets and liabilities of the associated company as one block in both the balance sheet and the profit and loss account. Alternatively, the individual items of the associated company could be grouped with the corresponding items in the accounts of the investing company, either with or without disclosure of the make up of the resulting figures.

Using the equity method of accounting we would value the investment in the balance sheet at cost plus the share of post-acquisition profits retained by the associated company.[8] Thus the balance sheet value of the investment would be increased year by year by the appropriate proportion of the increase in net assets of the associated company due to retained profits and the investing company's profit and loss account would be credited, not with dividends received and receivable, but with the appropriate proportion of the profits of the associated company. Conversely, the balance sheet value of the investment would be reduced if there was a decrease in the post-acquisition retained profits and the profit and loss account would be debited with the appropriate proportion of the losses of the associated company. The profit and loss account under both proportional consolidation and the equity method would be similar.

Let us explore these possible methods of accounting before considering the provisions of SSAP 1 in more detail.

---

8 Although the carrying value of the investment would be determined in this way, the revised SSAP 1 requires us to provide an analysis of the figure on a different basis which is explained below.

The summarized balance sheets of A Limited and B Limited on 31 December 19X1 are as follows:

Summarized balance sheets on 31 December 19X1

	A Limited (£)	B Limited (£)
Fixed assets		
Tangible assets	90 000	40 000
Investment in B Limited,		
5000 shares at cost	22 000	—
Net current assets	10 000	24 000
	122 000	64 000
Share capital, £1 shares	50 000	20 000
Retained profits	72 000	44 000
	122 000	64 000

A purchased its 25% holding in B Limited some years ago when the retained profits of B were £28 000. Providing there have been no changes in share cpaital, this tells us that B's summarized balance sheet at the date of acquisition was:

	£
Share capital	20 000
Retained profits	28 000
	48 000
Net assets	48 000

A purchased a 25% interest in these net assets for £22 000 and hence paid a premium on acquisition of £10 000 (i.e. £22 000 less 25% of £48 000).[9] Between the date of acquisition and 31 December 19X1 B has increased its retained profits by £16 000 (i.e. £44 000 less £28 000). A's share of this retained post-acquisition profit is 25% or £4 000. We may therefore replace the asset 'Investment in B Limited', shown in the balance sheet of A at £22 000, by the following items:

---

9 In computing this premium, it is necessary to consider the fair values of the net assets at the date of acquisition rather than the values of those net assets in the accounts of B Limited (revised SSAP 1, Para. 26). For ease of exposition, we have assumed that fair values are equal to the book values.

	£
Fixed assets	
Tangible assets, 25% × 40 000	10 000
Premium on acquisition	10 000
Net current assets 25% × 24 000	6 000
	26 000
less Retained profits (share of post-acquisition retained profits)	4 000
	22 000

Using proportional consolidation we would produce one of two balance sheets depending upon whether or not we group together items relating to the associated company.

Assuming first that we do keep all items relating to the associated company together, our summarized balance sheet would appear as follows:

A Limited
Summarized balance sheet on 31 December 19X1
(using proportional consolidation and grouping together assets and liabilities relating to associated company)

	£	£
Fixed assets		
Tangible assets		90 000
Investment in associated company		
Share of tangible assets	10 000	
Share of net current assets	6 000	
Premium on acquisition	10 000	
		26 000
Net current assets		10 000
		126 000
Share capital, £1 shares		50 000
Retained profits		
A Limited	72 000	
B Limited	4 000	
		76 000
		126 000

Alternatively we could group various items relating to the associated company with the corresponding items of A Limited, producing a balance sheet as follows:

A Limited
Summarized balance sheet on 31 December 19X1
(using proportional consolidation and grouping like items for investing
company and associated company together)

	£	£
Fixed assets		
Tangible assets		
A Limited	90 000	
B Limited	10 000	100 000
Premium on acquisition of investment in B Limited		10 000
Net current assets		
A Limited	10 000	
B Limited	6 000	16 000
		126 000
Share capital, £1 shares		50 000
Retained profits		
A Limited	72 000	
B Limited	4 000	76 000
		126 0000

Using the equity method of accounting the investment is simply
shown at cost plus the share of post-acquisition profits retained by
the associated company, that is at £26 000 (£22 000 plus £4000):

A Limited
Summarized balance sheet on 31 December 19X1
(using equity method of accounting)

	£	£
Fixed assets		
Tangible assets		90 000
Investment in associated company (see below)		26 000
Net current assets		10 000
		126 000
Share capital, £1 shares		50 000
Retained profit		
A Limited	72 000	
B Limited	4 000	76 000
		126 000

The carrying value of the investment may be calculated as follows:

	£
Cost of investment	22 000
add Share of post-acquisition profits retained by B Limited	4 000
	26 000

As discussed below, the revised SSAP 1 requires a more informative analysis of the carrying value:

	£
Share of net assets, 25% of £64 000	16 000
Premium on acquisition	10 000
	26 000

Comparison of the way in which the investment is shown using the equity method of accounting with the first of the two balance sheets using proportional consolidation makes it clear why the equity method is often referred to as a 'one line consolidation'. The investment is shown at a value equal to the appropriate proportion of the net assets of the associated company at the balance sheet date plus any premium or less any discount on acquisition.

In the USA it is common to write off any premium on acquisition so that the carrying value of the investment is always equal to the appropriate proportion of the net assets as shown in the balance sheet of the associated company. In the UK, SSAP 22, 'Accounting for goodwill', requires that such a premium on acquisition should normally be written off immediately against reserves although it also permits its amortization through the profit and loss account on a systematic basis over its useful economic life.[10]

It may be observed that proportional consolidation provides greater information about the underlying assets and liabilities[11] and it is possible to argue that it would be more useful, particularly in the case of an associated company formed by several companies as a joint venture.

The equity method of accounting and the revised SSAP 1

SSAP 1 requires the use of the equity method of accounting for associated companies.

10 SSAP 22, 'Acounting for goodwill', ASC, London, December 1984, Paras 32 and 34.
11 Revised SSAP 1, Para. 30, actually provides that more detailed information about the associated company's tangible and intangible assets should be given if the interests in the associated company is material and more detailed information would assist in giving a true and fair view.

Where the investing company prepares consolidated accounts, the equity method described in the previous section is applied. Where the investing company does not prepare consolidated accounts, it must prepare its own accounts following the traditional accounting principles for long-term investments. It must then either prepare a second set of accounts in which the full equity method of accounting is applied or provide supplementary information in the notes to its own accounts showing the relevant figures which would appear if the equity method had been used.[12]

To illustrate the approach of SSAP 1 let us first take the situation where the investing company, C Limited, does have subsidiaries and does prepare consolidated accounts. The consolidated accounts for the group, together with the accounts of the associated company D Limited, for the year ended 31 December 19X1 are given below.

Summarized profit and loss accounts for the year ended 31 December 19X1

	C Limited Consolidated P and L account (£)	D Limited associated company (£)
Turnover	1 040 000	720 000
Operating profit (consolidated profit includes a dividend receivable from D Limited amounting to £18 000)	210 000	180 000
less Taxation	100 000	60 000
	110 000	120 000
less Minority interest	10 000	—
	100 000	120 000
add Extraordinary profit (net of taxation and minority interest)	20 000	90 000
	120 000	210 000
less Dividends proposed	40 000	60 000
Retained profits for year	80 000	150 000

Movement on reserves for year	£	£
Retained profits brought forward	400 000	240 000
Retained profits for year	80 000	150 000
Retained profits carried forward	480 000	390 000

---

12 SSAP 1, Paras 24 and 35. This does not apply if the investing company is itself a wholly owned subsidiary.

The consolidated profit and loss account includes a dividend of £18 000 receivable from D Limited and in the consolidated balance sheet the long-term investment in D Limited is shown at its historical cost of £80 000.

Summarized balance sheet on 31 December 19X1

	C Limited Consolidated accounts (£)	D Limited Associated company (£)
Fixed assets		
Goodwill on consolidation	70 000	—
Tangible assets	510 000	420 000
Investment in associated company, 45 000 shares (30%) at cost	80 000	—
Net current assets	280 000	360 000
	940 000	780 000
less Long-term loans	100 000	150 000
	840 000	630 000
less Deferred taxation	80 000	60 000
	760 000	570 000
Share capital, £1 shares	200 000	150 000
Share premium	40 000	30 000
Retained profits	480 000	390 000
	720 000	570 000
Minority interests	40 000	—
	760 000	570 000

C Limited acquired its 30% interest in D Limited some years ago when the retained profits of D were £60 000. It therefore paid a premium on acquisition of £8000.[13]

13 This premium is calculated as follows:

Cost of investment		£80 000	
less Share of:			
Share capital	£150 000		
Share premium	30 000		
Retained profits	60 000		
30% of	240 000	72 000	
Premium on acquisition		8 000	

We are implicitly assuming that the fair value of the net assets at the date of acquisition was equal to their book value and that there have been no changes to the share capital or share premium since that date.

Let us concentrate first on the consolidated profit and loss account. At present this includes £18 000 in respect of the dividend receivable from D Limited. This must be removed and replaced by the share of the profits or losses of the associated company whether or not distributed:

	D Limited (£)	30% share (£)
Operating profit	180 000	54 000
less Taxation	60 000	18 000
	120 000	36 000
add Extraordinary profit (net of tax)	90 000	27 000
	210 000	63 000

Inclusion of these figures in the consolidated profit and loss account produces the following result:

Summarized consolidated profit and loss account for the year ended 31 December 19X1
(including results of associated company)

	£	£
Turnover (group only)		1 040 000
Operating profit		
Group (£210 000–£18 000)		192 000
Share of associated company		54 000
		246 000
less Taxation		
Group	100 000	
Share of associated company	18 000	118 000
		128 000
less Minority interests		10 000
		118 000
add Extraordinary profit		
Group	20 000	
Share of associated company	27 000	47 000
		165 000
less Dividends proposed		40 000
Retained profit for year		125 000
Retained by group	80 000	
Retained by associated company	45 000	
	125 000	

We have brought in the share of profits amounting to £63 000 to replace the dividend receivable of £18 000. Thus we have brought in an extra £45 000 which is, of course, the share of profits retained by the associated company in respect of the year as noted at the foot of the consolidated profit and loss account.

When we turn to the movement on reserves we must include the share of all post-acquisition profits retained by the associated company. This statement includes the workings:

Movement on reserves for the year ended 31 December 19X1
(with workings)

	£	£
Retained profits on 1 January 19X1		
Group		400 000
Share of associated company post-acquisition		
profits 30% × (£240 000 − £60 000)		54 000
		454 000
Retained profit for year, per consolidated profit		
and loss account		125 000
Retained profits on 31 December 19X1		
Group, per consolidated balance sheet	480 000	
Share of associated company		
30% × (£390 000 − £60 000)	99 000	
	579 000	579 000

At the end of the year we have therefore increased consolidated reserves by £99 000, the share of post-acquisition profits retained by the associated company, and we must therefore increase the carrying value of our investment by this figure in the consolidated balance sheet to keep it in balance. The carrying value of the investment is therefore £179 000, the cost of £80 000 plus £99 000.

C Limited
Summarized consolidated balance sheet on 31 December 19X1

	£
Fixed assets	
Goodwill on consolidation	70 000
Tangible assets	510 000
Investment in associated company	179 000
	759 000
Net current assets	280 000
Carried forward	1 039 000

	£
Brought forward	1 039 000
less Long-term loans	100 000
	939 000
Deferred taxation	80 000
	859 000
Share capital, £1 shares	200 000
Share premium	40 000
Reserves	579 000
	819 000
Minority interests	40 000
	859 000

The revised SSAP 1 requires that the investment in the associated company be analysed into three components:[14] (a) the investing group's share of the net assets other than goodwill of the associated company, (b) the investing group's share of the goodwill of the associated company and (c) the premium paid on the acquisition of the interest in the associated company after attributing fair values to the net assets acquired. In view of their intangible nature, (b) and (c) may be combined in one figure for disclosure purposes.

In our example there is no goodwill in the balance sheet of D Limited and, in the absence of details of the fair values of assets at the date of acquisition, an analysis would appear as follows:

	£
Investment in associated company	
Share of net assets other than goodwill	171 000
Premium on acquisition	8 000
	179 000

In order for the aggregation of net asset values of the associated companies with those of the investing group to be meaningful it is, of course, necessary for the accounting periods and policies of the associated company to coincide with those of the group. In practice this may pose problems requiring adjustment to the results of the associated company prior to aggregation. In addition further adjustments may

---

14 SSAP 1, Para. 26. Although not relevant to this particular example, readers should be aware of the other disclosure requirements of SSAP 1. Thus, for example, Paras 27 and 28 require disclosure of loans between associated companies and the group whilst Para. 29 requires disclosure, where material, of balances representing normal trading transactions.

be necessary to remove any unrealized profits due to intercompany trading.

When we turn to a company which does not prepare consolidated accounts, it is not possible to apply the equity method of accounting in the investing company's own accounts. In those accounts the profit and loss account will include dividends received and receivable, while, in the balance sheet, the investment will usually be shown at its historical cost.

In order to comply with the provisions of SSAP 1, the company must either prepare a second set of accounts in which the equity method of accounting is applied or provide similar information in notes to the accounts. In the former case, the treatment will be as illustrated above. In the latter case one or more supplementary notes will be necessary. Thus there must be a note to the balance sheet showing the carrying value of the investment if the equity method were applied, together with an appropriate analysis of that figure, and a note to the profit and loss account showing the effect of applying the equity method of accounting.

We shall conclude this section by illustrating a possible note to the profit and loss account.

E Limited holds 25% of the equity share capital of an associated company, F Limited, and has credited dividends received and receivable from F Limited in its own profit and loss account.[15] The summarized profit and loss accounts of the two companies are as follows:

Summarized profit and loss accounts for the year ended 31 December 19X1

	E Limited (£)	F Limited (£)
Operating profit	240 000	120 000
Dividends received and receivable from F Limited	20 000	—
	260 000	120 000
Taxation	80 000	40 000
Tax credit on dividends	6 000	—
	86 000	40 000

15 The dividends received and receivable from F Limited total £14 000 (25% of £56 000) but, in accordance with the provisions of SSAP 8, 'The treatment of taxation under the imputation tax system in the accounts of companies', the gross equivalent dividend (£20 000) and tax credit (£6000) have been disclosed (SSAP 8, Paras 22 and 25). The rate of tax credit is assumed to be three-sevenths of the net amounts received and receivable.

	E Limited (£)	F Limited (£)
Profit on ordinary activities after taxation	174 000	80 000
Extraordinary items (net of tax)	40 000	20 000
	214 000	100 000
Dividends paid and payable	100 000	56 000
Retained profit for year	114 000	44 000

A possible note to the profit and loss account, in summarized form, would be as follows:

Note to the profit and loss account of E Limited
The effect of applying the equity method of accounting as required by SSAP 1, 'Accounting for associated companies', is as follows:

	£	£
Share of profits of associated company (25% of £120 000)		30 000
Share of taxation of associated company (25% of £40 000)		10 000
		20 000
add Profit of E Limited		
Per profit and loss account	174 000	
less Dividends from associated company	14 000	160 000
Profit from ordinary activities after taxation		180 000
add Extraordinary items (net of tax)		
E Limited	40 000	
Share of associated company (25% of £20 000)	5 000	45 000
		225 000
less Dividends paid and payable		100 000
Retained profit		125 000
Retained in investing company	114 000	
Retained in associated company (20 000 + 5000 − 14 000)	11 000	
	125 000	

Accounting for groups

What is a group?

Subject to certain exceptions, a UK company is required to prepare group accounts when it has a subsidiary or subsidiaries at the end of its financial year.[16] Thus a group exists when a company has a subsidiary or subsidiaries and the Companies Act 1948 defined a subsidiary as follows:[17]

> For the purposes of this Act, a company shall, . . ., be deemed to be a subsidiary of another if, but only if, –
>
> (a) that other either –
>   (i) is a member of it and controls the composition of its board of directors; or
>   (ii) holds more than half in nominal value of its equity share capital; or
> (b) that first mentioned company is a subsidiary of any company which is that other's subsidiary.

The term equity capital is defined very widely to mean 'in relation to a company, its issued share capital excluding any part thereof which, neither as respects dividends nor as respects capital, carries any right to participate beyond a specified amount in a distribution'.[18]

Although this definition is based upon the existence of legal power of control, it gives rise to certain problems and may, in some cases, result in one company being the subsidiary of two separate holding companies at the same time. This will occur because ownership of more than half of the equity capital as defined above may not carry more than half of the voting power.

To illustrate, the total issued capital of G Limited is given in the first column below whilst the share capital held by F Limited is given in the second column:

	G Limited Issued share capital	F's holding in G
£1 voting ordinary shares	1 000 000	400 000
£1 non-voting ordinary shares	500 000	500 000
	1 500 000	900 000

---

16 Companies Act 1948, Sec. 150.
17 *Ibid.*, Sec. 154(1).
18 *Ibid.*, Sec. 154(5).

F holds 60% of the equity capital and hence G is its subsidiary. However, F holds only 40% of the voting power and would not normally have control of the composition of the board of directors.[19] Indeed, another company holding 550 000 £1 voting shares in G would have control and therefore also consider G to be its subsidiary. Such a problem with the legal definition of a subsidiary has long been apparent but has not so far been remedied.

As we have seen in Chapter 2, the EEC Council of Ministers adopted the Seventh Directive on Consolidated Accounts in June 1983. The provisions of the Directive must be introduced into national law before 1 January 1988 and subject to certain exceptions, the new rules must be effective for financial years beginning in 1990.

Early drafts of the Directive were heavily influenced by German accounting practice which adopts a rather different definition of a group.[20] Under German practice, the emphasis is not on the existence of legal power of control but on whether or not the companies, or other entities, are managed on a unified basis. If they are so managed there is a group irrespective of whether or not one company has legal power of control over another company. Thus the amended proposal, published in 1979, provided that:[21]

> For the purposes of this Directive, a dominant undertaking and one or more undertakings dependent on it shall constitute a group if the dominant undertaking exercises in practice its dominant influence to the effect that all such undertakings are managed on a unified basis by the dominant undertaking.

The term 'dependent undertaking' was defined in the following way:[22]

> For the purpose of this Directive, a dependent undertaking means an undertaking over which another undertaking, referred to as the dominant undertaking, is able, directly or indirectly, to exercise a dominant influence.

There is a presumption, but only a presumption, of dependence where one company holds the major part of the subscribed capital or controls the majority of the votes attaching to the issued shares or can appoint more than half of the members of the undertaking's administrative, managerial or supervisory body.[23] The essence of this group relationship

---

19 Where there is no control, Para. 21 of SSAP 14, 'Group accounts', requires that the subsidiary be excluded from consolidated accounts.
20 Two drafts of the Directive were published: 'Proposal for a Seventh Directive', *Official Journal of the European Communities*, No. C121/2, 2 June 1976 and 'Amended proposal for a Seventh Directive', *Official Journal of the European Communities*, No. C14/2, 14 January 1979.
21 'Amended proposal for a Seventh Directive', Article 3, Para. 1.
22 *Ibid.*, Article 2, Para. 1.
23 *Ibid.*, Article 2, Para. 2.

is the exercise of dominant influence by unified management, *de facto* control rather than *de jure* control.

Although this definition would seem to avoid the problem of the definition contained in the UK Companies Act, it also brings its own problems. Thus, unless we have regard to the shareholdings and legal powers of the investing company, it is difficult to establish whether or not a dominant influence exists. Indeed, even if we find that no dominant influence is exercised in practice, this may merely be due to the fact that the subsidiary is performing to the satisfaction of the holding company. Therefore, even in the absence of a dominant interest exercised in practice, we would not be justified in concluding that there is no group, for the dominant undertaking would perhaps exercise its dominant influence as soon as the performance of the subsidiary ceased to be satisfactory.

Such problems and pressures from other European countries have resulted in the actual Seventh Directive adopting a definition of a group which is much closer to the UK definition, that is one based upon the legal power of control rather than upon existence of a unified management.[24] However the Directive also accommodates the German approach by permitting Member States to require consolidated accounts where there is unified management.[25] The UK government is unlikely to require consolidated accounts in such circumstances and it is expected that the UK definition of a group will be firmly based upon the existence of legal power of control.

The form of group accounts

Although the law permits alternative presentations,[26] group accounts in the UK normally take the form of consolidated accounts. Indeed SSAP 14 requires[27] a single set of consolidated accounts for the group, although it also requires the exclusion of subsidiaries in certain cases. SSAP 14 therefore fetters the discretion which the law gives to directors to permit them to prepare group accounts in various forms and even to exclude subsidiaries from the group accounts altogether. It places the onus on the directors to justify the presentation of any group accounts other than consolidated accounts.[28]

24 'EEC Seventh Council Directive', 13 June 1983, Article 1, Para. 1. Published in the *Official Journal of the European Communities*, Volume L193/1, 18 July 1983.
25 *Ibid.*, Article 1, Para. 2.
26 Companies Act 1948, Sec. 151.
27 SSAP 14, Para. 15.
28 SSAP 14, Para. 22.

Preparation of a set of consolidated accounts involves the aggregation of amounts relating to different companies. In order to permit meaningful aggregation, it would seem to be necessary for the accounts of the companies in a group to be drawn up for the same accounting periods and on the basis of uniform accounting policies. Because of the enormous variety of situations found in practice, SSAP 14 recognizes that this will not always be possible and therefore requires appropriate disclosure.[29]

Whereas the law *permits* the exclusion of subsidiaries from *group* accounts in certain cases and requires certain information about the excluded subsidiaries,[30] SSAP 14 *requires* the exclusion of subsidiaries from the *consolidated* accounts in certain circumstances.[31] Thus, under the provisions of SSAP 14,

A subsidiary should be excluded from consolidation if:

(a) its activities are so dissimilar from those of other companies within the group that consolidated financial statements would be misleading and that information for that holding company's shareholders and other users of the statements would be better provided by presenting financial statements for such a subsidiary; or

(b) the holding company, although owning directly or through other subsidiaries more than half the equity share capital of the subsidiary, either:
(i) does not own share capital carrying more than half the votes; or
(ii) has contractual or other restrictions imposed on its ability to appoint the majority of the Board of Directors; or

(c) the subsidiary operates under severe restrictions which significantly impair control by the holding company over the subsidiary's assets and operations for the foreseeable future; or

(d) control is intended to be temporary.

Let us look at each of these four categories in turn.

Under (a) the statement envisages not merely the dissimilarity of activities found within manufacturing or trading groups but something more. An example would be a predominantly manufacturing group with a banking or insurance subsidiary. In such a case the combination of very different assets and liabilities may make the consolidated accounts difficult to understand. Exclusion is not, of course, the only answer and one alternative would be to group together all the items relating to the particular subsidiary in the consolidated accounts as envisaged by the relevant International Accounting Standard.[32]

29 SSAP 14, Paras 16–18.
30 Companies Act 1948, Sec. 150. Information required to be disclosed about subsidiaries excluded from group acounts may be found in the Companies Act 1967, Schedule 2, Para. 15.
31 SSAP 14, Para. 21.
32 IAS 3, Para. 9.

The situation referred to under (b) arises because of the particular definition of a group adopted by UK law, as discussed earlier. Although one company is legally a subsidiary of another, the holding company may not in fact possess control. In these circumstances it would be incorrect to include the results of the particular subsidiary as part of the results of the group; its assets and liabilities and the profits or losses thereon would not be under the control of the investing company.

Lack of control is also the reason for exclusion under heading (c), whilst under heading (d) inclusion of a temporary investment as a subsidiary in the consolidated accounts would be an incorrect treatment of a current asset.

SSAP 14 specifies the appropriate accounting treatment and information to be disclosed in respect of subsidiaries excluded for the above reasons. The required accounting treatments may be summarized as follows:[33]

(a) *Dissimilar activities*   Use the equity method of accounting for investment in subsidiary[34] but also include separate financial statements for the excluded subsidiary in the group accounts.

(b) *Lack of control*   Use the equity method of accounting, if the investment satisfies the criteria for treatment as an associated company laid down in SSAP 1. Otherwise show the investment at cost or valuation less any amounts written off.

(c) *Severe restrictions*   Show the investment at the amount that would have appeared if the equity method had been used at the date the restrictions came into force. Subsequently take credit only for dividends received.

(d) *Temporary investment*   Treat as a current asset, shown at the lower of cost and net realizable value.

Changes in the composition of a group

Consolidated accounts for a group are prepared to show the results of the group as a single economic entity. It follows that the consolidated

---

33 Readers are advised to consult the text of SSAP 14 for greater detail.

34 It is interesting to note a difference between the application of the equity method in SSAP 1 and SSAP 14. SSAP 1 requires investments in associated companies to be shown in a consolidated balance sheet as (a) the cost of the investments less any amounts written off; and (b) the investing company or groups share of the post-acquisition retained profits and reserves of the associated companies. SSAP 14 defines the equity method of accounting as a method under which the investment is shown on the consolidated balance sheet at: (a) the cost of the investment; and (b) the investing company or group's share of the post-acquisition retained profits and reserves of the company; less (c) any amount written off in respect of (a) and (b) above.

profit and loss account should include the profits or losses of all companies in the group for the relevant periods during which they were members of the group, whilst the balance sheet should show the combined assets and liabilities of companies which are members of the group at the accounting year end. This simple requirement gives rise to many accounting problems where there is an acquisition or disposal of a subsidiary during the course of a year.

The first problem is to decide exactly when an acquisition or disposal occurs. The negotiations which lead to such an event are often long and drawn out, involving preliminary discussions, agreement in principle, a drawing up of terms, an offer, an unconditional acceptance and then payment of the consideration. In practice various of these possible events have been selected as fixing the date of acquisition or disposal and often the selection of the date appears to have been influenced by a desire to show the largest possible profit in the consolidated accounts. Thus, where a new profit-making subsidiary is acquired, the earlier the selected date of acquisition, the greater the profits which will be included in the consolidated profit and loss account. Similarly, where the shares in a loss-making subsidiary are sold, the earlier the date of disposal the less the losses which serve to reduce the consolidated profits.

In order to reduce the choice of possible dates, SSAP 14 has now defined the effective date of acquisition or disposal quite clearly as 'the earlier of: (a) the date on which consideration passes; or (b) the date on which an offer becomes or is declared unconditional'.[35] The consolidated profits must therefore include the profits or losses of any new subsidiary from the date of acquisition to the end of the accounting year and the profits or losses of any subsidiary sold from the beginning of the year to the date of disposal.

Let us look first at the possible treatment of an acquisition of a subsidiary and then look at the various types of disposal which may occur.

Treatment of an acquisition
We have seen that the consolidated profit and loss account must include the results of a new subsidiary from the date of acquisition to the end of the accounting year and that the consolidated balance sheet must include the assets and liabilities of the new subsidiary which is a member of the group at the year end. Such a general statement

---

35 SSAP 14, Para. 32.

leaves us with various possible treatments which are best explored in the context of an example.

Let us take a company J Limited, which has many subsidiaries and makes up accounts to 31 December each year. J acquires a new wholly owned subsidiary, K Limited, during the year to 31 December 19X2. The offer is declared unconditional on 1 July and consideration passes on 31 August 19X2. Summarized consolidated accounts of the J group (excluding K) and accounts for K Limited are given below:

Summarized profit and loss accounts for the year ended 31 December 19X2

	J Group (£)	K Limited (£)
Turnover	2 000 000	500 000
Operating profit	500 000	80 000
less Taxation	200 000	36 000
	300 000	44 000
less Minority interest	40 000	—
	260 000	44 000
add Extraordinary profit (net of taxation and minority interest)	30 000	20 000
	290 000	64 000
less Dividends proposed	100 000	—
	190 000	64 000
add Retained profits on 1 January 19X2	310 000	82 000
Retained profits	500 000	146 000

Summarized balance sheets on 31 December 19X2

	J Group (£)	K Limited (£)
Share capital, £1 shares	250 000	40 000
Revaluation reserve (created 1 July 19X2)	—	20 000
Retained profits	500 000	146 000
	750 000	206 000
Minority interest	180 000	—
Long-term loans	170 000	50 000
	1 100 000	256 000

	J Group (£)	K Limited (£)
Fixed assets	500 000	156 000
Goodwill on consolidation	100 000	—
Investment in K Limited, 40 000 shares, at cost	200 000	—
Net current assets	300 000	100 000
	1 100 000	256 000

As K limited is deemed to have been acquired on 1 July 19X2, the date on which the offer became unconditional, the consolidated profit and loss account must include the results from that date. Let us assume that the sales and operating profit arose evenly over the year but that the extraordinary profit did not arise until October 19X2.

There would appear to be two ways of bringing in and disclosing the profits from 1 July to 31 December. First, it is possible merely to bring in profits made after 1 July. Second, we could bring in profits for the full year and deduct the proportion made prior to acquisition. These are illustrated, together with workings, which would, of course, not be published:

Consolidated profit and loss account for the year ended 31 December 19X2
Alternative 1

	£	£
Turnover		
J group	2 000 000	
K, ½ × £500 000	250 000	2 250 000
Operating profit		
J group	500 000	
K, ½ × £80 000	40 000	540 000
less Taxation		
J group	200 000	
K, ½ × £36 000	18 000	218 000
		322 000
less Minority interest (no change as new subsidiary is wholly owned)		40 000
Carried forward		282 000

	£	£
Brought forward		282 000
add Extraordinary profit (net of taxation and minority interest)		
J group	30 000	
K (all post-acquisition)	20 000	50 000
		332 000
less Dividends proposed		100 000
		232 000
add Retained profits on 1 January 19X2 J group only (K was not a member of the group at this date)		310 000
Retained profits on 31 December 19X2		542 000

Consolidated profit and loss account for the year ended 31 December 19X2
Alternative 2

	£	£
Turnover, as above		2 250 000
Operating profit		
J group	500 000	
K	80 000	580 000
less Taxation		
J group	200 000	
K	36 000	236 000
		344 000
less Minority interest	40 000	
Pre-acquisition profits of K Limited, $\frac{1}{2} \times (£80\,000 - £36\,000)$	22 000	62 000
		282 000
add Extraordinary profit, as above		50 000
		332 000
less Dividends proposed		100 000
		232 000
add Retained profits on 1 January 19X2, as above		310 000
Retained profits on 31 December 19X2		542 000

Under both alternatives we have effectively brought in the post-acquisition profits of K, that is one-half of the ordinary profits and the full amount of the extraordinary profits:

K Limited

	£	£
Ordinary profit		
Operating profit	80 000	
less Taxation	36 000	
50%	44 000 =	22 000
Extraordinary profit, all post-acquisition, 100%	20 000 =	20 000
		42 000

Note that the ordinary profits on which the earnings per share are calculated, £282 000, are the same under the two alternatives. Note also that the retained profits brought forward do not include any profits in respect of K; after all, K did not become a member of the group until 1 July so any of its profits prior to 1 July are pre-acquisition and represented by the net assets purchased on that date.

The first of the alternatives would seem to be the simpler of the two, although it would have to be accompanied by a note showing how the acquisition had affected the consolidated accounts. The second of the two alternatives does, however, have advantages. Many users are interested in predicting future profits. In future years K will be a member of the group and hence, *ceteris paribus*, a prediction based on accounts including the results of K for the full year is more likely to be correct than one based on accounts which include K for only part of a year. Apart from this, there seems little to choose between the alternative presentations.

We may now turn to the preparation of the consolidated balance sheet on 31 December 19X2. As K is a member of the group on that date the balance sheet must include its assets and liabilities together with any premium or discount on acquisition. In order to calculate the premium or discount on acquisition we need to know the net assets of K on 1 July 19X2. Alternatively we need to know the share capital and reserves on that date for this will tell us the net assets at the date of acquisition.

For the purpose of computing the premium or discount on acquisition, it is not sufficient merely to accept the book values in the accounts of K. From the point of view of the group it is purchasing net assets, and these must be valued, not on the basis of their past cost to K, but at their cost to the group on 1 July. In other words we must value the net assets acquired on the basis of their fair values on 1 July 19X2.[36]

36 This is required by SSAP 14, Para. 29.

The figures resulting from the revaluation should preferably be included in the accounting records of the subsidiary, and this is what has been done above. A revaluation reserve of £20 000 has been created for K on 1 July 19X2. Where it is not possible to make such adjustments in the accounting records of a subsidiary, they will have to be made on the consolidated working papers. This leads, in practice, to many complications as, for example, when subsequent depreciation is based on historical cost in the books of the subsidiary but on the revalued amount in the consolidated accounts.

Given that the subsidiary has revalued its assets, the share capital and reserves at the date of acquisition, 1 July 19X2, may be calculated as follows:

K Limited
Net assets on 1 July 19X2

	£	£
Share capital		40 000
Revaluation reserve		20 000
Retained profits		
On 1 January 19X2	82 000	
1 January to 30 June 19X2, $\frac{1}{2} \times$ £44 000	22 000	104 000
		164 000

J Limited has paid £200 000 to acquire net assets which have a value of £164 000 on 1 July 19X2. Hence it has paid a premium of £36 000.

The consolidated balance sheet on 31 December 19X2, together with appropriate workings, will appear as follows:

J Group
Summarized consolidated balance sheet on 31 December 19X2

	£	£
Share capital, £1 shares		250 000
Retained profits, per consolidated profit and		
loss account		542 000
		792 000
Minority interest, as before		180 000
Long-term loans		
Old J group	170 000	
K	50 000	220 000
		1 192 000

	£	£
Fixed assets		
Old J group	500 000	
K	156 000	656 000
Premium (or goodwill) on acquisition		
Old J group	100 000	
K	36 000	136 000
Net current assets		
Old J group	300 000	
K	100 000	400 000
		1 192 000

In order to show users of the consolidated accounts the effect of the acquisition on assets and liabilities it is necesary to append a note, usually as a footnote to the statement of source and application of funds. This will show the assets and liabilities of K Limited acquired on 1 July 19X2, consideration paid and the premium or goodwill on acquisition. On the basis of the information given above, the footnote would appear as follows:

Summary of effects of the acquisition of subsidiary K Limited

	£		£
Net assets acquired (itemized)	164 000	Consideration given (itemized)	200 000
Goodwill on acquisition	36 000		
	200 000		200 000

Now that we have examined the basic principles for dealing with the acquisition of a new subsidiary, readers should be in a position to cope with various complications. Thus the acquisition of a loss-making subsidiary or one in which profits do not arise evenly over the period should give few problems. Similarly, the acquisition of a partially owned subsidiary requires little modification to the approach we have adopted above.

Before we move on to examine disposals, there is one further point which we must consider, that is the notional interest adjustment.

As we have seen above, the effective date of acquisition will be the earlier of the date on which the offer becomes unconditional and the date on which consideration passes. Although this causes no problems where the consideration paid is in the form of shares ranking for dividends, it may cause problems where the consideration is loan stock or cash.

To illustrate, let us assume that we are dealing with a group which makes up its accounts to 31 December each year. An offer to acquire a new subsidiary becomes unconditional on 1 May 19X2 but the consideration of £1 million 15% loan stock is not issued until 1 July 19X2 and only ranks for interest from that date. When we consolidate the results of the new subsidiary with those of the old group we find that the consolidated profit and loss account includes profits of the new subsidiary for 8 months but that interest on the consideration is only charged for 6 months. This does not seem to comply with the accruals concept.

The consideration paid is not only for the net assets acquired on 1 May 19X2 but may be deemed also to include interest for the 2 months from 1 May to 1 July on the price paid. An adjustment is sometimes made for this 'notional interest' where it is material. Thus a notional charge is made in the consolidated profit and loss account and this reduces the premium or increases the discount on acquisition.

Where the consideration is loan stock we know the appropriate rate of interest. Where the consideration is cash we must estimate an appropriate rate of interest, which will normally be the rate payable by the investing company for a loan of the consideration for the particular period, two months in the above example.

Treatment of disposals

Just as companies acquire shares in subsidiaries, so too do they dispose of shares in subsidiaries. When we turn to disposals we may distinguish various categories of sales to outsiders[37] depending upon the shareholding, if any, which is retained:

(a) sale of total shareholding
(b) sale of part of shareholding such that the investee company becomes or remains
   (i) a subsidiary
   (ii) an associated company
   (iii) a simple investment

In all these cases it is necessary to recognize that different accounting treatments will be required in the books of the company which makes the sale and in the consolidation working papers.

---

37 Intragroup sales may occur, but these are not dealt with in this book.

Let us look at each category of disposal in turn, commencing with a sale of the total shareholding.

Sale of total shareholding
In the accounting records of the company which makes the sale it is necessary to match the book value of the investment with the proceeds of sale to ascertain the profit or loss on disposal. This will be an extraordinary item in the profit and loss account of the investing company which may, of course, attract a taxation liability. Once the investing company has recognized the extraordinary profit or loss and provided for any taxation liability, that is the end of the matter as far as that company is concerned.

When we turn to the consolidated accounts, matters are a little more complicated. In accordance with normal practice in the UK, post-acquisition profits of a subsidiary are credited to the consolidated profit and loss account year by year, whether or not they are distributed as dividend to the investing company. Hence, year by year, we recognize profits which are retained by the subsidiary company and hence increase the net assets shown in the consolidated balance sheet by these amounts. Having once recognized these profits we cannot then say that they never existed.

In the consolidated accounts, the profit or loss on disposal usually differs from that shown in the investing company's own profit and loss account. In the consolidated accounts the profit or loss on disposal will be the difference between the sale proceeds and the appropriate share of the underlying net assets of the subsidiary at the date of sale plus any premium or less any discount on acquisition. Thus the difference between the profit on disposal shown in the investing company's records and in the consolidated accounts will depend on the change in the net assets of the subsidiary since acquisition. To the extent that the net assets of the subsidiary have grown, due to the profits made and retained between acquisition and disposal, these have been recognized in the consolidated profit and loss account as part of the groups' results.

Let us start with a very simple example. L Limited has two wholly owned subsidiaries, M Limited and N Limited. The respective summarized balance sheets on 31 December 19X1 are given below:

Summarized balance sheets on 31 December 19X1

	L (£)	M (£)	N (£)
Share capital, £1 shares	100 000	20 000	30 000
Retained profits	125 000		
At date of acquisition		10 000	20 000
Post-acquisition		30 000	20 000
	225 000	60 000	70 000
Net assets	110 000	60 000	70 000
Investments in subsidiaries, at cost			
20 000 shares in M Limited	45 000		
30 000 shares in N Limited	70 000		
	225 000	60 000	70 000

If we assume that there are no unrealized intercompany profits, the summarized consolidated balance sheet, with relevant workings, on 31 December 19X1 would appear as follows:

Summarized consolidated balance sheet on 31 December 19X1

	£	£
Share capital, £1 shares		100 000
Retained profits		
L	125 000	
M post-acquisition	30 000	
N post-acquisition	20 000	175 000
		275 000
Net assets (£110 000 + £60 000 + £70 000)		240 000
Goodwill on consolidation		
M (£45 000 − £30 000)	15 000	
N (£70 000 − £50 000)	20 000	35 000
		275 000

From this consolidated balance sheet we can see that the consolidated retained profits have been credited with £30 000 of post-acquisition profit retained by M and £20 000 post-acquisition profit retained by N. Thus, since acquisition, the net assets of these two companies have increased by £30 000 and £20 000 respectively due to the making and retention of profits.

Let us now suppose that L sells its shareholding in M for £100 000 on 1 January 19X2. In the books of L it is necessary to compute the profit or loss on disposal by matching the book value of the investment, here its cost, against the sale proceeds. Sale proceeds are £100 000 and the cost was £45 000 so that the extraordinary profit on disposal is £55 000.

In order to concentrate on principles, we shall ignore taxation at this stage,[38] with the result that the profit and loss account of L for the year ended 31 December 19X2 will include an extraordinary profit on disposal of shares in subsidiary amounting to £55 000.

As the investment in M was sold on the very first day of 19X2, we shall prepare the consolidated profit and loss account for the year ended 31 December 19X2 by aggregating the profit and loss account items of L and N, the two companies in the group for this year. Assuming that we have profit and loss accounts, and concentrating only on the essential figures, we may produce a draft consolidated profit and loss account as follows:

Profit and loss accounts – year to 31 December 19X2

	L	N	Total
	(£)	(£)	(£)
Operating profit	80 000	60 000	140 000
less Taxation	40 000	20 000	60 000
			80 000
add Extraordinary profit on disposal of shares in M	55 000		55 000
			135 000
add Retained profits brought forward			
L	125 000		
N (post-acquisition)		20 000	145 000
Retained profits carried forward			280 000

Notice that the retained profits figure of £145 000 brought forward in this consolidated profit and loss account does not agree with the retained profits figure carried forward in the previous years' accounts and shown in the consolidated balance sheet on 31 December 19X1 as £175 000. The difference is, of course, the £30 000 post-acquisition retained profits of M Limited, which ceased to be a member of the group on 1 January 19X2. We cannot now say that this £30 000 never existed. What has happened is that we have previously taken credit for profits of £30 000 which are represented in the net assets of company

---

38 The taxation implications are discussed later in the chapter.

M. Any proceeds received for the shares are in respect of the underlying net assets at the date of disposal. What we must also do is to return our profits brought forward to £175 000 by adding £30 000 and correspondingly to reduce our extraordinary profit on disposal:

Workings for consolidated profit and loss account – year to 31 December 19X2

	Total (£)	Adjustment (£)	Draft consolidated P and L account (£)
Operating profit	140 000		140 000
less Taxation	60 000		60 000
	80 000		80 000
add Extraordinary profit on disposal of shares	55 000	− 30 000	25 000
	135 000		105 000
add Retained profits brought forward	145 000	+ 30 000	175 000
Retained profits carried forward	280 000		280 000

Notice that we have not changed the retained profits carried forward. These relate to L and its subsidiary N, the only two companies in the group at the year end. All we have done is to rearrange the items in the consolidated profit and loss account in order to give a true and fair view of what has happened:

	£	£
Sale proceeds		100 000
less Net assets of M at date of disposal	60 000	
Premium (goodwill) on acquisition	15 000	75 000
Extraordinary profit of group		25 000

The consolidated balance sheet on 31 December 19X2 poses no problems. At that date L has one subsidiary N and hence the consolidated balance sheet will be an aggregation for those two companies only.

Let us now complicate the example by assuming that the disposal occurs not on 1 January 19X2 but during the year to 31 December 19X2, for simplicity on 30 June 19X2. Let us assume that the proceeds on that date are £110 000 producing an extraordinary profit in the profit and loss account of L amounting to £65 000. Let us also assume that the profits of M arise evenly throughout the year.

M Limited
Summarized profit and loss account for the year to 31 December 19X2

	£
Operating profit	44 000
less Taxation	20 000
	24 000
add Retained profits brought forward	40 000
Retained profits carried forward	64 000

As explained above, we must make adjustments in the consolidated accounts to show the results as far as the group is concerned. First, we must restore the retained profits brought forward to £175 000 and reduce the profit on disposal by £30 000, as we did before. However, we must, in addition, make a second adjustment. The operating profit and taxation figures included in the total column above relate only to L and N. However, the group consisted of L, N and M for the first 6 months of the year. The profits made and retained by M during that first 6 months should therefore be included in the group profits. Such profits are, of course, represented by net assets at the date of disposal and hence we must also reduce our extraordinary profit on disposal. The appropriate adjustment will be as follows:

		£
Operating profits, $\frac{1}{2} \times$ £44 000	=	22 000
less Taxation, $\frac{1}{2} \times$ £20 000	=	10 000
		£12 000

Our consolidated profit and loss account will therefore be arrived at as follows:

Draft consolidated profit and loss account of L Limited and its subsidiary M Limited for the year ended 31 December 19X2

	Total (L and N) as above (£)	Adjustments (£)	Draft consolidated P and L account (£)
Operating profit	140 000	+ 22 000	162 000
less Taxation	60 000	+ 10 000	70 000
Carried forward	80 000	+ 12 000	92 000

	Total (L and N) as above (£)	Adjustments (£)	Draft con- solidated P and L account (£)
Brought forward	80 000	+ 12 000	92 000
add Extraordinary profit on disposal of shares in subsidiaries	65 000	$\left.\begin{array}{r}-12\,000 \\ -30\,000\end{array}\right\}$	23 000
	145 000		115 000
add Retained profits brought forward	145 000	+ 30 000	175 000
Retained profits carried forward	290 000		290 000

Notice again that the retained profit carried forward relates only to L and N, the companies in the group on 31 December 19X2. The extraordinary profit on disposal amounts to £23 000 and may be explained as follows:

	£	£
Sales proceeds		110 000
less Net assets at date of disposal:		
On 31 December 19X1	60 000	
Increase in 6 months to 30 June 19X2	12 000	
	72 000	
Premium on acquisition	15 000	87 000
Extraordinary profit		23 000

We have now examined the basic approach to the accounting treatment of disposals. Before we move on to partial disposals, let us look at two problems: first, the difficulty of obtaining information and, second, the treatment of taxation.

Information requirements

In order to give a true and fair view of the results of the group, we have seen that it is necessary to include as part of the ordinary profits, those relating to the subsidiary from the beginning of the year to the date of sale. If we had to rely on published accounts for this purpose, it might well be very difficult to obtain the necessary information.

Once the investing company sells its shares in the subsidiary, it has no power to obtain copies of the accounts of that subsidiary. Indeed under the new ownership the use of the assets and the choice of accounting policies of the subsidiary may well change. Thus, in order to find out the profits of the subsidiary to the date of sale, the investing company may have to wait until accounts for the ex-subsidiary are filed with the Registrar of Companies, and even then a different use of the assets and different accounting policies may make meaningful aggregation impossible.

In practice we do not, of course, have to wait for published accounts of the ex-subsidiary to be published. It is unlikely that any management is going to sell the shares in a subsidiary without knowing what the underlying assets are at the date of sale, in other words without knowing the profits or losses made in the current period up to the date of sale. It is the management's best estimate of the figures which should be used to make the relevant adjustment where there is any difficulty in obtaining published accounts.

Taxation

Under the UK taxation system, a chargeable gain or loss will occur when an investing company sells shares. Assuming that there is a gain, the extraordinary profit in the accounts of the selling company will be reduced by taxation.

When we turn to the consolidated profit and loss account the treatment is again a little more complicated.

Let us take the last example in the previous section and assume that company L faces a liability to taxation at 30% on the chargeable gain. Thus, on the gain of £65 000 in the accounts of L, the taxation would be £19 500 so that our extraordinary item in the profit and loss account of L would be as follows:

	£	£
Extraordinary profit on disposal of shares in subsidiary	65 000	
less Taxation	19 500	45 000

When we turn to the consolidated profit and loss account it would seem incorrect to set the whole taxation charge of £19 500 against the extraordinary profit of £23 000. An analysis of the component parts of the profit on disposal should be made as follows:

	£	£
Sale proceeds		110 000
less Net assets		
At date of acquisition	45 000	
Arising from post-acquisition profits retained		
to 31 December 19X1	30 000	
6 months to 30 June 19X2	12 000	87 000
Extraordinary profit		23 000

What is happening is that although the post-acquisition profits have already borne Corporation Tax, they are being taxed again as a result of the disposal. It may therefore be argued that we should recognize this by apportioning the taxation charge to the three components:

	£	£
Post-acquisition profit		
to 31 December 19X1	30 000 × 30%	9 000
6 months to 30 June 19X2	12 000 × 30%	3 600
Capital (extraordinary) profit	23 000 × 30%	6 900
	65 000	19 500

Such an approach requires rather clumsy disclosure in the consolidated profit and loss account. The ordinary profits must be reduced by part of the tax charge, £3600, retained profits brought forward must be reduced by £9000 and the extraordinary profit of £23 000 must be reduced by £6900. The approach, however, seems to give a clear view of what has happened as far as the group is concerned.

In order to keep this chapter to manageable proportions, taxation is ignored in future sections. The treatment suggested above would appear to provide the clearest picture of what has happened even though the necessary adjustment to retained profits brought forward is inconsistent with the provisions of SSAP 6.

Partial disposals
Where one company sells part of a holding in a subsidiary company, although the principles are the same, precise treatment depends upon the nature of the remaining investment. The investee company may remain a subsidiary or the holding may be sufficient merely to make it an associated company or a simple investment.

As before, it is essential to keep a clear distinction between the entries in the accounting records of the selling company and those in the consolidated working papers.

In the records of the investing company it is necessary to match the appropriate portion of the book value of the investment against the proceeds of disposal to produce an extraordinary profit or loss on disposal. This may be subject to taxation but, as discussed above, taxation will be ignored for the remainder of this chapter.

When we turn to the consolidated accounts the position is somewhat different. Let us look first at the situation where the remaining shareholding is sufficient to retain a subsidiary.

(1) *Retention of subsidiary company*   At the beginning of the year the consolidated retained profit will include the post-acquisition profits of all subsidiaries based on the respective holdings of those subsidiaries at that particular date. In order to give a true and fair view of the operations of the year, the consolidated profit and loss account must include the appropriate portion of profits or losses of all companies which were members of the group during the year. The consolidated balance sheet at the end of the year will be an aggregation of the balance sheets of all companies in the group as at that date.

This is best illustrated with an example. P Limited acquired an 80% interest in Q Limited many years ago when the reserves of Q were £20 000. The summarized balance sheets of the two companies, together with a summarized consolidated balance sheet on 31 December 19X1, were as follows:

Summarized balance sheets on 31 December 19X1

	P	Q	Consolidated
	(£)	(£)	(£)
Share capital, £1 shares	100 000	40 000	100 000
Retained profits	200 000		232 000
At date of acquisition		20 000	
Post-acquisition		40 000	
Minority interest			20 000
	300 000	100 000	352 000
Net assets	220 000	100 000	320 000
Investment in Q Limited, 32 000			
shares at cost	80 000		
Goodwill on consolidation			32 000
	300 000	100 000	352 000

P sells 4000 shares in Q on 30 June 19X2 for £16 000. This produces a profit in the records of P amounting to £6000, as shown below, and leaves P with a 70% shareholding in Q.

Sales of shares in subsidiaries

19X2		£	19X2	£
June 30 Investment account, cost of shares sold			June 30 Sale proceeds	£16 000
$\frac{1}{8} \times £80\,000$	10 000			
Profit on disposal	6 000			
	16 000			16 000

When we turn to the consolidated accounts our profit and loss account must include the result of Q as an 80% owned subsidiary for the first 6 months of the year and as a 70% owned subsidiary for the second 6 months. Our consolidated balance sheet on 31 December 19X2 will, of course, be based upon 70% holding at that date.

A simple approach is to prepare initially a consolidated profit and loss account on the basis of the holdings at the end of the year. Assuming that there are no unrealized profits on intercompany trading and that we have the individual profit and loss accounts as shown in the first two columns, we may proceed as follows:

Workings for consolidated profit and loss account for the year ended 31 December 19X2

	P (£)	Q (£)	Consolidated (£)
Operating profit	50 000	20 000	70 000
less Taxation	20 000	8 000	28 000
			42 000
less Minority interest, 30% × £12 000			3 600
			38 400
add Extraordinary profit on disposal of shares in Q Limited	6 000	—	6 000
			44 400
add Retained profit brought forward	200 000		228 000
Post-acquisition group share (70% × £40 000)		28 000	
Retained profit carried forward			272 400

As in the previous section we may now make adjustments to show what has happened as far as the group is concerned. First, we must restore the retained profits brought forward to the figure shown in the consolidated balance sheet on 31 December 19X1 by adding £4000 and reduce the extraordinary profit accordingly. Second, we must recognize that the minority interest was 20% rather than 30% for the first half of the year. Thus we must reduce the minority interest figure and also reduce the extraordinary profit figure by 10% of the profits of the first 6 months, which have of course increased the net assets underlying the shares sold. Assuming that the profits of Q arose evenly, we must therefore reduce the minority interest by £600 $(10\% \times \frac{1}{2} \times £12\,000)$:

Workings for consolidated profit and loss account – year to 31 December 19X2

	Total based on 70% holding as above (£)	Adjustment (£)	Draft consolidated P and L account (£)
Operating profit	70 000		70 000
less Taxation	28 000		28 000
	42 000		42 000
less Minority interest	3 600	− 600	3 000
	38 400		39 000
add Extraordinary profit on disposal of shares in Q Limited	6 000	−600⎫ −4 000⎭	1 400
	44 400		40 400
add Retained profits brought forward	228 000	+ 4 000	232 000
Retained profits carried forward	272 400		272 400

Having made these adjustments our ordinary profits of £39 000 on which the earnings per share calculation is based, may be analysed as follows:

	£	£
Operating profit before taxation		
P(£50 000 − £20 000)		30 000
Q		
6 months to 30 June 19X2,		
80% × (½ × £12 000)	4 800	
6 months to 31 December 19X2,		
70% × (½ × £12 000)	4 200	9 000
Per consolidated profit and loss account		39 000

As before, the closing consolidated balance sheet poses no problems. At 31 December 19X2 P has one subsidiary, Q, in which it has a 70% interest.

(2) *Retention of an associated company* We have seen earlier in this chapter how to account for an associated company and we have now seen how to account for a partial disposal. In this section we must put those pieces of knowledge together.

Let us take the same example that we used in the previous section but assume that P sells 16 000 shares in Q, thus leaving an investment of 16 000 shares, that is a holding of 40% which we shall assume constitutes Q an associated company. Let us assume, as before, that the sale occurs on 30 June 19X2 but that the proceeds are £90 000.

In the accounts of P we match the cost of 16 000 shares (½ × £80 000) with the proceeds to produce an extraordinary profit of £50 000. When we turn to the consolidated profit and loss account for the year to 31 December 19X2, we must reflect the fact that P has an 80% owned subsidiary for the first 6 months of the year but a 40% owned associated company for the second half of the year.[39] In order to facilitate reference, the summarized profit and loss accounts of P and Q for the year ended 31 December 19X2, with the revised extraordinary profit, are repeated below:

39 It may be argued that there is no technical requirement for group accounts as P has no subsidiary at the end of its financial year (Companies Act 1948, Sec. 150). We could, of course, expand the example to make Q one of many subsidiaries.

Summarized profit and loss accounts for the year ended 31 December 19X2

	P (£)	Q (£)
Operating profit	50 000	20 000
less Taxation	20 000	8 000
	30 000	12 000
add Extraordinary profit on sale of shares in Q	50 000	—
	80 000	12 000
add Retained profits brought forward	200 000	
At date of acquisition		20 000
Post-acquisition		40 000
Retained profits carried forward	280 000	72 000

Let us assume that the profits of Q arose evenly over the year and see what adjustments we must make to the profit and loss account of P to reflect what has happened.

For the first half of the year P had an 80% subsidiary, Q. Hence we must restore the opening retained profits to the figure included in the consolidated balance sheet on 31 December 19X1 in respect of the 80% owned subsidiary, that is we must add £32 000. In addition we must include, as part of the ordinary profits, 80% of 6 months profits of Q:

Q Limited profits for 6 months to 30 June 19X2

	£
Operating profit, $\frac{1}{2} \times$ £20 000	10 000
less Taxation, $\frac{1}{2} \times$ £8000	4 000
	6 000
less Minority interest, 20%	1 200
	4 800

Having brought in £32 000 plus £4800 we must recognize the fact that only half of these amounts relate to the holding sold and hence only one half must be deducted from the extraordinary profit. Column 2 below contains these adjustments:

Workings for consolidated profit and loss account for the year ended 31 December 19X2

	1	2	3
		Adjustment 6 months to 30 June	
	P Ltd	19X2	Total
	(£)	(£)	(£)
Operating profit	50 000	+ 10 000	60 000
less Taxation	20 000	+ 4 000	24 000
	30 000	+ 6 000	36 000
less Minority interest	—	+ 1 200	1 200
	30 000	4 800	34 800
add Extraordinary profit on disposal of shares	50 000	− 2 400 ⎫ − 16 000 ⎭	31 600
	80 000		66 400
add Retained profit brought forward	200 000	+ 32 000	232 000
Retained profit carried forward	280 000		298 400

The retained profits have been increased by £18 400, which is applicable to the holding in the associated company still retained. It is a 40% share of post-acquisition profits retained by the associated company between the date of acquisition and 30 June 19X2.

All we have to do finally is to add in the share of the associated company's profits from 1 July to 31 December 19X2, following the approach of SSAP 1:

P Limited
Consolidated profit and loss account (including workings) for the year ended 31 December 19X2

	£	£
Operating profit		
Group		60 000
Associated company (40% × 10 000)		4 000
		64 000
less Taxation		
Group	24 000	
Associated company (40% × £4000)	1 600	25 600
		38 400
less Minority interest		1 200
Carried forward		37 200

	£	£
Brought forward		37 200
add Extraordinary profit on disposal of shares		31 600
		68 800
add Retained profits brought forward		232 000
Retained profits carried forward		300 800
Retained by P Limited	280 000	
Retained by associated company	20 800	
	300 800	

If we are preparing a consolidated balance sheet or the supplementary balance sheet for an investing company which does not prepare consolidated accounts, the investment in Q Limited would appear at cost plus the share of post-acquisition profits retained by Q, that is at £60 800 (£40 000 + £20 800). If the investing company was not preparing a second set of accounts, then a note to the accounts should disclose this carrying value.

In either case, the carrying value would be analysed in the way required by SSAP 1 and the notes to the accounts would show clearly what has happened, as discussed in the final paragraphs of this chapter.

(3) *Retention of simple investment only*   The final disposal we are going to look at is one where the investing company retains only a simple investment. In this case the consolidated profit and loss account must reflect the fact that we have a subsidiary from the beginning of the year to the date of disposal but a simple investment thereafter.

As before, the approach is best illustrated by an example, so let us suppose that on 31 December 19X1 R Limited has two wholly owned subsidiaries, S Limited and T Limited. The summarized individual balance sheets and the consolidated balance sheet are given below:

Summarized balance sheets on 31 December 19X1

	R (£)	S (£)	T (£)	Consolidated (£)
Share capital, £1 shares	200 000	50 000	100 000	200 000
Retained profits	320 000			390 000
At date of acquisition		30 000	50 000	
Post-acquisition		40 000	30 000	
	520 000	120 000	180 000	590 000

	R (£)	S (£)	T (£)	Consolidated (£)
Net assets	220 000	120 000	180 000	520 000
Investment in subsidiaries				
S, at cost	100 000			
T, at cost	200 000			
Goodwill on consolidation				
S(£100 000				
− £80 000)				20 000
T(£200 000				
− £150 000)				50 000
	520 000	120 000	180 000	590 000

Let us suppose that R sells 90 000 shares in T Limited on 30 June 19X2 for £250 000. In the records of R Limited we will match the cost of 90 000 shares against the proceeds of sale to produce an extraordinary profit of £70 000. R will be left with an investment of 10 000 shares in T at a cost of £20 000.

When we come to prepare the consolidated profit and loss account, a simple approach is to commence by aggregating the results for the companies in the group at the year end, i.e. companies R and S. Let us assume that we have their profit and loss accounts and so are able to proceed as follows:

Summarized profit and loss accounts for the year ended 31 December 19X2

	R (£)	S (£)	Total (£)
Operating profit	150 000	25 000	175 000
less Taxation	70 000	12 000	82 000
			93 000
add Extraordinary profit on sale of shares	70 000		70 000
			163 000
add Retained profits			
Brought forward	320 000		360 000
Post-acquisition		40 000	
Retained profits carried forward			523 000

We must now recognize that, in respect of the 90% holding in T Limited sold, we had brought £27 000, that is 90% × £30 000, of post-acquisition retained profits into previous consolidated profit and loss accounts. Hence we must increase the retained profits brought forward and reduce the extraordinary profit on disposal by this amount. In addition we must increase the ordinary consolidated profits by 100% of those made between 1 January 19X2 and 30 June 19X2, recognizing that 90% of these have been realized in the sale proceeds by a deduction from the extraordinary profit. In order to do this let us assume that the profits of T, which arose evenly, are as follows:

T Limited
Profit and loss account for the year ended 31 December 19X2

	£
Operating profit	30 000
less Taxation	10 000
	20 000

We may now operate on the total column as before:

Workings for consolidated profit and loss account for the year ended 31 December 19X2

	Total (R and S) as before (£)	Adjustments in respect of T (£)	Consolidated P and L account (£)
Operating profit	175 000	+ 15 000	190 000
less Taxation	82 000	+ 5 000	87 000
	93 000	+ 10 000	103 000
add Extraordinary profit on disposal of shares	70 000	− 9 000 − 27 000	34 000
	163 000		137 000
add Retained profit brought forward	360 000	+ 27 000	387 000
Retained profits carried forward	523 000		524 000

This treatment poses two problems. First, we have brought in an additional £1000 of profit for the 6 months to 30 June 19X2 in respect of the 10% holding still retained in T Limited. Second, our retained profit of £387 000 brought forward does not agree with the retained profits carried forward at 31 December 19X1 as shown in the consolidated balance sheet at £390 000. Again the difference relates to the 10% holding in T which has been retained and which is now to be treated as a simple investment.

The appropriate accounting treatment would appear to be to remove these profits as follows:

Draft consolidated profit and loss account for the year ended 31 December 19X2

	£
Operating profit	190 000
less Taxation	87 000
	103 000
add Extraordinary profit on disposal of shares	34 000
	137 000
add Retained profits brought forward per last year's accounts	390 000
	527 000
less Retained profits included above in respect of 10% holding retained in T Limited which is no longer consolidated	4 000
Retained profit carried forward (R and S)	523 000

In the consolidated balance sheet on 31 December 19X2, the investment in T Limited would appear at its historical cost of £20 000, unless the directors considered the market value had fallen permanently below that figure. So, as in the case of all the disposals, preparation of the consolidated balance sheet poses no problems.

Disclosure

It is essential that the accounts should give sufficient information to enable users to understand the effects of a material disposal and Para. 30 of SSAP 14 specifically refers to this matter: 'In the case of material additions to or disposals from the group, the consolidated financial statements should contain sufficient information about the results of the subsidiaries acquired or sold to enable shareholders to appreciate the effect on the consolidated results.'

Such disclosure could take many forms depending on the precise circumstances. However, a note of the total profits, taxation charge, extraordinary items, etc., of the subsidiary sold, together with details of the extent to which these items have been included in the consolidated profit and loss account, would seem adequate as far as the profit and loss account is concerned. In addition, footnote disclosure of the effects of the disposal required by SSAP 10 would give adequate disclosure of the effect of the disposal on the consolidated balance sheet. Such a footnote would take the following form and show the assets and liabilities removed, the proceeds received and the profit or loss on disposal:

Effect of disposal of subsidiary

	£		£
Proceeds (itemized)	*X*	Net assets at date of	
		sale (itemized)	*X*
		Goodwill on original	
		acquisition	*X*
		Profit on disposal	*X*
	X		*X*

Recommended reading

J. C. Shaw, *Bogie on Group Accounts*, 3rd edn, Jordan, London, 1973.
R. M. Wilkins, *Group Accounts: The Fundamental Principles, Form and Content*, 2nd edn, ICAEW, London, 1979.
R. M. Wilkins, *Group Accounts*, Accountants Digest, No. 156, ICAEW, London, 1984.
S. M. McKinnon, *Consolidated Accounts: The Seventh EEC Directive*, (A. D. H. Newham, ed.), Arthur Young McClelland Moores, 1983.

Questions

12.1 **(a) Explain the term 'equity method of accounting' as defined in SSAP 14:** *Group Accounts* **and indicate two examples of where this method is generally used.** (8 marks)
(b) What are the advantages and disadvantages of preparing financial statements using this method? (7 marks)
(15 marks)
A. Cert. A. Level 2 The Regulatory Framework of Accounting, June 1982.

12.2 Public consideration has recently been given to the composition of a group for the purpose of presenting the group accounts of a commercial organization.

Consider the following data relating to the year ended 31 August 1981 of Octopus Ltd and Uncertain Ltd.

Balance Sheet	Octopus Ltd £'000	Uncertain Ltd £'000
Issued ordinary share capital	2 000	1 000
Reserves	3 450	2 000
Debentures	2 000	1 500
Current liabilities	4 550	2 500
	12 000	7 000
Fixed assets (net)	6 500	4 000
Investment in Uncertain Ltd at cost	2 000	—
Current assets	3 500	3 000
	12 000	7 000

Profit and loss account		
Trading profit before tax	1 100	500
Dividend from Uncertain Ltd, including tax credit	130	—
Taxation	(630)	(200)
Profit after tax	600	300
Dividends paid	300	(200)
Retained	300	100

Octopus Ltd acquired 50% of the ordinary share capital of Uncertain Ltd on 1 September 1980 for £2 000 000 when its reserves were £1 900 000 and sold this holding on 3 September 1981 for £2 050 000.

You are required to:

(a) **prepare the 'group' profit and loss account and balance sheet on three bases:**
   (i) **when Uncertain is treated as a subsidiary,**
   (ii) **when Uncertain is treated as an associated company,**
   (iii) **when Uncertain is treated as an investment** (9 marks),
(b) **calculate relevant financial ratios from the financial data produced by these three bases** (4 marks), **and**
(c) **comment on the validity of these three alternative bases** (7 marks).

(20 marks)

ICAEW PE II, Financial Accounting II, December 1981.

12.3 In the early days of group accounting (up to about 1929), the consolidation and equity methods were regarded as alternative accounting treatments for investments in subsidiaries and for the profits/losses generated by them. Since then the consolidation method has prevailed in this field.

You are required:

(a) to oultine the similarities, and differences, between the two methods;

(5 marks)

(b) to explain the conventional present-day uses of the two methods; and

(5 marks)

(c) to argue for OR against the general use of the equity method, in accounting for investments in subsidiaries.   (6 marks)

(16 marks)

A. Cert. A., Level 3, Advanced Financial Accounting December 1983.

12.4   On 31 March 1983 the balance sheet of Grasp Ltd showed an issued share capital of 200 000 ordinary shares of £1 each, fully paid, and a balance on revenue reserve of £97 000.

You also receive the following information:

(1) On 1 April 1982 Grasp Ltd had purchased 150 000 ordinary shares of 50p each in Palm Ltd for £100 000. Palm Ltd had an issued share capital of 200 000 ordinary shares of 50p each and a balance brought forward on revenue reserve of £30 000 at that time. In the year ended 31 March 1983 Palm Ltd had a profit after taxation of £49 000 out of which provision had been made for a dividend to be paid of 20p per share. The proposed dividend receivable has been included in the profit and loss account of Grasp Ltd.

(2) On 1 August 1982 Grasp Ltd had purchased 90 000 ordinary shares of £1 each in Digit Ltd for £20 000. Digit Ltd has an issued share capital of 100 000 ordinary shares of £1 each. On 1 April 1982 there had been a debit balance on revenue reserve account of £60 000 and during the year ended 31 March 1983 a loss after taxation was incurred of £39 000. Included in the stock of Grasp Ltd on 31 March 1983 was an amount of £6000 which had been purchased from Digit Ltd at a profit to that company of 25% on selling price. Digit Ltd had purchased plant and machinery from Grasp Ltd for £10 000 on 1 October 1982 and provided depreciation in its accounts on a straight line basis at 25% per annum, which commences in the month of purchase. Grasp Ltd had sold the plant and machinery to Digit Ltd at its normal selling price which gave a profit of 30% on selling price.

(3) On 1 January 1983 Grasp Ltd purchased 45 000 shares of 25p each in Wrist Ltd for £30 000. Wrist Ltd has an issued share capital of 100 000 ordinary shares of 25p each. On 1 April 1982 there had been a balance on revenue reserve of £36 000 and in the year ended 31 March 1983 the profit after taxation was £28 000. No dividend was paid or proposed for the year.

You are to assume that the profits and losses of Wrist Ltd and Digit Ltd have accrued evenly throughout the year.

You are required to show how the above items would be reflected in the consolidated balance sheet of Grasp Ltd on 31 March 1983, and to provide detailed schedules showing the make up of the relevant figures. (27 marks)

Note: Ignore Advance Corporation Tax.

ICAEW PEI Financial Accounting I, May 1983.

12.5 Grab Ltd, Hand Ltd, and Tight Ltd have issued share capital in ordinary shares of £1 each of £500 000, £250 000 and £200 000 respectively.

The summarized profit and loss accounts of the companies for the year ended 30 June 1983 showed the following:

	Grab Ltd £	Hand Ltd £	Tight Ltd £
Turnover	3 070 400	1 260 000	890 604
Deduct:			
Cost of sales	2 454 360	940 000	801 900
Gross profit	616 040	320 000	88 704
Deduct:			
Distribution costs	162 170	70 890	29 604
Administration expenses	156 890	71 860	16 296
Debenture interest (gross)		22 000	
	319 060	164 750	45 900
	296 980	155 250	42 804
Interim dividend received	24 000		
Proposed dividend receivable	46 000		
	366 980	155 250	42 804
Less:			
Provision for Corporation Tax	156 640	82 280	20 592
	210 340	72 970	22 212
Appropriations:			
Interim dividends paid	50 000	30 000	
Proposed dividends	125 000	35 000	20 000
	175 000	65 000	20 000
	35 340	7 970	2 212
Balance brought forward on 1 July 1982	115 670	47 860	14 800
	151 010	55 830	17 012

You also obtain the following information:

(1) Grab Ltd acquired 200 000 shares in Hand Ltd on 1 July 1980 when there had been a balance on profit and loss account of £40 000.

(2) On 1 October 1982 Grab Ltd acquired 180 000 shares in Tight Ltd whose profits accrue evenly throughout the year.

(3) Grab Ltd buys goods for resale from Hand Ltd which yield a profit to Hand Ltd of 25% on selling price. On 30 June 1983 Grab Ltd held in stock goods purchased from Hand Ltd for £20 000. On 30 June 1982 the amount of stock so held had been £28 000 and during the year ended 30 June 1983, sales made by Hand Ltd to Grab Ltd had totalled £220 000.

(4) Hand Ltd buys goods for resale from Tight Ltd on a regular basis at £20 000 per month. Tight Ltd achieves a profit on selling price of 10%. Stock of goods purchased from Tight Ltd and still held at 30 June 1983, amounted to £40 000 at cost to Hand Ltd. Stock of goods purchased from Tight Ltd held at 30 June 1982 had been £35 000.

You are required to prepare a consolidated profit and loss account of Grab Ltd and its subsidiaries for the year ended 30 June 1983 together with consolidation schedules. **(25 marks)**

Note: Ignore Advance Corporation Tax.

ICAEW PEI, Financial Accounting I, November 1983.

12.6   Below are the profit and loss accounts (in accordance with Format 2 in the Companies Act 1981) of Tweedle plc and its subsidiary Dum Ltd for the year to 30 June 1983.

From these and from the notes which follow, you are required:
(a) **to prepare a Consolidated Profit and Loss Account for the year to 30 June 1983, in accordance with Format 2 in the Companies Act 1981, avoiding the need to publish Tweedle plc's Profit and Loss Account, and showing the amounts added to group reserves, with suitable analysis between group companies; and** **(28 marks)**

(b) **to draft notes to the said Consolidated Profit and Loss Account, dealing with directors' remuneration, using such information as is given in the question, and indicating what further information is required to complete the published accounts in respect of directors' remuneration.** **(8 marks)**
(36 marks)

Tweedle plc
Profit and Loss Account for the year to 30 June 1983

	£	£
Turnover		10 000 000
Change in stocks of finished goods and in work in progress		300 000
Own work capitalized		200 000
Raw materials and consumables		(4 000 000)
Other external charges		(200 000)
Staff costs		(4 750 000)
Depreciation and other amounts written off tangible and intangible fixed assets		(500 000)
Other operating charges		(80 000)
Other operating income		60 000
Income from shares in group company		28 571
Income from shares in related company		160 714
Other interest receivable and similar income		20 000
Interest payable and similar charges		(200 000)
Profit on ordinary activities before taxation		1 039 285
Tax on profit on ordinary activities		(472 785)
Profit on ordinary activities after taxation		566 500
Extraordinary income	80 000	
Extraordinary charges	(60 000)	
Extraordinary profit	20 000	
Tax on extraordinary profit	(10 400)	
		9 600
Profit for the financial year		576 100
Dividends paid and proposed		(300 000)
Retained profits transferred to reserves		£276 100

Dum Ltd
Profit and Loss Account for the 15 months to 30 June 1983

	£	£
Turnover		7 500 000
Change in stocks of finished goods and in work in progress		200 000
Raw materials and consumables		(3 000 000)
Other external charges		(170 000)
Staff costs		(3 500 000)
Depreciation and other amounts written off tangible and intangible fixed assets		(350 000)
Other operating charges		(50 000)
Other operating income		10 000
Income from shares in related company		64 286
Interest payable		(10 000)
Profit on ordinary activities before taxation		694 286
Tax on profit on ordinary activities		(331 286)
Profit on ordinary activities after taxation		363 000
Extraordinary income	5 000	
Extraordinary charges	(20 000)	
Extraordinary loss	(15 000)	
Tax on extraordinary loss	7 800	
		(7 200)
Profit for the financial year		355 800
Dividends paid and proposed		(175 000)
Retained profits transferred to reserves		£180 800

Notes
(1) Tweedle plc, on 1 October 1982, acquired 80% of the 1 250 000 £1 ordinary shares of Dum Ltd for £2.00 per share in cash. Dum's latest accounts before acquisition, made up to its old year-end, 31 March 1982, showed total reserves of £1 008 680. As at acquisition, Dum's tangible fixed assets were revalued upwards by £600 000 net; no goodwill was taken on to its books. Dum's first accounting 'year' after acquisition was extended to secure conformity with Tweedle's accounting date.

(2) Dum Ltd had also in issue 500 000 £1 10% cumulative preference shares, whose dividends were payable on 31 March and 30 September. They were paid as usual in 1982–83. As at 1 November 1982, Dum also paid off dividend arrears for the year to 31 March 1982, when a loss was made and no dividends were paid. No preference shares have been acquired by Tweedle.

(3) Dum Ltd's ordinary dividends were paid thus: final, year to 31 March 1982, passed; interim, 15 months to 30 June 1983, 2% on 1 November 1982. A final dividend of 4% was provided for at 30 June 1983.

(4) During the 9 months to 30 June 1983, Dum Ltd invoiced Tweedle plc for £800 000 of goods supplied, at an average mark-up on cost of 25%. Of these goods, £70 000 (at selling price) were included in Tweedle's stock at 30 June 1983.

(5) Tweedle's policy on purchased goodwill is to amortize it by equal instalments over 5 years.

(6) Since 1981, Tweedle plc has held 25% of the equity share capital of Dee plc, whose results for the year to 30 April 1983 were: profit on ordinary activities before taxation, £1 500 000; after taxation, £750 000; extraordinary income, nil; extraordinary charges, £30 000; dividends – ordinary final, 1981–82, £300 000 (paid 1 August 1982); ordinary interim, 1982–83, £150 000 (paid 1 December 1982); ordinary final 1982–83, £350 000 (paid 1 August 1983).

(7) Dum Ltd, at acquisition by Tweedle plc, also owned 10% of the equity share capital of Dee plc, and has retained it since, treating Dee as a related company in its accounts since acquisition by Tweedle.

(8) Staff costs include the following amounts for directors' salaries and other benefits:
Tweedle plc: L. Carroll (chairman), £40 000; D. Redking (managing director), £60 000; B. Lion, £35 000; S. Tove, £30 000. The company contributed £50 000 to the directors' superannuation scheme during the year to 30 June 1983.
Dum Ltd: C. Dodgson (chairman), £30 000 for the 15 months to 30 June 1983; B. Lion (managing director), £20 000 for the 9 months to 30 June 1983; Miss A. Liddell, £15 000 for the 6 months to 30 September 1982; R. Whiteknight, £10 000 for the 6 months to 30 September 1982. Compensation for loss of office: Miss A. Liddell, £40 000; R. Whiteknight, £30 000. Dum Ltd has no superannuation scheme for its directors.

(9) In Dum Ltd's profit and loss account, 'depreciation and other amounts written off tangible and intangible fixed assets' includes £40 000 additional depreciation arising from revaluation of its fixed assets as at 1 October 1982.

(10) Except where otherwise indicated, all income and expenditure (including corporation tax) of Dum Ltd is deemed to accrue evenly over the 15 months to 30 June 1983.

(11) Corporation Tax, 52%; income tax basic rate, 30%.

A. Cert. A. Level 2 The Regulatory Framework of Accounting, June 1982.

12.7 Greater Combinations Ltd, and its subsidiary Cooperative Ltd, have produced the following summarized balance sheets as on 30 November 1975 and profit and loss accounts for the year ended on that date.

Summarized Balance Sheets as on 30 November 1975

	Greater Combinations £'000	Cooperative £'000
Issued share capital		
ordinary shares of £1	500	100
Reserves and unappropriated profits	800	260
Deferred taxation	100	90
	1 400	450
Fixed assets	600	100
Shares in subsidiary		
75 000 shares of £1	25	—
Patents and trade marks	75	20
Net current assets	700	330
	1 400	450

Summarized Profit and Loss Accounts for year ended 30 November 1975

	Greater Combinations £'000	Cooperative £'000
Trading profit	300	80
Taxation at 55%	165	44
	135	36
Proposed dividend	75	20
Retained	60	16

You have ascertained that:

(1) The entire issued share capital of Cooperative Ltd was acquired on 1 August 1966 at £1 per share. At this date total reserves and unappropriated profits of Cooperative Ltd were equivalent to £0.80 per share. There have not been any changes in the issued share capital since that date.

(2) On 31 May 1975 25 000 shares of Cooperative Ltd were sold at £3 per share.

(3) The sale had been recorded in the books of Greater Combinations Ltd by crediting the receipt against the cost of purchase.

(4) Trading and profit of Cooperative Ltd arise evenly throughout the year.

(5) Greater Combinations Ltd sells to Cooperative Ltd on the normal trade terms of cost plus 25%, goods to the value of £100 000 per month. Stock held by Cooperative Ltd at the end of the year represents one month's purchases.

(6) Both companies maintain the deferred taxation account under the deferral method.

(7) Greater Combinations Ltd does not take credit in its own acounts for dividends until they have been received.

You are required to:

(a) **prepare a consolidated balance sheet at 30 November 1975 which complies with the best current practice in so far as the information provided will allow,**

(b) **prepare a detailed analysis of the movements in the group 'reserves and unappropriated profits', and**

(c) **write a *brief* note with numerical illustration comparing the alternatives available to reflect in the group accounts the trading between parent and subsidiary.**   **(30 marks)**

ICAEW PE II, Financial Accounting II, December 1975.

13 Accounting for Overseas Involvement

The problems identified

Many firms based in the UK undertake transactions with firms in other countries and have branches, subsidiaries and associated companies overseas.

In the first case, transactions undertaken between the firms will often be expressed in foreign currencies and it will be necessary to translate these amounts into sterling in order to enter them in the accounting records of the UK firm. If the rate of exchange changes between the date of the transaction and the date of settlement it is necessary to decide how to deal with the resulting difference on exchange in the accounts of the UK company. If there is an intervening balance sheet date then it is necessary to decide which rate of exchange should be used at the balance sheet date and how the resulting difference on exchange should be treated.

In the second case, that is where there is an overseas branch, subsidiary or associated company, it is usual for the whole of the accounting records of the overseas unit to be kept in the local currency: indeed, the local law may require the preparation and publication of accounts in terms of the local currency. In order to combine the results of the overseas unit with the sterling results of the investing company and those of any similar UK units, the accounts expressed in foreign currency must be translated into sterling.[1] When exchange rates between currencies fluctuate over time, this need for translation poses two problems. First, it is necessary to decide what rates of exchange are appropriate for the individual assets, liabilities, revenues and expenses in the accounts of the overseas unit. No matter how this question is answered, the translation process invariably gives rise to differences on exchange. As a second problem, it is therefore necessary to decide

---

[1] Following the American terminology introduced in ED 21, the term 'conversion' is restricted to the exchange of one currency for another.

how these differences are to be dealt with in the aggregated financial statements. As we shall see, translation is a necessary but not sufficient condition for meaningful aggregation to take place.

Until the ASC attempted to standardize the accounting treatment of exchange differences in ED 16,[2] professional accountancy bodies in the UK had provided little guidance on how the above questions should be answered. Official pronouncements[3] tended to describe various methods and to emphasize that selection between them is a matter of professional judgement, without providing any guidance as to the principles on which that professional judgement should be based. As a result many different methods have been used in practice.

In this chapter, we look first at accounting for transactions denominated in foreign currencies and then turn our attention to the more complex subject of translating the accounts of an overseas unit for the purposes of aggregation. The accounting treatment of both topics is now regulated by SSAP 20, 'Foreign currency translation', which was issued in April 1983.

Accounting for foreign currency transactions

A UK company may purchase fixed assets, stocks or services from an overseas company and may, in addition, sell goods or services to an overseas company. It may also raise loans denominated in a foreign currency and make investments in the shares of an overseas company. Where the amounts involved are expressed in a foreign currency, it will be necessary to translate those amounts into sterling in order to incorporate them into the accounting records of the UK company. The approach which should be adopted is best illustrated by means of a number of examples.

EXAMPLE 13.1

Let us consider a UK company, Han Limited, which makes up its accounts to 31 December each year. On 12 September 19X1 it purchased a fixed asset, machinery, from a German company for 42 000 Deutschemarks when the rate of exchange was DM4.2 to £1. It paid

2 ED 16, 'Supplement to "Extraordinary items and prior year adjustments"', September 1975.
3 *See*, for example, recommendation N 25 of the ICAEW, issued in February 1968.

for this machinery on 15 November 19X1 when the rate of exchange was DM 4.0 to £1.[4]

At the date of purchase, 12 September 19X1, it is necessary to translate the foreign currency amount to record the cost of the fixed asset and the corresponding creditor in sterling. As there was no contractually agreed rate of exchange for settlement or forward exchange contract, the rate ruling on the date of purchase, that is DM 4.2 to £1, will be used.[5]

19X1
Sept. 12   *Dr* Machinery – at cost   £10 000
                  Cr Creditor – German company   £10 000

            Purchase of machinery for DM 42 000 at exchange rate of DM 4.2 to £1.

The sterling cost of the machinery is £10 000 and it is this figure which will be depreciated over the expected useful life of the asset. No further adjustment to this cost is necessary whatever subsequently happens to the rate of exchange.

In order to pay for the machinery, Han Limited must arrange with its bankers to convert sterling into Deutschemarks. If bank charges are ignored, the payment of DM 42 000 on 15 November 19X1 would require sterling of £10 500 given that the rate of exchange is DM 4.0 to £1. Settlement would be recorded as follows:

19X1
Nov. 15   *Dr* Creditor – German company   £10 500
                  Cr Cash   £10 500

            Being payment of DM 42 000 converted at DM 4.0 to £1.

The creditor is now settled but when we look at the account in the records of Han Limited, it shows a debit balance of £500.

Creditor – German company

19X1		£	19X1		£
Nov. 15	Cash	10 500	Sept. 12	Machinery	10 000

4 Although the currencies used in this and the following examples are often real currencies, the rates of exchange used are fictitious and movements are exaggerated to illustrate the principles involved.

5 SSAP 20, Para. 48, states that, where appropriate, contractually agreed rates of exchange for settlement *should* be used. It also *permits* the use of rates of exchange fixed in related or matching forward contracts.

This is a difference on exchange which, in this case, is a loss due to the fact that sterling has weakened (that is become less valuable) against the Deutschemark between the date of purchase and the date of settlement. The loss is, of course, realized and SSAP 20 requires that it be charged to the profit and loss account in arriving at the profit or loss from ordinary activities for the accounting year ended 31 December 19X1.

EXAMPLE 13.2
The next complication which may arise is that the purchase and the payment occur in different accounting years. To illustrate this, let us assume that Han Limited purchased stock from a French company for 200 000 French francs on 20 November 19X1 when the rate of exchange was 10 francs to £1. It subsequently paid for the goods on 15 January 19X2 when the rate of exchange was 12 francs to £1. The rate of exchange on 31 December 19X1, the intervening balance sheet date, was 11.5 francs to £1.

Following the principles explained in Example 13.1, the purchase would be recorded as follows:

19X1			
Nov. 20	*Dr* Stock	£20 000	
	Cr Creditor – French company		£20 000

Purchase of stock for 200 000 francs at 10 francs to £1.

The cost of stock is recorded at £20 000 and, as before, this figure is not affected by any subsequent changes in the exchange rate. If the stock is still held on 31 December 19X1 it is included in the balance sheet at the lower of cost and net realizable value. Cost will be determined in accordance with the company's normal accounting policy (e.g. FIFO, average cost, etc.).

When we turn to the creditor, a monetary amount, such an approach is not sensible and, in the absence of either contractually agreed exchange rates for settlement or forward exchange contracts, SSAP 20 requires that all monetary items are translated at the closing rate.[6] The closing rate is defined more precisely as follows:

> The closing rate is the exchange rate for spot transactions ruling at the balance sheet date and is the mean of the buying and selling rates at the close of business on the day for which the rate is to be ascertained.[7]

6 *See* preceding footnote.
7 SSAP 20, Para. 41.

On 31 December 19X1 the amount payable to extinguish the creditor is not £20 000 but a lower amount of £17 391, that is 200 000 francs, translated at the closing rate of exchange on that day – 11.5 francs to £1. When the liability is adjusted to this figure, the result is a gain on exchange:

Creditor – French company

19X1		£	19X1		£
Dec. 31	Balance c/d	17 391	Nov. 20	Stock	20 000
	Profit and				
	loss account				
	– gain on				
	exchange	2 609			
		20 000			20 000
			19X2		
			Jan. 1	Balance b/d	17 391

The gain on exchange has occurred because the sterling value of the liability has fallen between 20 November 19X1 and 31 December 19X1 which in turn is due to the strengthening of sterling against the French franc. SSAP 20 considers that, as there is objective evidence for the sterling value of the liability and, as such a gain on a short-term monetary item will shortly be reflected in cash flows, so the profit on exchange is a part of realized profit and hence should be included in the profit or loss from ordinary activities.

The gain recognized in 19X1 could, of course, be fully or partly offset by a loss in the subsequent year if sterling weakens against the franc between 31 December 19X1 and the date of settlement, 15 January 19X2. The treatment adopted is, of course, consistent with the accruals concept: the gain occurred in 19X1 and is reported in 19X1, whilst the loss would occur in 19X2 and be reported in 19X2.

In this particular example there is, of course, no loss in 19X2 but a further gain on exchange when settlement is made on 15 January 19X2. Ignoring bank charges, the amount payable in sterling is £16 667 (200 000 francs ÷ 12) so that the creditor's account appears as follows:

Creditor – French company

19X2		£	19X2		£
Jan. 15	Cash	16 667	Jan. 1	Balance b/d	17 391
15	Profit and loss account – gain on exchange	724			
		17 391			17 391

As in 19X1, the gain on exchange is credited to the profit and loss account, this time for the year ended 31 December 19X2.

SSAP 20 also requires similar adherence to the accruals principle in the case of long-term monetary liabilities as we shall see in the next example.

EXAMPLE 13.3

Let us suppose that Han Limited raised a long-term loan of 500 000 French francs on 1 October 19X1 when the rate of exchange was 10 francs to £1. The loan will be recorded in the accounting records of Han Limited at a figure of £50 000:

19X1
Oct. 1   *Dr* Cash   £50 000
               Cr Long-term loan   £50 000

Being loan of 500 000 French francs translated at
10 francs to £1.

If, on 31 December 19X1, the rate of exchange is 11.5 francs to £1 then, under the provisions of SSAP 20, the liability must be translated into sterling at that rate to produce a figure of £43 478 (500 000 ÷ 11.5):

Long-term loan

19X1		£	19X1		£
Dec. 31	Balance c/d	43 478	Oct. 1	Cash	50 000
	Profit and loss account – gain on exchange	6 522			
		50 000			50 000
			19X2		
			Jan. 1	Balance b/d	43 478

Restating the sterling liability at this figure produces a gain on exchange of £6522 and SSAP 20 requires that this be reported as part of the 'ordinary' profits of Han Limited.

Many accountants have argued that such a profit is not realized at the balance sheet date and, as a consequence, that the prudence concept required that it should not be included in the profit and loss account. Indeed, they may quote statutory support for their argument in that the Companies Act 1981 specifically states that: 'only profits realised at the balance sheet date shall be included in the profit and loss account'.[8] However, the law permits directors to depart from this principle if there are special reasons providing that the notes to the accounts give particulars of the departure, the reason for it and its effect.[9] SSAP 20 considers that such a departure from the realization principle is essential if exchange gains and losses are to be treated symmetrically in accordance with the accruals principle. Thus, in contravention of SSAP 2, SSAP 20 requires that the accruals concept takes precedence over the prudence concept.[10] Hence, in the same way as exchange losses on long-term liabilities during the period are debited to the profit and loss account, so exchange gains for the period are credited to the profit and loss account.

As explained above, relevant disclosure must be made. In addition any such unrealized profits credited to the profit and loss account should be removed when calculating legally distributable profits.

EXAMPLE 13.4

It is possible for a UK company to raise a foreign currency loan which it then invests in the shares of an overseas company. The loan and investment may be in the same currency or, alternatively, the loan may be raised in one currency whilst the investment is made in a country with a different currency. For ease of exposition we shall assume that only one currency is involved.

Let us assume that Han Limited raised a long-term loan of US $300 000 on 1 October 19X1 when the rate of exchange was US $1.5 to £1. It immediately invested the proceeds in the shares of a US corporation so that, if we ignore the receipt and payment of cash, the summarized journal entry will appear as follows:

---

8 Companies Act 1981, Schedule 1, Para. 12(a).
9 Companies Act 1981, Schedule 1, Para. 15.
10 SSAP 2, Para. 14(b), '. . . provided that where the accruals concept is inconsistent with the "prudence" concept, the latter prevails.'

19X1

Oct. 1   *Dr* Investment in US company   £200 000
                    Cr Long-term loan (US)   £200 000

Being loan of US$300 000 raised to finance investment in US company translated at $1.5 to £1.

The investment may constitute the US company a subsidiary, an associated company or merely a simple investment. Whichever is the case, the treatment in the accounting records of Han Limited will be exactly the same although the treatment in any consolidated accounts will differ.

Let us assume that the rate of exchange on 31 December 19X1 is $1.4 to £1. If Han Limited follows the rules explained in previous examples, certain difficulties will arise. Unless there had been a permanent fall in the value of the investment, the investment would be shown in the balance sheet at its cost of £200 000 whilst the loan, a monetary amount, would have to be translated at the closing rate of exchange and shown as a liability of £214 286 ($300 000 ÷ 1.4). Restating the loan at this amount produces a loss on exchange of £14 286 which would have to be charged to the profit and loss account.

Long-term loan – US dollars

19X1			19X1		
Dec. 31	Balance c/d	£214 286	Oct. 1	Cash	£200 000
			Dec. 31	Profit and loss account – loss on exchange	14 286
		214 286			214 286

It may be argued that to make such a one-sided adjustment is misleading. Because of our adherence to historical cost accounting, the investment is retained at its historical cost in sterling whilst the liability is shown at its current sterling equivalent. SSAP 20 recognizes the logic of this argument and permits, although it does not require, Han Limited to translate the investment at the closing rate of exchange rather than at the historical rate of exchange, thus:

Investment in US corporation

19X1				19X1		
Oct.	1	Cost	£200 000	Dec. 31	Balance c/d,	
					300 000 ÷ 1.4	£214 286
Dec. 31		Gain on				
		exchange	14 286			
			214 286			214 286

This produces a rather meaningless sterling figure for the investment, a figure which is neither the historical cost in sterling nor a current value in sterling, but it results in the creation of a gain on exchange which may be offset against the loss on exchange on the long-term loan. In this case the gain on the investment is exactly equal to the loss on the long-term loan and one may be offset against the other without any need to charge any gain or loss to the profit and loss account. If the loan and investment were for different currency amounts or in different foreign currencies, this equality of gain and loss is unlikely to exist. In such a case the provisions of SSAP 20 require that any exchange gain or loss on the investment should be taken direct to reserves. Any loss or gain on the loan should then be offset to the extent of the gain or loss on the investment. If the exchange loss/gain on the loan exceeds the gain/loss on the investment then it follows that the excess must be charged/credited to the profit and loss account.

The final problem we must address in this section is to what extent such an offset should be permitted. Should it be necessary to identify a particular loan with a particular investment? Should the offset be restricted to situations where the loan and investment are in the same currency? Where a large company has many loans denominated in various foreign currencies and many investments in various foreign currencies, should a global approach be permitted whereby any gains are set off against any losses? What criteria should be laid down to govern the use of this offset arrangement?

After receiving many different recommendations from those who commented on the offset arrangements included in ED 27, SSAP 20 has specified the following conditions:[11]

11 SSAP 20, Para. 51. Although ED 27, 'Accounting for foreign currency translations', issued in October 1980, considered this topic within the context of consolidated accounts, it did not even mention such offset arrangements within the accounts of the individual company.

(a) in any accounting period, exchange gains or losses arising on the borrowings may be offset only to the extent of exchange differences arising on the equity investments;

(b) the foreign currency borrowings, whose exchange gains or losses are used in the offset process, should not exceed, in the aggregate, the total amount of cash that the investments are expected to be able to generate, whether from profits or otherwise; and

(c) the accounting treatment adopted should be applied consistently from period to period.[12]

This must be recognized as a pragmatic solution to what is often a very difficult question to answer in practice: 'To what extent do foreign currency loans provide a hedge against foreign equity investments?'

Accounting for an overseas subsidiary

Where a UK company has an overseas branch, subsidiary or associated company which keeps its records in a foreign currency, it is necessary to translate the accounts in order to combine the figures with those of the UK company or group. In this chapter we assume that the overseas unit is a subsidiary although readers will appreciate that similar principles are appropriate for a foreign branch or associated company.

As explained in the first section of this chapter, when exchange rates are changing the existence of an overseas subsidiary requires us to answer two questions. First, what rate of exchange should be used to translate the individual items in the accounts of the overseas subsidiary? Second, how should the resulting differences on exchange be treated in the accounts?

Turning first to the balance sheet of the overseas subsidiary, there are at least two rates of exchange which could be applied to each asset or liability. These are the historical rate or the closing rate. The historical rate is the rate of exchange ruling at the date the transaction occurred or, where appropriate, the rate of exchange ruling at the date of a subsequent revaluation. The closing rate is the rate of exchange ruling on the balance sheet date.

The major methods of translation which have been used make use of a combination of these rates and the following table illustrates how four methods deal with the major categories of asset and liability:

12 SSAP 20, Para. 51.

Major methods of translation

	Current/ non- current		Monetary/ non- monetary		Temporal		Closing rate	
	H	C	H	C	H	C	H	C
Assets								
Fixed assets								
At cost less depreciation	*		*		*			*
At current value	*		*			*		*
Current assets								
Stock								
At cost		*	*		*			*
At current value		*	*			*		*
Debtors		*		*		*		*
Cash		*		*		*		*
Liabilities								
Long-term loans	*			*		*		*
Current liabilities		*		*		*		*

H = historical rate; C = closing rate.

Under the current/non-current method, current assets and liabilities are translated at the closing rate whilst fixed assets and long-term liabilities are translated at the appropriate historical rate.

Under the monetary/non-monetary method, monetary assets and liabilities are translated at the closing rate whilst non-monetary assets are translated at the historical rate.

Under the temporal method, which is discussed in more detail later in this chapter, the rate of exchange depends upon the basis of valuation used in the balance sheet of the overseas subsidiary. If items are shown at current value, which is automatically the case with monetary assets and liabilities, the closing rate is used.[13] Where items are shown at a figure based upon historical cost an historical rate is appropriate and where items are shown at a figure based on a valuation, the rate of exchange at the date of the valuation is used.

From the preceding table, it can be seen that there is very little difference between the temporal method and the monetary/non-monetary method within the context of historical cost accounts. The

13 This statement is only true within the confines of traditional accounts. Arguably the current value of a monetary item should take into account interest for the time period until maturity of the debt.

most frequent instance of a difference occurs where stock is shown at net realizable value.

Under the closing rate method all assets and liabilities are translated at the closing rate of exchange.

When we turn to the profit and loss account, three alternative translation rates may be distinguished: (a) historical rates, that is rates of exchange specific to each transaction; (b) average rate ruling during the year,[14] (c) closing rate on the balance sheet date. Under the first of these alternatives, the appropriate rate of exchange is determined as that ruling on the date of the transaction. So, if depreciation is based upon an historical cost, the rate of exchange at the date of acquisition of the asset is appropriate. If depreciation is based upon a revalued amount, the rate of exchange at the date of revaluation is appropriate. Where revenues and other expenses arise on a particular day, the rate of exchange on that day is appropriate. In practice, for recurrent items such as wages, power, directors' remuneration, etc., an average rate is used as an approximation to the historical or specific rate of exchange.

Under the second of the two alternatives, an average rate of exchange is used in its own right, whereas under the third alternative the closing rate of exchange is used for all items in the profit and loss account.

When we consider rates of exchange applied to balance sheet items and profit and loss account items, the following combinations have been found:

Balance sheet	Profit and loss account
Current/non-current	Historical or average
Monetary/non-monetary	Historical or average
Temporal	Historical or average
Closing rate	Average or closing rate

Thus there has been a wide choice in practice as to the appropriate combinations of rates of exchange.

Whichever combinations are used, there will inevitably be differences on exchange and there are various ways in which these may be dealt with in the consolidated accounts:

(i) Include as part of profit or loss from ordinary activities.
(ii) Include as an extraordinary item.

---

14 This should, of course, be an appropriate weighted average and not merely a simple average of the opening and closing rates.

(iii) Treat as a movement on reserves.
(iv) Some combination of (i) to (iii) above.

When the choice between relevant rates of exchange is coupled with the choice between the various ways of dealing with differences on exchange, there are a large number of possible combinations. Given such choice, it is not surprising that the ASC has felt it necessary to reduce the diversity in practice by producing an accounting standard on this topic.

The solution proposed by the ASC

ED 21, wrongly entitled 'Accounting for foreign currency transactions',[15] was issued in September 1972 as the first comprehensive attempt towards standardizing the accounting treatment of foreign currencies in the UK. It permitted companies to use either the temporal method or the closing rate method and laid down rules on the rates of exchange to be used for translation and the treatment of the differences on exchange.

If ED 21 had become a Statement of Standard Accounting Practice, it would certainly have reduced the choice of methods available to companies by outlawing the use of the current/non-current and the monetary/non-monetary methods. However, when applied to historical cost accounts, the temporal method and the closing rate method usually produce very different results and, hence, the degree of standardization proposed by ED 21 was limited and the Exposure Draft was heavily criticized for this.[16]

The subsequent ED 27, 'Accounting for foreign currency translations', issued in November 1980, and SSAP 20, 'Foreign currency translation', issued in April 1983, required the use of one method in most situations. The favoured method is now called the 'closing rate/net investment method' and this appears to be the method used by the majority of companies in the UK.[17]

The words 'net investment' have been added to the title of the method to indicate the view which the method implicitly takes of the investment

---

15 Wrongly entitled because it dealt almost exclusively with foreign currency translation and gave little attention to foreign currency transactions.

16 *See*, for example, D. Pendrill, 'Foreign currency and accounting', *The Certified Accountant*; February 1979.

17 'Financial reporting 1983–84: a survey of published accounts', ICAEW, shows that, of the companies surveyed in 1982/83 which had foreign operations, 93% used the closing rate/net investment method.

in the overseas subsidiary. The majority of overseas subsidiaries are thought to have a certain amount of autonomy and to operate primarily within the economic environment of an overseas country using the currency of that country. Using the terminology of the Financial Accounting Standards Board (FASB) Statement No. 52, the 'functional currency' of the overseas subsidiary is usually that of the country in which it operates.[18] The holding company is therefore regarded as having an investment in the net assets of the subsidiary rather than in its individual assets and liabilities. It follows that only the net investment is at risk from movements in the exchange rate and, as we shall see, use of the closing rate method is consistent with this position.

In some cases, however, the overseas subsidiary may not have significant autonomy. Thus the affairs of the overseas company may be closely linked with those of the parent company and its 'functional currency' may be sterling rather than the local currency. In such a case, SSAP 20 requires that the foreign accounts be translated using the temporal method so that the results are included as if the transactions had been undertaken by the parent company itself.

SSAP 20 provides little guidance on how to recognize situations where the temporal method is appropriate and, given the variety of situations found in practice, it will sometimes be extremely difficult to decide which method of translation to apply.

To summarize, under the provisions of SSAP 20, it is expected that the vast majority of companies should use the closing rate/net investment method whilst a small number of companies will be required to use the temporal method. It is therefore essential for us to look at both methods.

In the following two sections of this chapter we shall examine the principles of the closing rate/net investment method and temporal method using simple examples. In the following sections we shall compare and contrast the two methods before concluding, in the final section, with a more complex example of the closing rate/net investment method.

Closing rate/net investment method

As we have seen, any method for translating the accounts of an overseas subsidiary must specify which rates of exchange are to be used for

---

18 *See* Appendix A to Statement of Financial Accounting Standard No. 52 for factors which should be taken into account in determining the functional currency of an overseas subsidiary.

the various items in the accounts of that subsidiary and how the resulting differences on exchange are to be treated in the consolidated accounts.

The SSAP 20 version of the closing rate/net investment method lays down the following rules:

(a) All assets and liabilities in the balance sheet of the overseas subsidiary are to be translated at the closing rate. This, of course, determines the amount of the shareholders' interest although, as we shall see, it is sensible to translate the share capital and components of reserves at various rates of exchange.

(b) All profit and loss account items are to be translated at either the average rate or the closing rate.[19]

(c) All differences on exchange arising on translation are to be taken direct to reserves.

When the rate of exchange between sterling and the overseas currency is fluctuating, a difference on exchange will arise in respect of the opening net assets of the subsidiary; these are translated at a different rate at the year end to that used at the beginning of the year. A second difference will arise if the average rate of exchange is used to translate profit and loss account items for, in such a case, the increase in net assets as shown by the retained profit or loss is translated at the average rate whilst the resulting net assets are translated at the closing rate in the balance sheet. Both differences on translation are treated as movements on reserves.

Let us illustrate the method by means of a simple example.

EXAMPLE 13.5

Widening Horizons Limited, a UK company which owns and rents out properties, established a wholly owned overseas subsidiary, Foreign Venture Limited, on 31 December 19X1. Widening Horizons Limited subscribed £100 000 in cash for one million shares of 1 groucho each. On 31 December 19X1, the rate of exchange between currencies was 10 grouchos to £1.

---

19 ED 27 proposed the use of the average rate for profit and loss account items and, although this is standard practice in the USA and Canada, the comments on ED 27 showed that there was considerable opposition to the exclusive use of an average rate in the UK.

Foreign Venture Limited immediately raised a long-term loan of 500 000 grouchos and purchased freehold land and buildings, suitable for renting, at a cost of 1 200 000 grouchos.

After these transactions, the opening balance sheet of the new subsidiary, in both foreign currency and sterling, is therefore as given below:

Foreign Venture Limited

Opening balance sheet on 1 January 19X2

	Grouchos	Rate of exchange (grouchos to £1)	£
Share capital			
1 000 000 shares of 1 groucho	1 000 000	10	100 000
Freehold land and buildings			
At cost	1 200 000	10	120 000
Short-term monetary assets			
Cash	300 000	10	30 000
	1 500 000		150 000
less Long-term loan	500 000	10	50 000
	1 000 000		100 000

At this date only one rate of exchange is appropriate; it qualifies as both the historical rate and the closing rate. Once the balance sheet is translated into sterling, it is possible to match the cost of the investment shown in the records of Widening Horizons Limited at £100 000 against the share capital of Foreign Venture Limited to produce neither goodwill nor capital reserve on consolidation.

During the following year to 31 December 19X2 Foreign Venture Limited collects rentals and incurs expenses with the result that its profit and loss account for the year and balance sheet on 31 December 19X2 are as follows:

Foreign Venture Limited
Profit and loss account for the year ended 31 December 19X2

	Grouchos	Grouchos
Rentals received		400 000
less Expenses		
Management expenses	115 000	
Depreciation of buildings	50 000	
Interest on long-term loan	75 000	240 000
Profit before taxation		160 000
less Taxation payable		60 000
Retained profit for year		100 000

Balance sheet on 31 December 19X2

	Grouchos
Share capital	
1 000 000 shares of 1 groucho each	1 000 000
Retained profit	100 000
	1 100 000
Freehold land and buildings	
At cost	1 200 000
less Depreciation	50 000
	1 150 000
Short-term net monetary assets (debtors plus cash less creditors	450 000
	1 600 000
less Long-term loan	500 000
	1 100 000

Assuming that the relevant rates of exchange between grouchos and sterling are as given below, we may proceed to translate the accounts in accordance with the closing rate/net investment method:

	Grouchos to £1
1 January 19X2	10
Average for year to 31 December 19X2	8
31 December 19X2	6

The average rate, rather than the closing rate, has been applied in the profit and loss account.

Foreign Venture Limited
Profit and loss account for the year ended 31 December 19X2

	Grouchos	Rate of exchange	£
Rentals received	400 000	8	50 000
less Expenses			
Management expenses	115 000	8	14 375
Depreciation of buildings	50 000	8	6 250
Interest on long-term loan	75 000	8	9 375
	240 000		30 000
Profit before taxation	160 000		20 000
less Taxation payable	60 000	8	7 500
Retained profit for year	100 000		12 500

Balance sheet on 31 December 19X2

	Grouchos	Rate of exchange	£
Freehold land and buildings			
At cost	1 200 000	6	200 000
less Depreciation	50 000	6	8 333
	1 150 000		191 667
Short-term net monetary assets	450 000	6	75 000
	1 600 000		266 667
less Long-term loan	500 000	6	83 333
	1 100 000		183 334
Shareholders' interest:			
Share capital	1 000 000	10 (HR)	100 000
Retained profits	100 000	Per P and L a/c	12 500
			112 500
Difference on exchange	—	Balance	70 834
	1 100 000		183 334

The treatment of share capital merits special attention. It has been translated at the historical rate of exchange, that is the rate ruling at the date of acquisition.

If we assume for a moment that share capital had been translated at the closing rate of exchange of 6 grouchos to £1, this would have produced a sterling figure of £166 667 instead of the £100 000 shown. This would have reduced the difference on exchange, the balancing figure, by £66 667, but consideration must also be paid to the subsequent consolidation of the subsidiary's accounts with those of the parent company. In the consolidation workings the cost of the investment, £100 000, would be matched with the share capital of the subsidiary, £166 667 when translated at closing rate, to produce a capital reserve on consolidation of £66 667. This is clearly nonsensical since there was neither a capital reserve nor goodwill on acquisition and the apparent capital reserve would only have arisen because of the change in the exchange rate. In other words the £66 667 is a difference on exchange.

The wisdom of the method used in the example may now be seen. The application of the historical rate to share capital and, in a more general case, to pre-acquisition reserves as well, means, first, that the total difference emerges in the translation of the subsidiary's balance sheet and, second, that there is no risk that an erroneous adjustment will be made to the goodwill or capital reserve on consolidation. This should be retained at its original cost less any amounts written off in the normal way.

The total difference on exchange, a gain of £70 834, must be credited to consolidated reserves. It has arisen for two reasons. First, the opening net assets were translated at one rate on 1 January 19X2 and at a different rate on 31 December 19X2. Second, the increase in net assets, the retained profit, has been translated at one rate in the profit and loss account and at a different rate in the closing balance sheet. We may analyse the difference as follows:

Analysis of difference on exchange

	Grouchos	Opening balance sheet (10 grouchos to £1) (£)	Closing balance sheet (6 grouchos to £1) (£)	Difference (£)
Opening net assets				
Freehold land and buildings	1 200 000	120 000	200 000	80 000 (gain)

	Grouchos	Opening balance sheet (10 grouchos to £1) (£)	Closing balance sheet (6 grouchos to £1) (£)	Difference (£)
Cash	300 000	30 000	50 000	20 000 (gain)
	1 500 000	150 000	250 000	100 000
less Long-term loan	500 000	50 000	83 333	33 333 (loss)
	1 000 000	100 000	166 667	66 667

Increase in net assets during year
  Retained profit for year
    Per profit and loss account,
      100 000 grouchos at 8 grouchos to £1   £12 500
    Per closing balance sheet (part of net
      monetary assets), 100 000 grouchos
      at 6 grouchos to £1   16 667   4 167 (gain)

Total gain on exchange   70 834

It is hoped that the above analysis helps to explain why the words 'net investment' have been added in the name 'closing rate/net investment' method. The loss on the opening long-term loan has effectively been offset against the gains on the opening assets so that it is only the gain on the opening *net* assets which is taken to reserves with the second part of the gain in respect of the retained profit for the year. If the closing rate had been used for profit and loss account items, this second part of the gain would not occur.

Let us assume that the accounts of the parent company are as given in the left-hand column below. Provided there are no unrealized inter-company profits or similar consolidation adjustments, we may proceed to consolidate by adding the figures for the parent company with the translated figures for the overseas subsidiary, treating the difference on exchange of £70 834 as a movement on reserves.

Widening Horizons Limited
Workings for consolidated profit and loss account for the year ended 31 December 19X2

	Widening Horizons Limited (£)	Foreign Venture Limited (£)	Consolidated (£)
Rentals received	500 000	50 000	550 000
less Expenses			
Management expenses	120 000	14 375	134 375
Depreciation	60 000	6 250	66 250
Loan interest	100 000	9 375	109 375
	280 000	30 000	310 000
Profit before taxation	220 000	20 000	240 000
less Taxation	100 000	7 500	107 500
	120 000	12 500	132 500
less Dividends proposed	60 000	—	60 000
Retained profit for year	60 000	12 500	72 500

Workings for movement on reserves for year to 31 December 19X2

	Widening Horizons Limited (£)	Foreign Venture Limited (£)	Consolidated (£)
Reserves on 1 January 19X2	420 000	—	420 000
add Retained profit for year	60 000	12 500	72 500
Gain on exchange	—	70 834	70 834
Reserves on 31 December 19X2	480 000	83 334	563 334

Workings for consolidated balance sheet on 31 December 19X2

	Widening Horizons Limited (£)	Foreign Venture Limited (£)	Consolidated (£)
Freehold land and buildings			
At cost	2 000 000	200 000	2 200 000
less Depreciation	350 000	8 333	358 333
Carried forward	1 650 000	191 667	1 841 667

	Widening Horizons Limited (£)	Foreign Venture Limited (£)	Consoli- dated (£)
Brought forward	1 650 000	191 667	1 841 667
Investment in Foreign Venture Limited – at cost	100 000	—	—
Goodwill on consolidation – at cost	—	—	—
Short-term net monetary assets	330 000	75 000	405 000
	2 080 000	266 667	2 246 667
less Long-term loan	1 000 000	83 333	1 083 333
	1 080 000	183 334	1 163 334
Share capital	600 000	100 000	600 000
Reserves	480 000	83 334	563 334
	1 080 000	183 334	1 163 334

Once the translation has been undertaken, preparation of the consolidated accounts poses only the normal problems faced when con-
solidating a UK subsidiary and preparing the accounts using the formats
required by company law.

Temporal method

This method was first proposed by an American, Leonard Lorensen,
in a study published by the American Institute of Certified Public
Accountants.[20] It was the only method permitted by the US FASB
in their standard on the subject, Financial Accounting Standard
(FAS) 8, which was issued in October 1975. However, this standard
attracted a great deal of criticism in the USA and has now been replaced
by FAS 52, which was issued in December 1981 and, like SSAP 20,
favours the closing rate method.

Under the temporal method, the rates of exchange to be used for
translation are determined by the basis of measurement used for the
various items in the accounts of the overseas subsidiary.

In the balance sheet, assets which are shown at a figure based on
historical cost are translated at the relevant historical rate; assets which

---

20 L. Lorensen, *Reporting Foreign Operations of US Companies in US Dollars*, Accounting
Research Study No. 12, AICPA, New York, 1972.

are shown on the basis of a revalued amount at some past date are translated at the rate of exchange ruling when the revalued amount was established; assets and liabilities which are shown at a current value, which includes all monetary assets and liabilities, are translated at the closing rate.

In the profit and loss account the rate of exchange used is similarly determined by the underlying basis of measurement: depreciation based on historical cost is translated at the relevant historical rate, revenues and expenses which have accrued over the year are translated at an average rate whilst revenues or expenses which relate to amounts established in previous years or to merely a part of the current year are translated at a specific rate or an appropriate average rate.

It follows that more extensive records are necessary than those required under the closing rate/net investment method.

Under the SSAP 20 version of the temporal method, all differences on exchange are to be credited or charged to the consolidated profit and loss account as a part of the ordinary profits for the year.[21]

Let us examine the temporal method by applying it to the same simple facts used in the previous example.

EXAMPLE 13.6
The opening balance sheet of Foreign Venture Limited, the new subsidiary established by Widening Horizons Limited, in both grouchos and sterling is repeated below:

Foreign Venture Limited
Balance sheet on 1 January 19X2

	Grouchos	Rate of exchange	£
Share capital	1 000 000	10	100 000
Freehold land and buildings			
At cost	1 200 000	10	120 000
Short-term monetary assets			
Cash	300 000	10	30 000
	1 500 000		150 000
less Long-term loan	500 000	10	50 000
	1 000 000		100 000

---

21 Other variants of the temporal method exist. For example, the version of the temporal method required by the Canadian Institute of Chartered Accountants provides that unrealized gains and losses relating to long-term monetary assets and liabilities shall be amortized over the remaining life of the asset or liability.

Widening Horizons Limited paid £100 000 for the investment and hence at the date of acquisition there is no goodwill or capital reserve on consolidation.

The accounts of Foreign Venture Limited for the year ended 31 December 19X2 are given below. The left-hand column gives the accounts in foreign currency whilst the right-hand column shows the results translated into sterling. For ease of reference, the relevant exchange rates are repeated:

	Grouchos to £1
1 January 19X2	10
Average for year to 31 December 19X2	8
31 December 19X2	6

In the profit and loss account the historical rate, that ruling when the buildings were purchased on 31 December 19X1, is applied to depreciation. For other items the average rate is an appropriate approximation to the historical rate. A simple average of the opening and closing rates would only be appropriate if the revenue and expenses arose reasonably evenly over the year and the rate of exchange moved reasonably evenly. Otherwise an appropriate weighted average would have to be used.

Foreign Venture Limited
Profit and loss account for the year ended 31 December 19X2

	Grouchos	Rate of exchange (see note)	£
Rentals received	400 000	8 (AR)	50 000
less Expenses			
Management expenses	115 000	8 (AR)	14 375
Depreciation of buildings	50 000	10 (HR)	5 000
Interest on long-term loan	75 000	8 (AR)	9 375
	240 000		28 750
Profit before taxation	160 000		21 250
less Taxation payable	60 000	8 (AR)	7 500
Retained profit for year	100 000		13 750

Note   AR = average rate, HR = historical rate.

In the balance sheet, the freehold land and buildings, shown at depreciated historical cost, is translated at the historical rate of exchange on 1 January 19X2 whilst all monetary assets and liabilities are translated at the closing rate.

As explained in the previous example, it is sensible to translate the share capital and, in a more general case, any pre-acquisition reserves at the historical rate in order to maintain the goodwill or capital reserve on acquisition at its 'historical cost' in the consolidated accounts. It is also necessary to translate the retained profit for the year at the same sterling figure as shown for retained profit in the profit and loss account. When this has been done the difference on exchange emerges as the balancing figure:

Balance sheet on 31 December 19X2

	Grouchos	Rate of exchange (see note)	£
Freehold land and buildings			
At cost	1 200 000	10 (HR)	120 000
less Depreciation	50 000	10 (HR)	5 000
	1 150 000		115 000
Short-term net monetary assets	450 000	6 (CR)	75 000
	1 600 000		190 000
less Long-term loan	500 000	6 (CR)	83 333
	1 100 000		106 667
Shareholders' interest:			
Share capital			
1 000 000 shares of 1 groucho each	1 000 000	10 (HR)	100 000
Retained profit			
Per profit and loss account	100 000	Actual	13 750
			113 750
Difference on exchange	—	Balance	(7 083)
	1 100 000		106 667

Note   HR = historical rate, CR = closing rate.

As explained above, SSAP 20 requires any difference on exchange arising under the temporal method to be included in the ordinary profits and losses of the group.

If we assume that the accounts of the parent company are as given in the left-hand column below and that there are no consolidation adjustments for such matters as unrealized intercompany profits, we may proceed to consolidate. This requires adding the figures for the parent company with the sterling figures for the overseas subsidiary, treating the difference on exchange as part of the ordinary profits.

Widening Horizons Limited
Workings for consolidated profit and loss account for the year ended 31 December 19X2

	Widening Horizons Limited (£)	Foreign Venture Limited (£)	Consolidated (£)
Rentals received	500 000	50 000	550 000
less Expenses			
Management expenses	120 000	14 375	134 375
Depreciation	60 000	5 000	65 000
Loan interest	100 000	9 375	109 375
	280 000	28 750	308 750
Revenue less expenses	220 000	21 250	241 250
less Loss on exchange	—	7 083	7 083
Profit before taxation	220 000	14 167	234 167
less Taxation	100 000	7 500	107 500
	120 000	6 667	126 667
less Dividends proposed	60 000	—	60 000
Retained profit for the year	60 000	6 667	66 667

Workings for movement on reserves for year to 31 December 19X2

	Widening Horizons Limited (£)	Foreign Venture Limited (£)	Consolidated (£)
Retained profits on 1 January 19X2	420 000	—	420 000
add Retained profit for year	60 000	6 667	66 667
Retained profits on 31 December 19X2	480 000	6 667	486 667

Workings for consolidated balance sheet on 31 December 19X2

	Widening Horizons Limited (£)	Foreign Venture Limited (£)	Consolidated (£)
Freehold land and buildings			
At cost	2 000 000	120 000	2 120 000
less Depreciation	350 000	5 000	355 000
	1 650 000	115 000	1 765 000
Investment in Foreign Venture Limited			
At cost	100 000	—	—
Short-term net monetary assets	330 000	75 000	405 000
	2 080 000	190 000	2 170 000
less Long-term loan	1 000 000	83 333	1 083 333
	1 080 000	106 667	1 086 667
Share capital	600 000	100 000	600 000
Retained profits	480 000	6 667	486 667
	1 080 000	106 667	1 086 667

From workings similar to the above, it is quite straightforward to produce the consolidated accounts for publication, although attention would have to be given to providing the more-detailed information in accordance with the formats prescribed by company law.

As would be expected in this case, there is no goodwill or capital reserve on consolidation. The loss on exchange is charged in the profit and loss account and would only be disclosed if it were an exceptional item.

There is no need to analyse the difference on exchange for the purposes of preparing the consolidated accounts. However, it is instructive to do so.

No difference on exchange relates to the freehold land and buildings. In the opening balance sheet of Foreign Venture Limited the freehold land and buildings were shown at cost and translated at 10 grouchos to £1. In the profit and loss account, depreciation of 50 000 grouchos was provided and this was translated at 10 grouchos to £1. In the closing balance sheet the asset is shown at cost less depreciation, again translated at 10 grouchos to £1.

The difference arises first because monetary assets and liabilities are translated at different rates in the opening and closing balance sheet and second because for certain items, different rates are used in the profit and loss account and closing balance sheet. It may be analysed as follows:

Analysis of difference on exchange

1. Opening balance of
   Short-term net monetary assets   300 000 grouchos

In opening balance sheet, 10 grouchos to £1	£30 000	
In closing balance sheet, 6 grouchos to £1	£50 000	Gain £20 000

2. Opening balance on long-term loan   500 000 grouchos

In opening balance sheet, 10 grouchos to £1	£50 000	
In closing balance sheet, 6 grouchos to £1	£83 333	Loss £33 333

3. Increase in short-term net monetary assets during year
   Per profit and loss account

Retained profit	100 000 grouchos	
add Non-fund item; depreciation	50 000 grouchos	
	150 000 grouchos	
At 8 grouchos to £1	£18 750	
Per closing balance sheet as part of short-term net monetary assets, at 6 grouchos to £1	£25 000	Gain £6 250
Net loss		£7 083

The differences on exchange may therefore be understood by thinking in terms of a flow of funds statement, using net monetary items as the concept of funds:

Statement of source and application of funds for the year ended 31 December 19X2
(funds = net monetary assets/liabilities)

	Grouchos	Grouchos	Rate	£
Opening balance of net monetary liabilities				
Long-term loan		500 000		
Short-term monetary assets		300 000		
		200 000	10	20 000
less Source of funds				
Retained profit plus depreciation		150 000	8	18 750
				1 250
DIFFERENCE ON EXCHANGE – balance (loss)		—	—	7 083
Closing balance of net monetary liabilities				
Long-term loan	500 000			
Short-term monetary assets	450 000			
	50 000			
		50 000	6	8 333

A critical look at the two methods

Some substantial differences

We have now illustrated the mechanics of the two methods of translation, using the same facts but rather large movements in the hypothetical exchange rates.

When exchange rates between currencies change over time the methods produce very different results from the same set of foreign currency accounts. Thus if we compare the translated amount of the fixed assets of Foreign Venture Limited, in the simple examples in the two preceding sections, we find the following results:

Fixed assets of Foreign Venture Limited on 31 December 19X2

	Net book value £
Closing rate/net investment method	191 667
Temporal method	115 000

It is true that the rate of exchange moved from 10 grouchos to £1 at the beginning of the year to 6 grouchos at the end of the year, but there are substantial changes in practice in the exchange rates between currencies. The following table contains movements in the rate of exchange between sterling and a number of major currencies over a 10-year period:

	Rates to £1		*Change as a*
	---	---	---
	December 1973	*December 1983*	*percentage*
US dollars	2.3235	1.4520	−37.5
Belgian francs	95.95	80.70	−15.9
Swiss francs	7.549	3.1652	−58.1
French francs	10.914	12.0880	+10.8
Italian lire	1411.5	2397.3	+69.8
Deutschemarks	6.279	3.9515	−37.1

Source: CSO financial statistics.

To illustrate the effect of the differences between the two methods, let us suppose that a German subsidiary bought land in December 1973 and that this is shown in the balance sheet on 31 December 1983 as:

Land, at cost   1 000 000 Deutschemarks

Under the closing rate/net investment method this cost would be translated at the closing rate, whilst under the temporal method, it would be translated at the historical rate. Application of the two rates would produce very different sterling figures for the land:

Closing rate   1 000 000 ÷ 3.9515 = £253 068,
Historical rate   1 000 000 ÷ 6.279 = £159 261.

When we turn to differences on exchange, we again find substantial differences between the methods. Under the closing rate/net investment method differences on exchange are treated as a movement on reserves, whilst under the temporal method they are considered to be part of the ordinary profit or loss for the year.

What then are the respective advantages and disadvantages of the two methods and why has SSAP 20 favoured the use of the closing rate/net investment method?

Advantages and disadvantages

In order to evaluate the two methods of translation, we must bear in mind how the translated figures are going to be used. Thus, if we were studying the accounts of an overseas company for general interest or with a view to acquiring its shares, it might be useful to translate all items in the foreign currency accounts into sterling at the closing rate of exchange in order to produce figures which are meaningful in the home currency. Use of a constant rate of exchange for all items would maintain the same relationships in the sterling accounts as existed in the foreign currency accounts. Thus, for example, long-term liabilities would be the same proportion of fixed assets and the current ratio would be the same in sterling as in the foreign currency accounts.

However, when considering the translation of the accounts of a subsidiary company prior to consolidation, such a consideration would seem to be irrelevant. After all, we add the translated figures for the overseas subsidiary to those of the parent company and hence the relationship between items in the accounts of the overseas subsidiary will be completely lost. What would seem to be more important for meaningful aggregation in the consolidated accounts is that the bases of measurement used for the assets and liabilities are consistent.

If we accept the need to use consistent bases for consolidation then, in the context of historical cost accounting, it seems reasonable to aggregate the historical costs of fixed assets and stocks of the subsidiary with the historical costs of the fixed assets and stocks of the parent company. Similarly, the amounts payable and receivable at the balance sheet date for both companies should be dealt with in a consistent manner.

Stated in this way, it would seem to follow that only the temporal method of translation is conceptually consistent with the historical cost basis of accounting and indeed any basis of accounting. The translation of an historical cost at an historical rate produces the historical cost in sterling, that is the amount which would have been incurred if a sum of money had been dispatched from the UK to purchase the asset. The translation of an historical cost at a closing rate would seem to produce a conceptual nonsense.

It was arguments such as these which led the US FASB to require the exclusive use of the temporal method in FAS 8, and probably also to the ASC permitting a choice between the closing rate method or the temporal method in ED 21. However, the temporal method is not without its problems. First, there is the practical problem of keeping records. In order to translate fixed assets and stocks at historical rates of exchange, a detailed analysis of these items together with the respective rates of exchange has to be kept. Such a record is not required by those companies which use the closing rate method.

Second, the application of the method has caused large fluctuations in the reported profits of groups of companies from period to period, fluctuations which bear little relationship to the underlying operating performance of the overseas subsidiaries. Such volatility of reported earnings arises because of the requirement to include exchange gains and losses on long-term monetary items in the ordinary profits of the group and the problem could be solved by taking these particular exchange gains or losses direct to reserve or by spreading them over a period of years.

Third, the method produces misleading differences on exchange, which may in turn have adverse behavioural implications.

Let us take as an example a UK company which has an overseas subsidiary. In the balance sheet of the overseas subsidiary fixed assets and stocks are shown on the basis of historical cost whilst these are usually financed by net monetary liabilities and an equity interest. During a particular year sterling is weakening against the overseas currency, that is the other currency is becoming more valuable. In such a case the value of the overseas net assets to the UK company would be increasing and any potential dividends from the overseas subsidiary would be more valuable, as a given future dividend stream in the foreign currency would produce a greater amount of sterling. However, using the temporal method of translation, we would recognize no gains on the fixed assets but merely losses on the net monetary liabilities.

Thus, as a result of the movement in exchange rates, the overseas subsidiary is more valuable, but as a result of using the temporal method, the accounts show losses on exchange!

Under the provisions of both FAS 8 and the UK ED 21, such losses on exchange reduced the profits from ordinary activities and hence the earnings per share. Given that no board of directors wishes to undertake activities which reduce profits or produce losses in the accounts, there is considerable evidence to indicate that 'profitable' overseas projects have been rejected because of the subsequent accounting losses which resulted from the use of the temporal method of translation.[22]

---

22 *See*, for example, D. P. Walker, *An economic analysis of foreign exchange risk*, ICAEW Research Committee Occasional Paper No. 14, ICAEW, London, 1978.

The closing rate/net investment method does not produce these misleading differences. Because the closing rate is applied to non-monetary assets as well as monetary assets and liabilities, it is possible to set off exchange losses on foreign currency borrowings against exchange gains on real assets and therefore eliminate the need to charge such losses in the profit and loss account. The use of such a cover method is felt by many to reflect the reality of the situation where fixed assets and stocks are financed by money raised overseas. Indeed, under the offset arrangements included in SSAP 20, this cover method is extended to loans raised by the parent company or other companies in the group so that where foreign currency borrowings have been used to finance, or provide a hedge against, group equity investments in foreign enterprises exchange gains or losses on the borrowings may be set off against exchange differences arising on the retranslation of the net investment.[23]

To take into account exchange gains or losses on the monetary items without taking into account exchange losses or gains on real assets, as under the temporal method, is considered to be wrong by many accountants.

To summarize, the temporal method has the advantage of producing translated figures which are conceptually consistent with the underlying basis of measurement used whilst the closing rate method has the advantage of simplicity and manages to avoid the reporting of fluctuating profits and misleading differences on exchange by use of the cover or offset arrangements.

The ASC had to balance the respective advantages and disadvantages of the two methods in producing SSAP 20. As we have seen, it favoured the closing rate/net investment method for the majority of situations but required the use of the temporal method where the trade of the foreign enterprise is more dependent on the economic environment of the investing company's currency than that of its own reporting currency.

In the view of the authors, the use of the closing rate/net investment method is inconsistent with the subsequent consolidation of the resulting sterling figures.[24] In our view, the logic of the method should lead

---

23 SSAP 20, Para. 57 specifies the conditions under which this offset arrangement may be applied. As we shall see in the last section of this chapter, the exchange difference on the retranslation of the net assets in the consolidated accounts will usually differ from the exchange difference on the retranslation of the investment in the accounts of the parent company.

24 Such a criticism was made in several submissions to the ASC on ED 27. *See*, for example, those of C. Nobes, and Spicer and Pegler.

us to include the results of an overseas subsidiary in the consolidated accounts by using the equity method of accounting. In this way the consolidated profit and loss account would include the appropriate proportion of the profit or loss of the subsidiary whilst the consolidated balance sheet would show a net investment in the overseas subsidiary. This is surely what the title of the closing rate/net investment method implies!

One aspect of a larger problem
We have seen that both of the major methods of translation have advantages and disadvantages and that it has been difficult to choose between them.

The difficulties which we face here may be seen as part of the much larger problem discussed in the early part of this book. In Chapter 3 we have seen, for example, that the addition of historical costs which have been incurred at different points in time results in a rather unhelpful total when the value of the pound has been changing over time. The movement of exchange rates between currencies presents us with similar problems and, given that we have not yet solved the problem of the function of accounts where only one currency is involved, it is not surprising that there is considerable confusion when we introduce two or more currencies.

It might be suggested that the major stumbling block is the traditional reliance on historical cost accounts, which are known to have many defects. We cannot expect the choice of exchange rate to remedy these defects. If we were to depart from historical costs and instead to show assets and liabilities of the overseas company at their current values, only one rate of exchange would be appropriate. The closing rate is required by both the temporal method and the closing rate method and the resulting sterling figures may quite properly be aggregated with the current values of assets and liabilities of the parent company. It would still be necessary to determine the treatment of resulting differences on exchange but a major problem would have disappeared.

There would still, of course, be other problems in connection with foreign currencies. In all the examples we have assumed that our UK parent company prepares consolidated accounts so that sterling is the appropriate currency to use. Once we widen our horizons to look at a multinational company, which operates throughout the world and has shareholders in many countries, it is difficult to know even what the reporting currency should be, let alone what the resulting differences on exchange really mean.

To illustrate the sort of problem which we face, let us end this section with a very simple example:

Let us suppose that an individual habitually spends 6 months of every year in the UK and 6 months in the USA. On 1 January 19X2 he has wealth of $100 000 in the USA and £100 000 in the UK when the rate of exchange between the currencies is $2.5 to the £1. During the year he lives on income arising in the respective countries and ends the year with exactly the same money wealth in each country when the exchange rate has moved to $2 to £1.

Let us compare his wealth at the beginning and end of the year in dollars and sterling, respectively:

	$	£
Opening wealth – 1 January 19X2 (rate of exchange $2.5 to £1)		
UK, £100 000	250 000	100 000
USA, $100 000	100 000	40 000
	350 000	140 000
Closing wealth – 31 December 19X2 (rate of exchange $2 to £1)		
UK, £100 000	200 000	100 000
USA, $100 000	100 000	50 000
	300 000	150 000
Gain during year	—	£10 000
Loss during year	$50 000	—

As can be seen, if we ignore changes in the purchasing power of the respective currencies, the translation process produces a loss of $50 000 or a gain of £10 000 during the year, even though our individual has the same money wealth at the end as he did at the beginning.

Problems such as those discussed above obviously bedevil the multinational company. Although such companies prepare consolidated accounts in the currency of the country where the parent company is situated, it must be admitted that the figures produced are of dubious significance to many shareholders.

A more complex example

EXAMPLE 13.7: The closing rate/net investment method

A. Some years ago Home Country plc, a UK company, raised a

long-term loan of $400 000 which it used to help purchase 80% of the shares in Overseas Inc. at a total cost of $500 000.

B. Relevant rates of exchange were as follows:

	Dollars to £1
At date of acquisition	5
On 1 January 19X2	4
On 31 December 19X2	3

C. We shall first look at the treatment of the above transactions in the accounts of the parent company.

In accordance with the principles explained earlier in the chapter, the loan and investment would have originally been recorded at the following amounts:

Long-term loan ($400 000 ÷ 5)	£80 000
Investment in subsidiary ($500 000 ÷ 5)	£100 000

On 31 December 19X1 the loan would have been translated at the rate on that date and we shall assume that the company has also translated the investment at the closing rate at that date, as permitted by Para. 51 of SSAP 20. These items would have then appeared in the balance sheet as follows:

Home Country plc
Extract from balance sheet on 31 December 19X1
Long-term loan denominated in dollars
  $400 000 ÷ 4 .... £100 000

Investment in subsidiary
  $500 000 ÷ 4 .... £125 000

The difference on exchange between the date of acquisition and 31 December 19X1 would have been credited to reserves in past years, namely:

Exchange gain on equity investment	
£125 000 − £100 000	£25 000
less Exchange loss on dollar loan	
£100 000 − £80 000	20 000
Net gain	5 000

When the balance sheet on 31 December 19X2 is prepared the foreign currency amounts will be translated at the then closing rate of $3 to £1:

Home Country plc
Extract from balance sheet on 31 December 19X2
Long-term loan denominated in dollars
$400 000 ÷ 3   £133 333

Investment in subsidiary
$500 000 ÷ 3   £166 667

The difference on exchange to be treated as a movement on reserves in 19X2 in the accounts of the parent company is therefore as follows:

Home Country plc
Part of movement on reserves for 19X2
Exchange gain on equity investment
£166 667 − £125 000   £41 667
less Exchange loss on dollar loan
£133 333 − £100 000   33 333

Net gain   8 334

D. The above figures for 19X2 are incorporated in the summarized accounts of Home Country plc for the year ended 31 December 19X2 which appear below:

Home Country plc
Profit and loss account for the year ended 31 December 19X2

	£
Profit before taxation	112 000
Dividend receivable from Overseas Inc. (net) (80% of £20 000)	16 000
	128 000
less Taxation	60 000
	68 000
add Extraordinary profit, net of tax	5 000
	73 000
less Dividends payable	30 000
Retained profit for year	43 000

Home Country plc
Movement on reserves for the year ended 31 December 19X2

	£
Balance on 1 January 19X2	133 666
Retained profit for year	43 000
Difference on exchange	8 334
Balance on 31 December 19X2	185 000

Home Country plc
Balance sheet on 31 December 19X2

	£	£
Fixed assets		
Tangible assets		400 000
Investment in subsidiary (80% holding)		166 667
Current assets		
Stocks	60 000	
Debtors	40 000	
Dividend receivable from Overseas Inc.	16 000	
Cash	5 666	
	121 666	
less Current liabilities	70 000	51 666
		618 333
less Long-term loans:		
Denominated in dollars	133 333	
Denominated in sterling	100 000	233 333
		385 000
Share capital		200 000
Reserves		185 000
		385 000

E. We may now turn our attention to the accounts of the overseas subsidiary.

The balance sheet of Overseas Inc. on 31 December 19X1 in dollars is given in the left-hand column while the relevant rates of exchange and resulting sterling amounts are given in the second and third columns, respectively. It has been assumed that the assets of Overseas Inc. were revalued at their fair values at the date of acquisition to produce a revaluation reserve of $150 000. Other reserves at the date of acquisition are assumed to have been $100 000.

Overseas Inc.
Balance sheet on 31 December 19X1

	$	Rate of exchange	£
Fixed assets			
At revalued amounts at date of acquisition and subsequent cost less depreciation	1 000 000	4 (CR)	250 000
Current assets			
Stocks	300 000	4 (CR)	75 000
Debtors	200 000	4 (CR)	50 000
Cash	100 000	4 (CR)	25 000
	600 000		150 000
less Current liabilities	400 000	4(CR)	100 000
Net current assets	200 000		50 000
	1 200 000		300 000
less Long-term loan	600 000	4 (CR)	150 000
	600 000		150 000
Share capital	100 000	5 (HR)	20 000
Revaluation reserve – at date of acquisition by Home Country plc	150 000	5 (HR)	30 000
Reserves			
Pre-acquisition	100 000	5 (HR)	20 000
	350 000		70 000
Post-acquisition	250 000	Balance	80 000
	600 000		150 000

Notice that in translating the balance sheet, the share capital and pre-acquisition reserves have been translated at the historical rate at the date of acquisition with the intention of maintaining the goodwill or capital reserve on consolidation at its 'cost'. The balance of post-acquisition reserves, which is translated at £80 000, therefore includes all exchange differences which have arisen since the date of acquisition. The size of these exchange differences depend upon when the post-acquisition reserves were earned and the rates of exchange prevailing at those dates. The less the fluctuation in exchange rates since acquisition the lower will be the difference.

At first sight the use of historical rates for share capital and pre-acquisition reserves might be thought to be incorrect as far as the minority interest is concerned. However, the minority interest is 20% of the net assets or total share capital and reserves and the way in which the individual components of the share capital and reserves are translated has no effect on the total figure.

F. The accounts of Overseas Inc. for the year ended 31 December 19X2 are given below. The left-hand column is in dollars, the centre column gives the relevant rate of exchange and the right-hand column gives the resulting sterling figures.

The profit and loss account has been translated at the closing rate rather than the average rate and, as we have seen earlier in the chapter, this avoids one difference on exchange.

Overseas Inc.
Profit and loss account for the year ended 31 December 19X2

	$	Rate of exchange (closing rate)	£
Operating profit	300 000	3	100 000
less Taxation	150 000	3	50 000
	150 000		50 000
add Extraordinary profit, net of tax	30 000	3	10 000
	180 000		60 000
less Dividends payable	60 000	3	20 000
Retained profit for year	120 000		40 000

Overseas Inc.
Balance sheet on 31 December 19X2

	$	Rate of exchange	£
Fixed assets			
At revalued amount or cost			
less depreciation	960 000	3	320 000
Current assets			
Stock	360 000	3	120 000
Debtors	240 000	3	80 000
Cash	160 000	3	53 333
	760 000		253 333
less Current liabilities (including dividend payable)	400 000	3	133 333
Net current assets	360 000		120 000
	1 320 000		440 000
less Long-term loan	600 000	3	200 000
	720 000		240 000
Share capital	100 000	5 (HR)	20 000
Revaluation reserve (created at date of acquisition)	150 000	5 (HR)	30 000
Reserves			
Pre-acquisition	100 000	5 (HR)	20 000
Post-acquisition At 1 January 19X2	250 000	Per balance sheet 31.12.19X1	80 000
(Net assets on 1.1.19X2)	600 000	4	150 000
Post-acquisition Current year	120 000	Per P and L account	40 000
	720 000		190 000
Difference on exchange	—	Balance	50 000
	720 000		240 000

Note that the balance sheet contains a suitable analysis of reserves and, in particular, that it is necessary to translate the post-acquisition reserves so that they agree with the previous year's accounts and with the profit and loss account balance for the year ended 31 December 19X2, respectively. An exchange gain of £50 000 emerges as the balancing figure. As the profit and loss account has been translated at the closing rate rather than the average rate, the whole of the difference on exchange relates to the opening net assets:

Difference on exchange

Opening net assets	$600 000	
Translation at beginning of year		
$600 000 ÷ 4		£150 000
Translation at end of year		
$600 000 ÷ 3		200 000
Gain on exchange		50 000

G. Before it is possible to prepare consolidated accounts, it is necessary to provide the usual analysis of the shareholders' interest in Overseas Inc. and to decide how to deal with the difference on exchange. In practice there will usually be many other adjustments in respect of such matters as unrealized inter-company profits but these are problems faced on any consolidation and are therefore not dealt with here.

The shareholders' interest in Overseas Inc. may be analysed as follows:

Overseas Inc.
Analysis of shareholders' equity on 31 December 19X2

	Total (£)	Group 80%		Minority interest (£)
		Pre-acquisition (£)	Post-acquisition (£)	
Share capital	20 000	16 000		4 000
Revaluation reserve	30 000	24 000		6 000
Other reserves				
Pre-acquisition	20 000	16 000		4 000
Post-acquisition				
At 1.1.19X2	80 000		64 000	16 000
Retained profit 19X2	40 000		32 000	8 000
Difference on ex-				
change 19X2	50 000		40 000	10 000
	240 000	56 000	136 000	48 000
Cost of investment				
(original cost)		100 000		
Goodwill on consolidation		44 000		

H. Readers will recall, from Section C, that the accounts of Home Country plc for 19X2 include an exchange gain on the equity investment of £41 667 and an exchange loss on the dollar loan of £33 333, together producing a net gain of £8334 which has been credited to reserves.

When we turn to the consolidated accounts it is still possible to set the loss on the dollar loan, which appears in the parent company's accounts, against the gain on the investment as permitted by SSAP 20, Para. 57. However, the appropriate exchange gain in the consolidated accounts is the parent company's share of the exchange gain resulting from the translation of the subsidiary's accounts, in this case 80% of £50 000 = £40 000.

This treatment is in line with the general principle of consolidation whereby the cost of the investment in the parent company's balance sheet is replaced by the underlying net assets of the subsidiary.

As a consequence of this the net difference on exchange which is to be treated as a movement on reserves in the consolidated accounts below will be:

	£
Gain on exchange in 19X2 in respect of Home Country's share of net assets in Overseas Inc., 80% of £50 000	40 000
less Loss on exchange in 19X2 in respect of dollar loan – per accounts of Home Country plc (see C above)	33 333
Net gain	6 667

I. An adjustment similar to that discussed in H above is necessary to calculate the balance of consolidated reserves brought forward at 1 January 19X2.

It is insufficient just to add together the reserves of Home Country plc and 80% of the post-acquisition reserves of Overseas Inc. As shown in Section C, the reserves of Home Country plc on 31 December 19X1 include the following net exchange gain made since acquisition:

	£
Exchange gain on equity investment	25 000
less Exchange loss on dollar loan	20 000
Net gain	5 000

While the exchange loss on the dollar loan may be properly charged against consolidated reserves the appropriate exchange gain in the consolidated accounts is not that on the investment but the parent company's share of the gain on translating the subsidiary's accounts. We do not know the amount of this exchange gain but we do know that it is included in the figure of £80 000 for post-acquisition reserves shown in E above.

The balance of consolidated reserves on 31 December 19X1, that is brought forward on 1.1.19X2, may therefore be calculated as follows:

	£
Home Country plc	
Per company's own balance sheet	133 666
less Exchange gain on equity investment included in above figure	25 000
	108 666
Overseas Inc.	
Share of post-acquisition reserves at 1.1.19X2 including exchange differences on net assets since acquisition, 80% of £80 000	64 000
	172 666

J. We are now in a position to consolidate:

Home Country plc
Workings for consolidated profit and loss account for the year to 31 December 19X2

	£	£
Profit before taxation		
Home Country plc	112 000	
Overseas Inc.	100 000	212 000
less Taxation		
Home Country plc	60 000	
Overseas Inc.	50 000	110 000
		102 000
less Minority interest, 20% of		
(£100 000 − £50 000)		10 000
Carried forward		92 000

	£	£
Brought forward		92 000
add Extraordinary profit after tax		
Home Country plc	5 000	
Overseas Inc. net of minority interest,		
80% of £10 000	8 000	13 000
		105 000
less Dividends payable by parent company		30 000
Retained profit for the year		75 000

Workings for movement on reserves for year to 31 December 19X2

	£	£
Balance on 1 January 19X2 (per I above)		172 666
Retained profit for year – per consolidated profit and loss account above		75 000
Exchange gain (per H above)		
Gain on net assets	40 000	
less Loss on foreign currency borrowings	33 333	6 667
Balance on 31 December 19X2		254 333

Workings for consolidated balance sheet on 31 December 19X2

	£	£
Fixed assets		
Tangible assets – at net book value		
Home Country plc	400 000	
Overseas Inc. (see note (a))	320 000	720 000
Intangible assets		
Goodwill on consolidation – at cost per analysis of equity interest		44 000
Net current assets (see note (b))		
Home Country plc	51 666	
Overseas Inc.	120 000	171 666
		935 666
less Long-term loans		
Home Country plc	233 333	
Overseas Inc.	200 000	433 333·
		502 333

	£
Share capital	200 000
Reserves – as above	254 333
	454 333
Minority interest, per analysis of equity interest	48 000
	502 333

Notes

(a) Note that the revalued amount of the fixed assets of Overseas Inc. at the date of acquisition represents 'cost' to the group.

(b) An adjustment is necessary to cancel out the dividend receivable by Home Country plc. The amount is £16 000 but the effect on the total net current assets is, of course, nil.

It is now relatively straightforward to prepare the consolidated accounts for publication in the normal manner, although a greater amount of detail would be necessary to satisfy the disclosure requirements of company law and accounting standards. In order to simplify the example, goodwill on consolidation has not been written off.

Recommended reading

J. Pearcy, *Accounting for Foreign Currencies*, Macmillan, London, 1984.

John Flower with Arthur Andersen & Co., *Accounting Treatment of Overseas Currencies: A Background Study*, ICAEW, London, 1976.

K. J. Tuckwell and A. G. Piper, *Disclosure of overseas operations of U.K. companies*, ICAEW Research Committee Occasional Paper No. 11, ICAEW, London, 1977.

P. Wallace and B. D. G. Ogle, *Foreign Currency Translation*, Accountants Digest Number 150, ICAEW, London, Winter 1983/84.

Questions

13.1 SSAP 20: *Foreign Currency Translation* (1983) constitutes the first definitive statement of practice in this area.

You are required:

(a) to define concisely the two methods of currency translation specified in SSAP 20;   (4 marks)

(b) to explain the precise circumstances in which the use of each method is mandatory under SSAP 20; and   (8 marks)

(c) to justify the treatment prescribed in SSAP 20 for overseas investment financed by overseas borrowing.   (3 marks)

(15 marks)

A. Cert. A., Advanced Financial Accounting, June 1984.

13.2 An international oil company recently complained about the delay in issuing an internationally agreed accounting standard on foreign currency translation.

The results of a subsidiary for the year ended 31 August 1981 are shown below.

	1981 K's 000	1980 K's 000
Balance Sheet		
Issued ordinary share capital	20 500	20 500
Reserves	20 700	17 400
Debentures	10 000	5 000
Current liabilities	15 000	3 000
	66 200	45 900
Fixed assets (net)	38 700	22 400
Stock	17 543	19 389
Cash and bank balances	9 957	4 111
	66 200	45 900
Profit and Loss Account		
Trading profit	6 432	4 271
Taxation	2 789	1 164
Profit after taxation	3 643	3 107
Dividend paid to parent	343	300
Retained	3 300	2 807

Further information is provided below.	Exchange rate £1 =
(1) The shares were acquired by the investor company several years ago	5K
(2) Fixed assets were acquired as follows:	
10 000 000K in 1978/79	5K
16 000 000K in 1979/80	4K
12 000 000K in 1980/81	4K
9 000 000K in 1980/81	3K
(3) Depreciation is charged at the rate of 10% p.a. on cost including a charge for the whole year during the year of purchase	
(4) Dividend was paid during 1980/81	3K

	Exchange rate £1 =
(5) K5 million of debentures were raised in past years	5K
(6) K5 million of debentures raised in 1980/81	3K
(7) Average rate during the year	3.5K
(8) Rate at 31 August 1981	3K

You are required to:
  (a) **explain the terms translation, temporal method, closing rate method, net investment concept** (6 marks)**, and**
  (b) **translate the profit and loss account for the year ended 31 August 1981 and balance sheet at this date of the subsidiary using:**
     (i) **the temporal method, and**
     (ii) **the closing rate method** (12 marks)**.** **(18 marks)**
ICAEW Financial Accounting II, December 1981.

13.3 Rassendyll Public Limited Company has a wholly-owned subsidiary, Elphburg Limited, in Ruritania, whose currency is the dinar. The accounts of Elphburg Limited for the year ended 31 December 1981, drawn up in a form consistent with the British Companies Acts, are shown below (somewhat simplified).

Elphburg Limited
Profit and Loss Account for the year ended 31 December 1981

	Din. 000	Din. 000
Turnover		300 000
Net profit before interest and taxation		30 000
Interest on 15% debentures		7 500
Net profit before taxation		22 500
Ruritanian Corporation Tax		11 250
Net profit after taxation		11 250
Extraordinary items (*Dr.*) *less* tax		1 000
Net profit for year		10 250
Dividends:		
Ordinary – paid (4%)	2 800	
Ordinary – proposed (6%)	4 200	
		7 000
Retained earnings for year		3 250

Balance Sheet, 31 December 1981

Net assets	Cost Din. 000	Deprecia-tion Din. 000	Net Din. 000
Fixed assets			
Land	50 000	—	50 000
Buildings	30 000	5 550	24 450
Equipment and vehicles	35 000	15 000	20 000
	115 000	20 550	94 450
Current assets			
Stocks		60 000	
Debtors and prepayments		35 000	
Bank and cash balances		10 000	
		105 000	
less *Current liabilities*			
Creditors and accruals		25 000	
Ruritanian Corporation Tax –			
Current year		10 250	
Proposed dividend		4 200	
		39 450	
Net current assets			65 550
			160 000
Financed by			
Share capital – authorised, issued and fully paid			
Ordinary shares (20 Dinars)			70 000
Reserves			
Retained earnings			40 000
			110 000
15% Debentures			50 000
			160 000

Notes
(1) No fresh share or loan capital was issued in 1981.

(2) The 15% debentures are all held by the Ruritanian government. They were issued at par in payment for the company's land, and are secured on it, with an additional floating charge.

(3) Rates of exchange (Dinars to the £):

31 December 1980	30.00
31 December 1981	35.00
Average for 1981	32.50

You are required:
  (a) to translate Elphburg Limited's profit and loss account and balance sheet into sterling by the closing rate method (with profit for the year translated at the average rate), in a form suitable for consolidation with Rassendyll Public Limited Company's accounts; and (8 marks)
  (b) to reconcile the opening and closing *sterling* amounts of the net investment of Rassendyll in Elphburg. (8 marks)
  (16 marks)

A. Cert. A. Advanced Financial Accounting, June 1982.

13.4 Bigbite plc which trades in the UK has only one wholly owned subsidiary, Bigbite Inc. which trades in the USA. Both companies are engaged in the food industry.

The detailed profit and loss accounts for the year ended 31 May 1983 were:

	Bigbite plc £'000	Bigbite Inc $'000
Sales	5036	5486
less cost of sales		
Stock 1 June 1982	240	308
Purchases	2817	3322
Wages	554	617
Power	296	322
	3907	4569
less stocks 31 May 1983	263	287
	3644	4282
Gross profit	1392	1204
Other income – interest	67	—
discounts	28	—
	1487	1204

	Bigbite plc £'000	Bigbite Inc $'000
Wages and salaries – administration	88	38
delivery	275	304
National insurance and other social security		
costs	58	54
Motor expenses – administration	22	18
delivery	178	182
Pension costs	26	32
Rent, rates and local taxes	108	52
Insurance	18	21
Telephone, telex and postage	25	28
Laboratory costs	12	47
Bad debts	16	38
Depreciation – machinery	86	65
equipment	48	24
motor vehicles – administration	7	9
delivery	40	42
Bank overdraft interest	45	63
Hire of equipment	28	18
Audit fees	22	32
	1102	1067
Profit	385	137
Costs of retail closures	136	—
	249	137
Taxation	86	48
Net profit after tax	163	89

The following information is also given:

(1) The group's accounting policy on the translation of foreign currency is as follows: Profit and loss items are translated at the average exchange rate during the year. Other items are translated at the closing rate. Any differences arising are dealt with through reserves.

(2) The exchange rates were:

	$ to £1
31 May 1982	1.95
31 May 1983	1.52
Average for 1982/83	1.63

(3) The taxation computation of the parent company shows the following:

	£
Taxable profit	192 985
less losses brought forward	54 205
	138 780
Tax assumed payable at 50%	69 390

The deferred taxation adjustment for the UK is a charge of £17 600 and there is a prior year credit adjustment of £998. Tax relief on the retail closure costs, which should be treated as an extraordinary item and which are reflected in the taxable profits, amounts to £69 920. The charge in Bigbite Inc. is the taxation payable.

(4) Bigbite plc paid no interim but proposes to declare a final dividend of 0.85p per share amounting to £47 090. It is proposed to incorporate a dividend of $20 000 by Bigbite Inc. to the parent in the final accounts of both companies. Ignore any taxation consequences of these dividends.

(5) Bigbite Inc. trades with its parent and the sales in the year to 31 May 1983 amounted to $867 000 which were taken into Bigbite plc's purchases. None of these goods remained in stock at the year end.

You are required, in relation to Bigbite plc at 31 May 1983, to prepare in a form suitable for publication in £'000s the consolidated profit and loss account, including notes, complying with either of the vertical formats of the Companies Act 1981. Ignore comparatives, earning per share and information relating to directors' and higher paid employees' emoluments. **(18 marks)**
ICAEW Financial Accounting II, July 1983.

13.5 SSAP 20 deals with foreign currency translation. The overseas activities of two UK based companies are as follows:

(1) Terrier Ltd has two overseas branches as follows:
  (i) One branch in South America is concerned with buying raw materials for use in the company's UK manufacturing operation. The branch will arrange purchases from local suppliers settling the payments either on monthly accounts or on three month bills. The funds will be remitted from the UK on a monthly imprest system. The rates of exchange in the South American country have been volatile and local inflation has averaged 120% for the past three years. There are also restrictions on the export of currency. The branch's fixed assets consist of office equipment and motor vehicles and specific currency has been remitted from the UK for each item.

(ii) The other branch is based in West Germany. It assembles local components which are shipped back to the company in the UK for inclusion in its own products. All purchases are made locally with funds remitted from the UK. The expatriate manager is paid directly from the UK. A Swiss franc loan is outstanding from a bank in Switzerland which was used to purchase the factory in West Germany. The rates of exchange have been fairly constant but there has been some variation in the exchange rate between the franc and the mark.

(2) Spaniel plc has several subsidiaries. The following are its overseas subsidiaries:

(i) Alsatian is concerned with the manufacture of chains in Italy and was purchased four years ago. It is run by local management and all transactions take place in Italy.

(ii) Boxer is based in the Cayman Islands and is a captive insurance company for the UK parts of the group. In the UK companies' accounting records insurance premiums are credited in sterling to a current account with Boxer at the beginning of the financial year. Claims are debited to this current account as they arise and the resultant balance paid at the year end. When a premium is credited the appropriate foreign currency is brought forward at the year end rate and used to settle the balance due. Boxer, which carries on no business outside the UK group, enters each credit or debit in its accounting records in local currency translated at the daily spot rate.

You are required to:

(a) give the details of the two alternative treatments set out for the translation of financial statements in SSAP 20 and explain the circumstances in which they should be applied (9 marks), and

(b) state briefly how you would deal with the translation of foreign currencies arising in the cases of Terrier Ltd and Spaniel plc stating specifically the accounting treatment of any profit or loss arising (9 marks).

(18 marks)

ICAEW, Financial Accounting II, July 1984.

14 Expansion of the Annual Report

Introduction

The published annual reports of companies frequently include reports and statements other than those required by law. Some of these are required by accounting standard whilst others are supplied voluntarily. Traditionally the most common statement supplied voluntarily is the chairman's statement, which provides shareholders and others with a description of the company's progress during the year and frequently gives some indication of future prospects, but published reports now often also include a statement of source and application of funds, a highlights statement and, less frequently, a value added statement and employment report. In addition many companies produce a separate simplified report which may be intended for either shareholders or employees but may be a general purpose statement not aimed at any particular group of users. Since the mid 1970s, professional bodies and governments have taken a much greater interest in the utility of these and other statements.

In broad terms the objectives of all additional statements are the same – to assist users of accounts to obtain a more comprehensive view of the progress and future prospects of the company. This broad objective can be served in a number of ways and it is helpful to have a framework within which the statements can be analysed. Essentially the statements can be seen as constituting two groups depending on whether a statement:

(a) provides more data than is required by company law, or
(b) does not provide additional data but makes it easier to assimilate the data either by rearrangement of the figures or through the provision of simplified statements.

We might usefully refer to the first group as 'extended' statements and the second as 'rearranged and simplified' statements.

Extended statements include such documents as the Employment

Report as well as any statements which refer to corporate objectives and policies or the future prospects of the company.

Rearranged and simplified statements can be derived from the published accounts of the company, except in the case of smaller companies, and include such documents as statements of source and application of funds and, to a large extent, the simplified report to employees and the value added statement. It is interesting to question why companies should be required or choose to publish such rearranged and simplified statements. In part the reason may be behavioural in the sense that the publication of the document is intended to create better relations with employees and the community in general. Such an objective is clearly present in the case of simplified accounts prepared specially for employees. Another possible reason is the wish to remove the 'competitive advantage' possessed by investors and potential investors who have technical knowledge themselves or have ready access to professional advice.[1]

On the professional front, the first major developments in the drive towards the expansion of the annual report came in 1975 when the Accounting Standards Steering Committee issued both SSAP 10, 'Statements of source and application of funds' and *The Corporate Report*.[2] SSAP 10, which is discussed in detail below, required all but very small enterprises, to prepare a statement of source and application of funds as part of its audited financial accounts, a practice which is now well established. *The Corporate Report*, which was issued as a discussion paper, argued that current reporting practices did not fully meet the needs of the various users of accounts and recommended that all significant economic entities should publish the following additional statements:

(a) A statement of value added.
(b) An employment report.
(c) A statement of money exchanges with government.
(d) A statement of transactions in foreign currency.
(e) A statement of future prospects.
(f) A statement of corporate objectives.

The adoption of these recommendations would have resulted in the provision of substantially more information than that provided by the

1 Supporters of the 'efficient market hypothesis' which, in its semistrong form, states that all available data relevant to the price of a share is immediately reflected in the market price, would presumably take the view that there is nothing to be gained from any requirement for companies to publish otherwise available data in a different form.
2 *The Corporate Report*, Accounting Standards Steering Committee, London, 1975.

statutory financial accounts. Whilst *The Corporate Report* remains an important document worthy of study none of these recommendations have yet been accepted by the ASC.

The professional initiatives were followed by two Green Papers. The first, which was issued by a Labour administration in 1977[3] proposed that, for larger companies, the annual report and accounts should contain the following elements:

(a) an added value statement to show the wealth created by the company and the way in which that wealth is distributed;

(b) an employment statement, to indicate the manpower resources and policies of the company;

(c) more comprehensive financial accounts, based upon a new version of Schedule 8 of the Companies Act 1948, to include statements covering source and application of funds, short-term borrowings, leasing arrangements, obligations to pension funds and also giving more details of transactions in foreign currencies;

(d) more detailed disaggregation of the activities of the company by type of business and geographical area of operation;

(e) an international trade statement to show imports into as well as exports from the UK.

The second Green Paper, which was produced by a Conservative administration in 1979[4], proposed a three-tier classification of companies and recommended that disclosure requirements should differ between tiers. Thus it proposed that there should be a significant reduction in the amount of information to be disclosed by bottom-tier companies but an increase in the amount of information to be disclosed by the top tier, that is by large and listed companies.

In the context of such large and listed companies it considered the recommendations for additional disclosure contained in the previous Green Paper and, on the topics listed above, it came to the following conclusions:[5]

(a) *Added value statement*   The government believed that the presentation of a value added statement was a matter which should be the subject of accounting standard or recommendation rather than law. The Green Paper pointed out that implementation of the EEC Fourth Directive would in any case require compa-

---

3 *The future of company reports*, Cmnd 6888, HMSO, London, 1977.
4 *Company accounting and disclosure*, Cmnd 7654, HMSO, London, 1979.
5 *Ibid.*, Part A, Chap. III.

nies to disclose most of the information required to determine value added.

(b) *Employment statement* Although the government welcomed the moves towards producing employment reports, it did not consider that legislation had any part in encouraging these developments at that time.

(c) *More comprehensive financial accounts* It proposed the introduction of a legal requirement for companies to give additional details of short-term borrowings, leasing arrangements and pension commitments. It also envisaged a legal requirement for large companies to produce a statement of source and application of funds.

(d) *Disaggregated data* It proposed that larger companies should provide more disaggregated information about their activities and that such information should be subject to audit.

(e) *International trade statement* It did not propose a legal requirement for companies to prepare an international trade statement.

As we have seen in Chapter 2, the Companies Act 1981 did introduce a three-tier classification of companies and required much greater disclosure for companies in the top and middle tiers while requiring much reduced public disclosure, where desired, by small companies. As we shall see in Chapter 18, the Act also required the provision of disaggregated data as part of the audited financial statements of companies. However it now seems unlikely that there will be any legislative requirement for the value added statement, the employment statement, the statement of source and application of funds or the international trade statement.

Even in the absence of a legislative requirement, it is clear that the accountant must develop competence in producing and interpreting statements other than the traditional accounts, at least for large companies, and this chapter concentrates on two statements which pose both conceptual and practical problems for the accountant, namely the statement of source and application of funds and the value added statement. It concludes with a brief look at the subject of reporting about and to employees.

Statement of source and application of funds

Background

During the 1960s, there was a strong trend in the USA and Canada towards including an audited 'funds statement' as part of the annual financial statements of a corporation. In some cases such a statement merely rearranged information shown elsewhere in the accounts and hence reduced the work of the analyst, whilst, in other cases, it included information not available elsewhere in the accounts. The objective was to supplement the traditional accounts by showing how the corporation had acquired funds and how it had used them. So, whereas the profit and loss account shows changes in the equity interest of an enterprise for a period, the statement of source and application of funds shows changes, other than those caused by revaluations, in all balance sheet items.

ED 13, issued by the Accounting Standards Steering Committee in April 1974, recommended that audited financial accounts for all companies should include a statement of source and application of funds. The subsequent standard, SSAP 10, issued in July 1975, exempted small companies by requiring that only enterprises with a turnover or gross income of £25 000 or greater need prepare such a statement. Compliance with SSAP 10 automatically ensures compliance with the International Accounting Standard on this topic.[6]

Concepts of funds illustrated

In order to be able to prepare a meaningful statement of source and application of funds, it would seem to be essential to have a clear idea of what is meant by 'funds'. Like profit the term may be defined in various ways and three common definitions are as follows: (a) cash,[7] (b) working capital, (c) all financial resources. The choice of definition will, of course, determine what the statement seeks to explain and hence what appears as a source or application. To take a simple example, the receipt of cash from debtors is a source of funds if the cash concept is adopted whilst it is neither a source nor an application if the working capital concept is used. In this latter case funds are defined as working capital and hence there is no change in funds, merely a change in the constituent elements.

We may best explore the different concepts by looking at a simple example. The summarized accounts of Java Limited for the year 19X2, including the opening balance sheet, are given below:

---

6 IAS 7, 'Statement of changes in financial position', 1977.
7 The term 'cash' is usually taken to include both bank balances and cash in hand but is often extended to include cash equivalents such as short-term investments.

Summarized balance sheets on 31 December 19X1 and 19X2

	19X1 (£)	19X2 (£)
Fixed assets, at net book value (*see* note)	60 000	70 000
Current assets		
Stock	21 000	35 000
Trade debtors	40 000	52 000
Cash	17 000	14 000
	78 000	101 000
less Current liabilities		
Trade creditors	19 000	26 000
Corporation Tax payable	11 000	13 000
Dividend payable	8 000	10 000
	38 000	49 000
Net current assets (working capital)	40 000	52 000
Assets less current liabilities	100 000	122 000
less Deferred taxation	8 000	13 000
	92 000	109 000
Share capital	50 000	50 000
Retained profits	42 000	59 000
	92 000	109 000

Note   Fixed assets were purchased for £30 000 of cash during the year. No fixed assets were sold.

Summarized profit and loss account for the year ended 31 December 19X2

	£	£
Sales		410 000
less Cost of sales and expenses		
Depreciation	20 000	
Other	340 000	360 000
Profit before taxation		50 000
less Taxation		
Corporation Tax	13 000	
Deferred tax	5 000	18 000
Profit after taxation – carried forward		32 000

	£	£
Profit after taxation – brought forward		30 000
less Dividends		
Interim – paid	5 000	
Final – proposed	10 000	15 000
Retained profit for the year		17 000
add Retained profit on 1 January 19X2		42 000
Retained profits		59 000

Cash concept

If the cash concept of funds is adopted, the statement will seek to explain why the cash balance has fallen by £3000 from £17 000 to £14 000. Whilst it would, of course, be possible to do this by preparing a summary of receipts and payments in the company's cash account, it is also possible to prepare a funds statement using the balance sheets and profit and loss account. Cash is received from debtors and paid out to creditors and in cash expenses. Hence it is possible to identify a source of funds from the trading operations as follows:

Source of funds from operations	£	£
Sales per profit and loss account		410 000
less Increase in trade debtors (£52 000–£40 000)		12 000
Cash received from debtors		398 000
less Payments for goods and expenses		
Expenses per profit and loss account	340 000	
add Increase in stocks	14 000	
	354 000	
less Increase in creditors	7 000	
Cash paid to creditors		347 000
		51 000

An alternative approach would be to start with the profit before taxation and to make adjustments for items which do not affect cash, i.e.

Profit before taxation		50 000
Adjustments		
Depreciation	20 000	
Increase in trade and expense creditors	7 000	
Increase in stocks	(14 000)	
Increase in trade debtors	(12 000)	1 000
		51 000

Whichever way we arrive at the net cash amount generated by operations, this may be inserted in the statement of source and application of funds. Next it is necessary to deal with other sources and applications of cash. Working down the profit and loss account we find Corporation Tax and dividends, which have probably given rise to a payment during the year; deferred tax will obviously not affect the cash balance. Turning to the balance sheets we find there have been additions to fixed assets during the year. Hence, in this simple example, we must calculate cash paid for Corporation Tax, dividends and the purchase of fixed assets. This may easily be done by preparing ledger accounts from the available information and inserting cash paid as the balancing figure:

Corporation Tax

	£		£
Closing balance	13 000	Opening balance	11 000
Balance, cash	11 000	Profit and loss account	13 000
	24 000		24 000

Dividends

	£		£
Closing balance	10 000	Opening balance	8 000
Balance, cash	13 000	Profit and loss account	15 000
	23 000		23 000

Fixed assets (at net book value)

	£		£
Opening balance	60 000	Closing balance	70 000
Balance, cash	30 000	Profit and loss account, depreciation	20 000
	90 000		90 000

The statement may now be prepared:

Statement of source and application of funds for the year ended 31 December 19X2

(Funds = cash)

	£	£
Source of funds from operations		51 000
Application of funds		
Payment of Corporation Tax	11 000	
Payment of dividends	13 000	
Purchase of fixed assets	30 000	54 000
Reduction in cash balance		(3 000)

Working capital concept

If the working capital concept of funds is adopted, then the statement will seek to explain why working capital has increased by £12 000, from £40 000 to £52 000. It will therefore differ from the statement shown above.

If we commence with the source of funds from operations, all sales, whether for cash or credit, represent a source of funds since increases in cash and debtors both result in an increase in working capital. Similarly, the cost of goods sold and expenses incurred are reductions in funds whether paid in cash or incurred on credit since both a fall in cash and an increase in creditors are reductions in working capital. An exception to this is the depreciation expense, which does not affect funds at all. The book-keeping entry is, after all, a debit to the depreciation expense account and a credit to the provision for depreciation account, neither of which are components of working capital. We may therefore arrive at our source of funds from operations in two ways:

Source of funds from operations

	£
Sales	410 000
less Cost of sales and expenses other than depreciation	340 000
	70 000

Source of funds from operations

	£
Profit before taxation	50 000
add Item not involving a flow of funds	
Depreciation	20 000
	70 000

The latter 'bottom-up' approach is the one normally adopted in practice. It has the advantage that the starting figure is clearly identifiable in the profit and loss account. Against this, the addition of depreciation to the profit before taxation is misleading in that it mistakenly suggests that depreciation is a source of funds. This is, of course, not the case. The latter calculation is merely a short cut for arriving at the source of funds from operations and the calculation is, in the writers' view, best relegated to a note.

Once we have arrived at the source of funds from operations it is then necessary to examine other sources and applications. As before, funds are affected by Corporation Tax, dividends and purchases of fixed assets. However, in the first two cases the amounts differ from those previously shown. When the cash concept of funds was adopted, it was the payment of Corporation Tax and dividends which was an application of funds. When the working capital concept is adopted, such payments do not give rise to an application. The payment of tax, for example, causes a fall in cash and a corresponding fall in the current liability taxation so that working capital is unchanged. The application is therefore the amount of the liabilities for Corporation Tax and dividends created in the year which have reduced the working capital, that is the profit and loss account figures of £13 000 and £15 000, respectively.

Whether the fixed assets are purchased for cash or on short-term credit there is an application of funds. Here they were purchased for cash at a cost of £30 000.

The statement may now be prepared:

Statement of source and application of funds for the year ended 31 December 19X2

(Funds = working capital)

	£	£
Source of funds from operations (*see* note)		70 000
Applications		
Corporation Tax liability for year	13 000	
Dividends paid and payable for year	15 000	
Purchase of fixed assets	30 000	58 000
Increase in working capital		12 000

Note The source of funds from operations is calculated as follows:

	£
Profit before tax	50 000
add Item not involving flow of funds	
Depreciation	20 000
	70 000

Some writers would argue that the Corporation Tax liability for the year should be deducted in arriving at the source of funds from operations. Such an argument is based on the view that Corporation Tax is an expense over which the directors have little control. This is a valid argument but in practice Corporation Tax is almost always shown as an application.

All financial resources

The US Accounting Principles Board (APB), in Opinion no. 19,[8] took this broad concept as the basis of its funds statement, which was entitled 'Statement of changes in financial position'. Use of the concept requires that certain transactions which do not affect cash or working capital should be reflected in the funds statement. Thus, where a company acquires a fixed asset by issuing share capital or loan stock, neither cash nor working capital are affected but the financial resources of the company are affected. Using the 'all financial resources' approach, the issue of shares would be shown as a source of funds and the purchase of fixed assets as a use of funds.

The conversion of convertible loan stock into ordinary shares would require a similar treatment, the issue of shares being treated as a source and the redemption of loan stock as an application of funds. In our simple example there are no transactions of this sort.

APB Opinion no. 19 does not require a particular layout to be used. Hence an all inclusive funds statement might take either of the forms shown above[9] but with the inclusion of any transactions of the sort described here.

SSAP 10 and the simple company

We have seen that the term 'funds' may be defined in several ways and that statements based upon these definitions will differ from one another. Many people have therefore found it surprising that, in requiring all but very small enterprises to prepare a statement of source and application of funds, SSAP 10 does not define what it means by funds. Members of the ASC would no doubt argue that this omission provides necessary flexibility for directors to select that concept of funds which best explains to readers the important changes of a period. Others would criticize such a permissive approach on the grounds that it indicates a lack of agreement on what the funds statement is supposed to do.[10] If the term funds is not defined, it will be interpreted in different ways by different people so that difficulties may arise in making inter-company comparisons. That such differences have occurred in practice

---

8 Issued in March 1971.

9 In fact, like the later SSAP 10, APB Opinion no. 19 requires certain specific items to be disclosed.

10 *See*, for example, L. C. Heath, 'Let's scrap the funds statement', *Journal of Accountancy*, October 1978.

is evident from a casual examination of the statements of a few companies.

SSAP 10 merely defines one element of funds[11] and lists specific items which must be disclosed in the statement. Thus the statement must show the profit or loss for the period together with the adjustments required for items which did not use or provide funds and also disclose, where material, the following items:[12] (a) dividends paid; (b) acquisitions and disposals of fixed and other non-current assets; (c) funds raised by increasing, or expended in repaying or redeeming, medium- or long-term loans or the issued share capital of the company; (d) increases or decreases in working capital subdivided into its components, and movements in net liquid funds. In addition there is an Appendix to the statement containing three examples which are illustrative rather than prescriptive, although, as is often the case where such illustrations are given, the layout in these appendices has been applied almost mechanically by a large number of companies.

The layout in the examples adopts a hybrid of the concepts of funds discussed earlier and clearly tries to obtain the best of all concepts. Thus the illustrative statements basically attempt to explain changes in a 'modified' working capital, although they draw upon the 'all financial resources' concept to show items which do not affect such modified working capital and, in addition, focus attention on net liquid funds as one component of the modified working capital.

The illustrative statements may be approached as explaining changes in a modified working capital, that is current assets less current liabilities excluding taxation and dividends payable. The amounts actually paid in respect of taxation and dividends are treated as applications of funds for the period and thus current liabilities for these items are treated differently from other current liabilities. SSAP 10 provides no justification for this inconsistent treatment and it is difficult to see why these specific creditors should be dealt with on a different basis to any other creditors.

A statement of source and application of funds drawn up on the basis illustrated in the appendix examples to SSAP 10 would attempt to explain a change such as the following:

---

11 Paragraph 8 defines net liquid funds as: 'cash at bank and in hand and cash equivalents (e.g. investments held as current assets) less bank overdrafts and other borrowings repayable within one year of the accounting date'.
12 SSAP 10, Para. 11.

Extracts from balance sheets on 31 December 19X1 and 19X2

	19X1 (£)	19X2 (£)
Current assets		
Stocks	120 000	190 000
Debtors	160 000	150 000
Short-term investments	40 000	50 000
Cash	50 000	30 000
	370 000	420 000
less Current liabilities (except taxation and dividends	130 000	150 000
	240 000	270 000
Increase in funds		30 000

Although the examples in the appendix to SSAP 10 describe such a change as 'increase in working capital', this is not what is normally understood by the term 'working capital'. Let us nevertheless adopt this modified working capital concept of funds and proceed to consider what are sources and applications respectively in the context of a manufacturing or trading company which has no subsidiaries or associated companies.

Sources from operations
Just as with the working capital concept, it is possible to arrive at a source of funds from operations by using the 'bottom-up' approach. Thus it is usual to start with the profit before taxation and to add back or deduct any items which have not involved a flow of funds. We have already mentioned depreciation; other examples would be a profit or loss on disposal of a fixed asset, dealt with below, or an amount of deferred advertising expenditure or research and development expenditure written off, providing these have all been treated as ordinary items.

Although directors would hope that such a source of funds from operations would be positive, sometimes it will be negative. This means that operations have absorbed rather than generated funds. The treatment of such 'losses' from operations is sometimes confusing, particularly when we bear in mind the need to disclose comparative figures. Two possibilities exist. First, it is possible to show the losses, after adjustments for non-fund items, as a negative source. Second, and more correctly, the amount of the loss may be shown as an application of funds. Both methods are widely used in practice. In either case, much confusion can be avoided if the adjustments to the profit or loss before tax for non-fund items are relegated to a note.

Other sources

There are many other possible sources of funds. The proceeds of an issue of shares for cash or the raising of a medium- or long-term loan in cash would clearly provide sources of funds. A disposal of fixed assets for cash would also provide a source of funds to the extent of the sale proceeds. There is a complication in this case in that the proceeds of sale will rarely be equal to the net book value of the fixed assets sold. In order to avoid double counting, it will therefore be necessary to remove from the source of funds from operations any profit or loss on disposal which has been included in arriving at the profit before taxation.

To illustrate, suppose that fixed assets with a net book value of £4000 have been sold for £6000 and that the profit on disposal of £2000 has been taken into account in arriving at the profit before taxation of £25 000. It would be incorrect to show a source of funds from operations of £25 000 and also a source from the proceeds of disposal of £6000. The source of funds from operations is only £23 000, that is £25 000 less the profit on disposal, which may be thought of as negative depreciation. The source of funds from disposal of fixed assets is £6000.

Similarly, where a loss on disposal of fixed assets is deducted in arriving at the profit before taxation, this may be viewed as additional depreciation and should be added back in arriving at the source of funds from operations.

If a profit or loss on disposal has been treated as an extraordinary item, then it will be excluded from the statement.

Applications

Using the modified working capital concept of funds, funds are reduced when cash is paid out or a short-term creditor is established. Thus the purchase of fixed assets for cash or on credit and the redemption of a long-term loan or preference share capital by the payment of cash would clearly be applications of funds.

When we turn to taxation and dividends, we find that it is the payment of taxation or dividends, rather than the creation of a current liability, which is an application of funds. SSAP 10 specifically requires dividends to be treated in this way in that it states that dividends paid must be shown as an application of funds. Taxation is treated in a similar way in the appendix to SSAP 10 and thus, if the concept of funds used in the appendix examples is followed, taxation and dividends payable will be treated differently from other creditors.

If, instead, the working capital concept of funds is adopted and working capital is defined in the normal way as current assets less current liabilities, the application of funds would include taxation and dividends payable to the extent that these were treated as current liabilities. This emphasizes how important it is to be very clear about what is being explained by the statement, that is what concept of funds is being adopted.

Extraordinary items
These are treated in exactly the same way as ordinary items. If an extraordinary item increases or decreases funds it must be included in the appropriate part of the statement. If it does not affect funds then it must be excluded. This may best be illustrated with some examples, which will be based on the modified working capital concept of funds.

If a profit on disposal of a fixed asset is treated as an extraordinary item, this does not affect funds and should be excluded from the flow of funds statement altogether. The full proceeds of sale should be shown as a source of funds. If the extraordinary item represents the cash proceeds from the sale of 'know-how', this will have increased funds and hence should be shown as a source. If the extraordinary item is an amount of deferred advertising expenditure written off, it does not affect funds and should be excluded from the statement of source and application of funds altogether.

Components of 'modified' working capital
We have seen how the examples in the appendix to SSAP 10 seek to explain changes in 'modified' working capital. As stated earlier, SSAP 10 also requires the disclosure of 'increases or decreases in working capital subdivided into its components, and movements in net liquid funds'. Such an analysis is normally provided at the foot of the statement, as illustrated in the following example.

EXAMPLE 14.1
Summarized accounts of a manufacturing company, Kamina Limited, for the year ended 31 December 19X2, together with an opening balance sheet, are given below. The two right-hand columns by the balance sheet merely list differences between the opening and closing

balances. The + column contains increases in assets and reductions in liabilities, whilst the − column contains reductions in assets and increases in both liabilities and the shareholders interest.

Balance sheets on 31 December 19X1 and 19X2

	19X1	19X2	Change +	Change −
	(£000s)	(£000s)	(£000s)	(£000s)
Fixed assets (at net book value: note (a))				
Freehold properties	800	1140	340	
Plant and machinery	1100	1400	300	
	1900	2540		
Current assets				
Stock	1100	1680	580	
Debtors	640	980	340	
Cash	200	—		200
	1940	2660		
less Current liabilities				
Bank overdraft	—	85		85
Creditors	650	915		265
Taxation payable (note (b))	275	285		10
Proposed dividend	105	140		35
	1030	1425		
Net current assets	910	1235		
	2810	3775		
less Long-term loans	600	1000		400
	2210	2775		
less Deferred taxation (note (c))	380	472		92
	1830	2303		
Share capital and reserves				
£1 ordinary shares (note (d))	1000	1100		100
Share premium (note (d))	200	300		100
Retained profits	630	903		273
	1830	2303	1560	1560

Profit and loss account for the year ended 31 December 19X2

	£000s	£000s
Turnover		6250
Profit before taxation (note (e))		730
less Taxation		
Corporation Tax	180	
Deferred tax	95	275
		455
add Extraordinary profit on sale of freehold		
building	40	
less Taxation (deferred)	12	28
		483
less Dividends		
Paid	70	
Proposed	140	210
		273
add Retained profits brought forward		630
Retained profits		903

Extracts from the notes are also provided:

Notes

(a) Fixed assets movements:

	Freehold properties (£000s)	Plant and machinery (£000s)
Cost		
On 1 January 19X2	1000	2000
Additions during year	440	720
Cost of building sold	(60)	—
On 31 December 19X2	1380	2720
Depreciation		
On 1 January 19X2	200	900
Depreciation on building sold	(10)	—
Profit and loss account	50	420
On 31 December 19X2	240	1320
Net book value	1140	1400

(b) Taxation payable at 31 December 19X1 and 19X2 is made up as follows:

	19X1 (£000s)	19X2 (£000s)
Corporation Tax payable		
1 January 19X2	110	—
1 January 19X3	120	120
1 January 19X4	—	105
Advanced Corporation Tax (ACT) payable on proposed dividend	45	60
	275	285

(c) Deferred taxation:
  The deferred tax balance on 31 December 19X1 and 31 December 19X2 is made up as follows:

	19X1 (£000s)	19X2 (£000s)
Deferred taxation on all timing differences other than chargeable gain	425	520
less ACT recoverable	45	60
	380	460
Deferred taxation on chargeable gain on sale of property	—	12
	380	472

(d) 100 000 £1 ordinary shares were issued on 24 December 19X2 to acquire a freehold building valued at £200 000.

(e) Profit before taxation is after charging:

	£000s
Depreciation	
Freehold buildings	50
Plant and machinery	420
	470

(f) The ACT rate is three-sevenths of the distribution.

We will now consider the workings of this example in detail.

If we follow the approach adopted in the appendix examples to SSAP 10, we are attempting to explain the following change in modified working capital:

	Increase	Decrease	
	(£000s)	(£000s)	(£000s)
Increase in stock	580		
Increase in debtors	340		
Increase in creditors			265
Decrease in net liquid funds			
Cash		200	
Bank overdraft		85	285
	920		550
Net increase	370		

Such an analysis will appear at the foot of our statement.

We may now proceed to calculate the appropriate sources and applications.

(a) *Sources of funds from operations*

	£000s
Profit before tax, per profit and loss account	730
add Depreciation (from note (e))	470
	1200

(b) *Issue of shares*

100 000 shares issued to acquire freehold property

	£000s
Share capital	100
Share premium	100
	200

(c) *Long-term loan raised*   Providing no loans have been redeemed we may assume that new loans to the value of £400 000 have been raised.

(d) *Fixed assets*   Freehold buildings have been sold. Note (a) shows that the net book value was £50 000, that is £60 000 less £10 000, whilst the extraordinary profit on sale was £40 000. Hence our proceeds must have been £90 000. Taxation of £12 000 on the chargeable gain has been deferred due to roll over relief and has been credited to the deferred taxation account. There have been additions to both freehold properties and plant and machinery. The figures are £440 000 and £720 000 respectively as given in note (a).

(e) *Taxation*   The simplest way to deal with taxation is to have one large account including Corporation Tax, Advance Corporation Tax (ACT) and deferred tax.

Taxation

	£000s		£000s
Closing balances		Opening balances	
Corporation Tax		Corporation Tax	
and ACT, per		and ACT, per	
note (b)	285	note (b)	275
Deferred tax, per		Deferred tax, per	
note (c)	472	note (c)	380
		Profit and loss account	
Balance, cash paid	185	Corporation Tax	180
		Deferred tax	
		Ordinary	95
		Extraordinary	12
	942		942

It may strike readers as odd that deferred taxation balances have been included above. Whilst it is true that the profit and loss account charge or credit for deferred taxation does not involve a flow of funds, there may be transfers between the deferred taxation and Corporation Tax account for ACT recoverable in respect of proposed dividends. This is best dealt with in the above way. The amount paid can be analysed as follows:

	£000s
Corporation Tax paid 1 January 19X2 (assuming no adjustments)	110
ACT paid	
On final dividend for 19X1	45
On interim dividend for 19X2	30
	185

(f) *Dividends paid*   These may best be calculated using a ledger account:

Dividends

	£000s		£000s
Closing balance, per		Opening balance, per	
balance sheet	140	balance sheet	105
Balance, dividends paid	175	Profit and loss account	
		Paid	70
		Proposed	140
	315		315

The payment may be analysed as follows:

	£000s
Final dividend 19X1 per opening balance sheet	105
Interim dividend for 19X2	70
	175

We are now in a position to prepare our statement.

Kamina Limited
Statement of source and application of funds for the year ended 31 December 19X2

	£000s	£000s
Sources of funds		
From operations		
Profit before taxation		730
Adjustment for items not involving movement of funds		
Depreciation		470
		1200
From other sources		
Issue of 100 000 £1 shares at a premium to acquire freehold property	200	
Long-term loans raised	400	
Proceeds of sale of freehold property	90	690
		1890
less Applications		
Purchase of fixed assets		
Freehold property	440	
Plant and machinery	720	
	1160	
Payment of taxation	185	
Payment of dividends	175	1520
Increase in (modified) working capital		370

	Increase (£000s)	Decrease (£000s)	
Stock	580		
Debtors	340		
Creditors		265	
Net liquid funds		285	
	920	550	370

Group problems and associated companies

Introduction

Where a company has subsidiaries and prepares group accounts SSAP 10 requires that the statement of source and application of funds should be framed to reflect the operations of the group.[13] Thus, when consolidated accounts are prepared, the funds statement will be based upon the consolidated accounts. Following normal consolidation techniques, a consolidated balance sheet includes the whole of the assets and liabilities of the holding company and all subsidiaries, even where the subsidiary companies are only partially owned. It is important to appreciate that when working capital or modified working capital is extracted from the consolidated balance sheets it includes the current assets and the relevant creditors of all group companies. The funds statement must explain why this figure changed from one date to another.

Bearing this in mind, we may now turn to look at some of the problems involved in preparing a funds statement for a group of companies, namely the treatment of minority interests and the acquisition and disposal of a subsidiary.

Consolidated accounts often also include the results of associated companies and the methods of dealing with these are examined in this section. Finally, we look at the methods of dealing with foreign exchange differences relating to overseas subsidiaries.

Minority interests

As we have seen above, a simple company will have a source of funds from operations based upon the pre-tax profit of the period adjusted for certain non-fund items. The group will similarly have a source of funds from operations based upon a similarly adjusted consolidated profit before tax. If there is no minority interest that is the end of the matter, but, of course, many groups have minority interests.

Where a minority interest exists there is a deduction in the consolidated profit and loss account for the minority interest in the current after-tax profits, and it is necessary to decide how to deal with that in the funds statement.

The fact that the minority interests have been credited with their share of the current profits has not affected funds at all. It is only where a payment has been made to the minority interest that there is a use of funds. It follows that we may deal with the minority interest as follows:

13 SSAP 10, Para. 12.

Source of funds from operations
    Profit before taxation (per consolidated profit and loss account)   *X*
    Adjustment for non-fund items   *X*

    X

Application of funds
    Dividends paid to minority interests   *X*

    X

Examples 2 and 3 in the appendix to SSAP 10 adopt a different and unnecessarily confusing approach. Instead of commencing with the profit before taxation, an identifiable figure in the consolidated profit and loss account, they commence with the 'profit before tax and extraordinary items, less minority interests'. Thus they deduct from the profit before taxation the minority interest in those profits as shown in the consolidated profit and loss account. However, as explained above, this minority interest only represents a reduction in the source of funds to the extent that it is paid out as dividends. To the extent that the share of profits of minority interests is retained, it does not affect funds at all. Hence the examples add back as a non-fund item the minority interests in retained profits for the year.

A simple example will illustrate that the above two methods have the same net effect. Suppose that a simple consolidated profit and loss account contains the following entries:

Consolidated profit and loss account for the year ended 31 December 19X4

	£
Profit before taxation (after charging depreciation of £20 000)	100 000
less Taxation	40 000
	60 000
less Minority interest in profits	9 000
	£51 000

Let us assume that during the year, dividends of £4000 have been paid to minority interests so that £5000 of current profits applicable to those minority interests have been retained, that is, have resulted in an increase in the figure for minority interests shown in the consolidated balance sheets. A statement based on the first method would show:

	£
Source of funds from operations	
Profit before taxation	100 000
Non-fund item: depreciation	20 000
	120 000
Applications	
Dividends paid to minority interest	4 000
	£116 000

A statement based on the second method would show:

	£	£
Source of funds from operations		
Profit before taxation, less minority interest		
(£100 000–£9000)		91 000
Non-fund items		
Depreciation	20 000	
Minority interest in retained profit	5 000	25 000
		£116 000

Both have the same net effect, although the amounts shown as the source of funds from operations differ. The former seems to be a better explanation of why group funds have changed, and treats dividends paid to minority interests in a manner consistent with the treatment of dividends paid by the parent company.

Acquisition of subsidiary

When an investing company acquires a new subsidiary, the consolidated profit and loss account will include profits of that subsidiary from the date of acquisition to the end of the period and the consolidated balance sheet will include the whole of the assets and liabilities of the new subsidiary, whether it is wholly or partly owned.[14]

When we attempt to explain changes between entries in the opening consolidated balance sheet and the closing consolidated balance sheet, we find that part of the changes is due to the assets and liabilities of, and any minority interest in, the new subsidiary at the date of

---

14 *See* Chapter 12 for the treatment of an acquisition of a new subsidiary in the consolidated profit and loss account and balance sheet.

acquisition. Each change is made up of three components: first, changes in respect of those companies which were members of the group for the whole of the period; second, changes resulting from the introduction of the assets and liabilities of the new subsidiary at the date of acquisition; third, changes in the assets and liabilities of the new subsidiary from the date of acquisition to the end of the period. Although the first and last of these changes are easily dealt with in our funds statement, examples 2 and 3 in the appendix to SSAP 10 provide us with alternative methods of dealing with the second class of changes.

Let us illustrate by means of a simple example. Suppose that Timor Limited had one partly-owned subsidiary, Buru Limited, on 31 December 19X1 but acquired a new wholly owned subsidiary, Dili Limited, on 1 July 19X2, by issuing 25 000 £1 shares worth £50 000. The consolidated balance sheets for two companies on 31 December 19X1 and for the three companies on 31 December 19X2 are given below. The consolidated profit and loss account, which includes the results of Dili Limited for the six months 1 July 19X2 to 31 December 19X2, is also given.

Summarized accounts *Consolidated balance sheets*	31 December 19X1 (two companies) (£000s)	31 December 19X2 (three companies) (£000s)
Fixed assets		
Goodwill on consolidation	60	70
Tangible fixed assets	90	132
Working capital	50	77
	200	279
less Long-term loans	40	50
	160	229
£1 shares	50	75
Share premium	—	25
Retained profits	80	95
	130	195
Minority interests	30	34
	160	229

Consolidated profit and loss account for the year ended 31 December 19X2

	£000s
Profit before taxation (after charging depreciation of £12 000)	79
less Taxation	40
	39
less Minority interest	4
	35
less Proposed dividend	20
Retained profit for year	15
add Retained profits brought forward	80
Retained profits carried forward	95

The summarized balance sheets of Dili Limited at the date of acquisition and at 31 December 19X2 were as follows:

Dili Limited
Summarized balance sheet

	1 July 19X2 (£000s)	31 December 19X2 (£000s)
Fixed assets	15	22
Working capital	35	33
	50	55
less Long-term loans	10	10
	40	45
£1 shares	25	25
Retained profits	15	20
	40	45

In order to understand the effect of acquiring the new subsidiary we may analyse the change between consolidated balance sheets into three component parts:

	Timor and Buru, Consolidated balance sheet 31 Dec. 19X1 (£000s)	Timor and Buru, year to 31 Dec. 19X2 (£000s)	CHANGES Dili, on 1 July 19X2 (£000s)	Dili, 6 months to 31 Dec. 19X2 (£000s)	Timor, Buru and Dili, Consolidated balance sheet 31 Dec. 19X2 (£000s)
Fixed assets					
Goodwill on consolidation	60		+10		70
Tangible fixed assets	90	+20	+15	+7	132
Investment in Dili Limited	—	+50	−50		—
Working capital	50	−6	+35	−2	77
	200	+64	+10	+5	279
less Long-term loans	40	—	+10		50
	160	+64	—	+5	229
£1 shares	50	+25			75
Share premium	—	+25			25
Retained profits	80	+10		+5	95
	130	+60	—	+5	195
Minority interests	30	+ 4			34
	160	+64	—	+5	229

The first of the three 'change' columns shows changes in respect of the two companies in the group at the beginning of the year. It therefore includes the acquisition of an asset 'Investment in Dili Limited' and the corresponding credits to share capital and share premium account of Timor Limited. The second and third of the change columns show the assets and liabilities of Dili Limited at the date of acquisition and changes in those items from 1 July to 31 December 19X2, respectively.

From this data, and by making simplifying assumptions, for illustrative purposes only, that no ACT has been incurred nor any fixed assets sold, we may proceed to prepare a funds statement explaining why working capital has increased by £27 000, from £50 000 to £77 000.

The first method, which is illustrated in example 2 of the appendix to SSAP 10, is based upon the same principles as those used to record the treatment of the acquisition in the consolidated accounts. The second method, which is illustrated in example 3 of the appendix, follows the treatment of the acquisition in the accounts of the parent company. Let us take each in turn.

A statement following the first method would explain changes in this way:

Statement of source and application of funds for the year ended 31 December 19X2

	£000s	£000s
Sources of funds		
From operations		
Profit before taxation		79
Adjustment for item not involving movement		
of funds: Depreciation		12
		91
Other sources		
Shares issued to acquire new subsidiary*	50	
Long-term loan in new subsidiary at date of		
acquisition*	10	60
		151
Applications		
Purchase of fixed assets (£42 000 + £12 000)*	54	
Goodwill on consolidation*	10	
Taxation for the year[15]	40	
Dividend for the year[15]	20	
		124
Increase in working capital*		27

Such an approach would be consistent with the changes shown by a comparison of the opening and closing consolidated balance sheets. It would not, however, disclose the impact of the acquisition on the various items and hence a footnote on the following lines is required:

---

15 Because we are explaining the change in 'working capital' rather than the change in 'modified working capital' here, it is the taxation charge and dividend shown in the consolidated profit and loss account which appear as applications.

Summary of the effects of acquiring Dili Limited

	£000s		£000s
Fixed assets	15	Shares issued as consideration	50
Goodwill on consolidation	10		
Working capital	35		
Long-term loans	(10)		—
	50		50

The use of asterisks indicates clearly which items in the funds statement have been affected by the acquisition of the new subsidiary.

The assets owned by the subsidiary at the date of acquisition were in part financed by its long-term loans. As the total assets of the subsidiary are shown as applications the long-term loans outstanding on the date of acquisition must be included as a source of funds. If the new subsidiary is only partly owned then, for the same reason, any minority interest at the date of acquisition must be included as a source of funds.

The second method, which is illustrated in example 3 of the appendix to SSAP 10, would collect all the items relating to the acquisition of the new subsidiary together and show one application 'Purchase of shares in the new subsidiary: £50 000'. Thus the funds statement would take on a different form as follows:

Statement of source and application of funds for the year to 31 December 19X2

	£000s	£000s
Sources of funds		
From operations		
Profit before taxation		79
Adjustment for items not involving movement of funds		
Depreciation		12
		91
Other sources		
Shares issued to acquire new subsidiary*		50
Carried forward		141

	£000s	£000s
Brought forward		141
Applications		
Purchase of fixed assets (£20 000 + £7000 + £12 000)	39	
Purchase of shares in Dili Limited*	50	
Taxation for the year	40	
Dividend for the year	20	
		149
Decrease in working capital		(8)

This treatment follows the approach used to record the acquisition in the accounts of the parent company, Timor Limited, rather than with the treatment adopted in the consolidated accounts. Thus, although the consolidated balance sheets show an increase in working capital of £27 000 during the year, this type of statement shows a decrease in working capital of £8000. This is, of course, because the group working capital increased by £35 000 on the acquisition of Dili Limited, and reconciliation between the funds statement and the consolidated accounts is only possible it the same footnote as that shown above is included.

As explained earlier, in the case of a group, Para. 12 of SSAP 10 requires that the statement of source and application of funds should be so framed as to reflect the operations of the group. The method illustrated in example 2 of the appendix to SSAP 10 is therefore the preferred alternative. Indeed it may be argued that the method illustrated in example 3 of the appendix is not consistent with the consolidated accounts and therefore does not comply with the 'statement of standard accounting practice'.

Disposal of a subsidiary
When a holding company disposes of a subsidiary we have the reverse situation. Whereas the opening consolidated balance sheet includes the assets and liabilities of all companies in the group on that date, the closing consolidated balance sheet will exclude the assets and liabilities of the subsidiary sold. As far as the consolidated accounts are considered, the net assets of the subsidiary at the date of sale are exchanged for the sale proceeds. The sale proceeds must be shown as a source of funds and, as in the case of the disposal of fixed assets, any profit or loss on disposal must be excluded from the funds statement to avoid double counting.

When we look at the change in individual balance sheet items, we find that part of the change is explained by the removal of assets and liabilities of the subsidiary which existed at the date of disposal. This part of individual changes must be excluded from the funds statement and hence we have the problem that entries in the funds statement will not reconcile with the changes disclosed by the consolidated balance sheets. To enable users to understand what has happened, it is necessary to provide a footnote, similar to that used on an acquisition, which summarizes the effect of the disposal:

Summary of effects of disposal of subsidiary

	£000s		£000s
Consideration received		Net assets sold	
Shares	80	Fixed assets	40
Cash	20	Goodwill on consolidation	20
		Stock	20
		Debtors	30
		Creditors	(25)
		Profit on disposal	15
	__100__		__100__

Associated companies
Standard accounting practice for associated companies is contained in SSAP 1, which was revised in April 1982. This requires investing companies to take credit in their consolidated profit and loss accounts, not just for dividends received and receivable from an associated company, but for their full share of profits in that associated company.[16] An extract from a consolidated profit and loss account illustrates this treatment:

Consolidated profit and loss account for the year ended 31 December 19X2

	£	£
Operating profit of investing company and subsidiaries before taxation		100 000
Share of profits of associated company		10 000
Profit before taxation		110 000
Taxation		
Investing company and subsidiaries	40 000	
Associated company	4 000	44 000
		66 000

16 *See* Chapter 12 for a comprehensive coverage of this topic.

The treatment in the balance sheet depends upon whether or not a consolidated balance sheet is prepared. Where one *is* prepared, the investment in the associated company is usually shown at a value equal to cost plus the share of post-acquisition retained profits. Where a consolidated balance sheet *is not* prepared the investment is usually shown at cost with details of the value using the equity method of accounting included by way of note. In either case the balance sheet does not include the separate assets or liabilities of the associated company, so that when we look at the change in funds we calculate a figure which excludes the change in funds of the associated company.

The only way in which group funds, that is working capital or modified working capital, are affected by an associated company is when a dividend is received or receivable from that associated company. In the former case the cash balance increases whereas, in the latter case debtors increase. Both are an increase in funds.

Using the above consolidated profit and loss account for our example, let us assume that the investing company receives a dividend of £2500 from the associated company. A simple way to deal with this in the funds statement, ignoring any other complications, is as follows:

	£
Source of funds from operations	
Profit of investing company and subsidiaries before taxation	100 000
add Dividend received from associated company	2 500
	102 500

An alternative used in the illustrative examples contained in the appendix to SSAP 10 is to take as a starting point the profit before taxation of the investing company and subsidiaries including the share of profits of the associated company, that is £110 000 in our example. This, however, brings in profits which have not increased the funds of the investing company. The amount involved is £7500, made up as follows:

	£
Investing company's share of	
Tax charge of associated company	4000
Increase in profits retained by associated company	
(£6000 − £2500)	3500
	7500

The resulting statement would contain the following entries:

	£
Source of funds from operations	
Profit of investing company, subsidiaries and share of profits in associated company before taxation	110 000
less Non-fund item: share of profits retained in associated company	7 500
	102 500

Some companies have used a third alternative. As the investing company has, by definition, substantial influence over the associated company, and may therefore affect the level of dividends paid by that company, it may be argued that the full share of the profits should be brought in as above but that the £7500 share of profits retained should be shown as an application, a re-investment in the associated company. Such an alternative might be considered consistent with the 'all financial resources' approach to the statement. However, it perhaps overestimates the extent of significant influence, which is after all not control, and the authors prefer the first and simplest of the three alternatives.

The net effect in all three cases is, of course, to include as a source, or net source, the dividend received and/or receivable from the associated company.

Foreign currency differences

As we have seen in Chapter 13, exchange differences frequently arise both when a company engages in foreign transactions and when the accounts of an overseas entity are translated prior to the preparation of such statements as consolidated accounts. Although such differences on exchange must be dealt with consistently in the statement of source and application of funds, it is convenient to look at each type of difference in turn.

Exchange differences on transactions may relate to fund items, that is items within the definition of funds such as trade debtors and trade creditors, or to non-fund items such as long-term loans. Under the provisions of SSAP 20 exchange gains or losses on both types of items will usually be treated as part of the ordinary profits or losses of the company.

To the extent that the exchange differences relate to fund items they do, of course, partly explain the difference between funds shown in the balance sheet at the beginning of the year and funds shown in the balance sheet at the end of the year. This is best illustrated by a simple example.

Let us suppose that a company made a sale to an overseas company and that the sale was recorded in the accounting records at a sterling figure of £15 000. If the debt is outstanding at the ensuing balance sheet date, it will be retranslated at the closing rate of exchange to produce a different figure of, say, £16 500. Thus the closing debtors figure will include £16 500 and the difference in debtors as observed from the change in balance sheet figures will include this increase of £16 500. In the profit and loss account the amount will be shown in two parts:

Sale	£15 000
Gain on exchange	1 500
	16 500

Thus the gain on exchange explains in part the observed increase in debtors and there would seem to be three possible ways of dealing with such a difference in the statement of source and application of funds.

First, we may show any difference relating to the fund items as a source, if it is a profit, or as an application, if it is a loss. After all, these differences explain in part why the working capital has changed between balance sheet dates.

Second, we may exclude this profit or loss on exchange from the main body of the statement but instead show it as a subtraction from, or an addition to, the aggregate working capital changes shown at the foot of the statement.

Both of these methods mean that the changes in the individual components of working capital at the foot of the statement agree with the changes shown by comparing the opening and closing balance sheets.

The third possible method is to exclude the profit or loss on exchange from the statement and show the changes in the components of working capital net of exchange differences relating thereto. Under this approach the figures shown in the analysis of working capital at the foot of the funds statement will not agree with the changes reflected in the balance sheets.

On grounds of simplicity, the authors favour the first of the three methods.

Turning next to the exchange difference relating to non-funds items, let us suppose that a UK company had a loan of $1 million outstanding on both 31 December 19X1 and 31 December 19X2. If, during the year, the rate of exchange has moved from $4 to £1 to $5 to £1, the sterling value of the loan would have fallen from £250 000 to £200 000, producing a gain on exchange of £50 000. In the absence of any linked foreign equity investment, this gain would be treated as part of the ordinary profits for the year.

Since the loan is not part of the company's 'funds', the gain on exchange should not be reflected in the funds statement. Thus the gain should not be included in the figure showing the funds derived from operations whilst the offsetting reduction in the sterling value of the loan should not be shown as an application of funds. It should be noted that this is exactly the same principle as is applied in the case of the revaluation of a fixed asset such as land.

It has been assumed above that funds are defined as working capital or modified working capital. Different considerations apply if the 'all financial resources' approach is used as, in this case, the gain would be reflected in the statement. This is, actually, a good example of the virtues of the 'all financial resources' approach in so far as it permits the inclusion of an item which may have a significant effect on the future sterling cash flow in that less will be required to repay the debt.

When we turn to the translation of the accounts of an overseas subsidiary, the nature and treatment of the exchange differences will depend upon which method of translation is being used.

Under the closing rate/net investment method the whole of the difference on translation is taken direct to reserves. Part of the difference will usually relate to fund items and hence will partially explain changes in such items as debtors, creditors and cash balances as reflected in the consolidated balance sheet differences. Part of the difference will relate to non-fund items such as fixed assets and long-term loans.

With regard to the exchange gains or losses on fund items, the same three methods of dealing with them as were described in the context of differences on transactions are available. As before, it is suggested that any exchange gain or loss relating to non-fund items should be excluded from the funds statement, although it will then be necessary to disclose movements in such non-fund items during the year. Only then will it be possible for users to reconcile the opening and closing figures in the consolidated balance sheet and the actual sources and applications of funds shown in the funds statement.

When the temporal method of translation is used to translate the historical cost accounts of an overseas subsidiary, there will be no difference on exchange relating to fixed assets and any difference relating to other items will be dealt with as part of the ordinary consolidated profit or loss.

The treatment of this difference in the statement of source and application of funds is exactly the same as that outlined in connection with foreign currency transactions above. The differences relating to fund items may be treated in three different ways whilst the differences relating to non-fund items should not appear in the funds statement.

There are, then, a number of ways of dealing with foreign exchange differences in a statement of source and application of funds and a wide variety of treatments is found in practice.

Usefulness of the statement

Now that we have explored different concepts of funds and some of the problems of preparing a statement of source and application of funds, it is time to look briefly at the advantages or usefulness of such a statement.

As we have seen in Chapter 1, most users are concerned with the future performance of an enterprise and turn to the accounts, as well as to other sources, for help in making a judgement about likely future performance. In assessing the usefulness of the statement, it is therefore necessary to ask how it helps users in this task.

The statement supplements the traditional accounts by collecting together information regarding funds in a way which provides answers to many pertinent questions which a user might wish to ask. Examples of such questions are as follows: Has there been an increase or decrease in working capital? To what extent have funds been generated by operations and from other sources? Are payments of taxation and dividends covered by the funds generated from operations or have they been financed by long-term sources of funds and even perhaps by the proceeds from the sale of fixed assets? How have purchases of fixed assets been financed? What has happened to the individual components of working capital?

Answers to such questions as these undoubtedly help users to assess what has happened and what is likely to happen to the enterprise in future. Like all the figures shown in a set of traditional accounts, they cannot be used in isolation but must be interpreted as part of the whole collection of information. This may be illustrated by just one example. When a user looks at the relationship between sources of long-term funds and the purchase of fixed assets, it is essential for him to bear in mind the position shown in earlier statements of source and application of funds and in the opening and closing balance sheets. What appears to be a serious imbalance in one particular year may reflect a positive attempt to remedy an unsatisfactory position which existed previously.

The value added statement

Background

As we have seen in the introduction to this chapter, *The Corporate Report* recommended that all significant economic entities should publish a value added statement as part of their annual accounts. Contrary to the traditional legal position, but in keeping with many current organizational theories, such a statement regards the entity as being operated by and for the benefit of a team of interests. Such a team is usually taken to include employees, suppliers of long-term capital and the government but to exclude other firms which supply goods and services. Thus, whereas the profit and loss account has traditionally shown the profit or loss of a period from the point of view of the equity shareholders, the value added statement shows the income of the larger entity and how this has been divided between the wider team of contributors.

Concept of value added

Once the team has been specified, the value added may be calculated as the difference between the value of the goods or services produced by the team, i.e. sales revenue, less the value of the goods and services purchased from outsiders, i.e. the cost of bought-in materials and services.

The value added statement is normally in two parts, the first of which shows the value added by the team whilst the second shows how that value added has been divided between the team members. The illustrative layout proposed in *The Corporate Report* was as follows:

A manufacturing company. Statement of value added for the year to 31 December 19X9

	£	£
Turnover		X
Bought-in materials and services		X
Value added		X

	£	£
Applied the following way		
To pay employees		
Wages, pensions and fringe benefits		X
To pay providers of capital		
Interest on loans	X	
Dividends to shareholders	X	X
To pay government		
Corporation Tax payable		X
To provide for maintenance and expansion of assets		
Depreciation	X	
Retained profits	X	X
Value added		X

As may be seen from the above illustration, so far as large companies are concerned, the value added statement is largely a rearrangement of information disclosed elsewhere in the company's published accounts. For this reason many people consider it to be a mere cosmetic device to place less emphasis on the profit figure. Others would stress that presentation has an important role to play and that the arrangement of information in the value added statement provides a better means of understanding the contribution of a company to society. In particular, the inclusion of relevant percentages of value added by the side of items in the second part of the statement would make people aware of the respective shares of the various team members.

Simple company

Content of statement
For a manufacturing or trading company the first figure in the value added statement will usually be the turnover figure which appears in its profit and loss account. From this is deducted the cost of bought-in materials and services, which comprise the cost of materials and services consumed. Examples of such bought-in materials and services are raw materials, fuel costs, hire of computing facilities, printing and stationery and audit fees: these are all goods or services bought from non-team members. In practice the cost of bought-in materials and services will usually be calculated as a balancing figure.

Although the illustration in *The Corporate Report* does not deduct depreciation in arriving at value added, there is a very strong argument for doing so. The purchase of a fixed asset from another firm, a non-team member, is a bought-in item and it is only the fact that the asset has a long life which necessitates the charging of depreciation. Thus in arriving at value added, a preferred format would be:

	£	£
Turnover		X
less Bought-in materials and services	X	
Depreciation	X	X
		X

In order to avoid confusion it is perhaps sensible to talk of the illustration in *The Corporate Report* as a statement of gross value added and the illustration above as a statement of net value added. A similar distinction between gross national product and net national product is found in national income statistics.

In the lower part of the statement we need to show how the value added during the period has been shared between members of the team. Following the order to the illustrative layout of *The Corporate Report* we would start with amounts payable to all employees, that is gross pay, employers' National Insurance contributions, employers' pension contributions and pension payments and, to the extent that it is possible to arrive at them, fringe benefits. Theoretically we should disclose wages payable in respect of the sales of the year. However, most published statements show wages payable for the year and ignore the changes in the labour content of work-in-progress or finished goods stock, thus losing the difference in the balancing figure for 'bought-in materials and services'.

Some companies show as payable to employees merely the net pay of employees, grouping PAYE and both employers' and employees' National Insurance contributions under the heading 'To pay government'. Although one can understand companies wishing to emphasize how much is paid over to the government there seems a lot to be said for showing only Corporation Tax payable under the government heading for reasons which will be discussed below.

The second group of members of the team in the illustrative layout are providers of financial capital. Under this heading will be shown interest payable on loans and dividends payable to shareholders for the period. Where tax is deductible from interest payable, interest should be shown gross of tax for the company is merely accounting for the recipient's income tax liability at the basic rate of taxation.

It is when we turn to the heading 'To pay government' that we find the most variety in practice. Some companies merely show Corporation Tax payable in respect of the period, that is both Advance Corporation Tax and Mainstream Corporation Tax. Others show all taxes paid to the government whether paid over on behalf of others or not. In this case the heading 'To pay government' might include such taxes as the following: Corporation Tax, employees' PAYE, National Insurance contributions, taxation deducted from interest payable, VAT, local rates, motor vehicle license fees, Customs and Excise duties.

There seem to be arguments in favour of both treatments. To include just the figure for Corporation Tax payable avoids the need for arbitrary distinctions and time-consuming analysis of the accounts to ascertain the totals of the various taxes listed above. It also has the advantage of agreement with the profit and loss account figure. On the other hand, it may be argued that the inclusion of all taxes payable to the government would facilitate international comparison. The inclusion of only one direct tax, Corporation Tax, would make such international comparisons difficult in that countries have different mixes of direct and indirect taxes.

Although some writers have called for the standardization of treatment, the authors are of the opinion that it is much too early in the development of the statement for such standardization to be undertaken.

The final heading in the illustrative layout is 'To provide for maintenance and expansion of assets'. For the reasons stated above, depreciation is usually better classified as a bought-in cost. This leaves only retained profit, and some description such as 'available for investment' would then be more appropriate. Some people would argue that it is wrong to include such an abstraction as a member of the team, for, after all, retained profits belong to the equity shareholders.

Non-trading items
In the previous section we have examined the value added statement of a simple trading or manufacturing company. Most companies also have what may be loosely described as non-trading items, examples of which are investment income and extraordinary profits and losses. Although it may be argued that investment income is a share of the value added distributable by another company rather than a part of the value added by the company with which we are concerned, that investment income is certainly a part of the value added available to share between team members. Indeed it is impossible to eliminate

the investment income from the individual items in the second part of the statement and it must therefore either be deducted in total in the second part of the statement or, preferably, included separately in the first part of the statement. A similar treatment is appropriate for extraordinary items and, if this treatment is adopted, the first part of the value added statement would appear as follows:

	£	£
Sales		X
less Bought-in materials and services	X	
Depreciation	X	X
Value added by the company		X
add Investment income	X	
Extraordinary profits	X	X
Value added available		X

Group of companies – minority interests

Where a company prepares consolidated accounts, the value added statement will be based upon the consolidated profit and loss account rather than the profit and loss account of the parent company. It will therefore show value added by the group. The minority interests in subsidiary companies must therefore be treated as members of the team and their share of the value added included in the lower part of the statement. Two methods are commonly used in practice.

Some companies show, under the heading 'To pay providers of capital', the full share of minority interests in the current profits, whether or not these are distributable as dividends. Other companies split the share of profits applicable to minority interests, showing dividends paid and payable under the heading 'To pay providers of capital' and the retained profits applicable to the minority interest as a separate item under the heading 'Retained profits available for investment'. The latter would seem to be the better alternative as the treatment is consistent with that applied to the shareholders in the holding company.

Associated companies

Under SSAP 1 companies are required to include in their consolidated profit and loss accounts their full share of profits and losses of associated companies. Such an item should therefore be included as a separate component of value added in the top part of the statement.

In the second part of the statement there must be shown the share of the Corporation Tax payable by the associated company and the share of retained profits which will either be held by the investing company, to the extent that a dividend is payable by the associated company, or in the associated company itself. Tax payable should be shown under the heading 'To pay government' whereas the retained profits should be shown under the heading 'Retained to provide for investment'. Notice that no item appears under the heading 'To pay employees' because the figure we have included as value added is the share of profits in associated companies, after payments to employees.

Possible future developments

As discussed above, some people consider the value added statement to be a mere cosmetic device to divert attention from the profit figure. Others consider it to be an instrument for improving industrial relations in this country by emphasizing the team nature of the entity.[17] Whatever view is taken, a large number of companies do produce a value added statement as part of their annual report. A study of all listed companies in *The Times* 1000 for 1977/78[18] found that approximately 18% of such companies produced a value added statement. It also found that a significantly greater proportion of the larger companies in the study prepared the statement. However, recent ICAEW surveys of published accounts, which cover 300 large industrial and commercial companies, show that the proportion of such companies producing value added statements has never exceeded one-third and that the proportion has been declining. Only 21% of the 300 companies surveyed in 1982–83 provided value added statements.[19]

Although most companies which prepare such a statement appear to follow the layout illustrated in *The Corporate Report*, some companies have adopted very different presentations. Thus, in some cases the value added statement has been integrated with the profit and loss account or funds statement whilst pictorial representations, such as pie charts, have often been used.

We have seen that the value added statement is closely derived from the profit and loss account. It follows that, just as it is possible to prepare a profit and loss account using various concepts of profit and various levels of disaggregation, so too it is possible to prepare related value added statements. A few companies have provided value added

17 *See* M. F. Morley, *The Value Added Statement*, Gee, London, 1978, Chap. 3.
18 S. J. Gray and K. T. Maunders, 'Recent development in value added disclosures', *The Certified Accountant*, August 1979.
19 *Financial Reporting 1983–84*, ICAEW, London, 1983, p. 153.

statements based on their current cost accounts whilst a limited number have provided a geographical analysis of value added.

As the value added statement achieved a certain amount of popularity, there have been the inevitable calls for standardization of its presentation. In the view of the authors, such calls are misguided. Much experimentation is necessary before standardization is possible or desirable and, as discussed in the introduction to this chapter, the government has wisely decided not to introduce a legislative requirement.

Reporting about and to employees

As we have seen in the introduction to this chapter, both *The Corporate Report* and the subsequent Green Papers favoured the expansion of the annual report to include an employment report.

Companies and other entities employ a large number of people who look to those entities for employment security and prospects whilst society at large expects employers to maintain certain standards of conduct in relation to its employees. *The Corporate Report* therefore took the view that significant economic entities should report employment information and recommended that the annual report should be expanded to include an employment report which should provide the following information.[20]

(a)   Numbers employed, average for the financial year and actual on the first and last day.

(b)   Broad reasons for changes in the numbers employed.

(c)   The age distribution and sex of employees.

(d)   The functions of employees.

(e)   The geographical location of major employment centres.

(f)   Major plant and site closures, disposals and acquisitions during the past year.

(g)   The hours scheduled and worked by employees giving as much detail as possible concerning differences between groups of employees.

(h)   Employment costs including fringe benefits.

(i)   The costs and benefits associated with pension schemes and the ability of such schemes to meet future commitments.

(j)   The cost and time spent on training.

---

20 *The Corporate Report*, Para. 6.19. Appendix 3 to that document provides an example of the sort of employment report envisaged.

(k) The names of unions recognized by the entity for the purpose of collective bargaining and membership figures where available or the fact that this information has not been made available by the unions concerned.

(l) Information concerning safety and health including the frequency and severity of accidents and occupational diseases.

(m) Selected ratios relating to employment.

Such an employment report would provide much more information than that presently required to be disclosed by law but few companies have published such a report. Indeed the percentage of companies providing an employment report appears to be declining with less than 5% of the 300 companies surveyed in 1981–82 including one.[21] This may, in part, be due to the fact that there has been very little published work showing which users find the particular pieces of information useful and for what purposes they might be useful. An attempt has been made to remedy this dearth with the publication of a research study in 1984 by the ICAEW.[22]

While some writers have called for the ASC to issue guidelines specifying the detailed contents of an employment report, the authors are of the view that much more work is necessary before such action could be justified.

The employment report envisaged by *The Corporate Report* was of a general purpose nature to be included in the annual report of the relevant entities. It should not be confused with the employee report, a document separate from the annual report, intended for the use of employees. Whereas the publication of employment reports appears to be decreasing, the issue of employee reports appears to be increasing and, often, these are also issued to shareholders as a matter of course.

Employee reports usually contain a simplified set of accounts together with a narrative review of those accounts. The emphasis is on making the information as easy to understand as possible and such reports try to avoid technical language and frequently include charts and diagrams which might show, for example, the changes in sales or profits over a number of years or the distribution of value added between the team members.

In large companies the employees are primarily interested in a part, rather than the whole of the entity and frequently employee reports

21 *Financial Reporting 1982–83*, ICAEW, London, 1982.
22 K. T. Maunders, *Employment Reporting: An Investigation of User Needs, Measurement and Reporting Issues and Practice*, ICAEW, London, 1984.

are used to give more detailed segmental information about geographical areas, divisions or plants. They can thus be tailor made for the particular company and can be improved in response to suggestions from the users, that is the employees, themselves.

Recommended reading

R. W. Knox, *Statements of Source and Application of Funds: A Practical Guide to SSAP 10*, ICAEW, London, 1977.

M. F. Morley, *The Value Added Statement*, Gee, London, 1978.

M. Renshall, R. Allan and K. Nicholson, *Added Value in External Financial Reporting*, ICAEW, London, 1979.

S. J. Gray and K. T. Maunders, *Value Added Reporting: Uses and Measurement*, The Association of Certified Accountants, London, 1980.

Much useful information on current practice is included in the volume *Financial Reporting – A Survey of UK Published Accounts*, published annually by the ICAEW.

Questions

14.1 (a) **What do you consider to be the functions of source and application of funds statements in financial reporting?** (5 marks)

(b) **Explain briefly how you would account for the following five transactions in a statement of source and application of funds prepared in accordance with SSAP 10:** *Statements of Source and Application of Funds:*
  (i) Corporation Tax provided for the current accounting period and Corporation Tax paid for the previous period.
  (ii) The final dividend proposed for the current accounting period and last year's final dividend paid during the current period.
  (iii) The profit on the disposal of a fixed asset.
  (iv) The share of profits in an associated company.
  (v) The acquisition of a subsidiary paid for partly by an issue of shares and partly by a payment of cash. (10 marks)

(c) **How generally might alternative definitions of funds influence the preparation of source and application of funds statements?** (10 marks)
(**25 marks**)

A. Cert. A. Level 2, The Regulatory Framework of Accounting, Dec. 1983.

14.2 SSAP 10: *Statements of Source and Application of Funds*, suggests two ways for dealing with the effects of the acquisition of subsidiaries.

The following are extracts from the financial statements of Tastydeserts plc and one of its wholly owned subsidiaries, Custardpowders Ltd, the shares in which were acquired on 31 October 1982.

	Tastydeserts plc and subsidiaries 31 December		Custardpowders Ltd 31 October
	1982	1981	1982
	£'000	£'000	£'000
Balance sheet			
Fixed assets	4764	3685	694
Associated companies	2195	2175	—
Stocks	1735	1388	306
Debtors	2658	2436	185
Bank balances and cash	43	77	7
Creditors	(1915)	(1546)	(148)
Bank overdrafts	(176)	(343)	—
Taxation	(235)	(200)	—
Proposed dividend	(82)	(63)	—
Deferred taxation	(111)	(180)	—
	8876	7429	1044
Share capital	4896	4776	400
Reserves	2632	2000	644
Loans	1348	653	—
	8876	7429	1044

	Tastydeserts plc and subsidiaries 31 December 1982 £'000
Profit and loss account	
Net profit for year before taxation	546
Share of associated companies' profits	190
	736
Taxation	196
	540
Proposed dividend	82
Profit retained	458
In parent and subsidiaries	438
In associated companies	20
	458

The following information is also given:

(1) The consolidated figures at 31 December 1982 include Custardpowders Ltd.

(2) The amount of depreciation on fixed assets during the year was £78 000 and additions, excluding those on the acquisition of Custardpowders Ltd, were £463 000. There were no disposals.

(3) Dividends received during the year from associated companies were £100 000.

(4) The cost on 31 October 1982 of the shares in Custardpowders Ltd was £1 086 000 comprising the issue of £750 000 unsecured loan stock at par and 120 000 ordinary shares of £1 each at a value of 280p.

(5) During the year certain long-term loans have been repaid.

You are required to:

(a) **prepare a source and application of funds statement for Tastydeserts plc and subsidiaries for the year ended 31 December 1982 using either of the treatments suggested in SSAP 10** (13 marks),

(b) **redraft your statement so as to show the other treatment suggested in SSAP 10** (6 marks), **and**

(c) **explain briefly which of the treatments you consider is more appropriate in the case of Tastydeserts plc** (4 marks).

(23 marks)

ICAEW Financial Accounting II, December 1982.

14.3 Below is the (historical cost) consolidated profit and loss account of the Alphabeta Group for the year ended 31 December 1982, together with the (simplified) consolidated balance sheets as at 31 December 1981 and 1982, and notes amplifying these accounts.

You are required:

(a) **to prepare the Statement of Source and Application of Funds of the group for the year ended 31 December 1982, in a form suitable for publication and complying with SSAP 10: Statement of source and application of funds. Dividends and taxes PAID should be shown as applications, and an explanation of the effects of acquiring a subsidiary during the year ended 31 December 1982 should be given by way of a note to the Statement; and** (18 marks)

(b) **to explain the utility of the Statement of Source and Application of Funds, thus prepared, to an ordinary shareholder in Alphabeta plc, or to his or her financial adviser.** (8 marks)

(26 marks)

Alphabeta plc and its Subsidiaries

Consolidated Profit and Loss Account for the year ended 31 December 1982

	£'000s	£'000s	£'000s
Turnover			55 000
Change in stocks of finished goods and work in progress		4 700	
Own work capitalized		3 000	
Other operating income		2 000	
			9 700
			64 700
Raw materials and consumables	20 000		
Other external charges	1 000		
		21 000	
Staff costs		28 000	
Depreciation and amortization of fixed assets (net of gains/losses on disposals)		4 482	
Other operating charges		2 500	
			55 982
Net trading profit			8 718
Group's proportion of pre-tax profits of related companies			100
			8 818
Net profit before interest			
Interest payable and similar charges:			
On bank overdrafts		60	
On debenture loans of group companies (externally held)		1 050	
Amortization of discount on above debenture loans		200	
			1 310
Net profit before taxation			
Tax on profit on ordinary activities:			
Of group companies		2 500	
Transfers to deferred taxation:			
Of group companies		1 000	
Group's proportion of tax on ordinary activities of related companies		50	
		3 550	7 508

	£'000s	£'000s	£'000s
Brought forward		3 550	7 508
less Adjustment of previous year's tax charge		20	
			3 530
Profit on ordinary activities after taxation		3 550	3 978
Minority interests therein			540
Attributable to shareholders in Alphabeta plc			3 438
(of which £3 000 000 is dealt with in that company's accounts)			
Extraordinary income of group companies (less minority interest therein)		40	
Extraordinary charges of related companies (group's proportion)		(10)	
Extraordinary profit		30	
less Tax on extraordinary profit:			
Of group (less minority interests)	21		
Of related companies (group's proportion)	(5)		
		16	
			14
Profit for the financial year			3 452
Dividends of Alphabeta plc:			
Preference – paid		100	
Ordinary – paid		600	
do. – proposed		1 440	
			2 140
Retained earnings for the financial year:			
Of Alphabeta plc		870	
Of group companies (less minority interests)		422	
Of related companies (group's proportion)		20	
			1 312

Consolidated Balance Sheets, 31 December 1981 and 1982

		1981			1982	
	Gross	Depre-ciation	Net	Gross	Depre-ciation	Net
Net assets	£'000s	£'000s	£'000s	£'000s	£'000s	£'000s
Fixed assets						
Intangible assets:						
Patents and trade marks	100	50	50	140	60	80
Goodwill	400	250	150	710	392	318
	500	300	200	850	452	398
Tangible assets:						
Land	1 000	—	1 000	2 700	—	2 700
Buildings	6 000	2 000	4 000	13 000	3 983	9 017
Plant and machinery	12 000	6 000	6 000	16 700	8 040	8 660
Fixtures and fittings	3 000	1 200	1 800	3 850	1 185	2 665
	22 000	9 200	12 800	36 250	13 208	23 042
Investments:						
Shares in related companies (on equity basis)	350	—	350	1 070	—	1 070
Total fixed assets	22 850	9 500	13 350	38 170	13 660	24 510

Current assets						
Stocks:						
Raw materials and consumables	3 000			5 000		
Work in progress	1 000			1 700		
Finished goods	6 000			10 000		
		10 000			16 700	
Debtors:						
Trade debtors	4 700			5 654		
Prepayments	90			100		
		4 790			5 754	
Cash at bank and in hand		2 300			6 912	
			17 090			29 366

	£'000s	£'000s	£'000s	£'000s	£'000s
Creditors: Amounts falling due within one year					
Bank overdrafts	(600)			(1 014)	
Trade creditors	(2 500)			(3 000)	
Corporation Tax – current year (*less* ACT)	(1 000)			(1 806)	
Accruals	(400)			(450)	
Proposed dividend	(1 000)			(1 440)	
ACT on proposed dividend	(429)			(617)	
		(5 929)			(8 327)
Net current assets		11 161			21 039
		24 511			45 549
Financed by:					
Creditors: Amounts falling due after one year					
Debenture loans (externally held)	7 000			9 000	
less Unamortized discount	400			250	
		6 600			8 750
Provisions for liabilities and charges					
Deferred taxation		771			1 583
Minority interests in group companies		1 200			1 497
Capital and reserves					
Called up share capital:					
Preference (£1 shares)	1 000			1 000	
Ordinary (25p shares)	10 000			18 000	
		11 000			19 000
Reserves:					
Share premium account	1 500			6 300	
Revaluation reserve	—			3 667	
Profit and loss account	3 390			4 682	
Group's proportion of retained earnings of related companies since acquisition	50			70	
		4 940			14 719
		24 511			45 549

Notes

(1) The accounts were consolidated by the acquisition (purchase) method.

(2) Interests in related companies are accounted for by the equity method.

(3) During the year ended 31 December 1982 a new wholly-owned subsidiary, Zeta Limited, was acquired by the issue of 20 000 000 25p ordinary shares, whose fair market value was deemed to be 40p per share. Zeta Limited's identifiable assets (as revalued in its books before its acquisition by Alphabeta plc), and its liabilities, were:

	£
Land	300 000
Buildings (net)	1 500 000
Plant and machinery (net)	2 000 000
Fixtures and fittings (net)	500 000
Stocks: Raw materials and consumables	1 200 000
do. : Work in progress	400 000
do. : Finished goods	2 000 000
Debtors: Trade debtors	1 250 000
do. : Prepayments	20 000
Cash at bank and in hand	220 000
Creditors: Amounts falling due within one year:	
Trade creditors	800 000
Corporation Tax – current year (*less* ACT)	450 000
Accruals	100 000
Provisions for liabilities and charges: Deferred taxation	350 000

(4) During the year ended 31 December 1982, Alphabeta plc purchased a 25% interest in the equity of Mu plc for £700 000 in cash.

(5) As at 1 January 1982, the group's land was revalued in its books at market value, £2 000 000, and its buildings were revalued on the basis of gross replacement cost, £10 000 000. No deferred taxation adjustments were made in respect of these revaluations.

(6) During the year 1982, £3 000 000 of plant and machinery was constructed by group companies, and £1 200 000 was purchased from outside the group. Plant valued at 1 January 1982 at £1 500 000 gross, £200 000 net, was sold during 1982 for £225 000, the difference being included in 'depreciation and amortization', etc., in the consolidated profit and loss account.

(7) Corresponding movements on fixtures and fittings were: purchases, £800 000; disposals – gross, £450 000, net, £50 000, and proceeds, £70 000.

(8) All additions to land, buildings, and intangible assets were paid for in cash, unless otherwise accounted for.

(9) Minority interests in extraordinary income were £6 000 before taxation, and £3 000 after taxation.

(10) Corporation Tax 52%, payable nine months after the year-end. Basic rate of income tax 30%.

(11) All computations are to be made to the nearest £1 000.

A. Cert. A. Advanced Financial Accounting, June 1983.

14.4   The following balances have been extracted from the books of the company for the year ended 30 June 1979:

	£'000
Customs and excise duties (included in the turnover)	160.4
Depreciation charge for the year	13.5
Dividends to ordinary shareholders	6.7
Interest on borrowed money	7.3
Investment income received	6.2
Minority interests in subsidiaries (including dividends 2.5 payable by the subsidiaries)	4.0
Profit retained	16.5
Purchases of plant	120.4
Raw materials and bought-in services used	325.1
Stock and work-in-progress at 30 June 1979	62.7
Turnover (excluding value added tax)	642.7
United Kingdom and overseas corporation tax	15.4
Wages, salaries and retirement benefits	100.0

You are required to:
  (a) **prepare a value added statement for the year ended 30 June 1979, selecting the appropriate items from the list of balances** (9 marks), **and**
  (b) **state the purpose(s) of the value added statement now being presented by many public companies** (5 marks).

(14 marks)

ICAEW PE II, Financial Accounting II, July 1979.

14.5   The consolidated profit and loss account of Value Ltd has been drafted for the year ended 30 June 1982 with supporting notes as set out below:

	£'000	*1982* £'000	£'000
Sales		7 293	
Value Added Tax		432	6 861
Trading profit *(Note 1)*		537	
Deduct:			
Depreciation	71		
Interest *(Note 2)*	40		
		(111)	
Add:			
Investment and rent income *(Note 2)*	12		
Surplus on property disposal	4	16	
Profit before tax		442	
Taxation		105	
Profit after tax		337	
Deduct: (Note 3)			
Foreign currency differences	3		
Extraordinary items	7	10	
		327	
Dividends		141	
Retained profit		£186	

		£'000
Note 1.	Trading profit	
	After charging the following:	
	Directors emoluments	3
	Audit remuneration	1
	Hire of equipment	56
Note 2.	Interest, investment and rent income:	
	Interest paid on bank loans and overdrafts	43
	Interest received	(3)
		40
	Rent from let properties	12

		£'000
Note 3.	Extraordinary items:	
	Surplus on sale and leaseback of properties	8
	Reduction of interest in subsidiary to book value	(15)
		7

Note 4.   Payment to employees for wages and pension contributions totalled
£1 071.

Required:

(a) Prepare a Value Added Statement for the year ended 30 June 1982.

(15 marks)

(b) Select three of the items that appear in a statement of value added and briefly discuss possible alternative methods of disclosing these items within the statement. (10 marks)

(25 marks)

A. Cert. A. Level 2, Advanced Accounting Practice, June 1982.

14.6 There has been increasing concern in recent years that successive accounting standards and statutory requirements have made published financial statements understandable only by accountants and investment analysts and not by one of the groups most concerned, a company's employees.

You are required to:

(a) outline the content (without figures) of two additional statements, not at present required by either Company Law or Accounting Standard, which would be helpful to a company's employees as distinct from its shareholders (9 marks), and

(b) appraise the usefulness of your chosen statements for their intended purposes (5 marks).

(14 marks)

ICAEW Financial Accounting II, December 1983.

15 Accounting Standards I: Assets

Introduction

In this chapter and the following two chapters we will discuss a number of additional problems of accounting. We will do so by examining the various elements of a balance sheet and the associated treatment in the profit and loss account. In this chapter we concentrate on assets. In the second chapter (16), we look at accounting for leases and hire purchase contracts. In the third chapter (17) we look at liabilities, post balance sheet events, contingencies, extraordinary items and prior year adjustments.

All of the problems covered have been addressed by accounting standards and we shall focus more closely than in previous chapters on the approaches adopted by the particular standards. We will assume that readers have access to Statements of Standard Accounting Practice and Exposure Drafts and will only quote from these documents when we feel it will be helpful.

Fixed assets and depreciation

We will concentrate in this section on the problems associated with accounting for fixed assets and depreciation under the historical cost system. The treatment of these items under current cost accounting (CCA) was discussed in Chapter 6.

The determination of cost

An accounting standard (SSAP 12) has been issued on the subject of depreciation, but there is no UK standard on the subjet of how the cost of a fixed asset should be determined.[1] It may be thought

---

1 IAS 16, 'Accounting for property, plant and equipment', covers this topic as well as a number of other matters concerned with fixed assets.

that this is not surprising, as the determination of the historical cost of a fixed asset is not generally a difficult task. Further reflection, however, would suggest that there are numerous instances of cases where the cost of a fixed asset cannot be determined with exactitude.

Where a company purchases a business or shares in a subsidiary company, the collection of assets and liabilities acquired will invariably include fixed assets. The determination of the cost of these fixed assets for the accounts or consolidated accounts requires an allocation of the global cost to the individual assets and liabilities to be identified in the accounting system. To perform this allocation, accountants have recourse to that poorly defined concept 'fair value' and, at 1 January 1985, the ASC had a working party considering the preparation of a Statement of Recommended Practice on 'fair value in the context of acquisition accounting'.

Concentrating on the determination of the cost of an individual asset, perhaps the most common problem is the identification of the total cost incurred in establishing the asset in the location and condition required for it to provide service. Very often only the major identifiable costs, such as the cost of purchase of the asset and the costs of transportation and installation, are recorded, with other incidental costs being ignored on the grounds of materiality. There will, however, be cases where the additional costs are material and the determination of the cost of the asset for balance sheet purposes will be a difficult task.

Considerable uncertainty surrounds the question of whether interest costs should be capitalized where the asset (usually a building) is paid for in advance, often by a series of progress payments. The debate about whether or not interest should be capitalized is often conducted with a fervour reminiscent of the more extreme mediaeval religious conflicts, but the basic point is, however, extremely simple. The only point at issue is when interest should be charged to the profit and loss account. If interest is not capitalized interest will be charged over the life of the loan, while if it is capitalized the interest which is associated with the sums paid in advance will be charged to the profit and loss account over the life of the asset as part of the depreciation expense. On balance the authors would support the capitalization of interest on the grounds of consistency. The rationale for this view can best be demonstrated by the use of a simple example.

Assume that the client, A Limited, is offered the following choice by the builder, B Limited: 'The building will take 2 years to construct, you can either pay £1.0 million now or £1.2 million in 2 years time.'

If A Limited decides to select the first option it may well have to borrow the money on which it will have to pay interest. If A Limited selects the second option it will still have to pay interest, but in this case the interest will be included in the price paid to B Limited.

The above example is extreme, but it does highlight the principles involved. If we assume that both companies have to pay the same interest rate, then A Limited will be in exactly the same position at the end of 2 years whatever option is selected, and it does not seem sensible to suggest that the cost of the building is different because in one case the interest is paid directly by the client while in the second case the interest is paid via the builder.[2]

A fixed asset may be acquired for a consideration other than cash. The consideration may be goods – as part of a barter deal – or the issue of shares. In such cases the cost of the asset acquired is usually taken to be the current value of the asset exchanged, i.e. the price that could have been obtained if the goods were sold or shares issued for cash. The problems associated with the estimation of these amounts have been discussed earlier in this book in the sections concerned with CCA and the valuation of securities.

Finally we should mention the subject of assets constructed by the business for its own use (self-constructed assets). In general the cost of such assets should be determined in the same way as the cost of finished goods, which is the subject of a later section of this chapter. As will be seen in that section, it is impossible, even if it is desirable, to lay down specific rules about the treatment of overheads, and thus the cost of self-constructed assets would be subject to considerable variation depending on the methods used. One difference between finished goods and self-constructed assets is that in the former any 'errors' will generally be reversed in the next accounting period, while in the case of the self-constructed assets the effect of any errors will be retained in the accounting system for a much longer period. Thus if a 'self-constructed asset' is 'overvalued' the profit for the year of construction will be overstated. The consequence is that future depreciation charges will be overstated, but the 'excess profit' will not be totally eliminated until the asset is fully written off.

2 Readers who wish to study this topic in greater depth are referred to C. P. Rickwood, *Accounting treatment of capitalised interest*, Certified Bulletin, Association of Certified Accountants, London, 1983.

Depreciation

We will now turn to the question of depreciation, which is the subject of SSAP 12. This was issued in December 1977 and relates solely to the historical cost system. The ASC subsequently published a review of SSAP 12[3] as part of its programme of updating standards and reference will be made to this document in the course of this section.

The following definition is provided by the standard: 'Depreciation is a measure of the wearing out, consumption or other loss of value of a fixed asset whether arising from use, effluxion of time or obsolescence through technology and market changes' (SSAP 12, Para. 1).

This definition is acceptable as a description of the total depreciation charge over the life of a fixed asset, i.e. the difference between the value (the cost) of the asset on the date on which it is was acquired and the value (the sales proceeds) at the date of disposal. It is not, however, an adequate description of the annual depreciation process in the historical cost system, as with this system the annual depreciation charge does not generally represent a 'loss of value' if value is interpreted to mean any measure of economic worth. This is recognized by the ASC because the second sentence in the opening paragraph of SSAP 12 states, 'Depreciation should be allocated to accounting periods so as to charge a fair proportion to each accounting period during the expected life of the asset'.

There are, of course, a number of standard depreciation methods (with which we will assume readers are familiar), but the standard does not refer to the methods or give any but the vaguest guidance about the relative merits of the methods or the circumstances in which they should be used. The standard simply states that:

> The management of a business has a duty to allocate depreciation as fairly as possible to periods expected to benefit from the use of the asset and should select the method regarded as most appropriate to the type of asset and its use in the business. (SSAP 12, Para. 7)

It is unfortunate that the ASC did not feel that it was able to provide more specific guidance about the criteria that should be employed in selecting the accounting policy for depreciation. The depreciation charge may be one of the largest expense items in the profit and loss account of a company, particularly one which operates in a capital intensive industry. If the profit figure is to have any meaning, the choice of depreciation policy must be justifiable as something more than a random selection from a number of standard depreciation methods.

3 *A Review of SSAP 12 – Accounting for Depreciation*, ASC, London, 1982.

Although it would have been helpful to have some guidance on the choice of depreciation method, the omission of such guidance is really not surprising. Professor Arthur Thomas has argued very persuasively that the choice of depreciation method, like many other accounting allocations, must be arbitrary.[4] The need for depreciation rests upon the accruals concept and this requires, *inter alia*, the matching of costs against revenues. The revenues of virtually every business arise from the joint use of a number of assets, both tangible and intangible, and it follows that it will usually be impossible to determine how much of the total revenue is produced by one particular fixed asset. If it is impossible to determine the revenues produced by a particular fixed asset then it is impossible to select a depreciation policy which matches cost against those revenues.

One response to this difficulty would be to develop an accounting system which does not involve the use of arbitrary allocations,[5] but such an approach has not found favour with accountants. The alternative is to continue to make allocations, such as depreciation, but to recognize that there is no perfect answer. Rather, that it may be useful to find a method of reporting which provides a reasonable reflection of the underlying reality.

SSAP 12 is concerned both with the accounting treatment of depreciation and with its disclosure. We will deal with certain aspects of accounting treatment first.

Depreciation of buildings
Prior to the publication of SSAP 12 many companies did not provide depreciation on buildings. It was argued that the buildings appreciated in value and that this appreciation, which was generally not recorded in the balance sheet, more than offset the omitted depreciation charge. SSAP 12 lays down the principle that depreciation should be provided in respect of all assets which have a finite life and the only asset which does not need to be depreciated is freehold land which is not subject to depletion by the extraction of minerals, etc. The ASC did not justify its position, but it is likely that it would argue that the netting off of two figures of different amounts does not allow the accounts to show a 'true and fair view'. If managers wish to show the effect of

4 Arthur L. Thomas, *The Allocation Problem in Financial Accounting Theory*, Studies in Accounting Research no. 3, AAA, 1969.
5 One such system is CoCoA, Continuously Contemporary Accounting, which has been advocated by Professor Ray Chambers.

the appreciation of assets they should do so by revaluing the asset and then charge depreciation on the basis of the revalued amount.

The provision relating to buildings was fiercely contested by property companies whose profits would, of course, be substantially reduced if they had to provide for depreciation on their buildings. It was argued that the profits of property companies would be distorted if depreciation were charged to the profit and loss account while the surpluses on revaluation had, under the provisions of SSAP 6 ('Extraordinary items and prior year adjustments'), to be credited to reserves.

The ASC's response (which may, according to taste, be described as reflecting the committee's weakness or flexibility) was to allow property companies exemption from this provision and this exemption was confirmed with the issue, in 1981, of SSAP 19, 'Accounting for investment properties', which specified the conditions under which depreciation need not be charged with respect to properties held as investments (*see* page 579).

Changes in estimates of asset lives
The standard provides that, 'Where there is a revision of the estimated useful life of an asset, the unamortized cost should be charged over the revised remaining life' (Para. 17).

The purpose of this provision was to standardize practice in a way which accords with the accruals concept. Prior to the implementation of SSAP 12 some companies used an alternative method of accounting for a change in the estimate of the useful remaining life of the asset. With the alternative method an adjustment was made in the year in which the estimate was changed so that the asset's net book value was made equal to the figure which would have been shown had the asset been depreciated *ab initio* on the basis of the revised estimate. This is best illustrated by means of an example.

Suppose that a fixed asset was purchased for £12 000 on 1 January 19X0 and was depreciated over 10 years on a straight line basis, assuming a zero scrap value. The net book value of the asset at 31 December 19X3 (the end of the accounting period) would hence be six-tenths of £12 000, i.e. £7200. Assume that, at the end of 19X4, in the course of preparing the accounts for 19X4, it is decided that the asset will only last for another 3 years, i.e. the revised estimate of the total life of the asset is 8 years.

With the method specified in SSAP 12 the asset would be written down from £7200 (its net book value at 1 January 19X4) to zero over

4 years. Thus the new annual depreciation charge would be £1800 and the net book value at 31 December 19X4 would be £5400.

Under the rejected method the net book value of the asset at 31 December 19X4 would be three-eighths of £12000, i.e. £4500, and the annual depreciation charge for 19X4 would be £2700, while in 19X5 and subsequent years it would be £1500.

In the 1982 *Review* document support was given to the method specified in SSAP 12 for dealing with changes in the estimates of asset lives. However, the suggestion was made that if the correction of an erroneous estimate of the life of an asset is such as to distort materially the results of subsequent periods, then use could be made of the 'fundamental error' provision of SSAP 6 which would allow the results for a previous year to be restated. If this provision was included in a revised SSAP 12 a possible consequence would be a return to the situation of diversity in the way in which accountants deal with the problem.

In its review the ASC drew attention to the suggestion that in the context of historical cost accounting, many companies deliberately underestimated the lives of assets in order to show a higher depreciation charge. This was a crude way of overcoming one of the defects of historical cost accounting but as was pointed out in the *Review* this practice meant that depreciation was not charged fairly to the periods which benefited from the use of the assets and, as a result, many assets were still in use which had been fully depreciated.

The advent of CCA led some companies to review their estimates of asset lives and in some instances longer lives were assumed for the current cost accounts than for the historical cost accounts for the same period. The working party responsible for the review could find no logical reason for this and suggested that SSAP 12 should be revised to make it clear that the same realistic asset lives should be used for the same assets in both the historical and current cost accounts.

In the case of fully depreciated assets which are still in use the working party suggests that there should be a reassessment of the asset lives which should be reflected in the accounts thus ensuring that a depreciation charge is made in respect of all assets still in use.

Change in the method of depreciation
The standard requires that the same treatment as is employed where there is a change in the estimate of an asset life should be used where there is a change in the method of depreciation. Paragraph 19 states

Where there is a change from one method of depreciation to another, the unamortised cost of the asset should be written off over the remaining useful life on the new basis commencing with the period in which the change is made. The effect should be disclosed in the year of change, if material.

Changes in the book value of assets

If an asset is revalued the depreciation charge should be based on the revalued amount and, in the year in which the revaluation is made, the depreciation charges on the original and revalued amounts should be given (SSAP 12, Para. 9).

An asset should be written down if its net book value exceeds its *recoverable* amount. The standard does not give any guidance on how the recoverable amount should be evaluated. It is, of course, established that if the business can be regarded as being a going concern then the recoverable amount is not necessarily the same as the net realizable value. Thus it is acceptable for fixed assets to be stated in the balance sheet at an amount in excess of their net realizable value.

In general an asset's recoverable value will fall when it has become obsolescent or when there is a decline in the profitability of the business for which the asset is used. The estimation of recoverable value is difficult in either case, but it is especially difficult in the latter case because of the need to relate the effect of a general decline in profitability to individual assets.

There is no difference in principle between the writing down of an asset to its recoverable amount in the historical cost system and the recognition of a permanent diminution in the value of an asset under CCA; thus the considerations discussed in Chapter 6 will also be appropriate to this aspect of the historical cost system.

Disclosure

Depreciation is a very subjective figure which is heavily influenced by the methods used and estimates made by the business. Thus, in order to help users interpret financial statements and compare the results of companies which use different methods, SSAP 12 calls for the disclosure of more detailed information than is required by the Companies Acts. The standard requires that the following should be disclosed for each major class of depreciable asset:

(a) the depreciation methods used;
(b) the useful lives or the depreciation rates used;
(c) total depreciation allocated for the period;
(d) the gross amount of depreciable assets and the related accumulated depreciation.

(SSAP 12, Para. 21)

Investment properties

In response to the criticisms of the initial requirement that all companies should depreciate buildings, the ASC modified its position as evidenced by the issue in November 1981 of SSAP 19, 'Accounting for investment properties', to deal with the particular problem of properties which are not held for consumption as part of the business's operations but as investments. It was argued that, for the proper appreciation of the position of the enterprise, it was of prime importance for users of the accounts to be aware of the current value of the investment properties and the changes in their values which precludes the necessity to calculate a systematic depreciation charge. For this purpose investment properties are defined as an interest in land and/or buildings:

(a) in respect of which construction work and development have been completed; and
(b) which is held for its investment potential, any rental income being negotiated at arm's length.

The following are specifically excluded from the definition:

(a) A property which is owned and occupied by a company for its own purposes is not an investment property.
(b) A property let to and occupied by another group company is not an investment property for the purposes of its own accounts or the group accounts.

In outline the standard specifies:

(i) That investment properties should not be subject to a depreciation charge as otherwise required by SSAP 12 except that properties held on a lease which should be depreciated on the basis set out in SSAP 12 at least over the period when the unexpired term is 20 years or less. In other words leaseholds with more than 20 years to run can be depreciated whilst other leases must be depreciated.

(ii) Investment properties should be included in the balance sheet at their 'open market value'. The phrase 'open market value' is not defined in the standard but given that one of the objectives of the standard is to show changes in the value of assets held as investments, it would seem reasonable to suppose that the phrase is intended to mean the value the property would fetch, net of expenses, if sold on the open market. The bases of valuation should be disclosed in a note to the accounts (see (v) below).

   (iii) Changes in the value of investment properties should be shown as a movement on an investment revaluation reserve, unless a deficit on revluation exceeds the balance on the reserve in which case the deficit should be charged to the profit and loss account.[6]

   (iv) The value of the investment properties and of the investment revaluation reserve should be displayed prominently in the financial statements.

   (v) The names of the persons making the valuation, or particulars of their qualification, should be disclosed together with the bases of valuation used by them. If a person making a valuation is an employee or officer of the company or group which owns the property this fact should be disclosed.

Adherence to the provisions of SSAP 19 will, in the case of buildings, represent a departure from the specific requirement of the Companies Act 1981[7] that any fixed asset, which has a limited useful economic life, should be depreciated.

In justifying this departure the ASC draws attention to Sec. 1 of the Companies Act 1981 which states that the need to give a true and fair view in the financial statement overrides any particular specific requirement of the Act. The ASC believe that the treatment of investment properties required by SSAP 19 represents an example of a situation where the use of a method other than that specified in the Companies Act will more closely adhere to the overriding requirement of the disclosure of a true and fair view. In such circumstances the accounts must include a statement giving particulars of the departure from the specific requirements of the Act with the reasons for and effect of the departure.[8]

Not everyone would agree with the stance taken by the ASC in so far that it can be argued that a far fuller picture would be disclosed if, as under the provisions of SSAP 16, both the increase in value and the amount of the value that has been consumed by the passage of time are disclosed in the accounts.

---

6 There are exceptions for certain specialized types of enterprises. In the case of pension funds and the long-term business of insurance companies, changes in value are dealt with in the relevant fund account while investment trust companies and property unit trusts need not charge deficits to the profit and loss account. It should also be mentioned that the whole of the statement does not apply to charities.

7 Paragraph 18, 1st Schedule, Companies Act 1981.

8 Section 1(4), Companies Act 1981.

The accounting treatment of Government grants

It is convenient to discuss the accounting treatment of Government grants at this stage because the topic is closely related to the question of how one should account for fixed assets and depreciation. The topic is the subject matter of SSAP 4, 'The accounting treatment of Government grants' which was issued in 1974 following the passing of the Industry Act 1972 which, *inter alia*, regulated the award of regional development grants. It is pointed out in SSAP 4 that the Industry Act 1972 provides for grants related to both revenue expenditure and capital expenditure. The revenue related grants, according to SSAP 4, do not produce accounting problems 'as they clearly should be credited to revenue in the same period in which the revenue expenditure to which they relate is charged' (SSAP 4, Para. 2).

The very short SSAP 4 therefore concentrates on the treatment of capital-based grants and identifies three possible alternative methods.

(a) The total grant should be credited immediately to the profit and loss account.
(b) The total grant should be credited to a non-distributable reserve.
(c) The grant should be credited to the profit and loss account over the useful life of the asset concerned. This objective can be achieved by either:
  (i) reducing the cost of acquisition of the fixed asset by the amount of the grant thus reducing the depreciation to be charged on the asset so that the total grant will be credited to the profit and loss account when the asset is fully depreciated, or,
  (ii) treating the grant as a deferred credit, a portion of which is transferred to the profit and loss account each year over the life of the asset. (Although the point is not mentioned in SSAP 4 it would be logical to transfer the credit to the profit and loss account in a manner which is consistent with the selected method of depreciation.)

The third of the above methods is chosen on the following grounds:

Methods (a) and (b) provide no correlation between the accounting treatment of the grant and the accounting treatment of the expenditure to which the grant relates. Method (c) matches the application of the grant with the amortisation of the capital expenditure to which it relates and is therefore considered to be the most appropriate treatment. (SSAP 4, Para. 5)

This cannot be regarded as very convincing for it says little more than 'The third method is the best and the others must be rejected because they are different'. Why should the accounting treatment of the grant correlate with the treatment of the capital expenditure? While it is difficult (but not impossible) to make a case for method (a), a strong case can be made for method (b). A company acquires its finance to purchase its assets from a number of sources; a situation which is portrayed in any balance sheet which shows the assets of an enterprise and their sources – owners' equity and creditors. It can be argued that the government in providing grants is a third source of funds and that to credit the grant to a non-distributable reserve would reflect this economic reality. The counter argument which can be used to support the position adopted in SSAP 4 is that the government's intention in providing grants is to encourage investment by reducing the cost of using assets and that the gradual transfer of the grant to the profit and loss account over the life of the asset reflects the lower cost. In the view of the authors the argument is more evenly balanced than is implied by SSAP 4 and it is unfortunate that the alternatives were not discussed more fully.

The standard itself requires that method (c) be used, but allows either of the two alternative methods of presentation. If grants are treated as deferred credits the balance on the account should, if material, be shown separately in the balance sheet where it must not be included as part of shareholders' funds.

The main argument in favour of crediting the grant to fixed asset account is simplicity. The statement points out the advantages of the alternative method of presentation (the use of a deferred credit). The main one is that assets which are acquired at different times and locations are recorded on a uniform basis regardless of changes in government policy. It is pointed out that 'such comparability is often important to management in establishing price structures and investment policies' (SSAP 4, Para. 7).[9] Given the strength of the arguments advanced in favour of the use of the deferred credit alternative it is somewhat surprising that the other method is also permitted.

Investment grants and CCA

This topic is dealt with in Paras 60–62 of the guidance notes to SSAP 16.[10] The basic principle is that the current rates and availability of grants should be taken into account in the preparation of current cost accounts. Thus, if the grant is credited to the fixed asset account the gross current replacement cost of an asset will be stated after the deduction of available grants. This will be done automatically if an index is applied to the original net of grant historical cost of an asset but

---

9 It could be argued that the view that the total cost of the asset should be shown in the accounts seems rather more consistent with the argument that the grants should be credited to a non-distributable reserve.

10 Guidance notes on SSAP 16, 'Current cost accounting', ASC, 1980.

this method should only be used if there has been no change in the rates and conditions applying to the grant. If the deferred credit approach is used the balance on the account will need to be adjusted, probably by use of an index, so that the net charge to the current cost profit and loss will be the same as under the alternative approach. If grants are material the treatment adopted in the current cost accounts should be disclosed.

Intangible assets

Introduction

Accountants describe certain assets as intangible and, although it is difficult to develop a precise definition of this term, its meaning is well understood to encompass such capital assets as deferred research and development expenditure, goodwill and patents. Like tangible assets, these intangible assets have value because they are expected to produce future benefits for the entity. It would seem to follow that, in principle, the same accounting treatment should be applied to both tangible and intangible assets. If an entity purchases an intangible asset, this should be treated in the same way as a purchase of a tangible asset. Similarly, if a firm incurs expenditure to develop an intangible asset, such as research knowledge or a trained workforce, this should be treated in the same way as expenditure on the construction of a fixed asset.[11]

The main feature which characterizes intangible assets is the high degree of uncertainty about the future benefits which they will generate. Such benefits will, in any case, be generated jointly with other assets, so that it is extremely difficult to identify revenues, which is, of course, necessary to be able to apply the accruals concept. An additional problem under a system of CCA is the difficulty of determining replacement cost for what is often a unique asset.

The existence of this high level of uncertainty about the future benefits of a particular intangible asset gives rise to a conflict between two of the fundamental accounting concepts of SSAP 2. On the one hand, the accruals concept requires the matching of costs with appropriate

11 It is necessary to qualify the above statements. Although many accountants would agree with the principles expressed here, others would argue that a balance sheet should only include assets which are legally owned by the firm. If this view is taken it follows that, as many intangible assets are not legally owned, they should not be included as assets in the balance sheet.

revenues whilst, on the other hand, the prudence convention requires expenditure to be written off in the period in which it arises, unless its relationship to the revenue of a future period can be established with reasonable certainty. Thus, where an intangible asset is acquired or created, the accruals concept would require the capitalization of its cost and subsequent amortization or depreciation but, given that the future benefits are usually very uncertain, the prudence concept would require the expenditure to be written off. SSAP 2 is quite clear that where there is a conflict between the accruals concept and the prudence concept, the latter is to prevail.[12] With this conflict in mind we shall examine the accounting treatment of two intangible assets; first, research and development and then goodwill.

Accounting for research and development

Many organizations spend large sums of money on research and development in the hope that, by incurring such expenditure, future profits will be higher than they otherwise would be. In other words they incur expenditure on research and development in the expectation of creating an intangible asset which will yield benefits in the future. By the very nature of the process, some research and development activities will be unsuccessful and hence no asset will be created. Any expenditure on such projects must certainly be written off against profits of the year in which it is incurred. Other research projects will be successful and will result in the creation of an asset. Under historical cost accounting such an asset should be capitalized at an appropriate figure[13] and written off against profits of the periods in which benefits are expected to arise.

The accounting treatment proposed above seems quite clear, but two major problems arise as soon as an attempt is made to apply it. First, even where a project appears to have been successful, the size and timing of future benefits are often very uncertain; if such is the case the prudence convention would appear to require the expenditure to be written off. Second, the people who must make the decision on whether or not the research and development has been successful are not independent of the entity but are the directors who are interested in the outcome of the research and development. Because of their involvement, such directors may be susceptible to bias, either innocent or fraudulent, and, in view of the uncertainties involved, it

12 SSAP 2, Para. 14(b).
13 The appropriate figure will be cost or, if lower, the recoverable amount.

may be extremely difficult for an auditor to challenge the views of the directors.

In view of the difficulty and controversial nature of this topic, it is not surprising that the ASC issued two Exposure Drafts befôre issuing SSAP 13, 'Accounting for research and development'.[14] Let us see how the problem was tackled in the early Exposure Draft and how it has subsequently been resolved in SSAP 13.

ED 14, like its successors, followed the definition of research and development adopted by the Organization for Economic Co-operation and Development. This defines research and development expenditure as expenditure falling into one or more of the following broad categories:

(a) Pure (or basic) research: original investigation undertaken to gain new scientific or technical knowledge and understanding. Basic research is not primarily directed towards any specific practical aim or application.

(b) Applied research: original investigation undertaken in order to gain new scientific or technical knowledge and directed towards a specific practical aim or objective.

(c) Development: the use of scientific or technical knowledge in order to produce new or substantially improved materials, devices, products, processes, systems or services.

Although the Exposure Draft recognized that it might be possible to evaluate the future benefits to be produced by expenditure on development in certain circumstances, it ultimately proposed that research and development expenditure under all three categories should be written off and disclosed in the accounts for the year in which the expenditure was incurred.[15] Clearly the prudence convention triumphed in ED 14!

Although this approach may be simply applied and removes the need for judgement on the part of directors and auditors, many people would argue that it makes little economic sense. To take just one example, we may think of two similar companies which have spent an identical amount on research and development. The efforts of one company

---

14 The Exposure Drafts were: ED 14, 'Accounting for research and development' (January 1975) and ED 17, 'Accounting for research and development (revised)' (April 1976). The Statement of Standard Accounting Practice was issued in December 1977.

15 Exceptions were as follows: (a) expenditure incurred in locating and exploiting mineral deposits in the extractive industries (this was outside the scope of the Exposure Draft); (b) research and development expenditure reimbursible under a contract with a third party (this is in the nature of work in progress); (c) expenditure on fixed assets (such assets should be depreciated in the normal way and only the depreciation included as part of the expenditure on research and development).

have been successful whilst the efforts of the other company have not been successful. If both companies are required to write off all research and development expenditure as it is incurred then this essential difference between the two companies is not apparent from an examination of their accounts. An important element of business reality does not feature in the accounts.

The subsequent ED 17 and SSAP 13 took a somewhat less rigid approach to that of their predecessor. If we concentrate on the provisions of the standard, then (subject to the exceptions mentioned in footnote 15 on page 585) this now requires companies to write off all expenditure on pure and applied research as it is incurred. In this respect it is no different from ED 14. However, unlike ED 14, it permits certain development expenditure to be capitalized and carried forward to be matched against future revenues.[16]

The adoption of this permissive approach introduces the possibility of bias on the part of directors, who must decide whether or not an asset exists on a balance sheet date. In order to reduce this bias to a minimum, the standard proceeds to list the following conditions which must be satisfied before development expenditure may be carried forward: [17]

(a) there is a clearly defined project, and
(b) the related expenditure is separately identifiable, and
(c) the outcome of such a project has been assessed with reasonable certainty as to:
  (i) its technical feasibility, and
  (ii) its ultimate commercial viability considered in the likely market conditions (including competing products), public opinion, consumer and environmental legislation, and
(d) if further development costs are to be incurred on the same project, the aggregate of such costs together with related production, selling and administration costs are reasonably expected to be more than covered by related future revenues, and
(e) adequate resources exist, or are reasonably expected to be available, to enable the project to be completed and to provide any consequential increases in working capital.

The prudence convention is no longer the outright winner in SSAP 13, but it still has the upper hand and development expenditure may only be carried forward if the above, rather stringent conditions, are met.

16 Notice that SSAP 13 *permits* development expenditure to be carried forward where certain conditions are satisfied whilst ED 17 *required* development expenditure to be carried forward in those same circumstances.
17 SSAP 13, Para. 21.

In order to facilitate interpretation, the standard requires that the notes to the accounts contain a clear explanation of the accounting policy followed although this would, in any case, be required under the provisions of SSAP 2. It also requires the disclosure of movements on deferred development expenditure together with details of the balance at the beginning and end of the period.[18] Unlike ED 14 and the International Accounting Standard (IAS) 9, which both require such disclosure,[19] SSAP 13 does not require disclosure of the total cost of research and development charged to profit and loss account in each period. This would seem to be an important omission and makes it difficult for users to assess the adequacy of the company's research effort. The omission is defended on two grounds. First, the difficulty of defining research and development precisely makes it likely that figures disclosed by different companies would not be comparable. Second, it is argued that, if such information becomes available to competitors, it may damage the future interests of the company. It may be noted that similar arguments have been frequently rehearsed when there have been proposals for an extension of accounting disclosure, even though we now accept that extended disclosure as commonplace.

The Companies Act 1981 has, of course, been passed since SSAP 13 was issued. It requires that costs of research are charged to the profit and loss account but permits the carrying forward of development costs 'in special circumstances'.[20] Satisfaction of the criteria for the deferral of development expenditure in SSAP 13 is now generally accepted as providing the 'special circumstances' referred to in the Act.

The Act specifically requires that notes to the accounts explain why expenditure has been capitalized and the period over which the costs are being written off.[21]

Goodwill

Goodwill is the term used by accountants to describe the difference between the value placed upon a firm and the sum of the values of the individual net assets of that firm which are identified and recorded separately in the accounting system. If we think in terms of traditional

---

18 SSAP 13, Para. 27.
19 ED 14, 'Accounting for research and development', Para. 19, and IAS 9, 'Accounting for research and development activities', Para. 23.
20 Companies Act 1981, Schedule 1, Paras 3(2)(c) and 20(1).
21 Companies Act 1981, Schedule 1, Para. 20(2).

historical cost accounts, there would seem to be three reasons why the value of the firm will rarely be equal to the sum of the values of the individual net assets which are traditionally identified and included in a balance sheet. First, there is the obvious reason that the amounts at which individual assets are disclosed in a traditional balance sheet are based upon historical cost rather than current value. Second, most firms possess not only the predominantly tangible assets listed in a balance sheet but also such intangible assets as 'managerial ability', 'efficient staff' and 'regional monopoly' which contribute to the value of the firm and yet do not appear in a balance sheet. Third, there is the simple economic fact that assets operating together often have a much higher value than the sum of the values of those same assets operating separately.

Goodwill is usually only recorded in an accounting system when a company purchases another firm or acquires a subsidiary and prepares consolidated accounts. In the former case the goodwill arises in the accounting system of the purchasing company itself whilst, in the latter case, the goodwill arises only in the consolidated accounts. In both cases the goodwill is described as 'purchased goodwill' to distinguish it from internally generated goodwill.

In the past, goodwill has often been calculated as the difference between the price paid and the sum of the book values of the individually identified assets less liabilities in the books of the acquired firm or company. Although this may simplify calculations, it makes little economic sense as the values in the books of the acquired firm or company are irrelevant in determining the historical cost of assets to the acquiring company or group. In accounting for an acquisition it is essential for the acquiring company or group to value the individual assets and liabilities at their fair values, which determine their historical cost to the acquiring company or group.[22] Thus the total cost of the collection of net assets, tangible and intangible, must be apportioned between those assets and liabilities which are to be identified separately in the accounting system and those which are not so identified. The latter group are recorded in the accounting system as a balancing figure which is described as goodwill. Such goodwill will normally be positive

---

22 *See* SSAP 14, Para. 29, which requires the use of fair values when a subsidiary is acquired, and SSAP 1, Para. 26(a), which requires a similar treatment in the case of an associated company. As at 1 January 1985 the ASC had a working party considering the publication of a Statement of Recommended Practice on 'Fair value in the context of acquisition accounting'.

but SSAP 22 takes the view that it may be negative.[23] This may occur when the price paid for the collection of net assets is less than the sum of the fair values of the separable net assets. The standard warns us that, where negative goodwill appears, the amounts allocated to the separable net assets should be reviewed to ensure that their fair values have not been overstated.

Internally created goodwill is not recorded, while goodwill which results from a market transaction is. It is therefore important to recognize that when a goodwill figure appears in a set of accounts, it does not relate to the whole reporting entity but merely to one segment which has been acquired by purchase.[24] Once the purchase has been made that segment will usually be merged with the other assets of the enlarged entity and may, indeed, no longer be separately identifiable.

With this background we may proceed to examine the problem of accounting for goodwill, assuming for the most part that the goodwill figure is positive.

At the date of acquisition, goodwill represents the cost of acquiring certain intangible assets. As such is the case, the accruals concept would seem to dictate that the cost should be carried forward and matched against revenues of the periods expected to benefit from the use of such intangible assets. However, the future benefits may be extremely uncertain and there may be no way of determining which benefits arise from the particular collection of intangible assets. Hence the prudence convention would appear to suggest that no asset should be recognized, rather that the amount paid for goodwill should be written off.

Given that there is a conflict between fundamental accounting conventions, it is not surprising to find that various methods of accounting for goodwill have been proposed. If we ignore the impractical suggestions that goodwill for the whole entity be revalued on each balance sheet date, the various proposals may be summarized as follows:

(a) Retain goodwill at cost, unless there is a permanent fall in the value.

(b) Write off (amortize) the cost of goodwill over a period of years,

---

23 SSAP 22, 'Accounting for goodwill', ASC, London, December 1984, Para. 8. Some accountants would not admit this possibility, arguing that the price paid must place a ceiling on the sum of the 'costs' of the separable net assets.

24 An exception to this general position occurs when the net assets of one firm are purchased by a newly formed entity. An example is the conversion of a sole tradership or partnership into a limited company. Providing the limited company acquires only the net assets of the firm and owns no other assets, the goodwill figure will relate to the whole business.

which could be (i) its useful life, or (ii) a specific number of years, or (iii) its useful life subject to a maximum number of years.

(c) Write off goodwill immediately against reserves.

Some writers have argued that, in view of the unique nature of goodwill, the amount under (a) or (b) should appear, not as an asset, but as a 'dangling debit', that is as a deduction from share capital and reserves. This treatment can be regarded as a 'half-hearted' adoption of options (a) or (b) in that the information is provided but in such a way as to cast doubt upon its relevance. Whilst some companies have, in the past, adopted the approach, this method of disclosure is no longer permissible following the Companies Act 1981.

Let us look at each of the proposals in turn.

The retention of goodwill at cost would only seem to be justified if the asset has an indefinite life. It is expected that this would rarely be true in the case of the particular intangible assets purchased, although the purchased benefits may, of course, be replaced by subsequent activities. If the intangible assets acquired do not have an indefinite life, it is necessary to recognize the possibility of a fall in value of goodwill, but the determination of whether or not such a permanent fall has occurred will be an extremely difficult, if not impossible, task. It will certainly be impossible where the segment of the business which gave rise to the goodwill is no longer separately identifiable.

The amortization of goodwill over a period of years is also subject to difficulties. In the first case, it is usually impossible to determine the useful life of goodwill. In the second case, the selection of a specific number of years such as 5 or 40 is merely arbitrary, although the selection of a long period has the advantage that the results of no one period are significantly affected. The third case merely combines the impossibility of the first with the arbitrariness of the second.

The third proposal recognizes that, after the year of acquisition, the retention of a goodwill figure relating to part of the business is unlikely to provide information useful to those interested in the affairs of the entity. It therefore requires its removal from the balance sheet by a write-off immediately against reserves.

In view of the different proposals which have been made and their associated problems, it is not surprising that the ASC has experienced some difficulty in deciding upon an appropriate standard accounting practice.

Whereas the discussion paper, issued in June 1980, favoured the amortization of goodwill, ED 30, issued in October 1982, permitted a choice from two methods. Under that proposal, goodwill could be amortized through the profit and loss account on a systematic basis over its estimated useful economic life or written off immediately on acquisition directly against reserves. Either practice was considered equally acceptable.

By the time SSAP 22 was issued, in October 1984, the ASC had moved a long way from the tentative proposal in the 1980 Discussion Paper. Given the difficulties of estimating the useful economic life of goodwill, it is not surprising that SSAP 22 now favours the immediate write-off of goodwill to reserves. What is perhaps surprising is that the standard still permits the amortization of goodwill on a systematic basis over its useful economic life.[25] The authors find it difficult to comprehend how, in general, directors can possibly forecast the economic life of goodwill, a residual category of net assets measured by a balancing figure! In our view, any figures produced by applying such a policy are likely to be of dubious significance to any user of accounts.

Where negative goodwill arises, SSAP 22 requires that it be credited to reserves, a treatment which is consistent with the favoured treatment of positive goodwill. The standard lays down certain disclosure requirements and deals with the transitional problem of the accounting treatment of goodwill included in the balance sheet at the date on which the standard is first implemented; we shall look briefly at each of these.[26]

The standard reiterates the requirement of the law and SSAP 2 that the accounting policy followed for goodwill should be explained and specifically draws attention to the need to disclose the effect of adopting different accounting policies for goodwill existing at the date of implementing the standard (see below) and any other goodwill. It requires the separate disclosure of the amount of goodwill recognized on each acquisition during the year and, where goodwill is amortized, it requires the disclosure of the movement on goodwill account during the year (which is, of course, required by law) and the period selected for amortizing goodwill relating to each major acquisition. The law also requires

---

25 SSAP 22, Paras 32 and 34. The Companies Act 1981, Schedule 1, Para. 20 requires that, where an individual company treats goodwill as an asset (i.e. does not write it off immediately against reserves), the amount must be amortized systematically over a period chosen by the directors, which must not exceed the useful life of the goodwill.

26 The disclosure requirements are contained in Paras 39–42 while the rules concerning the treatment of existing goodwill are contained in Paras 36–38.

the disclosure of the reason for choosing that particular period.[27]

When the standard is first implemented, it is necessary to decide on the appropriate accounting treatment for any existing balance on a goodwill account. If the preferred policy of SSAP 22 is adopted, then the amount should be written off immediately against reserves. However, this may pose problems, particularly where the balance on goodwill account exceeds the balance of reserves. As a transitional provision, the standard therefore permits the write off of the balance at the date of implementation of the standard over the remaining useful economic life of the goodwill. This is permitted even though the goodwill arising on subsequent acquisitions is written off immediately to reserves.

If the alternative policy of amortization is adopted then the accounting treatment of existing goodwill depends upon what accounting policy has been employed in the past. If the policy has been to amortize goodwill over its useful economic life no change will be necessary. If, however, the goodwill has been retained at cost, it will be necessary to make a prior year adjustment to reflect the amount which would have been charged to profit and loss account using the new accounting policy. The balance should then be amortized over the remaining useful economic life of the goodwill.

Stock and work in progress

Introduction

It used to be said in jest that in drawing up the annual accounts of an enterprise, the first figure to be set down was that of profit, then all the other ascertainable figures, until finally the value of stock emerged as a balancing item. This sentiment is certainly echoed in the introductory remarks to SSAP 9, 'Stocks and work in progress', which was issued in May 1975:

> No area of accounting has produced wider differences in practice than the computation of the amount at which stocks and work in progress are stated in financial accounts. This statement of standard accounting practice seeks to define the practices, to narrow the differences and variation in those practices and to ensure adequate disclosure in the accounts.

---

27 Companies Act 1981, Schedule 1, Para. 21(4). Following the guidance given in Appendix 1 to SSAP 22, the reason will usually be that the period represents the economic life of the goodwill.

SSAP 9, like SSAP 12, relates specifically to historical cost accounting but, again like SSAP 12, it will have some impact on CCA.

SSAP 9 differs from most other statements in that a large proportion of the document is devoted to appendices which deal with practical problems. The ASC was of the view that the problems which arise in this area are of a practical rather than of a theoretical nature. This attitude can be exemplified by the following extract from the introduction to Appendix 1: 'Many of the problems involved in arriving at the amount at which stocks and work in progress are stated in accounts are of a practical nature rather than resulting from matters of principle.'

The statement includes two other appendices: Appendix 2, which consists of a glossary of terms, and Appendix 3, which reproduces a statement from the Board of Inland Revenue which was issued in response to a request for clarification of the Inland Revenue's practice on the publication of SSAP 9.

These appendices are important and need to be studied in their original version rather than in a summary. We will therefore not tempt readers by giving a summary but will instead concentrate on the few, but important, matters of principle which form the subject of SSAP 9. We will assume that readers are familiar with the basic approach to stock valuation and are aware of the different methods which are employed in the historical cost system.

The standard deals with (a) stocks and work in progress and (b) long-term contract work in progress and covers both accounting methods and disclosure. We will commence by discussing the treatment of stocks and work in progress other than long-term contract work in progress. We will quote and then comment on each section of the standard.

Stocks and other than long-term work in progress

> The amount at which stocks and work in progress, other than long-term contract work in progress, is stated in periodic financial statements should be the total of the lower of cost and net realisable value of the separate items of stock and work in progress or of groups of similar items.[28]

This provision can be divided into two parts. One says that the 'normal' basis of stock valuation is cost while the second is concerned with the 'abnormal' circumstances where the stock is to be written down.

To state that in historical cost accounting stock will, subject to the

---

28 SSAP 9, Para. 26.

lower of cost and net realizable value rule, be stated at cost does not take us very far, but as readers will be aware the determination of the cost of stock and work in progress is by no means a simple task and much of the statement, including the appendices, is devoted to the subject. The basic principle is that the cost of stock and work in progress should comprise 'that expenditure which has been incurred in the normal course of business in bringing the product or service to its present location and condition. Such costs *will* [our emphasis] include all related production overheads, even though these may accrue on a time basis.'[29]

The cost of stock and work in progress is to include costs of production and conversion (as defined in the statement). The specification of the treatment of overheads reflects one way in which the standard fulfils its objective of narrowing variations in practice. There has been much debate on the extent to which production overheads should be included in the costing of stock. At one extreme – the variable costing approach – is the view that overhead allocation is by its very nature arbitrary and that stock should be valued by reference to the costs (usually just direct material and labour), which can be directly related to the stock in question. A view which lies between this extreme and the ASC's position is that production overheads which relate to activity rather than time (e.g. cost of power) should be included in the cost of stock. These approaches are rejected by SSAP 9, which requires the inclusion of all production overheads, including those which accrue on a time basis. It appears that this alternative was adopted because the ASC felt that all production overheads, whether or not they arise on a time basis, are required to bring the stock to its 'present location and condition'.

Costs which include time-related production overheads will, all other things being equal, vary with the level of output, e.g. the lower the output the greater the cost of, say, rent per unit. Thus, the statement refers to the need to base the allocation of overheads on the company's normal level of activity.[30] Thus the cost of unused capacity should be written off in the current year. Appendix 1 of SSAP 9 provides some guidance on the question of how the normal level of activity should be determined, but it is clear that judgement will have to play a part in the resolution of this matter.

The ASC specifically rejected the argument that the omission of

---

29 SSAP 9, Para. 3.
30 *See* SSAP 9, Appendix 1, Para. 8.

production overheads can be defended on the grounds of prudence. This emerges from Appendix 1, Para. 10, which states:

The adoption of a conservative approach to the valuation of stocks and work in progress has sometimes been used as one of the reasons for omitting selected production overheads. In so far as the circumstances of the business require an element of prudence in determining the amount at which stocks and work in progress are stated, this needs to be taken into account in the determination of net realisable value and not by the exclusion from cost of selected overheads.

The conventional methods of stock valuation (FIFO, LIFO, etc.) are described in the glossary of terms. The actual standard does not give any guidance about the methods which should be used; but the ASC's view of the principle which should be followed is given in Appendix 1, where it is stated that 'management must exercise judgement to ensure that the methods chosen provide the fairest practicable approximation to "actual cost"'.[31] It can be seen that the ASC placed emphasis on the need to show as accurately as possible the cost of stock and rejected those methods such as LIFO which are used, especially in the United States, to produce a profit figure which approximates to a current cost operating profit.

We will now turn to the methods which must be adopted when stock is to be written down. We will not, however, at this stage refer to the problems of establishing the net realizable value which has been dealt with in Chapter 3.

SSAP 9 requires that stock should be written down to its net realizable value. Prior to the publication of the standard, some companies stated stock at replacement cost where this was lower than net realizable value and cost; this practice was given some support by the ICAEW's Recommendations on Accounting Principles no. 22, *Treatment of stock in trade and work in progress in financial accounts*. The use of replacement cost is rejected in SSAP 9 on the grounds that it may result in the recognition of 'a loss which is greater than that which is expected to be incurred'.[32]

Our final comment on the provisions of SSAP 9, Para. 26 quoted at the beginning of this section, relates to the requirement that the comparison of cost and net realizable value should be on an item by item basis or by reference to groups of similar items. The reason for this is that this provision is given in Para. 2, where it is stated that 'To compare the total realisable value of stocks with the total cost

---

31 SSAP 9, Appendix 1, Para. 12.
32 SSAP 9, Para. 6.

could result in an unacceptable setting off of foreseeable losses against unrealised profits'. In other words the practice contravenes the concept of prudence.

Long-term contract work in progress

We will now consider the next paragraph of the actual standard, which relates to long-term contract work in progress and which states:

> The amount at which long-term contract work in progress is stated in periodic financial statements should be cost plus any attributable profit, less any foreseeable losses and progress payments received and receivable. If, however, anticipated losses on individual contracts exceed cost incurred to date less progress payments received and receivable, such excess should be shown separately as provisions.[33]

The rationale for this provision is provided in Para. 7, which includes the following:

> Owing to the length of time taken to complete such (long-term) contracts, to defer taking profit into account until completion may result in the profit and loss account reflecting not so much a fair view of the activity of the company during the year but rather the results relating to contracts which have been completed by the year end.

This may well be an eminently practical and sensible view, but it does seem to be in conflict with the attitude adopted in SSAP 2, 'Disclosure of accounting policies', where it is stated 'that where the accruals concept is inconsistent with the prudence concept the latter prevails'.[34] The provision of SSAP 9 relating to long-term contracts does appear to suggest that the accruals concept should prevail over prudence.

The provision that attributable profit *should* (not might) be recognized in the financial statements was perhaps the most controversial aspect of SSAP 9. A number of large companies had consistently eschewed the recognition of profit on uncompleted contracts and some continued this practice after the implementation of SSAP 9, accepting the consequential qualifications in their audit reports.

In addition, there would appear to be a conflict between this requirement of SSAP 9 and the legal requirement that only realized profits may be credited to the profit and loss account (See Chapter 3). If attributable profit on long-term contract work in progress is not realized, then it may only be included in the profit and loss account if this is necessary to give a true and fair view. Our use of this true

---

33 SSAP 9, Para. 27.
34 SSAP 2, Para. 14(b).

and fair view override on a number of occasions in the UK has aroused considerable criticism from our partners in the EEC, who did not envisage that it would be used so often.

The statement, including its appendices, deals with a number of practical considerations which should be taken into account when deciding on the profit to be taken into account. The basic principle is summarized as follows: 'The amount to be reflected in the year's profit and loss account will be the appropriate proportion of this total profit by reference to the work done to date, less any profit taken up in prior years.'[35] It should be noted that this guidance does not support the unduly conservative approach which is sometimes advocated whereby only an arbitrarily determined proportion (e.g. two-thirds) of the profit deemed to have been earned to date is reflected in the accounts.

Disclosure

We shall conclude our discussion by reproducing the provisions of SSAP 9 relating to disclosure:

> The accounting policies which have been used in calculating cost, net realisable value, attributable profit and foreseeable losses (as appropriate) should be stated.[36]

> Stocks and work in progress should be sub-classified in balance sheets or in notes to the financial statement in a manner which is appropriate to the business and so as to indicate the amounts held in each of the main categories.[37]

> In relation to the amount at which long-term contracts are stated in the balance sheet there should be stated:
> (a) the amount of work in progress at cost plus attributable profits, less foreseeable losses;
> (b) cash received and receivable at the accounting date as progress payments on account of contracts in progress.[38]

It can be seen that SSAP 9 does to a limited extent fulfil its objective of narrowing the variation in practice. However, the standard could not be expected to settle all the problems in this area, and the estimation of the balance sheet values of stock and work in progress must still depend heavily on the application of judgement.

---

35 SSAP 9, Appendix 1, Para. 27.
36 SSAP 9, Para. 28.
37 SSAP 9, Para. 29.
38 SSAP9, Para. 30.

Recommended reading

Fixed assets and depreciation

W. T. Baxter, *Depreciation*, Sweet and Maxwell, London, 1970.
I. D. B. Campbell and C. Swinson, *Depreciation*, Accountant's Digest No. 135, ICAEW, London, 1983.

Intangible assets

M. C. Miller, 'Goodwill – an aggregation issue', *The Accounting Review*, April 1973.
G. W. Eccles and W. L. Lifford, *Accounting for Research and Development*, Accountants' Digest No. 74, ICAEW, London, 1979.

Stock and work in progress

R. W. Perks and E. Graham, *A Guide to Accounting Standards – Valuation of Stocks and Work in Progress*, Accountants' Digest No. 158, ICAEW, London, 1984.

Questions

15.1 In accounting for physical fixed assets, the use of 'cost' as a valuation basis is well established.
You are required to outline the difficulties that arise in applying the cost principle, and to justify the solutions normally adopted, in cases where:
(a) **physical fixed assets are acquired OTHERWISE THAN for a single cash payment (or on short-term credit) with IMMEDIATE transfer of the legal title to the assets; and** (12 marks)
(b) **more than one separately-identifiable item of physical fixed assets is acquired in the same transaction for a global sum of money, or for other valuable consideration that cannot be precisely apportioned.**
(4 marks)
(16 marks)
A. Cert. A., Advanced Financial Accounting, June 1983.

15.2 Motorhomes Ltd hires out motorized caravans for use on the continent and in the United Kingdom.
Only new vehicles are purchased and they have an effective life for continental use of either three years or 75 000 miles after which they are either sold or transferred for use in the United Kingdom, where they will have a further effective life of two years or 40 000 miles. Vehicles are always purchased on 1 April.

The vehicles carry fully comprehensive insurance cover against accidental damage when out on hire, and the company has a block maintenance and repair agreement with the vehicle suppliers.

Company practice has been to provide depreciation at 25% per annum on the reducing balance, but when three-year-old vehicles have been sold, usually for £4500, or five-year-old vehicles have been sold, usually for £2500, a book loss has had to be written off.

Details of the vehicles presently owned by the company are as follows:

Vehicle Number	Date of purchase 1 April	Cost £	Total recorded mileage (000's) 31 March	
			1983	1984
211	1979	12 000	95	110
212	1980	12 000	75	96
213	1981	12 000	50	74
214	1982	14 000	27	48
215	1982	14 000	26	56
216	1983	14 000	—	28
217	1983	14 000	—	24

Draft accounts for the year ended 31 March 1984 have been prepared in accordance with company practice but the directors have asked you to review the method of providing for depreciation before finalizing the financial statements.

You are required to:
  (a) write a short memorandum to the directors setting out the matters to be taken into consideration, stating the method of providing for depreciation which you would recommend, giving your reasons (11 marks);

  (b) draft the accounting policy note and the disclosure note on fixed assets that would appear in the company's financial statements for the year ended 31 March 1984 assuming your recommendations are accepted (8 marks); and

  (c) state how any additional depreciation charge should be dealt with (3 marks).

(22 marks)

ICAEW Financial Accounting I, November 1984.

15.3   The Companies Act 1981, Schedule 1 (the new Schedule 8 to the 1948 Act), SSAP 12: *Accounting for Depreciation* (1977, revised 1981), and SSAP 19: *Accounting for Investment Properties* (1981) are designed to regulate accounting for tangible fixed assets.

You are required:
  (a) **to assess the role of the above prescriptive documents in securing coherent methods of accounting for tangible fixed assets, comparable from company to company; and** (12 marks)
  (b) **to consider whether more should be done to standardize methods of depreciation for tangible fixed assets in particular industries.** (8 marks)
(20 marks)

A. Cert. A. Advanced Financial Accounting, December 1984.

15.4 On 1 January, 1984, Hideehigh Ltd was incorporated to acquire from a property development company a ready made holiday complex on the North Wales coast.

The complex is divisible into three distinct areas: a freehold site and two leasehold sites. The leases expire on 25 December, 2000, and 25 December, 2080. The developer designated these sites Meg I, II and III, respectively.

A schedule of the properties acquired describes the properties as:

Property Description	Meg I	Meg II	Meg III	Total
6-Room timber constructed chalets	38	48	66	152
3-Storey brick built 'town houses'	64	32	—	96

Hideehigh Ltd intend to lease the chalets and town houses. They have been advised that the chalets, which have a life of 25 years, and the town houses, which have a life of 50 years, should be let on 15-year leases.

You are required to discuss how Hideehigh Ltd should treat the properties in their annual accounts.

(13 marks)

ICAEW Financial Accounting I, May 1984.

15.5 Newtrade Ltd a manufacturing company, has prepared draft accounts as on 31 March 1983 for the purpose of producing its first year's financial statements.

Included in assets is a balance on suspense account of £165 808 made up as follows:

Purchases of:	£	Grants received:	£
plant and machinery	145 567	on cost of plant and machinery	25 316
motor lorries	48 898	for employment of local labour	15 600
motor cars	12 259		
		Balance	165 808
	206 724		206 724

All the amounts shown for the purchase of assets include VAT at 15%.

The directors wish to deal with capital grants on the deferred credit method and to depreciate all fixed assets at 20% per annum.

You are required to:
  (a) **prepare journal entries to incorporate the various items in the suspense account into the draft accounts** (9 marks), **and**
  (b) **write a short memorandum explaining your reasons for the journal entries and the effect they have on the accounts** (5 marks).

(14 marks)

ICAEW Financial Accounting I, May 1983.

15.6   Capsule Ltd is a chemical manufacturing company. The following items, in relation to the company's manufacturing processes, have been included in stocks and work in progress as on 31 July 1983:

(1) Stocks of Banoline have been valued at £426 000 based on the following amounts:

	£
Raw materials – cost	200 000
Other direct costs	144 000
Proportion of factory overheads	38 000
Proportion of selling office expenses	44 000
	426 000

Banoline is a steady selling product which shows reasonable profit margins.
(2) Laboratory costs to 31 July 1983 of £348 000 on research into a new tranquillizer called Calmdown. The research is being sponsored by a government agency on a one-year programme. The agency has agreed to reimburse the company on a cost plus 6% basis at the end of the programme, up to a maximum contribution of £500 000.
(3) Stocks of 1300 kg, held in bulk, of a chemical substance known as Apentone, and valued as follows:

	£
Raw materials – cost	340 000
Other direct costs	260 000
Proportion of factory overheads	47 000
Proportion of selling office expenses	59 000
	706 000

A competitor of Capsule Ltd has recently introduced to the market a similar substance, which it is selling in handy 100 g packs at £35 each.

To meet the competition, Capsule Ltd will also have to pack in 100 g containers. The cost of packing the stock held will be £20 000 and additional advertising costs, to clear the stock are estimated at £30 000.

(4) Laboratory costs to 31 July 1983 of £365 000 on research into a new chemical substitute for Supositone, of which demand exceeds the world supply. These costs include £100 000 for special items of plant required for the research programme.

You are required to state how you consider the above items should be dealt with in the company's accounts, giving your reasons in each case.

(20 marks)

ICAEW Financial Accounting I, November 1983.

15.7 **(a)** **How would you define goodwill?**   (5 marks)

(b) **Three accounting treatments of goodwill are:**

(i) **retain goodwill as an asset to be amortized over its estimated useful life;**

(ii) **retain goodwill as an asset indefinitely;**

(iii) **write off goodwill to reserves at the time of acquisition.**

Discuss briefly the principles underlying each of these three approaches.

(15 marks)

(20 marks)

A. Cert. A. The Regulatory Framework of Accounting, December 1983.

15.8 Two recently published accounts have included the following accounting policy in respect of work in progress.

(A) 'Work in progress is valued at cost plus two thirds of profits accrued to date less foreseeable losses to the completion of the contract. In arriving at this value, cost represents the cost of materials, subcontractors, plant and transport, and labour, together with related overheads.

In arriving at profits and losses to date, claims receivable are only recognized to the extent that they are agreed, but anticipated claims receivable are taken into account in calculating future losses.

For the purpose of balance sheet presentation, amounts received and due at the accounting date have been deducted from work in progress.'

(B) 'Until such time as the outcome of a contract or development can be foreseen with reasonable certainty, contract work in progress is valued at the lower of direct cost and net realizable value after deducting cash received or receivable on account. A proportion of profit is included in work in progress when contracts or developments have progressed to the point where a profitable outcome can prudently be foreseen.'

The following data relate to a fixed-price contract for £250 000 undertaken by your company whose accounting year ends on 31 October. When the contract was signed the company expected direct costs to be £150 000 and apportioned overheads to be £50 000.

| | up to 31 October | |
	1979	1980
Work certified	£75 000	£225 000
Invoiced	£70 000	£150 000
Cash received	£60 000	£150 000
Direct costs incurred	£60 000	£140 000
Central overheads apportioned	£20 000	£50 000
Percentage completed	30	90
Estimated further direct costs before completion	£110 000	£15 000

The contract includes a clause whereby any remedial work is covered by a performance bond so that no retentions are made.

When considering the accounts for 1979 the information relating to 1980 is not available.

The board of directors of your company is considering the accounting policy to be adopted and has asked your advice.

You are required to:
  (a) show how the contract would appear in the profit and loss account and balance sheet for 1979 and 1980 (excluding comparative figures) if policy A was adopted (5 marks),
  (b) show how the contract would appear in the profit and loss account and balance sheet for 1979 and 1980 (excluding comparative figures) if policy B was adopted with a working rule that 'prudently be foreseen' means when a contract is 70% or more completed and in these circumstances 80% of the profit is taken (5 marks),
  (c) indicate to what extent these two policies comply with the requirements of SSAP 9 in relation to long term work in process (5 marks), **and**
  (d) advise your board on the advantages and disadvantages of each policy
(5 marks).
(20 marks)

ICAEW Financial Accounting II, December 1980.

16 Accounting Standards II: Leases and Hire Purchase Contracts

Accounting for leases and hire purchase contracts

Introduction

Under a hire purchase agreement the user has the option to acquire the legal title to the asset upon the fulfilment of the conditions laid down in the contract, usually that all the instalments are paid. By contrast, under a leasing agreement in the UK no legal title passes to the lessee at any time during the currency of the lease. The lessor rents the asset to the lessee for an agreed period and, although the lessee has the physical possession and use of the asset, the legal title remains with the lessor.

In some cases a lease will be for a relatively short period in the life of the particular asset and the lessor may lease the same asset for many short periods to different lessees and in such cases he will usually be responsible for the repairs and maintenance of the asset. This type of lease is described as an *operating lease*. In other instances the lease may be for virtually the whole life of the asset with the lessor taking the whole of his profit from one transaction, such a lease is known as a *finance lease*. Typically, the lessee of a finance lease will in practical terms treat the leased asset in very much the same way as it would an owned asset, the lessee for example, will often be responsible for the asset's repair and maintenance.

The distinction between finance and operating leases is, however, not clear cut and we will return to the way in which they can be differentiated in our discussion of SSAP 21, 'Accounting for leases and hire purchase contracts' (*see* page 614).

For the accountant, operating leases pose few problems. Amounts are payable for the use of an asset. From the point of view of the lessee the amounts payable are for the cost of using an asset for particular periods and hence are charged to the profit and loss account using the accruals concept. So far as the lessor is concerned the amounts

604

receivable represents his revenue from leasing the asset and are credited to the profit and loss account. The leased asset is treated as a fixed asset by the lessor and depreciated in accordance with his normal policy.

It is the financing lease which poses problems for the accountant. Traditionally, prior to the introduction of SSAP 21, financing leases were treated by both the lessee and lessor in the same way as operating leases. However, it was widely recognized that such treatment, whilst being justified on a strict legal interpretation of the agreement, failed to recognize the financial reality or substance of the transaction. The substance of the transaction was that the lessee acquired an asset for his exclusive use with finance provided by the lessor; which in economic terms has few (if any) differences from the case of an asset purchased on credit. If accounts are to be 'realistic' as described in Chapter 1 it is necessary to find a way of accounting for finance leases which accords with the reality of the transaction rather than its legal form, a position which is supported by International Accounting Standard (IAS) 1 which specifically requires that the substance and financial reality of a transaction rather than its legal form, should determine the appropriate accounting treatment.[1]

The alternative treatment which accords with the substance of the transaction is, from the point of view of the lessee, to include in the lessee's balance sheet an asset representing the lease and a liability representing the obligation to make payments under the terms of the lease. At the inception of the lease the asset would be equal to the liability but this relationship does not hold thereafter. The asset would be written off over its life (or the length of the lease if shorter) whilst the liability would be eliminated by the payments. These payments are not, as in the case of an operating lease, charged entirely to the profit or loss account nor are they in general wholly set off against the liability. Instead the payments are split between that element which is regarded as representing the repayment of the liability and the remainder which is debited to the profit and loss account as the financing (or interest) charge. The alternative approach is referred to as the *capitalization* of the lease.

The lack of reality consequent upon the failure of a lessee to capitalize financial leases is highlighted by the problems experienced when comparing two companies, one of which leases most of its assets, with the other purchasing fixed assets using loans of one sort or another.

---

1 IAS 1, Paras 9b and 17.

The latter company's balance sheet would show the assets which it used to generate its revenue thus allowing users of accounts to estimate the rate of return earned on those assets, while the former company's balance sheet would understate its assets. Similarly, the latter company's balance sheet would indicate the liabilities which would have to be discharged if it is to continue in business with its existing bundle of assets while the former company's balance sheet would not.[2]

We have so far considered only how the lessee should treat a finance lease. Let us now consider the matter from the point of view of the lessor. The lessor's balance sheet would not include the physical asset but a debtor for the amounts receivable under the lease. Thenceforth the payments received under the terms of the lease should be split between that which goes to reducing the debt with the balance being credited to the profit and loss account. We shall see later in this section how the division can be made.

In order to understand part of the reason why leasing has become popular in recent years, the reluctance on the part of most companies to capitalize leases, and the provisions of SSAP 21, it is necessary to understand the way in which leases are treated for the purposes of taxation. Unlike hire purchase contracts and credit sales agreements, where the user obtains grants and capital allowances, in the case of a lease it is the legal owner, the lessor, who receives grants and capital allowances on the asset. The lessee receives no allowances but obtains tax relief on the amounts payable under the lease. Capital allowances are only of value to a company which has sufficient taxable profit. Hence, to their mutual advantage, one company with large taxable profits is able to lease assets to another company which does not have sufficient taxable profits to take full advantage of capital allowances. Thus the company with insufficient taxable profits can acquire fixed assets at a lower effective cost than would have been the case with alternative methods of financing.

The effect of what might well be described as the distortion of the tax system described above was undoubtedly one of the major causes of the growth of leasing in recent years. Hence, there was a good deal of opposition to the proposal that lessees should capitalize finance leases as it was feared that a change in accounting practice might precipitate changes in taxation law whereby finance leases would in the future be treated in the same way as hire purchase contracts.

---

2 It is for this reason that finance leases were described as providing on 'off balance sheet' source of finance.

Other factors which hindered the development of a standard requiring the capitalization of finance leases included concerns about the possible extension of the principle to other types of non-cancellable contracts, for example those for the regular supply of raw materials or labour, and fears about the potential complexity of any standard. However, the ASC did issue SSAP 21, 'Accounting for leases and hire purchase contracts', in August 1984 and, amongst other things, this requires lessees to capitalize finance leases and lessors to include in their balance sheets, not the fixed asset but the debtor for the net investment in the lease. It is perhaps somewhat ironic that, after studying the problem for some 9 years, the ASC issued this standard just after the Finance Act 1984 had reduced considerably the tax advantages of leasing.

We will start by examining the treatment of finance leases in the books of the lessee. This will not only enable us to show the basic principles involved but also introduce some terms which will make it easier to understand SSAP 21.

Let us start with a simple example.

Lonbok Limited, a company whose year end is 31 December, leases a machine from Salat Limited on 1 January 19X1. Under the terms of the lease Lonbok is to make four annual payments[3] of £35 000 payable at the start of the year. Lonbok Limited is responsible for all the maintenance and insurance costs, so these are not covered by the payments under the lease.

The first step is to decide the amount at which the leased asset should be capitalized, i.e. shown as an asset and a liability in the first instance. SSAP 21 requires that:

> At the inception of the lease the sum to be recorded both as an asset and as a liability should be the present value of the minimum lease payments, derived by discounting them at the interest rate implicit in the lease. (SSAP 21, Para. 32)

To do that we need to know what is meant by the minimum lease payments and the interest rate implicit in the lease. These terms are also defined in SSAP 21.

---

3 In practice lease payments are usually made at monthly, quarterly or 6-monthly intervals, but, in order to illustrate more clearly the principles involved, in our example we will assume that the payments are made at annual intervals. More realistic examples of the type of calculations that have to be made in practice, including leases which do not, conveniently, start on the first day of the year can be found in the guidance notes to SSAP 21.

Minimum lease payments

The minimum lease payments are the minimum payments over the remaining part of the lease term (excluding charges for services and taxes to be paid by the lessor) and:

(a) in the case of the lessee, any residual amounts guaranteed by him or by a party related to him; or

(b) in the case of the lessor, any residual amounts guaranteed by the lessee or by an independent third party. (SSAP 21, Para. 20)

In the Lonbok example we will assume that there are no residual amounts and thus the minimum lease payments at the inception of the lease are the four annual payments of £35 000.

Interest rate implicit in a lease

> The interest rate implicit in a lease is the discount rate that at the inception of a lease when applied to the amounts which the *lessor* expects to receive and retain produces an amount (the present value) equal to the fair value of the leased asset. The amounts which the lessor expects to receive and retain comprise (a) the minimum lease payments to the lessor (as defined above) plus (b) any unguaranteed residual value, less (c) any part of (a) and (b) for which the lessor will be accountable to the lessee. If the interest rate implicit in the lease is not determinable, it should be estimated by reference to the rate which a lessee would be expected to pay on a similar lease. (SSAP 21, Para. 24)

A key element in the above definition is fair value and hence we need to know how this is found:

Fair value

> Fair value is the price at which an asset could be exchanged in an arm's length transaction less, where applicable, any grants receivable towards the purchase or use of the asset. (SSAP 21, Para. 25)

Note that whilst knowledge of the implied interest rate is required to determine the appropriate accounting treatment in the books of the lessee it is found by reference to the cash flows of the lessor. In practice the lessee may not know or be able to estimate the various cash flows but we, at this stage, assume that the lessee can obtain all the necessary data.

If we let FV be the fair value, L_i be the lease payment in year i (assumed to be paid at the end of each year) and R_n the estimated residual values received at the end of year n, the last year of the lease, then using standard present value techniques the implied rate of interest r is found from the solution of the following equation:

$$FV = \sum_{j=0}^{n} \frac{L_j}{(1+r)^j} + \frac{R_n}{(1+r)^n}.$$

If we assume that in the case of the Lonbok/Salat lease that the fair value is £108 720 and that there is no residual value (i.e. $R_n = 0$) then substituting in the above equation we get:

$$£108\,720 = \sum_{j=0}^{3} \frac{£35\,000}{(1+r)^j}.$$

or

$$\sum_{j=0}^{3} \frac{1}{(1+r)^j} = 3.1064.$$

Inspection of tables showing the present value of an annuity shows that 3.1064 represents an interest rate of 20%.[4]

Thus the interest rate implicit in the lease is 20% and hence the present value PV of the minimum lease payments can be found as follows:

$$PV = £35\,000\,(3.1064)$$
$$= £108\,720.$$

This is of course equal to the fair value as in the simple case the only cash flows which the lessor will receive are the minimum lease payments. Later we will describe the circumstances where the two series of cash flows (i.e. the lessee's and the lessor's) might be different and the effect of these differences on the calculations.

We can now show how the lease will be treated in the books of Lonbok (the lessee).

The original entry recording the lease is:

Dr Leased asset	£108 720	
Cr Liability under lease		£108 720

From this time onwards the two accounts are dealt with separately. The leased machine will be depreciated over the shorter of the length of the lease or the asset's expected life, using the company's normal depreciation policy for assets of its type, whilst the liability will be

---

4 This and other necessary present value calculations can be made by use of standard computer packages.

gradually extinguished as payments are made during the primary period of the lease. The only problem which remains is how to spread the total interest charge over the primary period of the lease. This same problem is, of course, encountered in accounting for hire purchase transactions. The total interest charge may be calculated as follows:

Payments under lease, 4 × £35 000	£140 000
less 'Cost' as above	108 720
Interest	£31 280

Theoretically the best approach is to use the annuity method which produces a constant annual rate of interest (in this case 20%) on the outstanding balance on the liability account. This is the method specified in SSAP 21 which does, however, allow the use of any alternative method which is a reasonable approximation to the annuity method.

Assuming that all payments are made on the due dates, the liability account in books of Lonbok for the term of the lease can be summarized as followed:

	19X1	19X2	19X3	19X4
	£	£	£	£
1 Jan. opening balance (19X1 cost)	108 720	88 470	64 170	35 000
1 Jan. Cash	35 000	35 000	35 000	35 000
	73 720	53 470	29 170	—
31 Dec. Interest, 20% of above	14 750	10 700	5 830	—
31 Dec. Closing balance	£88 470	£64 170	£35 000	—

The account provides us with the interest charge to the profit and loss account for each year and the liability for inclusion in each balance sheet, although it is of course necessary to distinguish between the current portion of the liability (i.e. due within a year) and the rest for the purpose of balance sheet presentation. The amount of interest charged to the profit and loss account declines over the life of the lease because the outstanding balance is reduced by the annual payments.

One commonly used alternative to the annuity method is the 'sum of the year's digits' method or 'Rule of 78'.[5] If the sum of the digits method is used in the above illustration the results would be:

---

5 It is called the Rule of 78 because if the method is based on the monthly intervals and if the digit 1 is assigned to January, 2 to February and so on the sum of the digits for the year is 78.

Total interest charge   £31 280

Sum of the years' digits, 1 + 2 + 3   6

Interest charged to profit and loss account

	£
19X1, $\frac{3}{6}$ of £31 280	15 640
19X2, $\frac{2}{6}$ of £31 280	10 430
19X3, $\frac{1}{6}$ of £31 280	5 210
	£31 280

Although the use of the annuity method is conceptually superior, a comparison of the annual interest charges under the two methods reveals similar patterns of interest charge and thus the sum of the year's digit method is often used as a convenient approximation to the annuity method:

Year	Annuity method (£)	Sum of the years' digits method (£)
19X1	14 750	15 640
19X2	10 700	10 430
19X3	5 830	5 210
	£31 280	£31 280

The impact of residual values

Let us now complicate matters by assuming that the asset which is the subject of the lease has a residual value. We will assume that the manufacturer who originally supplied the asset to Salat has agreed to reacquire the asset at the end of the lease. The sum is dependent on the condition of the machine and the market factors at the end of the lease, but the manufacturer has guaranteed to pay £10 000 whatever the circumstances. Let us assume that at the inception of the lease it is anticipated that the manufacturer will actually pay £30 000. Let us also assume that Lonbok and Salat agree that they will divide any sums realized on the disposal of the asset in the ratio 60:40. Thus at the inception of the lease it is estimated that Lonbok will receive £18 000 (of which £6000 is guaranteed) and Salat £12 000 (£4000 guaranteed).

For the purposes of calculating the implicit interest rate the distinction between the guaranteed and unguaranteed elements of the residual value can be ignored as both have to be taken into the calculation but the distinction may be important when deciding whether the lease is a finance or operating lease (*see* page 614).

If we return to the equation on page 609 and substitute the estimated value on realization receivable by Salat the equation becomes:

$$108\,720 = \sum_{j=0}^{3} \frac{35\,000}{(1 + r)^j} + \frac{12\,000}{(1 + r)^3}.$$

Use of tables, or a programmable calculation on a computer shows that the above equation will be satisfied when $r = 25\%$. This is a higher rate of interest than the 20% which was previously calculated as Salat obviously earns a higher return due to the introduction of the residual value as an additional cash flow.

So far as Lonbok is concerned the minimum lease payments are unchanged but they will now be discounted at the higher rate of 25% which will produce an initial value of the leased asset of:

£35 000(2.952) = £103 320.

The annual payments of £35 000 are the same as in the original example except that the liability which is to be paid off is lower (£103 320 net £108 720). Hence the finance charge in the profit and loss account will be higher in the second example. This reflects the fact that in the first example the lease payments can be regarded as acquiring the whole of the productive use of the asset in that a zero residual value was assumed while in the second case the same annual lease payments only acquired a proportion of the asset's productive capacity.

It will be noted that the estimated realizable value which Lonbok expects to receive had no effect on the calculation of the amount by which the lease should be capitalized nor on the way in which the annual lease payments should be split. This is because these depend on the minimum lease payments. The recognition of the estimated realizable value does have an effect on the amount that has to be depreciated which is the present value of the minimum lease payments less the estimated realizable value. Thus the depreciation charges which would emerge from our two sets of assumptions are as follows (assuming the straight-line method is used):

Assumption 1 $\dfrac{£108\,720}{4} = £27\,180,$

Assumption 2 $\dfrac{£(103\,320 - 18\,000)}{4} = £21\,330.$

In the above examples we assumed that the lessee knows (or is able to find out from the lessor) the fair value of the asset and the estimated realizable value which the lessor expects to receive. In practice this may well not be the case and certain estimates will have to be made. Often the fair value will be known[6] and the interest rate estimated from a knowledge of other leases of a similar type.

SSAP 21, 'Accounting for leases and hire purchase contracts'

We are now in a position to discuss the specific requirements of SSAP 21. This is a detailed standard and we will not attempt to cover all its aspects but will instead concentrate on the important elements and those which might give rise to particular difficulties of understanding. The ASC has published guidance notes on SSAP 21 and readers should refer to this booklet for a more detailed explanation of the provisions of the standard.

We will first deal with a number of general issues before concentrating on the impact of the standard on the accounts of lessees and hirers. A discussion of the more specialized topic of accounting for lessors will be deferred to the concluding part of this chapter.

Scope
The standard covers leases and hire purchases contracts and is applicable to accounts based on both the historical cost and current cost conventions. The standard does not apply to leases of the rights to exploit natural resources such as oil or gas, nor does it apply to licensing agreement for items such as motion pictures, videos, etc. Stress is also laid on the point that the standard does not apply to immaterial items. Thus a company that leases some of its office equipment may not need to capitalize the lease but continue to treat a finance lease in the same way as an operating lease.

---

6 Unless the asset concerned is highly specific the prudent lessee will obviously wish to know how much it would cost him to purchase the asset before signing a lease.

Distinction between finance and operating leases
The basic distinction between the two different types of leases has already been explained (*see* page 604). The standard states that:

> A finance lease is a lease that transfers substantially all the risks and rewards of ownership of an asset to the lessee. (Para. 15)

It is presumed that a lease is a finance lease if at the start of the lease the present value of the minimum lease payments amounts to substantially all (normally 90% or more) of the fair value of the leased asset. The present value should be calculated by using the interest rate implicit in the lease. However, the standard recognizes that in exceptional circumstances this initial presumption may be rebutted if the lease in question does not transfer substantially all the risks and rewards of ownership to the lessee. It may sometimes be the case that the lessor will receive part of his return by way of a guarantee from an independent third party, possibly the manufacturer of the asset, in which case the lease may fail to be treated as a finance lease by the lessor but as an operating lease by the lessee.

Hire purchase contracts
With the vast majority of hire purchases contracts the 'risks and rewards' pass to the hirer and hence may be regarded as being akin to finance leases. In such cases the standard specifies that they should be treated in a similar way to finance leases. However, in exceptional circumstances a hire purchase contract may be accounted for on the same principles as an operating lease.

Accounting by lessees

Finance leases

A finance lease should be capitalized hence the lease should be recorded as an asset and an obligation to pay rentals. At the inception of the lease the asset will equal the liability (although this equality will not hold over the life of the lease) and will be the present value of the minimum lease payments, derived by discounting them at the interest rate implied in the lease.
The standard states:

> that the fair value of the asset will often be a sufficiently close approximation to the present value of the minimum lease payments and may in these circumstances be substituted for it. (Para. 33)

In most circumstances the fair value will be a sufficiently close approximation to be used, for, by definition, if the present value of the minimum lease payments does not equal 90% or more of the fair value, then it is presumed that the lease is an operating and not a finance lease.

If the fair value cannot be determined, possibly because the asset concerned is unique, then the present value can be found by discounting the minimum lease payments by the interest rate implicit in the lease. If the latter cannot be determined the rate may be estimated from that which applies in similar leases.

Total payments less than fair value
In some circumstances the combined impact of Regional Development Grants and taxation allowances received by the lessor may be such as to bring the total (i.e. not the present value) lease payments below the fair value. The standard specifies (Para. 34) that if this occurs the amount to be capitalized and depreciated should be reduced to the minimum lease payments. A negative finance charge should not be shown.

In other words if say the total of the payments to be made under the lease is £10 000 and the fair value of the asset is £12 000, the asset and liability on the inception of the lessee are both £10 000. The payments under the lease will all be applied to reducing the liability and no part of them will be charged to the profit and loss account as a finance charge. The only charge in the profit and loss account will be the annual depreciation charge.

Rentals
Rentals payable should be apportioned between the finance charge (if any) and a reduction of the outstanding obligation. The total finance charge should be allocated to accounting periods so as to produce a constant annual rate of charge (i.e. the annuity method), or a reasonable approximation thereto.

The guidance notes suggest that in most circumstances, especially where the lease is for 7 years or less and interest rates are not high that the Rule of 78 will be an acceptable approximation to the actuarial method. In the case of small (relative to the size of the companies) leases it is suggested that the straight-line method, whereby the total finance charge is recognized on a time basis, may be acceptable.

Depreciation
A leased asset should be depreciated over the shorter of the length of the lease or the asset's useful life. However, in the case of hire purchase contracts, because of the presumption that the asset concerned will be acquired by the hirer, the asset should be depreciated over its useful life.

Operating leases

The accounting treatment by the lessee in respect of operating leases is fairly straightforward in that the whole of the payments are charged to the profit and loss account. The only complication is that the standard requires the rental to be charged on a straight-line basis over the lease term (unless another systematic and rational basis is more appropriate) even if the payments are not made on such a basis. Hence, if the term of the lease requires a heavy initial payment a proportion of the payment can be treated as a pre-paid expense.

More commonly lessees are granted so-called 'rental holidays' in that they do not have to pay anything for an initial period. In such circumstances the standard would require a charge to be made to the profit and loss account for the period of the rental holiday which would be treated as an accrual in the balance sheet. Thereafter the charge to the profit and loss account would be less than the payments made in the year (as rental like other holidays have to be paid for) with the excess reducing the balance sheet accrual. Particularly significant examples of this type of arrangement are leases of buildings by government agencies to business in areas where the government want to encourage the creation of jobs.

Transitional arrangements
So far as lessees and hirers are concerned the accounting practices set out in the standard do not become mandatory until accounting periods beginning on or after 1 July 1987. Certain of the disclosure requirements, which will be identified in the following section, did, however, come into effect in respect of accounting periods commencing on or after 1 July 1984.

Disclosure requirements in the accounts of lessees and hirers

Finance leases
For disclosure purposes information relating to hire purchase contracts

with characteristics similar to finance leases should be included with the equivalent information regarding leases.

Those aspects of the disclosure requirements which came into force on 1 July 1984 are indicated by way of an asterisk in the following section.

1. *Fixed assets and depreciation*   The lessee may either:

(a) Show separately the gross amounts, accumulated depreciation and depreciation expense for each major class of leased asset, or

(b) Group the above information with the equivalent information for owned assets[7] but to show by way of a note how much of the net amount (i.e. net book value) and the depreciation expense relates to assets held under finance leases.

2. *Obligations*   The lessee must both:

(a) Disclose the obligations related to finance leases separately from other obligations and liabilities, and

(b) *Analyse the net obligations under finance leases into three components (the figures may be combined with other obligations):
    amounts payable in next year;
    amounts payable in second to fifth years;
    amounts payable thereafter.

3. *Finance charges*   The lessee must disclose the aggregate finance charge allocated to the period.

4. *Commitments*   The lessee must show by way of a note the amount of any commitment existing at the balance sheet date in respect of finance leases which have been entered into but whose inception occurs after the year end.

5. *Accounting policies*   Accounting policies adopted for finance leases must be stated.

Operating leases

All the disclosure requirements in respect of operating leases are standard accounting practice in respect of periods beginning on or after 1 July 1984.

---

7 Since it is the right to use the asset rather than the asset itself which is capitalized there is some doubt as to whether it should be called a tangible asset and included with the owned tangible assets. The ASC has ignored such niceties and for the purposes of balance sheet presentation the leases are regarded as tangible assets.

1. *Current rentals*   The lessee must disclose the total rentals charged as an expense, analysed between amounts payable in respect of the hire of plant and machinery and those charged in respect of other operating leases. (The Companies Act, of course, requires disclosure of the charge for the hire of plant and machinery.)

2. *Future rentals*   The lessee must show the payments which it is committed to make during the next year, analysed between those in which the commitment expires:

   (i) within that year,
   (ii) in the second to fifth years inclusive and
   (iii) over 5 years from the balance sheet date.

Commitments in respect of leases of land and buildings and other operating leases must be shown separately.

3. *Accounting policies*   The accounting policies adopted for operating leases must be stated.

Accounting for finance leases by lessors – general principles

The provisions of SSAP 21 regarding the accounting treatment of finance leases by lessors are relatively difficult for two main reasons. First, the basic method is not simple since – as will be shown – it depends on complex calculations of what constitutes the lessor's investment in a particular lease while, second, the standard permits the use of alternative methods and simplifying assumptions so that a host of different methods can be justified under the terms of the standard.

We will first describe the basic principles underlying the provisions of SSAP 21 with regard to the treatment of finance leases by lessors.

Balance sheet presentation – the measurement of net investment

Lessors should not include in their balance sheets the assets subject to the leasing contracts but instead record as a debtor the *net investment* in the lease after making any necessary provisions for bad and doubtful debts. In order to explain this term and describe how profit is recognized, we will need to reproduce certain definitions included in SSAP 21.

Net investment

The net investment in a lease at a point in time comprises:

(a) the gross investment in a lease (*see* below); less
(b) gross earnings allocated to future periods. (SSAP 21, Para. 22)

Thus we need to know what is meant by the gross investment and gross earnings.

Gross investment

The gross investment in a lease at a point in time is the total of the minimum lease payments [*see* page 608] and any unguaranteed residual value accruing to the lessor. (SSAP 21, Para. 21)

Gross earnings

Gross earnings comprise the lessor's gross finance income over the lease term, representing the difference between his gross investment in the lease [*see* above] and the cost of the leased asset less any grants receivable towards the purchase or use of the asset.[8] (SSAP 21, Para. 28)

In order to illustrate the effect of the above definitions assume that the details relating to a particular lease are as follows:

Cost of asset	£12 000
Grant receivable by lessor	£2 000
Lease term	5 years
Annual rental	£3 000
Estimated residual value accruing to the lessor	£500

Let us see how one measures the net investment at the inception of the lease and at the end of the first year.

	£
At inception:	
Minimum lease payments, 5 × £3000	15 000
Estimated residual value	500
Gross investment	15 500
less Gross earnings (£15 500 – £10 000)	5 500
Net investment	£10 000

Hence, at inception the net investment is equal to the cost of the asset less grants receivable by the lessor.

---

8 The paragraph goes on to modify the definition to deal with the use of a possible option available in SSAP 21 relating to the treatment of tax-free grants.

Assume that the gross earnings recognized in the profit and loss account in the first year is £2500 (we shall describe in the following section how this figure is calculated). Then the net investment at the end of the first year is:

	£
Minimum lease payments, 4 × £3000	12 000
Estimated residual value	500
	12 500
less Gross earnings allocated to future periods £5500 – £2500	3 000
Net investment	£9 500

The recognition of gross earnings

The total gross earnings on any lease is reasonably easy to calculate since the minimum lease payments will be known and, generally, the residual value, if any, can be estimated. The difficulty lies in allocating the gross earnings to the different accounting periods. The standard follows existing practice in the leasing industry by specifying that (other than in the case of hire purchase contracts) the interest should be allocated on the basis of the lessor's *net cash investment* in the lease and not on the basis of the net investment. Specifically Para. 39 of SSAP 21 states:

> The total gross earnings under a finance lease should normally be allocated to accounting periods to give a constant periodic rate of return on the lessor's *net cash investment* in the lease in each period. In the case of a hire purchase contract which has characteristics similar to a finance lease, allocation of gross earnings so as to give a constant periodic rate of return on the finance company's *net investment* will in most cases be a suitable approximation to allocation based on the net cash investment. In arriving at the constant periodic rate of return, a reasonable approximation may be made.

To an extent the above is familiar in that it is the counterpart of the annuity method prescribed for use by lessees in that the annual finance charge should be such as to produce a constant rate based on the decreasing obligation. The difference is that whilst the reduction in the obligation is relatively easy to calculate the determination of the net cash investment is somewhat more difficult.

The meaning of net cash investment

The meaning of the net cash investment can be more easily understood if one assumes that a separate company is established by the lessor for each lease and then measuring or estimating the cash flows in and out of that company. The net cash investment is then the balance of cash, which might be positive or negative, in the company at any point in time. The various cash flows may be summarized as follows:

Cash flows out	Cash flows in
1. Cost of the asset	a. Grants received against purchase or use of asset
2. Cost of setting up the lease	b. Rental income received
3. Tax payments on rental and interest received	c. Tax reductions on capital allowances[9] and on interest paid
4. Interest payments on cash invested in the lease	d. Interest earned when the net cash investment becomes a surplus
5. Profit withdrawn	e. Residual value at the end of the lease

If one thinks in terms of a single lease company and the cash flows associated with it, it can be seen that the company will start with an 'overdraft' – the cost of the asset and of setting up the lease – but that this will be reduced if a grant is received and as capital allowances for the purchase of the asset are received. The overdraft will be reduced as lease payments are received but will be increased by virtue of the interest payments made on the overdraft. Profit may also be withdrawn (and for this purpose profit may be regarded as including the contribution made by the 'single lease' company to the operating expenses of the enterprise of which it actually forms part) which will also increase the overdraft. At some stage the overdraft may be eliminated and replaced by a cash surplus on which interest may be deemed to be earned. The interest 'payments' and 'receipts' will also have taxation consequences which will respectively increase the cash surplus (or reduce the overdraft) or decrease the cash surplus. Finally, if the lessor receives a residual value this will increase the surplus.

---

9 Since in actuality the 'single-lease' company is not separate and distinct the reductions in tax payments due to the receipt of capital allowances and the charging of expenses can be treated as cash receipts since they are covered by tax payment otherwise payable by the lessor (if this were not the case the lessor should not be in the leasing business in the first place!).

It is on the basis of the above considerations that SSAP 21 defines net cash investment as follows:

> The *net cash investment* in a lease at a point in time is the amount of funds invested in a lease by a lessor, and comprises the cost of the asset plus or minus the following related payments and receipts:
>
> (a) government or other grants receivable towards the purchase or use of the asset;
> (b) rentals received;
> (c) taxation payments and receipts, including the effect of capital allowances;
> (d) residual values, if any, at the end of the lease term;
> (e) interest payments (where applicable);
> (f) interest received on cash surplus;
> (g) profit taken out of the lease.[10]

The actuarial method after tax

The guidance notes to SSAP 21 describe a number of ways of allocating the gross revenue to accounting periods based on the net cash investment. Of these the most accurate is the '*actuarial method after tax*'. This method produces a constant rate of return on the net cash investment over that period of the lease in which the lessor has a positive investment (i.e. before any cash surplus is generated). The phrase 'after tax' does not imply that it is after tax profit which is allocated but simply that the tax cash flows are included in the measurement of the net cash investment.

The actuarial method after tax is illustrated in Example 16.1.

EXAMPLE 16.1

Gasp plc, the lessor, acquired an asset for £7735 which it leased out on the following terms:

Period	5 years
Rental	£2000 per year payable in advance on 1 January of each year
Residual value	Zero

Gasp's year end is 31 December and tax in respect of any year is payable on 1 January of the next year but one. The tax rate is 50% and capital allowances of 100% are receivable in the first year.

The annual rate of return earned over the period when there is a net cash investment is 12% whilst it is estimated that surplus cash can be invested at 5% (both rates are before tax).

10 SSAP 21, Para. 23.

The interest paid by Gasp on the funds invested in the lease will be ignored.

The cash flows and the profit recognized on the lease are set out in Table 16.1.

Table 16.1
Hypothetical cash flows – figures in brackets represent cash flows out

Date	Cost (£)	Rent (£)	Tax (£)	Profit taken on lease (£)	Interest on cash surplus (£)	Net cash investment (£)
1 Jan. X0	(7735)	2000				(5735)
31 Dec. X0				(688)		(6423)
1 Jan. X1		2000				(4423)
31 Dec. X1				(531)		(4954)
1 Jan. X2		2000	2868			(86)
31 Dec. X2				(11)		(97)
1 Jan. X3		2000	(1000)			903
31 Dec. X3					45	948
1 Jan. X4		2000	(1000)			1948
31 Dec. X4					98	2046
1 Jan. X5			(1023)			1023
31 Dec. X5					52	1075
1 Jan. X6				(1049)		26
1 Jan. X7				(26)		—

Notes
(a) The profit taken on the lease has been calculated at 12% of the net cash investment at the start of each year (e.g. £688 = 0.12 × £5735) while the interest on the cash surplus has been calculated at 5% of the opening balance (e.g. £45 = 0.05 × £903). Interest on the cash surplus in 19X6 has been ignored (otherwise the calculation would never end).
(b) The tax computation for 19X0 (tax payable on 1 January 19X2) is as follows;

	£
Capital allowances (100%)	7735
less Rental income received	2000
Adjusted profit	£5735
Tax thereon, 50% of £5735 =	£2868

In subsequent years the tax payment is 50% of the sum of the rental income and the interest earned on the cash surplus.

Although the lease will generate an annual rental of £2000 for each of the five years after tax, profit recognized in respect of the lease is £688 in year 1, £531 in year 2 and £11 in year 3.[11] It may be thought that this is a very imprudent way of recognizing profit in that most of the profit is taken in the first 2 years of the lease. However, it must be recognized that the profit reported is that which is generated by the lessor's financing activities and is calculated by reference to the amount that he has invested in the lease. As Table 16.1 shows the investment falls to zero, to be replaced by a cash surplus, by 1 January 19X3.

Arithmetically all the figures in Table 16.1 can be found if you know the cash flows, which will be specified in the agreement, and either the profit on the lease (12%) or the re-investment rate (5%). Thus, if one of the two rates is known the other can be calculated, with the aid of a computer or a lot of patient trial and error. In practice, of course, the lessor will have made his calculations of these rates when agreeing the terms of the rental with the lessee. Thus he would start by deciding, on the basis of market conditions and competitive forces, the return he would require on the lease (taking into account the return on any surplus cash invested[12]) and hence work out the rent he would need to charge.

The next step is to calculate the proportion of the annual receipts of £2000 which is deemed to represent the reduction in the amount due from the lessee. The calculation is based on the figures in Table 16.2. This table also shows the necessary transfers to and from the deferred taxation account if it is judged necessary to establish such an account.

Table 16.2 is constructed from the bottom up. The figures in line 9 are taken from Table 16.1. The net profit is then grossed up at the appropriate tax rate (50%) to give line 5. Line 6 which shows the actual tax payments is also taken from Table 16.1 which means that line 8 (deferred tax) can be derived. Line 4 is taken from Table 16.1 and hence the gross earnings (line 3) and capital repayments (line 2) can be deduced. If, taking into consideration the affairs of the company

11 Observant readers will note that the sum of these is, at £1230, more than the 50% of the difference between the minimum lease payments and the cost of the asset, i.e. 50% of (£10 000 − £7735) = £1132. This is because the interest on the cash surplus is included in the total profit, i.e. £1230 = 50% of (£10 000 − 7735 + 45 + 98 + 52).

12 The surplus cash will probably be invested in another lease, thus the rate of return on the surplus cash will be the return from the new lease. The return on the new lease will *inter alia* depend on the return on any surplus cash it may generate which it may be presumed will be invested in yet another lease and so on *ad infinitum*. In practice, to avoid having to estimate returns on leases (or other investments) which will arise in the future, a prudent estimate of the return on surplus cash is used in the calculations.

Table 16.2

	19X0 (£)	19X1 (£)	19X2 (£)	19X3 (£)	19X4 (£)	19X5 (£)	Total (£)
1 Rental	2000	2000	2000	2000	2000		10 000
2 Capital repayments	(624)	(938)	(1978)	(2045)	(2098)	(52)	(7 735)
3 Gross earnings	1376	1062	22	(45)	(98)	(52)	2 265
4 Interest				45	98	52	195
5 Profit before tax	1376	1062	22	—	—	—	2 460
6 Taxation	2868	(1000)	(1000)	(1023)	(1049)	(26)	(1230)
7	4244	62	(978)	(1023)	(1049)	(26)	(1 230)
8 Deferred tax	(3556)	469	989	1023	1049	26	—
9 Net profit	£668	£531	£11	—	—	—	£1 230

as a whole, it is decided that it is not necessary to account for deferred tax, one could start Table 16.2 at line 5 and work up from there.

It must be emphasized that Table 16.2 is used only to calculate the capital repayment and, if appropriate, the deferred taxation transfers. For the purposes of the balance sheet presentation SSAP 21 requires that the amount due from the lessee should be the net investment (not the net cash investment) in the lease. Thus in the instance of Gasp plc the asset would be recorded as follows:

Balance sheet date	Gross investment (£)	Gross earnings allocated to future periods (£)	Net investment (£)
31 Dec. X0	8000	889	7111
31 Dec. X1	6000	(173)	6173
31 Dec. X2	4000	(195)	4195
31 Dec. X3	2000	(150)	2150
31 Dec. X4	—	(52)	52

The gross earnings allocated to future periods are found from row 3 of Table 16.2. Thus, for example, the figure at 31 December 19X0 is £(1062 + 22 − 45 − 98 − 52) = £889 and so on.

The method produces the apparently absurd result that the net investment at certain dates is greater than the remaining lease payments. The extreme case being that at 31 December 19X4 when a net investment of £52 is produced nothwithstanding the fact that the lease has terminated. This odd result derives from the fact that a larger profit is taken in the early years of the lease in consequence of the anticipated return on the surplus cash invested; thus, for example, the net investment at 31 December 19X3 of £2150 can be regarded as representing the final lease payment of £2000 plus the anticipated interest receipts of £150 (£98 in 19X4 and £52 in 19X5).

The above example assumed the existence of 100% first-year capital allowances and a high nominal rate of Corporation Tax as these assumptions make it easier to show the effect of tax on the net cash investment. The announced intention of the Chancellor in his 1984 Budget speech to remove first-year allowances and to reduce the Corporation Tax rate to 35% over a 2-year period will have a significant affect on the leasing industry. It is not expected that there will be any substantial reduction in the volume of activity although there may be a switch from finance to operating leases. From the point of view of the accountant the principles of lease accounting will be unchanged but there will be some transitional problems which, because of their specialized nature, will not be discussed in this book.

Alternative approaches to accounting for finance leases and hire purchase contracts

As stated on page 620, Para. 39 of SSAP 21 specifies that in the case of hire purchase contracts gross earnings can be allocated on the basis of the company's net investment. The reason for this is that in the case of hire purchase, capital allowances are granted to the hirer and hence the tax cash flows will not have the same significance to the hire purchase company as they have for a leasing company.

The same paragraph allows the use of alternative methods for both hire purchase and leasing companies which give 'reasonable approximations' to that which produces a constant rate of return on the net cash investment. A number of alternatives are described in the guidance notes to SSAP 21 which include the investment period method, which is similar to the actuarial method after tax. Other methods described are the 'Rule of 78' and the actuarial method before tax. These two methods are primarily intended for use with hire purchase contracts but they can be used for finance leases where the amounts concerned are not judged to be material.

A lessor may, if he chooses, write off the initial direct costs in arranging a lease over the period on a 'systematic and rational basis'.[13] This provision applies to both finance and operating leases.

Accounting for operating leases by lessors – general principles

The basic principles are contained in Paras 42–44 of SSAP 21. These are:

> An asset held for use in operating leases by a lessor should be recorded as a fixed asset and depreciated over its useful life. (Para. 42)

> Rental income from an operating lease, excluding charges for services such as insurance and maintenance, should be recognised on a straight-line basis over the period of the lease, even if the payments are not made on such a basis, unless another systematic and rational basis is more representative of the time pattern in which the benefit from the leased asset is receivable. (Para. 43)

> Initial direct costs incurred by a lessor in arranging a lease may be apportioned over the period of the lease on a systematic and rational basis. (Para. 44).

The accounting treatment of operating leases by the lessor is thus straightforward, subject only to the problems of dealing with cases where payment is not received on a straight-line basis and deciding on the circumstances where an alternative systematic and rational basis would be appropriate. These issues are similar to those faced by the lessee (*see* page 616).

Disclosure requirements for the lessor in respect of finance and operating leases and hire purchase contracts

In the case of lessors and finance companies, all the disclosure requirements come into effect in respect of accounting periods commencing on or after 1 July 1984. The requirements, contained in Paras 58–60 of SSAP 21 are as follows:

1. The net investment in (i) finance leases and (ii) hire purchase contracts should be disclosed. Note that separate totals need to be given for leases and hire purchase contracts. In the case of the remaining

13 SSAP 21, Para. 44.

disclosure requirements information regarding leases and hire purchase contracts can be combined.

2. The gross amount of assets held for use in operating leases and the related accumulated depreciation charge should be disclosed.

3. Disclosure should be made of:

(a) the policy adopted for accounting for operating leases and finance leases and, in detail, the policy for accounting for finance lease income;

(b) the aggregate rentals receivable in respect of an accounting period in relation to (i) finance leases and (ii) operating leases; and

(c) the cost of assets acquired, whether by purchase or finance lease, for the purpose of letting under finance leases.

Sale and leaseback transactions

The standard makes specific reference to sale and leaseback transactions which arise when the vendor/lessee sells an asset but continues to have the use of it on the basis of a lease granted by the purchaser/lessor. No problems arise with regard to the treatment of a sale and leaseback transaction in the accounts of the lessor who will record the asset purchased at cost and then, depending on the nature of the lease, follow the provisions of SSAP 21 in the usual way. The position regarding the vendor/lessee is different in so far that there are circumstances where the sales and leaseback transactions will have to be accorded special treatment. The nature of the circumstances depends on the type of lease.

Finance leases

The key characteristic of a finance lease is that the 'risk and reward' associated with the asset rests with the lessee. Hence when a vendor engages in a sale and finance leaseback transaction, he retains the 'risk and reward'. It is therefore argued that in such circumstances it would be wrong to recognize a profit or loss on the sale of the asset concerned in the year in which the sale and leaseback is effected.

Thus SSAP 21 states:

> In a sale and leaseback transaction which results in a finance lease, any apparent profit or loss (that is, the difference between the sale price and the previous carrying

value) should be deferred and amortised in the financial statements of the seller/ lessee over the shorter of the lease term and the useful life of the asset. (Para. 46)

If the asset was sold for its fair value, the provisions of Para. 46 could be avoided by revaluing the asset prior to sale and hence removing any difference between the sale price and the carrying value. However, to the extent that the vendor retains the 'risk and reward' any profit on the sale should not be regarded as being realized, but it would be reasonable to recognize gradually the realization of any profit over the shorter of the lease term and the useful life of the asset.

If the asset were not sold for its fair value it is likely that the consequence would be that the lease rental payments would be higher (if the asset were sold for more than its fair value) or lower than those which would be charged if the asset had been sold for its fair value. Hence it is reasonable to set the apparent profit or loss against the rental charges.

Operating leases

In the case of an operating lease the 'risks and rewards' are transferred along with the legal title to the asset. Hence any profit or loss on the sale of the asset should be recognized immediately as long as the asset was sold at its fair value.

If the asset is sold for an amount in excess of its fair value, the excess should be written back to the profit and loss account over the shorter of the remainder of the lease term or the period to the next rent review (if any).

Postscript

Since accounting for lessors is a specialized subject we have concentrated on the main principles. Interested readers will need to study SSAP 21 and the associated guidance notes to gain a full understanding of the topic.

Recommended reading

T. M. Clark, *Leasing*, McGraw-Hill, Maidenhead, 1978.
Deloitte, Haskins and Sells, *Accounting by Lessees following SSAP 21*, London, 1984.
Deloitte, Haskins and Sells, *Accounting by Lessors following SSAP 21*, London, 1984.

Questions

16.1 SSAP 21, *Accounting for Leases and Hire Purchase Contracts*, was recently published and incorporated, largely unchanged, the proposals made originally in ED29.

You are required to:
(a) state concisely the difference between operating and finance leases giving an example of each (5 marks);
(b) summarise the main requirements excluding those relating to disclosure and transitional arrangements affecting lessees (5 marks); and
(c) discuss the reasons which have led to the adoption of the requirements of SSAP 21 (8 marks).

(18 marks)

ICAEW Financial Accounting II, December 1984.

16.2 Two companies enter into an agreement whereby the lessor (Lessor Ltd) will lease on a capital (or financial) lease to the lessee (Lessee Ltd) for a period of five years from 1 September 1978 one item of plant, which will cost the lessor £1000 on 1 September 1978. The plant, to be depreciated on a straight line basis, is considered to have a nil residual value at the end of the agreement. The agreement specifies that a rental of £74 per quarter is payable in advance.

It is proposed that, in the lessor's accounts, profit should only be taken pro rata to the interest received and that the total interest element included in the rentals should be allocated over the period of the lease using the 'sum of digits' method (sometimes called the rule of 78). It is further proposed that, in the lessee's accounts, the lease should be capitalized.

You are required to:
(a) define a capital lease (sometimes, called a financial lease) and state the criteria which distinguish it from an operating lease (4 marks),
(b) show how these transactions would appear in the published accounts of both Lessor Ltd and Lessee Ltd for the year ending 31 August 1979 using the respective accounting treatments proposed above (16 marks), and
(c) compare the treatment used above for reporting the lease transactions in the lessee's accounts with the minimum legal disclosure requirements (4 marks).

(24 marks)

ICAEW Financial Accounting II, July 1978.

16.3 The Accounting Standards Committee first considered the proposed exposure drafts on leasing in 1978. Some of the proposals which have been considered include:

(1) Leases which are equivalent to the purchase of an asset (financial leases) should be capitalized in financial statements prepared by lessees and depreciated over their useful lives.

(2) Future lease rentals for financial leases which extend for more than one year beyond the balance sheet date should be disclosed separately for each of the next five years and in one sum thereafter.

(3) Lessors should account for financial leases as if they were equivalent to a loan of money. The finance charge should therefore be allocated over the period of the lease to give a constant rate of return on funds employed, and correspondingly lessees should account for the finance charge on a similar basis.

You are required to apply these proposals to the following case.

The Hard up Manufacturing Company Ltd whose year end is 31 December has acquired two items of machinery on leases, the terms of which would mean that they should be treated as financial leases.

Item A   10 annual instalments of £10000 each, the first payable on 1 January 1976. The machine was completely installed and first operated on 1 January 1976 and its purchase price on that date was £80000. The machine has an estimated useful life of 10 years at the end of which it will be of no value.

Item B   10 annual instalments of £15000 each, the first payable on 1 January 1978. The machine was completely installed and first operated on 1 January 1978 and its purchase price on that date was £117000. This machine has an estimated useful life of 12 years at the end of which it will be of no value.

The finance charges should be allocated over the period of the lease on the sum of the digits method.

The basic calculation for this allocation is shown below.

Item A
Sum the years $1 + 2 + 3 + 4 + 5 + 6 + 7 + 8 + 9 + 10 = 55$
Allocate finance charge £20000 (being £100000 – £80000) to each year

		Finance charge £	Total payment £	Capital repayment £
1976	$10/55 \times 20000 =$	3636	10000	6364
1977	$9/55$	3273	10000	6727
1978	$8/55$	2909	10000	7091
1979	$7/55$	2545	10000	7455
1980	$6/55$	2182	10000	7818
1981	$5/55$	1818	10000	8182
1982	$4/55$	1454	10000	8546
1983	$3/55$	1091	10000	8909
1984	$2/55$	727	10000	9273
1985	$1/55$	365	10000	9635
		20000		80000

Item B
Sum the years $1 + 2 + 3 + 4 + 5 + 6 + 7 + 8 + 9 + 10 = 55$
   Allocate finance charges £33 000 (being £150 000 – £117 000) to each year.

		Finance charge £	Total payment £	Capital Repayment £
1978	$10/55 \times 33\,000 =$	6 000	15 000	9 000
1979	$9/55$	5 400	15 000	9 600
1980	$8/55$	4 800	15 000	10 200
1981	$7/55$	4 200	15 000	10 800
1982	$6/55$	3 600	15 000	11 400
1983	$5/55$	3 000	15 000	12 000
1984	$4/55$	2 400	15 000	12 600
1985	$3/55$	1 800	15 000	13 200
1986	$2/55$	1 200	15 000	13 800
1987	$1/55$	600	15 000	14 400
		33 000		117 000

You are required to:
   (a) state briefly the terms that would make a lease a financial lease (4 marks),
   (b) calculate and state the charge to the profit and loss account for **1979** and **1980** if lease payments are charged thereto (2 marks),
   (c) calculate and state the charge to the profit and loss account for **1979** and **1980** if these leases are treated as financial leases and capitalised using the sum of the digits method for the finance charges (4 marks),
   (d) show how Items A and B would be incorporated in the balance sheet, and notes thereto, at **31 December 1980**, if capitalised (5 marks), and
   (e) comment on the necessity for the consideration of this topic and possible reasons for the delay in publishing a proposed standard (5 marks).

(20 marks)
Ignore taxation.
ICAEW Financial Accounting II, July 1980.

17 Accounting Standards III: Liabilities and Other Problems

Accounting for pensions

Introduction

The provision of occupational pension schemes for employees is now common practice in the UK. Some schemes are contributory, that is the cost is shared by both employees and employer, whilst others are non-contributory, that is the whole cost falls on the employer. In either case the cost to the employer may be both substantial and difficult to determine but the legal disclosure requirements are minimal and, although ED 32, 'Disclosure of pension information in company accounts', issued in May 1983, proposes a greater amount of disclosure, it does not deal with the much more controversial problem of how the cost of providing pensions should be measured.[1] We shall examine the disclosure requirements later in this section. The International Accounting Standard (IAS) 19 gives some guidance on the measurement of pension costs but, as might be expected, a large element of choice is still permitted.[2]

One distinction which may be made between pension schemes is whether they are funded or unfunded. In the case of the funded scheme, contributions are paid into a separate fund which is usually administered by trustees, who invest the contributions and meet the pension commitments. The contributions are invested in a portfolio of property and/or securities either directly or indirectly by the purchase of insurance policies. Under the unfunded schemes contributions are not placed in a separate fund but are re-invested in the employer's business and pensions are subsequently paid on a 'pay-as-you-go' basis. The unfunded pension scheme is obviously the more risky from the point

---

1 As at February 1985 the ASC has a working party studying this measurement problem.
2 IAS 19, 'Accounting for retirement benefits in the financial statements of employers', IASC, London, 1983.

of view of the employees and the vast majority of pension schemes in the UK are funded.

Another distinction which may be made is between 'defined contribution' schemes and 'defined benefit' schemes.

Under defined contribution schemes the contributions are determined and the employees receive pensions on the basis of whatever amounts are available from those contributions and the returns earned from their investment. Such a scheme poses few problems for the accountant. As the contributions are fixed the amount to be charged as the cost of providing pensions is clearly determinable as the amount payable by the employer in respect of a particular year.

Under a defined benefit scheme the retirement benefits are determined, sometimes on the basis of average salary over a period of service but more often on the basis of salary in the final year or years before retirement. For such a scheme the cost of pensions in a particular year is much more difficult to determine. It depends not upon the contribution payable in respect of a year but upon the pensions which will be paid in the future. The pensions payable depend on such factors as the future rate of increase in wages and salaries, the number of staff leaving the scheme before retirement and the life expectancy of pensioners and, where appropriate, their dependants. In addition the cost in the year of providing future pensions depends upon the rate of return to be earned on contributions and re-invested receipts. It is the need to take a very long-term view in the face of great uncertainties which makes accounting for defined benefit schemes such a difficult problem for the accountant.

Fortunately for employees, but unfortunately for accountants, all but a few small UK pension schemes are defined benefit schemes and we shall now concentrate on the problems to which they give rise. We will first deal with the treatment of pension costs in the accounts of employers and, later in the section, we will consider briefly the problem of accounting for pensions schemes.

Accounting for defined benefit schemes

The main problem
In the absence of any indication to the contrary, the going concern convention requires the accountant to assume that the company will continue to operate and that pensions to which employees are entitled, or will become entitled, will be paid. In other words he will not normally assume a discontinuance basis. In addition, the accruals convention requires that the profit and loss account be charged with the full cost

of pensions which have been earned as a result of work performed in the current period.

Where a company has a pension scheme, each participating employee usually earns an entitlement to pension during each year that he works for the company. Under a defined benefit scheme the amount of the pension which the employee receives will not be known until the date of retirement, when his salary for the final year or years of employment will be known, and the period for which a pension is payable will not be known until he or possibly his dependants die.

If the future were known with certainty, the amount of future pensions and the periods for which they are to be paid would be known. So too would the rates of return on contributions invested. As a result it would be possible to determine how much would have to be set aside in the pension fund in each period to meet the costs of pensions earned as a result of work done in that period. The amount of the contribution to the pension fund would be equal to the cost of pensions payable accruing in the particular year and could quite properly be charged as a staff cost in that year.

Even in this case of certainty, the employer may decide to contribute to the pension fund more or less than the cost of providing pensions in respect of that year. There are various methods of funding pensions and we must recognize that the funding or financing arrangements are different from the accounting problem of measuring pension costs and liabilities. It follows that, even in the case of certainty, the amount contributed to the pension fund in a particular year, would not necessarily measure the cost of providing pensions for that year.

Once we move from a word of certainty to a world of uncertainty, much greater problems arise.

In order to determine the necessary contributions, an actuary must look a very long way into the future and make both demographic and economic assumptions. The former include assumptions about the number and sex of employees, their life expectancies and the proportion of early leavers while the latter include assumptions about the rate at which salaries will increase in future and the rate of return which will be earned on the assets of the pension fund. Having considered these matters, the actuary will use a funding method to determine the amount of the contributions which must be made to the pension fund in respect of a particular year in order to be able to meet the increased pension liability arising in respect of that year.

If we assume that no contribution to the fund has been made in 19X5, the outline calculation for 19X5 might be made as follows:

	£
Actuarial liability to pay future pensions on 31 December 19X5	X
Net assets of the pension fund on 31 December 19X5	X
Contribution required for 19X5	$\overline{\overline{X}}$

If the accountant is to provide meaningful information on pension costs and liabilities he must rely on the calculation of the actuarial liability made by the actuary. Reliance on such a figure is, of course, disturbing. Not only is there the general problem of uncertainty and the fact that a small change in assumptions may lead to a very large change in the amount of the required contribution but there is also the problem that different actuaries may make different assumptions and adopt different funding methods. The funding method is the method for allocating the estimated cost of future pensions to particular periods and there are many acceptable funding methods which actuaries may employ.[3]

Even when the actuary has calculated the necessary contribution for a particular period, it does not automatically follow that the employer will pay that amount to the fund. Thus, particularly when there has been a large movement in the actuarial liability, perhaps due to reasons discussed in the next section, the employer may spread an increased contribution over a number of years rather than making it in one year. So, just as in the case of certainty, the contribution made to the fund in a particular year does not necessarily measure the cost of pensions relating to that year.

It follows that if the contributions are insufficient to meet the actuarial liability to pay expected future pensions, the profit and loss account charge should be greater than the contributions made and a provision established. Conversely, if the contributions to the fund are in excess of those needed to meet the expected costs of future pensions the profit and loss account charge should be less than the contributions made and a deferred asset should be created.

Some further problems
Two further problems need consideration: first, changes in actuarial assumptions and experience adjustments, and, second, past service costs. Experience adjustments are changes to actuarial assumptions

---

3 Readers who wish to explore this topic are referred to Christopher J. Napier, *Accounting for the Cost of Pensions*, ICAEW, London, 1983, Chapter 5. IAS 19, Para. 45(a) restricts the choice to an 'accrued benefit valuation method' or a 'projected benefit valuation method' and outlaws 'pay-as-you-go' and 'terminal funding'. However, this still leaves the actuary with an enormous amount of choice.

necessary as a result of one or more events which has actually occurred. Experience adjustments and past service costs are defined in IAS 19, as follows:[4]

> Experience adjustments are adjustments to retirement benefit costs arising from the differences between the previous actuarial assumptions as to future events and what actually occurred.

> Past service cost is the actuarially determined cost arising on the introduction of a retirement benefit plan, on the making of improvements to such a plan, or on the completion of minimum service requirements for eligibility in such a plan, all of which give employees credit for benefits for service prior to the occurrence of one or more of those events.

We have seen that in order to carry out an actuarial valuation it is necessary to make numerous assumptions about what is expected to happen in future. Given the existence of uncertainty, the assumptions made at one date and hence the valuations made at that date may need to be reassessed with the benefit of experience. Accordingly, previous assumptions and the resulting valuations may be revised at the next valuation date. How should we account for such changes?

If we think in terms of a one year period there would seem to be three possibilities:

(a) Charge or credit the whole difference in the current profit and loss account.

(b) Treat the difference between the valuation at the beginning of the year on the original assumptions and on the revised assumptions as a prior year adjustment.

(c) Spread the difference determined in (b) over a period of future years.

There is considerable difference of opinion on which of these options is appropriate. One school of thought is that, as the change of assumptions occurred in the current year, it should be reflected in the profit and loss account, a treatment which would seem to accord with the provisions of SSAP 6. Others argue that the incorporation of the revised assumptions should be treated as a prior year adjustment. However, unless the correction is of such a magnitude as to constitute a fundamental error this approach would not seem to comply with SSAP 6. Yet another view is that since changes in actuarial assumptions are bound to occur, in order to avoid erratic movements in pension costs, a smoothing process should be used.

---

4 IAS 19 Para. 5.

The International Accounting Standard permits one of two treatments. Either the adjustment should be charged or credited to the profit and loss account in the year in which it is made or it should be allocated systematically over a period not exceeding the expected remaining working lives of the participating employees.[5]

The second problem concerns past service costs. When a pension scheme is introduced or improved, it is common practice to give existing employees some credit for past periods of service. Thus such employees will become entitled to pensions or improved pensions in respect of past years in which no contributions or inadequate contributions have been made. How should we recognize the fact that there has been no charge for pension costs in past periods because no scheme existed and yet pensions will now be paid to reflect the service rendered in those past periods? Similarly, how should we recognize the fact that pension costs charged to the profit and loss account in the past, although correct at the time, are now seen to have been inadequate in view of changes which have improved the benefits under the scheme? If it is accepted that the pension cost is, like wages and salaries, a cost of employing labour, it is clear that such past service costs do not relate to prior periods. Employees have already worked and provided services on the terms which were offered and accepted in those past periods. The pensions or additional pensions are given as part of the rewards for current and future services. In view of this there is general agreement that these past service costs should not be treated as a prior year adjustment. The additional costs should therefore be treated either as a charge in the profit and a loss account for the year in which the change occurs or spread over some future period which should not exceed the expected remaining working lives of the participating employees.[6]

The disclosure requirements

Until the Companies Act 1981 the law did not even require a company to disclose the cost of pensions or the contribution payable under a pension scheme. It merely required that the financial statements disclosed 'the aggregate amount of directors' or past directors' pensions'.[7]

---

5 IAS 19, Para. 45(c).
6 IAS 19, Para. 45(c).
7 Companies Act 1948, Sec. 196, Para. 1(b). Even this requirement did not apply to any pension paid under a pension scheme where payments were substantially covered by contributions.

In accordance with the provisions of the EEC Fourth Directive, the Companies Act 1981 has extended the disclosure requirements and ED 32 proposes much greater disclosure. We shall look at the legal requirements and the ED 32 proposals in turn.

The law now requires that the financial statements of a company disclose the following:[8]

(a) Particulars of any pension commitments included as a provision in the company's balance sheet.

(b) Particulars of any pension commitments for which no provision has been made.

(c) The pension costs charged in the profit and loss account for the period.

The details given under paragraphs (a) and (b) must be analysed to show separately any pension commitments in connection with (i) a holding company or fellow subsidiary and (ii) any subsidiary of the reporting company. In addition pension commitments to past directors must be shown separately. Small companies are exempted from the requirement to disclose pension costs but group accounts must include the information required under (a), (b) and (c).[9]

In the absence of official guidance on the appropriate treatment of pensions in the accounts of the employer, it is not surprising that there is a wide variety in accounting practice. Even if it were to be agreed that the accounts should reflect the cost of pensions related to a particular accounting period rather than the contributions payable, there are a wide range of valuation approaches available to the actuary in determining the actuarial liability of the pension fund. In addition we have seen that there are different possible ways of accounting for changes in actuarial assumptions, experience adjustments and past service costs.

In view of the different possible approaches and the lack of agreement on which actuarial methods and accounting policies are appropriate, it would seem to be essential for companies to make adequate disclosure of what has been done: ED 32 lays down what the ASC considers to be adequate accounting disclosure:[10]

> Disclosure should be made in financial statements of sufficient information concerning pension arrangements to enable users of the statements to gain a broad understanding of the significance of pension costs in the accounting period and of actual contingent liabilities and commitments at the balance sheet date . . .

---

8 *See* Companies Act 1981, Schedule 1, Paras. 50(4), 50(6), 56(4) (c), 61 and 68.
9 Companies Act 1981, Sec. 6 and Schedule 1, Paras 61 and 68.
10 ED 32, Para. 38.

The Exposure Draft then provides a list of the minimum information which should be disclosed. In summary the list is as follows:

(a) Nature of the pension scheme(s).

(b) Details of the accounting policy and, if different, the funding policy, indicating the basis used for allocating pension costs to accounting periods.

(c) Date of the most recent actuarial valuation by a professional actuary.

(d) Amount charged in the profit and loss account, distinguishing between normal charges and other charges or credits.

(e) Any commitments to change contributions or make special contributions.

(f) Any provision or pre-payments in the balance sheet resulting from a difference between accounting and funding policies.

(g) Any deficiency if the fund is valued on a discontinuance basis and details of any proposed remedial action.

(h) The amount of any material self-investment (i.e. investment by the pension fund in the particular company).

(i) Information regarding any internally financed schemes.

(j) Effects on future financial statements of any changes which have been made.

While the provision of such information will undoubtedly help users of financial statements to appreciate the importance of pensions in the context of the company or group, little meaningful comparison between companies will be possible until there is agreement on the measurement of pension costs. Obtaining such agreement is likely to require the attention of the ASC for many years to come.

Pension scheme accounts

In the previous sections, we have considered the measurement of pension costs and the disclosure of pension information in the accounts of an employer. A related, although somewhat different, problem is the form and content of the accounts of the pension scheme and the ASC has issued an Exposure Draft of a Statement of Recommended Practice on this topic.[11] This is too specialized a topic for a general textbook on advanced financial accounting but, for completeness, we have decided to include a very brief summary of the problem and proposals.

11 'Exposure draft of SORP: pension scheme accounts', ASC, London, April 1984.

Reporting by pension funds is largely governed by trust law and, at the time of writing, no statutory framework for such reporting exists. The result is that considerable variety is found in the reports issued by different pension schemes and the quality of some of these reports leaves much to be desired. In view of this the ASC issued 'Pension scheme accounts: a discussion paper' in June 1982 and the Exposure Draft takes into account the comments received on that paper.

The Exposure Draft envisages that the annual report of a pension fund should comprise four elements:

(a) A trustees' report covering such matters as membership statistics, changes in benefits, financial growth of the scheme, the actuarial position and the investment policy and performance.

(b) Accounts designed to give a true and fair view of the financial transactions of the accounting period and a statement of the assets and liabilities at the accounting date.

(c) An actuarial report by a qualified actuary on the ability of the pension fund to meet accrued benefits.

(d) An investment report giving additional detail on investments, investment policy and performance.

Both the accounts under (b) and the actuarial report under (c) are prepared by experts and both are necessary for members and employers to appreciate the position of the pension scheme. Clearly the ASC has no authority to regulate the contents of the actuary's report so the Exposure Draft concentrates on the accounts.

The Exposure Draft recommends that the accounts should comprise (i) a revenue account which records the financial inflows and outflows of the fund and (ii) a net assets statement which discloses the disposition and composition of the net assets. Part 4 actually provides a detailed list of items which should be included in the accounts.

The Exposure Draft recommends the use of the accruals basis of accounting but also recommends the inclusion of assets at their current values. Needless to say, it also recommends that the accounts include a statement of all significant accounting policies.

Readers who wish to study this topic in greater detail are referred to the Exposure Draft.

Accounting for taxation

Introduction

The treatment of taxation in accounts is regulated not only by the Companies Acts, with which readers are assumed to be familiar, but also by three Statements of Standard Accounting Practice: SSAP 5, 'Accounting for value added tax' (April 1974); SSAP 8, 'The treatment of taxation under the imputation system in the accounts of companies' (amended version December 1977); and SSAP 15, 'Accounting for deferred taxation' (October 1978).

Although the treatment of value added tax may require complex book-keeping arrangements, it poses few theoretical problems and is therefore not dealt with in this book. The treatment of taxation under the imputation tax system does pose certain difficulties, whilst the appropriate treatment of deferred taxation is an extremely controversial subject. Both topics are covered in this section.

The treatment of taxation under the imputation tax system

The imputation tax system

Readers are assumed to be aware of the law relating to the taxation of companies and hence only a brief summary is provided. For simplicity it is assumed throughout this section that the rate of Corporation Tax is 50% and the rate of Advance Corporation Tax (ACT) is three-sevenths.[12]

When a company makes a distribution to shareholders in a particular period then, to the extent that the distribution has not been paid out of franked investment income of that same period, the company must pay over to the Inland Revenue ACT amounting to three-sevenths of the distribution or the excess of the distribution over franked investment income. For this purpose the year is divided into four quarters which run to 31 March, 30 June, 30 September and 31 December, although special rules are specified where a company's year does not end on one of these four dates. ACT must be paid within 14 days of the end of each quarter.[13] At the end of its accounting period the Corporation Tax payable on income (excluding franked investment income) and chargeable gains is computed. ACT in respect of distributions made during that accounting period is set against the Corporation

---

12 Until 31 March 1983 the rate of Corporation Tax was 52% but, under the provisions of the Finance Act 1984, Sect. 18, the rate is to be progressively reduced as follows:

Year to 31 March 1984	50%
1985	45%
1986	40%
1987	35%

As from 1 April 1983 the rate for small companies has been reduced from 38 to 30%.

13 Finance Act 1972, Schedule 14, Paras 1 and 3.

Tax payable on income (subject to an overriding maximum of 30% of that income) and the balance, known as Mainstream Corporation Tax, is payable at some date between 9 and 21 months after the end of the company's accounting period. The exact date of payment depends upon whether or not the company existed and was subject to income tax prior to the financial year which commenced on 1 April 1965.

Where a company resident in the UK carries on activities overseas, the profits made overseas will usually be subject to both overseas taxation and UK Corporation Tax, although, as we shall see, the UK tax payable may be reduced by all or part of the overseas tax payable.

SSAP 8
This Statement of Standard Accounting Practice requires that the following items should be included in the taxation charge in the profit and loss account and, where material, separately disclosed:[14]

(a) the amount of United Kingdom corporation tax specifying:
   (i) the charge for corporation tax on the income of the year (where such corporation tax includes transfers between the deferred taxation account these should also be separately disclosed where material);
   (ii) tax attributable to franked investment income;
   (iii) irrecoverable ACT;
   (iv) the relief for overseas taxation;
(b) the total overseas taxation, relieved and unrelieved, specifying that part of the unrelieved overseas taxation which arises from the payment or proposed payment of dividends.

We shall examine each of these items in turn, discussing both the treatment in the profit and loss account and the associated treatment in the balance sheet. Deferred taxation will be dealt with later.

Corporation Tax
At the end of each accounting period a company will compute the Corporation Tax payable on its profits, that is its income and chargeable gains, for the period using the known rate of Corporation Tax or the most recent rate if the actual rate is not known. The resulting liabilities will be deducted from the relevant ordinary or extraordinary profits in the profit and loss account and credited to a corporation tax payable account.

---

14 SSAP 8, Para. 22.

As mentioned above, the date of payment of such Corporation Tax will depend upon whether or not the company was within the charge to Income Tax prior to 1 April 1965. Where, for example, an established trading company makes up its accounts to 31 March each year, Income Tax for the year 1965/66, payable on 1 January 1966, was based upon its taxable profits for the accounting year ended in the preceding year of assessment 1964/65, that is the accounting year ended on 31 March 1965. Thus tax on the profits for the year ended 31 March 1965 was payable on 1 January 1966. The gap of 9 months would continue to apply and hence Corporation Tax for the year ended 31 March 1984 would be payable on 1 January 1985.

Where an established company makes up its accounts, not to 31 March, but to 30 April the position will be somewhat different. Here Income Tax for 1965/66, payable on 1 January 1966, would have been based upon the profits for the year ended 30 April 1964. Thus tax on profits for the year ended 30 April 1964 would not have been payable until 1 January 1966, an interval of 20 months. For such a company Corporation Tax for the year ended 30 April 1984 would not be payable until 1 January 1986.

It follows that, although the first company will only show one liability for Corporation Tax payable on any balance sheet date, the second company will show liabilities for Corporation Tax payable for two years. Using the circumstances given above, a company making up its accounts to 30 April 1984 would show the following liabilities:

Liabilities on 30 April 1984

	£
Corporation Tax on profits for year to 30 April 1983 payable 1 January 1985	X
Corporation Tax on profits for year to 30 April 1984 payable 1 January 1986	Y

The first of the two amounts is payable 9 months after the balance sheet date and is therefore a current liability. The second amount is not payable until 20 months after the balance sheet date and is therefore classified as a creditor falling due after more than 1 year. Although the balance sheet formats include appropriate headings for 'Other creditors including taxation and social security', the Companies Act 1981 specifically requires the disclosure of the amount of creditors for taxation and social security separate from other creditors.[15]

---

15 Schedule 1, Part 1, notes on the balance sheet formats (9).

Tax on franked investment income

Frequently a company which is resident in the UK receives dividends, more generally distributions, from one or more other companies also resident in the UK. The amount of such dividends plus the associated tax credits is known as 'franked investment income'. Thus, if a company receives a dividend of £700 and the relevant rate of tax credit is three-sevenths, the franked investment income is £1000. Such franked investment income is not subject to Corporation Tax.

Although it would be possible to ignore the tax credit altogether and merely to record as a source of income the amount of the dividend received, this would be inconsistent with the treatment of other sources of income. SSAP 8, Para. 13, therefore requires that the franked investment income, that is the 'gross' amount, should be shown as income whilst the tax credit should be shown as part of the taxation charge. Using the figures above, receipt of the dividend would be recorded as part of the profit and loss account entries as follows:

	£	£
Income from investments		1000
less Taxation:		
Corporation Tax, etc.	×	
Taxation on franked investment income	<u>300</u>	×

As we have seen, it is possible for a company which receives franked investment income to reduce the amount of ACT payable in respect of a distribution by the amount of the tax credit on that franked investment income for the same period. It should be noted that this merely affects the amount of ACT payable and does not alter the accounting treatment discussed above.

ACT

When a company pays a dividend it will, assuming it has received insufficient franked investment income, also have to pay an amount of ACT within 14 days of the end of the relevant quarter or other shorter period. It follows that whenever a company provides for a dividend in its accounts it must also provide for the associated ACT payable. Such ACT payable is a current liability and, like the dividend payable, is extinguished when payment is made. The creation of this liability for ACT involves a credit entry in an account for 'ACT payable' but it is, of course, necessary to have a debit entry in an account which may be described as 'ACT recoverable'. As explained earlier, the law proposes that this amount will in due course be set off against Corporation Tax payable on the income for the accounting period in which the dividend is paid. This treatment may best be illustrated by means of an example:

Let us suppose that we are dealing with a company which makes up its accounts annually to 31 December and pays Mainstream Corporation Tax 9 months after that date. In the year ended 31 December 19X1 it pays an interim dividend of £70 000 on 17 July and has a taxable income of £400 000. It follows that ACT amounting to £30 000 (three-sevenths of £70 000) becomes payable on 14 October 19X1, 14 days after the end of the quarter in which the dividend is paid. Mainstream Corporation Tax payable on 30 September 19X2 is computed as follows:

	£000s
Corporation Tax for accounting year ended 31 December 19X1, 50% of £400 000	200
less ACT on dividends paid in year ended 31 December 19X1	30
Mainstream Corporation Tax	170

The relevant book-keeping entries relating to taxation, assuming that all payments are made on the due dates, are

ACT payable

19X1	£	19X1	£
14 Oct. Cash	30 000	17 Jul. ACT recoverable	30 000

ACT recoverable

19X1	£	19X1	£
17 Jul. ACT payable	30 000	31 Dec. Corporation Tax payable	30 000

Corporation Tax payable

19X1	£	19X1	£
31 Dec. ACT recoverable	30 000	31 Dec. Profit and loss account	200 000
Mainstream CT c/d	170 000		
	200 000		200 000
		19X2	
		1 Jan. Balance b/d	170 000

The profit and loss account for 19X1 includes a Corporation Tax charge of £200 000 whilst the balance sheet on 31 December 19X1 contains a current liability for Mainstream Corporation Tax of £170 000 payable on 30 September 19X2.

The example may now be expanded to include not only the interim dividend paid but also a proposed final dividend of £105 000 payable on 20 March 19X2. The payment of this dividend will give rise to a payment of ACT of £45 000 on 14 April 19X2, 14 days after the end of the relevant quarter. As the final dividend is recognized as a current liability on 31 December 19X1, it is also necessary to provide for the current liability for ACT by crediting the 'ACT payable' account. Correspondingly it is necessary to debit the 'ACT recoverable' account.

It is the date of payment of the dividend[16] which determines the appropriate accounting year for set off. Thus, as the final dividend is not paid until 20 March 19X2, the ACT will be set off against the Corporation Tax payable on income for the year ended 31 December 19X2. In this example, such Corporation Tax is not payable until 30 September 19X3. In other words at 31 December 19X1 the ACT of £45 000 is not recoverable for 21 months. It therefore represents a deferred asset to be shown as a debtor in the balance sheet or, more usually, set against any credit balance in respect of income in the deferred taxation account.

The appropriate accounting entries in respect of taxation, repeating those dealt with above, are as follows:

ACT payable

19X1	£	19X1	£
14 Oct. Cash	30 000	17 Jul. ACT recoverable	30 000
		31 Dec. ACT recoverable (re proposed dividend)	45 000

ACT recoverable

19X1	£	19X1	£
		31 Dec. Corporation Tax	
17 Jul. ACT payable	30 000	payable	30 000
31 Dec. ACT payable	45 000		

16 Note that is the date of payment of the dividend, *not* the date of payment of the ACT, which determines the appropriate year for set off. Thus ACT in respect of a dividend paid on 14 November 19X1 may be set off against the Corporation Tax liability for the year to 31 December 19X1, even though it is not paid until 14 January 19X2.

Corporation Tax payable

19X1	£	19X1	£
31 Dec. ACT recoverable	30 000	31 Dec. Profit and loss	
Mainstream CT		account	200 000
c/d	170 000		
	200 000		200 000
		19X2	
		1 Jan. Mainstream CT	
		payable 30	
		Sep. 19X2	
		b/d	170 000

The profit and loss account for 19X1 will, as before, include the Corporation Tax charge of £200 000. The balance sheet on 31 December 19X1 will include two current liabilities in respect of taxation:

	£
ACT payable on 14 April 19X2 in respect of final dividend for 19X1	45 000
Mainstream Corporation Tax for 19X1 payable on 30 September 19X2	170 000
	215 000

It will also include the amount of £45 000 in respect of ACT recoverable either as a debtor due after more than one year or as a reduction in the credit balance on deferred taxation account.

So far it has been assumed that the company has sufficient income subject to Corporation Tax for the set off of ACT to be possible. Because successive governments have granted high initial capital allowances and stock relief, both of which reduce taxable profits, this has not been the case for many companies. Where such companies have no Corporation Tax liability against which to set ACT, it is necessary to consider whether or not any debit balance on ACT recoverable account should be regarded as an asset or instead written off to the profit and loss account as 'irrecoverable Advance Corporation Tax'.

In considering this question it is most important not to confuse the treatment of ACT recoverable for taxation purposes with its accounting treatment. For taxation purposes ACT unrelieved due to insufficient taxable income for the accounting period may be carried back for two years or carried forward indefinitely. If it is carried back then the ACT is, of course, recovered: If it is carried forward then nothing that is done in the accounts will remove the right of ultimate set off for taxation purposes. However, the ACT will only be recovered if there is sufficient taxable income in future years and, if the company is not expected to generate such taxable income, then it may be argued that prudence dictates that the ACT recoverable should no longer be regarded as an asset but should instead be written off to the profit and loss account. This need to write off ACT recoverable does not apply where it is set off against a credit balance on deferred taxation account but only where the ACT recoverable is treated as a separate deferred asset. In this case SSAP 8 states that it is prudent only to have regard to the immediate and forseeable future and suggests that this should normally not extend beyond the next accounting period.[17]

We have now explained why the tax charge shown in the profit and loss account may include 'irrecoverable Advance Corporation Tax'.

Overseas taxation

A company resident in the UK is liable to Corporation Tax on all its profits whether they arise in the UK or overseas. As profits which have arisen overseas are usually subject to taxation in the relevant overseas country they may therefore be subject to double taxation. Similarly, where a UK company receives dividends from the taxed profits of an overseas subsidiary, such dividends are neither franked investment income nor group income and hence are subject to UK Corporation Tax.

It is usually possible to obtain relief for such double taxation, although the precise nature of the relief depends upon whether or not a double taxation convention has been negotiated between the UK government and the relevant overseas government. Where there is no double tax convention, it is still possible to obtain unilateral relief for double taxation.[18]

In some cases it is possible to obtain relief against UK Corporation Tax for the whole of the overseas taxation payable. In other cases some of the overseas taxation may be unrelieved.

We shall examine two situations in which overseas taxation may be unrelieved. The first arises where the rate of overseas taxation on overseas profits exceeds the rate of UK Corporation Tax on those same profits. The second arises where the payment of a sufficiently large UK dividend restricts the relief for overseas taxation.

Let us suppose that a UK company has taxable profits of £300 000 overseas and an additional £800 000 in the UK. The rate of overseas Corporation Tax is 60% whilst the rate of UK Corporation Tax is 50%.

The Corporation Tax payable overseas is 60% of £300 000, that is

---

17 SSAP 8, Para. 6.
18 Income and Corporation Taxes Act 1970, Sec. 498, and Finance Act 1972, Sec. 100.

£180 000, whilst the Corporation Tax payable in the UK is 50% of £(800 000 + 300 000), that is £550 000. As the UK Corporation Tax payable on overseas income is only £150 000 (50% × £300 000) this is the maximum relief which may be given against the overseas taxation of £180 000.

Following the layout of Appendix 1 to SSAP 8, the taxation charge in the profit and loss account would therefore include the following;

	£000s
Corporation Tax on income at 50%	550
less Relief for overseas taxation	150
	400
Overseas taxation	180
	580

To illustrate the second situation, let us take a company which has a UK taxable income of £600 000 and an overseas taxable income of £400 000, subject to an overseas tax rate of 35%. If no dividend was paid or payable, the profit and loss account would have included the following tax charge:

	£000s
Corporation Tax on income at 50%	500
less Relief for overseas taxation, 35% of £400 000	140
	360
Overseas taxation (35% of £400 000)	140
	500

If, however, the company had paid a dividend of £700 000, part of the relief would have been lost. This is because, for accounting periods ending prior to 31 March 1984, the ACT had to be set off against Corporation Tax prior to calculating the relief for overseas tax. In this example, the effect would have been as follows:

	UK (£000s)	Overseas (£000s)	Total (£000s)
Income	600	400	1000
Corporation Tax at 50%	300	200	500
less ACT (max. 30%)	180	120	300
	120	80	200
less Overseas tax relief (£140 000) limited to	—	80	80
	120	—	120

As a result, the tax charge in the profit and loss account would have included the following items:

	£000s
Corporation Tax on income at 50%	500
less Relief for overseas tax	80
	420
Overseas tax, including £60 000 unrelieved due to payment of a dividend	140
	560

We have now illustrated all of the items which SSAP 8 require to be disclosed in the profit and loss account or notes to the accounts. However, for accounting periods ending on or after 1 April 1984, there will no longer be overseas taxation unrelieved as a result of payment of or provision for a dividend. The Finance Act 1984 now reverses the order of set off so that the Corporation Tax attributable to overseas income is first reduced by the overseas taxation and only then by the ACT.[19]

Accounting for deferred taxation

The case for comprehensive tax allocation
Although accounting profits form the basis for the computation of taxable profits in the UK, for most companies there are substantial differences between the two. Such differences may be divided into two categories: (a) permanent differences; (b) timing differences.

In the case of permanent differences certain items of revenue or expense properly taken into account in arriving at accounting profit are not included when arriving at taxable profit. Examples are amounts spent on entertainment, other than that afforded to overseas customers, and depreciation of non-industrial buildings.

In the case of timing differences, the same total amount is added or subtracted in arriving at both accounting profits and taxable profits over a period of years, but it is added or subtracted in different periods for accounting and taxation purposes. To give an example, the law grants capital allowances at specified rates in respect of capital expenditure on plant and machinery. For expenditure on or before 13 March 1984 there was a first-year allowance of 100% but this first-year allowance is now being phased out over a period of years so that eventually

19 Finance Act 1984, Sec. 53.

only a writing down allowance of 25% of the reducing balance will be granted. [20]

Whatever the tax allowance, for accounting purposes the plant and machinery is depreciated over its useful life in accordance with the provisions of SSAP 12. [21] The effect is that, although over the life of the asset the same amount of depreciation is charged for both taxation and accounting purposes, the amounts charged in each year will differ.

It is the existence of such timing differences which has supported the practice of accounting for deferred taxation and the provision for deferred taxation on all material timing differences may be described as comprehensive tax allocation. SSAP 15 identified five major categories of timing difference: [22]

(a) short-term timing differences from the use of the receipts and payments basis for taxation purposes and the accruals basis in financial statements: these differences normally reverse in the next accounting period;

(b) availability of capital allowances in taxation computations which are in excess of the related depreciation charges in financial statements;

(c) availability of stock appreciation relief in taxation computations for which there is no equivalent charge in financial statements;

(d) revaluation surpluses on fixed assets for which a taxation charge does not arise until the gain is realized on disposal;

(e) surpluses on disposals of fixed assets which are subject to rollover relief.

Since SSAP 15 was issued, the rules governing stock appreciation relief have been fundamentally changed on two occasions. In the Finance Act 1981 changes were made which resulted in stock relief effectively becoming a permanent difference, rather than a timing difference, for most companies. Then in the Finance Act 1984, stock relief was abo-

---

20 Finance Act 1984, Sec. 58 and Schedule 12. The rate of first-year allowance on plant and machinery has been fixed as follows:

Capital expenditure	Percentage
Up to 13 March 1984	100
14 March 1984 to 31 March 1985	75
1 April 1985 to 31 March 1986	50
From 1 April 1986	Nil

21 *See* Chapter 15
22 SSAP 15, Para. 6.

lished for all accounting periods beginning after 12 March 1984.[23] It follows that 'the availability of stock appreciation relief' will, in due course, be deleted from the list of major categories of timing difference.

In compensation for this deletion, SSAP 21, 'Accounting for leases and hire purchase contracts', introduces a new timing difference in respect of finance leases which are capitalized. If we concentrate on the lessee, he receives taxation relief each year on the rentals payable under the lease. However, in the accounts, the profit and loss account is charged with depreciation of the leased asset and interest on the finance provided. Over the life of the lease/asset the total amounts charged in the taxation computations and accounts will be exactly the same but in each individual year the amounts will differ.

An amended list of major categories of timing difference would therefore read as follows:

(a) short-term timing differences;
(b) capital allowances/depreciation;
(c) capitalization of finance leases;
(d) unrealized revaluation surpluses;
(e) realized surpluses subject to rollover relief.

One of the four fundamental accounting concepts listed in SSAP 2 is the 'accruals' concept, under which expenses are matched with revenues.[24] If taxation is regarded as an expense, then it may be argued that it is subject to this concept and that the taxation charge should therefore be matched against the accounting profit to which it relates, irrespective of the date on which the tax is paid. This may be illustrated by an example. Let us suppose that Sabah Limited makes up its accounts annually to 31 December and that on 1 January 19X1 it purchases a machine at a cost of £150 000. The machine has an expected life of 3 years and an expected scrap value of zero. Although it is eligible for a 100% first-year allowance for taxation purposes the straight-line method is considered appropriate for accounting purposes. Let us assume also that Sabah Limited has profits before depreciation and taxation of £200 000 each year. If no provision is made for deferred taxation, the profit and loss accounts for the three years of the machine's life would appear as follows:

---

23 *See* Finance Act 1981, Schedule 9 and Finance Act 1984, Sec. 48. ED 33 was issued in June 1983 to deal, *inter alia*, with the former of these changes.
24 *See* Chapter 2.

Profit and loss account for the three years ending 31 December 19X1, 19X2 and 19X3

	19X1 (£000s)	19X2 (£000s)	19X3 (£000s)
Profit before depreciation and taxation	200	200	200
less Depreciation	50	50	50
	150	150	150
less Corporation Tax			
50% × (£200 000 − £150 000)	25		
50% × £200 000		100	100
Profit after taxation	125	50	50

The picture shown by these profit and loss accounts is arguably misleading and, in particular, any predictions of profit after tax made using the accounts of 19X1 may tend to be too high. The purchase of a machine at a cost of £150 000 in 19X1 has given rise to a tax saving of £75 000. If the cost of the machine is spread over the accounts for the three years of its life then surely the tax saving should also be spread over that same period by the use of a deferred taxation account:

Profit and loss account for the three years ending 31 December 19X1, 19X2 and 19X3

	19X1 (£000s)	19X2 (£000s)	19X3 (£000s)
Profit before depreciation and taxation	200	200	200
less Depreciation	50	50	50
Profit before taxation	150	150	150
less Taxation			
Corporation Tax (as above)			
50% × (£200 000 − £150 000)	25		
50% × £200 000		100	100
Deferred tax			
On originating timing difference, 50% × (£150 000 − £50 000)	50		
On reversing timing differences, 50% × (£0 − £50 000)		(25)	(25)
	75	75	75
Profit after taxation	75	75	75

In 19X1 capital allowances exceed depreciation by £100000, so that taxable profit is lower than accounting profit. In both 19X2 and 19X3 the depreciation exceeds capital allowances by £50000, so that accounting profit is lower than taxable profit. As may be seen above, the use of a deferred taxation account in this simple situation results in a tax charge based upon the accounting profit of each period. In 19X1 the profit and loss account is debited and deferred taxation account credited with tax on the originating timing difference of £100000 whilst in each of the following two years, deferred taxation account is debited and profit and loss account credited with tax on the reversing timing difference of £50000.

In such simple circumstances it is possible to argue that the use of a deferred taxation account is necessay to comply with the accruals concept and, in addition, that deferred tax accounting provides useful information. However, it is important to bear in mind the simplifications which have been made.

First, we have looked at the purchase and use of just one machine and have not considered the position where a company regularly purchases machines. This will be examined in the next section.

Second, we have assumed that the rate of Corporation Tax is the same in each of the three years. Were the rate of tax to change then it would be necessary to make a choice on whether to apply the 'deferral' method or the 'liability' method of accounting for deferred taxation.

Under the deferral method all reversing timing differences in respect of an asset are, in principle, reversed at the same rate of tax as that applied to the originating timing difference on that asset. To apply this method strictly involves extensive record keeping and hence, when it is used in practice, it is usual to apply an approximate 'net change' method. Thus, where there is a net originating difference for a group of assets in a particular year it is dealt with at the current rate of tax. If, however, there is a net reversing difference in respect of those assets, it is reversed using some rule of thumb, such as FIFO or the average rate of tax on accumulated timing differences.

Under the liability method, whenever there is a change in the rate of tax the balance on the deferred taxation account is adjusted to that current rate of tax on accumulated timing differences. Subsequent reversing differences are made at the new rate of tax. It follows that, to operate the liability method, it is not necessary to keep such detailed records as those required for the deferral method as calculations may be made in total. To give one example: to calculate the balance on deferred taxation required because of the differences in capital allowances and depreciation on fixed assets, it is merely necessary to know the difference between the net book value and the tax written down value of the relevant assets and the current rate of tax on the balance sheet date. The liability method is therefore much simpler to apply than the deferral method and has been the more popular of the two methods.

The case against comprehensive tax allocation
Although comprehensive tax allocation seemed to provide useful information in the simple situation discussed above, its usefulness in more complex situations may be questioned. After all, most companies do not just purchase and use one machine. They purchase on a regular basis assets which have been eligible for accelerated tax allowances and have enjoyed both stock relief and rollover relief on chargeable gains. For such a company the originating timing differences regularly exceeded the reversing timing differences with the result that the balance on deferred taxation account grew over time to become a very large item in the company's balance sheet.

To illustrate this situation, let us suppose that a company, Kuching Limited, makes up its accounts to 31 December each year and buys one machine on 1 January each year. Each machine has an expected life of 3 years and an expected scrap value of zero. It qualifies for a 100% first-year allowance but is depreciated over its expected life using the straight-line method. Due to rising prices, the cost of the machine in successive years is as follows:

	£
1 January 19X1	150 000
19X2	180 000
19X3	216 000

The capital allowances and depreciation of Kuching Limited for 3 years may be summarized as follows:

Year ended 31 December:	19X1 (£000s)	19X2 (£000s)	19X3 (£000s)
Capital allowances			
Machine bought 1 January 19X1	150		
19X2		180	
19X3			216
Carried forward	150	180	216

	19X1 (£000s)	19X2 (£000s)	19X3 (£000s)
Capital allowances b/f	150	186	216
Depreciation			
Machine bought 1 January 19X1	50	50	50
19X2		60	60
19X3			72
	50	110	182
Net originating difference	100	70	34

Each year there is a net originating difference, with the result that the balance on deferred taxation account becomes larger and larger. An examination of the accounts of companies which used comprehensive tax allocation shows how rarely there was a 'draw down' or reduction in the deferred tax account balance from year to year and how large such a balance may become.[25]

The deferred taxation balance is normally disclosed as a separate item in the balance sheet of a company and certainly not as part of the shareholders' equity[26] If the balance is not part of the shareholders' equity, then a knowledge of elementary accounting would suggest that it is a liability. However, this may be questioned. As we have seen, for many companies it may well not be payable in the forseeable future and, in such cases, its inclusion in the balance sheet may therefore be regarded as inconsistent with the going concern concept.

The inclusion of an amount for deferred taxation in the balance sheet of a company undoubtedly poses problems of interpretation in many cases. If the amount is not part of the shareholders' equity then it must presumably be included as a part of other long-term capital in measuring gearing, although in this case many UK companies which used comprehensive tax allocation appeared to be rather highly geared!

Attempts at standardization: ED 11 to SSAP 15
The Accounting Standards Steering Committee made its first attempt at a standard method of accounting for deferred taxation when it issued ED 11, 'Accounting for deferred taxation', in May 1973. This proposed that companies should account for deferred taxation on all material timing differences using the deferral method; thus it favoured compre-

---

25 For example, the annual accounts of Thorn Electrical Industries Limited showed that deferred taxation was approximately one-third of the long-term capital in 1978. This fell considerably when the company adopted partial tax allocation in 1979.
26 Successive pronouncements of the ASC have emphasized this. *See*, for example, SSAP 15, Para. 37.

hensive tax allocation. The ensuing SSAP 11, which was published in August 1975, followed this approach, although it permitted companies to use either the deferral method or the liability method.

SSAP 11 came under such heavy criticism from industry that its starting date was postponed indefinitely and it was eventually withdrawn. The ASC was criticized for this withdrawal and many saw it as a manifestation of weakness, that is the ASC bending in the face of opposition rather than taking a strong line. Others saw it as an example of the ASC rightly responding to criticism, although even such supporters would argue that critics should make their views known during the exposure period rather than after a standard has been published.

ED 19, which was issued in May 1977, adopted a very different approach from SSAP 11. Instead of requiring comprehensive tax allocation, it permitted partial tax allocation in certain circumstances. Thus, instead of requiring companies to perfom a mechanical calculation to provide for deferred taxation on all timing differences, it recognized that not all timing differences would reverse in the foreseeable future and consequently permitted a more subjective approach which took into account the circumstances of the particular company. Even where a company took advantage of this permissive approach, it still required a note to the balance sheet showing the potential deferred taxation on all timing differences. This potential deferred taxation was to be calculated using the liability method.

SSAP 15, issued in October 1978, followed the approach of ED 19 and permits partial tax allocation providing certain conditions are satisfied. Similarly, where a partial provision is made, SSAP 15 requires a note of the potential deferred tax on all timing differences, distinguishing between the major categories of timing difference and showing for each category the amount actually provided in the accounts. Unlike ED 19, SSAP 15 does not require the use of the liability method for the purposes of the note.

Since SSAP 15 was issued in October 1978 there have been changes to both company law and taxation law and ED 33 was issued, primarily in response to these changes, in June 1983. Although we shall examine briefly the provisions of ED 33 later in this section, there have been yet further changes to taxation law since June 1983 and any revised standard will take these into account. Until a new standard is issued, SSAP 15 remains in force[27] so we shall now examine the provisions of that standard.

27 ED 33, Para. 39.

The approach of SSAP 15
SSAP 15 requires comprehensive tax allocation except where the tax effects of timing differences can be demonstrated with reasonable probability to continue in the future due either to recurring or continuing timing differences or, in the case of revalued assets, by the continuing use of the assets or the postponement of liability on their sale.[28]

Paragraphs 28–30 of the statement provide the criteria which must be satisfied before it is possible for a company to provide an amount less than that required by the application of comprehensive tax allocation:

> It will be reasonable to assume that timing differences will not reverse and tax liabilities will therefore not crystallise if, but only if, the company is a going concern and:
>
> (a) the directors are able to foresee on reasonable evidence that no liability is likely to arise as a result of reversal of timing differences for some considerable period (at least three years) ahead; and
> (b) there is no indication that after this period the situation is likely to change so as to crystallize the liabilities[29]

As we have seen, there are five major categories of timing difference, although the list now differs from that included in SSAP 15 itself. Let us apply the principles of SSAP 15 to each of these five categories of timing differences:

(a) *Short-term timing differences*   Deferred taxation must always be provided on these as they will normally reverse in the following accounting period.

(b) *Capital allowances and depreciation*   In the example of Kuching Limited given above we have seen that for a company which regularly purchases fixed assets subject to accelerated capital allowances, new originating timing differences may exceed reversing timing differences. Even if there is a reduction in the amount spent on fixed assets, the new originating differences will, at least, reduce the effect of reversing timing differences. In such cases, it may be possible for the company to provide less than the full potential amount of deferred taxation.

As we have seen, the statement provides that no provision will be required at a balance sheet date so long as, first, the company is a going concern; second, the directors are able to forecast on reasonable evidence that capital allowances will exceed depreciation for at least

---

28 SSAP 15, Paras 26 and 27.
29 SSAP 15, Para. 28.

the next 3 years; and, third, there is no evidence to suggest that the situation will change after this period. The decision on whether capital allowances are likely to exceed depreciation in the foreseeable future should be based upon the directors' intentions and plans for that period. It must be stressed that any decision not to provide for the full potential deferred taxation must be taken in the light of past experience and, in particular, the accuracy of past forecasts. If there is doubt on whether the three conditions are satisfied, full or partial provision must be made. A partial provision will be possible where, although net originating differences are expected in most years, some net reversing differences are expected in the foreseeable future. To illustrate, let us assume that a company, Teluk plc, is preparing its accounts for the year ended 31 March 1985 and, taking into account the expected rates of capital allowances and the company's depreciation policy, it has produced the following forecasts for the next 4 years:

Forecasts for the years ended 31 March 1986–89

	1986 (£000s)	1987 (£000s)	1988 (£000s)	1989 (£000s)
Capital allowances	100	100	60	120
Depreciation	80	90	95	100
Net originating differences	20	10	—	20
Net reversing differences	—	—	35	—

In the year ended 31 March 1988, the taxable profits are expected to exceed the accounting profits by £35 000 and, given that the rate of tax in the year to 31 March 1988 is expected to be 35%, the tax involved is 35% of £35 000 which is £12 250. The most prudent partial provision on 31 March 1985 would therefore be £12 250.

However, it may be argued that this is much too prudent and that it is necessary to take a cumulative view of the position in future years. On this basis the net reversing difference in the year to 31 March 1988 is preceded by net originating differences in the years 1985/86 and 1986/87. Thus it will be possible to make additional provisions in those two years so that the minimum amount to be provided at 31 March 1985 may be calculated as follows:

	£	£
Net reversing differences in 1987/88		35 000
less Future net originating differences:		
1985/86	20 000	
1986/87	10 000	
		30 000
		5 000
Minimum provision necessary at 31 March 1985:		
£5000 × 35%		£1 750

If this approach is adopted then the provision at 31 March 1985 will be £1750 and, providing the forecasts are met, provisions of £7000 (£20 000 × 35%) and £3500 (£10 000 × 35%) will be made in 1985/86 and 1986/87, respectively, so that, by the beginning of the year in which the net reversing difference occurs, there will be an accumulated provision equal to taxation on the net reversing difference, in this case £12 250.

SSAP 15 provides no guidance on how such a partial provision should be calculated but merely states 'The partial amount not provided for should be based upon substantiated calculations and assumptions which are explained in the financial statements.'[30]

(c) *Capitalization of finance leases*   As we have seen in the previous chapter, SSAP 21 requires a lessee to capitalize finance leases. A consequence of this is that the profit and loss account is charged with depreciation and finance charges (interest) rather than with the rentals payable. As taxation relief is granted on lease rentals payable, the capitalization of leases gives rise to a timing difference.

In order to determine the amount of provision required in accordance with the principles of SSAP 15, it is necessary to look into the future. Considering both finance leases already entered into before the balance sheet date and the finance leases which the company expects to enter into in the foreseeable future, forecasts of the depreciation of leased assets, finance charges and rentals payable in each year must be made. The forecast charges in the profit and loss account must then be compared with the rentals payable to determine whether or not a net reversing difference is expected to occur in the foreseeable future.

---

30 SSAP 15, Para. 30.

Let us suppose that Teluk plc is making up its accounts to 31 March 1985 and that the directors prepare the following forecasts for the next 4 years:

Forecasts for the years ended 31 March 1986–89

	1986 (£000s)	1987 (£000s)	1988 (£000s)	1989 (£000s)
Depreciation of leased assets	40	45	43	50
Finance charges re leased assets	16	20	18	15
	56	65	61	65
Rentals payable under finance leases	70	60	60	70
Net originating differences	14	—	—	5
Net reversing differences	—	5	1	—

Net reversing differences are expected in 1986/87 and 1987/88. In total these amount to £6000 and, if we assume that there are no net reversing differences expected after 31 March 1989, the most prudent partial provision at 31 March 1985 would be £6000 at the rate of corporation tax expected in 1986/87 and 1987/88, namely 35%. Hence the most prudent partial provision would be £2100 (£6000 × 35%).

However, it may be argued that this provision is too large in view of the fact that expected net originating timing differences in 1985/86 (£14 000) far exceed the expected net reversing differences (£6000) expected in the foreseeable future. If this view is taken then it follows that no provision for deferred taxation is required at 31 March 1985. Providing that there is no change in expectations an amount of £2100 (£6000 × 35%) would be provided in the following year 1985/86 and this would be sufficient to offset the higher tax charges in 1986/87 and 1987/88.

It would, of course, be necessary to explain how the amount not provided for has been calculated.[31]

(d) *Revaluation surpluses on fixed assets for which a taxation charge does not arise until the gain is realized on disposal* Taxation on a revaluation surplus only becomes payable when that surplus is realized, and then only if no rollover relief is available. It follows that a provision for deferred tax will only be necessary if the directors intend to sell

31 SSAP 15, Para. 30.

the revalued asset in the foreseeable future in circumstances where it is not possible to take advantage of rollover relief. If such a sale is not expected then no provision for deferred taxation is necessary.

(e) *Surpluses on disposals of fixed assets which are subject to rollover relief* As under (d) above, tax will only become payable on such a surplus if the replacement asset is sold and no rollover relief is possible at that time. Where such a sale is not envisaged in the foreseeable future no provision for deferred taxation is necessary.

It must be emphasized that where only a partial provision is made in the accounts, SSAP 15 requires the full amount of the potential deferred taxation to be stated by way of a note. The note should distinguish between the different categories of deferred taxation and also show for each category the amount that has been provided in the accounts.

We have now examined the approach of SSAP 15 to determining whether or not a provision for deferred taxation is required and how the amount of any partial provision for each category of timing difference may be calculated. One further problem remains. To what extent is it possible to set off expected reversing differences on one category of timing differences against originating differences on another category of timing differences? For example, to what extent is it possible to offset future net reversing differences in respect of capital allowances/ depreciation against future net originating differences on short-term items or revaluation surpluses in deciding whether or not a provision is necessary. A Statement of Intent (SOI) issued in April 1984 envisages that the standard will require that all differences should be considered together:[32]

> Short-term and other timing differences should be considered together when an assessment is made of whether a tax liability will crystallize; it will not be necessary to account for deferred tax on all short-term timing differences.

If the objective of deferred tax accounting is to arrive at a meaningful provision in respect of net reversing differences expected in the foreseeable future, such a global approach is undoubtedly sensible.

Proposed modifications to SSAP 15
As explained briefly above, ED 33 was issued in June 1983 primarily in response to changes in company law and revenue law, more specifically changes in the disclosure requirements made in the Companies Act 1981 and changes in stock relief made in the Finance Act 1981.

---

32 SOI, Para. 4(i), ASC, April 1984.

More substantial changes to taxation have been made in the Finance Act 1984 and, in response to these expected changes, the ASC issued a Statement of Intent in April 1984.

ED 33 and the Statement of Intent address a large number of detailed matters but the major change is one of emphasis.

As we have seen above, SSAP 15 requires a company to provide for deferred taxation in full unless certain criteria are satisfied. Directors may only make a zero or partial provision if that is supported by appropriate forecasts. In order to avoid the difficulties of making such forecasts in an uncertain world, it appears that many companies have decided not to concern themselves with such forecasts but rather to make a full provision. Thus, while some companies have tried to arrive at a meaningful partial provision, others, in similar circumstances, have provided for deferred taxation in full. The result has been a lack of comparability of post-tax profits.

To avoid this lack of comparability, ED 33 has proposed that all companies should make a meaningful provision. Thus all companies should make an assessment of their likely future position and should refrain from accounting for timing differences which are unlikely to give rise to a liability in the foreseeable future:[33]

> Deferred tax should be provided in respect of the tax effects arising from all timing differences of material amount to the extent that it is probable that a liability will crystallize.

> Deferred tax should not be provided to the extent that it is probable that a liability will not crystallize.

Thus, under the provisions in ED 33 it would no longer be permissible to make mechanical calculations and provide for deferred taxation in full. Whether or not this proposed approach will prove acceptable to the large number of small companies in the UK remains to be seen.

While ED 33 required that a note to the balance sheet should indicate the periods over which the liability was expected to crystallize, the Statement of Intent no longer envisages such a requirement. Both documents envisage a note showing the amount of the contingent liability for any deferred tax unprovided, analysed over its major components and the Statement of Intent envisages that the amount of the unprovided deferred tax will be calculated at the expected long-term tax rate.[34]

---

33 ED 33, Paras 20 and 21.
34 SOI, Para. 6(iv).

A postscript

For a going concern the application of the principles embodied in SSAP 15, as amended by ED 33, will undoubtedly provide a more meaningful balance sheet provision for deferred taxation. In spite of this the authors are concerned about the possible long-term effects of the adoption of partial provisions.

The deferred taxation which is not provided for in the accounts might be said to be like a time bomb which is triggered to explode at an inopportune moment. A company which runs into trading difficulties may well cut back its capital expenditure programme and may even make plans to sell off some of its assets. Such a course of action may well result in previously unexpected net reversing differences occurring with the consequence that a much larger provision for deferred taxation becomes necessary. The consequential charge to the profit and loss account and reduction of the ownership interest may be substantial and may well affect the confidence of investors and creditors, leading to even greater difficulties for the company.

This problem is mitigated to some extent by two factors. Firstly, by abolishing first-year allowances, the Finance Act 1984 has reduced the likely impact of timing differences and consequently the likely amount of deferred tax not provided for. Secondly, the requirement that the amount not provided for be disclosed in the notes to the accounts at least gives some warning to users of what might occur.

Accounting for post balance sheet events

One of the desirable characteristics of accounting reports discussed in Chapter 1 was 'timeliness', i.e. the need to publish accounts as quickly as possible. However, there will inevitably be some delay between the end of the accounting period and the date of publication (which is not to say that the duration of the delay could not often be reduced), and this leads one to the question of how the accountant should treat significant events which occur during this period.

The main principle underlying SSAP 17, issued in 1980, is that users should be presented with as up to date information as possible and be apprised of any significant events which have occurred since the end of the accounting period. The proposals are uncontroversial and straightforward and may therefore be briefly summarized.

A distinction is drawn between events which occur before and after the date on which the directors approved the financial statements, and the standard only covers those events which occurred prior to the date of approval. The point is made, however, that directors have a duty to ensure the publication of details of any events which occur after the date of approval if they have a material effect on the financial statements.

The date of approval is normally the date of the board meeting at which the financial statements are formally approved (or in the instance of an unincorporated association the corresponding date). In the case of group accounts the date is that on which the accounts are approved by the directors of the holding company.

Post balance sheet events are classified as either *adjusting* or *non-adjusting* events.

Adjusting events are those which provide additional evidence in respect of conditions existing at the balance sheet date and will therefore call for the revision of the amounts at which items are stated in the financial statements. A very obvious example of an adjusting event would be the receipt of cash from a debtor which could affect the provision against doubtful debts. Events such as the proposal of a dividend, a transfer to reserves and a change in the tax rate are also regarded as being adjusting events.

Non-adjusting events are those which do not relate to conditions existing at the balance sheet date and will not affect the figures included in the financial statements. Examples of non-adjusting events are the issue of shares; major changes in the composition of the company and the financial effect of the losses of fixed assets or stocks as a result of a disaster such as fire or flood. The last-mentioned instance is an example of a non-adjusting event because the fire or flood did not affect the condition of the asset concerned at the balance sheet date.

The standard also requires the disclosure, as a non-adjusting event, of the reversal after the balance sheet date of transactions undertaken before the year end with the prime intention of altering the appearance of the company's balance sheet. These alterations comprise those commonly referred to as 'window dressing', for example the borrowing of cash from an associated company to disguise an acute short-term liquidity problem.

It may be that some event occurs after the balance sheet date which because of its effect on the company's operating results or financial position, puts into question the application of the going concern convention to the whole (or to a significant part) of the company's accounts. The standard is to some extent inconsistent in respect of the treatment of such events in that in Part 1 of the standard it states that 'Consequently these [the events] may fall to be treated as adjusting events' (Para. 8). This suggests that a distinction should be drawn between events which represent the materialization of a situation which existed at the balance sheet date (adjusting events) and those which are constituted by completely fresh disasters which did not exist at the balance sheet date (i.e. non-adjusting events). However, the standard itself (Para. 22) requires that the accounts should be amended as a consequence of any material post balance sheet which casts doubt on the application of the going concern convention.

The actual standard may be summarized as follows:

(1) Financial statements should be prepared on the basis of conditions existing at the balance sheet date.

(2) A material post balance sheet event requires changes in the amounts to be included in financial statements where:

(a) it is an adjusting event, or
(b) it indicates that the application of the going concern concept to the whole or a material part of the company is not appropriate. (Note that for the reasons given above it might be argued that there is a conflict between requirements (1) and (2(b)).

(3) A material post balance sheet event should be disclosed where:

(a) its non-disclosure would hinder the users' ability to obtain a proper understanding of the financial position, or
(b) it is the reversal or maturity after the year end of a transaction, the substance of which was primarily to alter the appearance of the company's balance sheet (window dressing).

(4) In respect of any material post balance sheet event which has to be disclosed under the provisions of (3) above, the following should be stated in the notes to the accounts:

(a) the nature of the event, and
(b) an estimate of its financial effect or a statement that it is not practicable to make such an estimate. The financial effect should be shown without any adjustment for taxation but the taxation implications should be explained if such is necessary to enable a proper understanding of the financial position to be obtained.

(5) The date on which the financial statements are approved by the Board of Directors should be disclosed.

It should be noted that the Companies Act 1981 requires that all liabilities and losses in respect of the financial year (or earlier years) shall be taken into account including those which only became apparent between the balance sheet date and the date of the approval of the accounts.[35]

Accounting for contingencies

Company law has for many years required the disclosure by way of a note to the accounts of information concerning contingent liabilities. Such a practice can be argued to be asymmetric in that no regard is paid to contingent assets. Accounting for contingencies is the subject, and title of, SSAP 18 issued in 1980, the purpose of which is essentially twofold. It modified existing accounting practice by requiring disclosure of information relating to contingent assets as well as standardizing the methods used to define and disclose contingent liabilities and assets. The term contingency is defined as follows:

> Contingency is a condition which exists at the balance sheet date, where the outcome will be confirmed only on the occurrence or non-occurence of one or more uncertain future events. A contingent gain or loss is a gain or loss dependent on a contingency.[36]

There is obviously a close link between SSAP 18 and SSAP 17 ('Accounting for post balance sheet events') in that if what was an uncertain future event at the balance sheet date, crystallizes before the accounts are approved by the directors it would be regarded as an adjusting event which would result in the modification of the balance sheet value of the related asset or liability. Similarly, a material contingency which arises between the balance sheet date and the date of approval would be treated as a non-adjusting event and hence disclosed under the provisions of SSAP 17.

One of the major problems that may be experienced in the implementation of SSAP 18 is that the statement does not attempt to define what is meant by 'a condition which exists at the balance sheet date' although it goes some way towards this by explicitly excluding uncertainties associated with accounting estimates such as the lives of fixed assets and the amount of bad debts. Whilst some situation such as a pending legal action can clearly be identified as an existing condition there are many other situations which will require the application of judgement.

---

35 Companies Act 1981, Para. 12(b), 1st Schedule.
36 SSAP 18, Para. 14.

We will now summarize the provisions of SSAP 18 before providing further comment.

(1) A material contingent loss should be accrued in financial statements 'where it is probable that a future event will confirm a loss which can be estimated with reasonable accuracy on the date on which the financial statements are approved by the board'.

(2) A material contingent loss not accrued under (1) above should be disclosed except where the possibility of loss is remote.

(3) Contingent gains should not be accrued and should be disclosed only if it is probable that the gain will be realized.

(4) The following information should be given in respect of contingent items which are disclosed: (a) the nature of the item, (b) the uncertainties which are expected to affect the outcome, and (c) a prudent estimate of the potential financial effect (made at the date of the approval of the accounts) or a statement that it is not practicable to make such an estimate. In the case of a contingent loss the amount can be reduced by any amount which is accrued and by the amount of any component where the possibility of loss is remote.

(5) The financial effect should be stated before taking taxation into account but the taxation implication should be explained if such is necessary to give a proper understanding of the financial position.

(6) Where there are a large number of items of the same nature which are subject to the same uncertainties the financial effect of each contingency need not be estimated as the amount can be based on a group of similar transactions.

Item (1) begs the question of what should be done if the loss is probable but the amount cannot be estimated with reasonable accuracy. Should they simply be disclosed or should a provision be made in the accounts? In view of the requirement of Para. 12(b) of the 1st Schedule of the 1981 Act, which was enacted after the issue of SSAP 18, a provision should be made if a liability or loss is likely to occur.

SSAP 18 discloses an assymetrical approach to contingent gains and losses as shown below:

	Contingent	
Outcome	Loss	Gain
Probable	Accrue	Note
Possible	Note	Ignore
Remote	Ignore	Ignore

(Possible has been used by the authors to describe a situation which falls between 'probable' and 'remote'.)

Given the weight of opinion in favour of rejecting the traditional interpretation of prudence (*see* Chapter 1) it is unfortunate that the ASC did not, at the very least, require the disclosure of possible contingent gains.

The standard requires that the financial effect should be shown on a prudent basis. Presumably this means the maximum amount of any possible loss or, more strictly, the upper bound of the range of reasonable expectations, i.e. larger values which have a low probability of occurrence may be ignored. Similarly the lower bound of the range of reasonable expectation of possible gains should be disclosed. However, given the general movement towards more informative financial statements, it might be argued that it would be better to provide a more realistic estimate of the value of a contingent item. The point may be illustrated by the use of the following example:

Suppose that the company is facing litigation for damages and that the directors assess there is a probability of 0.4 of having to pay damages and costs. If the company wins the action it will be able to recover all its costs. If the company is penalized it must pay the total costs for both parties – say £40 000 – and damages which might with equal probability be £50 000, £100 000 or £150 000. The possible outcomes and their associated probabilities are as follows:

Outcome of action	Probability	Cost and damages
Win	0.6	Nil
Lose	$0.4 \times \frac{1}{3}$	£90 000
Lose	$0.4 \times \frac{1}{3}$	£140 000
Lose	$0.4 \times \frac{1}{3}$	£190 000

Thus the expected outcome is

$$£0.6 \times 0 + 0.4 \times (\tfrac{1}{3}) (90\,000 + 140\,000 + 190\,000) = £56\,000$$

It can be seen that the 'estimate of the financial effect' could be presented in a number of different ways. The maximum loss should the company lose the action, £190 000, could be stated; alternatively, the range of possible outcomes, £90 000 to £190 000, should the action be lost might be presented. A third alternative is the 'expected value' of £56 000 which takes account of the probabilities as well as the magnitudes of the possible outcomes. Accounting is not yet at the point where the concept of expected values can be used especially in the case of isolated events of the type used as the example. However, item (5) in the above summary of requirements appears to allow this approach to be used where there are a number of contingent items of a similar type. In the case of a company which had discounted a large number of bills of exchange, information about the likely loss will be equally if not more valuable than a note stating the total amount of bills outstanding at the balance sheet date.

Extraordinary items and prior year adjustments

Introduction

This section will be concerned with the provisions of SSAP 6, 'Extraordinary items and prior year adjustments' (issued in April 1974) and ED 16, 'Supplement to SSAP 6' (issued in September 1975). Reference will also be made to a Discussion Document 'A review of SSAP 6' (issued by the ASC in 1983).

The problem which gave rise to the issue of SSAP 6 was the variety of practice concerning the treatment of revenue (i.e. non-capital) items which were regarded as being of a 'non-recurring' nature. Two extreme positions could be identified. At one extreme all items were passed through the profit and loss account while at the other extreme any items which could be argued as not relating to the normal activities of the business (non-recurring items) were charged or credited direct to reserves or adjusted against the opening balance of retained profits. The latter methods are known as 'reserve accounting'.[37] In practice, most companies adopted a position between the two extremes.

The argument in favour of reserve accounting was that a profit or loss based only on the 'normal activities' of the business gave a fairer indication of the business's maintainable profit. It was suggested that such a profit figure would provide the more useful basis for estimating future profits than the profit resulting from a profit and loss account which included all items irrespective of their nature.

The view of the ASC, as evidenced by the provisions of SSAP 6, is that all revenue items should pass through the profit and loss account. The reasons for this view were as follows:

(a) The inclusion and disclosure of the non-recurring items enables the profit and loss account for the year to give a better view of a company's profitability and progress.

---

37 The two approaches are also often described, particularly in the USA, as 'all inclusive income' and 'current operating income', respectively.

(b) The exclusion of non-recurring items require the exercise of subjective judgement and may lead to variations in the treatment of similar items and hence to a loss of comparability between the accounts of different companies. The ASC did not refer to the suggestion that certain companies were more prepared to identify debits as being non-recurring than credits and hence used the device to boost reported profits.

(c) The exclusion of non-recurrent items could result in them being overlooked in any review of results over a series of years. Thus, while the nature of the items will, by definition, change, many businesses, especially larger ones, will often have items which are 'non-recurrent' and continually to exclude them from the profit and loss account would result in a distorted view of profit being shown.

The wholly sensible view of the ASC was that the legitimate advantages of reserve accounting can be obtained, without the drawbacks listed above, if adequate disclosure is provided in accounts. In essence SSAP 6 requires that all profits and losses recognized in the year should be shown in the profit and loss account. There are, however, two exceptions to the general rule in that two classes of adjustments – unrealized surpluses on the revaluation of fixed assets and prior year adjustments – can be dealt with directly through the reserves. We shall return to these exceptions a little later in this section.

Whilst the standard does in general reject the use of reserve accounting it does accept the notion that it is possible, and helpful to users, to distinguish between the results of *ordinary activities* of the business and *extraordinary* profits and losses. Thus the standard prescribes, if there are any extraordinary items, that the following elements should be included in the profit and loss account:

post-tax profit before extraordinary items,
extraordinary items (less taxation attributable thereto),
post-tax profit after extraordinary items.

Presumably, although this is not stated overtly in the standard, the ASC were of the view that knowledge of the profit on ordinary activities will be of assistance to users in understanding the trend of profits and, possibly, help forecast future profit levels.

In addition items of an abnormal size and incidence but which may be regarded as deriving from the ordinary activities of the business, *exceptional items*, should be disclosed but included in the derivation of the profit before extraordinary items.

The above provisions of SSAP 6 have been incorporated into statute law by the Companies Act 1981 but the Act does not attempt to define the various terms and hence the accountant must refer to SSAP 6 when deciding whether an item is an extraordinary, exceptional or ordinary item.

Extraordinary items

> Extraordinary items, for the purposes of this Statement, are those items which derive from events or transactions outside the ordinary activities of the business and which are both material and expected not to recur frequently or regularly. They do not include items which, though exceptional on account of size and incidence (and which may therefore require separate disclosure), derive from the ordinary activities of the business. Neither do they include prior year items merely because they relate to a prior year.[38]

The last sentence, which has to be read a few times to be understood, simply means that an item does not become extraordinary simply because it is recognized in the profit and loss account in a period following the one in which it occurred.

The definition of extraordinary items is not helpful and could indeed be said to be misleading. The problem is the phrase 'derive from events and transactions outside the ordinary activities of the business'. Taken literally this phrase means that an extraordinary item could only arise from the activities of a separate venture, e.g. if a chemical company used excess funds to develop an office block or a retail store decided to back a horse. However, it is clear that this was not intended by the ASC because the examples of extraordinary items provided include the following:

(a) the discontinuance of a significant part of a business
(b) the sale of an investment not acquired with the intention of resale
(c) writing off intangibles, including goodwill, because of unusual events or developments during the period; and
(d) the expropriation of assets.[39]

It does seem that a number of these examples, at least in part, derive from events which are associated with the normal course of business.

The authors would suggest that the definition would be improved if the phrase in question was deleted. The key elements in the definition are those which would remain. These relate to materiality, frequency and regularity. The distinction between frequency and regularity should

---

38 SSAP 6, Para. 11.
39 SSAP 6, Para. 3.

be noted. An item which occurs, say, every 5 or 6 years is infrequent but is regular, and thus would not constitute an extraordinary item.

The distinction between extraordinary items and those which might be termed exceptional or abnormal items is important. Exceptional items are described as follows:

> Items which, though abnormal in size and incidence, are not extraordinary items (as defined in paragraph 11 [of the standard]) because they derive from the ordinary activities of the business would include:
>
> (a) abnormal charges for bad debts and write-offs of stock and work in progress and research and development expenditure;
> (b) abnormal provision for losses on long-term contracts; and,
> (c) most adjustments of prior year taxation provisions.[40]

As mentioned earlier, we do not feel that the application of the test of whether the item derives from the normal course of business is all that helpful. We would suggest that the classification between extraordinary and exceptional items is better based on frequency and regularity. Thus the loss or profit from the discontinuance of a significant part of a business is extraordinary if the company closes down parts of its business at infrequent and irregular intervals. The provision for losses on long-term contracts is, on the other hand, a regular event in that each year a review must be made of the position to see whether any provision is necessary. It may well be that in most years a zero provision is made, but a review must still be made. Thus the provision for losses on long-term contracts may be abnormal in amount but does relate to an event (the review) which is both regular and frequent. We feel that the above basis for categorization is better than one which suggests that the discontinuance of a part of a business does not derive from the ordinary activities of the business while the provision for losses on long-term contracts does. In the view of the authors both derive from the ordinary activities of the business.

The working party responsible for the review of SSAP 6[41] reported that there had been considerable inconsistency in the way different companies had classified apparently similar items as exceptional or extraordinary items. They noted that although SSAP 6 had provided lists of examples of extraordinary and exceptional items the standard had recognized that the classification of items would depend on the particular circumstances. In the words of SSAP 6 'what is extraordinary in one business will not necessarily be extraordinary in another'.[42] The

---

40 SSAP 6, Para. 5.
41 *A review of SSAP 6*, ASC, London, 1983.
42 SSAP 6, Para. 3.

working party believed that this statement might have been responsible for the reported inconsistencies and suggested that in order to achieve greater consistency the definitions should be made more specific. Hence, the review document proposed that in a revised standard the definitions should be supplemented by a list defining by their nature whether items are normally to be treated as an ordinary, extraordinary or an exceptional item. Companies would be allowed to depart from the definition but they would have to justify any variation in treatment.

It appears to the authors that the review working party have placed too great an emphasis on the need for consistency and have overlooked the predictive value of the SSAP 6 provisions. The essence of the SSAP 6 requirements are that users are helped to distinguish between items which are likely to recur and those which are not expected to be repeated. Hence, it is the nature of the item in the context of the particular company which is important. For example, one company may, quite properly, treat redundancy costs as extraordinary because it has never paid and is not likely again to incur such costs, while another company may treat them as exceptional, or even as ordinary, items because it regularly and frequently incurs such costs as part of its ordinary activities.

The adoption of the approach suggested in the review document might result in greater comparability between the accounts of different companies but this would probably result in the provision of less useful information for predictive purposes in the accounts of individual companies.

Prior year adjustments

These are defined as follows: 'Prior year adjustments are those material adjustments applicable to prior years arising from changes in accounting policies and from the correction of fundamental errors. They do not include the normal recurring corrections and adjustments of accounting estimates made in prior years.'[43]

In many ways it is unfortunate that the ASC did not use a different name for this type of adjustment since it is clear that the vast majority of adjustments which are regularly made in accounts in respect of transactions which occurred in prior years do not constitute 'prior year adjustments' as defined in SSAP 6. It might have been better if the ASC had used a phrase such as 'fundamental prior year adjustments'.

---

43 SSAP 6, Para. 12.

A change in accounting policy gives rise to a prior year adjustment only, according to SSAP 6, Para. 8, if the new policy is adopted because it will give 'a fairer presentation of the results and of the financial position of the business'. An adoption or modification of an accounting basis necessitated by transactions or events that are clearly different in substance from those which occurred in the past is stated as not giving rise to a prior year adjustment. In other words the use of different policies because of different circumstances does not constitute a change of policy.

The ASC emphasizes that in order for the correction of an error to be regarded as a prior year adjustment the error must be one of major substance and of such significance that its inclusion in accounts would mean that a 'true and fair view' was not shown and would have led to the withdrawal of the accounts had the error been recognized in time.

The SSAP 6 review working party suggested that the definition of prior year adjustments be extended to include adjustments which would, if not dealt with through the reserves, materially distort the results of both the current and future periods.[44] The only example cited is a change in the estimate of the life of depreciating assets, due to an erroneous previous estimate. Thus, the SSAP 6 review supports the argument advanced in the previously published review of SSAP 12, 'Accounting for depreciation' (*see* page 577).

The provisions of SSAP 6

The provisions of the actual standard are reproduced below, together with our comments:

> The profit and loss account for the year should show a profit or loss after extraordinary items, reflecting all profits and losses recognized in the accounts of the year other than prior year adjustments as defined in Part 2 [of the statement] and unrealized surpluses on revaluation of fixed assets, which should be credited direct to reserves.[45]

The statement does not make any previous reference to the subject of unrealized surpluses on the revaluation of fixed assets. The subject is discussed in ED 16 ('Supplement to SSAP 6'), which will be considered later.

---

44 *Review of SSAP 6*, Para. 2.26.
45 SSAP 6, Para. 13.

Items of an abnormal size and incidence which are derived from the ordinary activities of the business should be included in arriving at the profit for the year before taxation and extraordinary items, and their nature and size disclosed.[46]

Extraordinary items as defined in Part 2 [of the statement] (less attributable taxation) should be shown separately in the profit and loss account for the year after the results derived from ordinary activities and their nature and size disclosed.[47]

The standard is silent on how the attributable taxation should be calculated. In practice the marginal tax figure is used, i.e. the change in tax charge resulting from the existence of the extraordinary item. This procedure is advocated in the *Review of SSAP 6*.

Prior year adjustments as defined in Part 2 [of the statement] (less attributable taxation) should be accounted for by restating prior years, with the result that the opening balance of retained profits will be adjusted accordingly. The effect of the change should be disclosed where practicable by showing separately in the restatement of the previous year the amount involved. Items which represent the normal recurring corrections and adjustments of accounting entries made in prior years should be included in the profit and loss account for the year and, if material, their nature and size should be disclosed.[48]

As a result of the foregoing the profit and loss account for the year should, if there are extraordinary items, include the following elements:
– profit before extraordinary items;
– extraordinary items (less taxation attributable thereto);
– profit after extraordinary items.
A statement of retained profits/reserves showing any prior year adjustments should immediately follow the profit and loss account for the year.[49]

ED 16: Supplement to SSAP 6

SSAP 6 is a brief document which did not discuss all aspects of the issues involved. It was clear that further statements would be required and ED 16 was intended to provide clarification on certain topics. These are detailed in ED 16, Para. 1, as follows: (a) accounting for deficits on the revaluation of fixed assets; (b) accounting for surpluses and deficits arising on the realization of revalued fixed assets; (c) accounting for the revenue effects of translating foreign currencies.

Revaluation of fixed assets
SSAP 6 requires that surpluses on revaluation of fixed assets should be credited direct to reserves. This provision is of course consistent

---

46 SSAP 6, Para. 14.
47 SSAP 6, Para. 15.
48 SSAP 6, Para. 16.
49 SSAP 6, Para. 17.

with current cost accounting in which surpluses are credited to the current cost reserve. SSAP 6, however, made no reference to the treatment of deficits on revaluation. ED 16 makes the obvious point that a deficit should be debited direct to reserves to the extent that it represents a reduction in previously recognized surpluses in respect of the same asset which had been credited to the reserves. If the deficit does not represent a reduction in a previously credited surplus, or if the deficit exceeds the surplus, the appropriate amount should be debited to the profit and loss account where it will be classified as an ordinary or extraordinary item according to its nature.

Realization of fixed assets
ED 16, Para. 14, states:

> When fixed assets are realized, the surpluses or deficits compared with the book value should be recognized in the profit and loss account for the year and classified as extraordinary items or otherwise according to their nature. Any reserve identified as being in respect of previously unrealized surpluses on the revaluation of those assets thereby becomes a realized surplus but should not be reported as part of the profit for the year.

The first part of the proposal is clearly reasonable. It suggests that all gains and losses should be taken through the profit and loss account and therefore disposes of the need to make artificial distinctions between those gains and losses which are part of the normal activities of the business and those which may be otherwise regarded and which are sometimes dealt with through the reserves rather than through the profit and loss account. The second part of the proposal does, however, appear to give rise to an inconsistency. If an asset is sold at a profit the profit will be passed through the profit and loss account if the asset had not been revalued in the past but would not be credited to the profit and loss account (at least in full) if the asset had been revalued. Thus, the same set of transactions, the sale of an asset, could give rise to different profit figures.

As is all too common, the ASC did not justify, or even discuss, the reasons for selecting the method proposed in the Exposure Draft. In the context of historical cost accounting the alternative of crediting all realized gains to the profit and loss account (noting where appropriate that the gain reflects the realization of a previously established revaluation surplus) would be more consistent with the principles enumerated in SSAP 6.

This problem is addressed in the SSAP 6 review which, on balance, but without giving a reason, supports the position taken in ED 16.

However, the authors of the review did recognize the resulting inconsistency and made a special request for comments on this point.

Foreign currency translation
This aspect of ED 16 has been overtaken by SSAP 20 ('Accounting for foreign currency transactions') which was discussed in Chapter 13.

The cost of reorganizations and terminated activities

One consequence of the economic problems faced by British industry in the first half of the 1980s was an increase in the reporting of the major reorganization or the termination of all, or a significant part, of a business, and the review document addresses a number of different aspects of this topic. One basic principle which flows from the prudence concept is that once the decision to reorganize or terminate is made the total net cost of the exercise should be provided in the accounts. This estimated net cost would include all anticipated future costs (less any expected surpluses) which will be incurred not just those which are borne in the period to which the accounts relate. The review document deals with three main related issues – the classification of the costs as exceptional or extraordinary items; the appropriate accounting treatment in cases where the decision to terminate or reorganize is made after the year end but before the date on which the accounts are approved for publication, and whether the losses incurred in the accounting period before the decision is made should be reported as part of the ordinary trading activities, or as part of the loss on termination.

A reorganization which does not involve the closure of an identifiable part of the business is intended to increase the efficiency of a continuing business and the review therefore considers that it should not be treated as an extraordinary item. Thus redundancy and other costs incurred on such a reorganization, if material, should be separately disclosed as an exceptional item. Where, however, redundancy and other costs are incurred in connection with the discontinuance of a business or businesses, the review proposes that they should be treated as extraordinary items.

As we have argued above, such a rigid classification without regard to the circumstances of the particular company would seem to have severe disadvantages.

Even more controversial is the review document's proposal regarding the appropriate treatment when the decision to reorganize or terminate is made after the year end but before the date on which the accounts are approved by the directors. The review proposes that in such circumstances the total anticipated net cost of the decision should be provided in the accounts. This could produce a conflict with one of the basic principles underlying SSAP 17, 'Accounting for post balance sheet events', that accounts should be prepared on the basis of conditions existing at the balance sheet date. Indeed, SSAP 17 specifically categorizes as a non-adjusting event (i.e. an event which should be noted but not reflected in the actual accounts) the closure of a significant part of a company's trading activities, where this was not anticipated at the year end.

Given the possible conflict the review working party specifically requested comments on their proposal. The authors believe that it would be unhelpful if the SSAP 6 review proposal was accepted without there being a complete review of SSAP 17 as the ASC should, having established a clear principle, not recommend departures therefrom. In any event the financial effects of the decision would be shown in the notes and hence brought to the attention of users. It should be noted that if the decision to terminate casts doubt on the application of the going concern concept then there would be no conflict with SSAP 17 in that that standard classifies, as an adjusting event, one which makes the going concern assumption doubtful.

On the question of whether the trading results of the appropriate part of the business for the period prior to the date of the termination decision should be reported together with the anticipated net costs of the closure the review document refers to the position in the USA. In that country Accounting Principles Board (APB) Opinion No. 30, 'Reporting the results of operations', requires companies to show the results for the year of discontinued operations, along with any loss (or gain) on disposal, as a separate item in the profit and loss account after post-tax profit but before extraordinary items. As is pointed out this practice clearly identifies the results of continuing operations and hence aids in the prediction of future earnings.

The review working party accepts that an analysis of the results between those relating to the continuing and those of the discontinued business would be useful. Nevertheless they rejected the US approach on the grounds that it would effectively treat as an extraordinary item what the working party would regard as part of the trading results for the period. In addition, attention is drawn to the emphasis placed in the UK on the single line of pre-tax profit or loss in the formats specified by the Companies Act 1981, which the working party contends should include the results of all operations prior to the date on which the termination is irrevocably decided. It should, however, be noted that the 1981 Act does not provide a definition of extraordinary items and that the accountancy profession is in a position to influence the way in which the term is defined. It appears, although the point is not made in the review, that the working party believed that the need to account for stewardship is of greater importance than the objective of providing useful information for prediction. The review document does point out, however, that in cases where the effect of the termination is material, information which would enable users to judge the effect should be given in a note to the profit and loss account.

Recommended reading

Accounting for pensions
C. Napier, *Accounting for the Cost of Pensions*, ICAEW, London, 1983.

Accounting for taxation
D. C. Hobson and R. J. Munson, *Deferred Taxation*, Accountants' Digest No. 70, ICAEW, London, 1978/79.

Accounting for post balance sheet events
A. T. Cabourne-Smith, *Accounting for Post Balance Sheet Events*, Accountants' Digest No. 101, ICAEW, London, 1981.

Accounting for contingencies
A. T. Cabourne-Smith and R. L. Cohen, *Accounting for Contingencies*, Accountants' Digest No. 113, ICAEW, London, 1981/82.

Extraordinary items and prior year adjustments
T. E. Cooke and J. Whittaker, *Extraordinary Items and Prior Year Adjustments*, Accountants' Digest No. 149, ICAEW, London, 1984.

Questions

17.1 The UK–Irish Accounting Standards Committee has recently been studying the question of accounting for the pension costs of a company.
You are required:
(a) to outline the conventional methods currently used to account for the pension costs of a company; and   (5 marks)

(b) to criticize the adequacy of such methods in the light of the accruals concept
   of accounting as set out in SSAP 2: Disclosure of Accounting Policies (1971).

(11 marks)

(16 marks)

A. Cert. A. Advanced Financial Accounting, First paper, December 1983.

17.2   It is the accounting policy of Forsters Ltd to provide for deferred taxation, in accordance with SSAP 15, only where there is a probability that
a liability will crystallize in the foreseeable future.

The following information is given in respect of the company's year ended
on 30 June 1982:

(1) The company has made a taxable profit for the year of £500 000.

(2) Its freehold property, which had cost £100 000 in 1970, was revalued at
   £200 000. This revaluation was incorporated in the financial statements
   at 30 June 1982.

(3) The other fixed assets comprised entirely plant and machinery on which
   100% capital allowances had been claimed in the year of purchase. The
   net book value of these assets at 30 June 1981 was £600 000.

(4) Depreciation is provided on the plant and machinery at 10% per annum
   on the reducing balance method and is provided for the full year in the
   year of purchase.

(5) During the year ended 30 June 1982 expenditure on similar plant and
   machinery was £100 000.

(6) The company's forecasts show that capital expenditure on similar plant
   and machinery, which will attract the 100% capital allowances, will be
   £10 000 in each of the next three years. After that it is anticipated that
   substantial replacement of scrapped plant will be required and annual
   expenditure of approximately £75 000 will be incurred. The scrapped plant
   will have no disposal value.

(7) At 30 June 1981, a timing difference arose through the accrual of loan
   interest receivable at the year end of £50 000. Receipt of this interest
   was on 5 July 1981. Equal amounts of interest were also received on
   5 January and 5 July 1982.

(8) On 1 April 1982 £125 000 with interest at 15% per annum was borrowed
   from a finance company. Although accrued at 30 June 1982 no payment
   of interest had been made. Six months interest was paid on 1st October
   1982.

(9) It was proposed to pay a dividend after the year end of £105 000.

Assume that the company continues to trade profitably and that there are no losses brought forward. The effective rates of Corporation Tax are 52% on trading profits and 30% on chargeable gains, and the rate of advance Corporation Tax is three-sevenths.

You are required to:
(a) **draft a suitable statement of accounting policy on deferred taxation for inclusion in the financial statements at 30 June 1982** (2 marks), **and**
(b) **draft the balance sheet note, omitting comparatives, on deferred taxation** (14 marks). **(16 marks)**

ICAEW Financial Accounting II, December 1982.

17.3   SSAP 15: *Accounting for Deferred Taxation* (1978) sought to lay down reasonable and enforceable rules for the area of accounting indicated by the title. ED 33: *Accounting for Deferred Tax* (1983) suggests changes that ought to be made to bring SSAP 15 into line with current thinking.

You are required:
(a) **to appraise critically the present requirements of SSAP 15, in relation to ascertainment of the total charge for taxation to be made in the profit and loss account of a UK (or Irish) company; and** (12 marks)
(b) **to state briefly what amendments to SSAP 15 are proposed in ED 33 in respect of ascertainment of the total tax charge as above, and to give the reasons for proposing them.** (8marks)
(20 marks)

A. Cert. A. Advanced Financial Accounting, December 1984.

17.4   The taxation consolidation schedules of County Manufacturing Ltd on 30 November 1984 show the following:

	Parent	Subsidiaries		
	County	Essex	Avon	Cumbria
	£	£	£	£
(1) Adjusted profits (losses)	25 140	286 360	(79 290)	21 660
Depreciation	—	36 340	16 480	8 120
Capital allowances	—	70 160	56 810	9 300
(2) Corporation Tax account: Corporation Tax provisions for year to 30 November 1983 brought forward	(3 680)	(40 600)	—	—

(cont. next page)

	Parent	Subsidiaries		
	County	Essex	Avon	Cumbria
(2) Corporation Tax account (*cont.*):	£	£	£	£
Payments during year:				
Agreed mainstream corporation tax liability for year to 30 November 1983	3 700	40 500	—	—
ACT on interim dividend paid 31 July 1984	4 650	—	—	—
Tax suffered on interest received	180	370	—	—
(3) Deferred taxation:				
Credit balance brought forward 1 December 1983	—	(90 880)	(12 960)	—
Credit balance carried forward 30 November 1984	—	(146 350)	(33 480)	—

The following information is also available:

(1) The three subsidiaries shown above are wholly owned. In addition there is another wholly owned subsidiary incorporated overseas whose charge against profits and liability to local tax for the year ended 30 November 1984 is £26 400. No double tax relief is available. There is no deferred taxation.

(2) County has a UK associated company in which it has a 25% holding. That company's Corporation Tax charge for the year ended 30 November 1984 is £37 080. There is no deferred taxation.

(3) All companies have been members of the group for many years and are trading companies. There have been no changes in their trades.

(4) Cumbria has available taxation losses of £45 600 brought forward at 1 December 1983.

(5) The adjusted profits (losses) shown above are those for the year ended 30 November 1984 adjusted for taxation purposes after taking account of depreciation and capital allowances.

(6) Depreciation is solely upon fixed assets which are eligible for capital allowances.

(7) It is intended to take advantage of the Group Relief provisions which are fully available.

(8) The rate of Corporation Tax applying for the year ended 30 November 1984 is 45% for all group companies with no small company rate.

(9) The deferred tax balances at 30 November 1984 have been provided at 45% and in accordance with SSAP 15. Following the March 1984 Budget, the deferred tax provision at 30 November 1984 includes an additional amount needed to make up provisions made in previous years. As from, and including, the year ended 30 November 1984 provision is to be made on the full difference between depreciation and capital allowances.

(10) A proposed final dividend will be payable on 31 March 1985 at the same rate as the interim paid on 31 July 1984. No change in the rate of ACT is expected and the ACT on the proposed dividend is considered to be recoverable against future liabilities.

You are required, in respect of the group financial statements of County Manufacturing Limited on 30 November 1984 to:
(a) state, with reasons, how you would deal with the additional amount of deferred taxation in the profit and loss account and notes thereto (5 marks);
(b) prepare the note supporting the taxation charge in the Profit and Loss Account (12 marks); **and**
(c) calculate the taxation liabilities to be included in creditors (3 marks).
(20 marks)

ICAEW Financial Accounting II, December 1984.

17.5   SSAP 17 and SSAP 18 deal with accounting for post balance sheet events and contingencies respectively.

In eight companies whose year ends were 31 December 1981, the financial statements were approved by their respective directors on 15 March 1982. During 1982, the following material events take place:

(1) Alpha Ltd sold a major property which was included in the balance sheet at £100 000 and for which contracts had been exchanged on 15 December 1981. The sale was completed on 15 February 1982 at a price of £250 000.
(2) On 28 January 1982, a wholly owned subsidiary of Beta Ltd paid a dividend of £300 000 in respect of its own year ended on 31 December 1981.
(3) On 28 February 1982 the mail order activities of Gamma Ltd, a retail trading group, were shut down with closure costs amounting to £2.5 million.
(4) On 1 April 1982 the discovery of sand under Delta Ltd's major civil engineering contract site causes the costs of the contract to increase by 25% for which there would be no corresponding recovery from the customer.
(5) A fire on 2 January 1982 completely destroyed a manufacturing plant of Epsilon Ltd. It was expected that the loss of £10 million would be fully covered by insurance.
(6) A damages claim of £8 million for breach of patent had been served on Phi Ltd prior to the year end. It is the directors' opinion, backed

by considered legal advice, that the claim will ultimately prove to be without foundation but that it will still involve the expenditure of considerable legal fees.

(7) The movement in a foreign exchange rate of 8% between 1 January 1982 and 1 March 1982 has resulted in Kappa Ltd's foreign assets being reduced by £1.3 million.

(8) An actuarial valuation of Lambda Ltd's pension fund on 1 February 1982 revealed that it was under funded by £800 000. The company paid this amount over to the pension fund trustees on 31 March 1982.

You are required to state, with reasons, how each of the above items numbered (1) to (8) should be dealt with in the financial statements of the various companies for the year ended 31 December 1981. You are not required to draft the relevant notes to the financial statements.   (16 marks)

ICAEW Financial Accounting II, July 1982.

17.6   In dealing with the annual accounts of three companies, the following information is available:

(1) At the balance sheet date Builditt Ltd has an overseas contract at cost, net of progress payments, of £2.6 million. Total work in progress is £13.7 million. Progress payments on the overseas contract are £1 million in arrears. Before the accounts are finalized there is a change of regime in the foreign country and the company suspended work on the contract. There is no export credit guarantee in force.

(2) Welditt Ltd has a contract to build an oil pipeline in the Middle East for a North American company. Part of the pipeline has been handed over. During unusual weather conditions, the pipeline has been damaged and this has resulted in considerable financial loss to the North American company. The latter company has indicated that it will take out civil actions in both the British and American courts claiming $16 million.

Welditt Ltd has obtained counsel's opinion that any case to be heard in the British courts will fail. Counsel is unable to give an opinion on the outcome of the case if heard in America until he has sight of the claimant's case. At the date the accounts were approved by the directors no case had been filed or legal proceedings commenced in either country.

(3) Clampitt Ltd specializes in design and construction of roller coasters. During 1983 it completed eight roller coasters and commenced work on a further seven. During the final commissioning checks on the first completed roller coaster, a stress fracture was discovered in a major structural girder. The cost of replacing the girders in all roller coasters is estimated to be £1.9million. All fifteen customers have been advised that the replacements will be carried out immediately at no cost to themselves and they have accepted that satisfactory completion of the work is the only redress they will seek.

The manufacturer of the girders, a substantial quoted company, has accepted liability and agreed to meet all costs incurred by Clampitt Ltd.

You are required to:
(a) **define a contingency and explain the principles of accounting for contingencies** (10 marks), **and**
(b) **discuss how Builditt Ltd, Welditt Ltd and Clampitt Ltd should deal with the above matters in their accounts** (10 marks).

(20 marks)

ICAEW Financial Accounting I, May 1984.

17.7 Waveprocessor Ltd is an electronic manufacturing company with an annual turnover of £15m and trading profits of £1.5m.

In preparing the financial statements for the year ended 30 April 1983 the following matters are brought to your attention:

(1) A factory was closed and the factory premises sold for £600 000 less than its book value.

(2) Goods exported overseas to the value of £300 000 have not been paid for due to the insolvency of the customer.

(3) Following a change in company policy all research expenditure on new technology will be written off in the year in which the expenditure arises. An amount of £425 000 has been written off in the year. This amount includes £125 000 of expenditure incurred during the year.

You are required to:
(a) **define what constitutes an extraordinary item in a company's financial statements, and indicate the distinction between extraordinary and exceptional items** (6 marks), **and**
(b) **discuss the treatment of the three items referred to above in the financial statements of Waveprocessor Ltd** (6 marks).

(12 marks)

ICAEW Financial Accounting I, May 1983.

17.8 Since SSAP 6 was originally published in 1974 there has been much discussion on the treatment of extraordinary items. Recently the Accounting Standards Committee has published a discussion paper reviewing the working of this standard. Set out below are details of events occurring in nine different companies. In each case, the financial effect is material in the context of the company's results.

(1) Redundancy and other costs relating to the closure of one of a manufacturing company's three factories.

(2) Amounts written off stock and additional depreciation following the removal of one shop of a chain of retail shops from one location to another.

(3) A substantial 'golden handshake' to a company's chief executive on his dismissal.

(4) Additional deferred taxation provision necessary following the acceptance that a company's profits would no longer fall within the small company rate of Corporation Tax. The provision is made on the liability method.

(5) The 'profits' arising in a manufacturing company on the maturity of a sinking fund endowment policy for the repayment of a back-to-back loan. The sum assured is sufficient to meet the principal due.

(6) The gain made on the sale of a minority shareholding in a company engaged in a similar trade.

(7) The loss made on the sale of a building company's land bank in order to repay borrowings.

(8) The costs of a complete re-roofing of a leasehold office block held by a manufacturing company on a full repairing lease at a full rent.

(9) The deliberate suppression of creditors, discovered by new management of a company.

You are required to explain, with reasons, the accounting treatment you consider should be adopted in respect of each event by the relevant company. You are not required to draft extracts for the financial statements.

(18 marks)

ICAEW Financial Accounting II, July 1983.

18 Interpretation of Accounts

Introduction

As we have seen in Chapter 1, there are many different groups of people who are interested in the affairs of a business entity and who are therefore likely to use its accounts. Although the government as tax collector is interested mainly in the past, most users, including the government in other roles, are more interested in what is likely to happen in the future. Such people will therefore use the accounts for a past period to help them make a judgement on the likely future success or otherwise of the entity.

As we explained in Chapter 1, relatively little is known about the way in which accounts are used in the process of decision making but at a general level, it is clear that different groups will place greater or lesser emphasis on particular aspects of a company's performance. To give an example, a potential long-term equity shareholder in a company will be interested in the potential returns and the riskiness of those returns in comparison with other investment opportunities, whilst a potential supplier of goods, that is a trade creditor, will be interested in whether or not he is likely to receive payment for goods supplied. Both users are interested in the future performance of the company but the emphasis of their interpretation will differ. When called upon to interpret a set of accounts, it is essential for the accountant to keep clearly in mind the purpose of the exercise.

Traditionally, textbooks on financial accounting have tended to concentrate on univariate analysis. Thus they examine and discuss one ratio at a time and show how it is possible to draw tentative conclusions by comparing the result for that ratio with some yardstick of comparison. By studying a number of ratios in this way, it is possible to piece together a picture of the company's performance and position. This is the predominant approach used in practice and occupies the second section of this chapter. In that section we shall assume that readers are familiar with the basic principles of ratio analysis.[1]

1 Readers who wish to revise this topic are referred to R. Lewis and M. Firth, *Foundation in Accounting*, Vol. 2, 2nd ed, Prentice-Hall, London, 1985.

In the 1970s there was a move towards the use of multivariate analysis, that is a consideration of the impact of several ratios at the same time by using such statistical techniques as multiple regression analysis and discriminant analysis. The third section of the chapter examines this approach.

Many companies and groups of companies are now highly diversified and it is often difficult to draw conclusions from one set of accounts covering all such diverse activities. The final section of this chapter therefore examines the case for segmental reports and discusses some of the problems which must be faced in the provision of such information.

Univariate analysis

Accounting systems

In this section we shall concentrate on the interpretation of historical cost accounts, although we shall refer to some differences in approach which may be necessary for the interpretation of current cost accounts.

In the case of historical cost accounts interpretation has become more difficult in a period of rapid price change. Many of the conclusions reached on the basis of the information contained in these accounts must be heavily qualified and many of the so called 'norms' for ratios, specified in traditional textbooks, are no longer relevant in a period where gains may be made from owing money and losses may be incurred by holding monetary assets.

Many large companies have now produced current cost accounts for a number of years, although the particular principles used have tended to change as the Hyde guidelines followed ED 18 and were themselves followed by ED 24, SSAP 16 and ED 35. Current cost accounts undoubtedly provide useful information for the purposes of interpretation but, not surprisingly, it has taken users a considerable amount of time to gain practical experience of and begin to understand such accounts.

Yardsticks of comparison

As readers will be aware, one figure in a set of accounts, or a ratio based on two figures in that set of accounts, are of little use unless the user has some yardstick of comparison. Although an internal user of accounts will have access to budgets as a suitable yardstick, the external user, with whom this book is concerned, must have recourse to other yardsticks. These are usually the results of previous periods, the results of other similar companies or industry averages for the same accounting period. Comparison with the results of previous periods is known as trend or time series analysis whilst comparison with the results of other firms, either individually or in terms of industry averages, is known as cross-sectional analysis. Both give rise to problems.

When trend analysis is employed, the results of each year will usually have been arrived at using consistent accounting policies.[2] Even so, the fixed asset values shown in historical cost accounts and the depreciation charges based on these tend to become more and more out of date as time passes.

In addition, comparisons are difficult when the value of the measuring rod, the pound, is changing over time. In current cost accounts the former of these problems is largely removed because fixed assets are shown at their value to the business; however, as we have seen in Chapter 6, the failure of SSAP 16 to incorporate adjustments for general inflation has made it difficult to compare results over time. In addition to these difficulties caused by the accounting principles used, there is the more fundamental problem that the company's environment will change over time, with the result that performance which was considered satisfactory in the past may no longer be so. Thus, for example, a current ratio which might be considered to be acceptable in a period when additional short-term credit can be obtained cheaply and easily might be regarded as being dangerously low when short-term loans are very difficult to obtain.

When cross-sectional analysis is employed, even greater problems must be faced. First, there is the problem of finding a comparable business. This may be difficult as businesses may be diversified to a greater or lesser extent. In addition, there can be substantial differences between businesses even when they operate within the same industry. Two examples will illustrate this point: (a) although two companies manufacture the same product, one company may own its own property while another company may rent its property; (b) two companies may manufacture a similar finished product but whereas one company uses bought-in components, the other may manufacture all its components from raw materials.

2 When this is not so, as in the case of a change in accounting policies, suitable adjustments must be made to render the figures comparable.

In addition to these underlying differences, the fixed asset values which appear in a set of historical cost accounts tend, as was pointed out above, to become more and more out of date as time passes. This introduces biases depending upon the date on which companies have purchased their assets although such biases are, of course, removed in current cost accounts.

In addition to the above difficulties, there is a wide choice of accounting policies available to reflect underlying business reality, with the result that one company may choose one set of policies whilst a second may choose a very different set.[3]

As readers may imagine, it is usually very difficult for an external user to make any adjustments for these differences, although he must bear them in mind when interpreting a set of accounts. Probably the best warning that may be given is that one must not be too dogmatic when interpreting accounts.

Aspects of performance

It is convenient to examine separately two aspects of performance of a company, profitability and liquidity. The continuance of a business depends both upon profitable operations and upon having enough cash to meet its commitments as they fall due. Although in the long run satisfactory profitability and liquidity are likely to accompany one another, in the short run it is quite possible for a company to be, on the one hand, profitable but illiquid or, on the other hand, liquid but unprofitable. In both cases there will be some doubt about the continuance of the business. Let us look at each of these aspects of performance in turn.

Profitability
Whether or not a company pursues profit maximization as its objective, the majority of users of accounts will be interested in its profitability, that is how well the directors are using the resources at their disposal. Return on capital employed is frequently used as a measure of profitability, although it is necessary to exercise care in interpreting such

---

3 The Centre for Interfirm Comparison Limited, which conducts interfirm comparison schemes for firms in a number of industries, goes to considerable lengths to adjust the accounting data of participants to a common set of accounting policies. Although the Centre conducts schemes for the benefit of management rather than external users, its requirements for extensive adjustments indicates the difficulties of making comparisons if these adjustments have not been made.

a ratio. In particular, it is essential to be wary of one ratio which attempts to summarize what may be an extremely complex business reality.

If a profit and loss account shows that a company has made a profit of, say, £100 000, it is impossible to draw any conclusion from this one figure on whether the company has performed well or badly. The conclusion would differ if, on the one hand, assets worth £500 000 had been used and, on the other hand, assets worth £10 000 000 had been used to generate the profit. In the former case the return on assets or capital employed is 20% whilst in the latter case it is only 1%.

A ratio of a measure of profit to a measure of capital employed is a first step towards assessing the profitability of most, although not all businesses.[4] Once such a return on capital employed has been calculated at, say, 20%, it is still impossible to draw any conclusion about profitability without reference to one of the yardsticks of comparison mentioned in the preceding section.

Bearing in mind this need for comparison, let us try to be a little more precise in what we mean by return on assets or capital employed. Should we take profit before interest and tax, profit available for shareholders, profit available for equity shareholders? Should we take gross assets or net assets, total capital employed whether short term or long term, long term capital employed or just equity capital employed? Whichever of these capital figures we select, should we use opening balance sheet figures, closing balance sheet figures or some average for the year?

Many combinations are possible and each may be useful for a specific purpose and also in helping us to build up a picture of the business. It is essential, however, that the numerator and denominator of each ratio are logically consistent.

We shall examine three ratios which measure different aspects of the return on capital employed:

(a) $\dfrac{\text{Profit available to equity shareholders}}{\text{Equity shareholders' interest}}$.

Equity shareholders and potential equity shareholders will be interested in the return which is being earned on equity capital employed in the business. This ratio provides an indication of the overall efficiency

4 As neither historical cost accounts nor current cost accounts include a value for human capital employed, such a ratio based on the accounting data would be unhelpful for assessing the profitability of, for example, a professional accountancy practice.

of the management not only in the operations of the business but also in arranging the financing position and taxation affairs of the company for the benefit of the equity shareholders.

When the ratio is calculated on the figures disclosed in historical cost accounts the profit to be taken is that after deducting interest, taxation and any preference dividends. The equity shareholders' interest is not just the equity share capital but the sum of equity share capital and all reserves. As the profits are earned over a period of time, it is preferable to use an appropriate average figure for the denominator.

Such a ratio based upon historical cost accounts suffers from the fact that the figure for equity interest shown in the balance sheet is based on out of date historical costs rather than current costs. Similarly, the profit figure is arrived at after charging out of date costs rather than current costs. These deficiencies are remedied to some extent where figures shown in current cost accounts are used to calculate the ratio.

When current cost accounts are used the numerator is the 'current cost profit attributable to shareholders' less any preference dividends.[5] The denominator is an appropriate average of the equity share capital plus all reserves, including the current cost reserve.

It is important to bear in mind that, although the equity shareholders' interest which appears in a current cost balance sheet will be based upon the current values of the assets which appear in that balance sheet, it will still exclude the value of many intangible assets, such as good management, which do not usually appear in balance sheets. It follows that, all other things being equal, a firm with a relatively high proportion of intangible assets will show a higher return on capital calculated on balance sheet figures than one with a low proportion of such assets. This point is also relevant to the following ratios.

$$\text{(b)} \quad \frac{\text{Profit before interest on long-term loans and taxation}}{\text{Long-term capital employed}}.$$

This ratio indicates the return on all long-term capital employed. Long-term capital comprises the equity shareholders' interest, preference share capital and any long-term loans. As profit is earned during

---

5 A current cost profit and loss account prepared in accordance with SSAP 16 provides a figure of 'current cost profit attributable to shareholders' rather than a 'current cost profit attributable to equity shareholders'. It follows that, in arriving at profit attributable to equity shareholders, it is theoretically necessary to make a second gearing adjustment to reflect any gain or loss which accrues to equity shareholders from using preference share capital to finance real assets which rise or fall in value.

a period an appropriate average figure should be employed for the denominator.

Where current cost accounts are available the numerator will usually be the 'current cost operating profit' of the company and the denominator will reflect the current values of the assets identified in the current cost balance sheet.

Difficulties may often occur with bank overdrafts which, although legally repayable on demand, are often in practice part of the long-term capital of a company. Here it is necessary to make a judgement upon whether overdrafts are or are not long-term capital and then to frame the ratio accordingly. If bank overdrafts are considered to be part of long-term capital, the denominator will include the average overdraft and the numerator must therefore be the profit before charging interest on overdrafts. If they are not considered to be part of long-term capital, they will be excluded from the denominator and the numerator will be the profit after bank interest but before interest on long-term loans and taxation.

$$(c) \quad \frac{\text{Profit before interest and taxation}}{\text{Total assets employed}}.$$

This ratio does not measure the overall success of the firm but abstracts from the financing and taxation position in order to measure what may be called operating efficiency. Thus it shows the rate of return which has been earned on the total assets at the disposal of the directors, irrespective of how those assets have been financed.

The denominator should be an average of the total assets employed by the firm, before the deduction of any current or long-term liabilities. The numerator should be the profit before interest on any sources of finance and before taxation.

Certain difficulties are likely to arise in calculating this ratio from a set of current cost accounts. At first it might be thought that current cost operating profit should be taken as the numerator whilst average total assets should be taken as the denominator. The current cost operating profit is, after all, the profit of the entity which abstracts from the way in which the entity has been financed. After more careful thought it is clear that this would be incorrect. The current cost operating profit is the profit after a monetary working capital adjustment has been made and, as we have seen in Chapter 6, this monetary working capital adjustment takes into account the necessary increased or reduced finance to be provided by short-term creditors and sometimes bank overdrafts. Such short-term creditors and bank overdrafts are not deducted in arriving at the total assets figure which is the denominator. In order to calculate a numerator which is logically consistent with the denominator, it is therefore necessary to 'add back' to the current cost operating profit that part of the monetary working capital adjustment which relates to current liabilities. It is unlikely that an analysis of the monetary working capital adjustment will be available in the accounts of most companies, and hence precise calculation of this ratio will not be possible within the context of current cost accounts.

When a set of detailed financial accounts is available, it is possible to carry out a systematic analysis using a pyramid of ratios like the one illustrated below.[6] We have designed a pyramid for a manufacturing company but it is, of course, possible to design all manner of pyramids depending upon the circumstances of the particular company and the information required. The simple pyramid for a manufacturing company might take the following form:

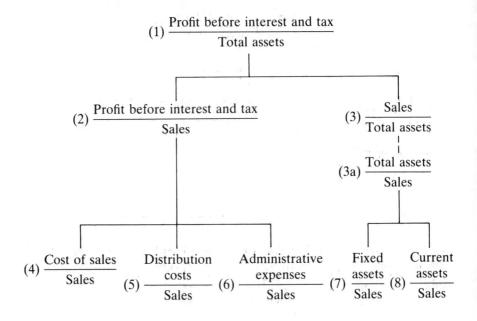

Ratio (1) provides the return on total assets expressed as a percentage. This may be analysed by examining ratios (2) and (3). Ratio (2) is the net profit margin on sales expressed as a percentage whilst

---

6 Such an analysis is only possible if companies adopt profit and loss account formats 1 or 3 specified in the Companies Act 1981, Schedule 1, Part 1.

ratio (3) is the asset turnover in times per year. The relationship between the three ratios is expressed as follows:

$$\frac{\text{Profit}}{\text{Assets}} = \frac{\text{Profit}}{\text{Sales}} \times \frac{\text{Sales}}{\text{Assets}},$$

i.e.

Ratio (1) = Ratio (2) × Ratio (3).

To give an example, if the result for ratio (2) is 10% and the result for ratio (3) is two times per year, the result for ratio (1) is 20%.

If the net profit margin on sales (ratio (2)) has deteriorated compared with previous years or is poor in comparison with the corresponding ratio of other companies, it is possible to move down the left-hand side of the pyramid to determine why this is so. By examining the results for ratios (4), (5) and (6), it is possible to see which ratios are increasing and hence causing ratio (2) to fall. If we assume that all ratios are expressed as percentages, the relationship between ratios (2), (4), (5) and (6) is expressed as follows:

Ratio (2) + Ratio (4) + Ratio (5) + Ratio (6) = 100%.[7]

The higher the result for ratios (4), (5) and (6), the lower will be the result for ratios (1) and (2). Hence at this stage we may say that high results for ratios (4), (5) and (6) are undesirable, although, as we shall see later in this section, even this statement will have to be modified when we consider the interrelationships between the two sides of the pyramid.

Turning now to the right-hand side of the pyramid, we may explore how well the firm is utilizing its assets to achieve sales. Ratio (3) shows

---

7 This may be easily demonstrated. Let S be sales and let C_4, C_5, C_6 be cost of sales, distribution costs and administrative expenses respectively, assuming that all operating costs of the company are included under one of these headings. Then

$$\text{Ratio (2)} = \frac{S - (C_4 + C_5 + C_6)}{S}$$

while

$$\text{Ratio (4)} = \frac{C_4}{S}, \qquad \text{Ratio (5)} = \frac{C_5}{S}, \qquad \text{Ratio (6)} = \frac{C_6}{S}.$$

It follows that

$$\frac{S - (C_4 + C_5 + C_6)}{S} + \frac{C_4}{S} + \frac{C_5}{S} + \frac{C_6}{S} = \frac{S}{S} = 1.$$

But $S/S = 1$ expressed as a percentage is 100%.

the gross asset turnover and, provided that ratio (2) is positive, the higher the result for this ratio the better. Many people find it conceptually difficult to think in terms of asset turnover, and it is therefore useful to express the same measures in a somewhat different way. Whereas ratio (3) shows sales divided by gross assets, ratio (3a) shows the value of gross assets per pound of sales. A result of two times per year for ratio (3) would therefore be equivalent to a result of £0.5 for ratio (3a). The relationship is

$$\text{Ratio (3a)} = \frac{1}{\text{Ratio (3)}}.$$

If similar measures are used for ratios (7) and (8), we have the advantage, for analytical purposes, that

$$\text{Ratio (7)} + \text{Ratio (8)} = \text{Ratio (3a)}.$$

Again we may tentatively say that the lower the results for ratios (7) and (8) the better.

It is possible to extend the pyramid downwards. Thus the utilization of the various categories of fixed assets and current assets may be explored. To take an example let us examine the utilization of current assets:

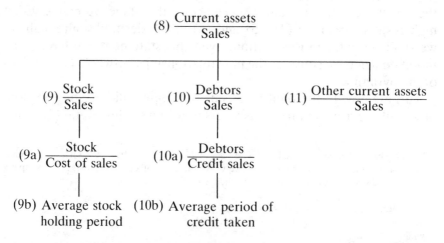

Current assets may be analysed into stocks, debtors and any other current assets and an examination made to determine to what extent a high value for ratio (8) is due to high results for ratios (9), (10) and (11). This may be the best that can be done with the information available in published accounts. The figures for stocks and debtors will, at best, be averages of the opening and closing balance sheet figures, and such simple averages may not be good approximations to the averages in the sense of typical values for the period. Similarly, ratios (9) and (10) are both logically inconsistent for the reasons given below and could be improved with better information.

Concentrating first on ratio (9), stocks are usually shown at cost whilst sales are at selling price. A consistent ratio would relate stocks to the cost of sales, as shown in ratio (9a), and from this we may arrive at the average stock holding period in days (ratio (9b)):

$$\text{Average stock holding period (ratio (9b))} = 365 \times \frac{\text{Stock}}{\text{Cost of sales}}.$$

A consistent ratio for 10 would relate debtors, not to total sales, but to credit sales. This is done in ratio (10a). Again we are able to arrive at an average period of credit taken by debtors, shown by ratio (10b):

$$\text{Average period of credit (ratio (10b))} = 365 \times \frac{\text{Debtors}}{\text{Credit sales}}.$$

We have now seen how, given sufficient data, it is possible to analyse performance in a systematic way. In addition we have seen that, looked at individually, high results for the cost ratios and for the asset utilization ratios (3a), (7) and (8) are unfavourable. It is, however, most important not to be too dogmatic here and to bear in mind that there are links *across* the pyramid. To give an example, a high result for ratio (5), selling and distribution costs to sales, is by itself unfavourable. However, high expenditure on selling may increase sales with a result that it is possible to use assets more effectively and hence achieve favourable results for the asset utilization ratios.

This emphasizes that interpretation of accounts is an art by which we look for clues to performance. It is an art in which one should never be rigid in one's thinking.

Liquidity
Even a very profitable company may be forced into liquidation if it is unable to meet its debts. In view of this, most users of accounts are concerned with the liquidity of a company, which may conveniently be divided into short-term liquidity and long-term solvency.

The short-term liquid position of a company has traditionally been assessed by looking at the relationship between current assets and current liabilities, or some components of current assets and current liabilities, on a balance sheet. These are essentially static measures, whereas debts are paid out of cash flows. A more recent tendency has been to look at ratios of a dynamic nature relating cash or funds flow to current liabilties. We shall look at these in turn, commencing with the static measures.

The current, or working capital, ratio relates current assets to current liabilities:

$$\text{Current ratio} = \frac{\text{Current assets}}{\text{Current liabilities}}.$$

A result greater than 1 suggests that a company is able to pay its current liabilities out of current assets. However, the composition of the current assets is important; two companies may have the same result of the current ratio although, in one case the major part of current assets is stock whilst, in the other case, the major part of current assets is debtors. Because of this it is usual to supplement the current ratio with a 'liquid' or 'quick' asset ratio, relating the more liquid current assets, such as debtors, cash and short-term marketable securities, to current liabilities:

$$\text{Liquid ratio} = \frac{\text{Debtors} + \text{Cash} + \text{Short-term marketable securities}}{\text{Current liabilities}}.$$

A ratio in excess of 1 is a much clearer indication, although still not conclusive evidence, that a company is able to meet its short-term debts.

Once the above ratios have been calculated it is usually still very difficult to say whether the results are good or bad. Although high results for the current ratio and the liquid ratio suggest a sound liquidity position, they may also suggest that an excessive amount of money is tied up unprofitably in stocks, debtors and cash. In addition, in an inflationary era, a large amount tied up in monetary assets will lead to monetary losses, that is losses of purchasing power, which most companies will be keen to avoid.

The above ratios are essentially static in nature and hence only give us indications of the short-term liquidity position to the extent that they are typical and that no window dressing has taken place. Window dressing occurs when action is taken to manipulate certain figures which appear in a set of accounts to produce more satisfactory results. The current ratio and liquid ratio are both particularly susceptible to such manipulation. This is best understood by recognizing that if a ratio is greater than 1, the subtraction of the same amount from both numerator and denominator will make it larger whereas, if it is less than 1, the subtraction of the same amount from both numerator and denominator will make it smaller.[8]

Let us provide an example. A company forecasts that it will have a liquid ratio of 0.7 on its balance sheet date calculated as follows:

$$\frac{\text{Liquid assets}}{\text{Current liabilities}} = \frac{700\,000}{1\,000\,000} = 0.70.$$

The firm realizes that this ratio is lower than that of previous years and considers that it is likely to have an adverse effect on the company's share price. It therefore delays the payment of creditors amounting to £300 000 so that the liquid ratio based on the reported results becomes

$$\frac{700\,000 + 300\,000}{1\,000\,000 + 300\,000} = 0.77.$$

The possibility of such window dressing emphasizes the dangers of assessing liquidity by taking the position at just one point in time. As current liabilities are paid out of cash flow, rather than out of a stock of current assets, analysts have developed ratios of a more dynamic nature. Several such ratios using funds flow have been suggested. Two of these are

(a) $\dfrac{\text{Funds generated by operations}}{\text{Current liabilities}}$;

(b) $\dfrac{\text{Quick assets}}{\text{Daily outflow of funds on operations}}$.

The former relates the source of funds from operations, as shown in the statement of source and application of funds, to the current liabilities at the close of a period. It therefore gives an indication of how long it takes to generate sufficient funds to pay off the stock of current liabilities. By dividing 365 days by the result for ratio (a), this information may be expressed in days. The second of the two ratios relates the quick assets, that is cash, debtors and marketable securities, to the average daily outlay of funds on operations. The former figure would be taken from the closing balance sheet whilst the latter would be arrived at by taking the total operating expenses from the profit and loss account and deducting depreciation. It indicates how many days the firm would be able to continue operations if there were no

---

8 If $A/B > 1$, then $(A - x)/(B - x) > A/B$. Conversely, if $A/B < 1$, then $(A - x)/(B - x) < A/B$. ($B > x > 0$.)

further inflow of funds and is usually referred to as a 'defensive interval measure' or sometimes a 'no credit interval'. Neither of these ratios are without fault, but they do attempt to focus on the flows out of which debts are paid rather than on what may be an atypical position at one point in time. Of course they still suffer from the possibility that the current liabilities or quick assets included in the ratios may themselves be atypical.

We have so far focused on the short-term liquidity of a company. It is also important to consider the longer-term solvency, in other words the ability of the company to meet debts in the future.

Two ratios are of particular help here: the first is the gearing or leverage ratio, that is the relationship between debt and equity capital.

$$(a) \ \frac{\text{Long-term debt and preference share capital}}{\text{Long-term debt, preference share capital and equity interest}}.$$

This ratio is often calculated on the basis of balance sheet values, although to have any economic meaning it should properly be based upon current values. The higher the result for this ratio, the greater the proportion of the assets which is financed by non-equity capital and hence the greater the risk of debt holders suffering a loss on a liquidation. In addition the higher the result for this ratio, the greater the potential volatility of the earnings stream attributable to the equity shareholders.

Of couse, this is a simple first conclusion because, on the one hand, different forms of debt have different rights and security and, on the other hand, the realizable values of the assets on a liquidation may bear little relationship to their balance sheet values in either historical cost accounts or current cost accounts. Nevertheless it is frequently used to compare the financial position of one company with that of another.

The second ratio is commonly called 'times interest covered', that is the relationship between operating income and interest and preference dividends payable.

$$(b) \ \frac{\text{Operating income before interest and taxation}}{\substack{\text{Interest payments (before taxation) and preference dividends} \\ \text{payable}}}.$$

This ratio tries to capture the same feature as ratio (a) above, that is the proportion of the total operating income which goes to suppliers of long-term capital other than equity shareholders. The lower the ratio the less certain are debt holders to receive their interest and preference shareholders their dividends; in other words, the greater the risk to lenders and preference shareholders.

In interpreting these ratios, it is, of course, essential to bear in mind the variability of the operating earnings. A company with stable earnings over time will be able to support a much higher level of debt than a company with variable earnings over time.

We must stress the undesirability of attempting to draw definite conclusions from the liquidity and solvency ratios. Instead the ratios should be used to help build up a picture of the company's overall position. Thus one should ask such questions as: Are the current and liquid ratios becoming larger or smaller over time? Is the gearing increasing or falling? How do the ratios of this company compare with those of other companies in the industry? If the ratios are out of line with those of other companies, what are the possible reasons?

Multivariate analysis

Introduction

In the preceding section we have concentrated on the univariate approach to interpretation. Under this approach one particular ratio is examined, comparisons are made with the results of previous years or of similar companies and tentative conclusions are drawn. This process is repeated in respect of another ratio and, gradually, by examining many ratios, a picture is built up of the position and likely future prospects of the company. The ratios are not combined together in any formal manner, but professional judgement is used to determine how much weight should be given to each of them.

A different approach involves considering several ratios simultaneously by means of multivariate analysis. Under this approach several ratios are combined by means of a formula to produce an index number and conclusions may be drawn by comparing that index number with the similar number for previous periods or for similar companies. One of the best documented areas in which such an approach has been applied is in the prediction of corporate failure and we shall concentrate on that particular application here.

The prediction of corporate failure

The failure[9] of a company will usually have serious repercussions for the individuals involved, such as shareholders, employees and creditors, and often for society at large. If it were possible to predict that a company was likely to fail, then it may well be possible for management to take steps to avoid failure and for other interested parties to take remedial action to mitigate the effects of failure in their own interests. A method which successfully predicts failure would therefore be very valuable, and considerable effort has been devoted to this problem by both institutional and academic researchers.[10] Both univariate and multivariate approaches have been used, although we shall concentrate on the latter approach here.[11] As will be seen it is not possible to predict whether a particular company is going to fail. Rather it appears possible to say whether or not a particular company exhibits characteristic similar to other companies which have failed in the past.

Although the multivariate approach had been used in this context before, the most influential work on the prediction of failure has been that of the American Professor E. I. Altman.[12] In a study published in 1968, he took a sample of 33 failed and 33 non-failed American manufacturing companies. He then examined many ratios to see which ratios taken together best discriminated between companies in the two groups. In the absence of any well-developed theoretical models which would explain why companies fail, he used a statistical technique known as 'multiple discriminant analysis'. By this means he found five ratios which could be combined to produce what is called a Z score, the level of which best captured differences between the failed and non-failed firms.

9 Failure may be defined (and has been defined) in many ways in different studies. This may include insolvency, entry into receivership, creditors' voluntary liquidation or compulsory liquidation, the need for a reconstruction or receipt of government aid as alternatives to liquidation.

10 In this section we concentrate on methods of predicting failure based on information contained in a set of accounts. These methods may be said to concentrate on the symptoms rather than on the more fundamental defects of the company and the mistakes of its management. John Argenti has developed an 'A' score, based on both accounting data and on qualitative judgements of management. Interested readers are referred to 'Company failure – long range prediction not enough', *Accountancy*, August 1977, and to the extremely readable book, J. Argenti, *Corporate Collapse*, McGraw-Hill, New York, 1976.

11 For an example of the univariate approach, *see* W. H. Beaver, 'Financial ratios as predictors of failure', in *Empirical Research in Accounting*, Supplement to *Journal of Accounting Research*, 1966.

12 *See*, for example, E. I. Altman, 'Financial ratios, discriminant analysis and the prediction of corporate bankruptcy', *The Journal of Finance*, 23 September 1968, or, E. I. Altman, *Corporate Bankruptcy in America*, Heath Lexington Books, New York, 1971.

The discriminant function took the form

$$Z = 0.012X_1 + 0.014X_2 + 0.033X_3 + 0.006X_4 + 0.010X_5.$$

The five ratios were

$$X_1 = \frac{\text{Working capital}}{\text{Total gross assets}},$$

$$X_2 = \frac{\text{Retained earnings}}{\text{Total gross assets}},$$

$$X_3 = \frac{\text{Earnings before interest and tax}}{\text{Total gross assets}},$$

$$X_4 = \frac{\text{Market value of equity}}{\text{Book value of debt}},$$

$$X_5 = \frac{\text{Sales}}{\text{Total gross assets}}.$$

Thus the Altman Z score combined ratios covering aspects of liquidity, re-invested earnings, profitability, gearing and asset turnover. There is no obvious economic reason why these emerged other than that, statistically, they gave the best results.

Having arrived at the above equation, Altman then found that all companies with a Z score greater than 2.99 were non-failed companies whilst all companies with a Z score below 1.81 were failed companies.[13] It was impossible to be so categoric with companies which had a score between 1.81 and 2.99. Altman tested his statistical model on different samples of companies and found that 1 year before failure his model correctly classified companies to the failed or non-failed group accurately in 96% of the cases. However, more generally he found that the percentage of correct classification declined considerably with data more than 1 year prior to failure.

It is important to bear in mind that Altman's researches and model relate to the manufacturing sector of the US economy in the period 1946–1965. It therefore does not follow that his results would be applicable to other sectors or at other times; nor does it follow that his results would be relevant in the different conditions of the UK economy. What he has done is to provide us with an approach to the prediction of failure which may be applied in other circumstances.

R. J. Taffler and H. Tisshaw have applied the approach to UK data

13 Strictly 'non-bankrupt' and 'bankrupt', respectively, using Altman's terminology.

and developed two 'Z scales', one for quoted manufacturing enterprises and one for non-quoted manufacturing enterprises with turnover above £$\frac{1}{2}$ million.[14] For the sample of quoted manufacturing enterprises, statistical analysis resulted in the following formula:

$$Z = C_0 + C_1 R_1 + C_2 R_2 + C_3 R_3 + C_4 R_4.$$

C_0 to C_4 are coefficients and R_1 to R_4 are the following ratios:

$$R_1 = \frac{\text{Profit before taxation}}{\text{Current liabilities}},$$

$$R_2 = \frac{\text{Current assets}}{\text{Total liabilities}},$$

$$R_3 = \frac{\text{Current liabilities}}{\text{Total assets}},$$

$R_4 = $ No credit interval

$$= \frac{\text{Immediate assets} - \text{Current liabilities}}{\text{Operating costs excluding depreciation}}.$$

Thus the four ratios combine together various aspects of profitability and solvency to produce a Z score. When they turn to the unquoted manufacturing enterprises the formula comprises not four but five ratios.

Taffler and Tisshaw claim very good results for their formula but, because of their proprietary interest, have not been willing to publish the coefficients for their equations. It has not therefore been possible for others working in the same area to test and comment on the particular models put forward.

In a general textbook on financial accounting we have only been able to provide a brief introduction to multivariate analysis. Such techniques are being used by various investment institutions and increasingly by large accounting practices to determine whether or not the going concern concept is or is not appropriate. It is undoubtedly an area which will receive more attention in future years.

Segmental reports and their problems

So far in this chapter we have been concerned with the interpretation of a set of accounts for a company or group and we have seen that

14 A brief account of this work appears in R. J. Taffler and H. Tisshaw, 'Going, going, gone – four factors which predict', *Accountancy*, March 1977, pp. 50–4.

such an interpretation is bedevilled with all manner of difficulties. These difficulties may be considerably increased in practice because many companies or groups operate in several industries and in different countries and the economic performance and outlook of these industries and countries may vary considerably.

If it is accepted that one of the functions of accounting is to 'assist financial statements users in analysing and understanding the enterprises' financial statements by permitting better assessment of the enterprises' past performance and future prospects',[15] then it may be argued that it is necessary for accountants to provide a more detailed analysis of the accounts to show the results of various segments of a business. Such a process is known by such terms as disaggregation, segmental reporting or analysed reporting.

Although most people would accept this in principle, many difficulties arise in its practical implementation. If, for example, the government or a standard-setting body is to require segmental reports, should it try to specify the appropriate segments itself or should it leave the determination of the segments to the company's directors? In the former case, it is extremely difficult to determine appropriate segments which are generally applicable and, given the diversity of business activity, information produced by some firms in accordance with standard segments may well be unhelpful.[16] In the latter case there is a possibility of bias, either innocent or fraudulent, in the choice of segments by directors. Another major problem is the treatment of joint assets, such as a head office computer, which are used by several segments of the business, and joint costs, such as the salary of a personnel director, which benefit several segments of the business.

Bearing these problems in mind, let us look at recent developments in this area in the UK.

For listed companies, the Stock Exchange has for many years required 'a geographical analysis of turnover and of contribution to trading results of those trading operations carried on by the company (or group) outside the United Kingdom'.[17] More generally, Sec. 17 of the Companies Act 1967 required that, where a company or group (for which consolidated accounts were prepared) carried on businesses

---

15 Taken from *Financial reporting for segments of a business enterprise*, FASB, New York, 1976.
16 For an introduction and criticism of the US approach to identifying reportable segments, *see* C. R. Emmanuel and S. J. Gray, 'Corporate diversification and segmental disclosure requirements in the USA', *Journal of Business Finance and Accounting*, Winter 1977.
17 Listing Agreement, Para. 10(c).

of two or more different classes, the directors' report had to contain a statement of the proportions of the turnover derived from each class and the extent or approximate extent of the profit or loss before taxation of each segment. Identification of segment was left to the discretion of directors and, as the directors' report was, and is, not subject to audit, the information disclosed in accordance with this requirement appears to have been of limited value.[18]

The Eighth Schedule to the Companies Act 1948, as amended by the Companies Act 1981, now requires that the notes to the accounts, rather than the directors' report, should contain the above segmental information.[19] In addition it requires an analysis of turnover between geographical markets and an analysis of the average number of employees between various categories of persons employed.[20] It is still left to directors to select the relevant segments. These notes are, of course, subject to audit and disclosure can only be avoided if the directors are of the opinion that it would be seriously prejudicial to the interests of the company, in which case the failure to disclose must be noted.

Although an International Accounting Standard was issued on this subject in 1983,[21] a UK standard is not expected in the foreseeable future as the topic, which appeared on the agenda of the ASC for many years, is no longer included in its work programme.

Recommended reading

D. Fanning and M. Pendlebury, *Company Accounts: A Guide*, George Allen and Unwin, London, 1984.

E. R. Farmer, *Understanding and Interpreting Company Reports and Accounts*, Van Nostrand Reinhold, Wokingham, 1983.

G. Foster, *Financial Statement Analysis*, Prentice-Hall, Englewood Cliffs, N.J., 1978.

---

18 *The future of company reports*, Cmnd 6888, HMSO, London, Para. 39.
19 Companies Act 1981, Schedule 1, Para. 55(1).
20 *Ibid.*, Para. 55(2) and 56(1).
21 IAS 14, 'Reporting financial information by segment', IASC, 1983. Paragraph 23 of this statement contains the useful requirement that reconciliations between the sum of the information on individual segments and the aggregated information should be provided.

Questions

18.1 The following extracts are taken from published financial statements of listed companies:

(1) Directors' report

Companies Act 1981
The company is not yet required to comply with the accounting and disclosure provisions of Part 1 of the Companies Act 1981.   (1 mark)

(2) Directors' report
Item No. 5 in the Notice of Meeting, which is a Special Resolution, is designed to give a limited release of the shareholders' statutory right of pre-emption. This release is limited to 5% of the authorized nominal value of the share capital of the Company, namely £11 250 000. The directors consider that this limited release is desirable in the interest of flexibility.   (3 marks)

(3) Directors' report

Intra group pricing
The prices agreed between Group companies for international sales of material and manufactured goods are based on normal commercial practices which would obtain between independent businesses.
                                          (2 marks)

(4) Accounting policies

Exploration and Development
During the initial exploration stage of projects, full provision is made in respect of the costs thereof by charge against profits of the year. Expenditure on projects after they have reached a promising stage, including the costs of extended evaluation programmes to establish their commercial viability, is carried forward and transferred to pre-production expenditure if the project proceeds. Property acquisition costs and entry premiums paid to gain access of interest are carried forward at cost where considered recoverable from resale or development or otherwise amortized over the expected period of evaluation.

Pre-production expenditure
Once development projects have been established as commercially viable, expenditure other than on property, plant and equipment is carried forward as pre-production expenditure and is charged against profit on the same basis as property, plant and equipment when commercial production commences.

Depreciation
Depreciation of property, plant and equipment and capitalized pre-production expenditure is calculated on a straight line basis with the exception of assets at certain mines in North America and capitalized North Sea oil expenditure which are depreciated on a depletion basis related to extraction.   (4 marks)

(5) Accounting policies

Translation of foreign currencies
Foreign currency assets and liabilities are translated into sterling at the rates ruling on the year end date, except for US dollar borrowings covered forward which are included at the forward cover rate.

Exchange differences arising in the Group's consolidated accounts on the retranslation to closing rates of exchange of its net investments in overseas subsidiaries and associated companies are recorded as movements on the Group's consolidated reserves. Where such net investments are matched in whole or in part by external foreign currency-borrowings by the parent company or a UK subsidiary, then the exchange differences arising on the retranslation of such matching borrowings are also recorded as movements on the Group's consolidated reserves. Average rates of exchange are used to translate the profit and loss account figures of foreign subsidiaries and associated companies in the consolidated profit and loss account, and differences arising between the translation of these figures at average and closing rates of exchange are recorded as movements on the consolidated reserves. All other exchange differences are dealt with through the profit and loss account.   (4 marks)

(6) Accounting policies

Pension contributions
Based on current actuarial advice, provision is made in respect of existing staff for pensions related to projected retirement salaries, taking into account an assessment of future salary increases and inflation. Any underprovision in previous years shown subsequently to have arisen from excessive inflation or other factors is recovered over future periods. Provision is similarly made for additional liabilities arising from increases in pensions to existing pensioners in excess of amounts stipulated in the rules of the funds.   (3 marks)

(7) Accounting policies

Interest
Interest is capitalized during the period of construction where it relates either to the financing of major projects with long periods of development or to dedicated financing of other projects. All other interest is charged against income.   (3 marks)

You are required to comment upon the treatment adopted in all of the above seven paragraphs explaining the rationale behind each. You should not consider or comment upon the taxation implications. **(20 marks)**
ICAEW Financial Accounting II, July 1983.

18.2 Below are summarized the published financial statements of a group of companies, drawn up on both the historical cost and current cost bases, with corresponding figures for the previous year.

You are required:
  (a) to compute FIVE significant accounting ratios, on EACH of the two bases, and for BOTH years or year-ends (i.e. 20 ratios in all). The five ratios must be separate and distinct; different versions of the same ratio will not be accepted; (10 marks)
  (b) to appraise the group's financial standing on the basis of the five ratios, and of other evidence. (6 marks)
  (16 marks)

Walsoken plc and Subsidiaries
Consolidated Profit and Loss Account to 30 September 1983

Y/t 30.9.82

HC £'000s	CC £'000s		Historical Cost £'000s	£'000s	Current Cost £'000s	£'000s
12 000	12 000	Turnover		15 000		15 000
(9 000)	(9 000)	Cost of sales		(10 950)		(10 950)
3 000	3 000	Gross profit		4 050		4 050
(600)	(600)	Distribution costs	(720)		(720)	
(1 300)	(1 300)	Administrative expenses	(1 550)		(1 550)	
(1 900)	(1 900)			(2 270)		(2 270)
1 100	1 100			1 780		1 780
100	100	Other operating income		120		120
1 200	1 200	*Historical cost operating profit*		1 900		1 900
		Current cost adjustments:				
	(200)	Depreciation adjustment			(400)	
	(300)	Cost of sales adjustment			(350)	
		Monetary working capital				
	40	adjustment			30	
	(460)				(720)	
	740	*Current cost operating profit*				1 180
200	130	Group's proportion of pre-tax				
		profits of related companies		240		160
1 400	870	*Net profit before interest*		2 140		1 340

Consolidated Profit and Loss Account – *continued*

Y/t 30.9.82   *Y/t 30.9.83*

HC £'000s	CC £'000s			*Historical Cost* £'000s	£'000s	*Current Cost* £'000s	£'000s
b/f 1 400	870		b/f		2 140		1 340
(100)	(100)	Interest on bank overdrafts		(20)		(20)	
(180)	(180)	Interest on debentures		(240)		(240)	
—	138	Gearing adjustment		—		187	
(280)	(142)				(260)		(73)
1 120	728	*Net profit before taxation*			1 880		1 267
(400)	(400)	Tax on profit on ordinary activities		(700)		(700)	
(50)	(50)	Transfer to deferred taxation		(100)		(100)	
(100)	(100)	Group's proportion of tax on ordinary activities of related companies		(120)		(120)	
10	10	Adjustment of previous year's taxation charge		15		15	
(540)	(540)				(905)		(905)
580	188	*Profit on ordinary activities*			975		362
(40)	(15)	Minority interests in group companies			(70)		(30)
540	173	*Attributable to shareholders in Walsoken plc*			905		332
(100)	(100)	Extraordinary charges		—		—	
52	52	Tax on extraordinary charges		—		—	
(48)	(48)				—		—
492	125	*Profit for the financial year* dividends of Walsoken plc			905		332
(50)	(50)	Preference – paid		(25)		(25)	
(50)	(50)	Ordinary – paid		(100)		(100)	
(150)	(150)	Ordinary – proposed		(300)		(300)	
(250)	(250)				(425)		(425)
242	(125)	*Retained earnings for the financial year*			480		(93)
6.1p	1.5p	*Earnings per share*			8.8p		3.1p

Consolidated Balance Sheet, 30 September 1983

30.9.82 HC £'000s	CC £'000s	Net assets	Historical Cost £'000s	£'000s	Current Cost £'000s	£'000s
		Fixed assets (net)				
400	400	Intangible assets		500		500
2 862	4 793	Tangible assets		3 549		5 915
		Investments:				
1 000	890	In related companies (equity basis)		1 070		880
4 262	6 083			5 119		7 295
		Current assets				
3 000	3 045	Stocks	3 800		3 838	
1 500	1 500	Trade debtors	2 000		2 000	
350	350	Cash at bank and in hand	464		464	
150	150	Prepayments	200		200	
5 000	5 045			6 464		6 502
		Creditors: Amounts falling due within one year				
(800)	(800)	Bank overdrafts	—		—	
(1 800)	(1 800)	Trade creditors	(2 100)		(2 100)	
(262)	(262)	Corporation tax – current year (*less* ACT)	(603)		(603)	
(250)	(250)	Accruals	(300)		(300)	
(150)	(150)	Proposed dividend	(300)		(300)	
(64)	(64)	ACT on proposed dividend	(129)		(129)	
(3 326)	(3 326)			(3 432)		(3 432)
1 674	1 719	*Net current assets*		3 032		3 070
5 936	7 802			£8 151		£10 365
		Financed by				
		Creditors: Amounts falling due after more than one year				
1 500	1 500	Debenture loans		2 000		2,000
		Provisions for liabilities and charges				
236	236	Deferred taxation		271		271
		Capital and reserves				
		Called up share capital of Walsoken plc				
500	500	Preference (£1 shares)		—		—
2 000	2 000	Ordinary (25p shares)	3000		3000	
2 500	2 500			3 000		3 000
c/f 4 236	4 236		c/f	5 271		5 271

Consolidated Balance Sheet, 30 September 1983 – *continued*

30.9.82				Historical Cost		Current Cost	
HC	*CC*						
£'000s	£'000s			£'000s	£'000s	£'000s	£'000s
b/f 4236	4236		b/f		5271		5271
		Reserves					
200	200	Share premium account		750		750	
—	—	Capital redemption reserve		500		500	
—	2326	Current cost reserve		—		3307	
700	500	Profit & loss account		610		(83)	
300	190	Group's proportion of retained earnings of related companies since acquisition		370		180	
1200	3216				2230		4654
500	350	*Minority interests in Group companies*			650		440
5936	7802				£8151		£10365

(1) Historical cost depreciation (included in administrative expenses): 1981–82, £400000; 1982–83, £600000.

(2) At 1 April 1983, the 500000 £1 preference shares were redeemed at par out of profits.

(3) During the year ended 30 September 1983, 4000000 25p ordinary shares were issued in exchange for ordinary shares in newly-acquired subsidiaries, for some of which cash was paid in addition.

(4) £500000 of debentures were issued at par during 1982–83. They are secured by a floating charge. The bank overdrafts were similarly secured in 1981–82.

(5) Stock at 30 September 1981 was £2600000 at historical cost, and £2650000 at current cost.

(6) Corporation Tax 52%; income tax basic rate 30%.

A. Cert. A., Advanced Financial Accounting, Second paper, December 1983.

18.3   The following is an extract from *Accountancy*, March 1977, p. 50:

'Take profit before tax divided by current liabilities; current assets as a proportion of total liabilities; current liabilities as a proportion of total tangible assets; take into account the no-credit interval; mix them in the right proportions and you can tell whether a company will go bust.'

The no-credit interval is defined as (current assets − current liabilities) ÷ (operating costs excluding depreciation).

The following are the summarized accounts of Go-go Products Ltd and Numerous Inventions Ltd for the years ended 30th April 1977 and 1976.

	Go-go Products		Numerous Inventions	
	1977	1976	1977	1976
	£	£	£	£
Turnover	30 067	25 417	9 734	8 044
Costs: depreciation	311	284	331	195
other	28 356	24 198	8 313	6 571
Profit before tax	1 400	935	1 090	1 278
	30 067	25 417	9 734	8 044
Intangible assets	918	937	—	—
Fixed assets	4 644	5 228	1 950	1 530
Stock	6 243	6 773	986	1 257
Debtors	4 042	4 580	3 234	2 236
Bank	516	184	2 578	1 366
	16 363	17 702	8 748	6 389
Creditors	5 261	5 144	1 297	972
Current taxation	312	379	483	321
Short term borrowing	2 357	4 447	2 577	1 174
Long term loans	1 409	1 168	55	38
Capital and Reserves	7 024	6 564	4 336	3 884
	16 363	17 702	8 748	6 389

You are required to:
  (a) **calculate three of the stated factors for the two companies and two others you consider relevant to their going-concern status.** (15 marks)
  (b) **compare the two companies stating clearly which of your calculated ratios have moved in an unfavourable direction, and** (5 marks)
  (c) **describe and discuss the limitations of ratio analysis as a predictor of failure.** (5 marks)
  (25 marks)

ICAEW Financial Accounting II, July 1977.

18.4 (a) **What do you understand by the term 'disaggregation/segmental reporting' and to what extent do you consider that financial reporting by companies would be improved by further disclosure of disaggregated/segmental information?** (12 marks)
  (b) **What objections and problems arise in the implementation of disaggregated/segmental reporting?** (8 marks)
  (20 marks)

A. Cert. A. The Regulating Framework of Accounting, June 1984.

Index